Internet and Technology Law Desk Reference

Internet and Technology Law Desk Reference
2002 Edition

Michael D. Scott

Aspen Law and Business
A Division of Aspen Publishers, Inc.
New York   Gaithersburg

This publication is designed to provide accurate and authoritative information in regard to the subject matter covered. It is sold with the understanding that the publisher is not engaged in rendering legal, accounting, or other professional services. If legal advice or other professional assistance is required, the services of a competent professional person should be sought.

—from a *Declaration of Principles* jointly adopted by
a Committee of the American Bar Association and
a Committee of Publishers and Associations

ISSN 1531-6947
ISBN 0-7355-2210-3

About Aspen Law & Business

Aspen Law & Business is a leading publisher of authoritative treatises, practice manuals, services, and journals for attorneys, corporate and bank directors, accountants, auditors, environmental compliance professionals, financial and tax advisors, and other business professionals. Our mission is to provide practical solution-based how-to information keyed to the latest original pronouncements as well as the latest legislative, judicial, and regulatory developments.

We offer publications in the areas of accounting and auditing; antitrust; banking and finance; bankruptcy; business and commercial law; construction law; corporate law; criminal law; environmental compliance; government and administrative law; health law; insurance law; intellectual property; international law; legal practice and litigation; matrimonial and family law; pensions, benefits, and labor; real estate law; securities; and taxation.

Other Aspen products treating law and technology issues include

Biotechnology: Law, Business, and Regulation
The Computer and Internet Lawyer
E-Business Legal Handbook
Federal Telecommunications Law
Intellectual Property for the Internet
Intellectual Property Legal Opinions
Journal of Internet Law
Law and the Information Superhighway
The Law of Electronic Commerce
Law of the Internet
Law of Internet Disputes
Multimedia Legal Handbook
Scott on Computer Law
Scott on Multimedia Law
Software Patents

ASPEN LAW & BUSINESS
A Division of Aspen Publishers, Inc.
A Wolters Kluwer Company
www.aspenpublishers.com

Subscription Notice

This Aspen Law & Business product is updated on a periodic basis with supplements to reflect important changes in the subject matter. If you purchased this product directly from Aspen Law & Business, we have already recorded your subscription for the update service.

If, however, you have purchased this product from a bookstore and wish to receive future updates and revised or related volumes billed separately with a 30-day examination review, please contact our Customer Service Department at 1-800-234-1660, or send your name, company name (if applicable), address, and title of the product to:

ASPEN LAW & BUSINESS
A Division of Aspen Publishers, Inc.
7201 McKinney Circle
Frederick, MD 21704

About the Author

Michael D. Scott is a partner in Perkins Coie LLP, Santa Monica, California. He has practiced computer and intellectual property law for the last 26 years. His practice currently focuses primarily on software, Internet, and electronic commerce law.

He is the author of the new *Licensing and Intellectual Property Law Desk Reference* (Aspen Law & Business, 2002), *Scott on Computer Law* (3d ed. Aspen Law & Business), *Scott on Multimedia Law* (3d ed. Aspen Law & Business), and *The Year 2000 Computer Crisis: Law, Business, Technology* (1998). He is also editor-in-chief of two monthly newsletters—*Cyberspace Lawyer* and *E-Commerce Law*.

Mr. Scott is an Adjunct Professor of Law at Pepperdine University School of Law, Malibu, California, a frequent speaker at various legal and industry conferences, and the author of hundreds of articles on computer, multimedia, and Internet law published worldwide in a variety of languages.

To my wife, Josie,
and my children, Michael,
Cindal, and Derek

Foreword

[L]awyers and courts need no longer feel ashamed or even sensitive about the charge, often made, that they confuse the issue by resort to legal "jargon," law Latin or Norman French. By comparison, the misnomers and industrial shorthand of the computer world make the most esoteric legal writing seem as clear and lucid as the Ten Commandments or the Gettysburg Address, and to add to this Babel, the experts in the computer field, while using exactly the same words, uniformly disagree as to precisely what they mean.[1]

[I]f there was one over-arching impression left on this court after the testimony given in this case it was that the computer industry is concerned with and depends upon accuracy. Thus, the testimony confirms our view that in an industry which depends upon accuracy, a lack of precision in the use of common terms, particularly in circumstances where those terms have the potential to be specific, would be anomaly.[2]

When I began studying computer programming in college in the 1960s, I was intimidated by the jargon used by my professors and peers. It was difficult enough to learn the technology and programming techniques. I felt that I should not be expected to further struggle just to ask a question or discuss an issue with a colleague.

In the 1970s, when I entered law school, I had the same feeling about the law. Where was Blackacre, anyway? What was the difference between interplead and implead? And why was the law so wedded to Latin, Norman French, and Middle English terms?

When I graduated from law school and began practicing computer law, I realized that there was a third, distinct vocabulary developing to describe the legal issues facing the computer industry. To help make sense of these myriad words and phrases that seemed to permeate the field, I began keeping a binder in which I placed photocopied pages from court decisions, statutes, and other sources, which contained "authoritative" definitions of terms I thought might be useful in my practice. When I bought my first personal computer, I transferred to my hard disk all of the definitions I had accumulated in what were now three overstuffed binders.

---

[1] *Honeywell, Inc. v. Lithonia Lighting, Inc.*, 317 F. Supp. 406, 408 (N.D. Ga. 1970).
[2] *See, e.g., Princeton Graphics Operating, L.P. v. NEC Home Elecs. (U.S.A.), Inc.*, 732 F. Supp. 1258, 1261 (S.D.N.Y. 1990).

Over the last 20 years, I have steadily added to that original database as the field has expanded to include terms from the telecommunications, entertainment, media, multimedia, Internet, and electronic commerce arenas. Over the years, I have also expanded that list from simple definitions to discussions of concepts and principles, related issues, sample contract clauses, summaries of the most important court decisions, and other materials that I personally find useful in my day-to-day practice.

The following materials were developed to make my practice easier and more efficient. I usually refer to the electronic version of this compendium at least once a day, and often more than once, for a definition, a concise discussion of a particular case, concept, or statute, or a sample clause for a contract. I usually add at least one new item daily to the database as well.

The most typical scenarios in which I refer to the compendium are when (i) drafting a definition for a contract, (ii) preparing a pleading or expert witness report for pending litigation, (iii) preparing an opinion letter for a client or a letter to opposing counsel, or (iv) responding to a telephone or e-mail query from a client or colleague. I find that opposing counsel and judges[3] are much more likely

---

[3] *See, e.g., Computer Assocs. Int'l, Inc. v. Altai, Inc.*, 982 F.2d 693, 696 (2d Cir. 1992) ("In recent years, the growth of computer science has spawned a number of challenging legal questions.... As scientific knowledge advances, courts endeavor to keep pace, and sometimes—as in the area of computer technology—they are required to venture into less than familiar waters"); *id.* at 706 ("[W]e are cognizant that computer technology is a dynamic field which can quickly outpace judicial decisionmaking"); *Digital Equipment Corp. v. Altavista Technology, Inc.*, 960 F. Supp. 456, 463 (D. Mass. 1997) ("Given the very new and unique nature of the technology, this Court will take heed of a Supreme Court plurality's recent recognition 'of the changes taking place in the law, the technology, and the industrial structure, related to telecommunications, [that] we believe [make] it unwise and unnecessary definitively to pick one analogy or one specific set of words now.' *Denver Area Education Telecommunications Consortium, Inc. v. FCC*, 135 L. Ed. 2d 888, 116 S. Ct. 2374, 2385 (1996) (Breyer, J., plurality opinion) (citation omitted)"); *American Library Association v. Pataki*, 969 F. Supp. 160, 161 (S.D.N.Y. 1997) ("Judges and legislators faced with adapting existing legal standards to the novel environment of cyberspace struggle with terms and concepts that the average American five-year-old tosses about with breezy familiarity"); *id.* ("Commentators reporting on the recent oral argument before the Supreme Court of the United States, which is considering a First Amendment challenge to the Communications Decency Act, noted that the Justices seemed bent on finding the appropriate analogy which would tie the Internet to some existing line of First Amendment jurisprudence: is the Internet more like a television? a radio? a newspaper? a 900-line?").

One judge has described his experience thus:

During a trial spanning two weeks on this matter the court was forced to "pass through the viewing screen" into a totally alien world of computer engineering and business terminology in which the conventional and comfortable concepts of "tangible" and "intanto accept a definition when it is taken directly from a reported case, statute, or government document, than from a book or other "unofficial" source. As you use this book, I am sure you will find other, practical uses for the materials.

Instead of a bulky, loose-leaf format, which is typical for law books in high-technology areas, I have asked the publisher to produce the compendium in a soft-bound format, so the book can be carried in a briefcase or backpack, or left on the desk for easy reference. And, with hundreds of new entries each year,[4] this book will be reissued regularly to make sure that the most recent terms are covered.

While every attempt has been made to be thorough, I am sure there are many definitions in judicial opinions, laws, and regulations that are not included in the current edition. If you know of a definition or discussion that should be included, please contact me directly at the e-mail address below.

Michael D. Scott
scotm@perkinscoie.com

---

gible" no longer have much meaning. Having "interfaced" for some weeks with a mountain of esoteric evidence in this strange world, the court reemerges at long last with its decision.

The significance of the word "Opinion" at the top of this decision takes on new meaning as the undersigned judge reflects upon his bruising encounter on the other side of the screen with the assorted Floppies, Stick-Figures, CPU's, CRT's, BIG's, PIX's, WMK's, RIP's and BITBLT's that exist in a new dimension involving "real time" in that dark and shadowy realm. As the evidence indicates, these strange creatures are wont to converse in "C-Language" over an Ethernet using "source codes" and "object codes" to "rasterize" into being "true fonts" with merged text and graphics wondrous to behold.

In re Bedford Corp., 62 Bankr. 555, 557 (D.N.H. 1986).

[4] "[W]e are mindful that computer technology, and the lexicon of terms that accompanies it, is changing rapidly." *Bernstein v. United States Dept. of Justice,* 176 F.3d 1132, 1140 n.10 (9th Cir. 1999).

Acknowledgments

The author would like to thank Warren S. Reid, principal of WSR Consulting Group, Encino, California, and James R. Black, partner in Perkins Coie LLP, San Francisco, for providing some of the "Annotations" contained in the following materials. Their contributions are noted by their initials ("wsr" and "jrb," respectively) at the end of the applicable Annotation.

I would also like to acknowledge and thank Richard Kravitz, Vice President of Aspen Law & Business, for his support for this book, and Frank Quinn, my editor, for his valuable assistance and helpful suggestions.

How to Use This Book

Unlike most law books, this deskbook is designed to let *you* determine the most effective way to use it in your practice. The content of this book is organized alphabetically, like a dictionary or encyclopedia. Most entries are a single word, but where a phrase is commonly used, the entire phrase may be included. The majority of entries are of the following form:

Sample Entry
(word or phrase)

Term/phrase
being defined

Field(s) of use
(see list below)

Definition
usually taken from an "official" source—court decision, statute, or government document; in some cases, where the term has not been officially defined, an authoritative "unofficial" definition is given

Annotation
a more expansive explanation of the term or phrase

Related issues
a discussion of other issues related to the term or phrase being defined

Cross-reference
to other defined terms

anonymous FTP *(Internet)*
A log-on convention that permits a user to access a computer on which it has no access rights, and to transfer files from publicly accessible areas of an FTP site to the user's computer by using the user name "anonymous" and the user's e-mail address as the password.

Annotation. "In addition to making files available to users with accounts, thousands of content providers also make files available for 'anonymous' retrieval by users who do not possess an account on the host computer. A content provider who makes files available for retrieval by anonymous FTP has no way of discerning who gains access to the files."
Shea v. Reno, 930 F. Supp. 916, 928 (S.D.N.Y. 1996).

Related issues. "To retrieve a file through anonymous FTP . . . the user must search for or know the address of a particular server."
Shea v. Reno, 930 F. Supp. 916, 930 (S.D.N.Y. 1996).
See also **anonymity; ftp.**

However, there are other types of entries as well, such as some important case decisions that are frequently cited in other cases, law review articles, conferences, etc. These court decisions are summarized in the following format:

Sample Entry

(case decision)

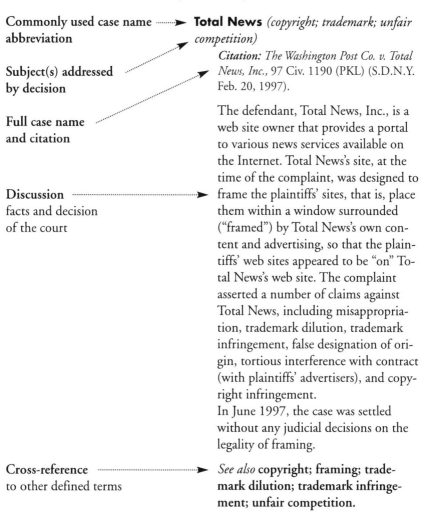

Commonly used case name abbreviation

Subject(s) addressed by decision

Full case name and citation

Discussion facts and decision of the court

Cross-reference to other defined terms

Total News *(copyright; trademark; unfair competition)*

Citation: *The Washington Post Co. v. Total News, Inc.*, 97 Civ. 1190 (PKL) (S.D.N.Y. Feb. 20, 1997).

The defendant, Total News, Inc., is a web site owner that provides a portal to various news services available on the Internet. Total News's site, at the time of the complaint, was designed to frame the plaintiffs' sites, that is, place them within a window surrounded ("framed") by Total News's own content and advertising, so that the plaintiffs' web sites appeared to be "on" Total News's web site. The complaint asserted a number of claims against Total News, including misappropriation, trademark dilution, trademark infringement, false designation of origin, tortious interference with contract (with plaintiffs' advertisers), and copyright infringement.

In June 1997, the case was settled without any judicial decisions on the legality of framing.

See also **copyright; framing; trademark dilution; trademark infringement; unfair competition.**

Other entries focus on statutes, government reports, and organizations. Their format is very similar to the formats noted above.

Fields of Use

Each definition indicates the field or fields of use of the term. These include

advertising
antitrust
broadcasting
business
computer technology
Constitution
contract
copyright
copyright infringement
copyright preemption
criminal
defamation
DMCA
economics
electronic commerce
entertainment
evidence
export
First Amendment
free speech
general
government
hardware
Internet
jurisdiction

law
manufacturing
mask work
mathematics
misappropriation
multimedia
obscenity
organization
patent
privacy
procedure
semiconductor chip
software
taxation
technology
telecommunications
tort
trade dress
trade secret
trademark
unfair competition
video
video game
Year 2000

"A" title *(entertainment; multimedia)*
A software, video game, or multimedia title that performs extremely well in the marketplace.

abandonment *(copyright)*
"It is well settled that rights gained under the Copyright Act may be abandoned. But abandonment of a right must be manifested by some overt act indicating an intention to abandon that right."
Micro Star v. FormGen, Inc., 154 F.3d 1107, 1112 (9th Cir. 1998).

above the fold *(advertising; technology)*
The portion of a web page that appears initially upon loading without scrolling.

Annotation. Advertisements that appear above the fold are generally more expensive than those that appear elsewhere on a web page.
See also **below the fold.**

above-the-line costs *(entertainment; multimedia)*
The portion of a production budget that covers the costs of content acquisition, as well as the salaries of the producer, director and principal cast members/actors. A concept also used by some multimedia companies.

abstraction-filtration-comparison method *(copyright)*
"This method of separating the protected from the unprotected in computer programs is referred to as the 'abstraction-filtration-comparison' method ('the A-F-C method'). This method is a three-step analysis which may be applied to any given computer program. First, the program should be dissected according to its varying levels of generality as provided in the abstractions test developed by Judge Learned Hand. Next, at the filtration stage, the court should examine each level of abstraction and 'filter' out those elements of the program which are unprotectable. This step should eliminate from comparison the unprotectable elements of ideas, processes, facts, public domain information, merger material, scenes à faire material, and other unprotectable

elements suggested by the particular facts of the program under examination. Finally, the court should compare the remaining protectable elements with the allegedly infringing program and determine whether the Defendant misappropriated substantial elements of the plaintiff's program."

DSC Com. Corp. v. DGI Technologies, Inc., 898 F. Supp. 1183, 1190 (N.D. Tex. 1995) (*citing Engineering Dynamics, Inc. v. Structural Software, Inc.,* 26 F.3d 1335, 1343 (5th Cir. 1995)), *aff'd,* 81 F.3d 597 (5th Cir. 1996).

See also **abstractions test; idea/expression dichotomy.**

abstractions test *(copyright)*

"Upon any work...a great number of patterns of increasing generality will fit equally well, as more and more of the incident is left out.... [T]here is a point in this series of abstractions where they are no longer protected, since otherwise the playwright could prevent the use of his 'ideas,' to which, apart from their expression, his property is never extended. Nobody has ever been able to fix that boundary, and nobody ever can.... As respects plays, the controversy chiefly centers upon the characters and sequence of incident, these being the substance."

Nichols v. Universal Pictures Corp., 45 F.2d 119, 121 (2d Cir. 1930), *cert. denied,* 282 U.S. 902 (1931), *cited approvingly in Atari, Inc. v. North Am. Philips Consumer Elecs. Corp.,* 672 F.2d 607, 615-16 (7th Cir.), *cert. denied,* 459 U.S. 880 (1982).

Annotation. "As applied to computer programs, the abstractions test will comprise the first step in the examination for substantial similarity. Initially, in a manner that resembles reverse engineering on a theoretical plane, a court should dissect the allegedly copied program's structure and isolate each level of abstraction contained within it. This process begins with the code and ends with an articulation of the program's ultimate function. Along the way, it is necessary essentially to retrace and map each of the designer's steps—in the opposite order in which they were taken during the program creation.

"As an anatomical guide to this procedure, the following description is helpful:

At the lowest level of abstraction, a computer program may be thought of in its entirety as a set of individual instructions organized into a hierarchy of modules. At a higher level of abstraction, the instructions in the lowest-level modules may be replaced conceptually by the functions of those modules. At progressively higher levels of abstraction, the functions of higher-level modules conceptually replace the implementations of those modules in terms of lower-level modules and instructions, until finally, one is left with nothing but the ultimate function of the program.... A program has structure at every level of abstraction at which it is viewed. At low levels of abstraction, a program's structure may be quite complex; at the highest level it is trivial.

Computer Assoc. Int'l, Inc. v. Altai, Inc., 982 F.2d 693, 707 (2d Cir. 1992).

"Judge Hand's abstraction analysis forces differentiation of the unprotectable idea and protectable expression. The abstraction method also properly recognizes that a computer program contains many distinct ideas.... By separating the program into manageable components, this method eases the court's task of discerning the boundaries of protectable expression."
Atari Games Corp. v. Nintendo of America, Inc., 975 F.2d 832, 839 (Fed. Cir. 1992) (citations omitted).
See also **abstraction-filtration-comparison method; idea/expression dichotomy.**

accelerator *(technology)*
"[A] security device which allowed [an individual] to 'access' certain... computer systems which were also equipped with accelerators...."
People v. Versaggi, 518 N.Y.S.2d 553, 554 (N.Y. Crim. 1987).

accept a certificate *(electronic commerce)*
"[E]ither: (a) To manifest approval of a certificate, while knowing or having notice of its contents; or (b) To apply to a licensed certification authority for a certificate, without canceling or revoking the application by delivering notice of the cancellation or revocation to the certification authority and obtaining a signed, written receipt from the certification authority, if the certification authority subsequently issues a certificate based on the application."
Wash. Rev. Code § 19.34.020(1).

accept a digital signature *(electronic commerce)*
"[T]o verify a digital signature or take an action in reliance on a digital signature."
Wash. Rev. Code § 19.34.020(2).

acceptable certification authorities *(electronic commerce)*
"[A] certification authority that meets the requirements of either Section 22003(a)6(C) or Section 22003(a)6(D)."
Cal. Code of Regs., tit. 2, div. 7, ch. 10, § 22003(a)(1)(A).

acceptable technology *(electronic commerce)*
"...must be capable of creating signatures that conform to requirements set forth in California Government Code Section 16.5, specifically,
1. It is unique to the person using it;
2. It is capable of verification;
3. It is under the sole control of the person using it;

4. It is linked to data in such a manner that if the data are changed, the digital signature is invalidated;

5. It conforms to Title 2, Division 7, Chapter 10 of the California Code of Regulations."

Cal. Code of Regs., tit. 2, div. 7, ch. 10, § 22002.

Annotation. "The technology known as Public Key Cryptography is an acceptable technology for use by public entities in California, provided that the digital signature is created consistent with the provisions in Section 22003(a)1-5."

Cal. Code of Regs., tit. 2, div. 7, ch. 10, § 22003(a).

acceptable use policy *(Internet)*

Abbreviated "AUP." An Internet service provider's policy statement on permissible uses of the service.

acceptance *(contract)*

"Under the UCC, goods are deemed accepted if the buyer (or, we think it clear though we cannot find any case, its delegate) fails, after having had a reasonable amount of time in which to inspect them, to communicate its rejection to the seller. This is a commonsensical rule. The seller is entitled to know where he stands, so that he can cure any defects in the goods. In addition, the rule saves on paperwork by allowing silence to count as acceptance. And it also discourages buyers who after receiving the goods decide they don't want them after all from trying to get out of their contract by making phony claims of nonconforming tender, perhaps when it is too late to verify the claims."

Micro Data Base Sys., Inc. v. Dharma Sys., Inc., 148 F.3d 649, 655 (7th Cir. 1998).

See also **acceptance of goods.**

acceptance of goods *(contract)*

"(1) Acceptance of goods occurs when the buyer

(a) after a reasonable opportunity to inspect the goods signifies to the seller that the goods are conforming or that he will take or retain them in spite of their non-conformity; or

(b) fails to make an effective rejection (subsection (1) of Section 2-602), but such acceptance does not occur until the buyer has had a reasonable opportunity to inspect them; or

(c) does any act inconsistent with the seller's ownership; but if such act is wrongful as against the seller it is an acceptance only if ratified by him.

(2) Acceptance of a part of any commercial unit is acceptance of that entire unit."

U.C.C. § 2-606.

See also **acceptance.**

acceptance testing *(contract)*
"Until a definite trade usage emerges defining the relation between beta testing and acceptance testing of custom software, parties to contracts for the sale of such software would be well advised to define 'beta testing' or 'acceptance' in the contract."
Micro Data Base Sys., Inc. v. Dharma Sys., Inc., 148 F.3d 649, 656 (7th Cir. 1998).
See also acceptance.

access
(copyright)
"[O]pportunity to review the copyrighted work."
E.F. Johnson Co. v. Uniden Corp. of America, 623 F. Supp. 1485, 1492 n.5 (D. Minn. 1985).
See also infringement.

(criminal)
"[T]o approach, instruct, communicate with, store data in, retrieve data from, or otherwise make use of any resources of a computer, directly or by electronic means."
Wash. Rev. Code 9A.52.010(6).

"The technical capability to interface with a communications facility, such as a communications line or switch, so that law enforcement can monitor and receive call setup information and call content."
Office of Technology Assessment, *Electronic Surveillance in a Digital Age,* Glossary (July 1995).

"[T]o gain entry to, instruct, or communicate with the logical, arithmetical, or memory function resources of a computer, computer system, or computer network."
Cal. Penal C. § 502.

(Internet)
"Individuals have a wide variety of avenues to access cyberspace in general, and the Internet in particular. In terms of physical access, there are two common methods to establish an actual link to the Internet. First, one can use a computer or computer terminal that is directly (and usually permanently) connected to a computer network that is itself directly or indirectly connected to the Internet. Second, one can use a 'personal computer' with a 'modem' to connect over a telephone line to a larger computer or computer network that is itself directly or indirectly connected to the Internet."
American Civil Liberties Union v. Reno, 929 F. Supp. 824, 832 (E.D. Pa. 1996), *aff'd, Reno v. American Civil Liberties Union,* 521 U.S. 844 (1997).

(technology)
To link up to a computer system, usually from a remote location.

Annotation (Internet). "It is estimated that as many as forty million individuals have access to the information and tools of the Internet, and that figure is expected to grow to 200 million by the year 1999. Access to the Internet can take any one of several forms. First, many educational institutions, businesses, libraries, and individual communities maintain a computer network linked directly to the Internet and issue account numbers and passwords enabling users to gain access to the network directly or by modem. Second, 'Internet service providers,' generally commercial entities charging a monthly fee, offer modem access to computers or networks linked directly to the Internet. Third, national commercial 'on-line services'—such as America Online, CompuServe, Prodigy, and Microsoft Network—allow subscribers to gain access to the Internet while providing extensive content within their own proprietary networks. Finally, organizations and businesses can offer access to electronic bulletin-board systems—which, like national on-line services, provide certain proprietary content; some bulletin-board systems in turn offer users links to the Internet."

> *Shea v. Reno,* 930 F. Supp. 916, 925-26 (S.D.N.Y. 1996) (citations omitted).

"Any internet user can access any website, of which there are presumably hundreds of thousands, by entering into the computer the internet address they are seeking. Internet users can also perform searches on the internet to find websites within targeted areas of interest. Via telephone lines, the user is connected to the website, and the user can obtain any information that has been posted at the website for the user. The user can also interact with and send messages to that website. Upon connecting to a website, the information is transmitted electronically to the user's computer and quickly appears on the user's screen. This transmitted information can easily be downloaded to a disk or sent to a printer."

> *Maritz, Inc. v. CyberGold, Inc.,* 947 F. Supp. 1328, 1330 (E.D. Mo. 1996).

See also **web site.**

Related issues
(copyright)
"In the absence of access, courts have required a showing of 'striking similarity' sufficient to 'preclude the possibility of independent creation.'"

> *E.F. Johnson Co. v. Uniden Corp. of America,* 623 F. Supp. 1485, 1492 n.5 (D. Minn. 1985) (citations omitted).

"[E]lectronic dissemination—unlike printing—does not involve the publication of copies. As a consequence, copyright ownership is transformed

from the right to reproduce a copyrighted work in copies for sale to the right to control access to the copyrighted work for any reason."
> Office of Technology Assessment, *Intellectual Property Rights in an Age of Electronics and Information* 204 (1986).

(criminal)
"[T]he Secret Service violated § 2701 when it [¶] intentionally accesse[d] without authorization a facility [the computer] through which an electronic communication service [the BBS] is provided...and thereby obtain[ed] [and] prevent[ed] authorized access [by appellants] to a[n]...electronic communication while it is in electronic storage in such system. 18 U.S.C. § 2701(a)."
> *Steve Jackson Games, Inc. v. United States Secret Serv.*, 36 F.3d 457, 462 (5th Cir. 1994).

(Internet)
"[W]ith the exception of e-mail, no content appears on a user's screen without the user having first taken some affirmative step. One wishing to read articles posted to a newsgroup must connect to a Usenet server and select the relevant group. To retrieve a file through anonymous PTP or access a gopher server, the user must search for or know the address of a particular server. To gain access to content on the World Wide Web, a user must know the URL of a relevant site or type a keyword into one of several available search engines."
> *Shea v. Reno*, 930 F. Supp. 916, 930 (S.D.N.Y. 1996).

"To transmit or gain access to Internet content, a user must specify a textual name; one cannot send e-mail without an e-mail address or the name of a mailing list; post an article to a newsgroup without specifying the name of the group; participate in the Internet Relay Chat without specifying a 'channel'; or access a file without its address."
> *Shea v. Reno*, 930 F. Supp. 916, 933 (S.D.N.Y. 1996).

access contract *(contract)*
"[A] contract to obtain by electronic means access to, or information from, an information processing system of another person, or the equivalent of such access."
> UCITA § 102(a)(1).

access device *(criminal)*
"[A]ny card, plate, code, account number, or other means of account access that can be used alone or in conjunction with another access device, to ob-

tain money, goods, services or any other thing of value, or that can be used to initiate a transfer of funds."
18 U.S.C. § 1029(c)(1).

Annotation. "This would cover credit cards, debit cards, account numbers, and combinations of these and other methods of obtaining money, goods and services. The definition of this term is broad enough to encompass future technological changes and the only limitation i.e. '(other than a transfer originated solely by paper instrument)' excludes such activities as passing forged checks. This definition, however, includes the invoices, vouchers, sales drafts, and other manifestations of access devices used between merchants and credit card companies for payment for access device transactions. Thus, any such paper medium would itself be an 'access device' quite apart from any card, plate or similar device that may have been used in creating such a paper instrument."
H.R. Rep. No. 894, 98th Cong., 2d Sess. 19 (1984), *reprinted in U.S. Code Cong. & Admin. News* 3182, 3705, *quoted approvingly in United States v. Brady,* 820 F. Supp. 1346, 1349 (D. Utah 1993).

access material *(contract)*
"[A]ny information or material, such as a document, address, or access code, that is necessary to obtain authorized access to information or control or possession of a copy."
UCITA § 102(a)(2).

access privileges *(technology)*
The scope of a user's right to use a computer system.

access time *(hardware)*
"...of a disk is the amount of time required to physically locate and retrieve stored data necessary for a program instruction (known as a 'disk read'), or to physically locate available, unoccupied space on the disk and write new data in that area (known as a 'disk write')."
USM Corp. v. Arthur D. Little, Inc., 28 Mass. App. 108, 112 n.5, 546 N.E.2d 888, 890-91 n.5 (1989).

account *(technology)*
The login and home directory of a user, generally accessible only with a password for security.

ACLU *(organization)*
See American Civil Liberties Union.

ACLU v. Reno *(free speech; Internet)*
Citation: *Reno v. American Civil Liberties Union,* 521 U.S. 844 (1997), *aff'g American Civil Liberties Union v. Reno,* 929 F. Supp. 824 (E.D. Pa. 1996).
See Reno v. ACLU; Communications Decency Act.

ActiveX *(technology)*
Technology developed by Microsoft that permits browsers to incorporate and execute other software applications seamlessly.

actual damages *(copyright)*
"The copyright owner is entitled to recover the actual damages suffered by him or her as a result of the infringement...."
17 U.S.C. § 504(b).

"This provision requires the plaintiff to demonstrate a 'causal connection' between the defendant's infringement and an injury to the market value of the plaintiff's copyrighted work at the time of infringement."
Montgomery v. Noga, 168 F.3d 1282, 1294 (11th Cir. 1999).

ad server *(advertising; technology)*
Software that delivers web advertisements to a user's browser.

adaptation *(copyright)*
"There is a dearth of both legislative history and case law interpreting the word 'adaptation' as used in § 117."
Foresight Resources Corp. v. Pfortmiller, 719 F. Supp. 1006, 1009 (D. Kan. 1989).

"The legislative history indicates that § 117 should be given a broader reading where the owner of a copy of a computer program adapts it for his own internal use."
RAV Comm., Inc. v. Philips Bros., Inc., Copyright L. Rep. (CCH) ¶ 26,263 (S.D.N.Y. 1988).

"The conversion of a program from one higher-level language to another to facilitate use would fall within this right, as would the right to add features to the program that were not present at the time of rightful acquisition."
CONTU Final Report 13 (1978).

"[Cases] which apply § 117 in a narrow manner are against the weight of recent authority and contrary to the intent of Congress. A better view is

that § 117 is designed to protect software purchasers who make modifications or enhancements to the software for their own use only."
Data Prods., Inc. v. Reppart, No. 89-1291-K, 1990 U.S. Dist. LEXIS 16,330 (D. Kan. Nov. 28, 1990).

add *(Internet)*
See subscribe.

add-in program *(software)*
"[A] program designed to be used in conjunction with another program."
Lotus Dev. Corp. v. Paperback Software Int'l, 740 F. Supp. 37, 78 (D. Mass. 1990).

address *(technology)*
[CANADA] "[T]he location (particular pigeon hole) of the memory from which an instruction or datum is sought."
Apple Computer, Inc. v. Mackintosh Computers Ltd. (1986), 28 D.L.R. (4th) 178 (Fed. T.D.).

adhesion contract *(contract)*
"[O]ne that is drafted unilaterally by the dominant party and then presented on a 'take-it-or-leave-it basis' to the weaker party who has no real opportunity to bargain about its terms. Such contracts are usually prepared in printed form, and frequently at least some of their provisions are in extremely small print. Common examples are tickets of various kinds and insurance policies."
Vault Corp. v. Quaid Software, Ltd., 655 F. Supp. 750, 760 (E.D. La. 1987), *quoting* Restatement (Second) of Conflict of Laws 187, com. (b), at 562 (1971).

"[A] standardized contract, which, imposed and drafted by the party of superior bargaining strength, relegates to the subscribing party only the opportunity to adhere to the contract or reject it.... Such an agreement does not issue from that freedom in bargaining and equality of bargaining which are the theoretical parents of the American law of contracts."
Neal v. State Farm Ins. Cos., 188 Cal. App. 2d 690, 694, 10 Cal. Rptr. 781, 784 (1961).

Annotation. "[F]orm contracts are a natural concomitant of our mass production-mass consumer society.... [A] rule automatically invalidating adhesion contracts would be completely unworkable."
Hartland Computer Leasing Corp. v. Insurance Man, Inc., 770 S.W.2d 525, 527 (Mo. App. 1989).

Related issues. "That the agreement was an adhesion contract... does not lead to the conclusion that it was unconscionable: parties routinely purchase products without expecting to negotiate the terms of sale with the seller and there is 'nothing unusual' in this limitation of damages, it being common in these types of commercial agreements."

Harper Tax Servs., Inc. v. Quick Tax Ltd., 686 F. Supp. 109, 112 (D. Md. 1988), *quoting Bakal v. Burroughs Corp.,* 74 Misc. 2d 202, 205, 343 N.Y.S.2d 541 (1972).

Administrative Law Judge *(general)*
Abbreviated as "ALJ." A nonjudicial hearing officer within a state or federal administrative agency who conducts formal hearings and issues initial decisions on appeals from agency rulings.

ADN *(telecommunications)*
Acronym for "Advanced Digital Network." This term usually refers to a 56-Kbps leased telephone line.

Adobe Photoshop *(software)*
"[A] graphics software package that allows a user to create drawings on a drawing window on a computer screen. Adobe Photoshop also has a tool palette that is displayed next to the drawing window, or may be positioned to overlap the drawing window. The palette is a menu of drawing commands or tools that can be selected by clicking on the icon in the palette for that function. A user may successively manipulate or click on the drawing window and the palette without changing the displayed ordering of these items. The palette will continue to float on top of the drawing window."

Apple Computer, Inc. v. Articulate Sys., Inc., 234 F.2d 14, 18 (Fed. Cir. 2000).

ADR *(general)*
Acronym for "Alternative Dispute Resolution." Any nonjudicial method for settling legal disputes. The most common are arbitration and mediation.

ADSL *(telecommunications)*
Acronym for "Asymmetric Digital Subscriber Line." A technology to allow for the faster movement of data over regular copper telephone lines between two specific locations. ADSL allows data transmission at 128 kilobits per second and data receipt at speeds of up to 1.544 megabits per second.

advance *(contract)*
An up-front payment for development of or the right to publish/distribute a title (software, multimedia work, web site). An advance is generally recoupable, meaning that it is recovered from payments otherwise due.

Sample clause. "[Commissioning Party] agrees to pay to Developer such advances against subsequently negotiated royalties as are specified in the Delivery Schedule attached as Appendix A within ten (10) business days of written approval of each Deliverable Item. Such advances shall be non-refundable, except as otherwise provided herein. No royalties will be paid to Developer under this or any other agreement between [Commissioning Party] and Developer with respect to the Product Design or the product based thereon until such royalties exceed the aggregate amount of the advances paid to Developer pursuant to all such agreements."

advance against royalties *(contract)*
See advance.

Advanced Intelligent Network *(criminal)*
Abbreviated as "AIN." "A system of interrelated computer-based components linked to a switched or wireless telecommunications network that provides a framework for services, e.g., call forwarding, credit card authentication, personal identification numbers, speed dialing, voice-dialing, etc."
Office of Technology Assessment, *Electronic Surveillance in a Digital Age,* Glossary (July 1995).

advertisement *(business; electronic commerce)*
"Advertisement on the Internet can reach as many as 10,000 Internet users within Connecticut alone. Further, once posted on the Internet, unlike television and radio advertising, the advertisement is available continuously to any Internet user."
Inset Sys., Inc. v. Instruction Set, Inc., 937 F. Supp. 161, 165 (D. Conn. 1996).

advertising *(business)*
The announcement of the availability of goods or services in a medium of mass communication directed at all or part of the actual or potential customers to induce them to buy the goods or services.

advertising copy *(business)*
The text of an advertisement.

AFAIK *(Internet)*
Abbreviation in electronic messages for "As Far As I Know."

affiliate *(electronic commerce)*
A web site that directs a user to an e-commerce site in exchange for a percentage of any purchases by that user.

affiliate label program *(business)*
A distribution arrangement whereby a software publisher markets the products of a developer under an exclusive arrangement. Generally, the developer is responsible for inventory costs, and some or all of the marketing costs.

age verification *(electronic commerce)*
A procedure for web site owners to verify the age of those requesting access to a web site or portions of a web site. Generally used before allowing users access to web sites containing adult-oriented materials.

Annotation. "The problem of age verification differs for different uses of the Internet. The District Court categorically determined that there 'is no effective way to determine the identity or the age of a user who is accessing material through e-mail, mail exploders, newsgroups or chat rooms.' The Government offered no evidence that there was a reliable way to screen recipients and participants in such fora for age. Moreover, even if it were technologically feasible to block minors' access to newsgroups and chat rooms containing discussions of art, politics or other subjects that potentially elicit 'indecent' or 'patently offensive' contributions, it would not be possible to block their access to that material and 'still allow them access to the remaining content, even if the overwhelming majority of that content was not indecent.'"
Reno v. American Civil Liberties Union, 521 U.S. 844, 856, 117 S. Ct. 2329, 2336-37 (1997), *quoting American Civil Liberties Union v. Reno,* 929 F. Supp. 824, 845, 846 (E.D. Pa. 1996).
See also **verification.**

agent
(entertainment)
One who acts by mutual consent for the benefit of another or represents the interests of another.
(software)
Also called "Intelligent Agent." A software program containing artificial in-

telligence that performs certain functions for a user, such as searches, and reports back to the user when it has completed the function. *See also* **electronic agent; software agent.**

aggrieved party *(contract)*
"[A] party entitled to a remedy for breach of contract."
UCITA §102(a)(3).

agreement *(contract)*
"[T]he bargain of the parties in fact as found in their language or by implication from other circumstances including course of dealing or usage of trade or course of performance as provided in this Act.... Whether an agreement has legal consequences is determined by the provisions of this Act, if applicable; otherwise by the law of contracts."
U.C.C. § 1-201(3).

"[U]nless the context otherwise requires 'agreement' [is] limited to those relating to the present or future sale of goods."
U.C.C. § 2-106(1).

"[T]he bargain of the parties in fact as found in their language or by implication from other circumstances, including course of performance, course of dealing, and usage of trade as provided in the [Act]."
UCITA § 102(a)(4).

algorithm
(copyright)
"A prescribed set of well defined rules or processes for the solution of a problem."
U.S. Copyright Office, *Compendium of Copyright Office Practices II,* § 326 (1984).

"The fundamental processes used by a program are called algorithms (mechanical computational procedures)."
Whelan Assocs., Inc. v. Jaslow Dental Lab., Inc., 797 F.2d 1222, 1229 (3d Cir. 1986), *cert. denied,* 107 S. Ct. 877 (1987).

(patent)
"A procedure for solving a given type of mathematical problem."
Gottschalk v. Benson, 409 U.S. 63, 65 (1972); *quoted in In re Chatfield,* 545 F.2d 152, 156 (C.C.P.A. 1976), *cert. denied,* 434 U.S. 875 (1977); *Parker v. Flook,* 437 U.S. 584, 585 n.1 (1978).

"1. A fixed step-by-step procedure for accomplishing a given result; usually a simplified procedure for solving a complex problem, also a full statement of a finite number of steps. 2. A defined process or set of rules that leads and assures development of a desired output from a given input. A sequence of formulas and/or algebraic/logical steps to calculate or determine a given task; processing rules."

> *Diamond v. Diehr*, 450 U.S. 175, 186 n.9 (1981) (suggested by the Patent Office); *In re Toma*, 575 F.2d 872 (C.C.P.A. 1978).

"A step-by-step procedure, or defined set of instructions, designed to solve a particular problem or to produce a particular result."

> *E.F. Johnson Co. v. Uniden Corp. of America*, 623 F. Supp. 1485, 1487 (D. Minn. 1985).

"Refer to methods of calculation, mathematical formulae, and mathematical procedures generally."

> *In re Walter*, 618 F.2d 758, 765 n.4 (C.C.P.A. 1980).

See also **mathematical algorithm(s)**.

Annotation (patent). "[A] recipe that contains instructions for completing a task. It can be expressed in any language, from natural spoken language to computer programming language."

> *Universal City Studios, Inc. v. Reimerdes*, 111 F. Supp. 2d 294, 309-10 n.59 (S.D.N.Y. 2000) (footnotes omitted).

"Unfortunately, the term 'algorithm' has been a source of confusion which stems from different uses of the term in the related, but distinct fields of mathematics and computer science. In mathematics, the word algorithm has attained the meaning of recursive computational procedure and appears in notational language, defining a computational course of events which is self contained, for example A2 + B2 = C2. In contrast, the computer algorithm is a procedure consisting of operations to combine data, mathematical principles and equipment for the purpose of interpreting and/or acting upon a certain data input. In comparison to the mathematical algorithm, which is self-contained, the computer algorithm must be applied to the solution of a specific problem. . . . Although one may devise a computer algorithm for the Pythagorean theorem, it is the step-by-step process which instructs the computer to solve the theorem which is the algorithm, rather than the theorem itself."

> *Paine, Webber, Jackson & Curtis, Inc. v. Merrill Lynch, Pierce, Fenner & Smith, Inc.*, 564 F. Supp. 1358, 1366-67 (D. Del. 1983).

"[A patent] claim drawn to subject matter otherwise statutory does not become nonstatutory simply because it uses a mathematical formula, computer program or digital computer. . . . [W]hen a claim containing a mathematical formula implements or applies that formula in a structure or process which, considered as a whole, is performing a function which the patent laws were designed to protect (e.g., transforming or reducing an article to a different state or thing), then the claim satisfies the requirements of §101."

Diamond v. Diehr, 450 U.S. 175, 192 (1981).

See also **mathematical algorithm.**

alias *(Internet)*
A short name, that represents a longer and more complicated name. Often used for e-mail addresses or domain names.

Annotation. "[A] user can avoid disclosing his true e-mail address by developing an e-mail 'alias.' . . ."

Shea v. Reno, 930 F. Supp. 916, 927 (S.D.N.Y. 1996).

aliasing *(technology)*
Distortion of the digital information due to an inadequate sampling rate. In graphics, it refers to the jagged appearance of diagonal or curved lines.

ALJ *(general)*
Acronym for "Adminstrative Law Judge."

Texas Instruments, Inc. v. United States Int'l Trade Comm'n, 805 F.2d 1558, 1561 (Fed. Cir. 1986); *In re Certain Personal Computers and Components Thereof,* 224 U.S.P.Q. (BNA) 270, 271 n.1 (U.S. Int'l Trade Comm'n 1984).

See also **Administrative Law Judge.**

allocation of risk *(contract)*
A contractual provision that designates which party (or parties) will accept the potential loss from a particular risk.

Annotation. "The possibilities that a computer system will not meet the buyer's needs and business opportunities will be lost are inherent risks that the parties as experienced commercial entities must be presumed to have known and allocated by their agreement, in the absence of conflicting evidence."

Ritchie Enters. v. Honeywell Bull, Inc., 730 F. Supp. 1041, 1048 (D. Kan. 1990).

Sample clause. "THE SECTIONS ON LIMITATION OF LIABILITY, DISCLAIMER OF WARRANTIES, AND WARRANTIES ALLOCATE THE RISKS OF THE AGREEMENT BETWEEN THE PARTIES.

THIS ALLOCATION IS REFLECTED IN THE PRICING OF THE SOFTWARE AND IS AN ESSENTIAL ELEMENT OF THE BASIS OF THE BARGAIN BETWEEN THE PARTIES."

alpha testing *(business)*
The initial testing of a computer program under actual usage conditions; can be done in-house by quality control personnel, or outside by customers or other testers.

alpha version *(business)*
An early version of an online database or service that contains all of the functions and content of the final version, but still contains bugs and other problems.

alphanumeric string *(technology)*
A sequence of letters of the alphabet (alphabetic), and numerals (numeric), or a combination of the two, plus other characters.

alt *(Internet)*
Abbreviation for "**alt**ernative." Refers to a type of newsgroup that can be created by anyone without having to be voted on, as is done with standard newsgroups. Alt newsgroups include every type of topic from noteworthy to frivolous and notorious.

alt text *(advertising; technology)*
Text that appears while a banner is loading or when a cursor moves over a banner.

Altai *(copyright)*
Citation: *Computer Associates International, Inc. v. Altai, Inc.,* 982 F.2d 693 (2d Cir. 1992).

This is the first case to clearly articulate the abstractions test (also known as the "abstraction-filtration-comparison method"), which is now used by most courts in evaluating software copyright infringement cases.
See also **abstraction-filtration-comparison method; abstractions test; idea/expression dichotomy.**

altered *(criminal)*
"[B]y issuing commands to the software which changed the instructions to the hardware, taking it off its normal course of action and shutting down the phone lines, defendant 'altered' a computer program...."
People v. Versaggi, 518 N.Y.S.2d 553, 557 (N.Y. Crim. 1987).

alternative dispute resolution *(general)*
Abbreviated as "ADR." *See* ADR.

ambiguous *(contract)*
"A contract is considered ambiguous if it is reasonably susceptible to more than one construction."
In re Sentry Data, Inc., 87 B.R. 943, 948 (Bankr. N.D. Ill. 1988).

America Online *(Internet)*
Abbreviated as "AOL."

"[A]n Internet service provider located in the Eastern District of Virginia."
America Online, Inc. v. IMS, 24 F. Supp. 2d 548, 549 (E.D. Va. 1998).

American Civil Liberties Union *(organization)*
Abbreviated as "ACLU."

"...is a national civil rights organization. The ACLU maintains a Web site on which it posts civil liberties information and resources, including material about art censorship, obscenity law, discrimination against lesbians and gays, and reproductive choice."
American Library Ass'n v. Pataki, 969 F. Supp. 160, 162 (S.D.N.Y. 1997).

Annotation. The ACLU was the lead plaintiff in the 1996 challenge to the Communications Decency Act, which resulted in the U.S. Supreme Court decision in *Reno v. ACLU,* 521 U.S. 844 (1997). Located at <www.aclu.org>.

American Registry for Internet Numbers *(organization)*
Abbreviated "ARIN." A nonprofit organization established to manage the allocation of Internet Protocol (IP) numbers for the areas currently served by the InterNIC's Registration Services—the Americas, the Caribbean, and sub-Saharan Africa. Located at <http://www.arin.net>.

analog(ue) *(technology)*
A type of signal characterized by a continuous, wavelike transmission, such as sound waves. An analog process seeks to produce an exact replica of the original signal. Analog signals can be converted to digital signals.

analog computer *(hardware)*
"Equipment that can, in the form of one or more continuous variables, accept data, process data, and provide output of data."
15 C.F.R. Part 379 (1988), Supp. 3, Advisory Note 12, at 385.

analog linear video *(technology)*
The traditional, linear storage format used on videotapes and laser discs.

analog modem *(hardware)*
A device that can be connected to standard telephone lines to send information between two computers.

analog recording *(technology)*
Recording of audio and/or visual content onto a magnetic tape or other analog media.

Annotation. "With analog recording each successive generation of copies suffers from an increasingly pronounced degradation in sound quality." *Recording Indus. Ass'n of America v. Diamond Multimedia Sys., Inc.,* 180 F.3d 1072, 1073 (9th Cir. 1999).

analog-to-digital converter *(hardware)*
A hardware device that allows a digital computer to use analog input, usually the output of laboratory instruments.

analog transmission *(technology)*
A method of communication that employs a continuous signal varied by amplification.

analytic dissection *(copyright)*
A procedure for analyzing a work for alleged copyright infringement, where the plaintiff's work is analyzed to determine which elements of that work are copyrightable, and then those elements are compared to the defendant's work to determine whether there are substantial similarities between the copyrightable elements and defendant's work.

Related issues. "Summary judgment is particularly appropriate where the idea and expression are inseparable or where analytic dissection determines that all similarities arise from standard elements derived from a common idea." *Interactive Networks, Inc. v. NTN Comm., Inc.,* 875 F. Supp. 1398, 1403 (N.D. Cal. 1995) (citations omitted).

animation *(multimedia)*
The process of creating moving images from drawings or three-dimensional objects recorded frame-by-frame, which provides the illusion of motion when played at normal speed.

anonymity *(Internet)*
The ability of Internet users to use the Internet without providing their name and other personal information about themselves. This feature is often used by political dissidents, corporate whistleblowers, and abused spouses or children to hide their identity and protect themselves from reprisals.

Annotation. "Anonymity is important to Internet users who seek to access sensitive information...."
American Civil Liberties Union v. Reno, 929 F. Supp. 824, 848 (E.D. Pa. 1996), *aff'd, Reno v. American Civil Liberties Union,* 521 U.S. 844 (1997).

"Many usernames are pseudonyms, known as 'handles,' which provide users with a distinct online identity and preserve anonymity."
American Library Association v. Pataki, 969 F. Supp. 160, 165 (S.D.N.Y. 1997).

"The username and e-mail address are the only indicators of a user's identity; generally speaking, neither datum discloses a party's age or geographic location."
American Library Association v. Pataki, 969 F. Supp. 160, 165 (S.D.N.Y. 1997).

Related issues. "Role playing and adopting assumed identities is common in on-line communities."
United States v. Baker, 890 F. Supp. 1375, 1386 n.17 (E.D. Mich. 1995).
See also **anonymous FTP.**

anonymous FTP *(Internet)*
A log-on convention that permits a user to access a computer on which it has no access rights, and to transfer files from publicly accessible areas of an FTP site to the user's computer by using the user name "anonymous" and the user's e-mail address as the password.

Annotation. "In addition to making files available to users with accounts, thousands of content providers also make files available for 'anonymous' retrieval by users who do not possess an account on the host computer. A content provider who makes files available for retrieval by anonymous FTP has no way of discerning who gains access to the files."
Shea v. Reno, 930 F. Supp. 916, 928 (S.D.N.Y. 1996).

"A content provider who makes files available on an anonymous FTP...has no way of knowing the identify of other participants who will have access to those servers."
Shea v. Reno, 930 F. Supp. 916, 941 (S.D.N.Y. 1996).

Related issues. "To retrieve a file through anonymous FTP...the user must search for or know the address of a particular server."
Shea v. Reno, 930 F. Supp. 916, 930 (S.D.N.Y. 1996).
See also **anonymity; ftp.**

anonymous remailer *(Internet)*

A computer programmed to serve as a relay station for electronic mail messages. Identifying information on the original message is removed and the message is then forwarded anonymously to its intended destination.

"[A] server that purges identifying information from a communication before forwarding it to its destination."
Shea v. Reno, 930 F. Supp. 916, 927 (S.D.N.Y. 1997).

Annotation. In general, posting a message to a Usenet newsgroup carries with it much less privacy than we expect. Even though a message may appear in the newsgroup for only a matter of days, some current Internet search engines, such as Deja News, permit searches of Usenet messages over the past several years. The results of these searches can list and show every message sent from a particular e-mail address. It would be easy to imagine sensitive situations in which Usenet participants' written views on controversial topics could be used against them years after they were posted.

Similar concerns may be shared by persons who participate in support groups via e-mail. Participants in such groups must send and receive e-mail messages to and from each other, but given the sensitive topics discussed, they may wish to retain their anonymity.

Simple methods of hiding the source of a message, such as configuring an e-mail or news reader computer program to provide an anonymous "return to" address, are ineffective, as the Internet message delivery system adds a "header" to each message that includes information regarding the source of the message.

However, an anonymous remailer can be used to hide this source information. The anonymous remailer will strip the return address information from a message, add a computer-generated code as a return address, then remail the message from its own server. The effect of this is that the recipient receives a message from an anonymous user name at the anonymous remailer's domain. In many cases, the anonymous remailer maintains the original return address information so that return mail may be forwarded to the original sender.

Using an anonymous remailer provides a greater degree of anonymity than sending a standard Usenet message, but it is not foolproof. The operator of a well-known anonymous remailer in Finland was forced by Finnish police and court order to disclose the identity of a user in connection with litigation involving the Church of Scientology. The user allegedly sent messages to newsgroups that included materials infringing copyrights held by the Church of Scientology.

For additional security, messages may be forwarded from one anonymous remailer to another, or several, before delivery to its ultimate addressee. Messages can also be encrypted in layers so that in each step along the chain of anonymous remailers only the next recipient is known. While still not foolproof, the discovery of a particular sender's identity could require disclosure by multiple anonymous remailers. In the alternative, anonymous remailers that do not retain any of the original message information can provide an even higher level of security. Discarding the original message information, however, precludes return mail to an anonymous sender or assignment of the same anonymous address to a sender's subsequent messages.

It should be noted that if an anonymous remailer is used, senders should disable any automatic signature feature in their e-mail programs. All of the precautions of a carefully sent anonymous message may be useless if the body of the message includes the sender's name, e-mail address or other information.

A list of anonymous remailers can be found at Ralph Levien's web site at <http://http.cs.berkeley.edu/~raph/remailer-list.html>. (jrb)

anonymous work *(copyright)*
"[A] work on the copies or phonorecords of which no natural person is identified as author."
U.S. Copyright Act, 17 U.S.C. § 101.

ANSI *(organization)*
Acronym for "American National Standards Institute." ANSI coordinates the U.S. private sector's voluntary standardization efforts. Its primary goal is to enhance U.S. global competitiveness by facilitating voluntary consensus standards. ANSI represents the interests of its nearly 1,400 company, organization, government agency, institutional and international members. ANSI does not itself develop American National Standards ("ANS"), but facilitates development by establishing a consensus among qualified groups.

anticipation *(patent)*
"[A] patent law term of art, means disclosure in the prior art of something substantially identical to the claimed invention."
Environmental Instruments, Inc. v. Sutron Corp., 688 F. Supp. 206, 214 (E.D. Va. 1988).

"It is well settled that a claim is anticipated if each and every limitation is found either expressly or inherently in a single prior art reference."
Celeritas Technologies, Ltd., v. Rockwell Int'l Corp., 150 F.3d 1354, 1361 (Fed. Cir. 1998).

Annotation. "Finding a patent 'anticipated' by a disclosure in the prior art results in the invalidation of the patent."
Environmental Instruments, Inc. v. Sutron Corp., 688 F. Supp. 206, 214 (E.D. Va. 1988).

"A patent is anticipated in the prior art 'only if each and every element as set forth in the claim is found, either expressly or inherently described, in a single prior art reference.'"
Environmental Instruments, Inc. v. Sutron Corp., 688 F. Supp. 206, 214 (E.D. Va. 1988) (citation omitted).

AOL *(Internet)*
Acronym for "American Online, Inc."

"The initials 'AOL' have been a registered trademark and service mark of America Online since 1996; AOL has used 'AOL' as a trademark and service mark to identify its products in various forms since 1989."
America Online, Inc. v. IMS, 24 F. Supp. 2d 548, 551 (E.D. Va. 1998).

AP *(organization)*
Acronym for "Associated Press." A major international news organization.

API *(software)*
Acronym for "Application Programming Interface." A set of subroutines that acts as an interface between an application program and the operating system, and which can be called by an application program to perform a specific function.
See **application programming interface(s).**

APNIC *(organization)*
Acronym for "Asia-Pacific Network Information Center."
See **Asia-Pacific Network Information Center.**

applet *(Internet; software)*
A small software application embedded in an HTML web page, which contains restrictions on access to certain network resources to prevent viruses and other potentially destructive programs from being introduced to a

computer system, and which are downloaded and run by a user on an "as needed" basis.

application(s) *(software)*
"[S]oftware programs . . . that perform specific user-oriented tasks."
> *United States v. Microsoft Corp.*, 65 F. Supp. 2d 1, 4 (D.D.C. 1999) (Finding of Fact 2).

Related issues. "Some Web resources are in the form of applications that provide functionality through a user's PC system but actually execute on a server."
> *United States v. Microsoft Corp.*, 65 F. Supp. 2d 1, 5 (D.D.C. 1999) (Finding of Fact 12).

See also **application software.**

application program(s) *(software)*
"[P]rograms that permit a user to perform some particular task such as word processing, database management, or spreadsheet calculations, or that permit a user to play video games."
> *Lotus Dev. Corp. v. Paperback Software Int'l,* 740 F. Supp. 37, 43 (D. Mass. 1990).

"In order to put the computer to a specific task . . . the user needs an application program. . . . Application programs must be keyed to a particular system software and work within that system's framework or environment to carry out a specific application or task, e.g., word processing, accounting, and charting."
> *Apple Computer, Inc. v. Microsoft Corp.,* 759 F. Supp. 1444, 1447 (N.D. Cal. 1991).

"[P]erform a task or set of tasks for the computer user, such as payroll accounting, data base operation, or word processing."
> *Computer Assocs. Int'l, Inc. v. Altai, Inc.,* 3 Computer Cas. (CCH) ¶ 46,505, (E.D.N.Y. 1991), *aff'd,* 982 F.2d 693 (2d Cir. 1992).

"[O]ne that directs the computer to perform specific functions the customer needs, for example, a payroll program."
> *Bruffey Contracting Co. v. Burroughs Corp.,* 522 F. Supp. 769, 770 n.1 (D. Md. 1981).

". . . usually perform a specific task for the computer user, such as word processing, checkbook balancing, or playing a game."
> *Apple Computer, Inc. v. Franklin Computer Corp.,* 714 F.2d 1240, 1243 (3d Cir. 1983), *cert. dism.,* 464 U.S. 1033 (1984).

"...has a specific task, ordinarily chosen by the user, such as to maintain records, perform certain calculations, or display graphic images. Application programs are normally written in high level languages which are designed to be easily used by the unsophisticated."

> *Apple Computer, Inc. v. Franklin Computer Corp.*, 545 F. Supp. 812, 814 (E.D. Pa. 1982), *rev'd,* 714 F.2d 1240 (3d Cir. 1983), *cert. dism.*, 464 U.S. 1033 (1984).

"[A] computer program which is designed to solve a particular problem; for example, to maintain personnel files or to handle a company's payroll. It is generally any computer program which is not a systems program."

> *Computer Sciences Corp. v. Commissioner of Internal Rev.*, 63 T.C. 327, 329 (1974).

"[T]hey enable the computer to achieve specific objectives, e.g., demand deposit accounting, commercial loan accounting, installment loan accounting, etc."

> *Alabama v. Central Computer Servs., Inc.*, 349 So.2d 1156, 1157 (Ala. Civ. App. 1977).

"[T]he particularized instructions adapted for an individual user."

> *Honeywell Information Systems v. Maricopa County,* 118 Ariz. 171, 575 P.2d 801, 808 (App. 1977).

[CANADA] "[A] set of instructions to the computer on how to do the particular tasks that it is going to be asked to perform. The instructions describe how the computer is to produce specific results in terms of output. Two identical computers may have entirely dissimilar application programs."

> *Continental Comm. Sys. Corp. v. R.* [1982], 5 W.W.R. 340 (B.C. C.A.).

[CANADA] "Application programs are designed for a specific task, such as the playing of a video game, preparation of a tax return, or the writing of text."

> *Apple Computer, Inc. v. Mackintosh Computers Ltd.* (1986), 28 D.L.R. (4th) 178 (Fed. T.D.).

[CANADA] "An application program is designed for a specific task, ordinarily chosen by the user, such as to maintain records, perform certain calculations or display graphic charts. Application programs are normally written in high-level languages that are designed to be easily used by the unsophisticated."

> *Apple Computer, Inc. v. Mackintosh Computers Ltd.* (1985), 3 C.I.P.R. 133 (Fed. T.D.).

[CANADA] "This consists of material programmed to the specific requirements of the user's business and may be prepared either by the user or as part of custom programming service done by experts on the user's instructions."

Clarke Irwin & Co. v. Singer Co. of Can., Ont. Div. Ct., Keith J., Dec. 3, 1979, *summarized at* [1979] 3 A.C.W.S. 807.
See also application software; integrated application program(s).

application program compatibility *(software)*

"The ability of customers to run application programs written for one party's operating system on another party's operating system."
IBM Corp. v. Fujitsu Ltd., Copyright L. Rep. (CCH) ¶ 20,517, at 11,392, 11,398-99 (American Arb. Ass'n 1988).
See also application program(s); application software; compatibility; integrated application program(s).

application programming interface(s) *(software)*

Abbreviated as "API(s)."

"These are synapses at which the developer of an application can connect to invoke prefabricated blocks of code in the operating system. These blocks of code in turn perform crucial tasks, such as displaying text on the computer screen."
United States v. Microsoft Corp., 65 F. Supp. 2d 1, 4 (D.D.C. 1999) (Finding of Fact 2).

Related issues. "[A]n application that relies on APIs specific to one operating system will not, generally speaking, function on another operating system unless it is first adapted, or 'ported', to the APIs of the other operating system."
United States v. Microsoft Corp., 65 F. Supp. 2d 1, 4 (D.D.C. 1999) (Finding of Fact 4).

"Theoretically, the developer of a non-Microsoft, Intel-compatible PC operating system could circumvent the applications barrier to entry by cloning the APIs exposed by the 32-bit versions of Windows (Windows 9x and Windows NT). Applications written for Windows would then also run on the rival system, and consumers could use the rival system confident in that knowledge. Translating this theory into practice is virtually impossible, however. First of all, cloning the thousands of APIs already exposed by Windows would be an enormously expensive undertaking. More daunting is the fact that Microsoft continually adds APIs to Windows through updates and new versions. By the time a rival finished cloning the APIs currently in existence, Windows would have exposed a multitude of new ones. Since the rival would never catch up, it would never be able to assure consumers that its operating system would run all of the applications written for Windows."

United States v. Microsoft Corp., 65 F. Supp. 2d 1, 15 (D.D.C. 1999) (Finding of Fact 52).

application service provider *(business; software)*
See ASP.

applications barrier to entry *(software)*

Related issues. "To the extent that developers begin writing attractive applications that rely solely on servers or middleware instead of PC operating systems, the applications barrier to entry could erode. . . . [H]owever, it remains to be seen whether server- or middleware-based development will flourish at all. Even if such development were already flourishing, it would be several years before the applications barrier eroded enough to clear the way for the relatively rapid emergence of a viable alternative to incumbent Intel-compatible PC operating systems. It is highly unlikely, then, that a firm not already marketing an Intel-compatible PC operating system could begin marketing one that would, in less than a few years, present a significant percentage of consumers with a viable alternative to incumbents."

United States v. Microsoft Corp., 65 F. Supp. 2d 1, 10 (D.D.C. 1999) (Finding of Fact 32).

See also "chicken-and-egg" problem.

application(s) software *(software)*
"[A] computer program which is designed to solve a particular problem; for example, to maintain personnel files or to handle a company's payroll. It is generally any computer program which is not a systems program."

Computer Sciences Corp. v. Commissioner of Internal Rev., 63 T.C. 327, 329 (1974).

"Application or customized 'software' refers to the logic and directions loaded into the machine that causes it to do certain things on command. It is the computer component which is designed to solve a particular problem; for example, to maintain personnel files or to handle a company's payroll."

Dreier Co. v. Unitronix Corp., 218 N.J. Super. 260, 527 A.2d 875, 879 (1986).

"Additional programs are . . . written, to be used 'on top of' the operating system, which tells the computer how to perform the finished tasks that a customer desires, whether it be the recording of journal entries, the preparation of a spread-sheet, or the creation of loan documents."

ISC-Bunker Ramo Corp. v. Altech, Inc., 765 F. Supp. 1310, 1318 (N.D. Ill. 1990).

"These are computer programs designed to perform a specific function, generally usable by an individual without knowledge of the internal operations of the computer system. These programs are usually written in a sophisticated computer language, and then translated by the operating system into machine language instructions."

Response of Carolina, Inc. v. Leasco Response, Inc., 537 F.2d 1307, 1326 (5th Cir. 1976).

"...is designed to perform specific data processing tasks."

In re Data Gen. Corp. Antitrust Litigation, 490 F. Supp. 1089, 1098 (N.D. Cal. 1980).

"Such software allows a computer to perform a specific function such as accounts payable or a general ledger analysis of financial information."

Cullinet Software, Inc. v. McCormack & Dodge Corp., 23 Mass. App. 231, 232, 500 N.E.2d 831, 832 (1986), rev'd, 511 N.E.2d 1101 (Mass. 1987).

"... consists of programs designed to perform a specific task, such as balancing an account."

Graphic Sales, Inc. v. Sperry Univac Div., Sperry Corp., 824 F.2d 576 (7th Cir. 1987).

"...consists of these further programs which enable the machine to apply itself to the task set for it."

Jostens, Inc. v. National Computer Sys., Inc., 318 N.W.2d 691, 695 n.3 (Minn. 1982).

"...consists of programs performing specific data processing tasks."

A.I. Root Co. v. Computer Dynamics, Inc., 806 F.2d 673, 675 (6th Cir. 1986).

See also **application program[s]; applications; integrated application program(s).**

application-specific integrated circuit *(hardware)*
Abbreviated "ASIC." An integrated circuit designed for a specific use. These circuits are often custom or semi-custom.

application system *(technology)*
"[A]n 'application system'—which is the use of that information and/or knowledge to build something constructive or to do something."

TRG Systems, Inc., 8 Computer L. Serv. Rep. 121 (R.I. Div. of Tax. 1980).

applicational program *(software)*

"[A] type of program designed to perform specific functions, such as preparation of the employee payroll, preparation of a loan amortization schedule, or any other specific job which the computer is capable of performing. Applicational programs instruct the central processing unit of the computer to perform the fundamental computations, comparisons, and sequential steps required to take incoming information and compute the desired output."

Commerce Union Bank v. Tidwell, 538 S.W.2d 405, 406 (Tenn. 1976).

"[A] set of instructions that will cause the machine to perform a specific task. An example from the banking field would be a program which listed certain information with respect to each installment loan account for which any payment was delinquent."

Comptroller of the Treasury v. Equitable Trust Co., 464 A.2d 248, 250 (Md. 1983).

". . . is designed to perform specific functions once the programming information is fed into the computer."

First Nat'l Bank of Springfield v. Department of Revenue, 421 N.E.2d 175, 176 (Ill. 1981); *Commerce Union Bank v. Tidwell,* 538 S.W.2d 405, 406 (Tenn. 1976).

See also **application program.**

approved list of certification authorities *(electronic commerce)*

"[T]he list of Certification Authorities approved by the Secretary of State to issue certificates for digital signature transactions involving public entities in California."

Cal. Code of Regs., tit. 2, div. 7, ch. 10, § 22003(a)(1)(B).

arbitrary mark(s) *(trademark)*

". . . are common words used in a manner which do not suggest or describe any 'quality, ingredient, or characteristic of the goods they serve. . .' Like fanciful marks, arbitrary marks are also inherently distinctive, receiving the fullest protection against infringement which the Lanham Act has to offer."

America Online, Inc. v. AT&T Corp., 64 F. Supp. 2d 549, 560 (E.D. Va. 1999) (citation omitted).

". . . are generally real words in common usage that do not describe any quality or characteristic of the products with which they are associated, such as 'Apple' computers."

Washington Speakers Bureau, Inc. v. Leading Authorities, Inc., 33 F. Supp. 2d 488, 494-95 (E.D. Va. 1999).

". . . have no intrinsic connection to the product with which the mark is used; . . . consists of words commonly used in the English language. . . ."
Brookfield Comm., Inc. v. West Coast Entertainment Corp., 174 F.3d 1036, 1058 n.19 (9th Cir. 1999).
See also **fanciful mark(s)**.

arbitration *(contract)*
A nonjudicial dispute resolution procedure. Generally, there is a hearing with testimony from witnesses before one or more arbitrators. At the end of the hearing, the arbitrator(s) issue an award, which is final and binding regarding all matter submitted to them.

Annotation. While an arbitration clause in a contract can be useful in many circumstances, it is important to understand the pros and cons of arbitration before such a clause is used. The most often quoted advantages of arbitration over litigation include speed, economy, flexibility, expertise, and privacy. The major disadvantages are the lack of the right to appeal, the inability of the arbitrator to issue injunctive orders, and the general prohibition on the award of punitive damages.

Sample clause. "Any controversy arising out of, or relating to, this contract or any modification or extension thereof, including any claim for damages or rescission, or both, shall be settled by arbitration in accordance with the rules then obtaining of the American Arbitration Association."

Archie *(Internet)*
"[A] remote computer capable of searching directories for file names containing a particular string of characters on FTP servers permitting anonymous retrieval."
Shea v. Reno, 930 F. Supp. 916, 928 n.8 (S.D.N.Y. 1997).

architecture *(hardware)*
The internal design of computer hardware or components. Differences in architecture are a primary reason for incompatibilities between different computer systems.

ARIN *(organization)*
Acronym for "American Registry for Internet Numbers."
See **American Registry for Internet Numbers**.

arithmetic/logical instructions *(hardware; software)*
[CANADA] "These instructions modify data in locations according to arithmetic or logical rules; these are instructions such as, for example, 'add,' 'subtract,' 'and,' 'or,' 'rotate,' 'clear,' etc."
Apple Computer, Inc. v. Mackintosh Computers Ltd. (1986), 28 D.L.R. (4th) 178 (Fed. T.D.).

ARPA *(Internet)*
"An acronym for the network developed by the Advanced Research Project Agency."
Reno v. American Civil Liberties Union, 521 U.S. 844, 850 n.3, 117 S. Ct. 2329, 2334 n.3 (1997).

Located at <www.darpa.mil>.

Annotation. "The Internet had its origins in 1969 as an experimental project of the Advanced Research Project Agency ('ARPA'), and was called ARPANET. This network linked computers and computer networks owned by the military, defense contractors, and university laboratories conducting defense-related research. The network later allowed researchers across the country to access directly and to use extremely powerful supercomputers located at a few key universities and laboratories. As it evolved far beyond its research origins in the United States to encompass universities, corporations, and people around the world, the ARPANET came to be called the 'DARPA Internet,' and finally just the 'Internet.'"
American Civil Liberties Union v. Reno, 929 F. Supp. 824, 831 (E.D. Pa. 1996), *aff'd, Reno v. American Civil Liberties Union*, 521 U.S. 844 (1997).

"Although 'the Internet' now formally describes a collection of more than 50,000 networks linking some nine million host computers in ninety countries, it has existed for nearly three decades on a much smaller scale. What we now refer to as the Internet grew out of an experimental project of the Department of Defense's Advanced Research Projects Administration ('ARPA') designed to provide researchers with direct access to supercomputers at a few key laboratories and to facilitate the reliable transmission of vital communications. ARPA supplied funds to link computers operated by the military, defense contractors, and universities conducting defense-related research through dedicated phone lines, creating a 'network' known as ARPANet.

* * *

"As faster networks developed, most network traffic shifted away from ARPANet, which formally ceased operations in 1990. What we know as

31

'the Internet' today is the series of linked, overlapping networks that gradually supplanted ARPANet. Because the Internet links together independent networks that merely use the same data transfer protocols, it cannot be said that any single entity or group of entities controls, or can control, the consent made publicly available on the Internet or limits, or can limit, the ability of others to access public content. Rather, the resources available to one with Internet access are located on individual computers around the world.
Shea v. Reno, 930 F. Supp. 916, 925 (S.D.N.Y. 1996).

ARPANET *(Internet)*
See ARPA; *see also* Internet.

article *(Internet)*
"New messages...posted to newsgroup...."
American Civil Liberties Union v. Reno, 929 F. Supp. 824, 835 (E.D. Pa. 1996), *aff'd, Reno v. American Civil Liberties Union,* 521 U.S. 844 (1997).

Article 2B *(contract)*
See U.C.C. Article 2B; UCITA.

Article 4 *(contract)*
See U.C.C. Article 4.

artifacts *(hardware)*
Video problems created by digitization and compression technologies. *See also* jaggies; pixelation.

artificial intelligence *(technology)*
Software and hardware that can be used in computer systems that learn, exhibit knowledge of themselves and their environment, make logical inferences, display creativity, or mimic other aspects of human intelligence. Such term includes expert systems, neural networks, natural language processing programs, translation programs, and high-level programming languages.

ASCII *(technology)*
Acronym for "American Standard Code for Information Interchange."

"ASCII language is an internationally understandable combination of control characters and alpha numeric [sic] characters established in the American Standard Code for Information Interchange."
E.F. Johnson Co. v. Uniden Corp. of Am., 623 F. Supp. 1485, 1492 (D. Minn. 1985).

[CANADA] "An acronym for the American Standard Code for Information Interchange. This is a standard whereby a unique 8-bit binary number is assigned for each upper- and lower-case letter, numeral, punctuation symbol, and other character of the typewriter keyboard."
Apple Computer, Inc. v. Mackintosh Computers Ltd. (1986), 28 D.L.R. (4th) 178 (Fed. T.D.).

ASCII Transfer *(technology)*
A file transfer protocol with no error-correcting or flow control.

Asia-Pacific Network Information Center *(organization)*
Abbreviated as "APNIC." A collaborative effort of national Network Information Centers (NICs) and Internet Service Providers in the Asian-Pacific region, which serves as a regional Internet Registry to allocate Internet Protocol (IP) address space to the Asian-Pacific region. Located at <www.apnic.net>.

ASIC *(hardware)*
Acronym for "Application-Specific Integrated Circuit."
See **application-specific integrated circuit.**

ASP *(business; software)*
Acronym for "Application Service Provider."

A company that provides customers with access to its software systems over a network—usually the Internet—for the entry and processing of a customer's data. The customer does not obtain a copy of the software, only the right to access it for the processing of the customer's data.

assembler *(software)*
"A computer program that changes assembly language into the language that the computer operates on directly—the object code."
U.S. Copyright Office, *Compendium of Copyright Office Practices II*, § 326 (1984).

"A program written in source code is translated into object code using a computer program called an 'assembler' or 'compiler.'..."
Sega Enters. Ltd. v. Accolade, Inc., 977 F.2d 1510, 1514 n.2 (1992).

Related issues. "Both assembly and disassembly devices are commercially available, and both types of devices are widely used within the software industry."
Sega Enters. Ltd. v. Accolade, Inc., 977 F.2d 1510, 1515 n.2 (9th Cir. 1992).

assembly language (or assembly code) *(software)*
"An 'intermediate'-level programming language...written in simple symbolic names, or alphanumeric symbols, more easily understandable by human programmers."
> *Lotus Dev. Corp. v. Paperback Software Int'l,* 740 F. Supp. 37, 44 (D. Mass. 1990).

"A somewhat lower level language..., which consists of alphanumeric labels (e.g., 'ADC' means 'add with carry'). Statements in...assembly language, are referred to as written in 'source code.'"
> *Apple Computer, Inc. v. Franklin Computer Corp.,* 714 F.2d 1240, 1243 (3d Cir. 1983), *cert. dism.,* 464 U.S. 1033 (1984).

"A language—verbs, nouns, syntax, etc.—used by programmers to write computer programs. It is relatively 'low level' in that the programmer must keep many machine details in mind. The source language for an assembler."
> U.S. Copyright Office, *Compendium of Copyright Office Practices II,* § 326 (1984).

"A computer program written in humanly-recognizable commands or mnemonics. An assembly language program is converted into machine-readable form by an assembler."
> *E.F. Johnson Co. v. Uniden Corp. of Am.,* 623 F. Supp. 1485, 1487 (D. Minn. 1985).

"The source code form is often translated into letters, numbers, and symbols sometimes called assembly language."
> *Apple Computer, Inc. v. Formula Int'l, Inc.,* 562 F. Supp. 775, 778 (C.D. Cal. 1983), *aff'd,* 725 F.2d 521 (9th Cir. 1984).

"A source language is then rewritten into 'assembly language,' consisting of brief mnemonics as a kind of bridge between human and computer language."
> *Jostens, Inc. v. National Computer Sys., Inc.,* 318 N.W.2d 691, 695 n.3 (Minn. 1982).

[CANADA] "Assembly codes may be said to be an intermediate level of language."
> *Apple Computer, Inc. v. Mackintosh Computers Ltd.* (1986), 28 D.L.R. (4th) 178 (Fed. T.D.).

See also **language.**

assembly program *(software)*
"[A] translation of the programming language into machine language, i.e., mechanically readable computer language. Unlike source programs, which

are readable by trained programmers, assembly programs are virtually unintelligible except by the computer itself."
Data Cash Sys., Inc. v. JS&A Group, Inc., 480 F. Supp. 1063, 1065 (N.D. Ill. 1979).

Annotation. "This type of code contains mnemonic abbreviations for each step and can be read by expert programmers. Once a programmer has access to the source code of a program, he is able to determine the construction of the program and write his own version. For this reason, source code programs are typically compiled (translated) into and sold as object code or machine language, which is not discernible to even an expert programmer, but which is readily usable by the computer."
United States v. Brown, 925 F.2d 1301, 1303 n.4 (10th Cir. 1991).

assignment *(contract)*

An agreement by which one transfers some or all of one's interest in a property to another.

Annotation. "[A] valid assignment vests in the assignee the same right, title or interest that the assignor had in the property assigned. In addition, an assignment does not absolve the assignor of its obligations under a contract."
In re Sentry Data, Inc., 87 B.R. 943, 948-49 (Bankr. N.D. Ill. 1988) (applying Minn. law) (citation omitted).

Sample clause. "The right of Lessee [Licensee] to hold and use the property of Lessor [Licensor] pursuant to this Agreement is restricted solely to Lessee [Licensee] and shall not be assigned, transferred, subleased [sublicensed], encumbered, or subject to any security interest without the written authorization of Lessor [Licensor]. Any attempted assignment will be void and of no effect."

assignor estoppel *(patent)*

"...prevents a party who assigns a patent to another from later challenging the validity of the assigned patent. This doctrine prevents the 'unfairness and injustice' of permitting a party 'to sell something and later to assert that what was sold is worthless.' This court explained that an assignment contains an 'implicit representation by the assignor that the patent rights that he is assigning (presumably for value) are not worthless.' "
Mentor Graphics Corp. v. Quickturn Design Sys., Inc., 150 F.3d 1374, 1377 (Fed. Cir. 1998) (citations omitted).

"...also prevents parties in privity with an estopped assignor from challenging the validity of the patent. Whether two parties are in privity depends on the nature of their relationship in light of the alleged infringement. 'The closer that relationship, the more the equities will favor

applying the doctrine' of assignor estoppel. Assessing a relationship for privity involves evaluation of all direct and indirect contacts."
Mentor Graphics Corp. v. Quickturn Design Sys., Inc., 150 F.3d 1374, 1379 (Fed. Cir. 1998) (citations omitted).

asymmetric cipher *(technology)*
"An encryption scheme using a pair of keys, one to encrypt and a second to decrypt a message."
U.S. Congress, Office of Technology Assessment, *Defending Secrets, Sharing Data: New Locks and Keys for Electronic Information* 176 (Oct. 1987).
See also **asymmetric cryptosystem; asymmetric key encryption.**

asymmetric compression *(technology)*
A compression methodology where compression of an image takes a great deal of time, but decompression of that image is extremely rapid.

asymmetric cryptosystem *(electronic commerce; technology)*
"[A] computer algorithm or series of algorithms which utilize two different keys with the following characteristics:
i. one key signs a given message;
ii. one key verifies a given message; and,
iii. the keys have the property that, knowing one key, it is computationally infeasible to discover the other key."
Cal. Code of Regs., tit. 2, div. 7, ch. 10, § 22003(a)(1)(C).

"[A]n algorithm or series of algorithms that provide a secure key pair."
Wash. Rev. Code § 19.34.020(3).
See also **asymmetric cipher; asymmetric key encryption; public key cryptography.**

asymmetric digital subscriber line *(telecommunications)*
Abbreviated "ADSL." *See* **ADSL.**

asymmetric key encryption *(technology)*
A method of encryption that uses two complementary keys—a private key and a public key. Each recipient has a private key which is kept secret and a public key which is published. A sender uses the recipient's public key to encrypt a message. The recipient uses its private key to decrypt the message.
See also **asymmetric cipher, asymmetric cryptosystem.**

asynchronous *(technology)*
A system in which the completion of one task initiates the next task.

asynchronous communications *(telecommunications)*
A method of communications where data is transferred sequentially with a start bit and stop bit to indicate the beginning and end of each data unit.

Asynchronous Transfer Mode *(telecommunications)*
See ATM.

AT&T *(organization)*
Acronym for "American Telephone & Telegraph Co." The world's largest telephone company. It provides voice, data and video telecommunications services to businesses, consumers, and government entities.

ATM *(technology)*
1. Acronym for "Asynchronous Transfer Mode." A method of delivering multiple multimedia programs over a single communications channel at speeds of 1.5 Mbps (T1 line) to 612 Mbps (OC12). The information is broken into small packets (53 bytes each), which are routed in order to their destination via high-speed cables. 2. Acronym for "Automated Teller Machine." [New Zealand] "ATM transactions involve the use of plastic cards which must be used in conjunction with a Personal Identification Number (PIN). After entry of the correct PIN by the customer using the card, the customer chooses the relative transaction."
Databank Sys. Ltd. v. Commissioner of Inland Revenue [1987], N.Z.L.R. 312 (H.C. Wellington).

attached document *(Internet)*
A binary file attached to an electronic mail message. On the Internet, attached documents often are coded using MIME.

attack *(criminal)*
Actions taken by individuals with malicious intent against a computer system that disrupt the system.

attorneys' fees *(contract)*
The fees charged a client by its attorneys. If provided by statute or contract, the attorneys' fees of one party can be ordered paid by another party in litigation or arbitration.

Annotation. *(patent)* "The award of attorney fees is within the informed discretion of the trial court. The statutory purpose of such award is to reach cases where the interest of justice warrants fee-shifting. Thus the trial court

has broad discretion in the criteria by which it determines whether to award attorney fees."
Brooktree Corp. v. Advanced Micro Devices, Inc., 977 F.2d 1555, 1582 (Fed. Cir. 1992).

Sample clause. "The prevailing party in any litigation or arbitration arising out of or relating to this Agreement shall be entitled to an award of its reasonable attorneys' fees and costs."

attract mode *(video game)*

"[T]he audiovisual effects displayed before a coin is inserted into the game. It repeatedly shows the name of the game, the game symbols in typical motion and interaction patterns, and the initials of previous players who have achieved high scores."
Williams Elecs., Inc. v. Artic Int'l, Inc., 685 F.2d 870, 872 n.2 (3d Cir. 1982).

"...refers to the audio-visual display seen and heard by a prospective customer contemplating playing the game; the video screen displays some of the essential visual characteristics of the game."
Stern Elecs., Inc. v. Kaufman, 669 F.2d 852, 854 n.2 (2d Cir. 1982).

"...in which a set pattern of sequences from the game is repeatedly shown in the video screen. The attract mode serves as a kind of advertising for the game as well as instruction in how to play it."
Midway Mfg. Co. v. Strohon, 564 F. Supp. 741, 743 (N.D. Ill. 1983).

attribution procedure *(contract)*

"[A] procedure to verify that an electronic authentication, display, message, record, or performance is that of a particular person or to detect changes or errors in information. The term includes a procedure that requires the use of algorithms or other codes, identifying words or numbers, encryption, or callback or other acknowledgment."
UCITA § 102(a)(5).

audio computer files *(copyright; technology)*

A computer file containing audio content stored in digital form.

Related issues. "In contrast to piracy, the Internet also supports a burgeoning traffic in legitimate audio computer files. Independent and wholly Internet record labels routinely sell and provide free samples of their artists' work online, while many unsigned artists distribute their own material from their own websites."
Recording Indus. Ass'n of America v. Diamond Multimedia Sys., Inc., 180 F.3d 1072, 1074 (9th Cir. 1999).

Audio Home Recording Act of 1992 *(copyright)*
"The Act does not broadly prohibit digital serial copying of copyright protected audio recordings. Instead, the Act places restrictions only upon a specific type of recording device. . . . [T]he Act provides that '[n]o person shall import, manufacture, or distribute any *digital audio recording device* . . . unless such person records the notice specified by this section and subsequently deposits the statements of account and applicable royalty payments.'"

> *Recording Indus. Ass'n of America v. Diamond Multimedia Sys., Inc.,* 180 F.3d 1072, 1075 (9th Cir. 1999) (citations omitted; emphasis in original).

Related issues. "[T]he Act's main purpose . . . [is] the facilitation of personal use."

> *Recording Indus. Ass'n of America v. Diamond Multimedia Sys., Inc.,* 180 F.3d 1072, 1079 (9th Cir. 1999).

audiotex *(telecommunications)*
"[A] service in which information is disseminated in audio form over voice telephone circuits. Such services range from entertainment services, such as 'Dial-A-Joke,' to sponsor-paid services offering health care and business information."

> *United States v. Western Elec. Co.,* 1 Computer Cas. (CCH) ¶ 46,156, at 61,489, 61,491 n.5 (D.D.C. 1989).

audiovisual display(s) *(hardware)*
Computer hardware that has the capability of displaying visual images as well as providing sound.

Related issues. "If a computer audiovisual display is copyrighted separately as an audiovisual work, apart from the literary work that generates it (i.e., the program), the display may be protectable regardless of the underlying program's copyright status. . . . Of course, the copyright protection that these displays enjoy extends only so far as their expression is protectable."

> *Computer Assocs. Int'l, Inc. v. Altai, Inc.,* 982 F.2d 693, 703 (2d Cir. 1992).

See also **audiovisual work(s)**.

audiovisual work(s) *(copyright)*
"[W]orks that consist of a series of related images which are intrinsically intended to be shown by the use of machines or devices such as projectors, viewers, or electronic equipment, together with accompanying sounds, if

any, regardless of the nature of the material objects, such as films or tapes, in which the works are embodied."
U.S. Copyright Act, 17 U.S.C. § 101.

"...has been held to cover the display of images from video games."
Interactive Networks, Inc. v. NTN Comm., Inc., 875 F. Supp. 1398, 1402 (N.D. Cal. 1995).

Annotation. "The definition demonstrates that 'audiovisual works' inherently requires some type of machine or device and that such machine shall embody as a 'copy' such work."
M. Kramer Mfg. Co. v. Andrews, 783 F.2d 421, 433 (4th Cir. 1986).

Related issues. "It is also unquestionable that video games in general are entitled to copyright protections as audiovisual works."
Midway Mfg. Co. v. Bandai-America, Inc., 546 F. Supp. 125, 139 (D.N.J. 1982). *Accord M. Kramer Mfg. Co. v. Andrews*, 783 F.2d 421, 436 (4th Cir. 1986); *Midway Mfg. Co. v. Artic Int'l, Inc.*, 704 F.2d 1009, 1012 (7th Cir. 1983); *Atari, Inc. v. North American Philips Consumer Elecs. Corp.*, 672 F.2d 607, 615 (7th Cir.), *cert. denied*, 459 U.S. 880 (1982); *Stern Elecs., Inc., v. Kaufman*, 669 F.2d 852, 856 (2d Cir. 1981); *Midway Mfg. Co. v. Dirkschneider*, 543 F. Supp. 466, 479 (D. Neb. 1981); *Atari, Inc. v. Amusement World, Inc.*, 547 F. Supp. 222, 226-27 (D. Md. 1981).

"A knock-off manufacturer could...write a computer program which would exactly duplicate the audiovisual display but which would not replicate the underlying program. In such an event, the registration of the computer program...would be ineffective since it is the audiovisual display which is sought to be protected."
Atari Games Corp. v. Oman, 888 F.2d 878, 885-86 (D.C. Cir. 1989) (citation omitted).

"Nor is copyright defeated because the audiovisual work and the computer program are both embodied in the same components of the game. The same thing occurs when an audio tape embodies both a musical composition and a sound recording."
Stern Elecs., Inc. v. Kaufman, 669 F.2d 852, 856 (2d Cir. 1982).
See also **audiovisual display(s).**

augmented reality *(technology)*
A virtual reality system in which computer-generated images and sounds merge with real surroundings.

AUP *(Internet)*
Acronym for "Acceptable Use Policy." *See* **acceptable use policy.**

authenticate *(contract; technology)*
"(A) [T]o sign, or
(B) with the intent to sign a record, otherwise to execute or adopt an electronic symbol, sound, message, or process referring to, attached to, included in, or logically associated or linked with, that record."
UCITA § 102(a)(6).

authentication *(technology)*
Verifying the identity of an individual or organization. Authentication insures that the sender is who he/she claims to be and that the message has not been modified after transmission, either accidentally or intentionally. Authentication in public key encryption systems uses digital signatures.

author *(copyright)*
"He to whom anything owes its origin; originator, maker."
Burrow-Giles Lithographic Co. v. Sarony, 111 U.S. 53, 58 (1884).

Annotation. "The computer, like a camera or a typewriter, is an inert instrument, capable of functioning only when activated either directly or indirectly by a human. When so activated it is capable of doing only what it is directed to do in a way that it is directed to perform.... The obvious answer is that the author is one who employs the computer."
CONTU Final Report, at 44.

authoring *(multimedia; software)*
The process of developing computer software, an interactive media title, or web site.

authoring system *(software)*
Software tools that simplify the development of interactive media products.

authorization *(technology)*
Determining whether a person requesting some action or access to a computer or certain information has the right to make the request. To enable authorization in a public key encryption system, an additional mechanism must be used, such as bilateral or multilateral trading agreements between the communicating parties.

"Authorization involves two steps—identification and authentication."
U.S. General Accounting Office, *Information Superhighway: An Overview of Technology Changes,* 20 n.9 (Jan. 1995).
See also **authentication; identification.**

automated transaction *(contract)*
"[A] transaction in which a contract is formed in whole or in part by electronic actions of one or both parties which are not previously reviewed by an individual in the ordinary course."
UCITA § 102(a)(7).

auto-responder *(Internet; software)*
An e-mail software package that automatically replies to e-mails with specific information.

auxiliary storage *(technology)*
"[T]he storage from which data are interchanged with the main memory for processing, temporary transfer, or more permanent storage. Auxiliary storage is usually accomplished in some one or more of the following: Large core storage (LCS), data cells, magnetic drums, magnetic disk devices, magnetic tape devices, paper tape devices and punch cards. The type of auxiliary storage used is dependent upon the applications and needs of the customer with reference to the stored data."
Telex Corp. v. IBM Corp., 367 F. Supp. 258, 274 (N.D. Okla. 1973), *aff'd in part, rev'd in part*, 510 F.2d 894 (10th Cir.), *cert. dism.*, 423 U.S. 802 (1975).

avatar *(technology)*
A three-dimensional, animated image that can be used to represent a user for purposes of online interactive conversations.

backbone *(Internet)*

A large-capacity, long-haul telecommunications line or series of lines that carry Internet communications between smaller networks.

backup *(technology)*

1. *(noun)* A copy of a file or data set that is kept for reference in case the original file or data set is destroyed. **2.** *(verb)* The process used to create a copy of certain files in the system (programs, data, etc.).

bad block *(technology)*

Message indicating that a block (a group of characters or records) was found with a number outside the bounds of the file system. May also indicate that a portion of the hard disk is damaged and a system malfunction has been located.

balance of hardships *(copyright)*

"[I]f the correct standard for balancing the hardships were whether the infringer would be forced out of business, then a knowing infringer could construct its business around an infringing product and effectively prevent the legitimate copyright holder from obtaining relief or enforcing its rights."

DSC Comm. Corp. v. DGI Technologies, Inc., 898 F. Supp. 1183, 1195 (N.D. Tex. 1995), *aff'd*, 81 F.3d 597 (5th Cir. 1996).

bandwidth *(technology)*

The speed at which data can flow through computer and communications systems without interference.

bankruptcy *(contract)*

A federal legal proceeding available to both individuals and organizations, which permits relief from or restructuring of debts under specific circumstances. In contract situations, such as licenses, the parties often want to specify what will happen to the agreement if a bankruptcy is filed. A sample clause is reprinted below.

Annotation. The bankruptcy laws favor the debtor over creditors and others with whom the debtor has dealt. The debtor generally has the right to confirm, assign, or reject any executory contract. A contract is considered executory if the "obligations of both the bankrupt and the other party to the contract are so far unperformed that the failure of either to complete the performance would constitute a material breach excusing the performance of the other."

However, under 11 U.S.C. § 365(n), if the bankruptcy trustee rejects an intellectual property or software license as executory, the licensee may either (i) treat the rejection as a termination and pursue whatever remedies are available for such rejection, or (ii) retain its rights under the license for the term of the license and any contractually permitted extensions by the licensee. If the licensee chooses to retain its rights under the license, the trustee must allow the licensee to exercise those rights, as long as the licensee makes all royalty payments as they become due and the licensee waives certain bankruptcy rights it otherwise would have.

The statute also imposes an obligation on the trustee to fulfill certain contractual rights between the licensee and the debtor on notice from the licensee and bars the trustee from blocking enforcement of contractual rights between the licensee and a third party (e.g., a software escrow company), which provide the licensee access to and possession of tangible things needed to exercise the license (e.g., the source code and documentation held in escrow).

Sample clause. "All rights and licenses granted under this Agreement (other than with respect to trademarks) by Licensor to Licensee are, and shall otherwise be deemed to be, for purposes of Section 365(n) of the U.S. Bankruptcy Code, licenses of rights to 'intellectual property' as defined under Section 101 of the Bankruptcy Code. The parties agree that Licensee, as a licensee of such rights under this Agreement, shall retain and may fully exercise all of its rights and elections under the Bankruptcy Code. The parties further agree that, in the event of the commencement of a bankruptcy proceeding by or against Licensor under the Bankruptcy Code, Licensee shall be entitled to a complete duplicate of (or complete access to, as appropriate) any such intellectual property and all embodiments of such intellectual property, and same, if not already in its possession, shall be promptly delivered to Licensee upon Licensee's written request (i) upon any such commencement of a bankruptcy proceeding, unless Licensor elects to continue to perform all of its obligations under this Agreement; or (ii) if not delivered under (i) above, upon the rejection of this Agreement by or on behalf of Licensor. [Licensee shall have the sublicensable right to modify, adapt and prepare derivative works based on such intellectual property [for any purpose] [only for maintenance and support purposes] [only for internal development purposes] [only for maintenance, support and internal development purposes].]"

banner ads *(Internet)*

"[A]dvertisements that are often active links to Web sites in which a product or service is advertised."

> *Digital Equipment Corp. v. Altavista Technology, Inc.*, 960 F. Supp. 456, 460 n.9 (D. Mass. 1997).

Annotation. Currently most banners are 468 x 60 pixels in size. Banners are usually located near the top of a web page and are linked to an advertiser's web site via a click-through URL.

Barker code *(technology)*

"A pattern of ones and zeros alternated in a prepatterned sequence."

> *E.F. Johnson Co. v. Uniden Corp. of America*, 623 F. Supp. 1485, 1494 (D. Minn. 1985).

barrier to entry *(business)*

"[U]nlike traditional media, the barriers to entry as a speaker on the Internet do not differ significantly from the barriers to entry as a listener. Once one has entered cyberspace, one may engage in the dialogue that occurs there. In the *argot* of the medium, the receiver can and does become the content provider, and vice-versa.

"The Internet is therefore a unique and wholly new medium of worldwide human communication."

> *American Civil Liberties Union v. Reno*, 929 F. Supp. 824, 843 (E.D. Pa. 1996) (paragraph numbers omitted), *aff'd, Reno v. American Civil Liberties Union*, 521 U.S. 844 (1997).

BASIC *(software)*

[CANADA] Acronym for "Beginners All-purpose Symbolic Instruction Code."

> *Apple Computer, Inc. v. Computermat, Inc. (1983)*, 1 C.I.P.R. 1 (Ont. H.C.) (Canada).

"A rather simple programming language that is widely used with the new micro-computers."
U.S. Copyright Office, *Compendium of Copyright Office Practices* II § 326 (1984).

basic input/output system *(software)*
See BIOS.

batch processing *(business)*
Where the computer is used to process data or accomplish tasks accumulated in advance, and where each task is completed before the next task is started.

"[T]he business of supplying to local customers a computer service rendered upon machines operated by, and either owned or leased by, the processor. The material fed to the computer is derived from a customer's original records, which he may deliver or which the processor may collect. Before such material is so fed, it is categorized according to a system devised by the processor to suit the requirements of the particular customer."
Kaplan v. Burroughs Corp., 426 F. Supp. 1328, 1330 (N.D. Cal. 1977).

baud *(technology)*
Acronym for "bits of audio data."

A measure of speed in sending or receiving data over telephone wires. Baud equals the binary units of information per second. 1200 baud means that approximately 1200 bits of data per second can be sent. 1200 baud is approximately 120 characters per second. *See also* **modem.**

baud rate *(technology)*
Actual rate of signaling (in bits per second). It is used as a measure of serial data flow between a computer and/or communication devices.

BBS *(technology)*
Acronym for "Bulletin Board System." *See* **bulletin board system; computer bulletin board.**

BCD *(technology)*
Acronym for "Binary-Coded Decimal."
Gottschalk v. Benson, 409 U.S. 63, 64 (1972).

"The BCD system using decimal numerals replaces the character for each component decimal digit in the decimal numeral with the corresponding four-digit binary numeral. . . ."
Gottschalk v. Benson, 409 U.S. 63, 66-67 (1972).

Bellcore *(organization)*
Acronym for "**Bell Communications Research, Inc.**" Originally part of AT&T, this computer and telecommunications research organization was subsequently sold to Scientific Applications International Corporation.

below the fold *(advertising; technology)*
That portion of a web page below the bottom of the initial page displayed on a user's screen, which requires the user to scroll down to see.
See also **above the fold.**

below-the-line costs *(entertainment; multimedia)*
The portion of a film budget relating to the labor and technical expenses in producing a film. A concept used by some multimedia companies.

benchmark *(technology)*
"A test designed to evaluate the performance of computer systems, programs and devices. The benchmark evaluates the performance of a computer relative to system specifications."
IBM Corp. v. Florida Dept. of Gen. Serv., 7 Computer L. Serv. Rep. (Callaghan) 495, 506 (1979).

BeOS *(software)*
"[A]n Intel-compatible PC operating system [developed and marketed by Be, Inc.] that is specially suited to support multimedia functions."
United States v. Microsoft Corp., 65 F. Supp. 2d 1, 14 (D.D.C. 1999) (Finding of Fact 49).

Berne Convention *(copyright)*
"[T]he Convention for the Protection of Literary and Artistic Works, signed at Berne, Switzerland, on September 9, 1886, and all acts, protocols, and revisions thereto."
U.S. Copyright Act, 17 U.S.C. § 101.

Berne Convention work *(copyright)*
"A work is a 'Berne Convention work' if—

(1) in the case of an unpublished work, one or more of the authors is a national of a nation adhering to the Berne Convention, or in the case of a published work, one or more of the authors is a national of a nation adhering to the Berne Convention on the date of first publication;

(2) the work was first published in a nation adhering to the Berne Convention, or was simultaneously first published in a nation adhering to the Berne Convention and in a foreign nation that does not adhere to the Berne Convention;

(3) in the case of an audiovisual work—

(A) if one or more of the authors is a legal entity, that author has its headquarters in a nation adhering to the Berne Convention; or

(B) if one or more of the authors is an individual, that author is domiciled, or has his or her habitual residence in, a nation adhering to the Berne Convention; or

(4) in the case of a pictorial, graphic, or sculptural work that is incorporated in a building or other structure, the building or structure is located in a nation adhering to the Berne Convention.

"For purposes of paragraph (1), an author who is domiciled in or has his or her habitual residence in, a nation adhering to the Berne Convention is considered to be a national of that nation. For purposes of paragraph (2), a work is considered to have been simultaneously published in two or more nations if its dates of publication are within 30 days of one another."

U.S. Copyright Act, 17 U.S.C. § 101.

best edition *(copyright)*

"[T]he edition, published in the United States at any time before the date of deposit, that the Library of Congress determines to be most suitable for its purposes."

U.S. Copyright Act, 17 U.S.C. § 101.

best efforts *(contract)*

A contractual provision that requires one of the parties to use its highest efforts to perform its obligations and to maximize the benefits to be received by the other party, although it does not generally require the party to achieve any specific goals.

Annotation. In a licensing or distribution arrangement, the party supplying the product is naturally interested in maximizing revenues. To reach that goal, the supplier wants the distributor to do whatever is necessary and prudent to market the product. This is particularly true when the agreement grants the distributor the exclusive marketing rights to the product.

Many distribution agreements either have no provision directed at the performance of the distributor or have a provision requiring that the distributor use its "best efforts" (or "reasonable efforts"). Unfortunately, in either situation, there are no objective criteria by which the distributor's performance can be judged.

When the contract is silent, a court would be required to decide whether there is an implied duty on the distributor to promote the product. The courts that have addressed this issue have had mixed results.

When the contract does provide for best efforts, a court must determine the enforceability of such a clause, and if enforceable, whether the distributor made sufficient effort to market the product under the circumstances. The courts have little trouble in finding a lack of best efforts when the distributor has done absolutely nothing to market the product. The more difficult question arises when the distributor has made some effort, but the supplier claims it was not enough.

Sample clause. "Distributor agrees to use its best efforts to advertise, market, promote, and license the interactive title in order to maximize sales volume. In that regard, Distributor agrees to the following minimum marketing commitment:

1. To spend not less than $ _____ in print advertising in major industry publications per calendar quarter for the first year; and

2. To include Developer's title in Distributor's annual catalog for a minimum of three issues, listed under Developer's name, name of software package and type of application in a typeface and style at least as prominent as all other listings in the catalog."

beta testing

(technology)
"[T]he final phase of operational testing prior to actual production release."

> *SAS Institute, Inc. v. S&H Computer Systems, Inc.,* 605 F. Supp. 816, 818 (M.D. Tenn. 1985).

Annotation (contract). "Until a definite trade usage emerges defining the relation between beta testing and acceptance testing of custom software, parties to contracts for the sale of such software would be well advised to define 'beta testing' or 'acceptance' in the contract."

> *Micro Data Base Sys., Inc. v. Dharma Sys., Inc.,* 148 F.3d 649, 656 (7th Cir. 1998).

beta version *(technology)*

An online database or service that has been tested, but which requires further testing and fine-tuning before it is ready for release. Beta versions of software are often sent to users (at beta sites) for "real-world" testing.

bias bar *(technology)*

"[A] solid stripe which runs horizontally across an input document to indicate that the form contains an ink used in the printing of the image that is beyond the tolerance of the machine for accurate reading [when it is programmed to do so by the purchaser of the document]."

> *Moore Bus. Forms, Inc. v. National Computer Sys., Inc.*, 211 U.S.P.Q. (BNA) 909, 912 (T.T.A.B. 1981).

Annotation. "The bar is not important if the ink is completely devoid of foreign matter. The stripe or bar is usually in the same color as the color in which the form is printed. It assertedly increases the machine reliability by adjusting the photocell sensitivity to the particular sheet being scored."

> *Moore Bus. Forms, Inc. v. National Computer Sys., Inc.*, 211 U.S.P.Q. (BNA) 909, 912 (T.T.A.B. 1981).

See also **input document.**

billing *(business)*

The size, position, and order of credits in the multimedia title and advertisements relating to the title. *See also* **credits.**

binary

(technology)

"A system of numeration consisting of only two digits, zero and one."

> *E.F. Johnson Co. v. Uniden Corp. of America*, 623 F. Supp. 1485, 1488 (D. Minn. 1985).

"[A] concept and system of reckoning…as simple as turning on and off a switch."

> *Telex Corp. v. IBM Corp.*, 367 F. Supp. 258, 267 (N.D. Okla. 1973), *aff'd in part, rev'd in part*, 510 F.2d 894 (10th Cir.), cert. dism., 423 U.S. 802 (1975).

[CANADA] "…a number system using only two digits, 1 and 0."

> *Apple Computer, Inc. v. Mackintosh Computers Ltd. (1986)*, 28 D.L.R. (4th) 178 (Fed. T.D.).

Annotation. "'Computers come down to one basic premise: They operate with a series of on and off switches, using two digits in the binary (base 2) number system—0 (for off) and 1 (for on).' All data and instructions input to or contained in computers therefore must be reduced to the numerals 1 and 0."

> *Universal City Studios, Inc. v. Reimerdes*, 111 F. Supp. 2d 294, 305 (S.D.N.Y. 2000) (footnote omitted).

See also **binary code; binary notation; binary signal(s); binary version.**

(Internet)
A type of newsgroup article containing encoded binary information.

binary code *(software)*

[CANADA] "[M]achine language represented in numeric form by a series of 1's (the presence of a signal) and 0's (the absence of a signal)."

> *IBM Corp. v. Ordinateurs Spirales, Inc.* (1984), 2 C.I.P.R. 56 (Fed. T.D.).

See also **binary; binary notation; binary signal(s); binary version; machine code; object code.**

binary digit *(technology)*

See **bit.**

binary notation *(technology)*

[CANADA] "...is based on a system having a base 2."

> *Apple Computer, Inc. v. Mackintosh Computers Ltd.* (1986), 28 D.L.R. (4th) 178 (Fed. T.D.).

See also **binary; binary code; binary signal(s).**

binary signal(s) *(hardware)*

"...are composed of a stream of zeros and ones usually transmitted in groups of eight."

> *Secure Servs. Technology, Inc. v. Time & Space Processing, Inc.*, 722 F. Supp. 1354, 1357 n.7 (E.D. Va. 1989).

See also **binary; binary code; binary notation; byte.**

binary system *(mathematics)*

"A pure binary system of positional notation uses two symbols as digits—0 and 1, placed in a numerical sequence with values based on consecutively ascending powers of 2. In pure binary notation, what would be the tens position is the twos position; what would be the hundreds posi-tion is the fours position; what would be the thousands position is the eights."

> *Gottschalk v. Benson*, 409 U.S. 63, 66 (1972).

binary version *(software)*
"A version of a computer program expressed in a language which is based on a two letter alphabet. It results from the translation of source code into machine instructions for operation of a computer."
Infosystems Technology, Inc. v. Logical Software, Inc., 8 Computer L. Serv. Rep. 689, 697 (D. Md. 1985).
See also **object code.**

binhex *(technology)*
Acronym for "**binary hex**adecimal." A method for converting nontext files (non-ASCII) into ASCII files. This is required since e-mail can handle only ASCII files. *See also* **ASCII; e-mail.**

biometrics *(technology)*
Automated methods of establishing identity using one's unique physiological or behavioral characteristics.

BIOS *(software)*
Acronym for "Basic Input/Output System."

[CANADA] "Bios is that series of instructions which can be described as fulfilling the role of taking information into and out of the operating portion of the computer."
IBM Corp. v. Ordinateurs Spirales, Inc. (1984), 2 C.I.P.R. 56 (Fed. T.D.).

bit *(Technology)*
Acronym for "binary digits."
Lotus Dev. Corp. v. Paperback Software Int'l, 740 F. Supp. 37, 43 (D. Mass. 1990).

"Each bit is equal to one binary decision—that is, to the designation of one of two possible and equally likely values, such as an 'on'-'off' or 'yes'-'no' choice. These binary decisions, the only kind that a typical computer can understand directly, are commonly represented by 0's and 1's."
Lotus Dev. Corp. v. Paperback Software Int'l, 740 F. Supp. 37, 43 (D. Mass. 1990).

"[A] single binary digit, i.e., a single zero or one."
Secure Servs. Technology, Inc. v. Time & Space Processing, Inc., 722 F. Supp. 1354, 1358 n.9 (E.D. Va. 1989).

"[B]inary digit."
Comptroller of the Treasury v. Equitable Trust Co., 464 A.2d 248, 250 (Md. 1983).

"The smallest unit of information used in a computer, represented as zero or one."

> *E.F. Johnson Co. v. Uniden Corp. of Am.*, 623 F. Supp. 1485, 1488 (D. Minn. 1985).

"'The smallest unit of memory in a computer,' a bit, 'is a switch with a value of 0 (off) or 1 (on).

> *Universal City Studios, Inc. v. Reimerdes*, 111 F. Supp. 2d 294, 305-06 (S.D.N.Y. 2000) (footnote omitted).

[CANADA] "Each digit of binary code (be it a 1 or 0) in computer terminology is called a bit."

> Apple Computer, Inc. v. Mackintosh Computers Ltd. (1986), 28 D.L.R. (4th) 178 (Fed. T.D.).

bitmap *(technology)*

A data file that describes the color/shade assigned to each pixel that comprises an image.

bitmapped character *(technology)*

"..., whether used on a computer screen or on a dot-matrix or laser printer, is a dotted representation of an analog letter or character image where dots are so close together that when reduced to actual printed or displayed size, they form an image or character without the need to connect the dots."

> Library of Congress, Copyright Office, 53 Fed. Reg. 38110 (Sept. 29, 1988).

bitmapping *(technology)*

"...refers to the technology that allows control of individual pixels on a display screen to produce graphic elements of superior resolution, permitting accurate reproduction of arcs, circles, sine waves, or other curved images."

> Library of Congress, Copyright Office, 53 Fed. Reg. 38110 (Sept. 29, 1988).

"...is a dot-by-dot representation of each character. A different bitmap is required for each size and style of character...."

> *Id.*

See also **bitmapped character; digital typefont; typeface.**

BITnet *(technology)*

Acronym for "Business Information Technology Students Network." A network of computers connecting approximately 560 CREN members in the U.S., including colleges and universities, research centers, and government agencies, for an electronic interchange of information via e-mail.

Annotation. "At the same time that ARPANET was maturing (it subsequently ceased to exist), similar networks developed to link universities, research facilities, businesses, and individuals around the world. These other formal or loose networks included BITNET, CSNET, FIDONET, and USENET. Eventually, each of these networks (many of which overlapped) were themselves linked together, allowing users of any computers linked to any one of the networks to transmit communications to users of computers on other networks. It is this series of linked networks (themselves linking computers and computer networks) that is today commonly known as the Internet."

American Civil Liberties Union v. Reno, 929 F. Supp. 824, 832 (E.D. Pa. 1996), aff'd, Reno v. American Civil Liberties Union, 521 U.S. 844 (1997).

bits per second *(technology)*
See bps.

black box *(technology)*
"[A]n electronic device or computer program that can be inserted in or removed as a unit from a larger assembly and perform some function by a method unknown to the user."

IBM Corp. v. Fujitsu Ltd., Copyright L. Rep. (CCH) ¶ 20,517, at 11,392, 11413 (Am. Arb. Ass'n 1988).

blank forms *(copyright)*
"...such as time cards, graph paper, account books, diaries, bank checks, score cards, address books, report forms, order forms and the like, which are designed for recording information and do not themselves convey information...."

35 C.F.R. § 202.1(c).

Annotation. "The basic principle behind denying copyright protection to 'blank forms' lies in the concern that providing such protection would give the copyright owner undue protection over the idea underlying the form, i.e., there are often very few methods to express the content of a form such as a calendar or time sheet and one individual could draw up these variations, copyright them, and thus obtain a virtual monopoly on such clearly useful ideas as a record of the days and of one's time and activities. Further, the majority of such forms are simple and require little ingenuity to design, so little incentive (protection) is required to motivate designers, while the use (communication) of the form is very important to society."

Digital Com. Assocs., Inc. v. Softklone Distrib. Corp., 659 F. Supp. 449, 461 (N.D. Ga. 1987).

"Although some courts have stated that the meaning of *Baker v. Selden* is that blank forms cannot be copyrighted, this circuit, like the majority of courts that have considered the issue, have rejected this position and instead have held that blank forms may be copyrighted if they are sufficiently innovative that their arrangement of information is itself informative.

"This is not to say that all blank forms or computer files are copyrightable. Only those that by their arrangement and organization convey some information can be copyrighted."

Whelan Assoc., Inc. v. Jaslow Dental Lab., Inc., 797 F.2d 1222, 1242-43 (3d Cir. 1986)(citations omitted).

blanket license *(contract)*
A license that allows the licensee to use a large number of copyright protected works without having to individually license them. This is often used in the field of music, where ASCAP and BMI issue blanket licenses for the use of any musical work in their repertoire.

blanking interval *(hardware)*
The period of time between images on a video display screen when there is no video signal being received.

block diagram format *(patent)*
"A group of hollow rectangles representing the elements of the system, functionally labelled and interconnected by lines."

U.S. Patent & Trademark Office, *Manual of Patent Examining Procedure*, § 2106.02, at 21005 (Rev. 6, Oct. 1987).

blocking software *(software)*
See filtering software; PICS.

blue screen *(entertainment; multimedia)*
A video process whereby actors are filmed in front of a blue background, and superimposed on computer-generated scenery or other materials. *See also* compositing.

blurring *(trademark)*
"...occurs when a defendant uses a plaintiff's trademark to identify the defendant's goods or services, creating the possibility that the mark will lose its ability to serve as a unique identifier of the plaintiff's product."

Panavision Int'l, L.P. v. Toeppen, 141 F.3d 1316, 1326 n.7 (9th Cir. 1998).

board *(hardware)*
See printed circuit board.

BOC *(business)*
Acronym for "(regional) Bell Operating Company." *See* RBOC.

bomb *(software)*
A computer or program failure, often due to a request for a process or command it cannot recognize.

bookends *(multimedia)*
Live-action video appearing at the beginning and end of a computer-generated game.

bookmark *(Internet)*
A feature on web browsers and other Internet software that permits the user to save a list of IP addresses for later use.

Annotation. "A bookmark is used to help users return quickly to web pages that he or she visits often."
  Malarkey-Taylor Assocs., Inc. v. Cellular Telecom. Indus. Ass'n, 929 F. Supp. 473, 477 (D.D.C. 1996).

boolean *(technology)*
A type of mathematical logic developed by George Boole, which is extensively used to perform keyword searches. Boolean logic contains various operators, such as AND, OR and NOT, which can be used to broaden or narrow a search.

booted up *(copyright; software)*
"[L]oading of software from some permanent storage medium, such as a floppy disk or a computer's hard drive, to the computer's random access memory ('RAM') when the software is 'booted up' causes a copy to be made."
  Stenograph L.L.C. v. Bossard Assocs., Inc., 144 F.3d 96, 101 (D.C. Cir. 1998).

booting *(technology)*
"... entails a transfer of the software program from a storage device such as a hard disk or floppy disk into the random access memory ('RAM') of the computer."
  Advanced Computer Serv. v. MAI Sys. Corp., 845 F. Supp. 356, 360 (E.D. Va. 1994).

bootleg *(copyright)*

"[A]n unauthorized copy of a commercially unreleased performance.... [T]he bootleg material may come from various sources. For example, fans may record concert performances, motion picture soundtracks, or television appearances. Outsiders may obtain copies of 'outtakes,' those portions of the tapes recorded in the studio but not included in the 'master,' that is, the final edited version slated for release...."

Dowling v. United States, 437 U.S. 207, 209 (1985).

bootstrap *(software)*

A program used for starting the computer. Booting usually results in clearing the memory, setting up devices such as terminals, and loading software information into the system's memory. The boot also causes the operating system to be loaded into memory.

boot-up *(software; technology)*

"[D]ownloads ... operating system software into ... random access memory."

Alcatel USA, Inc. v. DGI Technologies, Inc., 166 F.3d 772, 778 (5th Cir. 1999).

See also **bootstrap.**

-bot *(technology)*

Contraction of "**robot**." Often used as a suffix to designate something that has been automated. *See* **knowbot.**

bounce *(Internet)*

An e-mail message that indicates that a message sent by that user was not delivered. It usually includes an error code, routing information, and the text of the message that was not delivered.

box swap *(business)*

"[T]ypically refers to the purchase of a new machine and the sale of the old one, is the 'functional' and physical equivalent of an upgrade.... A box swap can also be performed with used machines; for example, with machines leased by leasing companies."

Allen-Myland, Inc. v. IBM Corp., 693 F. Supp. 262, 277 (E.D. Pa. 1988).

bps *(Internet; telecommunications)*

Acronym for "**bits per second.**" A measure of the amount of digital information transferred in one second.

branch concentrator *(technology)*
"[A] central [device] which in effect 'concentrated' the data that was being processed at each teller terminal."
ISC-Bunker Ramo Corp. v. Altech, Inc., 765 F. Supp. 1310, 1317 (N.D. Ill. 1990).

branching *(multimedia)*
Moving from one part of an interactive work to another in response to user interaction.

branding *(advertising; technology)*
The process of familiarizing a large group of online users with a product, service, or company name through extensive advertising and promotion.

breach of contract
(contract)
"If a license expressly limits use of the information or informational rights, use in any other manner is a breach of contract."
UCITA § 307(b).

(trade secret)
"The significance of breach of contract in this connection is that a commercial secret rarely has value if it is known only to one person. Others must be let in on the secret and the remaining secrecy preserved by contracts forbidding disclosure to still others who might exploit it commercially to the harm of the secret holder."
Micro Data Base Sys., Inc. v. Dharma Sys., Inc., 148 F.3d 649, 657 (7th Cir. 1998).

breakout box *(hardware)*
"[A] piece of test equipment that monitors the status of signals of each portion of the communications connector. The signals can be broken, patched, or cross connected. Breakout boxes are small in size, approximately 3″ × 3″ × 1/2″."
IRS Letter Ruling 8721016, Feb. 17, 1987.

brick and mortar *(electronic commerce)*
Traditional commercial ventures in the "real" world.

bridge
(hardware)
A hardware device that connects one part of a computer network to another.

(software; Year 2000)
Software written for the needs of a specific pair of applications that exchange date-sensitive data. This software converts the data (either incoming or outgoing) into compliant or noncompliant formats, depending on the compliance status of an application. For example, suppose Applications #1 and #2 exchange data, and #1 is Year 2000 compliant, while #2 is not. A bridge could be written and inserted between the two applications that will convert compliant data from #1 into a noncompliant format acceptable by #2, and vice versa. For many companies, especially those that get a late start on their compliance efforts, temporary bridges may be the difference between survival and system failure, until a more permanent solution can be implemented. (wsr)

broadband *(telecommunications)*
A type of communications channel offering a high bandwidth.

browser *(Internet)*
"Browser programs process information from Web sites and display the information using graphics, text, sound and animation."
Lockheed Martin Corp. v. Network Solutions, Inc., 985 F. Supp. 949, 951 (C.D. Cal. 1997).

"[C]lient software, such as Netscape Navigator, Mosaic, or Internet Explorer, capable of displaying documents formatted in 'hypertext markup language' ('HTML'), the standard Web formatting language."
Shea v. Reno, 930 F. Supp. 916, 929 (S.D.N.Y. 1996).

"[C]lient software permitting a user to view materials available on Web servers...."
Shea v. Reno, 930 F. Supp. 916, 945 (S.D.N.Y. 1996).

"[C]lient software designed to obtain access to material available on the World Wide Web."
Shea v. Reno, 930 F. Supp. 916, 946 (S.D.N.Y. 1996).

browser caching *(Internet; technology)*
See also caching.

brute force attack *(criminal)*
An effort to break an encryption system and decrypt one or more messages by trying every possible key, one by one, and checking the resulting decrypted message to see if it is meaningful.

BT cards *(hardware; telecommunications)*
". . . check and regulate the various circuits between the cards in a metal cabinet called a frame."
Alcatel USA, Inc. v. DGI Technologies, Inc., 166 F.3d 772, 778 n.3 (5th Cir. 1999).

BTB *(business)*
See **B2B.**

B2B *(business)*
Acronym for "Business-to-Business."

A type of business/web site/technology that focuses on transactions between businesses as opposed to business-to-consumer transactions.

BTC *(business)*
See **B2C.**

B2C *(business)*
Acronym for "Business-to-Consumer."

A type of business/web site/technology that focuses on transactions between businesses and consumers as opposed to business-to-business transactions.

BTW *(Internet)*
Abbreviation used in electronic messages for "By The Way."

bubble *(technology)*
"[T]he area designated on the input document for a respondent to place pencil marks to an array of potential responses [answers] to questions and generally consists of a small circle of some kind to be blacked in."
Moore Bus. Forms, Inc. v. National Computer Sys., Inc., 211 U.S.P.Q. (BNA) 909, 912 (T.T.A.B. 1981).
See also **input document.**

buddy list *(Internet)*
"[T]he brand for a service provided by AOL that provides real-time chat between two or more persons who are simultaneously using the AOL Service. Using this service, members can also learn when pre-selected users are online and available for real-time chat. AOL has been providing this one-to-one real-time chat service continuously since early 1997."
America Online, Inc. v. AT&T Corp., 64 F. Supp. 2d 549, 553 (E.D. Va. 1999).

buffer *(hardware)*
A part of a computer's memory where data can be temporarily stored until the computer is ready for it.

bug *(software)*
"A mistake or malfunction."
> U.S. Copyright Office, *Compendium of Copyright Office Practices* II, § 326 (1984).

"[A]n unexpected problem in a computer program which prevents the program from functioning properly."
> *Infosystems Tech., Inc. v. Logical Software, Inc.*, 1 Computer Cas. (CCH) ¶ 45,035, at 60,287 (4th Cir. 1987).

Annotation. "[E]very computer program has bugs...."
> *Micro Data Base Sys., Inc. v. Dharma Sys., Inc.*, 148 F.3d 649, 656 (7th Cir. 1998).

bug fix *(software)*
"An adjustment that corrects the bug."
> *Infosystems Tech., Inc. v. Logical Software, Inc.*, 1 Computer Cas. (CCH) ¶ 45,035, at 60,287 (4th Cir. 1987).

bug report *(software)*
"A written document which specifies in detail the subjective indications associated with a bug."
> *Infosystems Technology, Inc. v. Logical Software, Inc.*, 8 Computer L. Serv. Rep. 689, 697 (D. Md. 1985), *aff'd*, 1 Computer Cas. (CCH) ¶ 45,037, at 60,287 (4th Cir. 1987).

build *(multimedia)*
The process of premastering a disc. *See also* **premastering.**

bulletin board system *(technology)*
Abbreviated as "BBS."

"[A] bulletin board system (or BBS) is an electronic interface between two computer systems that allows users to download software onto their computer systems."
> *Montgomery v. Noga*, 168 F.3d 1282, 1286-87 n.2 (11th Cir. 1999).

"[L]ocal dial-in computer services...."
> *American Civil Liberties Union v. Reno*, 929 F. Supp. 824, 833 (E.D. Pa. 1996), *aff'd*, 521 U.S. 844 (1997).

[AUSTRALIA] "[A] BBS (Bulletin-Board System) is an electronic forum for exchanging electronic mail, reading notices and features, carrying on unstructured multilogs, and copying programs stored on the host computer. Bulletin-boards are videotext systems that provide quick access to information held in databanks. They can be used to transmit information back and forth. They can be used to provide information to a closed group or an open group. Bulletin-board services are sometimes provided as a free service, but may be subject to a charge. They function as electronic notice boards and as electronic mail services."

In re Application by International Computers Ltd. (1985), 5 I.P.R. 263 (Austrl. Pat. Office).

Annotation. "With an investment of as little as $2,000.00 and the cost of a telephone line, individuals, non-profit organizations, advocacy groups, and businesses can offer their own dial-in computer 'bulletin board' service where friends, members, subscribers, or customers can exchange ideas and information. BBSs range from single computers with only one telephone line into the computer (allowing only one user at a time), to single computers with many telephone lines into the computer (allowing multiple simultaneous users), to multiple linked computers each servicing multiple dial-in telephone lines (allowing multiple simultaneous users). Some (but not all) of these BBS systems offer direct or indirect links to the Internet. Some BBS systems charge users a nominal fee for access, while many others are free to the individual users."

American Civil Liberties Union v. Reno, 929 F. Supp. 824, 833-34 (E.D. Pa. 1996), *aff'd, Reno v. American Civil Liberties Union,* 521 U.S. 844 (1997).

Related issues. "[O]ne person can reach many other users through bulletin board services, newsgroups and numerous other Internet-based means of communication."

Lockheed Martin Corp. v. Network Solutions, Inc., 985 F. Supp. 949, 951 (C.D. Cal. 1997).

See also computer bulletin board; newsgroup.

bulletproof *(technology)*
A system or computer program that can withstand any external forces, e.g., hackers, and recover from any attempts to crash it.

bumpers *(multimedia)*
See bookends.

bundling *(business)*

"At that time Burroughs' practice was to sell the equipment and the programming under a 'bundled' price, i.e. the price for the equipment was the same whether Burroughs did the programming or not."

> *Carl Beasley Ford, Inc. v. Burroughs Corp.*, 361 F. Supp. 325, 328 n.1 (E.D. Pa. 1973), *aff'd*, 493 F.2d 1400 (3d Cir. 1974).

"Bundling in the computer industry is a practice by which a computer manufacturer charges a single price for the hardware and software, and other services provided, along with the sale of the computer system. Included in the single price is the hardware, all software that has been developed, future supportive systems, education services, and, to varying degrees, all future developments in software. This has been the practice in the computer industry since its inception, when there was little software available."

> *United Software Corp. v. Sperry Rand Corp.*, 5 Computer L. Serv. Rep. 1492, 1497 (E.D. Pa. 1974).

"Both parties agree that the lease of computer equipment involved a 'bundled' product, but they disagree as to the meaning of the term.... Graphic contends that Sperry's brochures indicated that application programs...were included with the 90/25 system hardware and the OS/3 operating system at no additional charge and were thus part of the bundled product.... Sperry claims that, in accordance with the custom and usage in the computer industry, the only software included in the bundle is the operating system and that application software is leased separately. In this case, where there are two permissible views of the evidence, the factfinder's choice between them cannot be clearly erroneous."

> *Graphic Sales, Inc. v. Sperry Univac Div., Sperry Corp.*, 824 F.2d 576, 578 (7th Cir. 1987). (Trial court ruled in favor of Sperry's interpretation.)

burden *(jurisdiction)*

"While [defendant] does have to cross the continent to appear in this Court, and this is somewhat 'onerous,' that may well be the price of its agreeing to do business involving the Internet under the circumstances of this case; if one does something that could cause a tort in another state, then this inconvenience should be considered by potential foreign defendants before they act."

> *Digital Equipment Corp. v. Altavista Technology, Inc.*, 960 F. Supp. 456, 471 (D. Mass. 1997).

burden of proof *(copyright)*
"[T]he burden of proof in an infringement case is on the party claiming infringement. . . ."
> *Interactive Networks, Inc. v. NTN Comm., Inc.*, 875 F. Supp. 1398, 1403 (N.D. Cal. 1995).

buried code *(Internet)*
". . . is another term for the HTML code that is used by search engines but that is not visible to users."
> *Brookfield Comm., Inc. v. West Coast Entertainment Corp.*, 174 F.3d 1036, 1062 n.23 (9th Cir. 1999).

See also **metatags.**

burning *(technology)*
Recording data, including music, onto a CD, CD-ROM, or DVD. CD-R (write once) and CD-RW (write multiple times) recorders are often used for this purpose.

bus terminator *(telecommunications)*
Abbreviated as "BT."
> *Alcatel USA, Inc. v. DGI Technologies, Inc.*, 166 F.3d 772, 778 n.3 (5th Cir. 1999).

See also **BT.**

business record *(evidence)*
"[E]mail is far less of a systematic business activity than a monthly inventory printout."
> *Monotype Corp. PLC v. International Typeface Corp.*, 43 F.3d 443, 450 (9th Cir. 1994).

business-to-business *(business)*
See **B2B.**

business-to-consumer *(business)*
See **B2C.**

button *(hardware)*
An area of a computer display screen that, when selected, will cause something to happen. The area is usually within a graphic or icon to designate where it is and what it does.

buyer *(contract)*

"[A] person who buys or contracts to buy goods."
U.C.C. § 2-103(1)(a).

BXA

Acronym for "*B*ureau of E*X*port *A*dministration."
Bernstein v. United States Dept. of Justice, 176 F.3d 1132, 1136 (9ᵗʰ Cir. 1999).

A U.S. federal government agency responsible for regulating the export of technology, particularly encryption technology.

byte *(technology)*

A contraction of "by eight."

"A group of eight bits is called a byte and represents a character—a letter or an integer."
Universal City Studios, Inc. v. Reimerdes, 111 F. Supp. 2d 294, 306 (S.D.N.Y. 2000) (footnote omitted).

"A sequence of eight bits (which allows 256 unique combinations of bits)."
Lotus Dev. Corp. v. Paperback Software Int'l, 740 F. Supp. 37, 43 (D. Mass. 1990).

"A grouping of eight bits."
E.F. Johnson Co. v. Uniden Corp. of Am., 623 F. Supp. 1485, 1488 (D. Minn. 1985).

"Each group of eight digits...."
Secure Servs. Technology, Inc. v. Time & Space Processing, Inc., 722 F. Supp. 1354, 1357 n.8 (E.D. Va. 1989).

[CANADA] "A string of eight digits...."
Apple Computer, Inc. v. Mackintosh Computers Ltd. (1986), 28 D.L.R. (4th) 178 (Fed. T.D.).

C *(software)*
"[A] high-level computer programming language. . . ."
Bernstein v. United States Dept. of Justice, 176 F.3d 1132, 1136 (9th Cir. 1999).

cable modem *(hardware; telecommunications)*
A hardware device that allows a computer to be connected to a cable TV network at much higher speeds than traditional telephone modems.

Related issues. "Cable modems also offer increased bandwidth."
Universal City Studios, Inc. v. Reimerdes, 111 F. Supp. 2d 294, 314 (S.D.N.Y. 2000) (footnote omitted).

cable system(s) *(copyright)*
"[A] facility, located in any State, Territory, Trust Territory, or Possession, that in whole or in part receives signals transmitted or programs broadcast by one or more television broadcast stations licensed by the Federal Communications Commission, and makes secondary transmissions of such signals or programs by wires, cables, microwave, or other communications channels to subscribing members of the public who pay for such service."
U.S. Copyright Act, 17 U.S.C. § 111(f).

cache busting *(Internet; technology)*
Web pages that do not allow a user's computer to store content from that page.

Annotation. There are two important benefits that web site owners achieve by using cache busting technology. First, it makes it more difficult for users and servers to make illegal copies of the work, thereby minimizing copyright infringement. Second, by preventing caching, the site owner will be able to determine exactly how many times users have accessed its web page.

cached *(Internet)*

"[T]emporarily stored. . . ."

> *American Civil Liberties Union v. Reno*, 929 F. Supp. 824, 848 (E.D. Pa. 1996), *aff'd*, *Reno v. American Civil Liberties Union*, 521 U.S. 844 (1997).

See **caching.**

caching *(Internet)*

A technique for temporarily storing digital information closer to a requesting computer on the Internet to speed up access to that information.

Annotation. "Because of the high cost of using the trans-Atlantic and trans-Pacific cables, and because the high demand on those cables leads to bottleneck delays, content is often 'cached', or temporarily stored, on servers in the United States. Material from a foreign source in Europe can travel over the trans-Atlantic cable to the receiver in the United States, and pass through a domestic caching server which then stores a copy for subsequent retrieval. This domestic caching server, rather than the original foreign server, will send the material from the cache to the subsequent receivers, without placing a demand on the trans-oceanic cables. This shortcut effectively eliminates most of the distance for both the request and the information and, hence, most of the delay. The caching server discards the stored information according to its configuration (e.g., after a certain time or as the demand for the information diminishes). Caching therefore advances core Internet values: the cheap and speedy retrieval of information.

"...Caching is not merely an international phenomenon. Domestic content providers store popular domestic material on their caching servers to avoid the delay of successive searches for the same material and to decrease the demand on their Internet connection. America Online can cache the home page of the New York Times on its servers when a subscriber first requests it, so that subsequent subscribers who make the same request will receive the same home page, but from America Online's caching service rather than from the New York Times's server."

> *American Civil Liberties Union v. Reno*, 929 F. Supp. 824, 848 (E.D. Pa. 1996), *aff'd*, *Reno v. American Civil Liberties Union*, 521 U.S. 844 (1997).

See also **cached.**

CAD *(technology)*

Acronym for "Computer-Aided Design."

Annotation. "[A] technology that is widely used in science and engineering. Using CAD systems, engineers may design new products, invent new processes, or even create other software programs that are based on interactions between their own experience and expertise with a CAD system."

Office of Technology Assessment, *Intellectual Property in an Age of Electronics and Information* 70 (Apr. 1986).

See **CAD/CAM.**

CAD/CAM *(technology)*

Also spelled "CAD-CAM." Acronym for "Computer-Aided Design/ Computer-Aided Manufacturing."

Lasercomb America, Inc. v. Reynolds, 911 F.2d 970, 976 n.2 (4th Cir. 1990); *Manufacturers Technologies, Inc. v. Cams, Inc.,* 706 F. Supp. 984, 987 (D. Conn. 1989); *Jostens, Inc. v. National Computer Sys., Inc.,* 318 N.W.2d 691, 694 (Minn. 1982).

"The computer system before us is called a CAD/CAM system, which stands for a computer-aided design and computer-aided manufacturing system. Jostens' CAD/CAM system consisted of three subsystems: (1) a digitizer or scanner subsystem, which translates positional data from artwork and three-dimensional models into computer-readable magnetic tape, which is then fed into, (2) the interactive computer graphics subsystem, in which an image is displayed in three dimensions on a screen where it can be manipulated and corrected by an operator; and (3) the engraving subsystem, where the computer, instructed by data from a magnetic tape, in a process called numeric control, guides a machine which engraves the design on the mold for the ring shanks."

Jostens, Inc. v. National Computer Sys., Inc., 318 N.W.2d 691, 694 (Minn. 1982).

"The CAD/CAM translates information from blueprints into numeric specifications that, at the time relevant to this assessment, were encoded on a paper tape. Upon its completion, the tape was physically removed from the CAD/CAM and inserted into a milling machine."

Plastic Tooling Aids Lab., Inc. v. Commissioner, 213 Conn. 365, 567 A.2d 1218, 1218-19 (1990).

CAE *(technology)*

Acronym for "Computer-Aided Engineering." Computer systems developed to assist engineers in doing their job.

call *(criminal)*

"Any wire or electronic signaling information generated by a human or a computer acting as an agent for a human to set up a physical or virtual connection to transit information to another or multiple users (humans and/or computer processes)."

Office of Technology Assessment, *Electronic Surveillance in a Digital Age*, Glossary (July 1995).

call content *(criminal)*

"The same as 'contents' as defined in 18 U.S.C. § 2510(8) and with respect to any electronic communication, includes any information concerning the substance, purport, or meaning of that communication."

Office of Technology Assessment, *Electronic Surveillance in a Digital Age*, Glossary (July 1995).

CAM *(technology)*

1. Acronym for "Computer-Aided Manufacturing." See **CAD/CAM**.
2. Acronym for "Content-Addressable Memory."

Intel Corp. v. Radiation, Inc., 184 U.S.P.Q. (BNA) 54, 55 (T.T.A.B. 1974).

cancel

(contract)
See **cancellation**.

(Internet)
Remove a posting from a newsgroup.

cancelbot *(Internet; software)*

Program that cancels posted messages, usually spam.

cancellation *(contract)*

"...occurs when either party puts an end to the contract for breach by the other and its effect is the same as that of 'termination' except that the cancelling party also retains any remedy for breach of the whole contract or any unperformed balance."

U.C.C. § 2-106(4).

"[T]he ending of a contract by a party because of a breach by the other party."

UCITA § 102(a)(8).

canned program *(software)*

"...existing, prepackaged programs of general application..."

Comptroller of the Treasury v. Equitable Trust Co., 464 A.2d 248, 250 (Md. 1983).

See also canned software.

canned software *(software)*
"…is prepared for a variety of users and is suitable for its purpose without modification."
Measurex Sys., Inc. v. State Tax Assessor, 490 A.2d 1192, 1195 (Me. 1985).

"…is sometimes called 'off the shelf' software."
Ridder v. Washington Mutual Savings Bank, 2 Computer L. Dec. (CCH) ¶ 60, 063, at 80,265 (Wash. Bd. Tax App. 1989).
See also **canned program.**

capacity *(hardware)*
The amount of data that can be stored in or on a storage device.

card-not-present-transaction *(electronic commerce)*
A credit card transaction in which the card holder does not or cannot present the physical credit card, such as orders placed by telephone or over the Internet.

cartridge *(hardware)*
"A very ambiguous term meaning some form of removable magnetic data storage medium, used along with a fixed (non-removable) medium. It may use magnetic tape or magnetic disk as the medium."
U.S. Copyright Office, *Compendium of Copyright Office Practices* II, § 326 (1984).
See also **storage device.**

CASE *(software)*
Acronym for "Computer-Aided Software Engineering." *See* **computer-aided software engineering.**

cassette *(hardware)*
"A small, self-contained volume of magnetic tape used for data storage. Similar to a sound-recording cassette."
U.S. Copyright Office, *Compendium of Copyright Office Practices* II, § 326 (1984).

CAT scan(ner) *(hardware)*
"A computerized x-ray device which prints out a picture display of the brain and surrounding tissue."
Beckman v. Mayo Foundation, 804 F.2d 435, 436 (8th Cir. 1986).

71

"...produces an image of internal bodily organs without invading the body."
> *Bridge C.A.T. Scan Assocs. v. Ohio-Nuclear, Inc.*, 608 F. Supp. 1187, 1189 (S.D.N.Y. 1985).

catalog *(technology)*

"A set of indices that contain file information and volume identifiers."
> *IBM Corp. v. Fujitsu Ltd.*, Copyright L. Rep. (CCH) ¶ 20,517, at 11,392 (Am. Arb. Ass'n 1988).

cathode-ray tube *(hardware)*

Abbreviated as "CRT." A vacuum tube display that uses a beam of electrons to form alphanumeric characters, symbols, or graphics on a screen.

"[A] typewriter-like device with a keyboard and display screen similar to a television screen upon which the information is displayed as it is sent and received."
> *United States v. Seidlitz*, 589 F.2d 152, 153 (4th Cir. 1978).

"[M]ore commonly known to laymen as a television picture tube."
> *Motorola, Inc. v. Computer Displays Int'l, Inc.*, 739 F.2d 1149, 1151 n.1 (7th Cir. 1984).

See also **display monitor.**

CATV *(broadcasting)*

Acronym for "Community Antenna Television." More recently, used as an acronym for "Cable Television."

"A television distribution system where a single antenna captures television signals and distributes them over a cable network to multiple television sets."
> *Fortnightly Corp. v. United Artists Television, Inc.*, 392 U.S. 390, 391 (1968).

CBT *(technology)*

Acronym for "Computer-Based Training." Training and educational services made available via computer.

CCITT *(organization)*

Acronym for "Comité Consultatif Internationale de Télégraphie et Téléphonie."

"[T]he standard abbreviation for the International Telephone and Telegraph Consultative Committee of the International Communications Union."
> *Secure Servs. Technology, Inc. v. Time & Space Processing, Inc.*, 722 F. Supp. 1354, 1357 n.6 (E.D. Va. 1989).

Annotation. A predecessor to the International Telecommunication Union—Telecommunication Standardization Bureau ("ITU-T").

CD *(hardware)*

Acronym for "Compact Disc." An audio recording format developed by Philips.

CDA *(Internet)*

Acronym for "Computer Decency Act." *See* **Communications Decency Act.**

CDMA *(telecommunications)*

Acronym for "Code-Division Multiple Access." A coding scheme in which multiple messages are independently coded so they can be transmitted over a broadband channel and individually retrieved at the receiving end. Currently this technology is used primarily in cellular telephone systems.

CD-ROM *(hardware)*

Acronym for "Compact Disc Read-Only Memory." This is a general term for compact disc technology used to store and retrieve digital information for use on computers. The term "read-only memory" (*see also* **ROM**) means that the disc can be read repeatedly, but cannot be written onto.

"[A] five-inch wide optical disk capable of storing approximately 650 MB of data."

> *Universal City Studios, Inc. v. Reimerdes*, 111 F. Supp. 2d 294, 307 (S.D.N.Y. 2000).

CD-ROM drive *(hardware)*

"To read the data on a CD-ROM, a computer must have a CD-ROM drive."

> *Universal City Studios, Inc. v. Reimerdes*, 111 F. Supp. 2d 294, 307 (S.D.N.Y. 2000).

CDT *(organization)*

Acronym for "Center for Democracy and Technology." The Center for Democracy and Technology is a nonprofit, public interest organization based in Washington, D.C. The center's mission is to develop and advocate public policies that advance democratic values and constitutional civil liberties in new computer and communications technologies. Located at <http://www.cdt.org>.

cell *(software)*

One discrete element in a two-dimensional array such as a spreadsheet.

Center for Democracy and Technology *(organization)*
Abbreviated as "CDT." *See* CDT.

central office *(telecommunications)*
"In telephone operations, the facility housing the switching system and related equipment that provides telephone services for customers in the immediate geographical area."
> Office of Technology Assessment, *Electronic Surveillance in a Digital Age,* Glossary (July 1995).

central processing unit *(hardware)*
Also abbreviated "CPU."

"...contains the electronic circuits that control the computer and perform the arithmetic and logical functions...."
> *Lotus Dev. Corp. v. Paperback Software Int'l,* 740 F. Supp. 37, 43 (D. Mass. 1990).

"...perform[s] the main logic and memory functions for the system."
> *In re Chatfield,* 545 F.2d 152, 153 n.1 (C.C.P.A. 1976).

"[G]enerally where most of the logical functions and calculations are performed."
> *Telex Corp. v. IBM Corp.,* 367 F. Supp. 258, 275 (N.D. Okla. 1973), *aff'd in part, rev'd in part,* 510 F.2d 894 (10th Cir.), *cert. dism.,* 423 U.S. 802 (1975).

"[T]he specialized integrated circuit that executes binary programs. The CPU does the primary calculations required of all programs and shifts answers to other parts of the system depending upon the requirements of the program controlling it."
> *Apple Computer, Inc. v. Franklin Computer Corp.,* 545 F. Supp. 812, 813 (E.D. Pa. 1982), *rev'd,* 714 F.2d 1240 (3d Cir. 1983), *cert. dism.,* 464 U.S. 1033 (1984).

"...can only follow instructions written in object code."
> *Apple Computer, Inc. v. Franklin Computer Corp.,* 714 F.2d 1240 (3d Cir. 1983), *cert. dism.,* 464 U.S. 1033 (1984).

"A 'digital computer is conveniently thought of functionally as composed of five elements: Input, Storage (sometimes called Memory), Control, Logic (sometimes called Arithmetic), and Output. Control and Logic are sometimes referred to jointly as the Central Processing Unit (CPU).'"
> *Computer Sys. of Am. v. Western Reserve Life Assur. Co. of Ohio,* 19 Mass. App. 430, 475 N.E.2d 745, 747 (1985).

[CANADA] "The CPU controls the operations of the computer, executes the instructions in the systems software and application programs and processes the data."

> *Clarke Irwin & Co. v. Singer Co. of Can.*, Ont. Div. Ct., Keith J., December 3,1979, *summarized at* [1979] 3 A.C.W.S. 807.

[CANADA] "It is the CPU which carries out the arithmetic and logic functions (e.g.: addition, subtraction, comparison of data presented as two fields of numbers)."

> *Apple Computer, Inc. v. Mackintosh Computers Ltd.* (1986), 28 D.L.R. (4th) 178 (Fed. T.D.).

See also **CPU**.

CEPT *(organization)*

Acronym for "Conference of European Postal and Telecommunications Administrations."

CERT *(Internet; organization)*

Acronym for "Computer Emergency Response Team."

> Office of the Comptroller of the Currency, Infrastructure Threats from Cyber-Terrorists 5 (March 19, 1999).

A group that analyzes Internet security vulnerabilities, provides incident response services, and publishes security alerts. Located at <www.cert.org>.

Annotation. "Located at Carnegie Mellon University, this incident response team offers advisories that contain enormous amounts of useful, specific security information."

> Office of the Comptroller of the Currency, Infrastructure Threats from Cyber-Terrorists 5 (March 19, 1999).

certificate *(electronic commerce)*

"[A] computer-based record which:

> i. identifies the certification authority issuing it;
>
> ii. names or identifies its subscriber;
>
> iii. contains the subscriber's public key; and
>
> iv. is digitally signed by the certification authority issuing or amending it, and
>
> v. conforms to widely-used industry standards, including, but not limited to ISO x.509 and PGP certificate standards."

> Cal. Code of Regs., tit. 2, div. 7, ch. 10, § 22003(a)(1)(D).

"[A] computer-based record that: (a) Identifies the certification authority issuing it; (b) Names or identifies its subscriber; (c) Contains the subscriber's public key; and (d) Is digitally signed by the certification authority issuing it."
Wash. Rev. Code § 19.34.020(4).

certification authority *(electronic commerce)*
Abbreviated "CA."

"[A] person or entity that issues a certificate, or in the case of certain certification processes, certifies amendments to an existing certificate."
Cal. Code of Regs., tit. 2, div. 7, ch. 10, § 22003(a)(1)(E).

"[A] person who issues a certificate."
Wash. Rev. Code § 19.34.020(5).

certification authority disclosure record *(electronic commerce)*
"[A]n on-line, publicly accessible record that concerns a licensed certification authority and is kept by the secretary. A certification authority disclosure record has the contents specified by rule by the secretary under RCW 19.34.030."
Wash. Rev. Code § 19.34.020(6).

certification practice statement *(electronic commerce)*
"[A] declaration of the practices that a certification authority employs in issuing certificates generally, or employed in issuing a material certificate."
Wash. Rev. Code § 19.34.020(7).

certification revocation list *(electronic commerce)*
Abbreviated as "CRL."
A list, maintained by a certification authority, of the certificates that have been revoked by the issuing certification authority.

certify *(electronic commerce)*
"[T]o declare with reference to a certificate, with ample opportunity to reflect, and with a duty to apprise oneself of all material facts."
Wash. Rev. Code § 19.34.020(8).

CGA *(hardware)*
Acronym for "Color Graphics Array." *See* **color graphics array.**

cgi
(technology)
Acronym for "computer-generated imagery." Technology that allows images to be generated by a computer and displayed on a computer display screen.

(Internet)
Acronym for "common gateway interface." *See* **common gateway interface script.**

channel *(business)*
A specific type of distribution system for hardware, software, video game and multimedia titles, e.g., the retail channel, the OEM channel. Each channel will have different economics and require different contracts.

channel capacity *(telecommunications)*
See **bandwidth.**

character *(technology)*
A single digit, letter, or symbol that a computer can recognize. Ordinarily represented in a one-byte combination of 1's and 0's.

character printer *(technology)*
A printer that transfers a fully formed letter, number or symbol with each impression stroke like a typewriter. The characters are generally more legible than those created by a dot matrix printer.

chat *(Internet)*
"[S]oftware, such as Internet Relay Chat ("IRC"), [which] permit[s] multiple users to converse by selecting one of many discussion 'channels' active at any time."
Shea v. Reno, 930 F. Supp. 916, 928 (S.D.N.Y. 1996).

Annotation. "Servers running so-called 'chat' software, such as Internet Relay Chat ("IRC"), permit multiple users to converse by selecting one of many discussion 'channels' active at any time. Commercial on-line services such as America Online, CompuServe, Prodigy, and the Microsoft Network offer their own chat systems for their members. Having joined a channel, the user can see and read messages transmitted by other users, each identified by a name the user selects upon joining the channel. Individual participants in IRC discussions know other participants only by the names they choose upon entering the discussion; users can participate anonymously by using a pseudonym."
Shea v. Reno, 930 F. Supp. 916, 928 (S.D.N.Y. 1996).
See also **chat room; chatting; relay chat.**

chat room *(Internet)*
"[T]wo or more individuals wishing to communicate more immediately can enter a chat room to engage in real-time dialogue—in other words,

by typing messages to one another that appear almost immediately on the others' computer screens. The District Court found that at any given time 'tens of thousands of users are engaging in conversations on a huge range of subjects.'"

Reno v. American Civil Liberties Union, 521 U.S. 844, 851-52, *quoting American Civil Liberties Union v. Reno,* 929 F. Supp. 824, 835 (3d Cir. 1996).

Annotation. "[A] service provided by Internet service providers, such as America Online Inc., where individuals can correspond with each other simultaneously."

United States v. Crow, 164 F.3d 229, 231 n.1 (5th Cir. 1999).

See also **chat; chatting.**

chatting *(Internet)*

A method of communication for two or more people online who can send real-time messages to each other. *See also* **chat; chat room.**

check disc *(multimedia)*

Once a manufacturer receives the gold master of a CD-ROM, it will prepare a sample disc containing all of the files and associated software. The check disc is then tested by both the manufacturer and the customer for any flaws or other problems.

"chicken-and-egg" problem *(software)*

Also referred to as "applications barrier to entry."

United States v. Microsoft Corp., 65 F. Supp. 2d 1, 9 (D.D.C. 1999) (Finding of Fact 30).

"The overwhelming majority of consumers will only use a PC operating system for which there already exists a large and varied set of high-quality, full-featured applications, and for which it seems relatively certain that new types of applications and new versions of existing applications will continue to be marketed at pace with those written for other operating systems. Unfortunately for firms whose products do not fit that bill, the porting of applications from one operating system to another is a costly process. Consequently, software developers generally write applications first, and often exclusively, for the operating system that is already used by a dominant share of all PC users. Users do not want to invest in an operating system until it is clear that the system will support generations of applications that will meet their needs, and developers do not want to invest in writing or quickly porting applications for an operating system until it is clear that

there will be a sizeable and stable market for it. What is more, consumers who already use one Intel-compatible PC operating system are even less likely than first-time buyers to choose a newcomer to the field, for switching to a new system would require these users to scrap the investment they have made in applications, training, and certain hardware."
United States v. Microsoft Corp., 65 F. Supp. 2d 1, 9 (D.D.C. 1999) (Finding of Fact 30).

Annotation. "The chicken-and-egg problem . . . would make it prohibitively expensive for a new Intel-compatible operating system to attract enough developers and consumers to become a viable alternative to a dominant incumbent in less than a few years."
United States v. Microsoft Corp., 65 F. Supp. 2d 1, 10 (D.D.C. 1999) (Finding of Fact 31).
See also **applications barrier to entry.**

Chief Information Officer *(business)*
See CIO.

child pornography *(criminal)*
Materials that depict minors engaged in actual or simulated sexual activity.

Annotation. "The Government could also completely ban obscenity and child pornography from the Internet. No Internet speaker has a right to engage in these forms of speech, and no Internet listener has a right to receive them. Child pornography and obscenity have 'no constitutional protection, and the government may ban [them] outright in certain media, or in all.'"
American Civil Liberties Union v. Reno, 929 F. Supp. 824, 865 (E.D. Pa. 1996), *aff'd, Reno v. American Civil Liberties Union,* 521 U.S. 844 (1997) (citation omitted).

"[A] social concern that has evaded repeated attempts to stamp it out. State legislatures and Congress have vigorously tried to investigate and enact laws to provide a basis to prosecute those persons involved in the creation, distribution, and possession of sexually explicit materials made by or through the exploitation of children."
Free Speech Coalition v. Reno, 198 F.3d 1083, 1087 (9th Cir. 1999).

children *(copyright)*
"A person's 'children' are that person's immediate offspring, whether legitimate or not, and any children legally adopted by that person."
U.S. Copyright Act, 17 U.S.C. § 101.

chip(s) *(hardware)*

"In microcircuitry, a single device, either a transistor or a diode, that has been cut from a larger wafer of silicon."

U.S. Copyright Office, *Compendium of Copyright Office Practices* II, § 326 (1984).

"[I]ndividual integrated circuits. Chips are mounted onto printed circuit boards (usually referred to as 'boards').... Chips, boards, and logic are all installed inside other units (personal computers, terminals, or control units)."

IRS Letter Ruling 8721016, Feb. 17, 1987.

[CANADA] "Silicon semiconductors."

Apple Computer, Inc. v. Mackintosh Computers Ltd. (1986), 28 D.L.R. (4th) 178 (Fed. T.D.).

See also **microchip; semiconductor.**

chip piracy *(mask work)*

"[T]he unauthorized copying and distribution of semiconductor chip products copied from the original creators of such works."

Brooktree Corp. v. Advanced Micro Devices, Inc., 977 F.2d 1555, 1561 (Fed. Cir. 1992) (*quoting* S. Rep. No. 425, 98th Cong., 2d Sess. 1 (1984)).

chirp signal *(technology)*

"[A] frequency-modulated continuous wave in which the frequency of vibration is varied as a function of time, usually a linear function, over a substantial period of time of as much as several seconds. Chirp signals are often referred to as 'sweep' signals, since the frequency is swept from one value to another. Chirp signals are generated by a mechanical apparatus which vibrates against the surface of the earth."

In re Walter, 618 F.2d 758, 760 (C.C.P.A. 1980).

choice of forum *(contract)*

A contractual provision that predetermines the forum for any dispute involving the contract. Usually, the forum will be one that is convenient to one of the parties.

Sample clause. "In the event of any dispute concerning this Agreement or the products [services] sold [licensed] hereunder, suit may be brought only in a court of competent jurisdiction in the State [Province][Country] of _____."

choice of law *(contract)*

A contractual provision that specifies that the laws of a mutually agreed upon jurisdiction are to govern the interpretation of the terms of the agreement.

Annotation. "Choice of law provisions in contracts are generally enforced by federal courts."
    Invacare Corp. v. Sperry Rand Corp., 612 F. Supp. 448, 451 n.4 (N.D. Ohio. 1984). *See also AMF, Inc. v. Computer Automation, Inc.*, 573 F. Supp. 924, 926 (S.D. Ohio 1983).

"The important thing, especially in a contractual setting, is that the parties should have a clear idea of which state's law will apply...since once they know this they can if they wish change the state whose law is to govern their relation by including a choice of law provision in their contract."
    Micro Data Base Sys., Inc. v. Dharma Sys., Inc., 148 F.3d 649, 653 (7th Cir. 1998).

Sample clause. "This agreement shall be governed by and construed in accordance with the laws of the United States and the State of California, as applied to agreements entered into and to be performed entirely within California between California residents. The application of the United Nations Convention for Contracts for the International Sales of Goods is hereby expressly excluded."

choose, then watch *(video game)*

A type of multimedia product in which the user chooses a course of action, then watches a linear movie or animation sequence during which the user cannot affect the action taking place on the screen.
See also lockout.

choreography *(copyright)*

"...has to do with the flow of steps in a ballet."
    Horgan v. MacMillan, Inc., 621 F. Supp. 1169, 1170 (S.D.N.Y. 1985), *rev'd on other grounds*, 789 F.2d 157 (2d Cir. 1986).

CIO *(business)*

Acronym for "Chief Information Officer." An executive who oversees all of the information technology and its operations within the company.

ciphertext *(technology)*

A message after it has been encrypted.

circuit switching *(telecommunications)*

"[W]hen a call is placed, telephone company equipment would set up an electrical path from calling party to called party. The entire conversation would flow over that same path; the path would be reserved for the use of the caller for the duration of the call."

I. Trotter Hardy, *Project Looking Forward: Sketching the Future of Copyright in a Networked World* 11 (May 1998).

See also **packet switching.**

circumvent a technological measure *(copyright)*

"[T]o descramble a scrambled work, to decrypt an encrypted work, or otherwise to avoid, bypass, remove, deactivate, or impair a technological measure, without the authority of the copyright owner."

17 U.S.C. § 1201(a)(3)(A).

circumvent protection afforded by a technological measure *(copyright)*

". . . means avoiding, bypassing, removing, deactivating, or otherwise impairing a technological measure."

17 U.S.C. § 1201(b)(2)(A).

circumvention *(copyright)*

"No person shall import, manufacture, or distribute any device, or offer or perform any service, the primary purpose or effect of which is to avoid, bypass, remove, deactivate, or otherwise circumvent any program or circuit which implements, in whole or in part, a [serial copyright management system or similar system]."

17 U.S.C. § 1002.

CISG *(contract)*

Acronym for the "United Nations Convention on Contracts for the International Sale of Goods."

See **United Nations Convention on Contracts for the International Sale of Goods.**

CIX *(organization)*

Acronym for "Commercial Internet Exchange Association." *See* **Commercial Internet Exchange Association.**

claim(s) *(patent)*

"Each claim component, recited as a 'means' plus its function, is to be read, of course, pursuant to §112, ¶ 6, as inclusive of the 'equivalents' of

the structures disclosed in the written description portion of the specification."

> *State Street Bank & Trust Co. v. Signature Financial Group, Inc.*, 149 F.3d
> 1368, 1372 (Fed. Cir. 1998).

classroom education *(general)*

"[C]onsists of courses designed to teach the operation and programming of
data processing equipment."

> *Honeywell Information Systems v. Maricopa County*, 118 Ariz. 171, 575 P.2d
> 801, 808 (App. 1977).

clean room *(technology)*

"[A] technique used in the software industry to prevent the direct
copying of a competitor's code during the development of a competing
product. The procedure usually consists of two teams of developers[;] one
team disassembles the code and describes its functional aspects, while the
other team takes the descriptions of the functional aspects and writes the
competing product's code. Ideally, this process represents the optimal way
to develop a competing product because the alleged infringer can demonstrate that the programmer who drafted the com-peting code had no access to the original copyrighted work. By showing no access the alleged
infringer could defeat the first requirement of a copyright infringement
action and thereby end both the analysis and the case."

> *DSC Com. Corp. v. DGI Technologies, Inc.*, 898 F. Supp. 1183, 1189 n.3 (N.D.
> Tex. 1995), *aff'd*, 81 F.3d 597 (5th Cir. 1996).

clear GIF *(technology)*

See **web bug.**

clearance *(Internet; multimedia)*

The process of obtaining permission to reuse a work owned or controlled
by another.

click *(Internet)*

"In Internet parlance, to 'click' is to point the mouse or cursor on a given
space or group of words and literally click by pushing a button; to click on
a 'link' on a Web site is to then be 'transported' to that spot."

> *Digital Equipment Corp. v. Altavista Technology, Inc.*, 960 F. Supp. 456, 460
> n.6 (D. Mass. 1997).

Annotation. "'Clicking' on a designated space on the initial page which
references the subsequent site by a picture, by some highlighted text or by

some other indication will take a person viewing the initial web page to a second page. In addition to their use in indexes, hyperlinks are commonly placed on existing web pages, thus allowing Internet users to move from web page to web page at the click of a button, without having to type in URLs."

Intermatic, Inc. v. Toeppen, 947 F. Supp. 1227, 1232 (N.D. Ill. 1996).

Related issues. "The government may well be right that sexually explicit content is just a few clicks of a mouse away from the user, but there is an immense legal significance to those few clicks."

American Civil Liberties Union v. Reno, 929 F. Supp. 824, 876 n.19 (E.D. Pa. 1996), *aff'd, Reno v. American Civil Liberties Union*, 521 U.S. 844 (1997).

click and mortar *(e-commerce)*

A business that combines traditional retailing ("brick and mortar") with e-commerce.

See **brick and mortar.**

click-through rate *(advertising; Internet)*

Abbreviated as "CTR."

The percentage of times users visiting a web page respond to an advertisement on that page by clicking on a specific button or banner.

Annotation. Click-through rates are one of the main statistics used by advertisers to gauge the success of a particular advertisement online.

click-through URL *(Internet; technology)*

The web page to which a user is directed when he/she clicks on a banner ad, button, or other link.

click-wrap license *(contract; Internet)*

A standard form software license that is displayed on a web site. The user must indicate assent to the license by clicking on an icon that indicates acceptance of the terms of the license before access will be granted to the software, data, or other digital content.

See also **shrinkwrap license.**

client *(Internet)*

1. A user of an Internet service provider; 2. A computer or software used to access a host server.

client-server architecture *(technology)*
A computer network in which processing is distributed among many
client computers (generally PCs) and a more powerful, central server
computer. Clients can share files and programs and retrieve data stored
on the server.

client software *(software)*
"...enables his [a user's] computer to communicate with and make requests
of remote computers where information is stored...."
Shea v. Reno, 930 F. Supp. 916, 927 (S.D.N.Y. 1996).

clip *(multimedia)*
A short amount of filmed or videotaped material.

cloning *(telecommunications)*
"Programming a cellular telephone to have an ESN and an MIN identical
to that of another cellular telephone having a valid ESN/MIN combination
assigned to a customer, thereby enabling the user to obtain telephone services through having access to that customer's account."
United States v. Brady, 820 F. Supp. 1346, 1348 n.6 (D. Utah 1993).

closed mailing list *(Internet)*
"Some mailing lists are 'closed': a user's request to join the list requires the
approval of an individual who maintains the list."
Shea v. Reno, 930 F. Supp. 916, 927 (S.D.N.Y. 1996).

Related issues. "There is no newsgroup equivalent of a 'closed' mailing list:
access to a particular newsgroup can only be limited by restricting the
number of servers participating in the newsgroup."
Shea v. Reno, 930 F. Supp. 916, 928 (S.D.N.Y. 1996).
See also **mailing list.**

closed network *(technology)*
"Some networks are 'closed' networks, not linked to other computers or
networks."
American Civil Liberties Union v. Reno, 929 F. Supp. 824, 831 (E.D.
Pa. 1996), aff'd, Reno v. American Civil Liberties Union, 521 U.S. 844
(1997).

Annotation. "Closed networks usually have proprietary access equipment,
which permit only those with the right equipment to access the informa-

tion in the network. LEXIS, the legal database network, and airline reservation systems are examples of closed networks."

> Solomon, *Intellectual Property and New Computer-based Media* (Office of Technology Assessment Report, Aug. 1, 1984).

CMOS *(hardware)*

Acronym for "Complementary Metal Oxide Semiconductor."

> *Pearl Sys., Inc. v. Competition Elecs., Inc.*, 8 U.S.P.Q.2d (BNA) 1520, 1521(S.D. Fla. 1988).

COBOL *(software)*

Acronym for "Common Business-Oriented Language."

> *Lotus Dev. Corp. v. Paperback Software Int'l*, 740 F. Supp. 37, 43 (D. Mass. 1990).

"A high-level language developed in the early 1960's and used primarily for business applications."

> U.S. Copyright Office, *Compendium of Copyright Office Practices* II, § 326 (1984).

"[A] computer language especially adapted for business applications. COBOL is written by human programmers. COBOL programs consist of words and characters resembling the English language, intelligible to humans but not to computers."

> *Teamsters Sec. Fund v. Sperry Rand Corp.*, 6 Computer L. Serv. Rep. (Callaghan) 951, 957 (N.D. Cal. 1977).

COBOL compiler *(software)*

"The COBOL compiler's function is to translate incoming coded application programs into machine-readable electronic impulses, which the computer can process under the direction of other systems software elements.... A COBOL compiler is an article of software that translates coded statements into machine instructions."

> *Teamsters Sec. Fund v. Sperry Rand Corp.*, 6 Computer L. Serv. Rep. (Callaghan) 951, 957 (N.D. Cal. 1977).

See also **compiler; compiler program.**

COCOM *(organization)*

Acronym for "Coordinating Committee on Multilateral Export Controls."

"[A]n international agency created to prevent the acquisition of certain western technology by the Soviet Union and its allies. COCOM maintains a list of items, the sale of which its members agree will be restricted and controlled."

Arjay Assocs., Inc. v. Bush, 1 Computer Cas. (CCH) ¶ 46,202, at 61,719 n.1
(Int'l Trade Comm'n 1989).

code *(software)*

"Can be used as verb or noun. As a noun, it can apply to (1) the data,
meaning the series of bits used to represent the characters, or (2) the
programs, meaning the computer instructions as written in the programming language. As a verb, it means creating the coded data or programs."

U.S. Copyright Office, *Compendium of Copyright Office Practices* II, § 326
(1984).

See also object code; source code.

code breakers *(technology)*

"...are products that operate to defeat protective devices and to permit a
possessor of a program to make copies."

Vault Corp. v. Quaid Software Ltd., 655 F.2d 750 (E.D. La. 1987), *aff'd*, 847
F.2d 255 (5th Cir. 1988).

code division multiple access *(telecommunications)*

See CDMA.

code generator program(s) *(software)*

Also called "code generator."

"...enable computer programmers to code sophisticated computer programs with added speed and relatively little creative or intellectual effort."

CMAX/Cleveland, Inc. v. UCR, Inc., 804 F. Supp. 337, 343 (M.D. Ga. 1992).

Annotation. "With the use of a code generator, which was described as a
sort of electronic paintbrush, a programmer can, for example, code a program to display a screen to reflect how he wishes the screen that will be
generated by the finished program to look. The programmer—using the
cursor and keyboard—'paints' upon the screen the features he wants the
program-generated field to display, including the data 'fields' that he wishes
to be included on the screen. Programs to develop reports and files can also
be created this way.

"Thereafter, with virtually the punch of a button, the code generator
produces a program that carries out the functions that the programmer
has requested. The code generator also produces documentation for the
resulting software program. Thus, when using a code generator, the development of a software system consists almost entirely of the design of the

system, while only a small portion of the process involves coding of the system."

CMAX/Cleveland, Inc. v. UCR, Inc., 804 F. Supp. 337, 343 (M.D. Ga. 1992).

CODEC *(technology)*

Acronym for "**C**ompression-**D**ecompression." Refers to the processes of compression and decompression of information, primarily video, to facilitate its storage and transmission.

coding *(software)*

"The act of actually writing program statements."

U.S. Copyright Office, *Compendium of Copyright Office Practices* II, § 326 (1984).

"Once each necessary module has been identified, designed, and its relationship to the other modules has been laid out conceptually, the resulting program structure must be embodied in a written language that the computer can read. This process is called 'coding.'..."

Computer Assocs. Int'l, Inc. v. Altai, Inc., 982 F.2d 693, 698 (2d Cir. 1992).

"...requires two steps. First, the programmer must transpose the program's structural blue-print into a source code.... Once the source code has been completed, the second step is to translate or 'compile' it into object code."

Computer Assocs. Int'l, Inc. v. Altai, Inc., 982 F.2d 693, 698 (2d Cir. 1992).

collaborative software *(software)*

Software that permits multiple users to work on the same document, database, or other materials at the same time. *See also* **groupware.**

collective-action problem *(economics)*

"Each ISV realizes that the new operating system could attract a significant number of users if enough ISVs developed applications for it; but few ISVs want to sink resources into developing for the system until it becomes established. Since everyone is waiting for everyone else to bear the risk of early adoption, the new operating system has difficulty attracting enough applications to generate a positive feedback loop. The vendor of a new operating system cannot effectively solve this problem by paying the necessary number of ISVs to write for its operating system, because the cost of doing so would dwarf the expected return."

United States v. Microsoft Corp., 65 F. Supp. 2d 1, 12 (D.D.C. 1999) (Finding of Fact 41).

Related issues. "Counteracting the collective-action phenomenon is another known as the 'first-mover incentive.'"
United States v. Microsoft Corp., 65 F. Supp. 2d 1, 12 (D.D.C. 1999) (Finding of Fact 42).

collective work *(copyright)*

"[A] work, such as a periodical issue, anthology, or encyclopedia, in which a number of contributions, constituting separate and independent works in themselves, are assembled into a collective whole."
U.S. Copyright Act, 17 U.S.C. § 101.

Annotation. "Copyright in each separate contribution to a collective work is distinct from copyright in the collective work as a whole, and vests initially in the author of the contribution. In the absence of an express transfer of the copyright or of any rights under it, the owner of copyright in the collective work is presumed to have acquired only the privilege of reproducing and distributing the contribution as part of that particular collective work, and revision of that collective work, and any later collective work in the same series."
U.S. Copyright Act, 17 U.S.C. § 201(c).

color dithering *(technology)*

A technique that uses the interaction between colors of adjoining pixels to trick the eye into seeing shades that are not there.

color graphics array *(hardware)*

Abbreviated as "CGA." A video display standard for IBM-compatible personal computers.
Princeton Graphics Operating L.P. v. NEC Home Elecs. (U.S.A.), Inc., 732 F. Supp. 1258, 1259 n.3 (S.D.N.Y. 1990).

.com *(Internet)*

The top-level domain originally intended for "commercial" entities. It is the most popular top-level domain name.

". . . identifies the user as a commercial entity."
Zippo Mfg. Co. v. Zippo Dot Com, Inc., 952 F. Supp. 1119, 1120 n.1 (W.D. Pa. 1997).

". . . for 'commercial,' which functions as the catchall domain for Internet users.
"Domain names with the .com designation must be registered on the Internet with Network Solutions, Inc. ('NSI')."
Panavision Int'l, L.P. v. Toeppen, 141 F.3d 1316, 1318 (9th Cir. 1998).

"...is short for 'commercial.'..."
> *Intermatic, Inc. v. Toeppen*, 947 F. Supp. 1227, 1231 (N.D. Ill. 1996).

Annotation. "Because most businesses with a presence on the Internet use the '.com' top-level domain name, as in 'acme.com.' Second-level domain names, the name just to the left of '.com,' must be exclusive. Therefore, although two companies can have non-exclusive trademark rights in a name, only one company can have a second-level domain name that corresponds to its trademark."
> *Lockheed Martin Corp. v. Network Solutions, Inc.*, 985 F. Supp. 949, 952 (C.D. Cal. 1997).

"Commercial entities generally use the '.com' top-level domain, which also serves as a catchall top-level domain."
> *Brookfield Comm., Inc. v. West Coast Entertainment Corp.*, 174 F.3d 1036, 1044 (9th Cir. 1999).

Related issues. *(trademark)* "Because many companies use domain names comprised of '.com' as the top-level domain with their corporate name or trademark as the second-level domain, . . . the addition of '.com' is of diminished importance in distinguishing the mark."
> *Brookfield Comm., Inc. v. West Coast Entertainment Corp.*, 174 F.3d 1036, 1055 (9th Cir. 1999).

command *(hardware; software)*
An order to the computer telling it what to do. A command can be typed on a keyboard, selected from a menu of selections, or chosen by a computer program from certain criteria.

command interpreter *(software)*
A program that reads lines typed at the keyboard and interprets them as requests to execute other programs.

comments *(software)*
"[L]ines of source code...describing the functioning of the accompanying code."
> *SAS Inst., Inc. v. S&H Computer Sys., Inc.*, 605 F. Supp. 816, 824 (M.D. Tenn. 1985).

Commerce Clause *(Constitution)*
A U.S. constitutional provision that grants to the federal government the power to regulate interstate and foreign commerce. Article 1, Section 8, Clause 3 provides in pertinent part, that "The Congress shall have the

Power...To regulate Commerce with foreign Nations, and among the several States, and with the Indian Tribes."

Annotation. "The unique nature of the Internet highlights the likelihood that a single actor might be subject to haphazard, uncoordinated, and even outright inconsistent regulation by states that the actor never intended to reach and possibly was unaware were being accessed. Typically, states' jurisdictional limits are related to geography; geography, however, is a virtually meaningless construct on the Internet. The menace of inconsistent state regulation invites analysis under the Commerce Clause of the Constitution, because that clause represents the framers' reaction to overreaching by the individual states that might jeopardize the growth of the nation—and in particular, the national infrastructure of communications and trade—as a whole."
American Library Ass'n v. Pataki, 969 F. Supp. 160, 169 (S.D.N.Y. 1997).

"The 'dormant implication of the Commerce Clause prohibits state . . . regulation . . . that discriminates against or unduly burdens interstate commerce and thereby "imped[es] free private trade in the national marketplace."' Moreover, the Supreme Court has long recognized that certain types of commerce are uniquely suited to national, as opposed to state, regulation."
American Civil Liberties Union v. Johnson, 194 F.3d 1149, 1160 (10th Cir. 1999) (citations omitted).

Related issues. "I find...that the Internet is analogous to a highway or railroad. This determination means that the phrase 'information superhighway' is more than a mere buzzword; it has legal significance, because the similarity between the Internet and more traditional instruments of interstate commerce leads to analysis under the Commerce Clause."
American Library Ass'n v. Pataki, 969 F. Supp. 160, 161 (S.D.N.Y. 1997).

"[T]he Internet is one of those areas of commerce that must be marked off as a national preserve to protect users from inconsistent legislation that, taken to its most extreme, could paralyze development of the Internet altogether.

* * *

"There is no compelling reason to find that local legal officials must take a 'hands off' approach just because a crook or a con artist is technologically sophisticated enough to sell on the Internet. Invocation of 'the Internet' is not the equivalent to a cry of 'sanctuary' upon a criminal's entry into a medieval church. It should be sufficient that the laws sought to be

applied, even if they might tangentially implicate interstate commerce, are 'media neutral' and otherwise pass constitutional muster."
American Library Ass'n v. Pataki, 969 F. Supp. 160, 169 (S.D.N.Y. 1997).

"The borderless world of the Internet raises profound questions concerning the relationship of the federal government to each state, questions that go to the heart of 'our federalism.'"
American Library Ass'n v. Pataki, 969 F. Supp. 160, 168 (S.D.N.Y. 1997).

"[T]he Internet represents an instrument of interstate commerce, albeit an innovative one; the novelty of the technology should not obscure the fact that regulation of the Internet impels traditional Commerce Clause considerations."

"The Internet is more than a means of communications; it also serves as a conduit for transporting digitized goods, including software, data, music, graphics, and videos which can be downloaded from the provider's site to the Internet user's computer."
American Library Association v. Pataki, 969 F. Supp. 160, 173 (S.D.N.Y. 1997).

"The Internet requires a cohesive national scheme of regulation.... The need for uniformity in this unique sphere of commerce requires that New York's law be stricken as a violation of the Commerce Clause."
American Library Ass'n v. Pataki, 969 F. Supp. 160, 182 (S.D.N.Y. 1997).
See also **in commerce.**

Commercial Internet Exchange Association *(organization)*
Abbreviated as "CIX." A nonprofit trade association of Public Data Internetwork service providers, which promotes the development of the public data communications internetworking services industry in both national and international markets. CIX provides a forum to exchange ideas, information, and experimental projects among suppliers of internetworking services. Located at <www.cix.org>.

Related issues. "Many [Internet service] providers—including the members of plaintiff Commercial Internet Exchange Association—are commercial entities offering Internet access for a monthly or hourly fee."
American Civil Liberties Union v. Reno, 929 F. Supp. 824, 833 (E.D. Pa. 1996), *aff'd, Reno v. American Civil Liberties Union*, 521 U.S. 844 (1997).

commercial on-line services *(Internet)*
"...such as America Online, CompuServe, Prodigy, and Microsoft Net-

work—allow subscribers to gain access to the Internet while providing extensive content within their own proprietary networks."

Shea v. Reno, 930 F. Supp. 916, 926 (S.D.N.Y. 1996).

"These on-line services offer nationwide computer networks (so that subscribers can dial-in to a local telephone number), and the services provide extensive and well organized content within their own proprietary computer networks."

American Civil Liberties Union v. Reno, 929 F. Supp. 824, 833 (E.D. Pa. 1996), *aff'd, Reno v. American Civil Liberties Union*, 521 U.S. 844 (1997).

Annotation. "In addition to allowing access to the extensive content available *within* each online service, the services also allow subscribers to link to the much larger resources of the Internet. Full access to the online service (including access to the Internet) can be obtained for modest monthly or hourly fees. The major commercial online services have almost twelve million individual subscribers across the United States."

American Civil Liberties Union v. Reno, 929 F. Supp. 824, 833 (E.D. Pa. 1996), *aff'd, Reno v. American Civil Liberties Union*, 521 U.S. 844 (1997).

See also **online service provider.**

commercial use *(trademark)*

Also called "use in commerce." The bona fide use of a trademark or service mark in either interstate or foreign commerce in the ordinary course of trade.

Related issues. "Registration of a trade[mark] as a domain name, without more, is not a commercial use of the trademark and therefore is not within the prohibitions of the Act."

Panavision Int'l, L.P. v. Toeppen, 945 F. Supp. 1296, 1303 (C.D. Cal. 1996), *aff'd on other grounds*, 141 F.3d 1316 (9th Cir. 1998).

"Toeppen's intention to arbitrage the 'intermatic.com' domain name constitute[d] a commercial use."

Intermatic, Inc. v. Toeppen, 947 F. Supp. 1227, 1239 (N.D. Ill. 1996).

commercially exploit *(mask work)*

". . . to distribute to the public for commercial purposes a semiconductor chip product embodying the mask work; except that such term includes an offer to sell or transfer a semiconductor chip product only when the offer is in writing and occurs after the mask work is fixed in the semiconductor chip product; . . . ."

17 U.S.C. § 901(a)(5).

common carrier *(telecommunications)*
A communications service provider that provides the means of transmitting messages to everyone on a nondiscriminatory basis.

common gateway interface script *(software)*
Abbreviated as "cgi."

"[T]he means by which a Web site can process a fill-in form and thereby screen visitors by requesting a credit card number or adult password."
> *American Civil Liberties Union v. Reno*, 929 F. Supp. 824, 845 (E.D. Pa. 1996), *aff'd, Reno v. American Civil Liberties Union*, 521 U.S. 844 (1997).

"...which enable creation of a document that can process information provided by a Web visitor."
> *American Civil Liberties Union v. Reno*, 929 F. Supp. 824, 854 (E.D. Pa. 1996), *aff'd, Reno v. American Civil Liberties Union*, 521 U.S. 844 (1997).

Communications Decency Act *(defamation; First Amendment; obscenity)*
Abbreviated as "CDA." The Communications Decency Act is part of the Telecommunications Act of 1996. There are two sections of the Act that address significant subject matter. One section attempted to control the content of the Internet by criminalizing "indecent" and "patently offensive" materials. That provision was struck down by the U.S. Supreme Court in *Reno v. American Civil Liberties Union*, 521 U.S. 844 (1997). The other section of the CDA provided a "safe harbor" for Internet service providers against claims for defamation arising from messages posted on or passing through their equipment. That section has been upheld in numerous cases. *See, e.g., Blumenthal v. Drudge*, 992 F. Supp. 44 (D.D.C. 1998).

Challenge to "Indecency" and "Patently Offensive" Provisions. "Title V [of the Telecommunications Act of 1996]—known as the 'Communications Decency Act of 1996' (CDA)—contains provisions that were either added in executive committee after the hearings were concluded or as amendments offered during floor debate on the legislation. An amendment offered in the Senate was the source of the two statutory provisions challenged in this case. They are informally described as the 'indecent transmission' provision and the 'patently offensive display' provision.
"The first, 47 U.S.C.A. § 223(a) (Supp. 1997), prohibits the knowing transmission of obscene or indecent messages to any recipient under 18 years of age. It provides in pertinent part:
'(a) Whoever—
(1) in interstate or foreign communications—...

(B) by means of a telecommunications device knowingly—
(i) makes, creates, or solicits, and
(ii) initiates the transmission of,
any comment, request, suggestion, proposal, image, or other communication which is obscene or indecent, knowing that the recipient of the communication is under 18 years of age, regardless of whether the maker of such communication placed the call or initiated the communication;...
(2) knowingly permits any telecommunications facility under his control to be used for any activity prohibited by paragraph (1) with the intent that it be used for such activity, "shall be fined under Title 18, or imprisoned not more than two years, or both.'"

"The second provision, §223(d), prohibits the knowing sending or displaying of patently offensive messages in a manner that is available to a person under 18 years of age. It provides:
'(d) Whoever—
(1) in interstate or foreign communications knowingly—
(A) uses an interactive computer service to send to a specific person or persons under 18 years of age, or
(B) uses any interactive computer service to display in a manner available to a person under 18 years of age,
any comment, request, suggestion, proposal, image, or other communication that, in context, depicts or describes, in terms patently offensive as measured by contemporary community standards, sexual or excretory activities or organs, regardless of whether the user of such service placed the call or initiated the communication; or
(2) knowingly permits any telecommunications facility under such person's control to be used for an activity prohibited by paragraph (1) with the intent that it be used for such activity,
shall be fined under Title 18, or imprisoned not more than two years, or both.'

"The breadth of these prohibitions is qualified by two affirmative defenses. See §223(e)(5). One covers those who take 'good faith, reasonable, effective, and appropriate actions' to restrict access by minors to the prohibited communications. §223(e)(5)(A). The other covers those who restrict access to covered material by requiring certain designated forms of age proof, such as a verified credit card or an adult identification number or code. §223(e)(5)(B)."

Reno v. American Civil Liberties Union, 521 U.S. 844, __, 117 S. Ct. 2329, 2338-39 (1997).

Annotation. "In an attempt to limit the availability of certain materials in interactive computer services, Congress enacted a statute of unprecedented sweep: the new § 223(d) purports to regulate not only how commercial purveyors of obscene or pornographic materials may advertise and sell their products on line, but also how private individuals who choose to exchange certain constitutionally protected communications with one another can do so."

> *Shea v. Reno*, 930 F. Supp. 916, 922 (S.D.N.Y. 1996).

"It is clear from the face of the CDA and from its legislative history that Congress did not intend to limit its application to commercial purveyors of pornography.

* * *

"The scope of the CDA is not confined to material that has a prurient interest or appeal, one of the hallmarks of obscenity, because Congress sought to reach farther. Nor did Congress include language that would define 'patently offensive' or 'indecent' to exclude material of serious value."

> *American Civil Liberties Union v. Reno*, 929 F. Supp. 824, 855 (E.D. Pa. 1996), *aff'd, Reno v. American Civil Liberties Union*, 521 U.S. 844 (1997).

"The evidentiary record in this case compels the conclusion that, given the current state of technology, most adult content providers wishing to engage in constitutionally protected indecent speech will be unable to avail themselves of these affirmative defenses. Only a limited subset of on-line content providers, commercial providers on the World Wide Web, can avail themselves of the defense set out in § 223(e)(5)(B), leaving both non-commercial providers of Web content and content providers using all other modes of on-line communication unprotected. The evidence further demonstrates that content providers' ability to comply with the terms of the second defense—the so called good-faith defense—depends on the actions of third parties, such as software manufacturers, whose cooperation is not required under the CDA or otherwise mandated. There is no feasible means, with our current technology, for someone to provide indecent content on line with any certainty that even his best efforts at shielding the material from minors will be 'effective,' as the language of the good-faith defense requires.

"Because neither of the affirmative defenses set out in § 223(e)(5) can, with our current technology, effectively protect adult content providers wishing to engage in constitutionally protected indecent communication, we reach the inescapable conclusion that § 223(d) will serve to chill protected speech. We therefore find that the plaintiff has demonstrated a likelihood of success on the merits of his claim that § 223(d) is unconstitutionally overbroad.

* * *

"In setting aside the challenged provisions, we do not question the legitimacy of the government's interest in safeguarding children from exposure to certain materials available on line nor suggest that other legislation on another day, carefully tailored to technological realities, may not pass constitutional muster. We also do not consider, nor attempt to delineate, the range of circumstances, if any, in which Congress could now or in the future constitutionally impose content-based restrictions upon communications in the developing medium we explore here."

Shea v. Reno, 930 F. Supp. 916, 923 (S.D.N.Y. 1996).

"Safe Harbor" Provisions Against Defamation Claims. "In February of 1996, Congress made an effort to deal with some of these challenges in enacting the Communications Decency Act of 1996. While various policy opinions were open to Congress, it chose to 'promote the continued development of the Internet and other interactive computer services and other interactive media' and 'to preserve the vibrant and competitive free market' for such service, largely 'unfettered by Federal or State regulation. . . .' 47 U.S.C. 230(b)(1) and (2). Whether wisely or not, it made the legislative judgment to effectively immunize providers of interactive computer services from civil liability in tort with respect to material disseminated by them but created by others. In recognition of the speed with which information may be disseminated and the near impossibility of regulating information content, Congress decided not to treat providers of interactive computer services like other information providers such as newspapers, magazines or television and radio stations, all of which may be held liable for publishing or distributing obscene or defamatory material written by others. While Congress could have made a different policy choice, it opted not to hold interactive computer services liable for their failure to edit, withhold or restrict access to offensive materials disseminated through their medium."

Blumenthal v. Drudge, 992 F. Supp. 44, 49 (D.D.C. 1998).

"By its plain language, sec. 230 creates a federal immunity to any cause of action that would make service providers liable for information originating with a third-party user of the service. Specifically, sec. 230 precludes courts from entertaining claims that would place a computer service provider in a publisher's role. Thus, lawsuits seeking to hold a service liable for its exercise of a publisher's traditional editorial functions—such as deciding whether to publish, withdraw, postpone or alter content—are barred.

"The purpose of this statutory immunity is not difficult to discern. Congress recognized the threat that tort-based lawsuits pose to freedom of speech in the new and burgeoning Internet medium. The imposition of tort liability on service providers for the communications of others presented, for Congress, simply another form of intrusive government regulation of speech. Section 230 was enacted, in part, to maintain the robust nature of Internet communication and, accordingly, to keep government interference in the medium to a minimum.

"None of this means, of course, that the original culpable party who posts defamatory messages would escape accountability. While Congress acted to keep government regulation of the Internet to a minimum, it also found it to be the policy of the United States 'to ensure vigorous enforcement of Federal criminal laws to deter and punish trafficking in obscenity, stalking, and harassment by means of computer.' Id. sec. 230(B)(5). Congress made a policy choice, however, not to deter harmful online speech through the separate route of imposing tort liability on companies that serve as intermediaries for other parties' potentially injurious messages." *Zeran v. America Online, Inc.*, 129 F.3d 327, 330-31 (4th Cir. 1997).

"Because it has the right to exercise editorial control over those with whom it contracts and whose words it disseminates, it would seem only fair to hold AOL to the liability standards applied to a publisher or, at least, like a book store owner or library, to the liability standard applied to a distributor. But Congress has made a different policy choice by providing immunity even where the interactive service provider has an active, even aggressive role in making available content prepare by others. In some sort of tacit quid pro quo arrangement with the service provider community, Congress has conferred immunity from tort liability as an incentive to Internet service providers to self-police the Internet for obscenity and other offensive material, even where the self-policing is unsuccessful or not even attempted.

"In Section 230(c)(2) of the Communications Decency Act, Congress provided:

"No provider or user of an interactive computer service shall be held liable on account of—
'(A) Any action voluntarily taken in good faith to restrict access to or availability of material that the provider or user considers to be obscene, lewd, lascivious, filthy, excessively violent, harassing, or otherwise objectionable, whether or not such material is constitutionally protected; or
'(B) any action taken to enable or make available to information content providers or others the technical means to restrict access to material described in paragraph (1).'

"47 U.S.C. sec. 230(C)(2). As the Fourth Circuit stated in Zeran: 'Congress enacted sec. 230 to remove...disincentives to self-regulation.... Fearing that the specter of liability would...deter service providers from blocking and screening offensive material...sect. 230 forbids the imposition of publisher liability on a service provider for the exercise of its editorial and self-regulatory functions.'"

Blumenthal v. Drudge, 992 F. Supp. 44, 51-52 (D.D.C. 1998).

See also **defamation; First Amendment; obscenity.**

communications protocol(s) *(Internet)*

"One who wishes to make certain articles, files, or software available to other users will set up a server, adhering to certain communications protocols, capable of retrieving and presenting stored information in response to a request from client software using the same communications protocols."

Shea v. Reno, 930 F. Supp. 916, 928 (S.D.N.Y. 1996).

"Having successfully implemented a system for the reliable transfer of information over a computer network, ARPA began to support the development of communications protocols for transferring data between different types of computer networks. Universities, research facilities, and commercial entities began to develop and link together their own networks implementing these protocols; these networks included a high-speed 'backbone' network known as NSFNet, sponsored by the National Science Foundation, smaller regional networks, and, eventually, large commercial networks run by organizations such as Sprint, IBM, and Performance Systems International (commonly known as 'PSI')."

Shea v. Reno, 930 F. Supp. 916, 926 (S.D.N.Y. 1996).

See also **Internet protocol.**

community standards *(obscenity)*

"[P]laintiff contends that Internet content providers are less well equipped to assess community indecency standards than those within the reach of previous statutes and regulations governing indecency; while entities engaging in the commercial traffic of pornographic materials (such as \ obscene or indecent telephone messages) may have legal staff to monitor FCC pronouncements on what is and is not patently offensive in communities across America, we are told, individuals engaged in an exchange of ideas over the Internet do not. Second, the plaintiff claims that even if those who use other communications media can tailor their messages to a particular community—as suggested by the Supreme Court in *Sable Communications*—Internet content providers simply cannot restrict the geographic area within which their messages are received.

"We are not persuaded. The plaintiff has offered no authority for the proposition that, so long as the providers of content targeted by a statute are private individuals, Congress cannot constitutionally link proscribed conduct to the community standards of various localities. While it is true that congressional action has directly targeted commercial dial-a-porn services, and restrictions on indecency in radio and television broadcasting or cable programming mainly affect for-profit enterprises, liability for violation of indecency restrictions has not been tied to the ability of a content provider to marshal its resources to explore various community indecency standards. Distributors of allegedly obscene materials may also be subjected to varying community standards; we know of no exemption for individuals whose primary motive is non-economic. Due process requires that a criminal statute 'give the person of ordinary intelligence a reasonable opportunity to know what is prohibited, so that he may act accordingly'; it does not require 'mathematical certainty,' or ' "impossible standards" of clarity,'... We have no basis for concluding that Internet content providers are any less capable than those subject to obscenity laws or other indecency restrictions to acquire a general familiarity with the relevant standards; indeed, one might conclude that a content provider's contact with others around the country and around the world through interactive computer services would cultivate a heightened awareness of regional and cultural differences.

"We turn to the plaintiff's claim that, even assuming a content provider can discern the appropriate community standards, the provider has no choice but to gear his message toward the least tolerant community. More specifically, unlike a provider of obscene or indecent telephone communications or cable programming, who might be able to prevent a message from being transmitted to certain geographical areas, an Internet content provider has no way of identifying the receiving community. It follows that, to comply with the CDA, a content provider must take steps to limit minors' access to all material that would be considered patently offensive in any community; only then could the content provider be sure that material considered inappropriate under the standards of a particular community is not available to minors in that community."

Shea v. Reno, 930 F. Supp. 916, 937-38 (S.D.N.Y. 1996).
See also **obscenity.**

compact disc *(hardware; multimedia; software)*
   See **CD.**

comparables *(business)*
Software, video game, or multimedia titles that are similar in quality and content to a specific title.

comparison *(copyright)*
"The third and final step of the test for substantial similarity that we believe appropriate for non-literal program components entails a comparison. Once a court has sifted out all elements of the allegedly infringed program which are 'ideas' or are dictated by efficiency or external factors, or taken from the public domain, there may remain a core of protectable expression. In terms of a work's copyright value, this is the golden nugget. At this point, the court's substantial similarity inquiry focuses on whether the defendant copied any aspect of this protected expression, as well as an assessment of the copied portion's relative importance with respect to the plaintiff's overall program."
Computer Assocs. Int'l, Inc. v. Altai, Inc., 982 F.2d 693, 710 (2d Cir. 1992).

Annotation. "To determine whether similarities result from unprotectable expression, analytic dissection of similarities may be performed. If . . . all similarities in expression arise from common ideas, then no substantial similarity can be found."
Data East USA, Inc. v. Epyx, Inc., 862 F.2d 204, 208 (9th Cir. 1988).
See also **abstraction-filtration-comparison method; abstractions test; idea/expression dichotomy.**

compatible *(technology)*
"[W]hen a clearly defined standard . . . exists and is widely accepted within the industry, a 'compatible' product must meet that standard or at least perform in a manner equivalent to the standard's requirements."
Princeton Graphics Operating, L.P. v. NEC Home Elecs. (U.S.A.), Inc., 732 F. Supp. 1258, 1262 (S.D.N.Y. 1990).
See also **compatibility.**

compatible software *(software)*
"[A] computer program which will perform the same overall task as an existing program."
SAS Inst., Inc. v. S&H Computer Sys., Inc., 605 F. Supp. 816, 825 (M.D. Tenn. 1985).

compatibility *(hardware; software)*
"'Compatibility' has no single definition, but instead suggests a broad range of possibilities. For mainframe processors, an operating system that is

truly 100 per cent compatible with another vendor's operating system—
that performs all functions offered by that system in exactly the same
way—might have to be virtually identical to that system."

> *IBM Corp. v. Fujitsu Ltd.*, Copyright L. Rep. (CCH) ¶ 20,517, at 11,392,
> 11,399 (Am. Arb. Ass'n 1988).

Annotation. "In order for an application program to run on an operating
system, the program must be able to request and utilize services provided
by the operating system. This is accomplished via interfaces between the
application program and the operating system. To use a simplified analogy,
the application program must contain 'plugs' that will fit properly into all
relevant 'sockets' offered by the operating system to allow the application
to run.

* * *

"If an operating system's interfaces have been clearly defined, then relatively little information beyond that defined by one vendor as its products'
customer interface specifications may be needed to independently develop a
compatible operating system that allows customers to run existing application programs written for the original operating system. However, if such
interfaces have not been clearly defined, then it may be the case that application programs have used more information, possibly including information
relating to the internal design of the operating system, in order to request
and utilize services offered by the operating system. As a result, application
programs may fail to operate on a compatible operating system that provides
only intended customer interfaces. Therefore, when interfaces have not been
clearly defined in the operating system, additional interface information
may be necessary to independently develop an operating system that meets
the primary requirements of application program compatibility."

> *IBM Corp. v. Fujitsu Ltd.*, Copyright L. Rep. (CCH) ¶ 20,517, at 11,392,
> 11,400 (Am. Arb. Ass'n 1988).

Related issues. "Compatibility and other functionality challenges to originality, if found to be applicable, are applied so as to deny copyright protection to a particular work or portion of a work."

> *Bateman v. Mnemonic, Inc.*, 79 F.3d 1532, 1546 n.28 (11th Cir. 1996).

See also **application program compatibility; multi-vendor interoperability.**

competitive advantage *(trade secret)*

Something that allows a company to do better than its competitor. The advantage may be short- or long-lived.

compilation

(copyright)

"[A] work formed by the collection and assembling of preexisting materials or of data that are selected, coordinated, or arranged in such a way that the resulting work as a whole constitutes an original work of authorship. The term 'compilation' includes collective works."

U.S. Copyright Act, 17 U.S.C. § 101.

"...results from a process of selecting, bringing together, organizing, and arranging previously existing material of all kinds, regardless of whether the individual items in the material have been or ever could have been subject to copyright."

M. Kramer Mfg. Co. v. Andrews, 783 F.2d 421, 437 n.16 (4th Cir. 1986) (citation omitted).

(technology)

"[I]nvolves an automatic process, performed by the computer under the control of a program called a 'compiler,' which translates the source code into 'object code.'..."

SAS Institute, Inc. v. S & H Computer Systems, Inc., 605 F. Supp. 816, 818 (M.D. Tenn. 1985).

Annotation (copyright). "The copyright in a compilation...extends only to the material contributed by the author of such work, as distinguished from the preexisting material employed in the work, and does not imply any exclusive right in the preexisting material. The copyright in such work is independent of, and does not affect or enlarge the scope, duration, ownership or subsistence of, any copyright protection in the preexisting material."

17 U.S.C. § 103(b).

"The use of one item retrieved from such a work—be it an address, a chemical formula, or a citation to an article—would not...conceivably constitute infringement of copyright. The retrieval and reduplication of any substantial portion of a data base, whether or not the individual data are in the public domain, would likely constitute a duplication of the copyrighted element of a data base and would be an infringement."

CONTU Final Report 42 (1978).

"A compilation of facts is not entitled to copyright protection unless the compilation itself possesses some degree of originality. Moreover, even if a compilation is original by virtue of the selection or arrangement of its component facts, the copyright is limited to that selection or arrangement and does not extend to the information contained in it."

> *Alcatel USA, Inc. v. DGI Technologies, Inc.,* 166 F.3d 772, 786 (5th Cir. 1999) (citations omitted).

"[W]e conclude that a CD-ROM disc infringes a copyrighted arrangement when a machine or device that reads it perceives the embedded material in the copyrighted arrangement or in a substantially similar arrangement. At least absent some invention, incentive, or facilitation not in the record here, a copyrighted arrangement is not infringed by a CD-ROM disc if a machine can perceive the arrangement only after another person uses the machine to *re*-arrange the material into the copyrightholder's arrangement."

> *Matthew Bender & Co. v. West Publ'g Co.,* 158 F.2d 693, 702 (2d Cir. 1998), *cert. denied,* 522 U.S. 3732 (1999) (emphasis in original).

"[I]n the case of compilations, the protected expression is the manner of selection, coordination, or arrangement of the information that constitutes the originality, not the information itself that is accumulated by the 'sweat of the brow.' Hence, copyright protection only extends to the selection, coordination and arrangement which comprises an original format of the compilation work. In the case of compilations, to satisfy the second element of the copyright infringement cause of action, there must be a substantial appropriation of the original format of the compilation to constitute the copying of protected material."

> *Bellsouth Advertising & Publishing Corp. v. Donnelley Info. Publ'g, Inc.,* 933 F.2d 952, 957 (11th Cir. 1991).

See also **originality.**

Related issues (copyright). "[I]f the compilation author clothes facts with an original collocation of words, he or she may be able to claim a copyright in this written expression. Others may copy the underlying facts from the publication, but not the precise words used to present them.... Where the compilation author adds no written expression but rather lets the facts speak for themselves, the expressive element is more elusive. The only conceivable expression is the manner in which the compiler has selected and arranged the facts. Thus, if the selection and arrangement are original, these elements of the work are eligible for copyright protection.

"This inevitably means that the copyright in a factual compilation is thin. Notwithstanding a valid copyright, a subsequent compiler remains free to use the facts contained in another's publication to aid in preparing a

competing work, so long as the competing work does not feature the same selection and arrangement."
  Feist Publications, Inc. v. Rural Tel. Serv. Co., 499 U.S. 340, 348-49 (1991).

compile *(software)*
"To prepare a machine language program from a computer program written in another programming language by making use of the overall logic structure of the program, or generating more than one machine instruction for each symbolic statement, or both, as well as performing the function of an assembler."
  U.S. Copyright Office, *Compendium of Copyright Office Practices* II, § 326 (1984).

Related issues. "Once a programmer has access to the source code of a program, he is able to determine the construction of the program and write his own version. For this reason, source code programs are typically compiled (translated) into and sold as object code or machine language, which is not discernible to even an expert programmer, but which is readily usable by the computer."
  United States v. Brown, 925 F.2d 1301, 1303 n.4 (10th Cir. 1991).

compiled data *(software)*
[CANADA] "This is precise and particular information that the application programme works on."
  Continental Comm. Sys. Corp. v. R., [1982] 5 W.W.R. 340 (B.C. C.A.).

compiler *(software)*
"A computer program that is used to change a high-level programming language into machine language. It is similar to an assembler."
  U.S. Copyright Office, *Compendium of Copyright Office Practices* II, § 326 (1984).

"Programs written in source code can be converted or translated by a 'compiler' program into object code for use by the computer."
  Apple Computer, Inc. v. Franklin Computer Corp., 714 F.2d 1240, 1243 (3d Cir. 1983), *cert. dism.*, 464 U.S. 1033 (1984).

"A program written in source code is translated into object code using a computer program called an 'assembler' or 'compiler,'..."
  Sega Enters. Ltd. v. Accolade, Inc., 977 F.2d 1510, 1514 n.2 (1992).

"[A]n automated, ruthlessly literal translator. . . ."
  Bernstein v. United States Dept. of Justice, 176 F.3d 1132, 1140 (9th Cir. 1999).

"To accomplish this, the source code is 'compiled.' This involves an automatic process, performed by the computer under the control of a program called a 'compiler,' which translates the source code into 'object code,' which is very difficult to comprehend by human beings. The object code version of the program is then loaded into the computer's memory and causes the computer to carry out the program function."

SAS Institute, Inc. v. S&H Computer Systems, Inc., 605 F. Supp. 816, 818 (M.D. Tenn. 1985).

See also **COBOL compiler; compiler program.**

Annotation. "Because source code is destined for the maw of an automated, ruthlessly literal translator—the compiler—a programmer must follow stringent grammatical, syntactical, formatting, and punctuation conventions. As a result, only those trained in programming can easily understand source code."

Bernstein v. United States Dept. of Justice, 176 F.3d 1132, 1140 (9th Cir. 1999).

compiler program *(software)*

"...translates the program once and for all into machine language, after which the translated program can be executed directly by the CPU without the need for any further resort to the compiler."

Lotus Dev. Corp. v. Paperback Software Int'l, 740 F. Supp. 37, 44 (D. Mass. 1990).

See also **COBOL compiler; compiler.**

completion bond *(entertainment; multimedia)*

Contractual commitment by a third-party guarantor to pay for completion of a multimedia or video game title according to the specifications if the developer fails to do so on time and within the agreed-upon budget.

compositing *(multimedia)*

The process of combining visual images from several sources into a single image. *See also* **blue screen.**

compression *(technology)*

See **data compression; video compression.**

compression algorithm(s) *(technology)*

Annotation. "[V]arious compression algorithms (which make an audio file 'smaller' by limiting the audio bandwidth) now allow digital audio files to be transferred more quickly and stored more efficiently."

> *Recording Indus. Ass'n of America v. Diamond Multimedia Sys., Inc.,* 180 F.3d 1072, 1073-74 (9th Cir. 1999).

compression ratio *(technology)*

A measure of data compression expressed as the ratio of the original size of a given amount of data to the compressed size.

computer

(criminal)

"[A]n electronic, mechanical, optical, electrochemical, or other high-speed data processing device performing logical, arithmetic, or storage functions, and includes any data storage facility or communications facility directly related to or operating in conjunction with such device, but such term does not include an automatic typewriter or typesetter, a portable hand held calculator, or other similar devices; . . ."

> 18 U.S.C. § 1030(e)(1).

See also **protected computer.**

(technology)

"An electronic, magnetic, optical, electrochemical, or other high speed data processing device performing logical, arithmetic, or storage functions, and includes any data storage facility or communications facility directly related to or operating in conjunction with such device, but such term does not include an automated typewriter or typesetter, a portable hand held calculator, or other similar device."

> 18 U.S.C. § 1030(e).

"A data processor that can perform substantial computation, including numerous arithmetic or logic operations, without intervention by a human operator during the run."

> U.S. Copyright Office, *Compendium of Copyright Office Practices* II, § 326 (1984).

"[A]n electronic device that accepts information in digital or similar form and manipulates it for a result based on a sequence of instructions."

> UCITA § 102(a)(9).

". . . is not mysterious to one skilled in the art; it is merely a distinct type of machine."

> *In re Walter,* 618 F.2d 758, 765 (C.C.P.A. 1980).

"...is nothing more than an electronic machine. It is characterized by its ability to process data, usually by executing mathematical operations on the data at high speeds. By virtue of the speeds with which computers operate, they are capable of executing complex or otherwise time-consuming calculations in fractions of a second. Their use in technology is analogous to the use of mechanical devices, such as levers, which provide mechanical advantages in inventions of a mechanical nature; they make possible, or practicable, the solution of mathematical problems which are impracticable to solve manually due to the inordinate amount of time a manual solution would consume."

In re Walter, 618 F.2d 758, 765 (C.C.P.A. 1980).

[CANADA] "Mechanical or electronic apparatus capable of carrying out repetitive and highly mathematical calculations at high speeds; a calculator especially designed for the solution of complex mathematical problems; specifically, a programmable electronic device that can store, retrieve, and process data; any of several devices for making rapid calculations in navigation or gunnery. Computers may be defined as systems of machines that process information in the form of letters, numbers, and other symbols, and that are self-directing within predetermined limits."

R. v. McLaughlin [1981], 1 W.W.R. 298 (S.C.C.).

[CANADA] "A complex system of interconnected, integrated electrical circuits. It consists of a circuit board (mother board) into which have been pinned or soldered a number of electronic components. The components communicate with one another by means of the traces (sometimes called buses, sometimes called wires) etched into the board. The main electronic components of the system are the input/output devices, the microprocessor (CPU) and the memory. The input/output devices connect, respectively, to whatever is being used to feed information into the computer (e.g., a keyboard, magnetic tape, punch cards) and to whatever is being used to display or otherwise make use of the information which results from the computers functioning (e.g., the screen of a monitor)."

Apple Computer, Inc. v. Mackintosh Computers Ltd. (1986), 28 D.L.R. (4th) 178 (Fed. T.D.).

[CANADA] "A highly complex miniaturized interconnected collection of electrical circuits."

Apple Computer, Inc. v. Mackintosh Computers Ltd. (1986), 28 D.L.R. (4th) 178 (Fed. T.D.).

[CANADA] "A device which is programmed to carry out a specified series of steps, but generally speaking it is the hardware itself which is usually referred to as the computer, or computing apparatus."

> *In re Application No. 096,284* (1978), 52 C.P.R. (2d) 96 (Can. Pat. App. Bd. & Pat. Comm'r).

[CANADA] "A repository for information stored in such manner that it may electrically or electronically be retrieved rapidly and, if necessary, selectively."

> *Canadian Real Estate Ass'n v. Charco Consultants Ltd.* (1976), 33 C.P.R. (2d) 15 (Reg. T.M.).

[UNITED KINGDOM] "A computer in its pristine state is merely an automatic programmable and reprogrammable, digital data processor."

> *Clinical Computing Ltd. v. Commissioners of Customs & Excise* [1983], V.A.T.T.R. 121 (London V.A.T. Trib.).

See also **general purpose computer.**

computer abuse *(criminal)*

"Criminal acts in the use of computers."

> *United States v. Jones*, 553 F.2d 351, 353 n.6 (4th Cir. 1977).

computer-aided retrieval system *(technology)*

Abbreviated as "CAR."

"[A] desk-top computer system which uses a keyword data base to interface with a micrographics reader/printer and retrieve information from microfilmed documents."

> *Property Growth Co. v. Commissioner of Internal Rev.*, T.C. Memo 1988-258, 55 TCM Dec. 44,835(M), 1073.

computer-aided software engineering *(software)*

Abbreviated as "CASE."

"'[F]ront end' Computer Aided Software Engineering [CASE] tools...are personal computer-based tools which run in the Disk Operating System [DOS] environment and are designed to automate the various stages of the software development tasks of defining user requirements, conducting system analysis activities, and creating a detailed design specification for the software system under development. There are a number of standardized engineering techniques which front-end CASE tools are designed to automate. These include techniques of 'structured analysis', 'structured design', and 'data modeling', among others. All front-end CASE tools are designed to produce logically validated and documented systems specifications, which in turn are used as detailed 'blueprints' for the actual writing of application codes. These front-end stages of the software development life cycle are contrasted with the 'backend' lifecycle stages of coding, testing, and maintenance."

> *Certain Computer Aided Software Engineering Products from Singapore*, ITA Docket C-559-804, 54 Fed. Reg. 37013, 37014 (Sept. 6, 1989).

computer bulletin board(s) *(Internet)*

"[A] computer program that simulates an actual bulletin board by allowing computer users who access a particular computer to post messages, read existing messages, and delete messages. The messages exchanged may contain a wide variety of information, including stolen credit card numbers, confidential business information, and information about local community events."

> *United States v. Riggs*, 739 F. Supp. 414, 417 n.4 (N.D. Ill. 1990).

"Computer bulletin boards generally offer both private electronic mail services and newsgroups. The latter is essentially email directed to the community at large, rather than a private recipient. A bulletin board is an interactive or bidirectional service that cannot currently be offered through cable television transmissions."

> *MTV Networks, Inc. v. Curry*, 867 F. Supp. 202, 204 n.3 (S.D.N.Y. 1994).

See also **bulletin board system.**

computer contaminants

(criminal)

"[A]ny set of computer instructions that are designed to modify, damage, destroy, record, or transmit information within a computer, computer system, or computer network without the intent or permission of the owner of the information. They include, but are not limited to, a group of computer instructions commonly called viruses or worms, that are self-replicating or self-propagating and are designed to contaminate other computer programs or computer data, or in some other fashion usurp the normal operation of the computer, computer system, or computer network."

> Cal. Penal C. § 502.

(software)

"[A]ny set of computer instructions that are designed to modify or in any way alter, damage, destroy or disrupt the proper operation of a computer system or computer network."

> Tenn. Code Ann. § 39-14-601(3) (1995).

See also **trapdoor; Trojan horse; worm.**

computer crime *(criminal)*

Annotation. "[T]he statutory [Cal. Penal C. § 502] intent [is] to comprehensively protect the integrity of private, commercial, and governmental computer systems and data."
> *People v. Lawton,* 48 Cal. App. 4th Supp. 11, 56 Cal. Rptr. 2d 521 (Cal. Super. Ct. 1996).

Related issues. "The Legislature finds and declares that the proliferation of computer technology has resulted in a concomitant proliferation of computer crime and other forms of unauthorized access to computers, computer systems, and computer data."
> Cal. Penal C. § 502(a).

"Public access computer terminals are increasingly common in the offices of many governmental bodies and agencies, from courthouses to tax assessors. We believe subdivision (c)(7) [of Cal. Penal C. § 502)] was designed to criminalize unauthorized access to the software and data in such systems, even where none of the other illegal activities listed in subdivision (c) have occurred."
> *People v. Lawton,* 48 Cal. App. 4th Supp. 11, 56 Cal. Rptr. 2d 521 (Cal. Super. Ct. 1996).

"To the extent that 'mere browsing' in this fashion may cause little or no harm, the statute appropriately sets modest penalties for unaggravated behavior."
> *People v. Lawton,* 48 Cal. App. 4th Supp. 11, 56 Cal. Rptr. 2d 521 (Cal. Super. Ct. 1996).

computer-generated *(technology)*
[UNITED KINGDOM] " 'Computer-generated,' in relation to a work, means that the work is generated by computer in circumstances such that there is no human author of the work."
> U.K. Copyright, Designs, and Patents Act 1988, c. 48.

computer graphics *(technology)*
"...use of a computer to create, transform, and display pictorial data...."
> *Jostens, Inc. v. National Computer Sys., Inc.,* 8 Computer L. Serv. Rep. 146, 148 (Minn. County Ct. 1981).

computer information *(contract)*
"[I]nformation, in electronic form which is obtained from or through the use of a computer or which is in a form capable of being processed by a

computer. The term includes a copy of the information and any documentation or packaging associated with the copy."

UCITA § 102(a)(10).

computer information transaction *(contract)*

"[A]n agreement or the performance of it to create, modify, transfer, or license computer information or informational rights in computer information. The term includes a support contract.... The term does not include a transaction merely because the parties' agreement provides that their communications about the transaction will be in the form of computer information."

UCITA § 102(a)(11).

computer language *(software)*

[CANADA] "A computer language, of which there are many, is a code for writing a program. A language is said to be higher or lower depending upon the ease with which it can be read. A high-level language has symbols and rules that correspond closely enough to ordinary mathematics and English (or other common language) and it may be read and understood with relative ease. Examples are languages such as BASIC, COBOL, Pascal, and FORTRAN. A second level of language, which can be referred to as an intermediate level, consists of mnemonics which correspond more explicitly to the operations the computer must perform. This intermediate level is referred to as assembly language. A third level of language, the lowest, is sometimes referred to as machine language or object code."

Apple Computer, Inc. v. Mackintosh Computers Ltd. (1986), 28 D.L.R. (4th) 178 (Fed. T.D.).

computer malpractice *(tort)*

"The novel concept of a new tort called 'computer malpractice' is premised upon a theory of elevated responsibility on the part of those who render computer sales and service. Plaintiff equates the sale and servicing of computer systems with established theories of professional malpractice. Simply because an activity is technically complex and important to the business community does not mean that greater potential liability must attach. In the absence of sound precedential authority, the Court declines the invitation to create a new tort. In view of the findings and conclusions, infra, the Court deems it unnecessary to rule explicitly on plaintiff's assertion of strict liability in tort."

Chatlos Sys., Inc. v. National Cash Register Corp., 479 F. Supp. 738, 740 n.1 (D.N.J. 1979), *aff'd in part, rev'd in part*, 635 F.2d 1081 (3d Cir. 1980), *cert. dism.*, 457 U.S. 1112 (1982).

Annotation. "If machinists, electricians, carpenters, blacksmiths, and plumbers are held to the ordinary standard of care in their professions, the Court fails to see why personnel in the computer industry should be held to any lower standard of care. [Plaintiff] simply alleges negligence in a business setting. This does not give rise to a new tort of 'computer malpractice.' Negligence is a business setting is clearly actionable."

> *Invacare Corp. v. Sperry Rand Corp.*, 612 F. Supp. 448, 453 (N.D. Ohio. 1984).

computer matching *(software)*

"A procedure in which a computer is used to compare two or more automated systems of records or a system of records with a set of nonfederal records to find individuals who are common to more than one system or set."

> U.S. Congress, Office of Technology Assessment, *Electronic Record Systems and Individual Privacy* 38 n.1 (June 1986).

computer memory *(hardware)*

[CANADA] "At the electrical level, the computer memory is an integrated circuit which is capable of holding, because of its circuitry, a pattern of high and low voltage states."

> *Apple Computer, Inc. v. Mackintosh Computers Ltd.* (1986), 28 D.L.R. (4th) 178 (Fed. T.D.).

See also **core; magnetic memory core; main memory; memory plane.**

computer network(s)

(criminal)

"[A]ny system that provides communications between one or more computer systems and input/output devices including, but not limited to, display terminals and printers connected by telecommunications facilities."

> Cal. Penal C. § 502.

(hardware; software)

"[A] configuration of hardware and software products connected for information interchange through communications facilities."

> *IBM Corp. v. Fujitsu Ltd.*, Copyright L. Rep. (CCH) ¶ 20,517, at 11,392, 11,403 (Am. Arb. Ass'n 1988).

Annotation. (criminal) "[T]he hardware and software which links one or more systems with each other and/or with terminals and printers."

> *People v. Lawton,* 48 Cal. App. 4th Supp. 11, 15, 56 Cal. Rptr. 2d 521, 523 (Cal. Super. Ct. 1996).

"[S]ystems of interconnected computers that allow the exchange of information between the connected computers."

> *United States v. Baker*, 890 F. Supp. 1375, 1379 n.1 (E.D. Mich. 1995), *cited approvingly in CompuServe Corp. v. Patterson*, 89 F.2d 1257, 1271 n.2 (6th Cir. 1996).

See also Internet; LAN; network.

computer printout *(technology)*

[SOUTH AFRICA] "Any statement or report which the computer may print."

> *Northern Office Micro Computers Ltd. v. Rosenstein* [1982], F.S.R. 124 (S.C. S. Africa).

computer-processed music *(technology)*

Music created or modified through the use of a computer system.

Annotation. "... permits the processing, editing, and resynthesis of sometimes costly preexisting works in the production of new works. Music can be sampled and manipulated in a process known as digital editing, and the notes and even the work itself can be rearranged and manipulated to create entirely new works."

> Office of Technology Assessment, *Intellectual Property in an Age of Electronics and Information* 70 (Apr. 1986).

computer program

(contract)

"[A] set of statements or instructions to be used directly or indirectly in a computer to bring about a certain result. The term does not include separately identifiable informational content."

> UCITA § 102(a)(12).

(copyright)

"[A] set of statements or instructions to be used directly or indirectly in a computer in order to bring about a certain result."

> U.S. Copyright Act, 17 U.S.C. § 101; *quoted in Stern Elecs., Inc. v. Kaufman*, 669 F.2d 852, 855 (2d Cir. 1982); *Pearl Sys., Inc. v. Competition Elecs., Inc.*, 8 U.S.P.Q.2d (BNA) 1520, 1521 n.1 (S.D. Fla. 1988).

"[A] set of statements or instructions to be used directly or indirectly in a computer in order to bring about a certain result."

> *Healthcare Affiliated Servs., Inc. v. Lippany*, 701 F. Supp. 1142, 1144 (W.D. Pa. 1988).

"[A] set of precise instructions that tells the computer how to solve a problem."
Data Cash Sys., Inc. v. JS&A Group, Inc., 480 F. Supp. 1063, 1065 (N.D. Ill. 1979), *aff'd*, 628 F.2d 1038 (7th Cir. 1980) (citation omitted).

"[A] set of detailed instructions by which the computer performs certain functions or delivers a desired result. While the program usually involves very complicated problems and procedures, these same problems and procedures could be solved with paper and pencil. The difference, of course, is the very long time it would require to perform the same functions manually that the computer, properly programmed, would perform in a matter of seconds."
Williams v. Arndt, 626 F. Supp. 571, 577 (D. Mass. 1985).

"[A] series of computer-intelligible messages which control the operation of the computer equipment in its performance. A program is introduced into the computer system and is retained therein electronically; it is often called software."
Central Trust Co. v. Lindley, 8 Computer L. Serv. Rep. 24, 34 (Ohio Bd. Tax App. 1979).

"... in a general sense instructs the computer regarding the things it is to do. In the industry, the physical machinery is referred to as hardware and the instructional material as software."
Synercom Technology, Inc. v. University Computing Co., 462 F. Supp. 1003, 1005 (N.D. Tex. 1978).

"... is made up of several different components, including the source and object code, the structure, sequence and/or organization of the program, the user interface, and the function, or purpose, of the program."
Johnson Controls, Inc. v. Phoenix Control Sys., Inc., 886 F.2d 1173, 1175 (9th Cir. 1989).

(criminal)
"[A] set of instructions or statements, and related data, that when executed in actual or modified form, cause a computer, computer system, or computer network to perform specified functions."
Cal. Penal C. § 502.

"... is property and means an ordered set of data representing coded instructions or statements that, when executed by computer, cause the computer to process data or direct the computer to perform one or more computer operations or both and may be in any form, including magnetic storage media, punched cards, or stored internally in the memory of the computer."
N.Y. Penal L. 156.00[2], *cited in People v. Versaggi*, 518 N.Y.S.2d 553, 556 (N.Y. Crim. 1987).

(patent)
"[A] set of instructions for carrying out pre-arranged operations on data by use of processing equipment."
  In re Ghiron, 442 F.2d 985, 986 (C.C.P.A. 1971).

"[A] sequence of coded instructions for a digital computer."
  Gottschalk v. Benson, 409 U.S. 63, 65 (1972).

(taxation)
"[A] list of instructions, one line at a time, each of which causes the computer to take a specific action. Once the program has been developed, it is preserved in the form of magnetic tapes, punch cards or some other recording medium."
  Computer Sciences Corp. v. Commissioner of Internal Rev., 63 T.C. 327, 329 (1974).

Annotation
(copyright)
"This 'set of statements or instructions,' in its literal or written manifestation, may be in the form of object code or source code. It may also be represented, in a partially literal manifestation, by a flowchart. A copyrightable work designed for use on a computer may include, as well, text that appears, for example, in a problem [sic] manual or a manual of instructions. These elements of text, however, ordinarily are not referred to in the industry as part of a 'computer program' unless they appear on the computer screen and serve a purpose like that of the components of a 'help screen' available to the user whenever needed."
  Lotus Dev. Corp. v. Paperback Software Int'l, 740 F. Supp. 37, 43 (D. Mass. 1990).

"Of signal difficulty in this case is the elasticity of the word 'program.' A computer program is a set of serial instructions that directs the computer to perform certain tasks. A user does not instruct the operating center of the machine. The user writes programs that are expressed in 'high level' languages resembling English. Depending on the circumstances, one or more special machine 'programs' will in turn translate or 'interpret' those instructions, given by the user, into a form of instruction that can be executed in the circuitry. At the level of the circuitry, programs are expressed in 'low level' languages. At the very lowest level, every program is eventually reduced to 'an object code,' which is expressed in binary (base 2) numbers, a series of zeroes and ones that represent open and closed switches within the computer's circuits."
  Apple Computer, Inc. v. Franklin Computer Corp., 545 F. Supp. 812, 813-14 (E.D. Pa. 1982), *rev'd*, 714 F.2d 1240 (3d Cir. 1983), *cert. dism.*, 464 U.S. 1033 (1984).

"In the industry, computer programs are referred to as 'software,' which term encompasses systems programs and application programs."

Computer Sciences Corp. v. Commissioner of Internal Revenue, 63 T.C. 327, 329 (1974).

(patent)
"Computer programs embodied in a tangible medium, such as floppy diskettes, are patentable subject matter under 35 U.S.C. §101 and must be examined...."

In re Beauregard, 53 F.3d 1583, 1584 (Fed. Cir. 1995).

(taxation)
"[T]he 'deck of cards'... that the banks bought, is a translation into computer language of a set of instructions to the computer. Each grid point can be given either a positive or a negative electrical charge. Particular sequences of charges process the factual data in the computer. When the cards are fed into the computer, the computer language on those cards causes the computer to arrange the factual data that it receives and stores, and to retrieve it, in particular ways. A particular use or particular uses of the data fed into the computer, and retrieved from it, is accomplished by a program properly designed to store and retrieve data in the desired manner. Thus, for example, the computer may be programmed to print out monthly bills, weekly sales volumes, etc."

First Security Bank of Idaho v. Commissioner of Internal Rev., 592 F.2d 1050, 1053 (9th Cir. 1979).

"[T]he instructions which make the data processing equipment perform tasks and include 'operational programs' which are the basic functions of the computer and 'application programs' which are the particularized instructions adapted for an individual user."

Honeywell Information Sys., Inc. v. Maricopa County, 118 Ariz. 171, 575 P.2d 801, 808 (App. 1977).

Related issues. (copyright). "There can no longer exist any doubt that computer programs are copyrightable."

S&H Computer Sys., Inc. v. SAS Inst., Inc., 568 F. Supp. 416, 422 (M.D. Tenn. 1983).

See also **computer software; software.**

computer program listing *(software)*

"A printout that lists in appropriate sequence the instructions, routines, and other contents of a program for a computer."

37 C.F.R. §1.96.

computer service(s) *(business)*

"...entail both the sale of computer programs to customers who own their own computer equipment, and leasing of time on in-house computers. This latter type of service is referred to as functioning on a 'service bureau basis' in the industry."

> *University Computing Co. v. Lykes-Youngstown Corp.*, 504 F.2d 518, 527 n.1 (5th Cir.), *rehearing denied*, 505 F.2d 1304 (5th Cir. 1974).

See also service bureau.

(criminal)

"... includes, but is not limited to, computer time, data processing, or storage functions, or other uses of a computer, computer system, or computer network."

> Cal. Penal C. § 502.

computer software

(criminal)

"[A] set of instructions or statements, and related data, that when executed in actual or modified form, cause a computer, computer system, or computer network to perform specified functions."

> Cal. Penal C. § 502.

(software)

"... consist of individual 'functions', which are contained in one or more 'files'."

> *Foresight Resources Corp. v. Pfortmiller*, 719 F. Supp. 1006, 1008 (D. Kan. 1989).

"...tells computer hardware to generate inWnitesimally brief, timed pulses of electricity according to a programmed sequence, hence the word program."

> *Jostens, Inc. v. National Computer Sys., Inc.*, 318 N.W.2d 691, 695 n.3 (Minn. 1982).

See also computer program; software.

Computer Software Act of 1980 *(copyright)*

See Copyright Act of 1980 Amendments.

computer system(s)

(criminal)

"[A] device or collection of devices, including support devices and excluding calculators that are not programmable and capable of being used in conjunction with external files, one or more of which contain computer programs, electronic instructions, input data, and output data, that performs functions including, but not limited to, logic, arithmetic, data storage and retrieval, communication, and control."

Cal. Penal C. § 502.

(hardware; software)
"The computer itself is the 'hardware'; the programming necessary to run it is the 'software'; together the hardware and software form the 'computer system.'"

Computer Systems Eng'g, Inc. v. Qantel Corp., 740 F.2d 59, 63 n.3 (1st Cir. 1984).

"...consists of a central processing unit (or 'mainframe') and peripheral equipment."

Greyhound Computer Corp. v. IBM Corp., 559 F.2d 488, 492 (9th Cir. 1977).

"[A] series of computer programs designed to accomplish specific business tasks. Normally this entails programming the computer to generate specific reports to be used in making business decisions."

University Computing Co. v. Lykes-Youngstown Corp., 504 F.2d 518, 527 n.2 (5th Cir. 1974).

"[A] group of devices designed: (a) to receive various forms of data (input); (b) to process the data in accordance with predesignated sets of instructions (programs); and (c) to produce the desired information (output)."

Dreier Co. v. Unitronix Corp., 218 N.J. Super. 260, 527 A.2d 875, 879 (1986).

[CANADA] "[A] device that, or a group of interconnected or related devices one or more of which, (a) contains computer programs or other data, and (b) pursuant to computer programs, (i) performs logic and control, and (ii) may perform any other function."

Criminal Code of Canada, R.S.C. 1985, c. C-46, s. 342.1(2) [en. R.S.C. 1985, c. 27 (1st Supp.), s. 45].

Annotation. (criminal). "To paraphrase the statute, a 'computer system' is a functioning combination of hardware and software."

People v. Lawton, 48 Cal App. 4th Supp. 11, 15, 56 Cal. Rptr. 2d 521, 523 (Cal. Super. Ct. 1996)

See also **EDP system; electronic data processing.**

computer tampering *(criminal)*

"[W]hen [a person] uses or causes to be used a computer or computer service and having no right to do so he intentionally alters in any manner or destroys computer data or a computer program of another person."

N.Y. Penal L. 156.20, *quoted in People v. Versaggi,* 518 N.Y.S.2d 553, 554 (N.Y. Crim. Ct. 1987).

computer text file *(technology)*

"A collection of stored data which, when retrieved from a disk or other computer storing device, presents typed English characters on a computer monitor, printer, or other media compatible with the computer storing the data."

United States v. Riggs, 739 F. Supp. 414, 416 n.2 (N.D. Ill. 1990).

computer virus *(criminal; software)*

"An unwanted computer program or other set of instructions inserted into a computer's memory, operating system, or program that is specifically constructed with the ability to replicate itself and to affect the other programs or files in the computer by attaching a copy of the unwanted program or other set of instructions to one or more computer programs or files."

Tex. Pen. Code § 33.01(9) (1989).

"[A] migrating program, [which] attaches itself to the operating system of any computer it enters and can infect any other computer that uses files from the infected computer."

United States v. Morris, 928 F.2d 504, 505 n.1 (2d Cir. 1991).

See also **virus.**

computerized reservation system *(business)*

Abbreviated as "CRS." *See* **CRS.**

computing *(technology)*

The processing of information by a computer.

Annotation. "…may involve both simple and complicated calculations, or the storage and sorting of large amounts of data."

Telex Corp. v. IBM Corp., 367 F. Supp. 258, 273 (N.D. Okla. 1973), aff'd in part, rev'd in part, 510 F.2d 894 (10th Cir.), cert. dism., 423 U.S. 802 (1975).

COMSAT *(organization)*

Acronym for "**Com**munications **Sat**ellite Corporation."

concurrent execution *(technology)*

"[T]he ability of a computer system to have two or more separate and unrelated programs running at the same time. The CPU works on a program for a time, then sets it aside and works on another, etc. Eventually it returns to the first program and picks up where it left off. This is made possible by the fact that a CPU processes data much faster than its peripherals operate. Also called multiprogramming."

In re Digital Research, Inc., 4 U.S.P.Q.2d (BNA) 1242, 1243 (T.T.A.B. 1987).

Conference on Fair Use *(copyright; government; organization)*
See CONFU.

configuration *(technology)*
The design or layout of a particular computer system with all its peripherals. To configure a system is to design a compatible system to meet the user's needs.

confirm *(electronic commerce)*
"[T]o ascertain through appropriate inquiry and investigation."
Wash. Rev. Code § 19.34.020(9).

conforming *(contract)*
"Goods or conduct including any part of a performance are 'conforming' or conform to the contract when they are in accordance with the obligations under the contract."
U.C.C. § 2-106(2).

CONFU *(copyright; government; organization)*
Acronym for "**Con**ference on **F**air **U**se." A conference convened by the Working Group on Intellectual Property of the Information Infrastructure Task Force to bring together copyright owner and user interests to discuss fair use issues and, if possible, to develop guidelines for uses of copyrighted works by librarians and educators.

connect time *(technology)*
"[E]ach unit of time that [s]ubscriber is in contact with [vendor's] entral computer, beginning with the transmission of an identification number and ending when connection with the computer is terminated."
Meites v. City of Chicago, 1 Computer Cas. (CCH) ¶ 46,115, at 61,314, 61,316 (Ill. App. 1989).

connectivity *(technology)*
"The capacity of one system or device to link to a second system or device to complete a connection and provide continuing service."

consequential damages

(contract)

"[A]ny loss[es] resulting from general or particular requirements and needs of which the seller at the time of contracting had reason to know and which could not reasonably be prevented," and "injur[ies] to person or property proximately resulting from any breach of warranty."

U.C.C. § 2-715(2).

"...resulting from breach of contract includes (i) any loss resulting from general or particular requirements and needs of which the breaching party at the time of contracting had reason to know and which could not reasonably be prevented and (ii) any injury to an individual or damage to property other than the subject matter of the transaction proximately resulting from breach of warranty. The term does not include direct damages or incidental damages."

UCITA § 102(a)(13).

(trade secret)

"Consequential damages, as long as they are reasonably foreseeable, are the norm in tort cases, and the misappropriation of a trade secret is a tort; we are just surprised not to have found any case in which consequential damages were awarded for such a misappropriation."

Micro Data Base Sys., Inc. v. Dharma Sys., Inc., 148 F.3d 649, 658 (7th Cir. 1998) (citation omitted).

Related issues (contract). "[T]he commercial context in which a contract is made is of substantial importance in determining whether particular damages flowing from its breach are direct or consequential."

Applied Data Processing, Inc. v. Burroughs Corp., 394 F. Supp. 504, 509 (D. Conn. 1974).

consequential damages, limitations on *(contract)*

"Consequential damages may be limited or excluded unless the limitation or exclusion is unconscionable. Limitation of consequential damages for injury to the person in the case of consumer goods is prima facie unconscionable but limitation of damages where the loss is commercial is not."

U.C.C. § 2-719(3) (1979).

"[I]nclude compensation for losses resulting from a party's general or particular requirements and needs of which the other party at the time of contracting had reason to know and which losses could not reasonably be prevented by the aggrieved party, and compensation for losses from injury to person or property proximately resulting from any breach of warranty. The term does not include direct or incidental damages."

U.C.C. 2B-102(a)(11) (proposed).

"The principle is one of the prevention of oppression and unfair surprise...and not of disturbance of allocation of risks because of superior bargaining power."

Harper Tax Servs., Inc. v. Quick Tax Ltd., 686 F. Supp. 106 (D. Md. 1988), *quoting* U.C.C. § 2-302, Official Comment 1.

"Limitations on consequential damages are generally valid under the U.C.C. unless they are unconscionable. Whether a limitation on consequential damages is unconscionable is a question of law. 'Exclusionary clauses in purely commercial transactions...are prima facie conscionable and the burden of establishing unconscionability is on the party attacking it.' If there is no threshold showing of unconscionability, the issue may be determined on summary judgment."

M.A. Mortenson Co., Inc. v. Timberline Software Corp., 998 P.2d 305, 314 (Wash. 2000), *aff'g* 93 Wash. App. 819, 970 P.2d 803 (1999).

Related issues. "The limited remedy of repair and a consequential damage exclusion are two distinct ways of attempting to limit recovery for breach of warranty.... The Code, moreover, tests each by a different standard. The former survives unless it fails of its essential purpose, while the latter is valid unless it is unconscionable. We therefore see no reason to hold, as a general proposition, that the failure of the limited remedy provided in the contract, without more, invalidates a wholly distinct term in the agreement excluding consequential damages. The two are not mutually exclusive."

Chatlos Sys., Inc. v. National Cash Register Co., 635 F.2d 1081, 1086 (3d Cir. 1980), *cert. dism.*, 457 U.S. 1112 (1982) (citations and footnote omitted).

"Comment 3 to [U.C.C.] sec. 2-719 generally approves consequential damage exclusions as 'merely an allocation of unknown or undeterminable risks.' Thus, the presence of latent defects in the goods cannot render these clauses unconscionable. The need for certainty in risk allocation is especially compelling where, as here, the goods are experimental and their performance by nature less predictable."

M.A. Mortenson Co., Inc. v. Timberline Software Corp., 998 P.2d 305, 315 (Wash. 2000), *aff'g* 93 Wash. App. 819, 970 P.2d 803 (1999).

console *(video game)*

"[A] base unit into which a user inserts game cartridges. These cartridges contain the various game programs for the NES. As dictated by the program on the cartridge, the console controls an image on a video monitor, often a television set."

> *Atari Games Corp. v. Nintendo of America, Inc.*, 975 F.2d 832, 835 (Fed. Cir. 1992).

conspicuous *(contract)*

"A term or clause is conspicuous when it is so written that a reasonable person against whom it is to operate ought to have noticed it.... Language in the body of a form is 'conspicuous' if it is in larger or other contrasting type or color.... Whether a term or clause is 'conspicuous' or not is for decision by the court."

> U.C.C. § 1-201(10).

"[W]ith reference to a term, means so written, displayed, or presented that a reasonable person against which it is to operate ought to have noticed it. A term in an electronic record intended to evoke a response by an electronic agent is conspicuous if it is presented in a form that would enable a reasonably configured electronic agent to take it into account or react to it without review of the record by an individual. Conspicuous terms include the following:

(A) with respect to a person:

(i) a heading in capitals in a size equal to or greater than, or in contrasting type, font, or color to, the surrounding text;

(ii) language in the body of a record or display in larger or other contrasting type, font, or color or set off from the surrounding text by symbols or other marks that draw attention to the language; and

(iii) a term prominently referenced in an electronic record or display which is readily accessible or reviewable from the record or display; and

(B) with respect to a person or an electronic agent, a term or reference to a term that is so placed in a record or display that the person or electronic agent cannot proceed without taking action with respect to the particular term or reference."

> UCITA § 102(a)(14).

consumer *(contract)*

"A buyer (other than for purposes of resale) of any consumer product, any person to whom such product is transferred during the duration of an implied or written warranty (or service contract) applicable to the product, and any other person who is entitled by the terms of such warranty (or service contract) or under applicable State law to enforce against the war-

rantor (or service contractor) the obligations of the warranty (or service contract)."
15 U.S.C. § 2301(3).

"[A]n individual who is a licensee of information or informational rights that the individual at the time of contracting intended to be used primarily for personal, family, or household purposes. The term does not include an individual who is a licensee primarily for professional or commercial purposes, including agriculture, business management, and investment management other than management of the individual's personal or family investments."
UCITA § 102(a)(15).

consumer contract *(contract)*
"[A] contract between a merchant licensor and a consumer."
UCITA § 102(a)(16).

consumer fraud *(tort)*
Fraudulent activities and unfair business practices directed at consumers.

Related issues. "[F]or Internet consumer fraud claims, the Internet medium is essentially irrelevant, for the focus is primarily upon the location of the messenger and whether the messenger delivered what was purchased. In some cases, it might be necessary to analyze the location of certain other business operations, such as the site used or the place orders were received."
People v. Lipsitz, 663 N.Y.S.2d 468, 474 (Sup. Ct. N.Y. Cty. 1997).
See also **fraud.**

consumer goods *(contract)*
"[Goods] used or bought for use primarily for personal, family or household purposes...."
U.C.C. § 9-109(1).

consumer products *(contract)*
"[A]ny tangible personal property which is distributed in commerce and which is normally used for personal, family, or household purposes (including any such property intended to be attached to or installed in any real property, without regard to whether it is so attached or installed)."
15 U.S.C. § 2301(1).

"[A]n agreement under which a consumer is the licensee."
U.C.C. 2B-102(a)(14) (proposed).

content *(criminal)*

"[W]hen used with respect to any wire, oral, or electronic communication, includes any information concerning the substance, purport, or meaning of that communication; . . ."
18 U.S.C. § 2510(8).

(Internet; multimedia)

"[A]ny text, data, sound, program, or visual image transmitted over or made available for retrieval on an interactive computer [service]."
Shea v. Reno, 930 F. Supp. 916, 925 n.2 (S.D.N.Y. 1996).

Related issues. "[W]ith the exception of e-mail, no content appears on a user's screen without the user having first taken some affirmative step."
Shea v. Reno, 930 F. Supp. 916, 931 (S.D.N.Y. 1996).

"It is no exaggeration to conclude that the content on the Internet is as diverse as human thought."
American Civil Liberties Union v. Reno, 929 F. Supp. 824, 842 (E.D. Pa. 1996), *aff'd, Reno v. American Civil Liberties Union*, 521 U.S. 844 (1997).

content development *(business; multimedia)*

The creation of information resources for the purpose of dissemination through one or more media, such as CD-ROM and online services.

content license *(contract)*

A license agreement for the use of content, either digital or nondigital, under specific terms and conditions.

Sample clause. "LICENSOR hereby grants to LICENSEE, its successors and assigns, an exclusive, irrevocable, perpetual (except as provided in the section defining 'Term') right, license and privilege worldwide ('Territory') to:

1. incorporate the WORK in the GAME and reproduce, distribute, import and sell the GAME on CD-ROM throughout the Territory on the following platforms: [describe platforms].

2. publicly perform and authorize others to perform the GAME (and those portions of the WORK incorporated therein) in connection with the advertising, publicizing, marketing and distribution of the GAME.

3. utilize the trademarks [identify trademarks] in connection with the advertising, publicizing, marketing and distribution, including on the packaging in which the GAME is distributed."

content packager *(business)*

An organization that combines ("packages") various content (sometimes its own, usually others) into a CD-ROM title or online service.

content provider(s) *(business)*

"[E]quivalent to the traditional 'speaker.'"
American Civil Liberties Union v. Reno, 929 F. Supp. 824, 843 (E.D. Pa. 1996), *aff'd, Reno v. American Civil Liberties Union*, 521 U.S. 844 (1997).

"[A]ny Internet 'speaker'—that is, a user who transmits or makes available any content over the Internet; . . . The phrase serves as a reasonable shorthand for the category of individuals targeted by the CDA—persons who send or display Internet content."
Shea v. Reno, 930 F. Supp. 916, 927 n.5 (S.D.N.Y. 1996).

Annotation. "[T]he Internet presents extremely low entry barriers to those who wish to convey Internet content or gain access to it. In particular, a user wishing to communicate through e-mail, newsgroups, or Internet Relay Chat need only have access to a computer with appropriate software and a connection to the Internet, usually available for a low monthly fee. The user then in a sense becomes a public 'speaker,' able to convey content, at relatively low cost, to users around the world to whom it may be of interest. Those who possess more sophisticated equipment and greater technical expertise can make content available on the Internet for retrieval by others (known and unknown) by running a server supporting anonymous FTP, a gopher server, or a Web server. Yet content providers need not necessarily run their own servers or have the programming expertise to construct their own sites; they can lease space on a Web server from another or create a 'home page' through an on-line commercial service."
Shea v. Reno, 930 F. Supp. 916, 929 (S.D.N.Y. 1996).

Related issues. "[D]istinctions in how Internet content is transmitted affect the degree of control that providers of content have over who will be able to gain access to their communications."
Shea v. Reno, 930 F. Supp. 916, 926-27 (S.D.N.Y. 1996).

"A content provider has no control over what client software a user installs, how the user reconfigures that software, or whether a minor can undo the reconfiguration. Thus, a content provider has no way of ensuring that a message posted to a newsgroup or a mailing list will not be available to persons under the age of eighteen; . . ."
Shea v. Reno, 930 F. Supp. 916, 946 (S.D.N.Y. 1996).

See also **information content provider.**

contingency plan *(business; Year 2000)*

A plan for responding to the loss of system use due to a disaster such as a flood, fire, computer virus, or major software failure. The plan contains procedures for emergency response, backup, and postdisaster recovery.

continuous processing *(technology)*

"[A] term commonly found in computer dictionaries to describe input systems that allow the introduction of information in a steady flow rather than in discrete chunks associated with 'batch processing.'"

Stratus Computer, Inc. v. NCR Corp., 2 U.S.P.Q. 2d (BNA) 1375, 1375 (D. Mass. 1987).

See also **fault-tolerant computers.**

contract *(contract)*

"[T]he total legal obligation which results from the parties' agreement as affected by this Act and any other applicable rules of law."

U.C.C. § 1-201(11).

"[U]nless the context otherwise requires 'contract' [is] limited to those relating to the present or future sale of goods."

U.C.C. § 2-106(1).

"[T]he total legal obligation resulting from the parties' agreement as affected by this [Act] and other applicable law.

UCITA § 102(a)(17).

Annotation. "[A] contract may be formed in any manner sufficient to show agreement...."

UCITA § 202(a).

contract fee *(contract)*

"[T]he price, fee, rent, or royalty payable in a contract under this Article."

UCITA § 102(a)(18).

contract for sale *(contract)*

"[I]ncludes both a present sale of goods and a contract to sell goods at a future time."

U.C.C. § 2-106(1).

contractual use term *(contract)*

"[A]n enforceable term that defines or limits the use, disclosure of, or access to licensed information or informational rights, including a term that defines the scope of a license."

UCITA § 102(a)(19).

contributory infringement

(copyright)

"'[O]ne who, with knowledge of the infringing activity, induces, causes or materially contributes to the infringing conduct of another,' may be held liable as a contributory infringer."

Sega Enters. Ltd. v. MAPHIA, 857 F. Supp. 679, 686 (N.D. Cal. 1994).

"A party is liable for contributory infringement when it, 'with knowledge of the infringing activity, induces, causes or materially contributes to infringing conduct of another.' "

Alcatel USA, Inc. v. DGI Technologies, Inc., 166 F.3d 772, 790 (5th Cir. 1999) (citation omitted).

"An act of direct infringement is a necessary predicate for any derivative liability on the part of [defendant]; absent direct infringement, there can be no contributory infringement."

DSC Comm. Corp. v. Pulse Comm., Inc., 170 F.3d 1354, 1359 (Fed. Cir. 1999).

"Notwithstanding the absence of substantial similarity, a database manufacturer may be liable as a contributory infringer (in certain circumstances) for creating a product that assists a user to infringe a copyright directly."

Matthew Bender & Co. v. West Publ'g Co., 158 F.3d 693, 706 (2d Cir. 1998), *cert. denied,* 522 U.S. 3732 (1999).

"[A] party 'who, with knowledge of the infringing activity, induces, causes, or materially contributes to the infringing conduct of another, may be held liable as a "contributory" infringer.' "

Matthew Bender & Co. v. West Publ'g Co., 158 F.3d 693, 706 (2d Cir. 1998), *cert. denied,* 522 U.S. 3732 (1999) (citations omitted).

(trademark)

"As to contributory infringement, there are two potential bases for liability. First, a defendant is liable if it intentionally induced others to infringe a mark. Second, a defendant is liable if it continued to supply a product to others when the defendant knew or had reason to know that the party receiving the product used it to infringe a mark."

Lockheed Martin Corp. v. Network Solutions, Inc., 985 F. Supp. 949, 951 (C.D. Cal. 1997) (citations omitted).

"Contributory infringement doctrine extends liability to reach manufacturers and distributors who do not themselves use the mark in connection with the sale of goods, but who induce such use by supplying goods to direct infringers. Liability for contributory infringement requires that the defendant either '(1) intentionally induces another to infringe on a trademark or (2) continues to supply a product knowing that the recipient is using the product to engage in trademark infringement.'"

Lockheed Martin Corp. v. Network Solutions, Inc., 985 F. Supp. 949, 951 (C.D. Cal. 1997).

***Annotation** (copyright).* "The absence of...express language in the copyright statute does not preclude the imposition of liability for copyright infringements on certain parties who have not themselves engaged in the infringing activity for vicarious liability is imposed in virtually all areas of the law, and the concept of contributory infringement is merely a species of the broader problem of identifying the circumstances in which it is just to hold one individual accountable for the actions of another."

Sony Corp. v. Universal City Studios, Inc., 464 U.S. 417, 435 (1984).

"[T]he sale of copying equipment, like the sale of other articles of commerce, does not constitute contributory infringement if the product is widely used for legitimate, unobjectionable purposes. Indeed, it need merely be capable of substantial noninfringing uses."

Sony Corp. v. Universal City Studios, Inc., 464 U.S. 417, 442 (1984).

Related issues
(copyright)
"Contributory infringement is a form of third party liability."

Lewis Galoob Toys, Inc. v. Nintendo of America, Inc., 964 F.2d 965, 970 (9th Cir. 1992).

"Where a BBS operator cannot reasonably verify a claim of infringement, either because of a possible fair use defense, the lack of copyright notices on the copies, or the copyright holder's failure to provide the necessary documentation to show that there is a likely infringement, the operator's lack of knowledge will be found reasonable and there will be no liability for contributory infringement for allowing the continued distribution of the works on its system."

Religious Technology Ctr. v. Netcom On-line Com. Servs., Inc., 907 F. Supp. 1361, 1374 (N.D. Cal. 1995).

"[I]t is fair, assuming Netcom is able to take simple measures to prevent further damage to plaintiffs' copyrighted work, to hold Netcom liable for contributory infringement where Netcom has knowledge of Erlich's infringing postings yet continues to aid in the accomplishment of Erlich's purpose of publicly distributing the postings."

Religious Technology Ctr. v. Netcom On-line Com. Servs., Inc., 907 F. Supp. 1361, 1374 (N.D. Cal. 1995).

"[The court] is not convinced that Usenet servers are directly liable for causing a copy to be made, and absent evidence of knowledge and participation or control and direct profit, they will not be contributorily or vicariously liable."

> *Religious Technology Ctr. v. Netcom On-line Com. Servs., Inc.*, 907 F. Supp. 1361, 1377 (N.D. Cal. 1995).

(trademark)
"[C]ontributory infringement doctrine does not impose upon NSI an affirmative duty to seek out potentially infringing uses of domain names by registrants."

> *Lockheed Martin Corp. v. Network Solutions, Inc.*, 985 F. Supp. 949, 951 (C.D. Cal. 1997).

contributory infringer *(copyright)*

"[O]ne who, with knowledge of the infringing activity, induces, causes or materially contributes to the infringing conduct of another...."

> *Sega Enters. Ltd. v. MAPHIA*, 857 F. Supp. 679, 686 (N.D. Cal. 1994).

"...is (i) a person who, with knowledge of the infringing activity, induces or materially contributes to the infringing conduct of a third party or (ii) a person who contributes machinery or goods to a third party with knowledge that the third party will use the machinery or goods to infringe a copyright."

> *Gershwin Publishing Corp. v. Columbia Artists Management, Inc.*, 443 F.2d 1159, 1162 (2d Cir. 1971).

control *(technology)*

"...directs the whole process, in accordance with predetermined instructions kept in Storage."

> *Computer Sys. of Am. v. Western Reserve Life Assur. Co.*, 19 Mass. App. 430, 431 n.2 (1985).

control character *(hardware)*

To create a control character, depress the 'ctrl' key along with another key. This results in a printing or nonprinting character that is used to specify information to the system, e.g., depressing control and C generates an interrupt that stops the execution of most programs.

control function *(technology)*

"...enables a computer system to perform a large number of consecutive instructions. The control function can usually understand or evaluate the various operations as they are concluded and perform alternate operations without human intervention based upon such evaluation. The control function directs and coordinates the operation of the various products making up the system and can be performed by a combination of hardware, microprogramming and software."

Telex Corp. v. IBM Corp., 367 F. Supp. 258, 274 (N.D. Okla. 1973), *aff'd in part, rev'd in part*, 510 F.2d 894 (10th Cir.), *cert. dism.*, 423 U.S. 802 (1975).

controller *(hardware)*

"[A]n electronic minicomputer which consists of many small components soldered to a printed circuit board."

Eaton Corp. v. Magnavox Co., 581 F. Supp. 1514, 1516 (E.D. Mich. 1984).

CONTU *(copyright; organization)*

"CONTU is an acronym for the National Commission on New Technological Uses of Copyright Works. That Commission was set up by Congress in 1974 to consider major public policy questions of concern to Congress in the copyright field. The Commission consisted of eminent experts in copyright law, public representatives and representatives of publishing and allied industries directly concerned with copyright matters. Among the problems Congress asked the Commission to consider was the extent to which computer programs should be protected by the copyright laws."

Apple Computer, Inc. v. Formula Int'l, Inc., 218 U.S.P.Q. (BNA) 47, 51 (C.D. Cal. 1983).

"The specific purpose of the Commission was to study and compile data on
(1) the reproduction and use of copyrighted works of authorship;
    (A) in conjunction with automatic systems capable of storing, processing, retrieving and transferring information, and
    (B) by various forms of machine reproductions, not including reproduction by or at the request of instructors for use in face-to-face teaching activities; and
(2) the creation of new works by the application or intervention of such automatic systems or machine reproduction."

CONTU Final Report 105 (1978).

Related issues. "[T]he Commission recognizes that the dynamics of computer science promise changes in the creation and use of authors' writings that cannot be predicted with any certainty."

CONTU Final Report 46 (1978).

"[T]he most valuable legislative history materials concerning the Copyright Act of 1976 and the Amendment of 1980 are the reports of CONTU...."

> *Apple Computer, Inc. v. Formula Int'l, Inc.*, 594 F. Supp. 617, 621 (C.D. Cal. 1984).

CONTU Final Report *(copyright)*

The results of the CONTU Commission hearings and recommendations are contained in the Final Report of the National Commission on the New Technological Uses of Copyright Works (1978), H.R. Rep. No. 1307, 96th Cong., 2d Sess., pt. 1, at 23.

Annotation. "The Final Report, published in 1978, is generally regarded as quasi-legislative history. While the relevance of the report is somewhat discounted or even ignored by some courts, it is used by many courts as an aid in interpreting the 1980 amendments."

> Office of Technology Assessment, *Finding a Balance: Computer Software, Intellectual Property, and the Challenge of Technological Change* 67 (May 1992) (citations omitted).

"The amendments of 1980 followed the Final Report of the Commission on New Technological Uses of Copyrighted Works (CONTU). That Report recommended:

> The new copyright law should be amended: (1) to make it explicit that computer programs, to the extent they embody an author's original creation, are proper subject matter of copyright; (2) to apply to all computer uses of copyrighted programs by the deletion of the present §117; and (3) to ensure that rightful possession [sic] of copies of computer programs may use or adopt these copies for their use.

"The Amendments of 1980 conform to these recommendations."

> *M. Kramer Mfg. Co. v. Andrews*, 783 F.2d 421, 432 n.8 (4th Cir. 1986).

Related issues. "[T]he most valuable legislative history materials concerning the Copyright Act of 1976 and the Amendment of 1980 are the reports of CONTU...."

> *Apple Computer, Inc. v. Formula Int'l, Inc.*, 594 F. Supp. 617, 626 (C.D. Cal. 1984).

convergence *(business)*

The process by which different technologies merge.

conversion *(technology)*

The process of making changes to databases or software, generally changes that will allow the databases or software to work on different computers or operating system software.

converter(s) *(technology)*

"Converters are sometimes called protocol converters. (Protocol refers to the procedure followed in sending and receiving control data.) Equipment manufactured by different companies can have different protocols. If machines have incompatible protocols, a converter can be used to make them compatible."

IRS Letter Ruling 8721016, Feb. 17, 1987.

cookie *(Internet)*

" 'Cookie' technology allows a Web site's server to place information about a consumer's visits to the site on the consumer's computer in a text file that only the Web site's server can read. Using cookies a Web site assigns each consumer a unique identifier (not the actual identity of the consumer), so that the consumer may be recognized in subsequent visits to the site. On each return visit, the site can call up user-specific information, which could include the consumer's preferences or interests, as indicated by documents the consumer accessed in prior visits or items the consumer clicked on while in the site."

Federal Trade Commission, *Privacy Online: A Report to Congress* n.4 (June 1998).

Annotation. A cookie (also known as a "Persistent Client State HTTP Cookie") is a small data text file that is transferred from a World Wide Web server computer to a client computer during a World Wide Web browsing session. The cookie is stored on the recipient computer and sent back to the server computer whenever an HTML file request is made. The cookie can be configured to last for only a single browsing session, or it can be configured to be stored on the client computer's hard drive for subsequent sessions. The cookie can include data such as the time of the client computer's last HTML file request from the server or the user name and password that the server assigned to the client computer.

With such information, a cookie can be used to personalize a World Wide Web site for each visitor by sending the server a list of the user's selected preferences during an earlier visit. A cookie can also permit a web server to track which web pages of its World Wide Web site were viewed during the client computer's last visit.

A cookie's primary purpose is to save and transmit information about a client computer to a server computer. At first impression, it may appear that transmission of such information results in a loss of privacy. It should be clarified, however, that a cookie is generated by the server computer based upon information the server already has regarding the client computer, and it is not designed to transfer additional information to the server from the client computer's RAM or hard drive. Further, as a security measure each cookie is designed to be read only by the server that originated it.

Cookies can do a great deal to enhance a browsing experience. Nevertheless, if a user does not have a taste for cookies, most popular browser programs can be configured to give the choice of whether to accept them. (jrb)

copier *(technology)*
"... [is] designed to copy the video game programs from a...game cartridge onto other magnetic media such as hard and floppy disks."
Sega Enters. Ltd. v. MAPHIA, 857 F. Supp. 679, 682 (N.D. Cal. 1994).

co-publish *(business)*
See affiliate label program.

copy(ies)
(contract)
"[T]he medium on which information is fixed on a temporary or permanent basis and from which it can be perceived, reproduced, used, or communicated, either directly or with the aid of a machine or device."
UCITA § 102(a)(20).

(copyright)
"[M]aterial objects, other than phonorecords, in which a work is fixed by any method now known or later developed, and from which the work can be perceived, reproduced, or otherwise communicated, either directly or with the aid of a machine or device. The term 'copies' includes the material object, other than a phonorecord, in which the work is first fixed."
U.S. Copyright Act, 17 U.S.C. § 101.

"[S]ince we find that the copy created in the RAM can be 'perceived, reproduced, or otherwise communicated,' we hold that the loading of software into the RAM creates a copy under the Copyright Act."
MAI Sys. Corp. v. Peak Computer, Inc., 991 F.2d 511, 519 (9th Cir. 1993).

"The act of loading of software into a computer constitutes the creation of a copy under the Copyright Act."

> *Vault Corp. v. Quaid Software Ltd.*, 847 F.2d 255, 260 (5th Cir. 1988).

"The placement of a work into a computer is the preparation of a copy."

> *CONTU Final Report*, at 13 (1978).

"[L]oading of software from some permanent storage medium, such as a floppy disk or a computer's hard drive, to the computer's random access memory ('RAM') when the software is 'booted up' causes a copy to be made."

> *Stenograph L.L.C. v. Bossard Assocs., Inc.*, 144 F.3d 96, 101 (D.C. Cir. 1998).

Related issues (jurisdiction). "Web-sites are modern analogs of national publications; potentially innumerable 'copies' can be (and are) regularly 'distributed' wherever there is access to the World-Wide Web."

> *Digital Equipment Corp. v. Altavista Technology, Inc.*, 960 F. Supp. 456, 470 (D. Mass. 1997).

copy protection *(technology)*

[United Kingdom] "... includes any device or means intended to prevent or to restrict copying of a work or to impair the quality of copies made."

> U.K. Copyright, Designs, and Patents Act 1988, c. 48.

copying *(copyright)*

"'[A] shorthand reference to any infringement of the copyright holder's exclusive rights' set forth in 17 U.S.C. §106."

> *Fonar Corp. v. Magnetic Resonance Plus, Inc.*, 920 F. Supp. 508, 515 n.6 (S.D.N.Y. 1996).

"Copying constitutes infringement if it conflicts with one of the specific exclusive rights conferred by the Copyright Act."

> *Michaels v. Internet Entertainment Group, Inc.*, 5 F. Supp. 2d 823, 830 (C.D. Cal. 1998) (citing *Sony Corp. v. Universal City Studios, Inc.*, 464 U.S. 417 (1984)).

Annotation. "Proof of copying may be shown either by direct evidence of the copying or, in the absence of such evidence, '[c]opying as a factual matter typically may be inferred from proof of access to the copyrighted work and "probative similarity."'"

> *Bateman v. Mnemonics, Inc.*, 79 F.3d 1532, 1541 (11th Cir. 1995).

"A plaintiff may prove...copying, either by direct evidence or by establishing that the defendant had access to the plaintiff's copyrighted work and that the defendant's work is substantially similar to the copyrightable material."

CMAX/Cleveland, Inc. v. UCR, Inc., 804 F. Supp. 337, 351 (M.D. Ga. 1992).

"A finding of actionable copying requires analysis of two separate components. First, a factual question regarding whether the alleged infringer actually used the copyrighted material to create its own work must be answered.... The second question that must be analyzed is whether the copying at issue is legally actionable."

DSC Comm. Corp. v. DGI Technologies, Inc., 898 F. Supp. 1183, 1187-88 (N.D. Tex. 1995), *aff'd*, 81 F.3d 597 (5th Cir. 1996).

"[T]he loading of copyrighted computer software from a storage medium (hard disk, floppy disk, or read only memory) into the memory of a central processing unit ('CPU') causes a copy to be made. In the absence of ownership of the copyright or express permission by license, such acts constitute copyright infringement."

MAI Sys. Corp. v. Peak Computer, Inc., 991 F.2d 511, 518 (9th Cir. 1993), *cert. dism.*, 510 U.S. 1033 (1994).

Related issues. "Copying deleted or so disguised as to be unrecognizable is not copying."

See v. Durang, 711 F.2d 141, 142 (9th Cir. 1983).

See also **copyright infringement.**

copyright *(copyright)*

"The purpose of copyright law is to create the most efficient and productive balance between protection (incentive) and dissemination of information, to promote learning, culture and development."

Whelan Assocs., Inc. v. Jaslow Dental Lab., 797 F.2d 1222, 1235 (3rd Cir. 1986).

"The purpose of copyright law is to promote and protect creativity."

Alcatel USA, Inc. v. DGI Technologies, Inc., 166 F.3d 772, 787 (5th Cir. 1999) (citations omitted).

"Copyright in a work created on or after January 1, 1978, subsists from its creation."

17 U.S.C. § 302(a).

"Copyright law does not admit of simple, bright-line rules."

Nihon Keizai Shimbun, Inc. v. Comline Business Data, Inc., 166 F.3d 65, 71 (2d Cir. 1999).

Annotation. "Such copyright, thus granted by the Copyright Office, is prima facie proof of the validity of plaintiff's copyright, including the existence of the elements of originality and fixation."
M. Kramer Mfg. Co. v. Andrews, 783 F.2d 421, 434 (4th Cir. 1986).

"[I]f a work is entitled to copyright protection, its author is granted exclusive rights over its reproduction, adaptation, distribution, performance, and display. Use of a copyrighted work by one who does not own the copyright constitutes infringement under federal law, provided the use falls within the scope of a copyright owner's exclusive rights."
Alcatel USA, Inc. v. DGI Technologies, Inc., 166 F.3d 772, 787-88 (5th Cir. 1999) (citations omitted).

"The grant to the author of the special privilege of a copyright carries out a public policy adopted by the Constitution and laws of the United States, 'to promote the Progress of Science and useful arts, by securing for limited Times to [Authors] . . . the exclusive Right . . .' to their 'original' works. United States Constitution, Art. I, § 8, cl. 8, 17 U.S.C. §102. But the public policy which includes original works within the granted monopoly excludes from it all that is not embraced in the original expression. It equally forbids the use of the copyright to secure an exclusive right or limited monopoly not granted by the Copyright Office and which is contrary to public policy to grant."
Alcatel USA, Inc. v. DGI Technologies, Inc., 166 F.3d 772, 793 (5th Cir. 1999) (citations omitted).

"For original computer programs and other original works of authorship created after 1977, copyright automatically inheres in the work at the moment it is created without regard to whether it is ever registered."
Montgomery v. Noga, 168 F.3d 1282, 1288 (11th Cir. 1999).

Related issues. "A copyright . . . is unlike an ordinary chattel because the holder does not acquire exclusive dominion over the thing owned. The limited nature of the property interest conferred by copyright stems from an overriding First Amendment concern for the free dissemination of ideas."
United States v. LaMacchia, 871 F. Supp. 535, 537 (D. Mass. 1994).

"The primary objective of copyright is not to reward the labor of authors, but '[t]o promote the Progress of Science and useful Arts.' . . . To this end, copyright assures authors the right to their original expression, but encourages others to build freely upon the ideas and information conveyed by a work. This principle, known as the idea/expression or fact/expression dichotomy, applies to all works of authorship. . . . This result is neither unfair nor unfortunate. It is the means by which copyright advances the progress of science and art."

Feist Publications, Inc. v. Rural Tel. Serv. Co., 499 U.S. 340, 349 (1991) (citations omitted).

"The interest of the copyright law is not in simply conferring a monopoly on industrious persons, but in advancing the public welfare through rewarding artistic creativity, in a manner that permits the free use and development of non-protectable ideas and processes."

Computer Assocs. Int'l, Inc. v. Altai, Inc., 982 F.2d 693, 711 (2d Cir. 1992).

"The copyright owner ... holds no ordinary chattel. A copyright, like other intellectual property, comprises a series of carefully defined and carefully delimited interests to which the law affords correspondingly exact protections."

Dowling v. United States, 473 U.S. 207, 216 (1985).

"The limited scope of the copyright holder's statutory monopoly, like the limited copyright duration required by the Constitution, reflects a balance of competing claims upon the public interest: Creative work is to be encouraged and rewarded, but private motivation must ultimately serve the cause of promoting broad public availability of literature, music, and the other arts.

"The immediate effect of our copyright law is to secure a fair return for an 'author's' creative labor. But the ultimate aim is, by this incentive, to stimulate artistic creativity for the general public good.... When technological change has rendered its literal terms ambiguous, the Copyright Act must be construed in light of this basic purpose."

Twentieth Century Music Corp. v. Aiken, 422 U.S. 151, 156 (1975) (citations and footnotes omitted).

"The judiciary's reluctance to expand the protections afforded by the copyright without explicit legislative guidance is a recurring theme. Sound policy, as well as history, supports our consistent deference to Congress when major technological innovations alter the market for copyrighted materials. Congress has the institutional authority and the institutional ability to accommodate fully the varied permutations of competing interests that are inevitably implicated by such new technology."

Sony Corp. of America v. Universal City Studios, Inc., 464 U.S. 417, 431 (1984) (citations omitted).

"There can no longer exist any doubt that computer programs are copyrightable."

S&H Computer Sys., Inc. v. SAS Inst., Inc., 568 F. Supp. 416, 422 (M.D. Tenn. 1983).

"[T]he legislative history explicitly states that copyright protects computer programs only 'to the extent that they incorporate authorship in programmer's expression of original ideas, as distinguished from the ideas themselves.'"

Computer Assocs. Int'l, Inc. v. Altai, Inc., 982 F.2d 693, 703 (2d Cir. 1992).

"[I]t is equally important to remember that there exists a distinction between the work and the copyright. The work—in this case a computer program—is separate and distinct from the copyright; the copyright is the rights to which the copyrighted work is subject. It is the rights, not the work, that the copyright holder owns. This distinction is manifest in view of the fact that when the copyright expires, the erstwhile copyright holder no longer owns any exclusive rights, but the work continues to exist without change. The copyright owner never owns the work because copyright is a series of specified rights to which a designated work is subject for a limited period of time, after which the work enters into the public domain unencumbered by copyright. Hence, the use of the work and the use of the copyright are distinct. One may use the work without using the copyright, but one cannot use the copyright without using the work—one does not infringe the work, rather one infringes the copyright.... Therefore, the basic issue in all copyright defense is whether the use involved was a use of the work or a use of the copyright."

Bateman v. Mnemonic, Inc., 79 F.3d 1532, 1542 n.23 (11th Cir. 1995).

"[P]atent and copyright law protect distinct aspects of a computer program. Title 35 protects the process or method performed by a computer program; title 17 protects the expression of that process or method. While title 35 protects any novel, nonobvious, and useful process, title 17 can protect a multitude of expressions that implement that process. If the patentable process is embodied inextricably in the line-by-line instructions of the computer program, however, then the process mergers with the expression and precludes copyright protection."

Atari Games Corp. v. Nintendo of America, Inc., 975 F.2d 832, 839-40 (Fed. Cir. 1992) (citations omitted).

See also **Copyright Act of 1976; Copyright Act 1980 Amendments; copyright clause; copyright, exclusive rights; copyright infringement; copyright misuse doctrine.**

Copyright Act of 1976 *(copyright)*

"In 1976, after a period of gestation over some twenty years, the Congress enacted a complete revision of copyright law which represented Congress' response at that time to the startling developments recently made in technology and science."

> *M. Kramer Mfg. Co. v. Andrews*, 783 F.2d 421, 432 (4th Cir. 1986).

Related issues. "[Y]ou can read the bill from beginning to end and you won't find in it any reference to computers.... [even though] these are one of the coming instruments of communication in the future. We have tried to phrase the broad rights granted in such a way that they can be adapted as time goes on to each of the new advancing media."

> *Copyright Law Revision: Hearings on H.R. 4347, 5680, 6831, 6835 Before Subcomm. No. 3 of the House Comm. on the Judiciary*, 89th Cong. 57 (1965) (testimony of George D. Cary, Deputy Register of Copyrights).

"We are of the opinion that the reason for finding that computer programs were copyrightable under the 1976 Act...are [sic] convincing. We agree that computer programs were copyrightable under the Act of 1976. Congress chose to make crystal clear by the Amendments of 1980 that fact...."

> *M. Kramer Mfg. Co. v. Andrews*, 783 F.2d 421, 432 n.9 (4th Cir. 1986).

Copyright Act 1980 Amendments *(copyright)*

Citation: Computer Software Act of 1980, Pub. L. No. 96-517, § 10, 94 Stat. 3015 (Act. of Dec. 12, 1980).

"Subsequently, in 1980, that [the 1976 Copyright] Act was amended to include expressly what had been generally assumed as implicit in the Act of 1976 itself that computer programs were proper subjects of copyright. The Amendment did this by including in the definitional section of copyrightable subject matter a definition of 'computer program.' This Amendment also replaced section 117 of the 1976 Act with a new section limiting the exclusive rights given 'authors' in copies of computer programs."

> *M. Kramer Mfg. Co. v. Andrews*, 783 F.2d 421, 432 (4th Cir. 1986).

Annotation. "The amendments of 1980 followed the Final Report of the Commission on New Technological Uses of Copyrighted Works (CONTU). That Report recommended:

> The new copyright law should be amended: (1) to make it explicit that computer programs, to the extent they embody an author's original creation, are proper subject matter of copyright; (2) to apply to all computer uses of copyrighted programs by the deletion of the present §117; and (3) to ensure that rightful possession [sic] of copies of computer programs may use or adopt these copies for their use.

"The Amendments of 1980 conform to these recommendations."

> *M. Kramer Mfg. Co. v. Andrews*, 783 F.2d 421, 432 n.8 (4th Cir. 1986).

"Prior to that amendment there has been some doubt whether a computer program was copyrightable under the Act of 1976 in view of the language of section 117 in that Act, which appeared to continue the status quo in copyright law for computer programs.

* * *

"We are of the opinion that the reason for finding that computer programs were copyrightable under the 1976 Act...are [sic] convincing. We agree that computer programs were copyrightable under the Act of 1976. Congress chose to make crystal clear by the Amendments of 1980 that fact...."

M. Kramer Mfg. Co. v. Andrews, 783 F.2d 421, 432 n.9 (4th Cir. 1986),

copyright clause *(copyright)*

"Congress shall have the Power to promote the Progress of Science and useful Arts, by securing for limited Times to Authors and Inventors the exclusive Right to their respective Writings and Discoveries."

U.S. Const., art. I, sec. 8.

Annotation. "The Supreme Court has stated that '[t]he economic philosophy behind the clause...is the conviction that encouragement of individual effort by personal gain is the best way to advance public welfare....' The author's benefit, however, is clearly a secondary consideration. '[T]he ultimate aim is by this incentive, to stimulate artistic creativity for the general public good.'

Thus, the copyright law seeks to establish a delicate equilibrium. On the one hand, it affords protection to authors as an incentive to create, and, on the other, it must appropriately limit the extent of that protection so as to avoid the effects of monopolistic stagnation. In applying the federal act to new types of cases, courts must always keep this symmetry in mind."

Computer Assocs. Int'l, Inc. v. Altai, Inc., 982 F.2d 693, 696 (2d Cir. 1992).

Related issues. "The Constitution thus gives Congress the authority to set the parameters of authors' exclusive rights."

Atari Games Corp. v. Nintendo of America, Inc., 975 F.2d 832, 838 (Fed. Cir. 1992).

copyright, exclusive rights *(copyright)*

"Section 106...affords a copyright owner the exclusive right to: (1) reproduce the copyrighted work; (2) prepare derivative works; (3) distribute copies of the work by sale or otherwise; and, with respect to certain artistic works, (4) perform the work publicly; and (5) display the work publicly."

Computer Assocs. Int'l, Inc. v. Altai, Inc., 982 F.2d 693, 716 (2d Cir. 1992).

copyright infringement *(copyright)*
"Any act that is inconsistent with the copyright holder's exclusive rights constitutes copyright infringement."
> *CMAX/Cleveland, Inc. v. UCR, Inc.*, 804 F. Supp. 337, 351 (M.D. Ga. 1992).

"Infringement is a technical concept describing interference with the statutorily defined rights of a copyright holder."
> *United States v. LaMacchia*, 871 F. Supp. 535, 545 n.19 (D. Mass. 1994).

"... occurs when a person violates any of the exclusive rights of the copyright owner as provided by Sections 106-118 of the Copyright Act."
> *Vault Corp. v. Quaid Software Ltd.*, 655 F. Supp. 750, 758 (E.D. La. 1987).

"Courts have long noted that a licensee infringes a copyright by exceeding his license."
> *S&H Computer Sys., Inc. v. SAS Inst., Inc.*, 568 F. Supp. 416, 422 (M.D. Tenn. 1983).

Annotation. "[I]t is as clear an infringement to translate a computer program from, for example, FORTRAN to ALGOL, as it is to translate a novel or play from English to French. In each case the substance of the expression (if one may speak in such contradictory language) is the same between original and copy, with only the external manifestation of the expression changing. Likewise, it would probably be a violation to take a detailed description of a particular problem solution, such as a flow chart or step-by-step set of prose instructions, written in human language, and program such a description in computer language."
> *Synercom Technology, Inc. v. University Computing Co.*, 462 F. Supp. 1003, 1013 (M.D. Tex. 1978).

"The legal or beneficial owner of an exclusive right under a copyright is entitled, subject to the requirements of section 411, to institute an action for any infringement of that particular right committed while he or she is the owner of it."
> 17 U.S.C. § 501(b).

Related issues. "... includes also the various modes in which the matter of any work may be adopted, imitated, transferred, or reproduced, with more or less colorable alterations to disguise the piracy."
> *Universal Pictures Co. v. Harold Lloyd Corp.*, 162 F.2d 354, 360 (9th Cir. 1947), *quoted approvingly in Atari, Inc. v. North Am. Philips Consumer Elecs. Corp.*, 672 F.2d 607, 618 (7th Cir.), *cert. denied*, 459 U.S. 880 (1982).

"The registration requirement is a jurisdictional prerequisite to an infringement suit."

> *M.G.B. Homes, Inc. v. Ameron Homes, Inc.*, 903 F.2d 1486, 1488 & n.4 (11th Cir. 1990).

"It is an affirmative defense to copyright infringement that the alleged infringer has received a license from the owner."

> *Michaels v. Internet Entertainment Group, Inc.*, 5 F. Supp. 2d 823, 831 (C.D. Cal. 1998).

"Two computer programs may be sufficiently dissimilar on the level of expression to defeat liability for copyright infringement, but they may be sufficiently similar on a more abstract or ideational level to establish liability for trade secret protection."

> *Comprehensive Technologies Int'l, Inc. v. Software Artisans, Inc.*, 3 F.3d 730, 736 nn. 6-7 (4th Cir. 1993).

"Such copyright, thus granted by the Copyright Office, is prima facie proof of the validity of plaintiff's copyright, including the existence of the elements of originality and fixation.... The defendants, in disputing the validity of such copyright on those grounds, have the burden of overcoming the presumption arising out of the granting of the copyright by the Copyright Office. 17 U.S.C. §410(c)."

> *M. Kramer Mfg. Co. v. Andrews*, 783 F.2d 421, 434 (4th Cir. 1986).

"The remedies for infringement 'are only those prescribed by Congress.'"

> *Sony Corp. of America v. Universal City Studios, Inc.*, 464 U.S. 417, 431 (1984).

"A single copy is sufficient to support a claim of copyright infringement."

> *Atari Games Corp. v. Nintendo of America, Inc.*, 975 F.2d 832, 840 (Fed. Cir. 1992).

"Even for works warranting little copyright protection, verbatim copying is infringement."

> *Atari Games Corp. v. Nintendo of America, Inc.*, 975 F.2d 832, 839-40 (Fed. Cir. 1992).

"In any suit for copyright infringement, the plaintiff must establish its ownership of a valid copyright, and that the defendant copied the copyrighted work."

> *Computer Assocs. Int'l, Inc. v. Altai, Inc.*, 982 F.2d 693, 701 (2d Cir. 1992).

"The plaintiff must prove defendant's copying either by direct evidence or, as is most often the case, by showing that (1) the defendant had access to the plaintiff's copyrighted work and (2) that defendant's work is substantially similar to the plaintiff's copyrightable material."

Computer Assocs. Int'l, Inc. v. Altai, Inc., 982 F.2d 693, 701 (2d Cir. 1992). *Accord Healthcare Affiliated Servs., Inc. v. Lippany,* 701 F. Supp. 1142, 1150 (W.D. Pa. 1988).

"[U]se of the ... program on a non-designated CPU, the making of unauthorized copies and use of the ... program after the license agreement was properly terminated all constitute a form of copyright infringement...."

S&H Computer Sys., Inc. v. SAS Inst., Inc., 568 F. Supp. 416, 422 (M.D. Tenn. 1983).

"'[C]opyright owner who grants a nonexclusive license to use his copyrighted material waives his right to sue the licensee for copyright infringement' and can sue only for breach of contract."

Graham v. James, 144 F.3d 229, 236 (2d Cir. 1998).

See also **contributory infringement; de minimis infringement; direct infringement; vicarious infringement.**

copyright license *(contract; copyright)*

"[A]n agreement of this nature may convey rights and interests in two, rather than only one form of property; the developer may transfer copyright rights in the software program (intellectual property rights) and at the same time transfer rights in the copy of the program through the material object that embodies the copyrighted work (personal property rights). Because technological developments that are the subject of such licensing agreements are relatively recent, the absence of clear legislative direction further complicates resolution of the issue. Furthermore, courts that have considered the question have not directly addressed the distinction between the two different forms of property rights involved."

Applied Info. Management, Inc. v. Icart, 976 F. Supp. 149, 150-51 (E.D.N.Y. 1997).

copyright management information *(copyright)*

"[A]ny of the following information conveyed in connection with copies or phonorecords of a work or performances or displays of a work, including in digital form, except that such term does not include any personally identifying information about a user of a work or of a copy, phonorecord, performance, or display of a work:

(1) The title and other information identifying the work, including the information set forth on a notice of copyright.

(2) The name of, and other identifying information about, the author of a work.

(3) The name of, and other identifying information about, the copyright owner of the work, including the information set forth in a notice of copyright.

(4) With the exception of public performance of works by radio and television broadcast stations, the name of, and other identifying information about, a performer whose performance is fixed in a work other than an audiovisual work.

(5) With the exception of public performance of works by radio and television broadcast stations, in the case of an audiovisual work, the name of, and other identifying information about, a writer, performance, or director who is credited in the audiovisual work.

(6) Terms and conditions for use of the work.

(7) Identifying numbers or symbols referring to such information or links to such information.

(8) Such other information as the Register of Copyrights may prescribe by regulation, except that the Register of Copyright may not require the provision of any information concerning the user of a copyrighted work."
17 U.S.C. § 1202(c).

copyright misuse doctrine *(copyright)*
"[A] copyright owner may not enforce its copyright to violate the antitrust laws or indeed use it in any 'manner violative of the public policy embodied in the grant of a copyright.'"
Advanced Computer Servs. v. MAI Sys. Corp., 845 F. Supp. 356, 366 (E.D. Va. 1994), *quoting Lasercomb America, Inc. v. Reynolds*, 911 F.2d 970, 978 (4th Cir. 1990).

"In an appropriate case a misuse of the copyright statute that in some way subverts the purpose of the statute, the promotion of originality, might constitute a bar to individual relief."
DSC Comm. Corp. v. DGI Technologies, Inc., 898 F. Supp. 1183, 1194 (N.D. Tex. 1995) (citation omitted), *aff'd*, 81 F.3d 597 (5th Cir. 1996).

Annotation. "The copyright misuse doctrine precludes injunctive relief based on that infringement. This doctrine—which has its historical roots in the unclean hands defense—"bars a culpable plaintiff from prevailing on an action

for the infringement of the misused copyright." It "forbids the use of the [copyright] to secure an exclusive right or limited monopoly not granted by the [Copyright] Office and which it is contrary to public policy to grant."
> *Alcatel USA, Inc. v. DGI Technologies, Inc.*, 166 F.3d 772, 793 (5th Cir. 1999) (citations omitted).

Related issues. "A finding of misuse does not, however, invalidate plaintiff's copyright. Indeed, the court in *Lasercomb* specified that '[plaintiff] is free to bring a suit for infringement once it has purged itself of the misuse.'"
> *Alcatel USA, Inc. v. DGI Technologies, Inc.*, 166 F.3d 772, 792 n.81 (5th Cir. 1999) (citation omitted).

"Copyright misuse is a defense to a claim of copyright infringement."
> *DSC Comm. Corp. v. Pulse Comm., Inc.*, 170 F.3d 1354, 1368 (Fed. Cir. 1999).

"While some cases have held that a plaintiff's violation of the antitrust laws may constitute a valid defense in a copyright infringement case, this misuse defense has only been upheld on the merits by the Fourth Circuit. *Lasercomb of America Inc. v. Reynolds*, 911 F.2d 970 (4th Cir. 1990) . . . ."
> *Microsoft Corp. v. BEC Computer Co.*, 818 F. Supp. 1313, 1316 (C.D. Cal. 1992) (citation omitted).

"In the absence of any statutory entitlement to a copyright misuse defense, however, the defense is solely an equitable doctrine. Any party seeking equitable relief must come to the court with 'clean hands.'"
> *Atari Games Corp. v. Nintendo of America, Inc.*, 975 F.2d 832, 846 (Fed. Cir. 1992).

copyright owner *(copyright)*
"[W]ith respect to any one of the exclusive rights comprised in a copyright, refers to the owner of that particular right."
> U.S. Copyright Act, 17 U.S.C. § 101.

copyright preemption *(copyright)*
See preemption.

copyright registration *(copyright)*
The process of registering the copyright for a work of authorship in the U.S. Copyright Office.

Annotation. "For original computer programs and other original works of authorship created after 1977, copyright automatically inheres in the work at the moment it is created without regard to whether it is ever registered."

Montgomery v. Noga, 168 F.3d 1282, 1288 (11th Cir. 1999).

"In order to bring an action for copyright infringement, however, the author must first register the copyright."

Montgomery v. Noga, 168 F.3d 1282, 1288 (11th Cir. 1999).

"The registration requirement is a jurisdictional prerequisite to an infringement suit."

M.G.B. Homes, Inc. v. Ameron Homes, Inc., 903 F.2d 1486, 1488 & n.4 (11th Cir. 1990).

Related issues. "This registration is prima facie evidence of the validity of the copyright and the facts stated in the certificate, including ownership."

E.F. Johnson Co. v. Uniden Corp. of America, 623 F. Supp. 1485, 1492 (D. Minn. 1985).

"Registration of the copyright is required even if the only relief sought in the action is injunctive in nature."

Healthcare Affiliated Servs., Inc. v. Lippany, 701 F. Supp. 1142, 1150 n.1 (W.D. Pa. 1988).

copyright, scope of protection *(copyright)*

"Congress has made clear that computer programs are literary works entitled to copyright protection. Of course, we shall abide by these instructions, but in so doing we must not impair the overall integrity of copyright law. While incentive based arguments in favor of broad copyright protection are perhaps attractive from a pure policy perspective,... ultimately, they have a corrosive effect on certain fundamental tenets of copyright doctrine."

Computer Assocs. Int'l, Inc. v. Altai, Inc., 982 F.2d 693, 712 (2d Cir. 1992) (citation omitted).

"We emphasize that, like all copyright infringement cases, those that involve computer programs are highly fact specific. The amount of protection due structural elements, in any given case, will vary according to the protectable expression found to exist within the program at issue."

Computer Assocs. Int'l, Inc. v. Altai, Inc., 982 F.2d 693, 715 (2d Cir. 1992).

copyrightability *(copyright)*

The ability of a work to be protected by copyright.

Annotation. "There are three types of work that are entitled to copyright protection—creative, derivative, and compiled. Copyrights in these three distinct works are known as creative, derivative, and compilation copyrights. An example of a creative work is a novel. An example of a derivative work is a screenplay based on a novel; it is called 'derivative' because it is based on a preexisting work that has been recast, transformed, or adapted.... The Act has created a hierarchy in terms of the protection afforded to these different types of copyrights. A creative work is entitled to the most protection, followed by a derivative work, and finally by a compilation. This is why the Feist Court emphasized that the copyright protection in a factual compilation is 'thin.'"

Warren Publ'g, Inc. v. Microdos Data Corp., 115 F.2d 1509, 1515 n.16 (11th Cir.) (en banc), *cert. denied*, 522 U.S. 963 (1997).

Related issues. "In judicial proceedings, a certificate of registration constitutes prima facie evidence of copyrightability and shifts the burden of proof to the defendant to show why the copyright is not valid."

DSC Comm. Corp. v. DGI Technologies, Inc., 898 F. Supp. 1183, 1187 (N.D. Tex. 1995), *aff'd*, 81 F.3d 597 (5th Cir. 1996); *Lotus Dev. Corp. v. Borland Int'l, Inc.*, 49 F.3d 807, 812-13 (1st Cir. 1995), *aff'd by an equally divided court*, 516 U.S. 233 (1996).

"That a computer program may be copyrightable as intellectual property does not alter the fact that once in the form of a floppy disc or other medium, the program is tangible, moveable, and available in the marketplace."

Advent Sys., Inc. v. Unisys Corp., 925 F.2d 670, 675 (3d Cir. 1991).

core *(hardware)*

The main memory that resides in the computer. This technology is no longer used.

[CANADA] "The area inside a computer where instructions are stored in order to be executed and is divided into a Common Area and one or more Partition Areas. The Common Area contains sets of instructions to perform routine tasks common to almost all application programs, such as preparing data to be sent to the math storage devices. The Partition Areas contain the application programs written to accomplish a particular function such as preparing a payroll."

Clarke Irwin & Co. v. Singer Co. of Can., Ont. Div. Ct., Keith J., December 3, 1979, *summarized at* [1979] 3 A.C.W.S. 807.

See also **computer memory; magnetic memory core; main memory; memory plane.**

CORE *(organization)*

Acronym for "Council for Registrars." A nonprofit organization formed in the fall of 1996 as a result of a plan developed by the Internet Society and Internet

Assigned Numbers Authority to "add new structure, free enterprise, and competition in the Internet Domain Name System when the old monopoly on .com, .org, and .net ends in 1998." Located at <www.corenic.org>.

core dump *(technology)*

When a program terminates abnormally, the system places an image of its current memory in a file named "core." This way, a programmer can examine the status of the program, along with a notation of the last instructions to be processed. In case of a system failure, the program can be traced to its start.

core memory board *(hardware)*

[CANADA] "The circuit board upon which the electronic components making up Core Memory are affixed."

> *Clarke Irwin & Co. v. Singer Co. of Can.*, Ont. Div. Ct., Keith J., Dec. 3, 1979, *summarized at* [1979] 3 A.C.W.S. 807.

correspond *(electronic commerce)*

"[W]ith reference to keys, means to belong to the same key pair."

> Wash. Rev. Code § 19.34.020(10).

cost per acquisition *(advertising; Internet)*.

Abbreviated as "CPA."

The total cost of the advertising divided by the total number of customers engaging in a transaction on the site.

Council for Registrars *(organization)*

See CORE.

counterfeit access device *(criminal)*

"[A]ny access device that is counterfeit, fictitious, altered, or forged, or an identifiable component of an access device or a counterfeit access device...."

> 18 U.S.C. § 1029(e)(2).

Annotation. "The definition is intended to be sufficiently broad to cover components of an access device or a counterfeit access device, but would exclude indistinguishable raw materials. The components would include elements of devices that are legitimate but obtained or used with an intent to defraud. Thus any identifiable component, whether it is in fact an actual component that has been obtained in some fashion by a perpetrator with intent to defraud or a false or counterfeit substitute for a legitimate component would fall within the definition of counterfeit access device. The Committee intends the term 'component' to include incomplete access devices or counterfeit access devices, such as any mag strips, holograms, signature panels, microchips, and blank cards of so-called 'white plastic.'"

H.R. Rep. No. 894, 98th Cong., 2d Sess. 19 (1984), *reprinted in* 1984 *U.S. Code Cong. & Admin. News* 3182, 3705, *quoted in United States v. Brady,* 820 F. Supp. 1346, 1350 (D. Utah 1993).

See also **access device.**

country of origin *(copyright)*

"The 'country of origin' of a Berne Convention work, for purposes of section 411 [of the U.S. Copyright Act], is the United States if—

(1) in the case of a published work, the work is first published—

(A) in the United States;

(B) simultaneously in the United States and another nation or nations adhering to the Berne Convention, whose law grants a term of copyright protection that is the same as or longer than the term provided in the United States;

(C) simultaneously in the United States and a foreign nation that does not adhere to the Berne Convention; or

(D) in a foreign nation that does not adhere to the Berne Convention, and all of the authors of the work are nationals, domiciliaries, or habitual residents of, or in the case of an audiovisual work legal entities with headquarters in, the United States;

(2) in the case of an unpublished work, all the authors of the work are nationals, domiciliaries, or habitual residents of the United States, or, in the case of an unpublished audiovisual work, all the authors are legal entities with headquarters in the United States; or

(3) in the case of a pictorial, graphic, or sculptural work incorporated in a building or structure, the building or structure is located in the United States.

For the purposes of section 411, the 'country of origin' of any other Berne Convention work is not the United States."

U.S. Copyright Act, 17 U.S.C. § 101.

course of dealing *(contract)*

"[A] sequence of previous conduct between the parties to a particular transaction which is fairly to be regarded as establishing a common basis of understanding for interpreting their expressions and their conduct."

U.C.C. §1-205.

"[A] sequence of previous conduct between the parties to a particular transaction which establishes a common basis of understanding for interpreting their expressions and other conduct."

UCITA § 102(a)(21).

Annotation. "[A] course of dealing between the parties and any usage of trade in a vocation or trade in which they are engaged or of which they are or should be aware give particular meaning to and supplement or qualify terms of an agreement."

U.C.C. §1-205.

See also **usage of trade.**

course of performance *(contract)*

"[R]epeated performances, under a contract that involves repeated occasions for performance, which are accepted or acquiesced in without objection by a party having knowledge of the nature of the performance and an opportunity to object to it."

UCITA § 102(a)(22).

court *(contract)*

"[I]ncludes an arbitration or other dispute-resolution forum if the parties have agreed to use of that forum or its use is required by law."

UCITA § 102(a)(23).

cover *(contract)*

"After a breach within the preceding section the *buyer* may 'cover' by making in *good faith* and without unreasonable delay any reasonable purchase of or *contract* to purchase *goods* in substitution for those due from the *seller.*"

U.C.C. § 2-712(1) (1979) (emphasis in original).

Annotation. "The *buyer* may recover from the *seller* as damages the difference between the cost of cover and the *contract* price together with any incidental or consequential damages as hereinafter defined (Section 2-715), but less expenses saved in consequence of the seller's breach.

"Failure of the *buyer* to effect cover within this section does not bar him from any other remedy."

U.C.C. § 2-712(2)-(3) (emphasis in original).

CPA *(advertising, Internet)*

Acronym for "cost per acquisition."

See **cost per acquisition.**

CPB *(organization)*
Acronym for "Corporation for Public Broadcasting." A nonprofit corporation created by the U.S. Congress in 1967 to promote noncommercial public television and radio. More recently it has expanded to noncommercial online and digital media as well.

CPC *(advertisement; Internet)*
Acronym for "cost per click-through."
See **cost per click-through.**

CPE *(telecommunications)*
Acronym for "Customer Premise Equipment." Telecommunications equipment that is physically located at the customer's premises.

CPL *(advertisement; Internet)*
Acronym for "cost per lead."
See **cost per lead.**

CPM *(advertisement; Internet)*
Acronym for "cost per thousand impressions" [where **M** is the Latin symbol for 1,000].

The total cost of advertising divided by the number of impressions delivered.

CPS *(advertisement; Internet)*
Acronym for "cost per sale."

CPT *(advertisement; Internet)*
Acronym for "cost per transaction."

CPU *(technology)*
Acronym for "Central Processing Unit."
> *Telex Corp. v. IBM Corp.*, 367 F. Supp. 258, 270 (N.D. Okla. 1973), *aff'd in part, rev'd in part,* 510 F.2d 894 (10th Cir.), *cert. dism.,* 423 U.S. 802 (1975).

"…which is the specialized integrated circuit that executes binary programs. The CPU does the primary calculations required of all programs and shifts answers to other parts of the system depending upon the requirements of the program controlling it."
> *Apple Computer, Inc. v. Franklin Computer Corp.*, 545 F. Supp. 812, 813 (E.D. Pa. 1982), *rev'd,* 714 F.2d 1240 (3d Cir. 1983), *cert. dism.,* 464 U.S. 1033 (1984).

"...is generally where most of the logical functions or calculations are performed."

> *Telex Corp. v. IBM Corp.*, 367 F. Supp. 258, 275 (N.D. Okla. 1973), *aff'd in part, rev'd in part*, 510 F.2d 894 (10th Cir.), *cert. dism.*, 423 U.S. 802 (1975).

See also **central processing unit.**

cracker *(criminal)*
One who breaks the security of a computer system.

crash *(technology)*
System failure, usually due to a hardware or software failure. A situation in which the computer gets misdirected or blocked. An unexpected shutdown or interruption of a working computer, occasionally due to power outages or a physical flaw in the hard disk. *See also* **hung.**

crawler *(software)*
See **spider.**

created *(copyright)*
"A work is 'created' when it is fixed in a copy or phonorecord for the first time; where a work is prepared over a period of time, the portion of it that has been fixed at any particular time constitutes the work as of that time, and where the work has been prepared in different versions, each version constitutes a separate work."

> U.S. Copyright Act, 17 U.S.C. § 101.

credit(s) *(entertainment; multimedia)*
A list of those people involved in development of a multimedia title. *See also* **billing.**

credit card system member *(criminal)*
"[A] financial institution or other entity that is a member of a credit card system, including an entity, whether affiliated with or identical to the credit card issuer, that is the sole member of a credit card system."

> 18 U.S.C. § 1029(e)(7).

critical path *(business)*
Those tasks in developing computer software that must be completed on time (i.e., are critical), lest completion of the entire project be delayed.

CRL *(electronic commerce)*
Acronym for "Certificate Revocation List."
See **certificate revocation list.**

cross-post *(Internet)*
To post a message on multiple newsgroups.

CRS *(business)*
Acronym for "Computerized Reservation System."

"…provides participating travel agents with schedule, fare, and seat availability information for every airline that subscribes to the CRS. Further, a CRS allows travel agents to send and receive airline booking data, book space on flights, and automatically prepare tickets and advance boarding passes."
Alaska Airlines, Inc. v. United Airlines, Inc., Part I, 948 F.2d 536, 538 (9th Cir. 1991).

"…is composed of computer terminals and printers in travel agents' offices which are telephonically linked to the vendor's computer. This equipment enables the travel agent to send and receive air transportation booking information, book flights and print out a ticket."
In re Air Passenger Computer Reservation Systems Antitrust Litigation, 694 F. Supp. 1443, 1449 (C.D. Cal. 1988); 727 F. Supp. 564, 565-66 (C.D. Cal. 1989).

CRT *(hardware)*
Acronym for "Cathode-Ray Tube."

"…a typewriter-like device with a keyboard and display screen similar to a television screen upon which the information is displayed as it is sent and received."
United States v. Seidlitz, 589 F.2d 152, 153 (4th Cir. 1978).
See also **cathode-ray tube.**

cryptographic algorithm *(electronic commerce)*
Also called "cipher." A mathematical formula used for encryption and decryption.

cryptography *(technology)*
". . . the science of secret writing, a science that has roots stretching back hundreds, and perhaps thousands, of years."

Bernstein v. United States Dept. of Justice, 176 F.3d 1132, 1136 (9th Cir. 1999).

"[A] technique for transforming ordinary text (plaintext) into unintelligible ciphertext through encryption."
U.S. General Accounting Office, *Information Superhighway: An Overview of Technology Changes* 20 n.10 (Jan. 1995).

Annotation. "For much of its history, cryptography has been the jealously guarded province of governments and militaries. In the past twenty years, however, the science has blossomed in the civilian sphere, driven on the one hand by dramatic theoretical innovations within the field, and on the other by the needs of modern communication and information technology. As a result, cryptography has become a dynamic academic discipline within applied mathematics. It is the cryptographer's primary task to find secure methods to encrypt messages, making them unintelligible to all except the intended recipients."
Bernstein v. United States Dept. of Justice, 176 F.3d 1132, 1136-37 (9th Cir. 1999).

Related issues. "By utilizing source code, a cryptographer can express algorithmic ideas with precision and methodical rigor that is otherwise difficult to achieve. This has the added benefit of facilitating peer review—by compiling the source code, a cryptographer can create a working model subject to rigorous security tests."
Bernstein v. United States Dept. of Justice, 176 F.3d 1132, 1141 (9th Cir. 1999).

"[C]ryptographic ideas and algorithms are conveniently expressed in source code. That this should be so is, on reflection, not surprising. As noted earlier, the chief task for cryptographers is the development of secure methods of encryption. While the articulation of such a system in layman's English or in general mathematical terms may be useful, the devil is, at least for cryptographers, often in the algorithmic details. By utilizing source code, a cryptographer can express algorithmic ideas with precision and methodological rigor that is otherwise difficult to achieve. This has the added benefit of facilitating peer review—by compiling the source code, a cryptographer can create a working model subject to rigorous security tests. The need for precisely articulated hypotheses and formal empirical testing, of course, is not unique to the science of cryptography; it appears, however, that in this field, source code is the preferred means to these ends.

"Thus, cryptographers use source code to express their scientific ideas in much the same way that mathematicians use equations or economists use graphs. Of course, both mathematical equations and graphs are used in other fields for many purposes, not all of which are expressive. But mathematicians and economists have adopted these modes of expression in order to facilitate the precise and rigorous expression of complex scientific ideas. Similarly, the undisputed record here makes it clear that cryptographers utilize source code in the same fashion.

"In light of these considerations, we conclude that encryption software, in its source code form and as employed by those in the field of cryptography, must be viewed as expressive for First Amendment purposes, and thus is entitled to the protections of the prior restraint doctrine."

Bernstein v. United States Dept. of Justice, 176 F.3d 1132, 1140-41 (9th Cir. 1999).

See also **decryption; encryption.**

CSNet *(Internet)*

Acronym for "Community Schools Network." A network that connected various schools. CSNet has changed its name to WINSTAR for Education.

Annotation. "At the same time that ARPANET was maturing (it subsequently ceased to exist), similar networks developed to link universities, research facilities, businesses, and individuals around the world. These other formal or loose networks included BITNET, CSNET, FIDONET, and USENET. Eventually, each of these networks (many of which overlapped) were themselves linked together, allowing users of any computers linked to any one of the networks to transmit communications to users of computers on other networks. It is this series of linked networks (themselves linking computers and computer networks) that is today commonly known as the Internet."

Reno v. American Civil Liberties Union, 929 F. Supp. 824, 832 (E.D. Pa. 1996), *aff'd*, 521 U.S. 844 (1997).

C-SPAN *(broadcasting; organization)*

Acronym for "Cable Satellite Public Affairs Network." A private, nonprofit public service company created by the cable television industry to provide public affairs programming distributed primarily on cable.

CSS *(technology)*

Acronym for "Content Scramble System."

"[A]n access control and copy prevention system for DVDs developed by the motion picture companies, including plaintiffs. It is an encryption-based system that requires the use of appropriately configured hardware such as a DVD player or a computer DVD drive to decrypt, unscramble and play back, but not copy, motion pictures on DVDs. The technology necessary to configure DVD players and drives to play CSS-protected DVDs has been licensed to hundreds of manufacturers in the United States and around the world."

> *Universal City Studios, Inc. v. Reimerdes*, 111 F. Supp. 2d 294, 308 (S.D.N.Y. 2000) (footnotes omitted).

Annotation. "CSS involves encrypting, according to an encryption algorithm, the digital sound and graphics files on a DVD that together constitute a motion picture. A CSS-protected DVD can be decrypted by an appropriate decryption algorithm that employs a series of keys stored on the DVD and the DVD player. In consequence, only players and drives containing the appropriate keys are able to decrypt DVD files and thereby play movies stored on DVDs."

> *Universal City Studios, Inc. v. Reimerdes*, 111 F. Supp. 2d 294, 309-10 (S.D.N.Y. 2000) (footnotes omitted).

Related issues. "One cannot gain access to a CSS-protected work on a DVD without application of the three keys that are required by the software. One cannot lawfully gain access to the keys except by entering into a license with the DVD CCA under authority granted by the copyright owners or by purchasing a DVD player or drive containing the keys pursuant to such a license. In consequence, under the express terms of the statute, CSS 'effectively controls access' to copyrighted DVD movies. It does so, within the meaning of the statute, whether or not it is a strong means of protection."

> *Universal City Studios, Inc. v. Reimerdes*, 111 F. Supp. 2d 294, 317-18 (S.D.N.Y. 2000) (footnotes omitted).

CTR *(advertising; Internet)*
Acronym for "Click-Through Rate."
See **click-through rate.**

cursor *(technology)*
A movable icon on a display screen that indicates the location at which the next action will take place. The cursor can be moved about the screen by the operator through a variety of commands.

custom application software *(software)*
"[Software] specifically designed for the customer's individual needs."

> *Triangle Underwriters, Inc. v. Honeywell, Inc.*, 457 F. Supp. 765, 767 (E.D.N.Y. 1978), *aff'd in part, rev'd in part*, 604 F.2d 737, 739 (2d Cir. 1979).

See also **custom program(s); custom software.**

custom circuit *(hardware)*
An integrated circuit designed and manufactured for a particular customer. Contrasts with semi-custom, which has only the last few manufacturing steps tailored to customer specifications. Also contrasts with integrated circuits of standard design, which are produced in volume for many users. *See also* **semi-custom circuit.**

custom program(s) *(software)*
"…are uniquely created for an individual user and an individual system. Virtually 100% of a custom program is written for the user."
> *Health Micro Data Sys., Inc. v. Wisconsin Dep't of Revenue*, 2 Computer Cas. (CCH) ¶ 60,056, at 80,228 (Tax. App. Comm'n 1989).
See also **custom application software; custom software.**

custom software *(software)*
"…is prepared for a specific customer's needs and is not easily transferable to other customers. Custom software is often canned software which has been modified to fit the needs of a particular customer."
> *Ridder v. Washington Mutual Savings Bank*, 2 Computer Cas. (CCH) ¶ 60,063, at 80,265 (Wash. Bd. Tax. App. 1989).
See also **custom application software; custom program(s).**

customer lists *(trade secret)*
A list of names and related information (e.g., addresses, e-mail addresses, telephone numbers) of customers of a particular organization.

Annotation. "There is some authority for the proposition that non-specialized customer lists are not property…and therefore an employer may not prevent an employee from using such a list in the absence of a contract. However, it does not follow that a rule of questionable origins should be extended to customer information that may be found on more sophisticated media such as an employer's microfiche or in its computer databases."
> *Equifax Servs., Inc. v. Examination Management Servs., Inc.*, 216 Ga. App. 35, 453 S.E.2d 488, 494 (1994) (citations omitted).

cyber pirate *(Internet)*
"[One] who steals valuable trademarks and establishes domain names on the Internet using these trademarks to sell the domain names to the rightful trademark owners."
> *Panavision Int'l, L.P. v. Toeppen*, 141 F.3d 1316, 1318 (9th Cir. 1998).
See also **cybersquatter.**

cybercoupons *(Internet)*
Downloadable "coupons" for savings on goods or services.

cyberpunk *(criminal; video game)*
"[A] science fiction literary genre which became popular in the 1980s, which is characterized by the fictional interaction of humans with technology and the fictional struggle for power between individuals, corporations, and government."
> *Steve Jackson Games, Inc. v. United States Secret Serv.*, 36 F.3d 457, 459 n.1 (5th Cir. 1994).

cybersmear *(Internet)*
Posting false rumors and negative comments on web sites and bulletin boards, primarily to drive down the price of stocks.

cyberspace *(Internet; trademark)*
A word coined by science fiction author William Gibson in the short story "Burning Chrome," and later used in his novel *Neuromancer* (1984) to refer to the virtual world created within a computer and the network to which it is attached (also called a "computer-generated reality"). It includes the internal computer memory and wiring, and the networks to which the computer is connected. The prefix "cyber" is derived from the Greek word *kybernan*, which means to steer or control.

Annotation. "[R]efers to the interaction of people and businesses over computer networks, electronic bulletin boards, and commercial online services. The largest and most visible manifestation of cyberspace is the Internet...."
> *Blumenthal v. Drudge*, 992 F. Supp. 44, 49 n.8 (D.D.C. 1998) (citation omitted).

"[L]ocated in no particular geographical location but available to anyone, anywhere in the world, with access to the Internet."
> *Reno v. American Civil Liberties Union*, 521 U.S. 844 (1997).

"Some of the computers and computer networks that make up the Internet are owned by governmental and public institutions, some are owned by non-profit organizations, and some are privately owned. The resulting whole is a decentralized, global medium of communications—or 'cyberspace'—that links people, institutions, corporations, and governments around the world."
> *American Civil Liberties Union v. Reno*, 929 F. Supp. 824, 831 (E.D. Pa. 1996), *aff'd, Reno v. American Civil Liberties Union*, 521 U.S. 844 (1997).

"[S]ome of our cases have recognized special justifications for regulation of the broadcast media that are not applicable to other speakers.... In these cases, the Court relied on the history of extensive government regulation of the broadcast medium...the scarcity of available frequencies at its inception...and its 'invasive' nature. Those factors are not present in cyberspace. Neither before nor after the enactment of the CDA have the vast democratic fora of the Internet been subject to the type of government supervision and regulation that has attended the broadcast industry."

   Reno v. American Civil Liberties Union, 521 U.S. 844, 868-69 (1997) (citations omitted).

"The Government estimates that '[a]s many as 40 million people use the Internet today, and that figure is expected to grow to 200 million by 1999.' This dynamic, multifaceted category of communication includes not only traditional print and news services, but also audio, video, and still images, as well as interactive, real-time dialogue. Through the use of chat rooms, any person with a phone line can become a town crier with a voice that resonates farther than it could from any soapbox. Through the use of Web pages, mail exploders, and newsgroups, the same individual can become a pamphleteer. As the District Court found, 'the content on the Internet is as diverse as human thought.'...We agree with its conclusion that our cases provide no basis for qualifying the level of First Amendment scrutiny that should be applied to this medium."

   Reno v. American Civil Liberties Union, 521 U.S. 844, 870-71 (1997).

"The record demonstrates that the growth of the Internet has been and continues to be phenomenal. As a matter of constitutional tradition, in the absence of evidence to the contrary, we presume that governmental regulation of the content of speech is more likely to interfere with the free exchange of ideas than to encourage it. The interest in encouraging freedom of expression in a democratic society outweighs any theoretical but unproven benefit of censorship."

   Reno v. American Civil Liberties Union, 521 U.S. 844, 885 (1997).

"Because it is no more than the interconnection of electronic pathways, cyberspace allows speakers and listeners to mask their identities. Cyberspace undeniably reflects some form of geography; chat rooms and Web sites, for example, exist at fixed 'locations' on the Internet. Since users can transmit and receive messages on the Internet without revealing anything about their identities or ages …, however, it is not currently possible to exclude persons from accessing certain messages on the basis of their identity. Cyberspace differs from the physical world in another basic way: Cyberspace is malleable. Thus, it is possible to construct barriers in cyberspace and use them to screen for identity, making cyberspace more like the physical world and, consequently, more amenable to zoning laws. This transformation of cyberspace is already underway…. Internet speakers (users who post material on the Internet) have begun to zone cyberspace itself through the use of 'gateway' technology."

Reno v. American Civil Liberties Union, 521 U.S. 844, 889-90 (1997) (O'Connor, J., concurring in part, dissenting in part).

"It is probably safe to say that more ideas and information are shared on the Internet than in any other medium. But when we try to pin down the location of this exchange, we realize how slippery our notion of the Internet really is. Perhaps this is because 'cyberspace' is not a 'space' at all. At least not in the way we understand space. It's not located anywhere; it has no boundaries; you can't 'go' there. At the bottom, the Internet is really more idea than entity. It is an agreement we have made to hook our computers together and communicate by way of binary impulses and digitized signals sent over telephone wires.

* * *

"[T]he Internet is fundamentally different from traditional forms of mass communications in at least three important respects. First, the Internet is capable of maintaining an unlimited number of information sources…. Second, the Internet has no 'gatekeepers'—no publishers or editors controlling the distribution of information…. Finally, the users of Internet information are also its producers. But every person who taps into the Internet is his [or her] journalist. In other words, the Internet has shifted the focus of mass communications to the individual…. Never before has it been so easy to circulate speech among so many people."

Blumenthal v. Drudge, 992 F. Supp. 44, 48 n. 7 (D.D.C. 1998).

Related issues. "[I]t takes several steps to enter cyberspace. At the most fundamental level, a user must have access to a computer with the ability to reach the Internet (typically by way of a modem). A user must then direct the computer to connect with the access provider, enter a password, and enter the appropriate commands to find particular data."

American Civil Liberties Union v. Reno, 929 F. Supp. 824, 844 (E.D. Pa. 1996), *aff'd, Reno v. American Civil Liberties Union*, 521 U.S. 844 (1997).

"In the medium of cyberspace, however, anyone can build a soap box out of web pages and speak her mind in the virtual village green to an audience larger and more diverse than any the Framers could have imagined. In many respects, unconventional messages compete equally with the speech of mainstream speakers in the marketplace of ideas that is the Internet, certainly more than in most other media."

    American Civil Liberties Union v. Reno, 31 F. Supp. 2d 473, 476 (E.D. Pa. 1999).

"While no one should lose sight of the inventiveness that has made this complex of resources available to just about anyone, the innovativeness of the technology does not preclude the application of traditional legal principles—provided that those principles are adaptable to cyberspace."

    American Library Ass'n v. Pataki, 969 F. Supp. 160, 166 (S.D.N.Y. 1997).

". . . a medium of 'virtual reality' that invites fantasy and affords anonymity. . . ."

    McVeigh v. Cohen, 983 F. Supp. 215, 219 (D.D.C. 1998).

"With the Web becoming an important mechanism for commerce . . . companies are racing to stake out their place in cyberspace."

    Brookfield Comm., Inc. v. West Coast Entertainment Corp., 174 F.3d 1036, 1044 (9th Cir. 1999).

See also **Internet, cybersquatting.**

cybersquatter *(Internet; trademark)*

"[A]n entrepreneur who made a business of registering trademarks as domain names for the purpose of selling them later to the trademarks' owners."

    Lockheed Martin Corp. v. Network Solutions, Inc., 985 F. Supp. 949, 959 (C.D. Cal. 1997).

Annotation. "These individuals attempt to profit from the Internet by reserving and later reselling or licensing domain names back to the companies that spend millions of dollars developing the goodwill of the trademark. While many may find patently offensive the practice of reserving the name or mark of a federally registered trademark as a domain name and then attempting to sell the name back to the holder of the trademark, others may view it as a service. Regardless of one's view as to the morality of such conduct, the legal issue is whether such conduct is illegal."

    Intermatic, Inc. v. Toeppen, 947 F. Supp. 1227, 1233-34 (N.D. Cal. 1996).

"Congress and the states have been slow to respond to the activities of the cyber-squatters. Some commentators take an extremely dim view of their activities.... However, becoming rich does not make one's activity necessarily illegal. Speculation and arbitrage have a long history in this country."

> *Intermatic, Inc. v. Toeppen,* 947 F. Supp. 1227, 1234 (N.D. Cal. 1996).

See also cyber pirate; cybersquatting.

cybersquatting *(trademark)*

"[U]se [domain name] registration as a club to extort payment.... [C]onstitutes continuing infringement."

> *Washington Speakers Bureau, Inc. v. Leading Authorities, Inc.,* 49 F. Supp. 2d 496, 498 (E.D. Va. 1999).

See also cybersquatter.

cyber-terrorism *(criminal)*

"The use of computing resources against persons or property to intimidate or coerce a government, the civilian population, or any segment thereof, in furtherance of political or social objectives."

> Office of the Comptroller of the Currency, Infrastructure Threats from Cyber-Terrorists 2 (Mar. 19, 1999).

Annotation. "As commercial technologies create advantages, their increasingly indispensable nature transforms them into high value targets of cyber-terrorists and cyber-criminals. The Year 2000 problem has served to heighten the awareness of our nation's critical reliance on technology and permeates all industries through the interdependence of our infrastructures. These critical infrastructures include telecommunications, energy, banking and finance, transportation, water systems, and emergency services, both government and private.

"Recent advances in computer hardware, software, and communications technologies have made these infrastructures highly automated and capable. While technological advances have promoted greater efficiency and improved service, they have also made these infrastructures potentially more vulnerable to disruption or incapacitation by a wide range of physical or computer-based (cyber) threats. The infrastructures are much more interdependent than in the past, with the result that the debilitation or destruction of one could have cascading destructive effects on others. Electronic transactions within the financial services infrastructure underpin the entire national economy, as well as the operations of the other infrastructure sectors."

> Office of the Comptroller of the Currency, Infrastructure Threats from Cyber-Terrorists 2 (Mar. 19, 1999).

". . . can be one catastrophic attack on our infrastructure, or a series of co-ordinated, seemingly independent attacks."

> Office of the Comptroller of the Currency, Infrastructure Threats from Cyber-Terrorists 2 (Mar. 19, 1999).

". . . includes acts of commercial espionage and employee sabotage."

> Office of the Comptroller of the Currency, Infrastructure Threats from Cyber-Terrorists 2 (Mar. 19, 1999).

See also **cyber-terrorist(s)**; **cyber-terrorist attack(s)**.

cyber-terrorist(s) *(criminal)*

". . . can be an individual, a criminal organization, a dissident group or faction, or another country."

> Office of the Comptroller of the Currency, Infrastructure Threats from Cyber-Terrorists 2 (Mar. 19, 1999).

Annotation. "The basic attack tools of the cyber-terrorist are a computer, modem, telephone, and user-friendly hacker software."

> Office of the Comptroller of the Currency, Infrastructure Threats from Cyber-Terrorists 3 (Mar. 19, 1999).

See also **cyber-terrorism**; **cyber-terrorist attack(s)**.

cyber-terrorist attack(s) *(criminal)*

". . . can take the form of:

Denial or disruption of computer, cable, satellite, or telecommunications services.

Monitoring of computer, cable, satellite, or telecommunications systems.

Disclosure of proprietary, private, or classified information stored within or communicated through computer, cable, and satellite or telecommunications systems.

Modification or destruction of computer programming codes, computer network databases, stored information, or computer capabilities.

Manipulation of computer, cable, satellite, or telecommunications services resulting in fraud, financial loss or other federal criminal violation.

Threats to destroy data or program files.

The ultimate threat to computer security is the insider. These individuals may be disgruntled employees, or represent some group or country. Thus, security clearance checks should be required."

> Office of the Comptroller of the Currency, Infrastructure Threats from Cyber-Terrorists 3 (Mar. 19, 1999).

See also **cyber-terrorist(s)**; **cyber-terrorism**.

C³I *(business)*

Acronym for "Command, Control, Communications and Intelligence."

cycle time *(business)*

The total time it takes to build a product.

cyclic validity checks *(technology)*

"Reconfirmations of each incoming message for validity."

> *OAO Corp. v. United States*, 1 Computer Cas. (CCH) ¶ 46,080, at 61,142 (Ct. Cl. 1989).

daisy wheel *(technology)*

A wheel-like print head used on some printers. The type characters are on small keys circling the center of the head, and resemble daisy petals. This wheel is used to print typewriter-quality characters on paper. This type of printing technology has been supplanted by laser printers and ink-jet printers in most applications, except where multiple copies of a form must be printed simultaneously.

damage limitations *(contract)*

See consequential damages, limitations on.

damages

(contract)

"[G]eneral damages are such as naturally and ordinarily follow the breach, whereas special damages are those that ensue, not necessarily or ordinarily, but because of special circumstances."

Applied Data Processing, Inc. v. Burroughs Corp., 394 F. Supp. 504, 509 (D. Conn. 1975).

(criminal)

"[A]ny impairment to the integrity or availability of data, a program, a system, or information, that—

(A) causes loss aggregating at least $5,000 in value during any 1-year period to one or more individuals;

(B) modifies or impairs, or potentially modifies or impairs, the medical examination, diagnosis, treatment, or care of one or more individuals;

(C) causes physical injury to any person; or

(D) threatens public health or safety."

18 U.S.C. § 1030(e)(8).

Annotation

(contract)

"An award not reduced by the benefit received by the plaintiff would be too large to be compensatory, and so it would be punitive, and punitive damages are rarely, and in New Hampshire never, awarded in contract cases;

and so a victim of a breach of contract who wants to keep the contract breaker's money above and beyond the amount necessary to compensate for the breach may be said to be 'unjustly enriched,' entitling the contract breaker to restitution."

> *Micro Data Base Sys., Inc. v. Dharma Sys., Inc.*, 148 F.3d 649, 656 (7th Cir. 1998).

(copyright)

"The copyright owner is entitled to recover... any profits of the infringer that are attributable to the infringement and are not taken into account in computing the actual damages. In establishing the infringer's profits, the copyright owner is required to present proof only of the infringer's gross revenue, and the infringer is required to prove his or her deductible expenses and the elements of profit attributable to factors other than the copyrighted work."

> 17 U.S.C. § 504(b).

Related issues

(criminal)

"Damages for violations involving damage as defined in subsection (e)(8)(A) are limited to economic damages."

> 18 U.S.C. § 1030(g).

(semiconductor)

"The Semiconductor Chip Protection Act, like the Copyright Act, contains no provision authorizing or prohibiting the enhancement of damages. The patent statute, in contrast, authorizes the court to increase damages up to three times the amount assessed as actual damages."

> *Brooktree Corp. v. Advanced Micro Devices, Inc.*, 977 F.2d 1555, 1581 (Fed. Cir. 1992).

damages, proof of *(trade secret)*

"There is no rule that damages can be proved only by documents, only by experts, or only by disinterested third parties. The only pertinent rules are that damages must be based on evidence rather than guesswork, wishful thinking, and pie-in-the-sky dreaming, and that costs must be netted from revenues to determine the plaintiff's actual loss."

> *Micro Data Base Sys., Inc. v. Dharma Sys., Inc.*, 148 F.3d 649, 657-58 (7th Cir. 1998) (citations omitted).

DARPA *(Internet; organization)*

Acronym for "Defense Advanced Research Project Agency." *See* ARPA.

DASD *(hardware)*
Acronym for "Direct-Access Storage Device."
> *IBM Corp. v. Fujitsu Ltd.,* Copyright L. Rep. (CCH) ¶ 20,517, at 11,392 (Am. Arb. Ass'n 1988).

data

(criminal)
"[A] representation of information, knowledge, facts, concepts, computer software, computer programs or instructions. Data may be in any form, in storage media, or as stored in the memory of the computer or in transit or presented on a display device."
> Cal. Penal C. § 502.

(technology)
[CANADA] "[R]epresentations of information or of concepts that are being prepared or have been prepared in a form suitable for use in a computer system."
> Criminal Code of Canada, R.S.C. 1985, c. C-46, s. 342.1(2) [en. R.S.C. 1985, c. 27 (1st Supp.), s. 45].

[CANADA] " 'Data' is commonly used in the electronics field to refer to information provided by electronic equipment."
> *Smiths Indus. Ltd. v. Ventek Computer Sys. Ltd.* (1978), 42 C.P.R. (2d) 139 (T.M. Opp. Bd.).

data attribute *(technology)*
Refers to a characteristic of a data element, such as length, value, etc.

data center *(business)*
"[A]n establishment having a computer installation which permits customer personnel to operate the computer equipment for a fee."
> *Telex Corp. v. IBM Corp.,* 367 F. Supp. 258, 273 (N.D. Okla. 1973), *aff'd in part, rev'd in part,* 510 F.2d 894 (10th Cir.), *cert. dism.,* 423 U.S. 802 (1975).

data compression *(technology)*
A technique for reducing the amount of CD-ROM storage required for a given amount of data.

data converter(s) *(software)*
See data translator(s).

data element *(technology)*
Any single item of data.

data glove *(hardware)*
A glove fitted with position- and/or motion-sensitive sensors, which is primarily used in connection with virtual reality systems.

data mining *(technology)*
The process of locating previously unknown data within existing databases.

data processing *(technology)*
The recording, handling, and manipulating of data by means of electronic equipment. Data processing applications include such tasks as telephone system control and satellite operation, office functions including word processing and financial calculations, and data reduction for large research projects, etc.

data recovery *(encryption; software)*
See **key recovery.**

data transfer protocol *(technology)*
A formal set of standards governing the format and control of data, which allows it to be transferred from one computer to another.

Annotation. "No single entity—academic, corporate, governmental, or non-profit—administers the Internet. It exists and functions as a result of the fact that hundreds of thousands of separate operators of computers and computer networks independently decided to use common data transfer protocols to exchange communications and information with other computers (which in turn exchange communications and information with still other computers)."
　　Reno v. American Civil Liberties Union, 929 F. Supp. 824, 832 (E.D. Pa. 1996), *aff'd, American Civil Liberties Union v. Reno,* 521 U.S. 844 (1997).

data transfer rate *(technology)*
A measure of the amount of data that can be transferred from one location in a data processing system to another.

data translator(s) *(software)*
". . . are common in the CAD [computer aided design] market because users of CAD products commonly employ more than one CAD system to perform their necessary tasks and, as a result, often transfer information between various CAD systems. This need has created a demand for translators of all kinds in the CAD market. . . ."
　　Baystate Technologies, Inc. v. Bentley Sys., Inc., 946 F. Supp. 1079, 1081 (D. Mass. 1996).

data warehouse *(technology)*
A location in which business information is collected and stored.

database *(technology)*
"A collection of data elements that the user puts into the computer; the term refers also to how these elements are organized in records, and how they [are] organized in files."
> *Dental Office Computer Sys., Inc. v. Clutting*, No. CV-86-5613DT (Mich. App. filed Aug. 13, 1987).

[EUROPE] "A collection of information stored and accessed by electronic means. It may be a collection of full text material, that is to say, existing copyright works, in which case it is an analogy between the database and a generalized or specialized library. It may be a compilation of extracts of works, similar to an anthology or a documentation centre, from which relevant parts of works may be obtained. It may be a collection of material that is in the public domain, such as a list of names and addresses, prices, and reference numbers. There is here a similarity with catalogs, time tables, price lists, and other such reference material in printed form. Lastly, it may consist of the electronic publishing of a single but voluminous work, such as an encyclopedia."
> EEC, *Green Paper on Copyright and the Challenge of Technology,* COM (88)172 Final (1988).

database management system *(software)*
"A program used to store, retrieve, and manipulate data within a computer."
> *Infosystems Tech., Inc. v. Logical Software, Inc.,* 1 Computer Cas. (CCH) ¶ 45,035, at 60,287 (4th Cir. 1987).

"... is designed to permit the user of a computer to store, update, and retrieve information in an organized and efficient fashion."
> *Cullinet Software, Inc. v. McCormack & Dodge Corp.,* 23 Mass. App. 231, 232 n.2, 500 N.E.2d 831, 832 n.2 (1986), *rev'd,* 511 N.E.2d 1101 (Mass. 1987).

"A computer software program which is used to store, retrieve, and manipulate data within a computer."
> *Infosystems Technology, Inc. v. Logical Software, Inc.,* 8 Computer L. Serv. Rep. 689, 697 (D. Md. 1985).

database program *(software)*
"A program that allows the user to access within the program itself a variety of technical materials and data incorporated into the program's logic and

analysis that one would otherwise have to provide on one's own or by reference to some type of data compilation."

> *Manufacturers Technology, Inc. v. Cams, Inc.,* 706 F. Supp. 984, 991 (D. Conn. 1989).

DBS

(computer technology)
Acronym for "Database System" or Database Software."

(telecommunications)
Acronym for "Direct Broadcast Satellite."

deal memo *(business)*

A short document that sets forth the salient terms of the "deal," often in the form of a letter. The parties normally anticipate that a comprehensive written agreement will be negotiated and drafted, incorporating the terms of the deal memo.

debug *(technology)*

See debugging.

debugging *(technology)*

"The process of detecting and removing the errors in a computer program or set of programs. Typically, errors are detected by trying to run a program with a series of transactions designed to test the main portions of the program, and observing the correctness of results."

> U.S. Copyright Office, *Compendium of Copyright Office Practices II,* § 326 (1984).

"[A] term of art used in the computer software business to describe the correction of errors in a program."

> *Georgetown College of Science and Arts Ltd. v. Microsystems Eng'g Corp.,* 8 Computer L. Serv. Rep. 342, 343 (D.D.C. 1984).

"The testing is generally called 'debugging.'"

> *Pezzillo v. General Tel. & Elecs. Information Sys., Inc.,* 414 F. Supp. 1257, 1259 (M.D. Tenn. 1976).

Annotation. "Debugging, or error removal, is frequently a lengthy process, for any moderately difficult task may require a fairly detailed and complex program.... The program demands arduous debugging not only because of its complexity, but also because of its delicacy. Even slight and perhaps obvious errors can hinder a program, for a computer has no way of recognizing errors. Like a perfect soldier, it takes instructions without questioning them."

> *Whelan Assocs., Inc. v. Jaslow Dental Lab., Inc.,* 797 F.2d 1222, 1231 n.21 (3d Cir. 1986) (citations omitted), *cert. denied,* 107 S. Ct. 877 (1987).

"After the coding is finished, the programmer will run the program on the computer in order to find and correct any logical and syntactical errors. This is known as 'debugging' and, once done, the program is complete."

> *Computer Assocs. Int'l, Inc. v. Altai, Inc.,* 982 F.2d 693, 698 (2d Cir. 1992).

decimal system *(mathematics)*

"The decimal system uses as digits the 10 symbols 0, 1, 2, 3, 4, 5, 6, 7, 8, and 9. The value represented by any digit depends, as it does in any positional system of notation, both on its individual value and on its relative position in the numeral. Decimal numerals are written by placing digits in the appropriate positions or columns of the numerical sequence. . . ."

> *Gottschalk v. Benson,* 409 U.S. 63, 66 (1972).

decompilation *(software)*

"[T]he process by which a machine language program is placed in another programming language which is more readily understood by human beings."

> *Vault Corp. v. Quaid Software Ltd.,* 655 F. Supp. 750, 755 (E.D. La. 1987).

See also decompiler; disassembler; disassembly; disassembly program; reverse engineering.

decompile *(software)*

See decompilation; decompiler; disassembler; disassembly; disassembly program; reverse engineering.

decompiler *(software)*

"Devices called 'disassemblers' or 'decompilers' can reverse this process by 'reading' the electronic signals for '0' and '1' that are produced while the program is being run, storing the resulting object code in computer memory, and translating the object code into source code."

> *Sega Enters. Ltd. v. Accolade, Inc.,* 977 F.2d 1510, 1515, n.2 (9th Cir. 1992).

decompression *(technology)*

The process of restoring compressed data to its original form.

decryption *(technology)*

The opposite of encryption. The process of decoding encryption information using a special code.

DeCSS *(software)*

"[A] software utility, or computer program, that enables users to break the CSS copy protection system and hence to view DVDs on unlicensed players and make digital copies of DVD movies. The quality of motion pictures decrypted by DeCSS is virtually identical to that of encrypted movies on DVD."

> *Universal City Studios, Inc. v. Reimerdes*, 111 F. Supp. 2d 294, 308 (S.D.N.Y. 2000) (footnotes omitted).

Annotation. "DeCSS is a free, effective and fast means of decrypting plaintiffs' DVDs and copying them to computer hard drives. DivX, which is available over the Internet for nothing, with the investment of some time and effort, permits compression of the decrypted files to sizes that readily fit on a writeable CD-ROM. Copies of such CD-ROMs can be produced very cheaply and distributed as easily as other pirated intellectual property. While not everyone with Internet access now will find it convenient to send or receive DivX'd copies of pirated motion pictures over the Internet, the availability of high speed network connections in many businesses and institutions, and their growing availability in homes, make Internet and other network traffic in pirated copies a growing threat."

> *Universal City Studios, Inc. v. Reimerdes*, 111 F. Supp. 2d 294, 315 (S.D.N.Y. 2000) (footnotes omitted).

dedicated *(technology)*

A computerized device with a single purpose, i.e., a cash register, a video game, etc.

dedicated line *(technology)*

See leased line.

dedicated server *(hardware)*

A computer system devoted to a specific Internet web site.

defamation *(tort)*

A wrongful action wherein a false and malicious statement is made that damages the name and/or reputation of an individual.

Related issues. "No provider or user of an interactive computer service shall be treated as the publisher or speaker of any information provided by another information content provider."

47 U.S.C. § 230(e)(1).

default settings *(technology)*

When no explicit choice is specified by the user, the system sets guidelines such as tab settings, line width, and characters per inch.

delegation of duties *(contract)*

A contractural clause by which one party to the contract transfer its duties under the contract to another party.

Annotation. When a duty is delegated, the delegator remains liable to the obligee (the person to whom the duty is owed). The delegatee is also liable to the obligee to render performance. Thus, when a duty is delegated, both the delegator and delegatee are liable to the obligee for the performance due under the contract.

There are nondelegable duties, including duties that relate to personal services or to the exercise of personal skill or discretion, or are such that the obligee has a substantial interest in having the original promisor perform or supervise performance.

Sample clause. "None of the duties, responsibilities or conditions of either party to this Agreement may be delegated or subcontracted except as explicitly stated in this Agreement, unless there is an express authorization in writing signed by the party to whom the duty is owed."

delivery *(contract)*

"[W]ith respect to instruments, documents of title, chattel paper, or certificated securities means voluntary transfer of possession."

U.C.C. § 1-201(14).

"[W]ith respect to a copy, means the voluntary physical or electronic transfer of possession or control."

UCITA § 102(a)(24).

de minimis infringement *(copyright)*

"Copyright law does not admit of simple, bright-line rules."

Nihon Keizai Shimbun, Inc. v. Comline Business Data, Inc., 166 F.3d 65, 71 (2nd Cir. 1999).

See also **copyright infringement.**

demo *(software)*

An abbreviation for "demonstration." In relation to computer software, a limited version of a computer software package, which is distributed to potential licensees so that they can use it prior to obtaining a license to the complete version.

demographics *(advertising)*

Statistical data that describes the makeup of a given user base, such as age, gender, educational level, and average household income.

Annotation. Demographics are a tool used to match ad space with an advertising campaign. Most media buyers purchase only ad space supported by substantiated demographic data.

DEMS *(telecommunications)*

Acronym for "Digital Electronic Messaging Services."

Wireless communication services providing local, broadband data transmission.

deposit *(copyright)*

[T]he owner of copyright or of the exclusive right of publication in a work published in the United States shall deposit, within three months after the date of publication—(1) two complete copies of the best edition. . . ."

17 U.S.C. § 407(a).

deprive *(criminal)*

". . . includes making unauthorized use or an unauthorized copy of records, information, data, trade secrets or computer programs. . . ."

Wash. Rev. Code § 9A.56.010(5).

derivative work *(copyright)*

"[A] work based upon one or more preexisting works, such as a translation, musical arrangement, dramatization, fictionalization, motion picture version, sound recording, art reproduction, abridgment, condensation, or any other form in which a work may be recast, transformed, or adapted. A work consisting of editorial revisions, annotations, elaborations, or other modifications which, as a whole, represent an original work of authorship, is a 'derivative work.'"

U.S. Copyright Act, 17 U.S.C. § 101.

Annotation. "To constitute a violation of section 106(2) the infringing work must incorporate in some form a portion of the copyrighted work."

> *Vault Corp. v. Quaid Software Ltd.*, 655 F. Supp. 750, 758 (E.D. La. 1987), *quoting Litchfield v. Spielberg*, 736 F.2d 1352, 1357 (9th Cir. 1984), *cert. denied*, 470 U.S. 1052 (1985).

"A derivative work must incorporate a protected work in some concrete or permanent 'form.'"

> *Lewis Galoob Toys, Inc. v. Nintendo of America*, 964 F.2d 965, 967 (9th Cir. 1992).

"Such a work—if it is non-infringing and sufficiently original—qualifies for a separate copyright, although this copyright does not protect the preexisting material employed in the derivative work."

> *Montgomery v. Noga*, 168 F.3d 1282, 1290 (11th Cir. 1999).

"The copyright in a…derivative work extends only to the material contributed by the author of such work, as distinguished from the preexisting material employed in the work, and does not imply any exclusive right in the preexisting material. The copyright in such work is independent of, and does not affect or enlarge the scope, duration, ownership or subsistence of, any copyright protection in the preexisting material."

> 17 U.S.C. § 103(b).

"The statutory language is hopelessly overbroad, however, for '[e]very book in literature, science and art, borrows and must necessarily borrow, and use much which was well known and used before.' To narrow the statute to a manageable level, we have developed certain criteria a work must satisfy in order to qualify as a derivative work. One of these is that a derivative work must exist in a 'concrete or permanent form,' and must substantially incorporate protected material from the preexisting work…."

> *Micro Star v. FormGen, Inc.*, 154 F.3d 1107, 1110 (9th Cir. 1998) (citations omitted).

"The requirement that a derivative work must assume a concrete or permanent form was recognized without much discussion in *Galoob*. There, we noted that all the Copyright Act's examples of derivative works took some definite, physical form and concluded that this was a requirement of the Act."

> *Micro Star v. FormGen, Inc.*, 154 F.3d 1107, 1111 (9th Cir. 1998).

Related issues. "A derivative work must be fixed to be protected under the Act…but not to infringe."

> *Lewis Galoob Toys, Inc. v. Nintendo of America*, 964 F.2d 965, 968 (9th Cir. 1992) (citation omitted; emphasis in original).

"...requires a process of recasting, transforming, or adopting 'one or more preexisting works.'..."

> *M. Kramer Mfg. Co. v. Andrews,* 783 F.2d 421, 437 n.16 (4th Cir. 1986), *citing* H.R. Rep. No. 1476, 94th Cong., 2d Sess. (1976), U.S. Code & Cong. Ad. News 5659, 5670 (1976).

"[T]o the extent an author's work is derived from preexisting materials in the public domain, copyright protection is afforded only to the non-trivial, original features contributed by the author to the derivative work."

> *E.F. Johnson Co. v. Uniden Co. of America,* 623 F. Supp. 1485, 1499 (D. Minn. 1985).

DES *(technology)*

Acronym for "Data Encryption Standard." The National Standard algorithm for symmetric block encryption adopted by the U.S. federal government in the 1970s.

description metatags *(Internet)*

"... are intended to describe the web site. ..."

> *Brookfield Comm., Inc. v. West Coast Entertainment Corp.,* 174 F.3d 1036, 1045 (9th Cir. 1999) (citation omitted).

See also **metatag.**

descriptive mark(s) *(trademark)*

" ... identifies the characteristics and qualities of the article, such as its color, odor, functions, dimensions or ingredients."

> *Washington Speakers Bureau, Inc. v. Leading Authorities, Inc.,* 33 F. Supp. 2d 488, 495 (E.D. Va. 1999).

"... which are not inherently distinctive, are those which identify some function, use, characteristic, size or intended purpose of the product. In order for a descriptive mark to be accorded protection, it must be shown that it has acquired what is known as 'secondary meaning'."

> *America Online, Inc. v. AT&T Corp.,* 64 F. Supp. 2d 549, 560 (E.D. Va. 1999) (citations omitted).

"... are not inherently distinctive, but 'merely describe a function, use, characteristic, size, or intended purpose of the product.' ... Descriptive marks are the weakest category of protectible marks; they are not accorded trademark protection unless they have acquired 'secondary meaning'."

> *Washington Speakers Bureau, Inc. v. Leading Authorities, Inc.,* 33 F. Supp. 2d 488, 494-95 (E.D. Va. 1999).

Annotation. "For a descriptive mark to merit trademark protection, the party claiming that protection must demonstrate that the mark has gained secondary meaning among the relevant consuming public. In the case of geographically descriptive marks, this occurs when 'the mark no longer causes the public to associate the goods with a particular place, but to associate the goods with a particular source.' In other words, the mark merits protection when its primary significance to the consuming public is not the descriptive information it imparts, but the mark's association with a particular business or product."

> *Washington Speakers Bureau, Inc. v. Leading Authorities, Inc.,* 33 F. Supp. 2d 488, 496 (E.D. Va. 1999) (citations omitted).

Related issues. "While acronyms or initials can be entitled to protection if they are descriptive . . . if the initials have become so generally understood as being substantially synonymous with the words they represent, they are not protectible."

> *America Online, Inc. v. AT&T Corp.,* 64 F. Supp. 2d 549, 566 (E.D. Va. 1999).

See also **descriptive term(s).**

descriptive term(s) *(trademark)*

". . . directly describe the quality or features of the product."

> *Brookfield Comm., Inc. v. West Coast Entertainment Corp.,* 174 F.3d 1036, 1058 n.19 (9th Cir. 1999).

See also **descriptive mark(s).**

design phase *(software)*

"[I]ncludes interviewing the user, determining input and output, and structuring files and reports."

> *CMAX/Cleveland, Inc. v. UCR, Inc.,* 804 F. Supp. 337, 346 n.5 (M.D. Ga. 1992).

Annotation. "Weinstock stated that the design phase accounts for up to ninety percent of the time and intellectual input required to develop a system when a code generator is used. Both the coding phase and the final testing phase account for a relatively small portion of the overall process."

> *CMAX/Cleveland, Inc. v. UCR, Inc.,* 804 F. Supp. 337, 346 (M.D. Ga. 1992) (footnote reference omitted).

destination path *(technology)*

The path through a computer network that a packet of information follows to get from the source computer to the destination computer. There are generally many possible destination paths possible for each packet.

device-making equipment *(criminal)*

"[A]ny equipment, mechanism, or impression designed or primarily used for making an access device or a counterfeit access device...."
18 U.S.C. §1029(e)(6).

See also **access device; counterfeit access device.**

diagnostic system *(software)*

Also called "diagnostics."

"Software to isolate or detect software or equipment malfunctions."
15 C.F.R. Part 379 (1988), Supp. 3, Advisory Note 12, at 385.

"...is used to diagnose problems in central processing units and other computer equipment. Diagnostics are used in the design and manufacture of computers as well as in their field service maintenance and repair."
Service & Training, Inc. v. Data Gen. Corp., 737 F. Supp. 334, 337 (N.D. Ill. 1990).

"These programs do not instruct the computer on how to process information for the customer's use.... Rather [they] instruct the computer on how to locate, diagnose, and even correct malfunctions."
ISC-Bunker Ramo Corp. v. Altech, Inc., 765 F. Supp. 1310, 1318 (N.D. Ill. 1990).

dial-a-porn *(telecommunications)*

"[A] shorthand description of 'sexually oriented prerecorded telephone messages.'"
Reno v. American Civil Liberties Union, 929 F. Supp. 824, 868 n.4 (E.D. Pa. 1996), *aff'd, American Civil Liberties Union v. Reno,* 521 U.S. 844 (1997).

dial-up *(telecommunications)*

A type of network connection where the user dials a telephone number and communicates with a computer via modem.

die *(hardware)*

The small piece of the wafer on which an individual semiconductor device has been formed.

diffusion *(manufacturing)*

A semiconductor manufacturing process in which desired impurities are introduced into the silicon by baking the silicon wafers at high temperatures and pressures in chemically altered atmospheres. A less precise alternative to ion implantation.

digerati *(general)*

A concatenation of "**dig**ital lite**rati**. A group of people viewed as knowledgeable and hip with regard to the social, cultural, and economic implications of the digital revolution.

digit *(technology)*

A single integer used to represent a specific quantity of information. In the decimal numerical system, 0 through 9 are the digits used, whereas in the binary system, 0 and 1 are used.

digital *(technology)*

A type of signal characterized by a series of on/off pulses, that correspond to the binary states 0 and 1. Any information can be stored in digital form and can be manipulated by microprocessors. Digital signals can be converted into analog(ue) signals.

digital audio copied recording *(copyright)*

"[A] reproduction in a digital recording format of a digital musical recording, whether that reproduction is made directly from another digital musical recording or indirectly from a transmission."

17 U.S.C. § 1001(1).

Annotation. "[A] device falls within the [Audio Home Recording] Act's provisions if it can indirectly copy a digital music recording by making a copy from a transmission of that recording."

Recording Indus. Ass'n of America v. Diamond Multimedia Sys., Inc., 180 F.3d 1072, 1081 (9th Cir. 1999).

digital audio interface device *(copyright)*

"[A]ny machine or device that is designed specifically to communicate digital audio information and related interface data to a digital audio recording device through a nonprofessional interface."

17 U.S.C. § 1001(2).

digital audio recording device *(copyright)*

"[A]ny machine or device of a type commonly distributed to individuals for use by individuals, whether or not included with or as part of some other machine or device, the digital recording function of which is designed or marketed for the primary purpose of, and that is capable of, making a digital audio copied recording for private use. . . ."

17 U.S.C. § 1001(3).

Annotation. The legislative history thus expressly recognizes that computers (and other devices) have recording functions capable of recording digital musical recordings, and thus implicate the home taping and piracy concerns to which the Act is responsive. Nonetheless, the legislative history is consistent with the Act's plain language—computers are *not* digital audio recording devices.

"In turn, because computers are not digital audio recording devices, they are not required to comply with the SCMS requirement and thus need not send, receive, or act upon information regarding copyright and generation status."

> *Recording Indus. Ass'n of America v. Diamond Multimedia Sys., Inc.,* 180 F.3d 1072, 1078 (9th Cir. 1999) (citations omitted; emphasis in original).

digital audio recording medium *(copyright)*

"[A]ny material object in a form commonly distributed for use by individuals, that is primarily marketed or most commonly used by consumers for the purpose of making digital audio copied recordings by use of a digital audio recording device."

"Such term does not include any material object—

(i) that embodies a sound recording at the time it is first distributed by the importer or manufacturer; or

(ii) that is primarily marketed and most commonly used by consumers either for the purpose of making copies of motion pictures or other audiovisual works or for the purpose of making copies of nonmusical literary works, including computer programs and data bases."

17 U.S.C. § 1001(4).

digital certificate *(electronic commerce)*

See certificate.

digital computer(s) *(technology)*

"...is conveniently thought of functionally as composed of five elements: Input, Storage (sometimes called Memory), Control, Logic (sometimes called Arithmetic), and Output. Control and Logic are sometimes referred to jointly as the Central Processing Unit (CPU). The function of Input is to get instructions and data, prepared in some computer-readable form, into the computer. Storage retains the data and instructions so entered as well as the intermediate and final results of processing. Control directs the whole process in accordance with predetermined instructions kept in Storage. Logic performs the arithmetic and logical operations.

Output disgorges the requisite information in accordance with instructions."

> *Computer Sys. of Am. v. Western Reserve Life Assur. Co. of Ohio,* 475 N.E.2d 745, 747 n.2, 19 Mass. App. 430, 431 n.2 (1985).

"A digital computer, as distinguished from an analog computer, operates on data expressed in digits, solving a problem by doing arithmetic as a person would do it by head and hand. Some of the digits are stored as components of the computer. Others are introduced into the computer in a form which it is designed to recognize. The computer operates then upon both new and previously stored data. . . ."

> *Gottschalk v. Benson,* 409 U.S. 63, 65 (1972). *See also Synercom Technology, Inc. v. University Computing Co.,* 462 F. Supp. 1003, 1005 (N.D. Tex. 1978).

". . . [M]achines currently used to perform three types of functions electronically: (1) arithmetic calculations; (2) logical operations (e.g., comparing values to determine whether one is larger; and (3) storage and display of the results."

> *Lotus Dev. Corp. v. Paperback Software Int'l,* 740 F. Supp. 37, 42 (D. Mass. 1990). *See also* **computer.**

digital files *(hardware)*
"Digital files may be stored on several different kinds of storage media, some of which are readily transportable. Perhaps the most familiar of these are so called floppy disks or 'floppies,' which now are 3½ inch magnetic disks upon which digital files may be recorded. For present purposes, however, we are concerned principally with two more recent developments, CD-ROMs and digital versatile disks, or DVDs."

> *Universal City Studios, Inc. v. Reimerdes,* 111 F. Supp. 2d 294, 307 (S.D.N.Y. 2000) (footnote omitted).

digital imaging *(technology)*
The process of using computer technology to capture, transmit, create, enhance, and/or manipulate images.

Digital Millennium Copyright Act *(copyright)*
Abbreviated as "DMCA."

Annotation. The Digital Millennium Copyright Act was enacted in 1998 to update copyright law to reflect the emergence of digital technology and to comply with certain international copyright treaties. It contains a series of related but independent provisions that amend the U.S. Copyright Act.

• **Copyright circumvention.** The new law prohibits circumvention of technological measures that control access to copyrighted works (such as copy-protection systems and encryption technologies). Limited exceptions to the prohibition apply for reverse engineering, legitimate encryption research, and good-faith security testing. The manufacture of, sale of, and trafficking in devices whose primary purpose is to circumvent technological access control measures are prohibited. There are both criminal and civil sanctions for any violation.

• **Service providers' limitation on liability.** The DMCA limits the liability of online or Internet service providers for copyright infringement based on passive activities, such as the transmission of infringing material by a user, the making of automatic, transitory copies (e.g., caching), and the provision of information-location tools (e.g., search engines or links) that facilitate infringement. To benefit from these provisions, a service provider must comply with certain requirements, including appointing a designated agent to receive claims of infringement and, upon receipt of notice of a claim, acting expeditiously to remove or prevent access to infringing material.

• **Overrules *MAI v. Peak*.** The DMCA also amends copyright law so that a third-party service organization can load the operating systems and diagnostic software onto a computer system for maintenance purposes.

"The DMCA contains two principal anticircumvention provisions. The first, Section 1201(a)(1), governs 'the act of circumventing a technological protection measure put in place by a copyright owner to control access to a copyrighted work,' an act described by Congress as 'the electronic equivalent of breaking into a locked room in order to obtain a copy of a book.' The second, Section 1201(a)(2)... 'supplements the prohibition against the act of circumvention in paragraph (a)(1) with prohibitions on creating and making available certain technologies...developed or advertised to defeat technological protections against unauthorized access to a work.'"

Universal City Studios, Inc. v. Reimerdes, 111 F. Supp. 2d 294, 316 (S.D.N.Y. 2000) (footnotes omitted).

"[T]he statute [DMCA] expressly provides that 'a technological measure "effectively controls access to a work" if the measure, in the ordinary course of its operation, requires the application of information or a process or a treatment, with the authority of the copyright owner, to gain access to a work.'"

Universal City Studios, Inc. v. Reimerdes, 111 F. Supp. 2d 294, 317 (S.D.N.Y. 2000) (footnote omitted).

"Technological access control measures have the capacity to prevent fair uses of copyrighted works as well as foul. Hence, there is a potential tension between the use of such access control measures and fair use. Defendants are not the first to recognize that possibility. As the DMCA made its way through the legislative process, Congress was preoccupied with precisely this issue. Proponents of strong restrictions on circumvention of access control measures argued that they were essential if copyright holders were to make their works available in digital form because digital works otherwise could be pirated too easily. Opponents contended that strong anticircumvention measures would extend the copyright monopoly inappropriately and prevent many fair uses of copyrighted material.

"Congress struck a balance. The compromise it reached, depending upon future technological and commercial developments, may or may not prove ideal. But the solution it enacted is clear. The potential tension to which defendants point does not absolve them of liability under the statute."

Universal City Studios, Inc. v. Reimerdes, 111 F. Supp. 2d 294, 304 (S.D.N.Y. 2000) (footnote omitted).

See also encryption research.

digital musical recording *(copyright)*

"[A] material object —

(i) in which are fixed, in a digital recording format, only sounds, and material, statements, or instructions incidental to those fixed sounds, if any, and

(ii) from which the sounds and material can be perceived, reproduced, or otherwise communicated, either directly or with the aid of a machine or device."

17 U.S.C. § 1001(5)(A).

Annotation

"[T]he term 'digital musical recording' does not include":
"A material object—

(i) in which the fixed sounds consist entirely of spoken word recordings, or

(ii) in which one or more computer programs are fixed, except that a digital recording may contain statements or instructions constituting the fixed sounds and incidental material, and statements or instructions to be used directly or indirectly in order to bring about the perception, reproduction, or communication of the fixed sounds and incidental material."

Recording Indus. Ass'n of America v. Diamond Multimedia Sys., Inc., 180 F.3d 1072, 1076 (9th Cir. 1999), *citing* 17 U.S.C. § 1001(5)(B).

"[A] hard drive is a material object in which one or more programs are fixed; thus, a hard drive is excluded from the definition of digital music recordings."

> *Recording Indus. Ass'n of America v. Diamond Multimedia Sys., Inc.,* 180 F.3d 1072, 1076 (9th Cir. 1999).

"There are simply no grounds in either the plain language of the definition or in the legislative history for interpreting the term 'digital musical recording' to include songs fixed on computer hard drives."

> *Recording Indus. Ass'n of America v. Diamond Multimedia Sys., Inc.,* 180 F.3d 1072, 1077 (9th Cir. 1999).

"The plain language of the exemption at issue does not exclude the copying of programs from coverage by the Act, but instead, excludes copying from various types of material objects. Those objects include hard drives, which indirectly achieve the desired result of excluding copying of programs. But by its plain language, the exemption is not limited to the copying of programs, and instead extends to any copying from a computer hard disk.

* * *

. . . The legislative history thus expressly recognizes that computers (and other devices) have recording functions capable of recording digital musical recordings, and thus implicate the home taping and piracy concerns to which the Act is responsive. Nonetheless, the legislative history is consistent with the Act's plain language—computers are *not* digital audio recording devices."

> *Recording Indus. Ass'n of America v. Diamond Multimedia Sys., Inc.,* 180 F.3d 1072, 1078 (9th Cir. 1999) (citations omitted; emphasis in original).

digital object *(electronic commerce)*
A unit of information in digital form that can be easily indexed, located, and used. It generally consists of two portions—an unencrypted portion (known as the "wrapper") that describes the content and its conditions for use, and can be used to locate and identify the data, and an encrypted portion. *See also* **wrapper.**

Digital Performance Right in Sound Recordings Act *(copyright)*
Citation: Pub. L. No. 104-39, 109 Stat. 336 (EV. Feb. 1, 1996).

The Act creates an exclusive right for copyright owners of sound recordings to perform publicly the sound recordings by means of certain digital audio transmissions.

digital phonorecord delivery *(copyright; Internet)*
"[E]ach individual delivery of a phonorecord by digital transmission of a sound recording which results in a specifically identifiable reproduction by or for any transmission recipient of a phonorecord of that sound recording."
17 U.S.C. § 115(d).

digital readout system *(hardware)*
Sometimes abbreviated as "DRO."

"DRO systems provide linear or rotational displacement information for high-precision industrial equipment such as metalworking machine tools, and generally consist of an electronic console and one measurement transducer for each axis of linear or rotational displacement to be measured."
54 Fed. Reg 2236 (Jan. 19, 1989).

digital recording *(technology)*

Annotation. "With digital recording . . . there is almost no degradation in sound quality, no matter how many generations of copies are made. Digital copies thus allow thousands of perfect or near perfect copies (and copies of copies) to be made from a single original recording. Music 'pirates' use digital recording technology to make and to distribute near perfect copies of commercially prepared recordings for which they have not licensed the copyrights."
Recording Indus. Ass'n of America v. Diamond Multimedia Sys., Inc., 180 F.3d 1072, 1073 (9th Cir. 1999).

digital reproduction of a digital musical work *(copyright)*
Annotation. "The term 'digital reproduction of a digital musical recording' does not include a digital musical recording as distributed, by authority of the copyright owner, for ultimate sale to consumers."
17 U.S.C. § 1001(11).

digital sampler *(technology)*
A device that digitizes and stores sounds, usually music in digital form. The stored materials can then be modified using a digital signal processor. Sampling is used extensively in much modern music, including rock, hip-hop, rap, house, and industrial.

digital sampling *(copyright; technology)*
See also **sampling.**

"[T]he conversion of analog sound waves into a digital code. The digital code that describes the sampled music…can then be reused, manipulated or combined with other digitalized or recorded sounds using a machine with digital data processing capabilities, such as a…computerized synthesizer."
Jarvis v. A&M Records, 27 U.S.P.Q.2d (BNA) 1812, 1813 (D.N.J. 1993).

digital signal processor *(hardware)*
See DSP.

digital signature *(electronic commerce)*
"[A] transformation of a message using an asymmetric cryptosystem such that a person having the initial message and the signer's public key can accurately determine: (a) Whether the transformation was created using the private key that corresponds to the signer's public key; and (b) Whether the initial message has been altered since the transformation was made."
Wash. Rev. Code § 19.34.020(11).

"[A] transformation of a message using an asynchronous cryptosystem such that a person having the initial message and the signer's public key can accurately determine: (a) whether the transformation was created using the private key that corresponds to the signer's public key; and (b) whether the message has been altered since the transformation was made."
Utah Digital Signatures Act, 46 Utah Code Ann., ch. 3, Utah Adm. Code RI 54-2-103(10).

Annotation. "For a digital signature to be valid for use by a public entity, it must be created by a technology that is accepted for use by the State of California."
Cal. Code of Regs., tit. 2, div. 7, ch. 10, § 22001(a).
See also **signature.**

digital tone detector *(telecommunications)*
Abbreviated as "DTD."
See DTD.
Alcatel USA, Inc. v. DGI Technologies, Inc., 166 F.3d 772, 778 n.4 (5th Cir. 1999).

digital transmission *(copyright)*
"[A] transmission in whole or in part in a digital or other non-analog format."
17 U.S.C. § 101.

digital trunk interface *(telecommunications)*
Abbreviated as "DTI."
See DTI.

digital typefont *(technology)*
"[A] bitmapped digital representation of an actual analog typeface design, stored in binary form on magnetic or optical media, or Read-Only Memory (ROM) mounted on a circuit board. Sometimes, the ROM on the circuit board is assembled into a plastic cartridge which is inserted into a laser printer or other microprocessor-driven device. When decoded and interpreted by the 'bitmapping code' software, the digital representation of the design will reproduce the appropriate character."
Library of Congress, Copyright Office, 53 Fed. Reg. 38110 (Sept. 29, 1988).
See also bitmapping; typeface.

digital video disk *(technology)*
Abbreviated "DVD." A new industry standard for supplying high-quality video on CD-ROMs; utilizes the MPEG-2 standard.

digital watermark *(technology)*
"[A] small, almost unnoticeable alteration to a digital work like an image, a photograph, or a sequence of sounds. The watermark cannot be perceived with the human eye, but can be detected with a computer program designed for the purpose. Watermarks can be used to embed identifying information into the digital work."
I. Trotter Hardy, *Project Looking Forward: Sketching the Future of Copyright in a Networked World* 14 (May 1998).

digitally-signed communication *(electronic commerce)*
"[A] message that has been processed by a computer in such a manner that ties the message to the individual that signed the message."
Cal. Code of Regulations, tit. 2, div. 7, ch. 10, § 22000(a)(1).

digitization *(technology)*
"[T]he process of converting information (text, pictures, music, etc.) into a series of ones and zeros, which can be read by computers and transmitted over telephone lines."
Ohio v. Perry, 41 U.S.P.Q.2d 1989 (1997) *aff'd,* 697 N.E.2d 624 (Ohio Supreme Ct. 1998).

digitize[d] *(technology)*
"[T]ranslated into a digital code (usually a series of zeros and ones)."
Working Group on Intellectual Property Rights, *Intellectual Property and the National Information Infrastructure* (Sept. 1995)
See also **digitization.**

dilution *(trademark)*
"... [means] the lessening of the capacity of a famous mark to identify and distinguish goods or services, regardless of the presence or absence of (1) competition between the owner of the famous mark and other parties, or (2) likelihood of confusion, mistake or deception."
15 U.S.C. § 1127.

Annotation. "The concept of trademark dilution dates back to an article written by Frank I. Schechter and published in the Harvard Law Review. Schechter explained that the true function of a trademark is 'to identify a product as satisfactory and thereby to stimulate further purchases by the consuming public.' Schechter rejected the theory that the exclusive role of a trademark was to serve as a source identifier. . . . He argued that injury occurs to a trademark owner whenever a trademark is used by another, even when used on non-competing goods. He explained that an injury to the trademark owner occurs when there is 'a gradual whittling away or dispersion of the identity and hold upon the public mind of the mark or name by its use upon non-competing goods. The more distinctive or unique the mark, the deeper is its impress upon the public consciousness, and the greater is its need for protection against vitiation or dissociation from the particular product in connection with which it has been used.' This argument that the trademark laws should protect owners in connection with non-competing goods was novel.

* * *

"The serious push for a federal trademark dilution law began in 1987 with the publication of 'The United States Trademark Association Review Commission Report and Recommendations to USTA President and Board of Directors.' In that report, the Commission proposed the adoption of a new federal trademark dilution law. Trademark dilution provisions were included in S. 1883, the proposed Trademark Law Revision Act of 1987. However, while most of the bill's provisions eventually became law, concerns—raised by the broadcast industry and rallied by Rep. Robert Kastenmeier (D.Wis.)—that dilution protection would impinge on the First Amendment resulted in the deletion of the dilution provisions from the final legislation.

"In 1991, the United States Trademark Association (USTA) Board of Directors adopted a resolution supporting a federal trademark dilution provision. The American Bar Association Patent, Trademark and Copyright Law Section, in its 1991-92 Annual Report, voted overwhelmingly in favor of adding a dilution section to the Lanham Act.

"On March 22, 1995, the Federal Trademark Dilution Act of 1995 was introduced in the House of Representatives as H.R. 1295. With changes largely designed to make the bill applicable to the owners of both federally registered and common law trademarks, the bill was signed into law on January 16, 1996 as Public Law 104-98, creating a new Section 43(c) to the Lanham Act."

Intermatic, Inc. v. Toeppen, 947 F. Supp. 1227, 1236-37 (N.D. Ill. 1996).

"[The] federal dilution statute is necessary because famous marks ordinarily are used on a nationwide basis and dilution protection is currently only available on a patch-quilt system of protection, in that only approximately 25 states have laws that prohibit trademark dilution."

H.R. Rep. No. 374, 104th Cong., 1st Sess. 4 (1995).

"The definition is designed to encompass all forms of dilution recognized by the courts, including dilution by blurring, by tarnishment and disparagement, and by diminishment. In an effort to clarify the law on the subject, the definition also recognizes that a cause of action for dilution may exist whether or not the parties market the same or related goods or whether or not a likelihood of confusion exists. Thus, a mark protected against dilution can have acquired its fame in connection with one type of good or service and, as a result, be so famous as to be entitled to protection against dilution when used on or in connection with an unrelated good or service."

H.R. Rep. No. 374, 104th Cong., 1st Sess. 3 (1995).

"In order to state a cause of action under the Act a party must show that the mark is famous and that the complainant's use is commercial and in commerce which is likely to cause dilution."

Intermatic, Inc. v. Toeppen, 947 F. Supp. 1227, 1238 (N.D. Ill. 1996).

"To find dilution, a court need not rely on the traditional definitions such as 'blurring' and 'tarnishment.' Indeed, in concluding that Toeppen's use of Panavision's trademarks diluted the marks, the district court noted that Toeppen's conduct varied from the two standard dilution theories of blurring and tarnishment. The court found that Toeppen's conduct diminished

'the capacity of the Panavision marks to identify and distinguish Panavision's goods and services on the Internet.'"
Panavision Int'l, L.P. v. Toeppen, 141 F.3d 1316, 1326 (9th Cir. 1998).

"Likelihood of injury to business reputation or of dilution of the distinctive quality of a mark registered under this Act, or a mark valid at common law, shall be a ground for injunctive relief notwithstanding the absence of competition between the parties or the absence of confusion as to the source of goods or services."
Model State Trademark Bill § 12 (USTA 1964).

"Under the [Federal] Act, the owner of a famous mark is only entitled to injunctive relief unless the person against whom the injunction is sought willfully intended to trade on the owner's reputation or to cause dilution of the famous mark. The Act does not preempt state dilution claims. The Act specifically provides that noncommercial use of the mark is not actionable."
Intermatic, Inc. v. Toeppen, 947 F. Supp. 1227, 1238 (N.D. Ill. 1996).

Related issues. "[I]t is my hope that this anti-dilution statute can help stem the use of deceptive Internet addresses taken by those who are choosing marks that are associated with the products and reputations of others."
141 Cong. Rec. § 19312-01 (daily ed. Dec. 29, 1995) (statement of Sen. Leahy); *quoted in Panavision Int'l, L.P. v. Toeppen,* 141 F.3d 1316, 1326 (9th Cir. 1998).

"All prior domain name registrations corresponding to words in a trademark impede the trademark owner's use of the same words for use as a domain name. The Internet, however, is not exclusively a medium of commerce. The non-commercial use of a domain name that impedes a trademark owner's use of that domain name does not constitute dilution."
Lockheed Martin Corp. v. Network Solutions, Inc., 985 F. Supp. 949, 960 (C.D. Cal. 1997).

"The California Anti-dilution statute is similar [to the federal statute]. See Cal. Bus. & Prof. Code §14300. It prohibits dilution of 'the distinctive quality' of a mark regardless of competition or the likelihood of confusion. The protection extends only to strong and well recognized marks."
Panavision Int'l, L.P. v. Toeppen, 141 F.3d 1316, 1324 (9th Cir. 1998).
See also **Federal Trademark Dilution Act.**

diode *(hardware)*
A semiconductor device that allows electricity to flow only in one direction.

direct-control video characters *(video game; technology)*

A type of interactive product where the user can directly control the character appearing in the video. Such games require video clips for all permissible actions of the character(s).

direct damages *(contract)*

"[C]ompensation for losses measured by Section 808(b)(1) or 809(a)(1). The term does not include consequential damages or incidental damages." UCITA § 102(a)(25).

Related issues. "[T]he commercial context in which a contract is made is of substantial importance in determining whether particular damages flowing from its breach are direct or consequential." *Applied Data Processing, Inc. v. Burroughs Corp.*, 394 F. Supp. 504, 509 (D. Conn. 1974).

direct infringement *(copyright)*

"To succeed on a claim for direct copyright infringement, a plaintiff must prove two elements: (1) ownership of the copyrighted material and (2) copying by the defendant. A copy is legally actionable if (1) the alleged infringer actually used the copyrighted material to create his own work, and (2) substantial similarity exists between the two works." *Alcatel USA, Inc. v. DGI Technologies, Inc.*, 166 F.3d 772, 790 (5th Cir. 1999) (citations omitted).

Related issues. "Netcom's actions, to the extent that they create a copy of plaintiffs' works, were necessary to having a working system for transmitting Usenet postings to and from the Internet. Unlike the defendant in *MAI*, neither Netcom nor Klemsrud initiated the copying...Netcom's and Klemsrud's systems can operate without any human intervention. Thus, unlike *MAI*, the mere fact that Netcom's system incidentally makes temporary copies of plaintiffs' works does not mean Netcom has caused the copying. The court believes that Netcom's act of designing or implementing a system that automatically and uniformly creates temporary copies of all data sent through it is not unlike that of the owner of a copying machine who lets the public make copies with it. Although some of the people using the machine may directly infringe copyrights, courts analyze the machine owner's liability under the rubric of contributory infringement not direct infringement.

* * *

"The court does not find workable a theory of infringement that would hold the entire Internet liable for activities that cannot reasonably be deterred. Billions of bits of data flow through the Internet and are necessarily stored on servers throughout the network and it is thus practically impossible to screen out infringing bits from noninfringing bits. Because the court cannot see any meaningful distinction (without regard to knowledge) between what Netcom did and what every other Usenet server does, the court finds that Netcom cannot be held liable for direct infringement."

> *Religious Technology Ctr. v. Netcom On-line Com. Servs., Inc.,* 907 F. Supp. 1361, 1367-68, 1372-73 (N.D. Cal. 1995).

"[The court] is not convinced that Usenet servers are directly liable for causing a copy to be made, and absent evidence of knowledge and participation or control and direct profit, they will not be contributorily or vicariously liable."

> *Religious Technology Ctr. v. Netcom On-line Com. Servs., Inc.,* 907 F. Supp. 1361, 1377 (N.D. Cal. 1995).

"[B]ecause Sega has not shown that Sherman directly caused the copying, Sherman cannot be liable for direct infringement."

> *Sega Enters. Ltd. v. MAPHIA,* 948 F. Supp. 923, 932 (N.D. Cal. 1996).

See also **copyright infringement.**

directory *(technology)*

Analogous to a file drawer or a book with chapters and subchapters, the directory is an index that contains the names and addresses of each file in the data storage system. Many levels of directories can exist.

See also **file system; pathname.**

disassembler *(software)*

"Devices called 'disassemblers' or 'decompilers' can reverse this process by 'reading' the electronic signals for '0' and '1' that are produced while the program is being run, storing the resulting object code in computer memory, and translating the object code into source code."

> *Sega Enters. Ltd. v. Accolade, Inc.,* 977 F.2d 1510, 1515, n.2 (9th Cir. 1992).

See also **decompiler; disassembly; reverse engineering.**

disassembly *(software)*

"[T]he process by which a machine language program is placed in another programming language which is more readily understood by human beings."

> *Vault Corp. v. Quaid Software Ltd.,* 655 F. Supp. 750, 755 (E.D. La. 1987).

"Disassembly of a computer program is done by translating the machine or object code into humanly-readable assembly language."

> *E.F. Johnson Co. v. Uniden Corp. of Am.,* 623 F. Supp. 1485, 1490 (D. Minn. 1985).

"Disassembling a program consists of translating the firmware code, or instructions, from machine readable object code to human (at least computer programmer) readable form."

> *DSC Comm. Corp. v. DGI Technologies, Inc.,* 898 F. Supp. 1183, 1186 (N.D. Tex. 1995), *aff'd,* 81 F.3d 597 (5th Cir. 1996).

"[W]hen good reason exists for studying or examining the unprotected aspects of a copyrighted program, disassembly for the purpose of study or examination of the disassembled program constitutes fair use."

> *DSC Comm. Corp. v. DGI Technologies, Inc.,* 898 F. Supp. 1183, 1189 (N.D. Tex. 1995), *aff'd,* 81 F.3d 597 (5th Cir. 1996).

"Allowing a computer programmer to hide his ideas, processes and concepts in copyrighted object code defeats the fundamental purpose of the Copyright Act—to encourage the creation of original works by protecting the creator's expression while leaving the ideas, facts and functional concepts in the free marketplace to be built upon by others."

> *DSC Comm. Corp. v. DGI Technologies, Inc.,* 898 F. Supp. 1183, 1189 (N.D. Tex. 1995), *aff'd,* 81 F.3d 597 (5th Cir. 1996).

"[C]onvert the firmware into human-readable form."

> *Alcatel USA, Inc. v. DGI Technologies, Inc.,* 166 F.3d 772, 779 (5th Cir. 1999).

"[T]he translation of machine code into human-readable form."

> *Alcatel USA, Inc. v. DGI Technologies, Inc.,* 166 F.3d 772, 784 (5th Cir. 1999) (citation omitted).

Related issues. "Without disassembling the program there is no way to tell what is protected expression and what is an unprotected idea or process."

> *DSC Comm. Corp. v. DGI Technologies, Inc.,* 898 F. Supp. 1183, 1190-91 (N.D. Tex. 1995), *aff'd,* 81 F.3d 597 (5th Cir. 1996).

"Section 117 does not purport to protect a user who disassembles object code, converts it from assembly into source code, and makes printouts and photocopies of the refined source code version."

> *Sega Enters. Ltd. v. Accolade, Inc.,* 977 F.2d 1510, 1520 (9th Cir. 1992).

"If disassembly of copyrighted object code is per se an unfair use, the owner of the copyright gains a de facto monopoly over the functional as-

pects of his work—aspects that were expressly denied copyright protection by Congress."
Sega Enters. Ltd. v. Accolade, Inc., 977 F.2d 1510, 1525 (9th Cir. 1992).

"Both assembly and disassembly devices are commercially available, and both types of devices are widely used within the software industry."
Sega Enters. Ltd. v. Accolade, Inc., 977 F.2d 1510, 1515 n.2 (9th Cir. 1992).

"[W]here disassembly is the only way to gain access to the ideas and functional elements embodied in a copyrighted computer program and where there is a legitimate reason for seeking such access, disassembly is a fair use of the copyrighted work, as a matter of law."
Sega Enters. Ltd. v. Accolade, Inc., 977 F.2d 1510, 1527-28 (9th Cir. 1992).
See also **decompiler; disassembler; reverse engineering.**

disassembly program *(software)*
"One which converts machine language code into humanly-readable assembly language."
E.F. Johnson Co. v. Uniden Corp. of Am., 623 F. Supp. 1485 (D. Minn. 1985).
See also **decompiler; disassembler; disassembly; reverse engineering.**

disclosure *(trade secret)*
"[U]pon disclosure, even if inadvertent or accidental, the information ceases to be a trade secret and will no longer be protected."
Kewanee Oil Co. v. Bicron Corp., 416 U.S. 470, 475-76 (1974).

Annotation. "[T]rade secret rights do not survive when otherwise protectable information is disclosed to others, such as customers or the general public, who are under no obligation to protect its confidentiality."
Advanced Computer Servs., Inc. v. MAI Sys. Corp., 845 F. Supp. 356, 370 (E.D. Va. 1994).

Related issues. "Despite RTC and the Church's elaborate and ardent measures to maintain the secrecy of the Works, they have come into the public domain by numerous means.... The evidence also showed portions of the Works have been made available on the Internet...with the potential for downloading by countless users."
Religious Technology Ctr. v. F.A.C.T.Net, Inc., 901 F. Supp. 1519, 1526 (D. Colo. 1995).

"While the Internet has not reached the status where a temporary posting on a newsgroup is akin to publication in a major newspaper or on a television network, those with an interest in using the Church's trade secrets to compete with the Church are likely to look to the newsgroup. Thus, posting works to the Internet makes them 'generally known' to the relevant people...."

> *Religious Technology Ctr. v. Netcom On-line Com. Servs., Inc.,* 923 F. Supp. 1231, 1256 (N.D. Cal. 1995).

"The court is troubled by the notion that any Internet user, including those using 'anonymous remailer' to protect their identity, can destroy valuable intellectual property rights by posting them over the Internet, especially given the fact that there is little opportunity to screen postings before they are made.... [O]ne of the Internet's virtues, that it gives even the poorest individuals the power to publish to millions of readers...can also be a detriment to the value of intellectual property rights. The anonymous (or judgment proof) defendant can permanently destroy valuable trade secrets, leaving no one to hold liable for the misappropriation.... Although a work posted to an Internet newsgroup remains accessible to the public for only a limited amount of time, once that trade secret has been released into the public domain there is no retrieving it."

> *Religious Technology Ctr. v. Netcom On-line Com. Servs., Inc.,* 923 F. Supp. 1231, 1256 (N.D. Cal. 1995) (citations and footnotes omitted).

See also **public domain; secret; trade secret.**

disintermediation *(business)*

"Cutting out the middleman." Disintermediation is the process of removing intermediaries from the marketing and distribution channels. Many commentators have opined that the growth of electronic commerce will see the disappearance of middlemen as vendors set up web sites and sell their products and services directly to the end user/consumer. Others, such as Paul Saffo, Institute for the Future, believe that it is not necessarily in a company's best interest to get too close to the customer, and that it is often useful and important to place one or more layers of "cultural brokers" between the vendor and the customer. "The essence is that computers make it easier than ever to be an intermediary. That's why we will have more intermediaries, not less," said Saffo. One type of intermediary is a "vortex" business. *See also* **vortex business.**

disk *(hardware)*

Also spelled "disc."

"[A] magnetic data storage device."

> *USM Corp. v. Arthur D. Little, Inc.,* 28 Mass. App. 108, 112 n.5, 546 N.E.2d 888, 891 n.5 (1989).

"The popular form of bulk data storage with rapid access capabilities. Data is recorded in tracks on a magnetic medium on the disk surface. The two main forms are 'floppy disks' and 'hard disks.'"

> U.S. Copyright Office, *Compendium of Copyright Office Practices* II, § 326 (1984).

"[A]n object which looks like a phonograph record but stores data in a form that can be read by a computer."

> *National Union Elec. Corp. v. Matsushita Elec. Indus. Co.,* 7 Computer L. Serv. Rep. 1181, 1186-87 (E.D. Pa. 1980).

"[A] thin, circular piece of synthetic material, not unlike a 45 r.p.m. record, on which computer programs are stored electronically. When one wishes to use a program, the disk is inserted into a mechanism called a disk drive, and the computer is instructed to transfer the program from the disk into its memory."

> *Micro-Sparc, Inc. v. Amtype Corp.,* 592 F. Supp. 33, 33 n.1 (D. Mass. 1984).

"[S]torage devices and/or components within these devices attached to data processing systems on which a large volume of data is stored providing a quick retrieval source. Disk drives on [mini computers and personal computers] can be located either inside the computer or outside the computer and can use either hard disks or floppy disks."

> 60-1 IRS Letter Ruling 8721016, Feb. 17, 1987.

See also **disk drive; diskette; floppy disk; hard disk.**

disk access *(hardware)*

"[A] disk read or disk write."

> *USM Corp. v. Arthur D. Little, Inc.,* 28 Mass. App. 108, 112 n.5, 546 N.E.2d 888, 891 n.5 (1989).

disk array *(hardware)*

Multiple disk drives that function as a single storage device and provide massive storage and/or rapid data transfer rates (ideal for video playback).

disk drive *(hardware)*

"...consists of a stack of magnetic disks on a spindle. Heads which move laterally across the disk can either record on or read information from the disk as it rotates beneath the head."

> *Mukerji v. Commissioner of Internal Rev.,* 87 T.C. No. 61, Tax Court Decisions (CCH) ¶ 43,469, at 3701 (Tax Ct. 1986).

See also **diskette; floppy disk; hard disk.**

disk products *(hardware)*

"...are part of a broader category of what is known as peripheral equipment, such as disks, tapes, printers, and terminals, which is connected to the central processing unit ('CPU') to enable the data processing system to perform particular functions. Included in the reference to disk products are disk drives, devices using magnetic disks similar in appearance to phonograph records to store information, and controllers, used for communication between disk drives and the CPU. Occasionally these devices are built into the CPU; alternatively, they exist as external components that may be 'plugged into' the CPU."

California Computer Prods., Inc. v. IBM Corp., 613 F.2d 727, 731 (9th Cir. 1979).

See also **disk; disk drive; diskette; floppy disk; hard disk.**

disk read *(hardware)*

"[To] physically locate and retrieve stored data necessary for a program instruction...."

USM Corp. v. Arthur D. Little, Inc., 28 Mass. App. 108, 112 n.5, 546 N.E.2d 888, 891 n.5 (1989).

disk utilization *(hardware)*

See **disk access.**

disk utilization factor *(hardware)*

"A calculation which is used to help predict response time.... The calculation expresses the number of disk accesses required in a particular time period as a percentage of the total number of disk accesses available during the time period."

USM Corp. v. Arthur D. Little, Inc., 28 Mass. App. 108, 112 n.5, 546 N.E.2d 888, 891 n.5 (1989).

disk write *(hardware)*

"[T]o physically locate available, unoccupied space on the disk and write new data in that area."

USM Corp. v. Arthur D. Little, Inc., 28 Mass. App. 108, 112 n.5, 546 N.E.2d 888, 891 n.5 (1989).

diskette *(hardware)*

"[A]n auxiliary memory device consisting of a flexible magnetic disk that can be inserted into the computer and from which data or instructions can be read."

Apple Computer, Inc. v. Franklin Computer Corp., 714 F.2d 1240 (3d Cir. 1983), *rev'g and remanding*, 545 F. Supp. 812 (E.D. Pa. 1982).

"[A] storage medium for data. Sometimes called a 'floppy disk,' it is used in conjunction with computers. Computer programs are recorded on diskettes. Some diskettes are blank when sold and the buyer records thereon such computer programs as he chooses. Others are sold with computer programs already recorded thereon."

Apple Computer, Inc. v. Formula Int'l, Inc., 594 F. Supp. 617, 620 (C.D. Cal. 1984).
See also **disk; disk drive; floppy disk; hard disk.**

display *(copyright)*

"[T]o show a copy of it [a work], either directly or by means of a film, slide, television image, or any other device or process or, in the case of a motion picture or other audiovisual work, to show individual images nonsequentially."

U.S. Copyright Act, 17 U.S.C. § 101.

display monitor *(hardware)*

Also called "display screen."

"An electronic device used to display data on the screen of a CRT."

Motorola, Inc. v. Computer Displays Int'l, Inc., 739 F.2d 1149, 1151 n.1 (7th Cir. 1984).

See also **cathode-ray tube.**

dispute resolution *(contract)*

Any of many legal means available to settle an existing dispute, including litigation, arbitration, and mediation. Many contracting parties decide to set forth the type of procedures to be used in resolving any disputes arising out of the performance of the contract. If no means of dispute resolution are identified in the agreement, it is assumed that the parties intend to resolve any disputes arising from the contract by litigation.

Sample clause. "a. In the event of a dispute arising out of or in relation to the terms of this Agreement, representatives of Vendor and Licensee shall meet and endeavor to settle the dispute in an amicable manner through mutual consultation. If such persons are unable to resolve the dispute in a satisfactory manner within ten (10) business days, either party may seek binding arbitration.

b. Upon receipt of written notice by either party calling for arbitration with respect to any dispute arising out of or in relation to the terms of this Agreement, the matter shall be submitted to binding arbitration under the commercial rules of the American Arbitration Association in [designate location], by a single arbitrator appointed by the American Arbitration Association. Insofar as possible, such arbitrator shall be, at the time of his or her selection, a partner or manager of a national or regional accounting firm (including the information processing, management support, and merger and acquisitions operations or affiliates thereof) not regularly employed by Vendor or Licensee. Such arbitrator shall be required to have substantial experience in the field of computer software technology and licensing.

c. A decision of the arbitrator shall be final and binding on the parties and may be entered and enforced in any court of competent jurisdiction by either party.

d. The prevailing party in any arbitration shall be awarded reasonable attorneys' fees, expert witness costs and expenses, and all other costs and expenses incurred directly or indirectly in connection with the proceedings, unless the arbitrator for good cause determines otherwise."

distortion *(technology)*
Anomalies in an analog signal introduced by the recording, processing, or playback processes.

distribute *(copyright)*
"[T]o sell, lease, or assign a product to consumers in the United States, or to sell, lease, or assign a product in the United States for ultimate transfer to consumers in the United States.
17 U.S.C. §1001(6).

distributed data processing *(technology)*
Data processing in which some or all of the processing and storage activities and input/output functions are situated in different places and are connected by transmission facilities.

distributed message databases *(Internet)*
"Similar in function to listservs—but quite different in how communications are transmitted—are distributed message databases such as 'USENET newsgroups.'"
American Civil Liberties Union v. Reno, 929 F. Supp. 824, 834 (E.D. Pa. 1996), *aff'd, Reno v. American Civil Liberties Union,* 521 U.S. 844 (1997).
See also Usenet.

distribution
(copyright)
"The copyright holder's distribution right is the right to distribute *copies.*"
National Car Rental Sys., Inc. v. Computer Assocs. Int'l, Inc., 991 F.2d 426, 430 (8th Cir. 1993) (emphasis in original).

(jurisdiction)
"Web-sites are modern analogs of national publications; potentially innumerable 'copies' can be (and are) regularly 'distributed' wherever there is access to the World-Wide Web."
Digital Equipment Corp. v. Altavista Technology, Inc., 960 F. Supp. 456, 470 (D. Mass. 1997).

Annotation (copyright). "Distribution of the Tape on the Internet would conflict with the plaintiffs' exclusive rights to distribute copies of the Tape to the public. 17 U.S.C. § 106(4)."
Michaels v. Internet Entertainment Group, Inc., 5 F. Supp. 2d 823, 830-31 (C.D. Cal. 1998).

Related issues (copyright). "The author's control of first public distribution implicates not only his personal interest in the creative control but his property interest in exploitation of prepublication rights, which are valuable in themselves and serve as a valuable adjunct to publicity and marketing."
Harper & Row, Publishers, Inc. v. Nation Enters., 471 U.S. 539, 555 (1985).

distribution, right of *(copyright)*
The exclusive right of a copyright owner to distribute copies of the copyrighted work to third parties.

Related issues. "Among the exclusive rights given to the owner of a copyrighted work is the right to distribute copies of the work by lending.... Therefore, [defendant's] loaning of [plaintiff's] software, if established, would constitute a violation of the Copyright Act."
MAI Sys. Corp. v. Peak Computer, Inc., 991 F.2d 511, 519 (9th Cir. 1993), *cert. dism.,* 510 U.S. 1033 (1994).

distributor *(business)*
One who purchases packaged products and resells them to retailers, OEMs, and sometimes directly to end users.

DivX *(software)*
"[A] compression program available for download over the Internet. It compresses video files in order to minimize required storage space, often to facilitate transfer over the Internet or other networks."
Universal City Studios, Inc. v. Reimerdes, 111 F. Supp. 2d 294, 308 (S.D.N.Y. 2000) (footnotes omitted).

"DivX, a compression utility available on the Internet that is promoted as a means of compressing decrypted motion picture files to manageable size."
Universal City Studios, Inc. v. Reimerdes, 111 F. Supp. 2d 294, 313 (S.D.N.Y. 2000) (footnote omitted).

Annotation. "DivX is capable of compressing decrypted files constituting a feature length motion picture to approximately 650 MB at a compression ratio that involves little loss of quality. While the compressed sound and graphic files then must be synchronized, a tedious process that took plaintiffs' expert between 10 and 20 hours, the task is entirely feasible. Indeed, having compared a store-bought DVD with portions of a copy compressed and synchronized with DivX (which often are referred to as 'DivX'd' motion pictures), the Court finds that the loss of quality, at least in some cases, is imperceptible or so nearly imperceptible as to be of no importance to ordinary consumers."
Universal City Studios, Inc. v. Reimerdes, 111 F. Supp. 2d 294, 313-14 (S.D.N.Y. 2000) (footnotes omitted).

"DivX effects what is known as 'lossy' compression—it achieves its reduction in file size by eliminating some of the data in the file being compressed. The trick, however, is that it seeks to do so by eliminating data that is imperceptible, or nearly so, to the human observer."
Universal City Studios, Inc. v. Reimerdes, 111 F. Supp. 2d 294, 313 n.107 (S.D.N.Y. 2000) (footnotes omitted).

DMCA *(copyright)*
Acronym for the "Digital Millennium Copyright Act." *See* **Digital Millennium Copyright Act.**

DNS *(Internet)*
Acronym for "Domain Name System." *See* **domain name system.**

document *(general)*
Anything printed, written upon, or otherwise recorded that generally has permanence and that can be read by humans or machines; in word processing, text that can be named and stored as a separate entity. Documents can be stored, retrieved, edited, and printed via computer programs.

documentation *(general)*
"[T]he general term for the material that a programmer must give to a user to explain how the program runs. Programs frequently come with pam-

phlets that explain the program's powers and limitations. The documentation must anticipate as many potential questions and exigencies as the programmer can imagine the user will face because most people do not understand computers and programs fully, and it would therefore be very difficult for users to solve their problems themselves."

> *Whelan Assocs., Inc. v. Jaslow Dental Lab., Inc.,* 797 F.2d 1222, 1231 n.21 (3d Cir. 1986), *cert. denied,* 107 S. Ct. 877 (1987).

"[M]eans manuals and other media, such as printed matter, magnetic tapes, discs, and microfiche, that have been or are developed for subject software by or for either party, on which is transferred to customers a description of, but not including, any computer program and shall include manuals that describe architectures implemented or intended to be implemented in subject software."

> *IBM Corp. v. Fujitsu Ltd.,* Copyright L. Rep. (CCH) ¶ 20,517, at 11,392 (Am. Arb. Ass'n 1988).

See also **supporting documentation.**

DoD *(organization)*
Acronym for "U.S. Department of Defense."

DoJ *(organization)*
Acronym for "U.S. Department of Justice."

domain address *(Internet)*
"[A]n identifier somewhat analogous to a telephone number or street address."

> *Brookfield Comm., Inc. v. West Coast Entertainment Corp.,* 174 F.3d 1036, 1044 (9th Cir. 1999).

See also **domain name.**

domain name(s) *(Internet)*
". . . consist of a second-level domain—simply a term or series of terms (e.g., westcoastvideo)—followed by a top-level domain, many of which describe the nature of the enterprise."

> *Brookfield Comm., Inc. v. West Coast Entertainment Corp.,* 174 F.3d 1036, 1044 (9th Cir. 1999).

"Domain names—e.g., bettyandnicks.com—consist of at least two groups of alphanumeric characters, each known as a string, separated by a period or dot. The last string—the farthest to the right—denotes the top-level domain. The second-to-last string is the second-level domain name and identifies the person's or organization's Internet computer site.

Each string may contain up to 63 characters but the overall domain name must be less than 256 characters. For the domain name system to function, each domain name must be unique and correspond to a unique Internet Protocol number. A new user who wishes to have an Internet site with a domain name address first obtains an Internet Protocol number (e.g., 1.23.456.7). The user then registers a domain name and it becomes linked with that Internet Protocol number."

Thomas v. Network Solutions, Inc., 176 F.3d 500, 503 (D.C. Cir. 1999) (citations omitted).

"[N]ames identifying and accessing particular websites on the Internet."

Washington Speakers Bureau, Inc. v. Leading Authorities, Inc., 33 F. Supp. 2d 488, 491. n.4 (E.D. Va. 1999).

"[F]unctions as an address on the Internet. . . . Those who are connected to the Internet can access a Web-site or a person's electronic mail address by way of its domain name."

Digital Equipment Corp. v. Altavista Technology, Inc., 960 F. Supp. 456, 459 n.3 (D. Mass. 1997) (citations omitted).

". . . is similar to a 'vanity number' that identifies its source."

Panavision Int'l, L.P. v. Toeppen, 141 F.3d 1316, 1325 (9th Cir. 1998).

". . . often consists of a person's name or a company's name or trademark."

Panavision Int'l, L.P. v. Toeppen, 141 F.3d 1316, 1318 (9th Cir. 1998).

Annotation. *(Internet)* "Internet domain names are similar to telephone number mnemonics, but they are of greater importance, since there is no satisfactory Internet equivalent to a telephone company white pages or directory assistance, and domain names can often be guessed. A domain name mirroring a corporate name may be a valuable corporate asset, as it facilitates communication with a customer base. The uniqueness of Internet addresses is ensured by the registration services of the Internet Network Information Center ('Internic'), a collaborative project established by the National Science Foundation."

MTV Networks, Inc. v. Curry, 867 F. Supp. 202, 203-04 n.2 (S.D.N.Y. 1994).

"Domain names are arranged so that reading from right to left, each part of the name points to a more localized area of the Internet. For example, in the domain name 'cacd.uscourts.gov,' 'gov' is the top-level domain, reserved for all networks associated with the federal government. The 'uscourts' part specifies a second-level domain, a set of the networks used by the federal courts. The 'cacd' part specifies a sub-network or computer used by the United States District Court for the Central District of California.

"If a user knows or can deduce the domain name associated with a Web site, the user can directly access the Web site by typing the domain name into a Web browser, without having to conduct a time-consuming search."

> *Lockheed Martin Corp. v. Network Solutions, Inc.*, 985 F. Supp. 949, 952 (C.D. Cal. 1997).

"A given domain name, the exact alphanumeric combination in the same network and using the same suffix, can only be registered to a single entity."

> *Intermatic, Inc. v. Toeppen*, 947 F. Supp. 1227, 1232 (N.D. Ill. 1996).

"Before using a domain name to locate an Internet computer site in 'cyber-space,' a computer must match the domain name to the domain name's Internet Protocol number. The match information is stored on various Internet-connected computers around the world known as domain name servers. The computer attempts to find the match information by sending out an address query. The goal of the address query is to find the particular domain name server containing the match information the user seeks.

"When ordered to translate an unknown domain name into an Internet Protocol number, a computer will ask its Internet Service Provider's server if it knows the domain name and corresponding Internet Protocol number. If that server lacks the information, it will pass the query to a 'root server,' also called a 'root zone' file, the authoritative and highest level of the domain name system database. The root zone file directs the query to the proper top-level domain zone file, which contains the domain names in a given domain and their corresponding Internet Protocol numbers. In the case of someone searching for the 'bettyandnicks.com' home page, the root zone file sends the query to the top-level domain zone file with information about '.com' domain names. The '.com' zone file then refers the query to a second-level domain name file with all the second-level domain names under '.com.' This is where the 'bettyand-nicks.com' query ends: the second-level domain name file has the information matching the domain name to its associated Internet Protocol number. With the Internet Protocol number, the user's computer can connect the user to the requested Internet site. The 'bettyandnicks.com' home page will appear, just as if the user had typed in the Internet Protocol number instead of the domain name."

> *Thomas v. Network Solutions, Inc.*, 176 F.3d 500, 503-04 (D.C. Cir. 1999) (citations and footnotes omitted).

"A domain name does not signal where a computer is physically located. A computer may be moved from one place to another while retaining the same domain name. Thus a domain name is not an address as typically understood but instead is a mark identifying a specific person's or organization's site on the Internet."

Thomas v. Network Solutions, Inc., 176 F.3d 500, 503 n.2 (D.C. Cir. 1999).

"A domain name is the simplest way of locating a web site. If a computer user does not know a domain name, she can use an Internet 'search engine.' To do this, the user types in a key word search, and the search will locate all of the web sites containing the key word. Such key word searches can yield hundreds of web sites. To make it easier to find their web sites, individuals and companies prefer to have a recognizable domain name."

Panavision Int'l, L.P. v. Toeppen, 141 F.3d 1316, 1319 (9th Cir. 1998).

"A significant purpose of a domain name is to identify the entity that owns the web site."

Panavision Int'l, L.P. v. Toeppen, 141 F.3d 1316, 1327 (9th Cir. 1998).

"A customer who is unsure about a company's domain name will often guess that the domain name is also the company's name."

Cardservice Int'l v. McGee, 950 F. Supp. 737, 741 (E.D. Va. 1997).

". . . serve as a primary identifier of an Internet user."

Zippo Mfg. Co. v. Zippo Dot Com, Inc., 952 F. Supp. 1119, 1120 n.1 (W.D. Pa. 1997).

"They are, in effect, the addresses for websites, which are computer data files that can include names, words, messages, pictures, sounds, and links to other information. Use of a domain name takes an Internet user directly to the particular website associated with that domain name. Often domain names consist of some memorable or intuitive name or phrase related to the content of the website. In many instances, the domain name of a corporate website will consist of or incorporate the company's name or trademark. Such domain names can be valuable to a company because a domain name is the most direct way of locating a website."

Washington Speakers Bureau, Inc. v. Leading Authorities, Inc., 33 F. Supp. 2d 488, 491. n.4 (E.D. Va. 1999).

"To obtain a domain name, an individual or entity files an application with Network Solutions listing the domain name the applicant wants. Because each web page must have a unique domain name, Network Solution[s] checks to see whether the requested domain name has already been assigned to someone else. If so, the applicant must choose a different domain name. Other than requiring an applicant to make certain representations,

Network Solutions does not make an independent determination about a registrant's right to use a particular domain name."
> *Brookfield Comm., Inc. v. West Coast Entertainment Corp.*, 174 F.3d 1036, 1044 (9th Cir. 1999).

"A specific web site is most easily located by using its domain name. Upon entering a domain name into a web browser, the corresponding web site will quickly appear on the computer screen. Sometimes, however, a Web surfer will not know the domain name of the site he is looking for, whereupon he has two principal options: trying to guess the domain name or seeking the assistance of the Internet 'search engine.'

"Oftentimes, an Internet user will begin by hazarding a guess at a domain name, especially if there is an obvious domain name to try. Web users often assume, as a rule of thumb, that the domain name of a particular company will be the company name followed by '.com.' . . . Sometimes, a trademark is better known than the company itself, in which case a Web surfer may assume that the domain address will be ' "trademark".com.' "

* * *

"Guessing domain names, however, is not a risk-free activity. The Web surfer who assumes that ' "X".com' will always correspond to the web site of company X or trademark X will, however, sometimes be misled.

* * *

"A Web surfer's second option when he does not know the domain name is to utilize an Internet search engine, such as Yahoo, Altavista, or Lycos."
> *Brookfield Comm., Inc. v. West Coast Entertainment Corp.*, 174 F.3d 1036, 1044-45 (9th Cir. 1999) (citation omitted).

(trademark)
"[A]ny alphanumeric designation which is registered with or assigned by any domain name registrar, domain name registry, or other domain name registration authority as part of an electronic address on the Internet."
> 15 U.S.C. § 1127.

"When a domain name is used only to indicate an address on the Internet and not to identify the source of specific goods and services, the name is not functioning as a trademark."
> *Data Concepts, Inc. v. Digital Consulting, Inc.*, 150 F.3d. 620, 627 (6th Cir. 1998) (Merritt, J., concurring).

Related issues. "In short, the exclusive quality of second-level domain names has set trademark owners against each other in the struggle to establish a commercial presence on the Internet, and has set businesses against domain name holders who seek to continue the traditional use of the Internet as a non-commercial medium of communication."

Lockheed Martin Corp. v. Network Solutions, Inc., 985 F. Supp. 949, 952 (C.D. Cal. 1997).

"Domain names present a special problem under the Lanham Act because they are used for both a non-trademark technical purpose, to designate a set of computers on the Internet, and for trademark purposes, to identify an Internet user who offers goods or services on the Internet. When a domain name is used only to indicate an address on the Internet, the domain name is not functioning as a trademark. Like trade names, domain names can function as trademarks, and therefore can be used to infringe trademark rights. Domain names, like trade names, do not act as trademarks when they are used merely to identify a business entity; in order to infringe they must be used to identify the source of goods or services.

* * *

"Domain names and vanity telephone numbers both have dual functions. Domain names, like telephone numbers, allow one machine to connect to another machine. Domain names, like telephone numbers, are also valuable to trademark holders when they make it easier for customers to find the trademark holder. Where the holder of a vanity telephone number promotes it in a way that causes a likelihood of confusion, the holder has engaged in an infringing use. But, where...the pure machine-linking function is the only use at issue, there is no trademark use and there can be no infringement.

* * *

"In the domain name context, the domain name registration itself does not infringe the trademark. Infringement occurs when the domain name is used in certain ways."

Lockheed Martin Corp. v. Network Solutions, Inc., 985 F. Supp. 949, 956, 958 (C.D. Cal. 1997) (citations omitted).

"It is important to note that impending access to a domain name is not the same thing as impending access to the Internet. Even if the trademark owner cannot establish a 'vanity' domain name, the owner remains free to promote the trademark on the Internet by using the trademark in the content of a web site. A web site's content is not connected to or restricted by the domain name under which it is accessed. In addition, the trademark owner may use the trademarked words as a third-level domain name, or as a second-level domain name in combination with letters that distinguish it from previously registered second-level domains."

> *Lockheed Martin Corp. v. Network Solutions, Inc.,* 985 F. Supp. 949, 960 n.4 (C.D. Cal. 1997) (citations omitted).

"If the Internet were a technically ideal system for commercial exploitation, then every trademark owner would be able to have a domain name identical to its trademark. But the parts of the Internet that perform the critical addressing functions still operate on the 1960s and 1970s technologies that were adequate when the Internet's function was to facilitate academic and military research. Commerce has entered the Internet only recently. In response, the Internet's existing addressing systems will have to evolve to accommodate conflicts among holders of intellectual property rights, and conflicts between commercial and non-commercial users of the Internet. 'In the long run, the most appropriate technology to access Web sites and e-mail will be directories that point to the desired Internet address. Directory technology of the necessary scale and complexity is not yet available, but when it is developed it will relieve much of the pressure on domain names.' No doubt trademark owners would like to make the Internet safe for their intellectual property rights by reordering the allocation of existing domain names so that each trademark owner automatically owned the domain name corresponding to the owner's mark. Creating an exact match between Internet addresses and trademark will require overcoming the problem of concurrent uses of the same trademark in different classes of goods and geographical areas. Various solutions to this problem are being discussed, such as a graphically-based Internet directory that would allow the presentation of trademark in conjunction with distinguishing logos, new top-level domains for each class of goods, or a new top-level domain for trademarks only. The solution to the current difficulties faced by trademark owners on the Internet lies in this sort of technical innovation, not in attempts to assert trademark rights over legitimate non-trademark uses of this important new means of communication."

> *Lockheed Martin Corp. v. Network Solutions, Inc.,* 985 F. Supp. 949, 967-68 (C.D. Cal. 1997) (citations omitted).

"Without domain name service, the domain name is effectively removed from the Internet, because users who attempt to access Internet resources associated with the domain name receive only an error message."

> *Lockheed Martin Corp. v. Network Solutions, Inc.,* 985 F. Supp. 949, 966 n.11 (C.D. Cal. 1997).

"Most web browsers will show somewhere on the screen the domain name of the web page being shown and will automatically include the domain name in any printout of the web page. There is no technical connection or relationship between a domain name and the contents of the corresponding web page."

Intermatic, Inc. v. Toeppen, 947 F. Supp. 1227, 1231 (N.D. Ill. 1996).

"We agree that simply registering someone else's trademark as a domain name and posting a web site on the Internet is not sufficient to subject a party domiciled in one state to jurisdiction in another.... [T]here must be 'something more' to demonstrate that the defendant directed his activity toward the forum state."

Panavision Int'l, Inc. v. Toeppen, 141 F.3d 1316, 1322 (9th Cir. 1998).

"A customer who is unsure about a company's domain name will often guess that the domain name is also the company's name."

Cardservice Int'l v. McGee, 950 F. Supp. 737, 741 (E.D. Va. 1997).

"[A] domain name mirroring a corporate name may be a valuable corporate asset, as it facilitates communication with a customer base."

MTV Networks, Inc. v. Curry, 867 F. Supp. 202, 203-03 n.2 (S.D.N.Y. 1994).

"Businesses using the Internet commonly use their business names as part of the domain name (e.g., IBM.com)."

Zippo Mfg. Co. v. Zippo Dot Com, Inc., 952 F. Supp. 1119, 1120 n.1 (W.D. Pa. 1997).

"Once a domain-name combination is reserved, it cannot be used by anybody else, unless the first registrant voluntarily or otherwise relinquishes its registration."

Avery Dennison Corp. v. Sumpton, 189 F.3d 868, 872 (9th Cir. 1999). *See also Zippo Mfg. Co. v. Zippo Dot Com, Inc.,* 952 F. Supp. 1119, 1120 n.3 (W.D. Pa. 1997) ("Once a domain name is registered to one user, it may not be used by another.").

"The registrar of Internet domain names, Network Solutions, Inc. [NSI], maintains a database of registrations and translates entered domain-name combinations into Internet protocol addresses."

Avery Dennison Corp. v. Sumpton, 189 F.3d 868, 872 (9th Cir. 1999).

"Domain names ending in '.com,' '.net,' or '.org,' among others, are registered through NSI on a first-come-first-served basis. Anyone may register any unused domain name upon payment of a fee. Of course, this registration in no way trumps federal trademark law, registration of a mark or name with NSI does not itself confer any federal trademark rights on the registrant."

> *Washington Speakers Bureau, Inc. v. Leading Authorities, Inc.,* 33 F. Supp. 2d 488, 491 n.3 (E.D. Va. 1999) (citation omitted).

See also **domain address; fully qualified domain name; Internet domain name; trademark; trademark infringement.**

domain name server *(Internet)*

"Specialized computers known as 'domain name servers' maintain tables linking domain names to IP numbers."

> *Lockheed Martin Corp. v. Network Solutions, Inc.,* 985 F. Supp. 949, 952 (C.D. Cal. 1997).

See also **name server.**

domain name service *(Internet)*

"A given host looks up the IP addresses of other hosts on the Internet through a system known as domain name service.

"Domain name service is accomplished as follows: The Internet is divided into several 'top level' domains. . . . Each domain name active in a given top-level domain is registered with the top level server which contains certain hostname and IP address information.

". . . If an Internet user desires to establish a connection with a web page . . . , the Internet user might enter into a web browser program the URL. . . . [A]ll queries for addresses are routed to certain computers, the so-called 'top level servers.' The top level server matches the domain name to an IP address of a domain name server capable of directing the inquiry to the computer hosting the web page. Thus, domain name service ultimately matches an alphanumeric name . . . with its numeric IP address."

* * *

"Domain name service can be operated by the domain name holder or obtained from any entity with the proper computer equipment, including hundreds of Internet service providers."

> *Intermatic, Inc. v. Toeppen,* 947 F. Supp. 1227, 1231 (N.D. Ill. 1996).

See also **domain name system.**

domain name system *(Internet)*

Abbreviated as "DNS." A distributed database used to translate alphanumeric domain names into Internet Protocol (IP) numbers used by computers to find a site on the Internet.

"The DNS controls the way in which each component of the Internet identifies and communicates with one another."
  Name.Space, Inc. v. Network Solutions, Inc., 202 F.3d 573, 576 (2d Cir. 2000).

"The current DNS has a hierarchical tree structure of names. A domain name, such as <www.uscourts.gov>, comprises a series of alphanumeric fields, or 'domains,' separated by periods or 'dots.' The alphanumeric field to the far right of a domain name is the Top Level Domain ('TLD'), and each prior field to the left of the period preceding the TLD is the Second Level Domain ('SLD'), the Third Level Domain, and so on. Thus, TLDs are the highest subdivisions of Internet domain names, and SLDs and other lower level domain names identify the host computers and individual websites under each TLD."
  Name.Space, Inc. v. Network Solutions, Inc., 202 F.3d 573, 577 (2d Cir. 2000).

"Web sites, like other information resources on the Internet, are currently addressed using the Internet 'domain name system.' A numbering system called the 'Internet Protocol' gives each individual computer or network a unique numerical address on the Internet. The 'Internet Protocol number,' also known as the 'IP number,' consists of four groups of digits separated by periods, such as '192.215.247.50.' For the convenience of users, individual resources on the Internet are also given names. Specialized computer known as 'domain name servers' maintain tables linking domain names to IP numbers."
  Lockheed Martin Corp. v. Network Solutions, Inc., 985 F. Supp. 949, 952 (C.D. Cal. 1997).

Related issues. "On July 1, 1997, in response to growing domestic and international concerns regarding the future of the DNS, President Clinton directed the Secretary of Commerce to privatize the DNS. On February 20, 1998, after a consultative process whereby the Department of Commerce solicited public comments on various issues regarding the DNS, including whether new gTLDs should be added, the National Telecommunications and Information Administration—a part of the Commerce Department—published a proposed rule and request for public comment, the so-called 'Green Paper.' That document recommended that the DNS be managed by a private, non-profit corporation which would determine, inter alia, the circumstances under which gTLDs should be added to the root server system. The Green Paper contemplated that up to five new gTLDs be added during the period of transition to private management of the DNS, in order to enhance competition and enable other entities to enter the Internet registry business.

"After considering the numerous public comments that were received in response to the Green Paper, the Commerce Department published a final policy statement known as the 'White Paper' on June 10, 1998. The White Paper affirmed the basic proposals of the Green Paper with some modifications, including a determination that no new gTLDs would be added to the Internet during the transition period, as such decisions would be best made by the new, globally representative non-profit corporation with input from the international community. The White Paper stated that any expansion of new gTLDs should proceed at a deliberate pace, in order to maintain the stability and promote the controlled evolution of the DNS.

"As part of the policy set forth in the White Paper, NSF and the Commerce Department entered into a Memorandum of Agreement on September 8, 1998, pursuant to which NSF transferred responsibility for administering its Cooperative Agreement with NSI to the Commerce Department, while expressly agreeing to remain responsible for defending this lawsuit. In October 1998, NSI and the Commerce Department entered into Amendment No. 11 to the Cooperative Agreement, which provides for NSI's recognition of the new non-profit corporation described in the White Paper, and the programmatic transfer of various DNS management functions to this corporation. Amendment No. 11, which extends the Cooperative Agreement though September 30, 2000, also provides for the continued operation of the master root zone server by NSI until this function is transferred to the new private corporation or another entity, and states that NSI must request written direction from an authorized Commerce Department official before making any changes to the root zone file.

"In the fall of 1998, the Internet Corporation for Assigned Names and Numbers ('ICANN') was incorporated as a non-profit public benefit corporation in California, in order to assume the management of the DNS as contemplated in the White Paper. ICANN's bylaws state that it is to be aided by three supporting organizations, one of which is the Domain Name Supporting Organization ('DNSO'), the entity responsible for making policy recommendations to ICANN regarding the DNS, including, among other things, new TLDs. On November 25, 1998, ICANN and the Commerce Department entered into a Memorandum of Understanding, pursuant to which they agreed jointly to develop and test the mechanisms and procedures that should be in place in the new, privatized DNS. Specifically, ICANN and the Commerce Department agreed to collaborate on "written technical procedures for operation of the primary root server including procedures that permit modifications, additions or deletions to the root zone file."

> *Name.Space, Inc. v. Network Solutions, Inc.*, 202 F.3d 573, 578-79 (2d Cir. 2000) (citations omitted).

See also **domain name; IP number.**

DOS *(hardware)*
Acronym for "Disk Operating System." General term used to refer to an operating system that runs on IBM and IBM-compatible computers.

dot *or "." (Internet)*
The symbol used to separate various portions of a domain name.

dot com *(Internet)*
See .com.

dot gov *(Internet)*
See .gov.

dot matrix *(technology)*
A method used in some printers to transfer images to paper. The printed characters are made up of small dots, like lights on an electric scoreboard. Clarity of characters is determined by how close the dots are spaced to each other. *See also* **printer.**

dot matrix printer *(hardware)*
A printer that creates characters by printing a pattern of dots.

dot net *(Internet)*
See .net.

dot org *(Internet)*
See .org.

down time *(hardware)*
See **downtime.**

download *(software)*
"...generally begins with the appearance of a dialog box, or small window, prompting the user to confirm the location on the user's computer hard

drive where the downloaded software will be stored. The actual download does not begin until the user provides the computer with this information."

> *Universal City Studios, Inc. v. Reimerdes*, 111 F. Supp. 2d 294, 312 n.88 (S.D.N.Y. 2000).

Annotation. "[M]uch software is ordered over the Internet by purchasers who have never seen a box. Increasingly software arrives by wire. There is...only a stream of electrons."

> *ProCD, Inc. v. Zeidenberg*, 39 U.S.P.Q.2d (BNA) 1161, 1164 (7th Cir. 1996).

Related issues. "It is possible also to create a link that commences the download immediately upon being clicked."

> *Universal City Studios, Inc. v. Reimerdes*, 111 F. Supp. 2d 294, 312 n.88 (S.D.N.Y. 2000).

See also **downloading.**

downloading *(technology)*

"[T]he process of transferring files, programs, or other computer-stored information from a remote computer to one's own computer."

> *United States v. Riggs*, 739 F. Supp. 414, 417 n.3 (N.D. Ill. 1990).

"Third party users can also retrieve information from the electronic bulletin board to their own computer memories by a process known as 'downloading.'"

> *Sega Enters. Ltd. v. MAPHIA*, 857 F. Supp. 679, 683 (N.D. Cal. 1994).

Related issues. "The Internet is more than a means of communications; it also serves as a conduit for transporting digitized goods, including software, data, music, graphics, and videos which can be downloaded from the provider's site to the Internet user's computer."

> *American Library Association v. Pataki*, 969 F. Supp. 160, 173 (S.D.N.Y. 1997).

See also **download.**

downside *(business)*

The risk inherent in a particular project that it will lose money/value.

downstream use problem *(contract; copyright)*

Use of a copyrighted work in excess of a license or in violation of copyright by the purchaser of a multimedia product containing that work.

downtime *(technology)*

Also "down time."

"[T]ime during which the system was not functioning."
Liberty Fin. Management Corp. v. Beneficial Data Processing Corp., 670 S.W.2d 40, 46 (Mo. App. 1984).

[CANADA] "[T]he time that the machine is not working due to its own failure."
Public Utilities Comm'n (Waterloo) v. Burroughs Business Machines Ltd. (1973), 34 D.L.R. (3d) 320 (Ont. H.C.), *aff'd,* (1974), 6 O.R. (2d) 257 (Ont. C.A.).

DPI *(technology)*
Acronym for "**D**ots **P**er **I**nch." Refers to the number of pixels per inch. The more pixels per inch, the better the video representation of the original image.

DRAM *(hardware)*
Acronym for "**D**irect **R**andom **A**ccess **M**emory." "[A] memory device in a computer in which information is stored and from which it is retrieved. It is an acronym for direct random access memory. The symbol 'K' represents the potential amount of memory stored in the DRAM."
Texas Instruments, Inc. v. International Trade Comm'n, 871 F.2d 1054, 1058 (Fed. Cir. 1989).

"DRAMs are 'dynamic' because they must be repeatedly 'refreshed' with an electrical charge or they will lose the information stored within them."
Advanced Computer Servs., Inc. v. MAI Sys. Corp., 845 F. Supp. 356, 362 (E.D. Va. 1994).

dramatic right *(copyright)*
The right to perform a work on stage plus the live broadcast rights (but not the recording rights).

drive *(hardware)*
The electromechanical device that rotates the storage disk while the magnetic sensor reads and transfers data to and from the disk. *See also* **disk drive.**

droit moral *(copyright)*
French for "moral rights." *See* **moral rights.**

DSL *(technology)*
"DSL lines, which increasingly are available to home and business users, offer transfer rates of 7 megabits per second."
Universal City Studios, Inc. v. Reimerdes, 111 F. Supp. 2d 294, 314 (S.D.N.Y. 2000) (footnote omitted).

DSP *(technology)*
Acronym for "Digital Signal Processor." A computer chip that takes analog signals and translates and compresses them into digital form for use in computer and other digital systems.

DTD cards *(hardware; telecommunications)*
". . . detect and handle dial tones."
> *Alcatel USA, Inc. v. DGI Technologies, Inc.,* 166 F.3d 772, 778 n.4 (5th Cir. 1999).

DTI *(telecommunications)*
Acronym for Digital Trunk Interface.
> *Alcatel USA, Inc. v. DGI Technologies, Inc.,* 166 F.3d 772, 778 n.2 (5th Cir. 1999).

See **DTI cards.**

DTI cards *(hardware; telecommunications)*
". . . translate incoming signals from the format of the incoming trunk line that carries long distance calls to the switch format and back."
> *Alcatel USA, Inc. v. DGI Technologies, Inc.,* 166 F.3d 772, 778 n.2 (5th Cir. 1999).

dual media format *(hardware)*
A CD-ROM based product that will work on both IBM-based and Apple Macintosh-based computer systems. *See also* **hybrid.**

due process
(Constitution)
"If free speech is at the heart of our democracy, then surely due process is the very lifeblood of our body politic; for without it, democracy could not survive. Distilled to its essence, due process is, of course, nothing more and nothing less than fair play. If our citizens cannot rely on fair play in their relationship with their government, the stature of our government as a shining example of democracy would be greatly diminished."
> *Reno v. American Civil Liberties Union,* 929 F. Supp. 824, 859 (E.D. Pa. 1996), *aff'd, American Civil Liberties Union v. Reno,* 521 U.S. 844 (1997).

(criminal)
"Where a federal statute or regulation fails to supply a fair warning of what will give rise to criminal liability, it violates the Due Process Clause of the Fifth Amendment; . . ."
> *Shea v. Reno,* 930 F. Supp. 916, 935 (S.D.N.Y. 1996).

(jurisdiction)
"To determine whether personal jurisdiction exists over a defendant, federal courts apply the law of the forum state, subject to the limits of the Due Process Clause of the Fourteenth Amendment."
  CompuServe, Inc. v. Patterson, 89 F.3d 1257, 1262 (6th Cir. 1996)

"To satisfy the Due Process Clause of the Fourteenth Amendment, a plaintiff must show that the defendant has 'minimum contacts' with the forum state 'such that the maintenance of the suit does not offend "traditional notions of fair play and substantial justice."'" *International Shoe Co. v. Washington,* 326 U.S. 310, 316, 66 S. Ct. 154, 158 (1945) (*quoting Milliken v. Meyer,* 311 U.S. 457, 463, 61 S. Ct. 339, 343 (1940). There must be 'some act by which the defendant purposefully avails itself of the privilege of conducting activities within the forum State, thus invoking the benefits and protections of its laws.' *Hanson v. Denckla,* 357 U.S. 235, 253, 78 S. Ct. 1228, 1240 (1958)."
  State v. Granite Gate Resorts, Inc., 568 N.W.2d 715, 718 (Minn. App. 1997),
  aff'd per curiam, 576 N.W.2d 747 (Minn. 1998).

"Due process is satisfied where the defendant has enough 'minimum contacts' with the forum state such that requiring him to defend his interests there would not 'offend traditional notions of fair play and substantial justice.' Furthermore, the minimum contacts with the state must be such that the defendant could 'reasonably anticipate being haled into court there.' 'It is essential in each case that there be some act by which the defendant purposefully avails itself of the privilege of conducting activities within the forum state, thus invoking the benefits and protection of its laws.'"
  Coastal Video Comm. Corp. v. Staywell Corp., 59 F. Supp. 2d 562, 565 (E.D. Va. 1999) (citations omitted).

"The Due Process Clause of the Fourteenth Amendment permits the exercise of personal jurisdiction over a nonresident defendant when (1) that defendant has purposefully availed himself of the benefits and protections of the forum state by establishing 'minimum contacts' with the forum state; and (2) the exercise of jurisdiction over that defendant does not offend 'traditional notions of fair play and substantial justice.'"
  Mink v. AAAA Dev. LLC, 190 F.3d 333, 336 (5th Cir. 1999).
See also **minimum contact(s); personal jurisdiction.**

(procedure)
"Today governments collect great quantities of data about their citizens, data which, when stored on computers, potentially are available to large

numbers of people. The dangers presented by governmental possession and use of inaccurate information are greater than ever. The principles of due process are our most effective shield against these dangers."

In re Bagley, 513 A.2d 331, 338 (N.H. Supreme Ct. 1986).

dumb terminal *(hardware)*

A computer terminal, usually including keyboard and video monitor, that can be used only when connected to a main computer for processing and calculations.

dump *(technology)*

"The term applied to the process of making a copy of some or all data stored in a storage device, usually for backup purposes."

U.S. Copyright Office, *Compendium of Copyright Office Practices* II, § 326 (1984).

See also **core dump.**

dump-restore program(s) *(software)*

". . . enable a computer user to transfer information to (the 'dump' function) and from (the 'restore' function) computer disks and tapes."

Innovation Data Processing, Inc. v. IBM Corp., 585 F. Supp. 1470, 1472 (D.N.J. 1984).

duplex feature *(technology)*

"[O]ne which would allow a system user speaking over the LTR radio to simultaneously hear transmissions directed to the user from other radios."

E.F. Johnson Co. v. Uniden Corp. of America, 623 F. Supp. 1485, 1495 (D. Minn. 1985).

duration *(contract; trade secret)*

"[T]his court finds that the one-year duration of EarthWeb's restrictive covenant is too long given the dynamic nature of this [Internet] industry, its lack of geographical borders, and Schlack's former cutting-edge position with EarthWeb where his success depended on keeping abreast of daily changes in content on the Internet."

EarthWeb, Inc. v. Schlack, 71 F. Supp. 2d 299, 313 (S.D.N.Y. 1999).

DVD *(hardware)*

Acronym for "Digital Video Disc."

"[F]ive-inch wide disks capable of storing more than 4.7 GB of data."

Universal City Studios, Inc. v. Reimerdes, 111 F. Supp. 2d 294, 307 (S.D.N.Y. 2000).

Annotation. "In the application relevant here, they are used to hold full-length motion pictures in digital form. They are the latest technology for private home viewing of recorded motion pictures and result in drastically improved audio and visual clarity and quality of motion pictures shown on televisions or computer screens."

Universal City Studios, Inc. v. Reimerdes, 111 F. Supp. 2d 294, 307 (S.D.N.Y. 2000) (footnote omitted).

e- *(electronic commerce)*

An all-purpose prefix added to virtually any word which can be used for some facet of electronic commerce. Refers to "e-commerce."

EAR *(export)*

Acronym for Export Administration Regulations.

"The EAR contain specific regulations to control the export of encryption software, expressly including computer source code. Encryption software is treated differently from other software in a number of significant ways."
Bernstein v. United States Dept. of Justice, 176 F.3d 1132, 1137 (9th Cir. 1999).

Annotation. "First, the term 'export' is specifically broadened with respect to encryption software to preclude the use of the Internet and other global mediums if such publication would allow passive or active access by a foreign national within the United States or anyone outside the United States. Second, the regulations governing the export of nonencryption software provide for several exceptions that are not applicable to encryption software. In addition, although printed materials containing encryption source code are not subject to EAR regulation, the same materials made available on machine-readable media, such as floppy disk or CD-ROM, are covered. The government, moreover, has reserved the right to restrict source code in printed form that may be easily 'scanned,' thus creating some ambiguity as to whether printed publications are necessarily exempt from licensing."
Bernstein v. United States Dept. of Justice, 176 F.3d 1132, 1137 (9th Cir. 1999) (citations omitted).

"[I]nsofar as the EAR regulations on encryption software were intended to slow the spread of secure encryption methods to foreign nations, the government is intentionally retarding the progress of the flourishing science of cryptography. To the extent the government's efforts are aimed at interdicting the flow of scientific ideas (whether expressed in source code or otherwise), as distinguished from encryption products, these efforts would appear to strike deep into the heartland of the First Amendment. In this regard, the EAR regulations are very different from content-neutral time, place and manner restrictions that may have an incidental effect on expression while aiming at secondary effects."

Bernstein v. United States Department of Justice, 176 F.3d 1132, 1145 (9th Cir. 1999).

early adopters *(business)*
The group of people who purchase new technologies first.

Easter eggs *(video game)*
Hidden surprises that players find as they play a video game or explore a multimedia product.

e-cash *(electronic commerce)*
An electronic form of currency that substitutes for money in online transactions, including secured credit cards, electronic checks, and digital coins.

echo *(technology)*
When a keyboard character is typed, it does not automatically display on the screen. The character is first sent to the system, then the program copies what is typed and "echos" it back on the screen. Echoing is turned off for activities such as entering one's password, so that others do not see it displayed on the screen.

e-commerce *(electronic commerce)*
See electronic commerce.

economic loss *(tort)*
"[T]he diminution in the value of the product because it is inferior in quality and does not work for the general purposes for which it was manufactured and sold."

Budgetel Inns, Inc. v. Micro Sys., Inc., 8 F. Supp. 2d 1137, 1140-41 (E.D. Wis. 1998) (citations omitted).

" . . . encompasses direct economic loss, based upon the difference in value between what was received as compared to what was represented, together with costs of replacement and repair. It also includes consequential, or indirect, economic losses attributable to the product defect, such as lost profits resulting from the inability to make use of the product."

Budgetel Inns, Inc. v. Micro Sys., Inc., 8 F. Supp. 2d 1137, 1141 (E.D. Wis. 1998).
See also economic loss doctrine.

economic loss doctrine *(tort)*

"[A] judicially created doctrine providing that a commercial purchaser of a product cannot recover from a manufacturer under tort theories damages that are solely economic losses. When contractual expectations are frustrated because of a defect in the subject matter of a contract, a party's remedy instead lies exclusively in contract.

"The doctrine does not bar claims involving physical injury or physical harm to property, however, as those are considered proper tort claims."

> *Budgetel Inns, Inc. v. Micro Sys., Inc.*, 8 F. Supp. 2d 1137, 1141 (E.D. Wis. 1998) (citations omitted).

ECPA *(criminal; privacy)*

Acronym for "Electronic Communications Privacy Act."

"The Electronic Communications Privacy Act of 1986 (the 'Electronic Communications Act') provides a system of privacy protections for electronic communications (i.e., email messages), as well as procedures for government access to the communications and related records. In general, when the Government seeks to obtain information from a provider of electronic communication or remote computing services, the Government must demonstrate specific and articulable facts showing that there are reasonable grounds to believe that the requested information is relevant and material to an ongoing criminal investigation. The procedures required differ depending on whether the Government seeks to discover the contents of electronic communications or merely records related to them (i.e., personal information of subscribers, user activity logs, billing records and so on). Most notably, when the Government seeks only the related information, notice is not required to be given to the affected customer or subscriber. Any provider of electronic communication or remote computing services that discloses information in accordance with section 2703 is shielded from liability for any cause of action relating to the disclosure."

> *In re Application of the United States of America for an order pursuant to 18 U.S.C. 2703(d)*, 8 Computer Cas. (CCH) ¶ 47,897 (D. Mass. 1999) (citations omitted).

Related issues. "[T]here is no case law interpreting the word 'public' as used in the ECPA."

> *Andersen Consulting LLP v. UOP*, 991 F. Supp. 2d 1041, 1042 n.1 (N.D. Ill. 1998).

See also **Electronic Communications Privacy Act.**

EDI *(electronic commerce)*
Acronym for "Electronic Data Interchange."
See **electronic data interchange.**

edit *(software)*
To revise the contents of a document by moving, adding, deleting, or rearranging text.

EDP *(technology)*
Acronym for "Electronic Data Processing."
> *Telex Corp. v. IBM Corp.,* 367 F. Supp. 258, 270 (N.D. Okla. 1973), *aff'd in part, rev'd in part,* 510 F.2d 894 (10th Cir.), *cert. dism.,* 423 U.S. 802 (1975).

See **electronic data processing.**

EDP machine *(technology)*
"[A] machine or device and attachments thereof used primarily in or with an electronic data processing system."
> *Honeywell, Inc. v. Sperry Rand Corp.,* 1974 Trade Cases (CCH) ¶ 74,874, at 95,875, 95,923 (D. Minn. 1973).

See also **EDP system.**

EDP system *(technology)*
"[A]ny machine or group of automatically inter-communicating machine units capable of entering, receiving, storing, classifying, computing and/or recording alphabetic and/or numeric accounting and/or statistical data without intermediate use of tabulating cards, which system includes one or more central data processing facilities and one or more storage facilities, and has either (a) the ability to receive and retain in the storage facilities at least some of the instructions for the data processing operations required, or (b) means, in association with storage, inherently capable of receiving and utilizing the alphabetic and/or numeric representation of either the location or the identifying name or number of data in storage to control access to such data, or (c) storage capacity for 1,000 or more alphabetic and/or decimal numeric characters in or with an electronic data processing system."
> *Honeywell, Inc. v. Sperry Rand Corp.,* 1974 Trade Cases (CCH) ¶ 74,874, at 95, 875, 95,923 (D. Minn. 1973).

"…consists of products which perform five basic functions. These are 'processing,' 'storage,' 'input,' 'output' and 'control.' Input is the entering of data into storage. The input devices convert data from an 'ordinary' language form (i.e., English and numbers) to 'machine' language or electronic signals which are then understandable to a computer. Output is the opposite. Output devices convert the 'machine' language or electronic signals to the output form desired, such as printed or typed in humanly understandable language on paper, recorded on magnetic tape or magnetic disk, punched as a hole in a punched card, or displayed on a television-like screen. Output devices can also be used to open or close a valve, or to transfer electrical impulses to another computer system."

> *Telex Corp. v. IBM Corp.,* 367 F. Supp. 258, 274 (N.D. Okla. 1973), *aff'd in part, rev'd in part,* 510 F.2d 894 (10th Cir.), *cert. dism.,* 423 U.S. 802 (1975).

Related issues. "The first EDP system—the Univac I—was delivered in 1951 to the Bureau of the Census."

> *Telex Corp. v. IBM Corp.,* 367 F. Supp. 258, 271 (N.D. Okla. 1973), *aff'd in part, rev'd in part,* 510 F.2d 894 (10th Cir.), *cert. dism.,* 423 U.S. 802 (1975).

See also **EDP machine.**

.edu *(Internet)*

"A [top level] domain reserved for educational institutions...."

> *Intermatic, Inc. v. Toeppen,* 947 F. Supp. 1227, 1231 (N.D. Ill. 1996).

edutainment *(multimedia)*

A concatenation of the words "**edu**cation" and "enter**tainment.**" Refers to a species of interactive media works that incorporates both educational materials and entertainment techniques, which is supposed to facilitate learning.

EEA *(criminal; trade secret)*

Acronym for "Electronic Espionage Act of 1996." *See* **Electronic Espionage Act of 1996.**

effectively controls access to a work *(copyright)*

"[A] technological measure 'effectively controls access to a work' if the measure, in the ordinary course of its operation, requires the application of information, or a process or a treatment, with the authority of the copyright owner, to gain access to a work."

> 17 U.S.C. § 1201(a)(3)(B).

effectively protects a right of a copyright owner under this title

(copyright)

"[A] technological measure 'effectively protects a right of a copyright owner under this title' if the measure, in the ordinary course of its operation, prevents, restricts, or otherwise limits the exercise of a right of a copyright owner under this title."

17 U.S.C. § 1201(b)(2)(B).

effects doctrine *(jurisdiction)*

"In tort cases, jurisdiction may attach if the defendant's conduct is aimed at or has an effect in the forum state.... [P]ersonal jurisdiction can be based upon (1) intentional actions (2) expressly aimed at the forum state (3) causing harm, the brunt of which is suffered—and which the defendant knows is likely to be suffered—in the forum state."

Panavision Int'l, Inc. v. Toeppen, 141 F.3d 1316, 1321 (9th Cir. 1998) (citations omitted).

See also **personal jurisdiction.**

efficiency *(copyright)*

The ability of a computer program to work quickly, without wasted operations, and within a relatively small amount of memory.

Annotation. "In the context of computer program design, the concept of efficiency is akin to deriving the most concise logical proof or formulating the most succinct mathematical computation. Thus, the more efficient a set of modules are, the more closely they approximate the idea or process embodied in that particular aspect of the program's structure.

"While, hypothetically, there might be a myriad of ways in which a programmer may effectuate certain functions within a program—i.e., express the idea embodied in a given subroutine—efficiency concerns may so narrow the practical range of choices to make only one or two forms of expression workable options.

* * *

"It follows that in order to determine whether the merger doctrine precludes copyright protection to any aspect of a program's structure that is so oriented, a court must inquire 'whether the use of *this particular set* of modules is necessary efficiently to implement that part of the program's process' being implemented. If the answer is yes, then the expression represented by the programmer's choice of a specific module or group of modules has merged with their underlying idea and is unprotected.

"Another justification for linking structural economy with the application of the merger doctrine stems from a program's essentially utilitarian nature and the competitive forces that exist in the software marketplace. Working in tandem, these factors give rise to a problem of proof which merger helps to eliminate.

"Efficiency is an industry-wide goal. Since, as we have already noted, there may be only a limited number of efficient implementations for any given program task, it is quite possible that multiple programmers, working independently, will design the identical method employed in the allegedly infringed work. Of course, if this is the case, there is no copyright infringement.

"Under these circumstances, the fact that two programs contain the same efficient structure may as likely lead to an inference of independent creation as it does to one of copying. Thus, since evidence of similarly efficient structure is not particularly probative of copying, it should be disregarded in the overall substantial similarity analysis."

Computer Assocs. Int'l, Inc. v. Altai, Inc., 982 F.2d 693, 708-09 (2d Cir. 1992) (emphasis in original; citations omitted).

"A program's efficiency depends in large part on the arrangement of its modules and subroutines; although two programs could produce the same result, one might be more efficient because of different internal arrangements of modules and subroutines. Because efficiency is a prime concern in computer programs (an efficient program being obviously more valuable than a comparatively inefficient one), the arrangement of modules and subroutines is a critical factor for any programmer."

Whelan Assocs., Inc. v. Jaslow Dental Lab., Inc., 797 F.2d 1222, 1230 (3d Cir. 1986).

EFT-POS *(electronic commerce)*
Acronym for "Electronic Funds Transfer—Point of Sale."

[NEW ZEALAND] *Databank Systems Ltd. v. Commissioner of Inland Revenue* [1987], N.Z.L.R. 312 (H.C. Wellington).

EGA *(hardware)*
Acronym for "Enhanced Graphics Array."

Princeton Graphics Operating L.P. v. NEC Home Elecs. (U.S.A.), Inc., 732 F. Supp. 1258, 1259 n.3 (S.D.N.Y. 1990).

See **enhanced graphics array.**

electronic *(contract; technology)*
"[R]elating to technology having electrical, digital, magnetic, wireless, optical, electromagnetic, or similar capabilities."

UCITA § 102(a)(26).

electronic agent *(contract; Internet)*
"[A] computer program, or electronic or other automated means, used independently to initiate an action, or to respond to electronic messages or per-

formances, on the person's behalf without review or action by an individual at the time of the action or response to the message or performance."

UCITA § 102(a)(27).

See also agent; software agent.

electronic bulletin board *(Internet)*

"...consists of electronic storage media, such as computer memories or hard disks, which [are] attached to telephone lines via modem devices, and controlled by a computer."

Sega Enters. Ltd. v. MAPHIA, 857 F. Supp. 679, 683 (N.D. Cal. 1994).

See also electronic bulletin board system.

electronic bulletin board system *(Internet)*

"..., which, like national on-line services, provide certain proprietary content; some bulletin-board systems in turn offer users links to the Internet."

Shea v. Reno, 930 F. Supp. 916, 926 (S.D.N.Y. 1996).

See also electronic bulletin board.

electronic commerce *(electronic commerce)*

Also called "e-commerce" and "Internet commerce."

"Electronic Commerce integrates communications, data management, and security services, to allow business applications within different organizations to automatically interchange information. Communications services transfer the information from the originator to the recipient. Data management services define the interchange format of the information. Security services authenticate the source of information, verify the integrity of the information received by the recipient, prevent disclosure of the information to unauthorized users, and verify that the information was received by the intended recipient."

Information Infrastructure Technology and Applications (IITA) Task Group, National Coordination Office for High Performance Computing and Communications 13-4 (Feb. 1994).

"[A] means of conducting transactions that, prior to the evolution of the Internet as a business tool in 1995, would have been completed in more traditional ways—by telephone, mail, facsimile, proprietary electronic data interchange systems, or face-to-face contact."

U.S. Dept. of Commerce, The Emerging Digital Economy II, at 1 (June 1999).

"[E]lectronic techniques for accomplishing business transactions including electronic mail or messaging, World Wide Web technology, electronic bulletin boards, purchase cards, electronic funds transfer, and electronic data interchange."

Federal Acquisition Regulation 2.101 (1999).

Annotation. "The Internet is more than a means of communications; it also serves as a conduit for transporting digitized goods, including software, data, music, graphics, and videos which can be downloaded from the provider's site to the Internet user's computer."

American Library Association v. Pataki, 969 F. Supp. 160, 173 (S.D.N.Y. 1997).

"Commerce on the Internet could total tens of billions of dollars by the turn of the century. For this potential to be realized fully, governments must adopt a non-regulatory, market-oriented approach to electronic commerce, one that facilitates the emergence of a transparent and predictable legal environment to support global business and commerce. Official decision makers must respect the unique nature of the medium and recognize that widespread competition and increased consumer choice should be the defining features of the new digital marketplace."

The White House, *A Framework for Global Electronic Commerce* 2 (July 1, 1997).

Related issues. "The Federal Government shall use electronic commerce whenever practicable or cost-effective. The use of terms commonly associated with paper transactions (e.g., 'copy,' 'document,' 'page,' printed,' 'sealed envelope,' and 'stamped') shall not be interpreted to restrict the use of electronic commerce. Contracting officers may supplement electronic transactions by using other media to meet the requirements of any contract action governed by the FAR [Federal Acquisition Regulations](e.g., transmit hard copy of drawings)."

Federal Acquisition Regulations 4.502(a).

"Before using electronic commerce, the agency head shall ensure that the agency systems are capable of ensuring authentication and confidentiality commensurate with the risk and magnitude of the harm from loss, misuse, or unauthorized access to or modification of the information."

Federal Acquisition Regulations 4.502(c).

electronic communication(s) *(criminal)*

"[A]ny transfer of signs, signals, writing, images, sounds, data, or intelligence of any nature transmitted in whole or in part by a wire, radio, electromagnetic, photoelectronic or photooptical that affects interstate or foreign commerce, but does not include—(A) the radio portion of a cordless telephone communication that is transmitted between the cordless telephone handset and the base unit; (B) any wire or oral communication; (C) any communication made through a tone-only paging device; or (D) any communication from a tracking device (as defined in section 3117 of this title)…."

18 U.S.C. § 2510(12).

Related issues. The term includes "wireless communication," as defined in 18 U.S.C § 2510(1).

electronic communication service *(criminal; telecommunications)*

"[A]ny service which provides to users thereof the ability to send or receive wire or electronic communications."

18 U.S.C. § 2510(15).

See Electronic Communications Privacy Act.

Electronic Communications Privacy Act *(criminal; privacy)*

Abbreviated as "ECPA."

"The ECPA, enacted by Congress to address privacy concerns on the Internet, allows the government to obtain information from an online service provider…but only if a) it obtains a warrant issued under the Federal Rules of Criminal Procedure or state equivalent; or b) it gives prior notice to the online subscriber and then issues a subpoena or receives a court order authorizing disclosure of the information in question."

McVeigh v. Cohen, 983 F. Supp. 215, 219 (D.D.C. 1998).

"A person or entity providing any electronic communication service to the public shall not knowingly divulge to any person or entity the contents of a communication while in electronic storage by that service."

18 U.S.C. § 2702(a)(1).

Annotation. "ECPA was enacted in 1986 to address new technologies not anticipated by the 1968 wiretap law. While that law generally prohibits eavesdropping and the interception of the content of electronic mail, radio communications, data transmissions, and telephone calls without consent, it imposes no restrictions on the internal use by providers of an 'electronic communications service' of transactional records pertaining to such communications. As a consequence, such providers are free to make any use of the identity of the parties to the communication or the fact of the communication. Moreover, while the ECPA specifies standards and procedures for court authorized electronic surveillance by government entities, and government access to stored electronic communications, it does not restrict the dissemination of transactional data that is maintained in electronic storage to non-governmental entities. Indeed, a service provider is expressly permitted to disclosure transaction information concerning a subscriber to any person, for any purpose, without notice or subscriber consent."

> Department of Commerce, *Inquiry on Privacy Issues Relating to Private Sector Use of Telecommunications-Related Personal Information,* 59 Fed. Reg. 6841, 6844-48 (Feb. 11, 1994) (footnotes omitted).

Related issues. "[I]t is elementary that information obtained improperly can be suppressed where an individual's rights have been violated. In these days of 'big brother,' where through technology and otherwise the privacy interests of individuals from all walks of life are being ignored or marginalized, it is imperative that statutes explicitly protecting these rights be strictly observed.

* * *

"With literally the entire world on the world-wide web, enforcement of the ECPA is of great concern to those who bare the most personal information about their lives in private accounts through the Internet."

> *McVeigh v. Cohen,* 983 F. Supp. 215, 220, 221 (D.D.C. 1998).

electronic communications system *(criminal)*

"[A]ny wire, radio, electromagnetic, photooptical or photoelectronic facilities for the transmission of electronic communications, and any computer facilities or related electronic equipment for the electronic storage of such communications; . . ."

> 18 U.S.C. § 2510(15).

Electronic Copyright Management Systems *(copyright; technology)*

Abbreviated as "ECMS." Technical schemes to make the copying of digital works more difficult without a license.

electronic data interchange *(technology)*

Abbreviated as "EDI." The exchange of business information in a standard electronic format between computers via a network. "Business information" includes a full range of information associated with high-volume, repetitive, commercial, and business transactions, but is most often used for purchasing and distribution transactions.

"[A] technique for electronically transferring and storing formatted information between computers utilizing established and published formats and codes, as authorized by the applicable Federal Information Processing Standards."
Federal Acquisition Regulations 4.501 (1999).

electronic data processing *(technology)*
Abbreviated as "EDP."

"[T]he conversion of words, letters, numbers or combinations of words, letters and numbers, or other types of data, into electronic signals; the data is then collected, stored, sorted, analyzed, compared or computed."
Telex Corp. v. IBM Corp., 367 F. Supp. 258, 273 (N.D. Okla. 1973), *aff'd in part, rev'd in part,* 510 F.2d 894 (10th Cir.), *cert. dism.,* 423 U.S. 802 (1975).

electronic data processing industry *(business)*
"[A]n industry based upon a concept and system of reckoning (binary) as simple as turning on or off a switch; in which transmissions are timed in billionths of seconds (nano-seconds), storage capacity (memory), measured in millions of combinations of bits of information (megabytes); in which numerous problems involving logic or arithmetic functions are separately but simultaneously worked upon and instantly solved within a single system; in which in their own peculiar language machines communicate with one another (multiprocessing) and then in words understandable by humans may present printouts of results at the rate of as much as 2,000 lines per minute; in which devices facilitate maintenance by the detection and isolation of their own malfunctions or mistakes (diagnostic programs); upon which most other industries of the country and countless businesses, as well as science and space explorations, vitally depend; in which products and market developments seem almost kaleidoscopic when viewed from outside; which appears unique in monopoly context by reason of its youth and apparent dynamics, but which by the same token in this ultramodern setting may be unprecedented also because of increased inducements for, and vulnerability to, sophisticated submarket control on the one hand, and massive industrial espionage on the other."
Telex Corp. v. IBM Corp., 367 F. Supp. 258, 267 (N.D. Okla. 1973), *aff'd in part, rev'd in part,* 510 F.2d 894 (10th Cir.), *cert. dism.,* 423 U.S. 802 (1975).

electronic database *(copyright)*
See also database.

Related issues. "Section 201(c) does not permit the Publisher to license individually copyrighted works for inclusion in the electronic databases."
Tasini v. New York Times Co., 206 F.3d 161, 165 (2d Cir. 2000).

Electronic Espionage Act of 1996 *(criminal; trade secret)*
Abbreviated as "EEA."

Citation: 18 U.S.C. § 1831 et seq.

"The EEA became law in October 1996 against a backdrop of increasing threats to corporate security and a rising tide of international and domestic economic espionage. The end of the Cold War sent government spies scurrying to the private sector to perform illicit work for businesses and corporations,... and by 1996, studies revealed that nearly $24 billion of corporate intellectual property was being stolen each year.

"The Problem was augmented by the absence of any comprehensive federal remedy targeting the theft of trade secrets, compelling prosecutors to shoehorn economic espionage crimes into statutes direct at other offenses."
United States v. Hsu, 155 F.3d 189, 194 (3d Cir. 1998).

electronic form *(technology)*
[UNITED KINGDOM] "[I]n a form usable only by electronic means."
U.K. Copyright, Designs, and Patents Act 1988, c. 48.

Electronic Frontier Foundation *(organization)*
Abbreviated as "EFF." A national, nonpartisan organization advocating civil liberties in the online medium. Located at <http://www.eff.org>.

electronic mail *(Internet)*
Electronic transmission of messages or requests for information through a central communications network. The messages are received and sorted according to recipient.

Related issues. "Electronic mail systems may be available for public use or may be proprietary, such as systems operated by private companies for internal correspondence."
S. Rep. No. 99-541, at 8 (1986), *reprinted in* 1986 U.S.C.C.A.N. 3555, 3562.
See also **electronic message; e-mail; one-to-one messaging.**

electronic message *(contract)*
"[A] record or display that is stored, generated, or transmitted by electronic means for the purpose of communication to another person or electronic agent."
UCITA § 102(a)(28).
See also **electronic mail; e-mail; one-to-one messaging.**

Electronic Privacy Information Center *(organization)*
Abbreviated as "EPIC." This is a research organization advocating free speech and privacy rights in the online medium.

electronic publishing *(business)*
"[T]he provision of any information which a provider or publisher has, or has caused to be originated, authored, compiled, collected, or edited, or in which he has a direct or indirect financial or proprietary interest, and which is disseminated to an unaffiliated person through some electronic means."
> *United States v. American Tel. & Tel. Co.,* 552 F. Supp. 131, 181 (D.D.C. 1982), *aff'd sub nom. Maryland v. United States,* 460 U.S. 1001 (1983).

electronic purse *(electronic commerce)*
A microchip on which cash value is stored electronically and which can be used to purchase goods or services by the transfer of some or all of the cash value to another electronic purse.

electronic serial number *(telecommunications)*
"A coded serial number assigned by the manufacturer to the mobile unit."
> Office of Technology Assessment, *Electronic Surveillance in a Digital Age,* Glossary (July 1995).

See also **ESN.**

electronic signature *(electronic commerce)*
Data appended to a message or a transformation of a message that allows the recipient to verify the source and integrity of the message.

electronic storage *(hardware)*
"(A) any temporary, intermediate storage of a wire or electronic communication incidental to the electronic transmission thereof; and

(B) any storage of such communication by an electronic communication service for purposes of backup protection of such communication...."
> 18 U.S.C. § 2510(17).

"[U]nlike the definition of 'wire communication,' *the definition of 'electronic communication' does not include electronic storage of such communications.*"
> *Steve Jackson Games, Inc. v. United States Secret Serv.,* 36 F.3d 457, 461 (5th Cir. 1994) (emphasis in original).

electronic surveillance *(criminal)*

"The statutory-based process and the associated technical capability and activities of law enforcement agencies related to the interception and monitoring of electronic communications."

Office of Technology Assessment, *Electronic Surveillance in a Digital Age,* Glossary (July 1995).

electronically *(contract)*

See electronic.

e-mail *(Internet)*

Also written as "email."

"...enables an individual to send an electronic message—generally akin to a note or letter—to another individual or to a group of addressees. The message is generally stored electronically, sometimes waiting for the recipient to check her 'mailbox' and sometimes making its receipt known through some type of prompt."

Reno v. American Civil Liberties Union, 521 U.S. 844, 851 (1997).

"...allows computer network users to send messages to each other which are received at an 'electronic mailbox' identified by the recipient's unique user name and address."

CompuServe, Inc. v. Patterson, 89 F.3d 1257, 1261 n.5 (6th Cir. 1996); *United States v. Baker,* 890 F. Supp. 1375, 1379 n.1 (E.D. Mich. 1995).

Annotation. "One method of communication on the Internet is via electronic mail, or 'e-mail,' comparable in principle to sending a first class letter. One can address and transmit a message to one or more other people. E-mail on the Internet is not routed through a central control point, and can take many and varying paths to the recipients. Unlike postal mail, simple e-mail generally is not 'sealed' or secure, and can be accessed or viewed on intermediate computers between the sender and recipient (unless the message is encrypted)."

American Civil Liberties Union v. Reno, 929 F. Supp. 824, 834 (E.D. Pa. 1996), *aff'd, Reno v. American Civil Liberties Union,* 521 U.S. 844 (1997).

"E-mail is 'comparable in principle to sending a first-class letter.'... Both the sender and the recipient have 'an address (rather like a telephone number).'... Such an e-mail address represents a individual user's chosen identifying name at a particular computer system, for example, 'mailbox-name@host.com,'... with the 'host computer providing Internet services ("site") [having] a unique Internet address which is an alphanumeric "domain name" [registered with] the Internet Network Information Center ("Internic"), a collaborative project established by the National Science Foundation.'"

People v. Lipsitz, 663 N.Y.S.2d 468, 475 (Sup. Ct. N.Y. Cty. 1997).

"The term 'e-mail' commonly is used as a noun, verb, and adjective."

People v. Lipsitz, 663 N.Y.S.2d 468, 470 (Sup. Ct. N.Y. Cty. 1997).

"The analogy [to a letter] is not a perfect one, however, for two reasons. First, the sender directs his message to a logical rather than geographic address, and therefore need not know the location of his correspondent in real space. Second, most programs provide for a 'reply' option which enables the recipient to respond to the sender's message simply by clicking on a button; the recipient will therefore not even need to type in the sender's e-mail address. A further distinction concerns the level of security that protects a communication. While first-class letters are sealed, e-mail communications are more easily intercepted."

American Library Ass'n v. Pataki, 969 F. Supp. 160, 165 (S.D.N.Y. 1997).

"The Internet allows one-to-one communication via electronic mail ('e-mail')."

Lockheed Martin Corp. v. Network Solutions, Inc., 985 F. Supp. 949, 951 (C.D. Cal. Nov. 17, 1997).

"The BBS also offered customers the ability to send and receive private E-mail. Private E-mail was stored on the BBS computer's hard disk drive temporarily, until the addressees 'called' the BBS (using their computers and modems) and read their mail. After reading their E-mail, the recipients would choose to either store it on the BBS computer's hard drive or delete it."

Steve Jackson Games, Inc. v. United States Secret Serv., 36 F.3d 457, 458 (5th Cir. 1994).

Related issues. "[W]hen a sender transmits an e-mail message, the message is accompanied by the sender's address, which contains a 'user name' identifying a particular user and a 'domain name' assigned to a computer or set of computers."

Shea v. Reno, 930 F. Supp. 916, 933 (S.D.N.Y. 1996).

See also **electronic mail; electronic message; one-to-one messaging.**

e-mail address *(Internet)*

A string of characters, generally of the form "username@server.com," which specifies a unique source or destination of an electronic message.

Annotation. "An e-mail address provides no authoritative information about the addressee, who may use an e-mail 'alias' or an anonymous remailer. There is also no universal or reliable listing of e-mail addresses and corresponding names or telephone numbers, and any such listing would be incomplete or rapidly become so."

American Civil Liberties Union v. Reno, 929 F. Supp. 830, 845 (3d Cir. 1996), *aff'd, Reno v. American Civil Liberties Union,* 521 U.S. 844 (1997).

emoticon *(Internet)*

Also called a "smiley." Faces made out of keyboard characters to express the writer's emotions, e.g., smile :-), wink ;-), frown :-(.

employee sabotage *(criminal)*

Common examples of computer-related employee sabotage include:

Entering data incorrectly.
Changing data.
Deleting data.
Destroying data or programs with logic bombs.
"Crashing" systems.
Holding data hostage.
Destroying hardware or facilities.

Office of the Comptroller of the Currency, Infrastructure Threats from Cyber-Terrorists 3 (Mar. 19, 1999).

emulator *(software)*

"Object code often is directly executable by the computer into which it is entered. It sometimes contains instructions, however, that are readable only by computers containing a particular processor, such as a Pentium processor, or a specific operating system such as Microsoft Windows. In such instances, a computer lacking the specific processor or operating system can execute the object code only if it has an emulator program that simulates the necessary processor or operating system or if the code first is run through a translator program that converts it into object code readable by that computer."

Universal City Studios, Inc. v. Reimerdes, 111 F. Supp. 2d 294, 306 n.18 (S.D.N.Y. 2000) (footnotes omitted).

enablement *(patent)*

Annotation. "If the claimed subject matter is inoperable, the patent may indeed be invalid for failure to meet the utility requirement of §101 and the enablement requirement of §112."

Brooktree Corp. v. Advanced Micro Devices, Inc., 977 F.2d 1555, 1571 (Fed. Cir. 1992).

encapsulation *(Year 2000)*
A technique in which the current date is time-shifted backward 28 years during processing, and time shifted forward 28 years after processing. Twenty-eight years is used because every 28 years the days of the week match the dates.

encoding *(software)*
The process of creating a compressed or encrypted file.

encryption *(technology)*
"The process of systematically turning messages (information) into gibberish, as a security measure. The inverse process of decryption is needed for recovering the original messages."
U.S. Copyright Office, *Compendium of Copyright Office Practices* II, § 326 (1984).

". . . basically involves running a readable message known as 'plaintext' through a computer program that translates the message according to an equation or algorithm into unreadable 'ciphertext.' Decryption is the translation back to plaintext when the message is received by someone with an appropriate 'key.'"
Bernstein v. United States Dept. of State, 974 F. Supp. 1288, 1292 (N.D. Cal. 1997).

Annotation. "The applications of encryption, however, are not limited to ensuring secrecy; encryption can also be employed to ensure data integrity, authenticate users, and facilitate nonrepudiation (e.g., linking a specific message to a specific sender)."
Bernstein v. United States Dept. of Justice, 176 F.3d 1132, 1137 (9th Cir. 1999).

Related issues. "It is, of course, encryption's secrecy applications that concern the government. The interception and deciphering of foreign communications has long played an important part in our nation's national security efforts. In the words of a high-ranking State Department official:
"Policies concerning the export control of cryptographic products are based on the fact that the proliferation of such products will make it easier for foreign intelligence targets to deny the United States Government access to information vital to national security interests. Cryptographic products and software have military and intelligence applications. As demonstrated throughout history, encryption has been used to conceal foreign military communications, on the battlefield, aboard ships and submarines, or in other military settings. Encryption is also used to conceal

other foreign communications that have foreign policy and national security significance for the United States. For example, encryption can be used to conceal communications of terrorists, drug smugglers, or others intent on taking hostile action against U.S. facilities, personnel, or security interests."

Bernstein v. United States Dept. of Justice, 176 F.3d 1132, 1137 (9th Cir. 1999).

"As increasingly sophisticated and secure encryption methods are developed, the government's interest in halting or slowing the proliferation of such methods has grown keen."

Bernstein v. United States Dept. of Justice, 176 F.3d 1132, 1137 (9th Cir. 1999).

"[T]he government's efforts to regulate and control the spread of knowledge relating to encryption may implicate more than the First Amendment rights of cryptographers. In this increasingly electronic age, we are all required in our everyday lives to rely on modern technology to communicate with one another. This reliance on electronic communication, however, has brought with it a dramatic diminution in our ability to communicate privately. Cellular phones are subject to monitoring, email is easily intercepted, and transactions over the Internet are often less than secure. Something as commonplace as furnishing our credit card number, social security number, or bank account number puts each of us at risk. Moreover, when we employ electronic methods of communication, we often leave electronic 'fingerprints' behind, fingerprints that can be traced back to us. Whether we are surveilled by our government, by criminals, or by our neighbors, it is fair to say that never has our ability to shield our affairs from prying eyes been at such a low ebb. The availability and use of secure encryption may offer an opportunity to reclaim some portion of the privacy we have lost. Government efforts to control encryption thus may well implicate not only the First Amendment rights of cryptographers intent on pushing the boundaries of their science, but also the constitutional rights of each of us as potential recipients of encryption's bounty. Viewed from this perspective, the government's efforts to retard progress in cryptography may implicate the Fourth Amendment, as well as the right to speak anonymously, . . . While we leave for another day the resolution of these difficult issues, it is important to point out that Bernstein's is a suit not merely concerning a small group of scientists laboring in an esoteric field, but also touches on the public interest broadly defined."

Bernstein v. United States Dept. of Justice, 176 F.3d 1132, 1145-46 (9th Cir. 1999) (citations omitted).

"…means that Snuffle can be used for interactive communications because it encrypts and decrypts on a character-by-character basis—the users need not complete an entire message before encrypting and sending."
> *Bernstein v. United States Dept. of Justice*, 176 F.3d 1132, 1135-36 n.1 (9th Cir. 1999).

See also ciphertext; cryptography; key; plaintext.

encryption research *(copyright)*

"[A]ctivities necessary to identify and analyze flaws and vulnerabilities of encryption technologies applied to copyrighted works, if these activities are conducted to advance the state of knowledge in the field of encryption technology or to assist in the development of encryption products."
> 17 U.S.C. § 1201(g)(1)(A).

"In determining whether one is engaged in good faith encryption research, the Court is instructed to consider factors including whether the results of the putative encryption research are disseminated in a manner designed to advance the state of knowledge of encryption technology versus facilitation of copyright infringement, whether the person in question is engaged in legitimate study of or work in encryption, and whether the results of the research are communicated in a timely fashion to the copyright owner."
> *Universal City Studios, Inc. v. Reimerdes*, 111 F. Supp. 2d 294, 321 (S.D.N.Y. 2000) (footnotes omitted).

See also DMCA.

encryption software *(encryption; technology)*

A set of operating instructions to a computer that allows for the execution of an encryption function on a computer.

Annotation. "If encryption software falls within the ambit of the relevant EAR provisions, the 'export' of such software requires a prepublication license."
> *Bernstein v. United States Dept. of Justice*, 176 F.3d 1132, 1138 (9th Cir. 1999).

See also cryptography; encryption; encryption source code.

encryption source code *(encryption; technology)*

"A precise set of operating instructions to a computer, that when compiled, allows for the execution of an encryption function on a computer."
> 15 C.F.R., pt. 722.

Annotation. "Like much computer software, encryption source code is inherently functional; it is designed to enable a computer to do a designated task. Encryption source code does not merely explain a cryptographic theory or describe how the software functions. More than describing encryption, the software carries out the function of encryption. The software is essential to carry out the function of encryption. In doing this function, the encryption software is indistinguishable from dedicated computer hardware that does encryption.

"In the overwhelming majority of circumstances, encryption source code is exported to transfer functions, not to communicate ideas. In exporting functioning capability, encryption source code is like other encryption devices. For the broad majority of persons receiving such source code, the value comes from the function the source code does."

Junger v. Daley, 8 F. Supp. 3d 708, 716 (N.D. Ohio 1998).

See also **cryptography; encryption; encryption source code.**

encryption technology *(copyright)*

"[T]he scrambling and descrambling of information using mathematical formulas or algorithms."

17 U.S.C. § 1201(g)(1)(B).

end user *(business)*

"...any purchaser other than an OEM."

Data Gen. Marketing Practices, 1980-1 Trade Cas. (CCH) ¶ 63,045 at 77,198 n. 4 (1979).

"[T]he ultimate purchaser . . . ."

Universal Computers (Systems) Ltd. v. Datamedia Corp., 653 F. Supp. 518, 521 (D.N.J. 1987).

end-user interface *(technology)*

"In general, this is the information that the program's vendor provides to customers to install and use the program and to write programs that use the program's services which shall be clearly differentiated from other information about the program available from the vendor, and the information necessary to allow user-written programs that use only those interfaces to execute on a party's programs after compilation, assembly, pre-processing or link-editing by the other party's programs."

IBM Corp. v. Fujitsu Ltd., Copyright L. Rep. (CCH) ¶ 20,517 (Am. Arb. Ass'n 1988).

See also **look and feel; user interface.**

engine *(software)*

A software program that can be reused with different content, thereby avoiding the cost of creating new software for each interactive product.

enhanced graphics array *(hardware)*
Abbreviated as "EGA."

"IBM video standard."
> *Princeton Graphics Operating L.P. v. NEC Home Elecs. (U.S.A.), Inc.,* 732 F. Supp. 1258, 1259 n.3 (S.D.N.Y. 1990).

See also **EGA.**

enhancements
(copyright)
"The conversion of a program from one higher-level language to another to facilitate use would fall within this right, a would the right to add features to the program that were not present at the time of rightful acquisition."
> *CONTU Final Report* 13 (1978).

"[Cases] which apply § 117 in a narrow manner are against the weight of recent authority and contrary to the intent of Congress. A better view is that § 117 is designed to protect software purchasers who make modifications or enhancements to the software for their own use only."
> *Data Prods., Inc. v. Reppart,* No. 89-1291-K, 1990 U.S. Dist. LEXIS 16,330 (D. Kan. Nov. 28, 1990).

(software)
"Changes or refinements made to an existing computer program."
> U.S. Copyright Office, *Compendium of Copyright Office Practices* II, § 326 (1984).

"Software systems such as Model 204 are constantly evolving. The technical support staff continuously improves the system in consultation with the users of the product. Improvements in the system are termed 'enhancements.'
"Some enhancements simply add a new feature to the software, while others modify its basic capability. Although features can be optional with the buyer, most enhancements are marketed with the standard system."
> *Thomas Bradshaw Assocs., Inc. v. Computer Corp. of America,* 7 Computer L. Serv. Rep. 1103, 1104 (D.D.C. 1980).

"..., which is not defined anywhere in the contract and has no standard meaning in the industry, is ambiguous.... Enhancements here can only mean improvements made to...systems, not to include a separate marketable product."
> *Infosystems Tech., Inc. v. Logical Software, Inc.,* 1 Computer Cas. (CCH) ¶ 45,035, at 60,289 (4th Cir. 1987).

"[T]he court found that the parties intended the term 'enhancement to LOGIX' to refer only to improvements made to the product LOGIX *itself,* not to products that, like Softshell, could be used and marketed quite independently from LOGIX."

> *Infosystems Tech., Inc. v. Logical Software, Inc.,* 1 Computer Cas. (CCH) ¶ 45,035, at 60,289 (4th Cir. 1987) (emphasis in original).

enterprise resource planning *(software)*
Abbreviated as "ERP." An integrated system of applications combining logistics, production, distribution contract and order management, sales forecasting, and financial and human resources management.

entirety clause *(contract)*
See integration clause.

entrepreneur *(business)*
A person who is willing to take a risk in starting a new business in exchange for equity in the company.

EPROM *(hardware)*
"Anagram for 'Erasable Programmable Read Only Memory.'"

> *E.F. Johnson Co. v. Uniden Corp. of America.,* 623 F. Supp. 1485, 1488 (D. Minn. 1985). *See also United States v. Brady,* 820 F. Supp. 1346, 1356 n.20 (D. Utah 1993).

"A type of computer memory device for storing data within a computer; can be erased and reprogrammed."

> U.S. Copyright Office, *Compendium of Copyright Office Practices* II, § 326 (1984).

"...on which the stored information can be erased and the chip reprogrammed...."

> *Apple Computer, Inc. v. Franklin Computer Corp.,* 714 F.2d 1240, 1243 (3d Cir. 1983), *cert. dism.,* 464 U.S. 1033 (1984).

"A microchip on which data can be stored, and which may be erased and reprogrammed."

> *E.F. Johnson Co. v. Uniden Corp. of America,* 623 F. Supp. 1485, 1488 (D. Minn. 1985).

"(Erasable Programmable Read Only Memory) on which the stored information can be erased and the chip reprogrammed, but the district court found that for purposes of this proceeding, the difference between ROMs and EPROMs is inconsequential."

> *Apple Computer, Inc. v. Franklin Computer Corp.,* 714 F.2d 1240, 1243 (3d Cir. 1983), *rev'g,* 545 F. Supp. 812 (E.D. Pa. 1982), *cert. dism.,* 104 S. Ct. 890 (1984).

"[A] monolithic integrated circuit containing thousands of metal oxide semiconductor transistor cells on which encoded binary information can be stored. In addition to memory cells an EPROM has various other electronic elements that operate as sensing devices, operating circuits buffers, etc. EPROMs can be programmed, then erased by the application of ultraviolet radiation and reprogrammed, as the needs of the user dictate."
ITC Opinion re Certain EPROMs ¶ 60,030.

[CANADA] "An electronic chip that is programmable, the most important constituent of it being a piece of silicon which has a certain number of memory locations, that is, bits. This chip, when programmed, is then used by being plugged directly into the main board of a computer, incorporated into a cartridge of the type used with a video game unit, or in a piece of prototype hardware. It is a piece of industrial equipment roughly equivalent to an industrial video copying machine in the video industry. It is typically used by manufacturers of computers and computer programs and research and development organizations and software houses."
Elan Digital Sys. Ltd. v. Elan Computers Ltd. [1984], F.S.R. 373 (C.A.).

[CANADA] "Generic chips that anyone with a simple device, known as an EPROM burner, can program."
Apple Computer Inc. v. 115778 Can., Inc. (1988), 23 C.P.R. (3d) 22 (Fed. T.D.).

EPROM programmer *(technology)*
[CANADA] "A piece of equipment that enables the operator to set the bits of a EPROM on or off electrically so that the EPROM will contain a computer program in object code, that is, in its binary form."
Elan Digital Systems Ltd. v. Elan Computers Ltd. [1984], F.S.R. 373 (C.A.).

equipment *(hardware)*
"…includes all equipment used to deliver the service to the customer, including the main computer, the terminal lines, and the terminal."
Telerate Sys., Inc. v. Caro, 689 F. Supp. 221, 226 (S.D.N.Y. 1988).

ergonomic *(hardware)*
The design of machines specifically suited to the worker. For example, chairs can be ergonomically designed to afford workers the most comfort. Keyboards can be ergonomically designed to minimize strain, fatigue, and repetitive stress.

error message *(technology)*
A message displayed by hardware or software describing an error condition, or a command that instructs the system to carry out a previously defined action.

ESN *(hardware)*
Acronym for "Electronic Serial Number."

"[A] unique numerical code embedded in each cellular telephone by the manufacturer identifying that particular instrument."
United States v. Brady, 820 F. Supp. 1346, 1348 n.2 (D. Utah 1993).

essential *(copyright)*
". . . means indispensable and necessary."
Apple Computer, Inc. v. Formula Int'l, Inc., 594 F. Supp. 617, 622 (C.D. Cal. 1984).

etching *(manufacturing)*
A semiconductor manufacturing process in which acid is used to remove previously defined portions of the silicon oxide layer covering the wafer to expose the silicon underneath. Removing the oxide layer permits introducing desired impurities into the exposed silicon through diffusion or ion implantation or the deposition of aluminum paths for electrical interconnection of circuit elements.

Ethernet *(technology)*
A 10-Mbps network technology, which is currently the most popular technology for LANs.

Eudora *(Internet)*
The name of one company's e-mail reader software.

European Union *(organization)*
Abbreviated "EU." The European Union currently consists of 15 member states (The Netherlands, Belgium, France, Luxembourg, Germany, Italy, the U.K., Ireland, Denmark, Greece, Spain, Portugal, Austria, Finland, and Sweden). The EU is based upon the "Four Freedoms"—free movement of goods, persons, services, and capital. The goal is to create a closer integration among the member states. The EU began in 1951 with the execution of the Treaty of Paris establishing the European Coal and Steel Community. In 1957 the Treaty of Rome established the European Economic Community ("EEC") and the European Atomic Community. Various amendments to these treaties include the Single Europe Act, 1987, the Treaty on European Union, 1992 (the "Maastricht Treaty"), and the Treaty of Amsterdam, 1997.

event horizon *(Year 2000)*
The earliest point at which a company is impacted by the Year 2000 problem. For example, a mortgage lender writing a 25-year note would have

been impacted in 1975—the payment schedule would have spanned the Year 2000, which could have affected the amortization calculations.

exceeds authorized access *(criminal)*

"[T]o access a computer with authorization and to use such access to obtain or alter information in the computer that the accessor is not entitled so to obtain or alter; . . ."

18 U.S.C. § 1030(e)(6).

exclusive rights *(copyright)*

See copyright; exclusive rights.

expert *(electronic commerce)*

"[A] person with demonstrable skill and knowledge based on training and experience who would qualify as an expert pursuant to California Evidence Code § 720."

Cal. Code of Regs., tit. 2, div. 7, ch. 10, § 22003(b)(1)(C).

See also **expert opinion; expert witness.**

expert opinion *(copyright infringement)*

"Thus, in deciding the limits in which expert opinion may be employed in ascertaining the substantial similarity of computer programs, we cannot disregard the highly complicated and technical subject matter at the heart of these claims. Rather, we recognize the reality that computer programs are likely to be somewhat impenetrable by lay observers—whether they be judges or juries—and seem to fall outside the category of works contemplated by those who engineered the *Arnstein* test.

* * *

"In making its finding on substantial similarity with respect to computer programs, we believe that the trier of fact need not be limited by the strictures of its own lay perspective.

* * *

"[W]e leave it to the discretion of the district court to decide to what extent, if any, expert opinion, regarding the highly technical nature of computer programs, is warranted in a given case."

Computer Assocs. Int'l, Inc. v. Altai, Inc., 982 F.2d 693, 713 (2d Cir. 1992) (citations omitted).

See also **expert; expert opinion.**

expert witness *(litigation)*

"If scientific, technical, or other specialized knowledge will assist the trier of fact to understand the evidence or to determine a fact in issue, a witness qualified as an expert by knowledge, skill, experience, training, or education, may testify thereto in the form of an opinion or otherwise."

Fed. R. Evid. 702.

See also **expert; expert opinion.**

expired *(Internet)*

An article that has been deleted from a newsgroup and is no longer available.

export *(export)*

". . . even as applied to software generally, is defined quite broadly to include any release, including oral exchanges of information and visual inspections, in a foreign country or to a foreign national within the United States. 15 C.F.R. § 734.2(b)(2) & (3)."

Bernstein v. United States Dept. of Justice, 176 F.3d 1132, 1137 n.5 (9th Cir. 1999).

". . . includes: downloading or causing the downloading of, such software to locations (including electronic bulletin boards, Internet file transfer protocol, and World Wide Web sites) outside the U.S., or making such software available for transfer outside the United States, over wire, cable, radio, electromagnetic, photo-optical, photoelectric or other comparable communications facilities accessible to persons outside the United States, including transfers from electronic bulletin boards, Internet file transfer protocol and World Wide Web sites, unless the person making the software available takes precautions adequate to prevent unauthorized transfer of such code outside the United States."

Bernstein v. United States Dept. of Justice, 176 F.3d 1132, 1137-38 n.6 (9th Cir. 1999), *quoting* 15 C.F.R. § 734.2(b)(9)(B)(ii).

See also **EAR; export control.**

Export Administration Regulations *(export)*

Abbreviated as "EAR."

See **EAR.**

export control *(export)*

Annotation. "Policies concerning the export control of cryptographic products are based on the fact that the proliferation of such products will make it easier for foreign intelligence targets to deny the United States Government access to information vital to national security interests. Cryptographic products and software have military and intelligence applications. As demonstrated throughout history, encryption has been used to conceal foreign military communications, on the battlefield, aboard ships and submarines, or in other military settings. Encryption is also used to conceal other foreign communications that have foreign policy and national security significance for the United States. For example, encryption can be used to conceal communications of terrorists, drug smugglers, or others intent on taking hostile action against U.S. facilities, personnel, or security interests."

Bernstein v. United States Dept. of Justice, 176 F.3d 1132, 1137 (9th Cir. 1999).

"[T]he government's efforts to regulate and control the spread of knowledge relating to encryption may implicate more than the First Amendment rights of cryptographers. In this increasingly electronic age, we are all required in our everyday lives to rely on modern technology to communicate with one another. This reliance on electronic communication, however, has brought with it a dramatic diminution in our ability to communicate privately. Cellular phones are subject to monitoring, email is easily intercepted, and transactions over the Internet are often less than secure. Something as commonplace as furnishing our credit card number, social security number, or bank account number puts each of us at risk. Moreover, when we employ electronic methods of communication, we often leave electronic 'fingerprints' behind, fingerprints that can be traced back to us. Whether we are surveilled by our government, by criminals, or by our neighbors, it is fair to say that never has our ability to shield our affairs from prying eyes been at such a low ebb. The availability and use of secure encryption may offer an opportunity to reclaim some portion of the privacy we have lost. Government efforts to control encryption thus may well implicate not only the First Amendment rights of cryptographers intent on pushing the boundaries of their science, but also the constitutional rights of each of us as potential recipients of encryption's bounty. Viewed from this perspective, the government's efforts to retard progress in cryptography may implicate the Fourth Amendment, as well as the right to speak anonymously, ... While we leave for another day the resolution of these difficult issues, it is important to point out that Bernstein's is a suit not merely concerning a small group of scientists laboring in an esoteric field, but also touches on the public interest broadly defined."

Bernstein v. United States Dept. of Justice, 176 F.3d 1132, 1145-46 (9th Cir. 1999) (citations omitted).

"The EAR contain specific regulations to control the export of encryption software, expressly including computer source code. Encryption software is treated differently from other software in a number of significant ways. First, the term 'export' is specifically broadened with respect to encryption software to preclude the use of the internet and other global mediums if such publication would allow passive or active access by a foreign national within the United States or anyone outside the United States. Second, the regulations governing the export of nonencryption software provide for several exceptions that are not applicable to encryption software. In addition, although printed materials containing encryption source code are not subject to EAR regulation, the same materials made available on machine-readable media, such as floppy disk or CD-ROM, are covered. The government, moreover, has reserved the right to restrict source code in printed form that may be easily 'scanned,' thus creating some ambiguity as to whether printed publications are necessarily exempt from licensing."

> *Bernstein v. United States Dept. of Justice*, 176 F.3d 1132, 1137 (9th Cir. 1999) (citations omitted).

"In December 1996, President Clinton shifted licensing authority for non-military encryption commodities and technologies from the State Department to the Department of Commerce. The Department of Commerce then promulgated regulations under the EAR to govern the export of encryption technology, regulations administered by the Bureau of Export Administration ('BXA')."

> *Bernstein v. United States Dept. of Justice*, 176 F.3d 1132, 1136 (9th Cir. 1999) (citations omitted).

"[I]nsofar as the EAR regulations on encryption software were intended to slow the spread of secure encryption methods to foreign nations, the government is intentionally retarding the progress of the flourishing science of cryptography. To the extent the government's efforts are aimed at interdicting the flow of scientific ideas (whether expressed in source code or otherwise), as distinguished from encryption products, these efforts would appear to strike deep into the heartland of the First Amendment. In this regard, the EAR regulations are very different from content-neutral time, place and manner restrictions that may have an incidental effect on expression while aiming at secondary effects."

> *Bernstein v. United States Dept. of Justice*, 176 F.3d 1132, 1145 (9th Cir. 1999).

See also **EAR; export.**

export restrictions *(contract)*

Government laws and regulations that limit, and often prohibit, the exportation of certain technology considered by that government to have strategic value to its enemies.

Sample clause. "You agree that none of the Software or underlying information or technology may be downloaded or otherwise exported or reexported (i) into (or to a national or resident of) Cuba, Iraq, Libya, Yugoslavia, North Korea, Iran, Syria, or any other country to which the U.S. has embargoed goods; or (ii) to anyone on the U.S. Treasury Department's List of Specially Designated Nationals or the U.S. Commerce Department's Table of Denial Orders. You further represent and warrant that you are not located in, under the control of, or a national or resident of any such country or on any such list."

express warranty *(contract)*

"Any affirmation of fact or promise made by the seller to the buyer which relates to the goods and becomes part of the basis of the bargain...."

U.C.C. § 2-313(1)(a).

See also written warranty.

expression *(copyright)*

"It is a fundamental principle of copyright law that a copyright does not protect an idea, but only the expression of the idea."

Computer Assocs. Int'l, Inc. v. Altai, Inc., 982 F.2d 693, 703 (2d Cir. 1992), *citing Baker v. Selden,* 101 U.S. 99 (1879) & *Mazer v. Stein,* 347 U.S. 201, 217 (1954).

external information *(technology)*

"A term related to the interface information that is normally provided to customers so that they can use programming material."

IBM Corp. v. Fujitsu Ltd., Copyright L. Rep. (CCH) ¶ 20,517 (Am. Arb. Ass'n 1988).

externalities *(copyright).*

"...such as the memory constraints of the computer upon which the program will be run."

Computer Assocs. Int'l, Inc. v. Altai, Inc., 982 F.2d 693, 698 (2d Cir. 1992).

See also extrinsic considerations; scenes à faire doctrine.

extra element *(copyright preemption)*

"Section 301 thus preempts only those state law rights that 'may be abridged by an act which, in and of itself, would infringe one of the exclusive rights' provided by federal copyright law. But if any 'extra element' is 'required instead of or in addition to the acts of reproduction, performance, distribution or display, in order to constitute a state-created cause of action, then the right does not lie "within the general scope of copyright," and there is no preemption.'

"A state claim is not preempted if the 'extra element' changes the 'nature of the action so that it is *qualitatively* different from the copyright infringement claim.'"

Computer Assocs. Int'l, Inc. v. Altai, Inc., 982 F.2d 693, 716 (2d Cir. 1992) (emphasis in original; citations omitted).

Related issues. "Following this 'extra element' test, we have held that unfair competition and misappropriation claims grounded solely in the copying of a plaintiff's protected expression are preempted by section 301. We also have held to be preempted a tortious interference with contract claims grounded in the impairment of a plaintiff's right under the Copyright Act to publish derivative works.

"However, many state law rights that can arise in connection with instances of copyright infringement satisfy the extra element test, and thus are not preempted by section 301. These include unfair competition claims based upon breaches of fiduciary duties and trade secrets."

Computer Assocs. Int'l, Inc. v. Altai, Inc., 982 F.2d 693, 717 (2d Cir. 1992) (citations omitted).

See also **preemption.**

extranet *(technology)*

A system based upon Internet protocols that allows users outside of an organization to access some parts of an organization's network via the Internet.

Annotation. Extranets are private networks designed to serve more that one enterprise; such as a network serving an organization and its customers. An extranet may also include features such as e-mail, web sites, and FTP file transfers. Unlike an intranet, an extranet may be reached from the Internet. Access to an extranet from the Internet, however, is usually limited by use of passwords or other security devices, such as "tunneling" a secure path across the Internet using point-to-point tunneling protocol ("PPTP"). An extranet with a high degree of security is sometimes referred to as a virtual private network, because it is nearly private, notwithstanding its use of a public network such as the Internet. (jrb)

See also **intranet.**

extrinsic considerations *(copyright)*

"Professor Nimmer points out that 'in many instances it is virtually impossible to write a program to perform particular functions without employing standard techniques.' This is a result of the fact that a programmer's freedom of design choice is often circumscribed by extrinsic considerations

such as (1) the mechanical specifications of the computer on which a particular program is intended to run; (2) compatibility requirements of other
programs with which a program is designed to operate in conjunction;
(3) computer manufacturers' design standards; (4) demands of the industry
being serviced; and (5) widely accepted programming practices within the
computer industry."

> *Computer Assocs. Int'l, Inc. v. Altai, Inc.*, 982 F.2d 693, 709-10 (2d Cir. 1992)
> (citations omitted).

See also **externalities; scenes à faire doctrine.**

facilities management *(business)*
"Facilities management companies, or system engineering consultants, . . . provide the customer with systems engineering and design services as well as services for the actual operation of the end-user's computer facilities."
Telex Corp. v. IBM Corp., 367 F. Supp. 258, 273 (N.D. Okla. 1973), *aff'd in part, rev'd in part,* 510 F.2d 894 (10th Cir.), *cert. dism.,* 423 U.S. 802 (1975).

facsimile machine *(technology)*
"In general, . . . devices that transmit and receive printed or pictorial matter on documents from one location to another, typically over telephone lines."
Secure Servs. Technology, Inc. v. Time & Space Processing, Inc., 722 F. Supp. 1354, 1356 (E.D. Va. 1989).

Annotation. "The facsimile devices . . . transmit the material by scanning input documents and producing a series of digital pulses electrically related to the scanned printed or pictorial images. The digital pulses are sent via wire to a receiving machine which, when synchronized with the sending machine, is able to reproduce the transmitted document."
Secure Servs. Technology, Inc. v. Time & Space Processing, Inc., 722 F. Supp. 1354, 1356 (E.D. Va. 1989).

fact/expression dichotomy *(copyright)*
"The 'fact/expression dichotomy' is a bedrock principle of copyright law that 'limits severely the scope of protection in fact-based works.' *Feist Publications, Inc. v. Rural Tel. Service Co.,* 499 U.S. 340, 350 (1991). '"No author may copyright facts or ideas. The copyright is limited to those aspects of the work—termed 'expression'—that display the stamp of the author's originality."' *Id. (quoting Harper & Row, Inc. v. Nation Enter.,* 471 U.S. 539, 547-48 (1985))."
National Basketball Ass'n v. Motorola, Inc., 105 F.3d 841, 847 (2d Cir. 1997).
See **idea/expression dichotomy.**

facts *(copyright)*

"That copyright does not extend to facts is a 'most fundamental axiom of copyright law.' *Feist Publications, Inc. v. Rural Tel. Serv. Co.*, 499 U.S. 340, 344 (1991). The reason for this rule is that the law of copyright is founded on originality of expression — facts, by their nature, are never original to an author."

> *Nihon Keizai Shimbun, Inc. v. Comline Business Data, Inc.*, 166 F.3d 65, 70 (2d Cir. 1999).

failure of essential purposes *(contract)*

"Where circumstances cause an exclusive or limited remedy to fail of its essential purpose, remedy may be had as provided by [Article 2 of the Uniform Commercial Code]."

> U.C.C § 2-719(2) (1979).

"In other words, when unexpected circumstances presently prevent the agreed remedy from yielding its purported and expected relief[,] then the remedy has failed of its essential purpose."

> *Ritchie Enters. v. Honeywell Bull, Inc.*, 730 F. Supp. 1041, 1048 (D. Kan. 1990).

Annotation. "The limited remedy of repair and a consequential damage exclusion are two distinct ways of attempting to limit recovery for breach of warranty. . . . The Code, moreover, tests each by a different standard. The former survives unless it fails of its essential purpose, while the latter is valid unless it is unconscionable. We therefore see no reason to hold, as a general proposition, that the failure of the limited remedy provided in the contract, without more, invalidates a wholly distinct term in the agreement excluding consequential damages. The two are not mutually exclusive."

> *Chatlos Sys., Inc. v. National Cash Register Co.*, 635 F.2d 1081, 1086 (3d Cir. 1980), *cert. dism.*, 457 U.S. 1112 (1982) (citations and footnote omitted).

"[A] seller who fails to comply with its obligations under the warranty, such as its repair or replacement duties, cannot receive the benefit of the other provisions, which in part at least were premised on the assumption that the seller would fulfill its obligations. The failure of the limited remedy in this case would materially alter the balance of risk set by the parties in the agreement. In such situations we conclude that the other limitations and exclusions on the seller's warranties and liability must also be disregarded and that the general provisions of the U.C.C. should govern the rights of the parties."

> *Clark v. International Harvester Co.*, 99 Idaho 326, 343, 581 P.2d 784, 801-02 (1978).

"Under certain circumstances, when a contract, including its damage limitation provision, entirely fails of its essential purpose and the product in question cannot be remedied through the means provided in the contract, the Court will disregard the contract, thereby allowing traditional damages."

Invacare Corp. v. Sperry Rand Corp., 612 F. Supp. 448, 454 (N.D. Ohio. 1984).

Sample clause. "[Seller] warrants that this product is free of defects in materials and workmanship for one year from the date of sale. [Buyer]'s sole and exclusive remedy for breach of this agreement is the repair or replacement of defective parts. If [Seller] is unable to repair the product after a reasonable number of attempts, [Seller] will provide either a refund of the monies paid under this Agreement or a replacement unit, at [Seller's] option. [Seller] shall not in any case be liable for special, incidental, consequential or exemplary damages arising from breach of warranty, breach of contract, negligence, or any other legal theory."

fair use *(copyright)*

"Notwithstanding the provisions of sections 106 and 106A, the fair use of a copyrighted work, including such use by reproduction in copies or phonocopies or by any other means specified in that section, for purposes such as criticism, comment, news reporting, teaching . . . scholarship, or research is not an infringement of copyright. In determining whether the use made of a work in any particular case is a fair use the factors to be considered shall include—

(1) the purpose and character of the use;

(2) the nature of the copyrighted work;

(3) the amount and substantiality of the portion used in relation to the copyrighted work as a whole; and

(4) the effect of the use upon the potential market for or the value of the copyrighted work."

U.S. Copyright Act, 17 U.S.C. § 107.

"Stated in its most general terms, the doctrine, now codified in Section 107 of the Copyright Act, limits the exclusive rights of a copyright holder by permitting others to make limited use of portions of the copyrighted work, for appropriate purposes, free of liability for copyright infringement. For example, it is permissible for one other than the copyright owner to reprint or quote a suitable part of a copyrighted book or article in certain circumstances. The doctrine traditionally has facilitated literary and artistic criticism, teaching and scholarship, and other socially useful forms of expression. It has been viewed by courts as a safety valve that accommodates the exclusive rights conferred by copyright with the freedom of expression guaranteed by the First Amendment."

Universal City Studios, Inc. v. Reimerdes, 111 F. Supp. 2d 294, 321-22 (S.D.N.Y. 2000) (footnotes omitted).

(mask work)
"Notwithstanding the provisions of section 905, it is not an infringement of the exclusive rights of the owner of a mask work for—

(1) a person to reproduce the mask work solely for the purpose of teaching, analyzing, or evaluating the concepts or techniques embodied in the mask work or the circuitry, logic flow, or organization of components used in the mask work; or

(2) a person who performs the analysis or evaluation described in paragraph (1) to incorporate the results of such conduct in an original mask work which is made to be distributed."

17 U.S.C. § 906(a).

***Annotation** (copyright).* "These statutory factors are not exclusive. Rather, the doctrine of fair use is in essence an equitable rule of reason."

DSC Comm. Corp. v. DGI Technologies, Inc., 898 F. Supp. 1183, 1188 (N.D. Tex. 1995); *Sega Enters. Ltd. v. Accolade, Inc.,* 977 F.2d 1510, 1521 (9th Cir. 1992).

"Fair use is an 'equitable rule of reason,' allowing courts to find certain uses noninfringing where such uses benefit the public and further the overall purpose of the Copyright Act. The rationale for the fair use doctrine is that, when the free flow of information is sufficiently vital, it should override the copyright holder's interest in the exclusive control of the work."

Advanced Computer Servs., Inc. v. MAI Sys. Corp., 845 F. Supp. 356, 364 (E.D. Va. 1994) (citations omitted).

"The legislative history of section 107 suggests that courts should adapt the fair use exception to accommodate new technological innovations."

Atari Games Corp. v. Nintendo of America, Inc., 975 F.2d 832, 843 (Fed. Cir. 1992).

"Analyzing the affirmative defense of fair use is not to be simplified with bright-line rules. The statute, like the doctrine it recognizes, calls for a case-by-case analysis. In conducting this case-by-case analysis, the Court may not treat the four factors in isolation. Instead, all of the factors are to be explored, and the results weighted together, in light of the purposes of the Copyright Act."

> *DSC Comm. Corp. v. DGI Technologies, Inc.,* 898 F. Supp. 1183, 1189 (N.D. Tex. 1995).

"[T]he fact that an entire work was copied does not preclude a finding of fair use."

> *DSC Comm. Corp. v. DGI Technologies, Inc.,* 898 F. Supp. 1183, 1191 (N.D. Tex. 1995).

"When the nature of a work requires intermediate copying to understand the ideas and processes in a copyrighted work, that nature supports a fair use for intermediate copying."

> *Atari Games Corp. v. Nintendo of America, Inc.,* 975 F.2d 832, 843 (Fed. Cir. 1992).

"The fourth factor is the 'most important, and indeed, central fair use factor.'"

> *Lewis Galoob Toys, Inc. v. Nintendo of America, Inc.,* 964 F.2d 965, 971 (9th Cir. 1992).

"Whether a use of copyrighted materials is a 'fair use' is a mixed question of law and fact."

> *Lewis Galoob Toys, Inc. v. Nintendo of America, Inc.,* 964 F.2d 965, 969 (9th Cir. 1992).

"Fair use is an affirmative defense."

> *Campbell v. Acuff-Rose Music, Inc.,* 510 U.S. 569, 590 (1994).

"Although the traditional approach is to view 'fair use' as an affirmative defense, this writer, speaking only for himself, is of the opinion that it is better viewed as a right granted by the Copyright Act of 1976. Originally, as a judicial doctrine without any statutory basis, fair use was an infringement that was excused—this is presumably why it was treated as a defense. As a statutory doctrine, however, fair use is not an infringement. Thus, since the passage of the 1976 Act, fair use should no longer be considered an infringement to be excused; instead, it is logical to view fair use as a right."

> *Bateman v. Mnemonic, Inc.,* 79 F.3d 1532, 1542 n.22 (11th Cir. 1995).

"Regardless of how fair use is viewed, it is clear that the burden of providing fair use is always on the putative infringer."

> *Bateman v. Mnemonic, Inc.,* 79 F.3d 1532, 1542 n.22 (11th Cir. 1995).

"The doctrine of fair use allows a holder of the privilege to use copyrighted material in a reasonable manner without the consent of the copyright owner."

Lewis Galoob Toys, Inc. v. Nintendo of America, Inc., 964 F.2d 965, 969 (9th Cir. 1992).

"[T]he mere fact that all of a work is copied is not determinative of the fair use question, where such total copying is essential given the purpose to the copying."
Religious Technology Ctr. v. Netcom On-line Com. Servs., Inc., 907 F. Supp. 1361, 1380 (N.D. Cal. 1995).

"Technological access control measures have the capacity to prevent fair uses of copyrighted works as well as foul. Hence, there is a potential tension between the use of such access control measures and fair use. Defendants are not the first to recognize that possibility. As the DMCA made its way through the legislative process, Congress was preoccupied with precisely this issue. Proponents of strong restrictions on circumvention of access control measures argued that they were essential if copyright holders were to make their works available in digital form because digital works otherwise could be pirated too easily. Opponents contended that strong anticircumvention measures would extend the copyright monopoly inappropriately and prevent many fair uses of copyrighted material.

"Congress struck a balance. The compromise it reached, depending upon future technological and commercial developments, may or may not prove ideal. But the solution it enacted is clear. The potential tension to which defendants point does not absolve them of liability under the statute."
Universal City Studios, Inc. v. Reimerdes, 111 F. Supp. 2d 294, 304 (S.D.N.Y. 2000) (footnote omitted).

"Any alleged positive impact of defendant's activities on plaintiff's prior market in no way frees defendant to usurp a further market that directly derives from reproduction of the plaintiffs' copyrighted works. This would be so even if the copyrightholder had not yet entered the new market in issue, for a copyrightholder's 'exclusive' rights . . . include the right, within broad limits, to curb the development of such a derivative market by refusing to license a copyrighted work or by doing so only on terms the copyright owner finds acceptable."
UMG Recordings, Inc. v. MP3.com, Inc., 92 F. Supp. 2d 349, 350 (S.D.N.Y. 2000) (citations omitted).

(trademark)
"[T]he Lanham Act provides that 'the use of the name, term or device charged to be an infringement in a use, otherwise than as a mark . . . of a term or device which is descriptive of and used fairly and in good faith only to describe the goods or services of such party, or their geographic origin' is

fair use of the name, term, or device and cannot constitute infringement. 15 U.S.C. §1115(b)(4)."

> *Washington Speakers Bureau, Inc. v. Leading Authorities, Inc.,* 33 F. Supp. 2d 488, 501 (E.D. Va. 1999).

Related issues (copyright). "With regard to the ideas, procedures, processes, systems, methods of operation or concepts which may be embodied in a computer program, the fact that these unprotected items are usually found in object code precludes examining the unprotected portions of the program. . . . [T]he only means of gaining access to the unprotected aspects of [plaintiff's] firmware was through the program's disassembly. [Defendant] has a legitimate interest in gaining access to the unprotected aspects of the firmware in order to create a compatible . . . microprocessor with which it could compete with [plaintiff]. . . . [T]his Court holds that when good reason exists for studying or examining the unprotected aspects of a copyrighted program, disassembly for the purpose of study or examination of the disassembled program constitutes fair use."

> *DSC Comm. Corp. v. DGI Technologies, Inc.,* 898 F. Supp. 1183, 1189 (N.D. Tex. 1995).

"[A]lthough there has been some uncertainty as to whether reverse engineering constitutes copyright infringement, the one federal circuit court that has squarely addressed the issue has concluded that reverse engineering may be a fair use. *See Sega Enters. Ltd. v. Accolade, Inc.,* 977 F.2d 1510, 1527-28 (9th Cir. 1992) (holding that 'where disassembly is the only way to gain access to the ideas and functional elements embodied in a copyrighted computer program and where there is a legitimate reason for seeking such access, disassembly is a fair use of the copyrighted work, as a matter of law'). Another federal circuit court has addressed the issue, although its highly unusual factual posture seems to limit its precedential value. *See Atari Games Corp. v. Nintendo of America, Inc.,* 975 F.2d 832, 843 (Fed. Cir. 1992) (concluding that 'reverse engineering object code to discern the unprotectable ideas in a computer program is a fair use,' although denying the defendant's fair use claim, based on the fact that it was wrongfully in possession of the source code)."

> *Bateman v. Mnemonics, Inc.,* 79 F.3d 1532, 1539-40 n.18 (11th Cir. 1995).

"As to [defendant's] assertion that its copying of the software constitutes fair use under 17 U.S.C. § 107, the Court again considers the manner in which the [defendant] obtained the operating system software is relevant."

> *DSC Comm. Corp. v. DGI Technologies, Inc.,* 898 F. Supp. 1183, 1193 (N.D. Tex. 1995).

"To invoke the fair use exception, an individual must possess an authorized copy of a literary work."

  Atari Games Corp. v. Nintendo of America, 975 F.2d 832, 843 (Fed. Cir. 1992).

"Principles of fair use would be applicable in limited instances to excuse an unauthorized input of a work into computer memory. Exemplifying such fair uses could be the creation of a copy in a computer memory to prepare a concordance of a work or to perform a syntactical analysis of a work, which but for the use of a computer would require a prohibitive amount of human time and effort. To satisfy the criteria of fair use, any copies created for such research purposes should be destroyed upon completion of the research project for which they were created. Should the individual or institution carrying on this research desire to retain the copy for archival purposes or future use, it should be required to obtain permission to do so from the copyright proprietor."

  CONTU Final Report 40 (1978).

"The example of a copyrighted work placed in a computer memory solely to facilitate an individual's scholarly research has been cited as a possible fair use. The Commission agrees that such a use, restricted to individual research, should be considered fair. To prevent abuse of fair use principles, any copy created in a machine memory should be erased after completion of a particular research project for which it was made."

  CONTU Final Report 40 n.166 (1978).

"[T]he issue of how much is enough to constitute a copyright violation would likely entail analysis on a case-by-case basis with consideration of fair use bearing on whether the unauthorized copying of a limited portion of a data base would be held noninfringing. Fair use should have very limited force when an unauthorized copy of a data base is made for primarily commercial use."

  CONTU Final Report 42 (1978).

"[W]here disassembly is the only way to gain access to the ideas and functional elements embodied in a copyrighted computer program and where there is a legitimate reason for seeking such access, disassembly is a fair use of the copyrighted work, as a matter of law."

  Sega Enters. Ltd. v. Accolade, Inc., 977 F.2d 1510, 1527-28 (9th Cir. 1992).

See also **transformative use.**

false designation of origin *(trademark)*

"Any person who, on or in connection with any goods or services, or any container for goods, uses in commerce any word, term, name, symbol, or device, or any combination thereof, or any false designation of origin, false or misleading description of fact, or false or misleading representation of fact, which

(A) is likely to cause confusion, or to cause mistakes, or to deceive as to the origin, sponsorship, or approval of his or her goods, services, or commercial activities by another person, or

(B) in commercial advertising or promotion, misrepresents the nature, character, qualities, or geographic origin of his or her or another person's goods, services, or commercial activities, shall be liable in a civil action by any person who believes that he or she is or is likely to be damaged by such act."

15 U.S.C. § 1125(a)(1)(A).

Annotation. "The Lanham Act has been held to protect the 'trade dress,' of the total image of a product, to the same extent as an unregistered trademark.

"Section 43(a) protection depends on nonfunctionality because, otherwise, the protection would grant a perpetual monopoly."

Interactive Networks, Inc. v. NTN Comm., Inc., 875 F. Supp. 1398, 1406 (N.D. Cal. 1995).

"[U]nder the Lanham Act, false designation of origin does not have a scienter requirement."

America Online, Inc. v. IMS, 24 F. Supp. 2d 548, 551 (E.D. Va. 1998).

See also **trademark infringement.**

famous mark *(trademark)*

"The FTDA provides a nonexclusive list of eight factors courts must consider in determining whether a mark is 'distinctive and famous':

"(A) the degree of inherent or acquired distinctiveness of the mark; (B) the duration and extent of use of the mark in connection with the goods or services with which the mark is used; (C) the duration and extent of advertising and publicity of the mark; (D) the geographical extent of the trading area in which the mark is used; (E) the channels of trade for the goods or services with which the mark is used; (F) the degree of recognition of the mark in the trading areas and channels of trade used by the mark's owner and the person against whom the injunction is sought; (G) the nature and extent of use of the same or similar marks by third parties; and (H) whether the mark was registered under the Act of March 3, 1881, or the Act of February 20, 1905, or on the principal register."

Washington Speakers Bureau, Inc. v. Leading Authorities, Inc., 33 F. Supp. 2d 488, 502-03 (E.D. Va. 1999), *citing* 15 U.S.C. § 1125(c)(1).

fanciful mark(s) *(trademark)*

". . . are made-up words which serve as a product's brand name. Fanciful marks are inherently distinctive, thus receiving the greatest protection against infringement."

> *America Online, Inc. v. AT&T Corp.,* 64 F. Supp. 2d 549, 560 (E.D. Va. 1999) (citation omitted).

". . . are usually coined words expressly designed to serve as a trademark, such as 'Kodak' or 'Exxon'."

> *Washington Speakers Bureau, Inc. v. Leading Authorities, Inc.,* 33 F. Supp. 2d 488, 493 (E.D. Va. 1999).

". . . have no intrinsic connection to the product with which the mark is used; . . . are wholly made-up terms."

> *Brookfield Comm., Inc. v. West Coast Entertainment Corp.,* 174 F.3d 1036, 1058 n.19 (9th Cir. 1999).

See also **arbitrary mark(s).**

FAQs *(general)*

Acronym for "Frequently Asked Questions," and pronounced "facks." Answers to commonly asked questions on many topics on the Internet. Most newsgroups on the Usenet include FAQs to quickly bring new users up to speed and to avoid the frequent reposting of common questions. FAQs are also used on web sites. (jrb)

fault-tolerant computers *(technology)*

"Computers that are able to continue functioning even when a part of the system breaks down. Often associated with the term 'continuous processing' computers."

> *Stratus Computers, Inc. v. NCR Corp.,* 2 U.S.P.Q.2d (BNA) 1375, 1375 (D. Mass. 1987).

See also **continuous processing; fault-tolerant processing.**

fault-tolerant processing *(technology)*

"[S]maller computers are used essentially in parallel to ensure continuous processing capability. . . ."

> *Allen-Myland, Inc. v. IBM Corp.,* 693 F. Supp. 262, 275 (E.D. Pa. 1998).

See also **continuous processing; fault-tolerant computers.**

FCC *(telecommunications)*

Acronym for "Federal Communications Commission." *See* **Federal Communications Commission.**

FCS *(business)*

Acronym for "First Customer Shipment." The first date on which a title is actually shipped to a customer.

Annotation. The FCS date is important in various types of license agreements, since that date is often used to calculate dates on which royalty payments and sales reports are due. It may also be the starting date for the term of the license.

FDDI *(hardware; telecommunications)*

Acronym for "Fiber Distributed Data Interface." A standard for fiber-optic-based digital communications.

features *(software)*

"Particular capabilities or functions of a given computer program."

> U.S. Copyright Office, *Compendium of Copyright Office Practices* II, § 326 (1984).

Federal Arbitration Act *(government)*

A federal law that sets forth the procedures for and enforceability of arbitration provisions contained in contracts.

> *Citation:* 9 U.S.C. § 2.

". . . [C]onstitutes a congressional declaration of a liberal federal policy favoring arbitration agreements and preempts state arbitration law for contracts involving interstate commerce."

> *Yale Materials Handling Corp. v. White Storage & Retrieval Sys., Inc.,* 240 N.J. Super. 370, 376, 573 A.2d 484, 487 (1990), *citing Southland Corp. v. Keating,* 465 U.S. 1, 10-16 (1984).

Federal Communications Commission *(government; organization)*

Abbreviated as "FCC." An independent U.S. government agency established to encourage competition in all communications markets and to protect the public interest. Located at <www.ftc.gov>.

federal preemption *(copyright)*

See preemption.

Federal Trademark Dilution Act *(trademark)*

> *Citation:* 15 U.S.C. § 1125(c).

"The owner of a famous mark shall be entitled . . . to an injunction against another person's commercial use in commerce of a mark or trade name, if such use begins after the mark has become famous and causes dilution of the distinctive quality of the mark. . . ."

15 U.S.C. § 1125(c).

"In order to prove a violation of the Federal Trademark Dilution Act, a plaintiff must show that (1) the mark is famous; (2) the defendant is making a commercial use of the mark in commerce; (3) the defendant's use began after the mark became famous; and (4) the defendant's use of the mark dilutes the quality of the mark by diminishing the capacity of the mark to identify and distinguish goods and services. 15 U.S.C. § 1125(c)."

Panavision Int'l, L.P. v. Toeppen, 141 F.3d 1316, 1324 (9th Cir. 1998).

"Trademark dilution laws protect 'famous' marks from certain unauthorized uses regardless of a showing of competition, relatedness or likelihood of confusion. The federal dilution statute entitles the owner of a famous mark to enjoin 'another person's commercial use in commerce of a mark or trade name, if such use begins after the mark has become famous and causes dilution of the distinctive quality of the mark. . . .' 15 U.S.C. § 1125(c)(1). Dilution is defined as 'the lessening of the capacity of a famous mark to identify and distinguish goods or services, regardless of the presence or absence of— (1) competition between the owner of the famous mark and other parties, or (2) likelihood of confusion, mistake or deception.' 15 U.S.C. § 1127. The Federal Trademark Dilution Act specifically excludes non-commercial use of a mark from its coverage. 15 U.S.C. § 1125(c)(4)(B)."

Lockheed Martin Corp. v. Network Solutions, Inc., 985 F. Supp. 949, 959 (C.D. Cal. 1997).

Related issues. "Registration of a trade[mark] as a domain name, without more, is not a commercial use of the trademark and therefore is not within the prohibitions of the Act."

Panavision Int'l, L.P. v. Toeppen, 945 F. Supp. 1296, 1303 (C.D. Cal. 1996), *aff'd on other grounds,* 141 F.3d 1316 (9th Cir. 1998).

"Toeppen's intention to arbitrage the 'intermatic.com' domain name constitute[d] a commercial use."

Intermatic, Inc. v. Toeppen, 947 F. Supp. 1227, 1239 (N.D. Ill. 1996).

Feist *(copyright)*

Citation: *Feist Publications, Inc. v. Rural Telephone Service, Inc.,* 499 U.S. 340 (1991).

"[T]he seminal Supreme Court decision on copyrights in compilations. In *Feist,* the publisher of a telephone book claimed that a competitor had infringed its compilation copyright by copying some of its white pages listings. The Court clarified the scope of a copyright in compilations: 'A factual compilation is eligible for copyright if it features an original selection or arrangement of facts, but the copyright is limited to the particular selection or arrangement. In no event may copyright extend to the facts themselves.' Because of this limitation on protectability, 'the copyright in a factual compilation is thin. Notwithstanding a valid copyright, a subsequent compiler remains free to use the facts contained in another's publication to aid in preparing a competing work, so long as the competing work does not feature the same selection and arrangement.' The Court expressly rejected the 'sweat of the brow' doctrine, which had justified the extension of copyright protection to the facts and other non-original elements of compilations on the basis of the labor invested in obtaining and organizing the information."

> *Matthew Bender & Co. v. West Publ'g Co.*, 158 F.3d 693, 698-99 (2d Cir. 1998), *cert. denied*, 522 U.S. 3732 (1999).

Annotation. "While the *Feist* decision deals primarily with the copyrightability of purely factual compilations, its underlying tenets apply to much of the work involved in computer programming. *Feist* put to rest the 'sweat of the brow' doctrine in copyright law. The rationale of that doctrine 'was that copyright was a reward for the hard work that went into compiling facts.' The Court flatly rejected this justification for extending copyright protection, noting that it 'eschews the most fundamental axiom of copyright law—that no one may copyright facts or ideas.'

"*Feist* teaches that substantial effort alone cannot confer copyright status on an otherwise uncopyrightable work. As we have discussed, despite the fact that significant labor and expense often goes into computer program flow-charting and debugging, that process does not always result in inherently protectable expression."

> *Computer Assocs. Int'l, Inc. v. Altai, Inc.*, 982 F.2d 693, 711 (2d Cir. 1992) (citations omitted).

See also **sweat of the brow doctrine.**

fidonet *(Internet)*

A worldwide network of computer systems that allows the exchange of electronic mail and files via modem using a proprietary communications protocol.

Annotation. "At the same time that ARPANET was maturing (it subsequently ceased to exist), similar networks developed to link universities, research facilities, businesses, and individuals around the world. These other formal or loose networks included BITNET, CSNET, FIDONET, and USENET. Eventually, each of these networks (many of which overlapped) were themselves linked together, allowing users of any computers linked to any one of the networks to transmit communications to users of computers on

other networks. It is this series of linked networks (themselves linking computers and computer networks) that is today commonly known as the Internet."
American Civil Liberties Union v. Reno, 929 F. Supp. 824, 832 (E.D. Pa. 1996), *aff'd, Reno v. American Civil Liberties Union,* 521 U.S. 844 (1997).

field(s) *(technology)*
"[S]pecific locations within files for storing individual pieces of information."
CMAX/Cleveland, Inc. v. UCR, Inc., 804 F. Supp. 337, 342 n.1 (M.D. Ga. 1992).

"A specific area within a record for storing particular information concerning the subject."
Dickerman Assocs., Inc. v. Tiverton Bottled Gas Co., 594 F. Supp. 30, 34 n.2 (D. Mass. 1984).

file *(technology)*
"[D]esignated areas for storing information on a computer system."
CMAX/Cleveland, Inc. v. UCR, Inc., 804 F. Supp. 337, 344 n.3 (M.D. Ga. 1992).

"[T]he physical area on a magnetic disc where information is stored."
Dickerman Assocs., Inc. v. Tiverton Bottled Gas Co., 594 F. Supp. 30, 34 n.2 (D. Mass. 1984).

"[A] storage place for data . . . it's like a manila folder that contains all the data on a particular subject category in a computer."
Whelan Assocs., Inc. v. Jaslow Dental Lab., Inc., 797 F.2d 1222, 1242 (3d Cir. 1986), *cert. denied,* 107 S. Ct. 877 (1987).

Annotation. "There are no standards for determining which files are needed to accomplish a particular task. The determination of how to store data in files is a crucial element in the design process of a computer software system. This layout or blueprint for data storage is the foundation upon which a computer system is built, and is the result of a creative thought process."
CMAX/Cleveland, Inc. v. UCR, Inc., 804 F. Supp. 337, 344 n.3 (M.D. Ga. 1992).

file access permission *(technology)*
Permission to read, write, execute, or delete a file. File access permissions determine the type of access a user has to a file.

file system *(software)*
Refers to the organization or hierarchies of directories and rules. *See also* directory; pathname.

file transfer protocol *(technology)*
Abbreviated as "ftp" or "FTP."

"One type of software implements a set of conventions for copying files from a host computer known as 'file-transfer protocol' ("FTP"). With appropriate client software, a user with an account on the host computer can contact the server, view a directory of available files, and copy one or more of those files to his own computer. In addition to making files available to users with accounts, thousands of content providers also make files available for 'anonymous' retrieval by users who do not possess an account on the host computer. A content provider who makes files available for retrieval by anonymous FTP has no way of discerning who gains access to the files."
    Shea v. Reno, 930 F. Supp. 916, 928 (S.D.N.Y. 1996) (citations omitted).
See also **anonymous FTP; data transfer protocol; ftp.**

file wrapper *(patent)*
"The folder in which the PTO maintains the application papers is referred to as a file wrapper or prosecution history."
    U.S. Patent & Trademark Office, *Manual of Patent Examining Procedure*
    § 717, at 700 85 (Rev. 6, Oct. 1987).

filename *(software)*
Alphanumeric characters (letters or numbers) used to identify a particular file. The name given to a file.

film clip *(entertainment)*
See clip.

filter *(software)*
See filtering software.

filtering software *(software)*
Also called **filter, blocking software.** Application software that blocks or filters web sites containing objectionable materials.

Annotation. The Communications Decency Act encourages, but does not require, Internet service providers to implement filtering software on behalf of their subscribers.

"Because it has the right to exercise editorial control over those with whom it contracts and whose words it disseminates, it would seem only fair to hold AOL to the liability standards applied to a publisher or, at least, like a book store owner or library, to the liability standard applied to a distributor. But Congress has made a different policy choice by providing immunity even where the interactive service provider has an active, even aggressive role in making available content prepared by others. In some sort of tacit quid pro quo arrangement with the service provider community, Congress has conferred immunity from tort liability as an incentive to Internet service providers to self-police the Internet for obscenity and other offensive material, even where the self-policing is unsuccessful or not even attempted.

"In Section 230(c)(2) of the Communications Decency Act, Congress provided:

'No provider or user of an interactive computer service shall be held liable on account of—

(A) any action voluntarily taken in good faith to restrict access to or availability of material that the provider or user considers to be obscene, lewd, lascivious, filthy, excessively violent, harassing, or otherwise objectionable, whether or not such material is constitutionally protected; or

(B) any action taken to enable or make available to information content providers or others the technical means to restrict access to material described in paragraph (1).'

"47 U.S.C. sec. 230(C)(2). As the Fourth Circuit stated in Zeran: 'Congress enacted sec. 230 to remove . . . disincentives to self-regulation. . . . Fearing that the specter of liability would . . . deter service providers from blocking and screening offensive material . . . sect. 230 forbids the imposition of publisher liability on a service provider for the exercise of its editorial and self-regulatory functions.'"

Blumenthal v. Drudge, 992 F. Supp. 44, 51-52 (D.D.C. 1998).

"It is the policy of the United States to remove disincentives for the development and utilization of blocking and filtering technologies that empower parents to restrict their children's access to objectionable or inappropriate online material."

47 U.S.C. § 230(b)(4).

Related issues. "As the Internet has become accessible to more households, several commercial on-line services and software companies have developed features and packages designed to enable parents to limit children's exposure to potentially inappropriate Internet material. For example, America On-line, Prodigy, and Microsoft Network, which permit their subscribers to obtain access to Internet material, offer parental control options free of charge to their members. America Online, for example, allows parents to establish a separate account for their children limited to the service's own proprietary content. In addition, at least one type of screening software, SurfWatch, has a feature allowing parents to block access to all Internet sites except for those that parents choose to make available to their children.

"The Government offered testimony and a demonstration regarding SurfWatch (configured to act as a screening tool, rather than to block all Internet access) and a second type of screening software, Cyber Patrol. SurfWatch and Cyber Patrol maintain lists of sites known to contain sexually explicit material; when operating while a user attempts to retrieve Internet material, access to sites identified on their programs will be blocked. In addition, the programs block access to sites whose URLs contain particular character patterns or words, such as 'xxx' or 'sex,' and block any searches including those character patterns or words.

"Because of the constant change in the number and location of Internet sites, both SurfWatch and Cyber Patrol offer regular subscription or update services. But even where a parent has properly installed screening software and the software is operational (and configured to block access to certain sites rather than to the entire Internet), it is possible to retrieve some sexually explicit material. The Government's witness was able to run searches using 'Babe' and 'Little Women' as key words with screening software running in the background. As with searches performed in the absence of screening software, the searches returned links to sexually explicit materials. Some of the links were not blocked by the screening tool. In addition, the Government's witness obtained access to sexually explicit material by directly entering URLs obtained from earlier searches conducted without blocking software in the background. The record also shows that blocking software is not widely owned by or used in households with access to the Internet: nearly seventy percent of SurfWatch's 1,500 subscribers are schools rather than individual households."

Shea v. Reno, 930 F. Supp. 916, 931-32 (S.D.N.Y. 1996).

See also **PICS.**

filtration test *(copyright)*

"This process entails examining the structural components [of a computer program] at each level of abstraction to determine whether their particular inclusion at that level was 'idea' or was dictated by considerations of efficiency, so as to be necessarily incidental to that idea; required by factors external to the program itself; or taken from the public domain and hence is nonprotectable expression. . . . The structure of any given program may reflect some, all, or none of these considerations. Each case requires its own fact specific investigation."

Computer Assocs. Int'l, Inc. v. Altai, Inc., 982 F.2d 693, 707 (2d Cir. 1992).

"After separating the program into manageable components, the court must next filter the unprotectable components of the program from the protectable expression. The court must filter out as unprotectable the ideas, expression necessarily incident to the idea, expression already in the public domain, expression dictated by external factors (like the computer's mechanical specifications, compatibility with other programs, and demands of the industry served by the program), and expression not original to the programmer or author."

Atari Games Corp. v. Nintendo of America, Inc., 975 F.2d 832, 839 (Fed. Cir. 1992) (citations omitted).

See also **abstraction-filtration-comparison method; abstractions test; idea/expression dichotomy.**

Final Report *(copyright)*

See CONTU Final Report.

financial accommodation contract *(contract)*

"[A]n agreement under which a person extends a financial accommodation to a licensee and which does not create a security interest governed by [Article 9 of the Uniform Commercial Code]. The agreement may be in any form, including a license or lease."

UCITA § 102(a)(29).

financial institution *(electronic commerce)*

"[A] national or state-chartered commercial bank or trust company, savings bank, savings association, or credit union authorized to do business in the state of Washington and the deposits of which are federally insured."

Wash. Rev. Code § 19.34.020(12).

financial services transaction *(contract)*

"[A]n agreement that provides for, or a transaction that is, or entails access to, use, transfer, clearance, settlement, or processing of:

(A) a deposit, loan, funds, or monetary value represented in electronic form and stored or capable of storage by electronic means and retrievable and transferable by electronic means, or other right to payment to or from a person;

(B) an instrument or other item;

(C) a payment order, credit card transaction, debit card transaction, funds transfer, automated clearinghouse transfer, or similar wholesale or retail transfer of funds;

(D) a letter of credit, document of title, financial asset, investment property, or similar asset held in a fiduciary or agency capacity; or

(E) related identifying, verifying, access-enabling, authorizing, or monitoring information."

UCITA § 102(a)(30).

financier *(contract)*

"[A] person that provides a financial accommodation to a licensee under a financial accommodation contract and either (i) becomes a licensee for the purpose of transferring or sublicensing the license to the party to which the financial accommodation is provided or (ii) obtains a contractual right under the financial accommodation contract to preclude the licensee's use of the information or informational rights under a license in the event of breach of the financial accommodation contract. The term does not include a person that selects, creates, or supplies the information that is the subject of the license, owns the informational rights in the information, or provides support for, modifications to, or maintenance of the information."

UCITA § 102(a)(31).

finger *(software)*

A software tool used to locate people on other Internet sites.

finger demon *(software)*

"[A] program that permits a person to obtain limited information about the users of another computer."

United States v. Morris, 928 F.2d 504, 506 (2d Cir. 1991).

See also **finger.**

fingerprint *(hardware)*

"[A] small mark physically placed on the magnetic surface of each . . . diskette which contains certain information that cannot be altered or erased."

Vault Corp. v. Quaid Software Ltd., 847 F.2d 255, 256 (5th Cir. 1988).

firewall *(security; software)*

"A system or combination of hardware and software solutions that enforces a boundary between two or more networks."

Office of the Comptroller of the Currency, Infrastructure Threats from Cyber-Terrorists 5 (Mar. 19, 1999).

firmware *(technology)*

"[S]oftware embedded in a memory chip on the card. . . ."

Alcatel USA, Inc. v. DGI Technologies, Inc., 166 F.3d 772, 778 (5th Cir. 1999).

"This term is applied to computer programs that are stored in a type of memory (a ROM) that can in general only be read, not erased or changed easily. Firmware are chips that contain information beyond the minimum necessary to turn on the computer. They contain attributes of both hardware and software. Like hardware, they are integral to the machine as a form of circuitry through which electric current passes directly. But, like software, they do serve as repositories for computer instructions in object code. Firmware is used both for protection and for higher speed."

U.S. Copyright Office, *Compendium of Copyright Office Practices* II, §326 (1984).

"[S]oftware which is imbedded in a computer chip. Firmware cannot be modified by the user or owner of the card."

DSC Comm. Corp. v. DGI Technologies, Inc., 898 F. Supp. 1183, 1186 (N.D. Tex. 1995).

"[A] term of art in the computer field and refers to microinstructions permanently embodied in hardware elements."

In re Bradley, 600 F.2d 807, 810 n.3 (C.C.P.A. 1979), *aff'd sub nom. Diamond v. Bradley,* 450 U.S. 381 (1981).

"[H]ardware elements permanently programmed with a microcode, which directs the data transfers, between the scratchpad registers and the system base located in main memory, which are necessary to effect the alteration.

In re Bradley, 600 F.2d 807, 809, *aff'd by an equally divided court sub nom. Diamond v. Bradley,* 450 U.S. 381 (1981).

". . . controls the computer equipment in conjunction with instructions of application programs."

Bruffey Contracting Co., Inc. v. Burroughs Corp., 522 F. Supp. 769, 770 n.1 (D. Md. 1981).

". . . generally regarded as hardwired software, and that it can be considered to be both hardware and software."

In re Sperry Rand Corp., 56 Comp. Gen. 312, 315 (1977).

Annotation. "A ROM chip, actually, is neither strictly 'hardware,' a purely mechanical component of a computer, nor 'software,' a 'drive' or set of instructions external to the machine. Such chips, which are part of every modern computer, are generally designated 'firmware,' when they contain information beyond the minimum necessary to turn the machine on, reflecting the fact that they share attributes of both: like hardware, they are integral to the machine as a form of circuitry through which electric current passes directly; but like software, they do in fact serve as repositories for computer instructions in object code."

Midway Mfg. Co. v. Strohon, 564 F. Supp. 741, 751 (N.D. Ill. 1983).

See ROM.

First Amendment *(Constitution)*

"Congress shall make no law . . . abridging the freedom of speech."

U.S. Const. amend. I.

Annotation. "Cutting through the acronyms and *argot* that littered the hearing testimony, the Internet may fairly be regarded as a never-ending worldwide conversation. The Government may not, through the CDA, interrupt that conversation. As the most participatory form of mass speech yet developed, the Internet deserves the highest protection from governmental intrusion. True it is that many find some of the speech on the Internet to be offensive, and amid the din of cyberspace many hear discordant voices that they regard as indecent. The absence of governmental regulation of Internet content has unquestionably produced a kind of chaos, but as one of plaintiffs' experts put it with such resonance at the hearing:

'What achieved success was the very chaos that the Internet is. The strength of the Internet is that chaos.'

"Just as the strength of the Internet is chaos, so the strength of our liberty depends upon the chaos and cacophony of the unfettered speech the First Amendment protects."

American Civil Liberties Union v. Reno, 929 F. Supp. 824, 883 (E.D. Pa. 1996), *aff'd, Reno v. American Civil Liberties Union,* 521 U.S. 844 (1997).

"Although there is no complete consensus on the issue, most courts and commentators theorize that the importance of protecting freedom of speech is to foster the marketplace of ideas. If speech, even unconventional speech that some find lacking in substance or offensive, is allowed to compete unrestricted in the marketplace of ideas, truth will be discovered. Indeed, the First Amendment was design to prevent the majority, through acts of Congress, from silencing those who would express unpopular or unconventional views.

"Despite the protection provided by the First Amendment, unconventional speakers are often limited in their ability to promote such speech in the marketplace by the costs or logistics of reaching the masses, hence, the adage that freedom of the press is limited to those who own one. In the medium of cyberspace, however, anyone can build a soap box out of web pages and speak her mind in the virtual village green to an audience larger and more diverse that any the Framers could have imagined. In many respects, unconventional messages compete equally with the speech of main-

275

stream speakers in the marketplace of ideas that is the Internet, certainly more than in most other media."

American Civil Liberties Union v. Reno, 31 F. Supp. 2d 473, 476 (E.D. Pa. 1999).

"The Senate's recent passage of a telecommunications bill including Senator Exon's measure criminalizing the distribution of 'filthy' material over computer networks suggests that the First Amendment's applicability to on-line communications has not been well considered."

United States v. Baker, 890 F. Supp. 1375, 1387 n.19 (E.D. Mich. 1995).

"Baker is being prosecuted under 18 U.S.C. § 875(c) for his use of words, implicating fundamental First Amendment concerns. Baker's words were transmitted by means of the Internet, a relatively new communications medium that is itself currently the subject of much media attention. The Internet makes it possible with unprecedented ease to achieve world-wide distribution of material, like Baker's story, posted to its public areas. When used in such a fashion, the Internet may be likened to a newspaper with unlimited distribution and no locatable printing press—and with no supervising editorial control. But Baker's e-mail messages, on which the superseding indictment is based, were not publicly published but privately sent to Gonda. While new technology such as the Internet may complicate analysis and may sometimes require new or modified laws, it does not in this instance qualitatively change the analysis under the statute or under the First Amendment."

United States v. Baker, 890 F. Supp. 1375, 1390 (E.D. Mich. 1995) (citations omitted).

"The First Amendment is concerned with expression, and we reject the notion that the admixture of functionality necessarily puts expression beyond the protections of the Constitution."

Bernstein v. United States Dept. of Justice, 176 F.3d 1132, 1142 (9th Cir. 1999).

"We emphasize the narrowness of our First Amendment holding. We do not hold that all software is expressive. Much of it surely is not. Nor need we resolve whether the challenged regulations constitute content-based restrictions, subject to the strictest constitutional scrutiny, or whether they are, instead, content-neutral restrictions meriting less exacting scrutiny. We hold merely that because the prepublication licensing regime challenged here applies directly to scientific expression, vests boundless discretion in government officials, and lacks adequate procedural safeguards, it constitutes an impermissible prior restraint on speech."

Bernstein v. United States Dept. of Justice, 176 F.3d 1132, 1145 (9th Cir. 1999).

"Computer code is expressive. To that extent, it is a matter of First Amendment concern. But computer code is not purely expressive any more than the assassination of a political figure is purely a political statement. Code causes computers to perform desired functions. Its expressive element no more immunizes its functional aspects from regulation than the expressive motives of an assassin immunize the assassin's action."

Universal City Studios, Inc. v. Reimerdes, 111 F. Supp. 2d 294, 304 (S.D.N.Y. 2000).

"[I]nsofar as the EAR regulations on encryption software were intended to slow the spread of secure encryption methods to foreign nations, the government is intentionally retarding the progress of the flourishing science of cryptography. To the extent the government's efforts are aimed at interdicting the flow of scientific ideas (whether expressed in source code or otherwise), as distinguished from encryption products, these efforts would appear to strike deep into the heartland of the First Amendment. In this regard, the EAR regulations are very different from content-neutral time, place and manner restrictions that may have an incidental effect on expression while aiming at secondary effects."

Bernstein v. United States Dept. of Justice, 176 F.3d 1132, 1145 (9th Cir. 1999).

Related issues. "We are mindful that the Internet is a communication medium that lacks historical parallel in the potential extent of its reach and that regulation across jurisdictions may implicate fundamental first amendment concerns. It will undoubtedly take some time to determine the precise balance between the rights of those who use the Internet to disseminate information and the powers of the jurisdictions in which receiving computers are located to regulate for the general welfare."

State v. Granite Gate Resorts, Inc., 568 N.W.2d 715, 718 (Minn. App. 1997), aff'd per curiam, 576 N.W.2d 747 (Minn. 1998).

"The purpose of this statutory immunity [under the CDA] is not difficult to discern. Congress recognized the threat that tort-based lawsuits pose to freedom of speech in the new and burgeoning Internet medium. The imposition of tort liability on service providers for the communications of others represented, for Congress, simply another form of intrusive government regulation of speech. Section 230 was enacted, in part, to maintain the robust nature of Internet communication and, accordingly, to keep government interference in the medium to a minimum. In specific statutory findings, Congress recognized the Internet and interactive computer services as offering 'a forum for a true diversity of political discourse, unique opportunities for cultural development, and myriad avenues for intellectual activity.' . . . It also found that the Internet and interactive computer services 'have flourished, to the benefit of all Americans, *with a minimum of government regulation.*' . . . Congress further stated that it is 'the policy of the United States . . . to preserve the vibrant and competitive free market that presently exists for the Internet and other interactive computer services, *unfettered by Federal or State regulation.*' "

> *Zeran v. America Online, Inc.,* 129 F.3d 327, 330 (4th Cir. 1997) (citations omitted; emphasis in original).

"[T]he Internet presents extremely low entry barriers to those who wish to convey Internet content or gain access to it. In particular, a user wishing to communicate through e-mail, newsgroups, or Internet Relay Chat need only have access to a computer with appropriate software and a connection to the Internet, usually available for a low monthly fee. The user then in a sense becomes a public 'speaker,' able to convey content, at relatively low cost, to users around the world to whom it may be of interest. Those who possess more sophisticated equipment and greater technical expertise can make content available on the Internet for retrieval by others (known and unknown) by running a server supporting anonymous FTP, a gopher server, or a Web server. Yet content providers need not necessarily run their own servers or have the programming expertise to construct their own sites; they can lease space on a Web server from another or create a 'home page' through an on-line commercial service."

> *Shea v. Reno,* 930 F. Supp. 916, 929 (S.D.N.Y. 1996).

"[W]here a statute or regulation purports to limit freedom of expression, its vagueness will also 'operate[] to inhibit the exercise' of that freedom and violate the First Amendment."

> *Shea v. Reno,* 930 F. Supp. 916, 935 (S.D.N.Y. 1996).

"In a case in which the injury alleged is a threat to First Amendment interests, the finding of irreparable injury is often tied to the likelihood of success on the merits."

> *American Civil Liberties Union v. Reno,* 929 F. Supp. 824, 851 (E.D. Pa. 1996), *aff'd, Reno v. American Civil Liberties Union,* 521 U.S. 844 (1997).

"No provider or user of an interactive computer service shall be treated as the publisher or speaker of any information provided by another information content provider."

> 47 U.S.C. § 230(e)(1).

"[O]therwise criminal conduct is not protected under the First Amendment simply because it involves the use of speech."

> *United States v. Kufrovich,* 977 F. Supp. 246, 254 (D. Conn. 1997); *see also United States v. Riggs,* 743 F. Supp. 556, 559-60 (N.D. Ill. 1990).

"We emphasize the narrowness of our First Amendment holding. We do not hold that all software is expressive. Much of it surely is not."

> *Bernstein v. United States Dept. of Justice,* 176 F.3d 1132, 1145 (9th Cir. 1999).

"The First Amendment is concerned with expression, and we reject the notion that the admixture of functionality necessarily puts expression beyond the protections of the Constitution."

> *Bernstein v. United States Dept. of Justice,* 176 F.3d 1132, 1142 (9th Cir. 1999).

"Sexual expression which is indecent but is not obscene is protected by the First Amendment."

> *American Civil Liberties Union v. Johnson,* 194 F.3d 1149, 1156 (10th Cir. 1999) (citation omitted).

"[T]he First Amendment prohibits Congress from enacting a statute that makes criminal the generation of images of fictitious children engaging in imaginary but explicit sexual conduct."

> *Free Speech Coalition v. Reno,* 198 F.3d 1083, 1086 (9th Cir. 1999).

"[T]he government's efforts to regulate and control the spread of knowledge relating to encryption may implicate more than the First Amendment rights of cryptographers. In this increasingly electronic age, we are all required in our everyday lives to rely on modern technology to communicate with one another. This reliance on electronic communication, however, has brought with it a dramatic diminution in our ability to communicate privately. Cellular phones are subject to monitoring, email is easily intercepted, and transactions over the Internet are often less than secure. Something as commonplace as furnishing our credit card number, social security number, or bank account number puts each of us at risk. Moreover, when we employ electronic methods of communication, we often leave electronic 'fingerprints' behind, fingerprints that can be traced back to us. Whether we are surveilled by our government, by criminals, or by our neighbors, it is fair to say that never has our ability to shield our affairs from prying eyes been at such a low ebb. The availability and use of secure encryption may offer an opportunity to reclaim some portion of the privacy we have lost. Government efforts to control encryption thus may well implicate not only the First Amendment rights of cryptographers intent on pushing the boundaries of their science, but also the constitutional rights of each of us as potential recipients of encryption's bounty. Viewed from this perspective, the government's efforts to retard progress in cryptography may implicate the Fourth Amendment, as well as the right to speak anonymously, ... While we leave for another day the resolution of these difficult issues, it is important to point out that Bernstein's is a suit not merely concerning a small group of scientists laboring in an esoteric field, but also touches on the public interest broadly defined."

> *Bernstein v. United States Dept. of Justice*, 176 F.3d 1132, 1145-46 (9th Cir. 1999) (citations omitted).

"In an era in which the transmission of computer viruses—which . . . are simply computer code and thus to some degree expressive—can disable systems upon which the nation depends and in which other computer code also is capable of inflicting other harm, society must be able to regulate the use and dissemination of code in appropriate circumstances. The Constitution, after all, is a framework for building a just and democratic society. It is not a suicide pact."

> *Universal City Studios, Inc. v. Reimerdes*, 111 F. Supp. 2d 294, 304-05 (S.D.N.Y. 2000).

See also **freedom of speech; prior restraint.**

first-mover incentive *(economics)*

Also called the "first mover advantage."

"For an ISV interested in attracting users, there may be an advantage to offering the first and, for a while, only application in its category that runs on a new PC operating system. The user base of the new system may be small, but every user of that system who wants such an application will be compelled to use the ISV's offering. Moreover, if demand for the new operating system suddenly explodes, the first mover will reap large sales before any competitors arrive. An ISV thus might be drawn to a new PC operating system as a 'protected harbor.'"

> *United States v. Microsoft Corp.*, 65 F. Supp. 2d 1, 12 (D.D.C. 1999) (Finding of Fact 42).

Related issues. "Counteracting the collective-action phenomenon is another known as the 'first-mover incentive.'"

> *United States v. Microsoft Corp.*, 65 F. Supp. 2d 1, 12 (D.D.C. 1999) (Finding of Fact 42).

first-person perspective *(video game)*

"[T]he player assumes the personality and point of view of the title character, who is seen on the screen only as a pair of hands and an occasional boot, much as one might see oneself in real life without the aid of a mirror."

> *Micro Star v. FormGen, Inc.*, 154 F.3d 1107, 1109 (9th Cir. 1998).

"This form of play was pioneered by a company called id Software with its classic Wolfenstein 3D character."
Micro Star v. FormGen, Inc., 154 F.3d 1107, 1109 n.1 (9th Cir. 1998).

first sale doctrine *(copyright)*

"Notwithstanding the provisions of section 106(3), the owner of a particular copy . . . lawfully made under this title, or any person authorized by such owner, is entitled, without the authority of the copyright owner, to sell or otherwise dispose of the possession of that copy. . . ."
U.S. Copyright Act, 17 U.S.C. § 109(a).

Related issues. "By its very terms, the statute codifying the first sale doctrine, 17 U.S.C. § 109(a), is limited in its effect to the distribution of the copyrighted work. It prohibits the owner of the copyright in a work who has sold a copy of the work to another from preventing or restricting the transferee from a further sale or disposition of possession of the copy. Thus, by its own terms, § 109(a) has no application to the other four rights of a copyright owner, including the right to perform the work publicly."
Red Baron-Franklin Parks, Inc. v. Taito Corp., 883 F. Supp. 275, 280 (4th Cir. 1989).

"[T]he first sale doctrine has no application to the rights of the owner of a copyright guaranteed by § 106, except the right of distribution."
Red Baron-Franklin Parks, Inc. v. Taito Corp., 883 F. Supp. 275, 281 (4th Cir. 1989).

(mask work)
"Notwithstanding the provisions of section 905(2), the owner of a particular semiconductor chip product made by the owner of the mask work, or by any person authorized by the owner of the mask work, may import, distribute, or otherwise dispose of or use, but not reproduce, that particular semiconductor chip product without the authority of the owner of the mask work.
17 U.S.C. § 906(b).

fixation *(copyright)*

See **fixed.**

fixed *(copyright)*

"A work is 'fixed' in a tangible medium of expression when its embodiment in a copy or phonorecord, by or under the authority of the author, is sufficiently permanent or stable to permit it to be perceived, reproduced, or otherwise communicated for a period of more than transitory duration. A work consisting of sounds, images, or both, that are being transmitted, is 'fixed' for purposes of this title if a fixation of the work is being made simultaneously with its transmission."

U.S. Copyright Act, 17 U.S.C. § 101.

(mask work)
"A mask work is 'fixed' in a semiconductor chip product when its embodiment in the product is sufficiently permanent or stable to permit the mask work to be perceived or reproduced from the product for a period of more than transitory duration."

17 U.S.C. § 901(a)(3).

Annotation. "Under the 1976 Act, copyright protection is granted 'in original works of authorship fixed in a tangible medium of expression, now known or later developed, from which they can be perceived, reproduced, or otherwise communicated, either directly or with the aid of a machine or device.' Section 102(a). One of the important purposes of this section, as declared in the legislative history, was to broaden the scope of fixation, an essential requirement for copyright medium of expression and, specifically to abrogate the 'artificial' rule enunciated in *White-Smith Co. v. Apollo Co.,* 209 U.S. 1, 28 S. Ct. 319, 52 L.Ed. 655 (1908), which precluded protection for works not embodied in human-readable medium."

M. Kramer Mfg. Co. v. Andrews, 783 F.2d 421, 432-33 (4th Cir. 1986).

"The sole purpose of §101's definitions of the words 'copies' and 'fixed' is to explicate the 'fixation' requirement, i.e., to define the material objects in which copyrightable and infringing works may be embedded and to describe the requisite fixed nature of that work within the material object."

Matthew Bender & Co. v. West Publ'g Co., 158 F.3d 693, 702 (2d Cir. 1998), *cert. denied,* 522 U.S. 3732 (1999).

"That definition [of fixation]—intended to clarify that a work stored on a disk or tape can be a copy of the copyrighted work even if it cannot be perceived by human senses without technological aid—means that CD-ROM discs can infringe a copyright even if the information embedded upon them is not perceptible without the aid of a CD-ROM player."

Matthew Bender & Co. v. West Publ'g Co., 158 F.3d 693, 703 (2d Cir. 1998), *cert. denied,* 522 U.S. 3732 (1999).

"[T]he Copyright Law is not so much concerned with the temporal 'duration' of a copy as it is with what that copy does, and what it is capable of doing, while it exists. 'Transitory duration' is a relative term that must be interpreted and applied in context. This concept is particularly important in cases involving computer technology where speed and complexity of machines and software is rapidly advancing, and where the diversity of computer architecture and software design is expanding at an ever increasing rate."

> *Triad Sys. Corp. v. Southeastern Express Co.*, 64 F.3d 1330, 1334 (9th Cir. 1995).

"The fixation requirement . . . does not require that the work is written down or recorded somewhere exactly as it is perceived by the human eye. Rather, all that is necessary for the requirement to be satisfied is that the work is capable of being 'reproduced . . . with the aid of a machine or device.'"

> *Midway Mfg. Co. v. Artic Int'l, Inc.*, 547 F. Supp. 999, 1007-08 (N.D. Ill. 1982), *aff'd*, 704 F.2d 1009 (7th Cir.), *cert. denied*, 464 U.S. 823 (1983).

Related issues. "[T]he definition of 'fixation' would exclude . . . purely evanescent or transient reproductions such as those projected briefly on a screen, shown electronically on a television or other cathode ray tube, or captured momentarily in the 'memory' of a computer."

> H.R. Rep. No. 1476, 94th Cong., 2d Sess. 52 (1976).

"[B]y showing that [defendant] loads the software into RAM and is then able to view the system error log and diagnose the problem with the computer, [plaintiff] has adequately shown [fixation]. . . ."

> *MAI Sys. Corp. v. Peak Computer, Inc.*, 991 F.2d 511, 518 (9th Cir. 1993), *cert. dism.*, 510 U.S. 1033 (1994).

"Beyond materiality is the question whether the program, in the form of electrical impulses in RAM, is adequately 'fixed' to qualify as a 'copy' for purpose of the Act. . . . Once a software program is loaded into a computer's RAM, useful representations of the program's information and intelligence can be displayed on a video screen or printed out on a printer. And this can be done virtually instantaneously once loading is completed. Given this, it is apparent that a software program that resides in RAM is 'stable enough to be perceived, reproduced, or otherwise communicated for a period of more than transitory duration.' 17 U.S.C. § 101.

". . . [O]ne need only imagine a scenario where the computer with the program loaded into RAM, is left on for extended periods of time, say months or years, or indeed left on for the life of the computer. In this event, the RAM version of the program is surely not ephemeral or transient; it is, instead, essentially permanent and thus plainly sufficiently fixed to constitute a copy under the Act. . . . In sum, where, as here, a copyrighted program is loaded into RAM and maintained there for minutes or longer, the RAM representation of the program is sufficiently 'fixed' to constitute a 'copy' under the Act."

Advanced Computer Servs., Inc. v. MAI Sys. Corp., 845 F. Supp. 356, 363 (E.D. Va. 1994).

"Whether located in the PROM for this particular game or elsewhere in the total assembly, all portions of the program, once stored in memory devices anywhere in the game, are fixed in a tangible medium of expression within the meaning of the Act."

Stern v. Kaufman, 669 F.2d 852, 855-56 (2d Cir. 1982).

"(a) Anyone who, without the consent of the performer or performers involved—

(1) fixed the sounds or sounds and images of a live musical performance in a copy . . . , or reproduced copies . . . of such performance from an unauthorized fixation, or

(2) transmits or otherwise communicates to the public the sounds or sounds and images of a live musical performance, or

(3) distributes or offers to distribute, sells or offers to sell, rents or offers to rent, or traffics in any copies . . . fixed as described in paragraph (1), regardless whether the fixations occurred in the United States

(b) shall be subject to the remedies provided in sections 502 through 505, to the same extent as an infringer of copyright."

17 U.S.C. § 1101.

[EUROPE] "The copyright owner of a computer program shall have the right to do and to authorize the permanent or temporary reproduction of a computer program by any means and in any form, in part or in whole. Insofar as loading, displaying, running, transmission or storage of the computer program necessitate such reproduction, such acts shall be subject to authorization by the rightholder."

Council Directive on the Legal Protection of Computer Programs, 91/250/EEC, O.J. (L 122) (May 17, 1991).

flame *(Internet)*
1. *(noun)* An angry e-mail or newsgroup posting that strongly attacks someone or someone's opinion. 2. *(verb)* To communicate with someone online in an abusive or vitriolic manner. Often such messages are printed in all capital letters. *See also* **flamer; flaming.**

flamer *(Internet)*

One who flames someone else. *See also* **flame; flaming.**

flaming *(Internet)*

"[T]he practice of users sending electronic mail messages that confront and chastise the addressee."

> Department of Commerce, *Inquiry on Privacy Issues Relating to Private Sector Use of Telecommunications-Related Personal Information,* 59 Fed. Reg. 6841, 6848 n.55 (Feb. 11, 1994).

Annotation. Flaming is a "hot" reply to an online message that can range from sarcastic, constructive criticism (pointing out spelling or grammatical errors) to severe personal attacks. As the responses are often posted publicly for all Usenet members to read, the flames can sometimes provoke reply flames or third-party flames and lead to what is referred to as a "flame war," involving many participants and lasting for many weeks.

In response to flaming and flame wars, some Internet service providers police their services to keep flaming in check, and some jurisdictions have attempted to address the issue of flaming with statutes. For example, Connecticut has amended its criminal harassment statute to prohibit sending an electronic message with "intent to harass, annoy or alarm another person." (jrb)

See also **flame; flamer.**

flat-panel display *(hardware)*

A type of video display that is relatively thin (usually less than three inches), unlike the cathode ray tube found in most home television receivers and computer desktop monitors. Most commonly used in portable personal computers and portable television sets.

floppies *(hardware)*

See floppy disk.

floppy disk *(technology)*

Also referred to as "floppy diskette."

" . . . or 'floppies,' which now are 3 ½ inch magnetic disks upon which digital files may be recorded."

> *Universal City Studios, Inc. v. Reimerdes,* 111 F. Supp. 2d 294, 307 (S.D.N.Y. 2000).

"Not too many years ago, the most common transportable storage media were 5 ¼ inch flexible magnetic disks. Their flexibility led to their being referred to as 'floppies.' They have been replaced almost entirely with today's 3 $\frac{1}{2}$ inch disks, which are enclosed in hard plastic housings and which therefore are not flexible or 'floppy.' The earlier name, however, has stuck."

> *Universal City Studios, Inc. v. Reimerdes*, 111 F. Supp. 2d 294, 307 n.25 (S.D.N.Y. 2000) (footnotes omitted).

"A thin plastic disk, usually 5-1/4 inches or 8 inches in diameter, enclosed in a square, protective envelope, with a magnetic surface for storing information on a diskette."

> U.S. Copyright Office, *Compendium of Copyright Office Practices* II, §326 (1984).

"[A]n auxiliary memory device consisting of a flexible magnetic disk resembling a phonograph record, which can be inserted into the computer and from which data or instructions can be read."

> *Apple Computer, Inc. v. Franklin Computer Corp.*, 714 F.2d 1240, 1243 (3d Cir. 1983), *cert. dism.*, 464 U.S. 1033 (1984).

"[A] thin, circular piece of synthetic material, not unlike a 45 r.p.m. record, on which computer programs are stored electronically. When one wishes to use a program, the disk is inserted into a mechanism called a disk drive, and the computer is instructed to transfer the program from the disk into its memory."

> *Micro-Sparc, Inc. v. Amtype Corp.*, 592 F. Supp. 33 (D. Mass. 1984).

"[A] thin pliant magnetic disk capable of storing computer information."

> *Tandon Corp. v. U.S. Int'l Trade Comm'n*, 831 F.2d 1017, 1020 n.1 (Fed. Cir. 1987).

". . . serve[s] as a medium upon which computer companies place their software programs. To use a program, a purchaser loads the diskette into the disk drive of a computer, thereby allowing the computer to read the program into memory. The purchaser can then remove the diskette from the disk drive and operate the program from the computer's memory. This process is repeated each time a program is used."

> *Vault Corp. v. Quaid Software, Ltd.*, 847 F.2d 255, 256 (5th Cir. 1988).

See also **diskette.**

FLOPS *(hardware)*

Abbreviation for "Floating-Point Operations Per Second." A unit of measurement of the performance of a computer for certain scientific and engineering calculations.

flow chart *(software; technology)*
Also written as "flowchart."

"[A] graphic representation for the definition, analysis or solution of a problem in which symbols are used to represent operations, data flow, or equipment."
CONTU Final Report, at 21 n.109 (1978).

"[A] graphic representation of a computer program that is written in symbols, rather than in bits or symbolic names, and with a syntax that is graphic rather than grammatical. . . . A flowchart can be thought of as a kind of symbolic outline or schematic representation of a computer program's logic, which is written by a programmer once he or she has a conceptualization of the goals of the program."
Lotus Dev. Corp. v. Paperback Software Int'l, 740 F. Supp. 37, 44 (D. Mass. 1990).

"[A] graphic representation of the fundamental idea for solving a problem; it is the first expression of the programmer's ideas, and breaks down a given problem by determining the sequence in which the data is to be operated upon by the computer. The fundamental idea represented by the flowchart is known as an algorithm and is capable of being expressed in differing forms and by differing symbolizations. The flowchart is not literally a computer program, but a diagram of the logical operations that will be performed by the computer."
Paine, Webber, Jackson & Curtis, Inc. v. Merrill Lynch, Pierce, Fenner & Smith, Inc., 564 F. Supp. 1358, 1363-64 (D. Del. 1983).

"[A] schematic representation of the program's logic. It sets forth the watchful steps involved in solving a given problem."
Data Cash Sys., Inc. v. JS&A Group, Inc., 480 F. Supp. 1063, 1065 (N.D. Ill. 1979), *aff'd,* 628 F.2d 1038, 1040 (7th Cir. 1980).

"Flow charts map the interactions between modules that achieve the program's end goal."
Computer Assocs. Int'l, Inc. v. Altai, Inc., 982 F.2d 693, 697 (2d Cir. 1992).

Related issues (copyright). "[I]t would probably be a violation [of copyright law] to take a detailed description of a particular problem solution, such as a flow chart or step-by-step set of prose instructions, written in human language, and program such a description in computer language."
Synercom Technology, Inc. v. University Computing Co., 462 F. Supp. 1003, 1013 (M.D. Tex. 1978).

FMV *(technology)*
Acronym for "Full Motion Video." Video shown at 24 to 30 frames per second. Any playback at a slower rate appears jerky.

FOB *(contract)*
Acronym for "Freight On Board." Indicates that the buyer pays for shipping from the location designated in the agreement.

focus group *(multimedia)*
A number of people brought together to view and discuss the design for, prototype of, or completed version of a multimedia title or video game.

focus testing *(multimedia)*
Before or during production of an interactive media title, various aspects of the title (e.g., the user interface) will be tested with groups of potential users to determine ease of use, understandability of the interface and rules, appropriateness for the target age group, etc.

font *(hardware; software)*
A set of alphanumeric characters with a uniform appearance. *See also* **typeface**.

footprint *(hardware)*
[CANADA] "[T]he area occupied by a video terminal, such as on a desk."
Digital Equip. Corp. v. C. Itoh & Co. (Can.) Ltd. (1985), 6 C.P.R. (3d) 511 (Fed. T.D.).

force majeure *(contract)*
A general clause included in most contracts to deal with unanticipated situations where events beyond a party's control prevent or delay that party's performance of its obligation under the contract.

Annotation. Although the doctrine of impossibility excuses performance of a contractual act when, due to circumstances beyond the control of a party, it is unable to perform, such protection should be specifically set forth in the contract through the use of a force majeure (or excusable delay) clause. Such a clause excuses performance when, under a particular set of circumstances, there is an interference that cannot be overcome and that could not have been prevented by diligence or due care.

It must be understood, however, that a force majeure clause only excuses a delay in performance; it does not excuse performance entirely. If performance after the date originally negotiated may cause a problem, then the clause should be modified to take into account the effect of an unexpected delay, such as giving one or both parties the right to terminate the contract.

Sample clause. "Neither party to this contract is in default hereunder by reason of its delay in the performance of or failure to perform, in whole or in part, any of its obligations hereunder, if such delay or failure resulted from acts of God or other occurrences beyond its reasonable control and without its fault or negligence. [Such acts or occurrences shall include, but not be limited to, earthquakes, floods, fire, power failures, communications failures, epidemics, strikes, lockouts, war, terrorist activity or government regulations which go into effect after the effective date of this Agreement.]"

foreseeability *(jurisdiction)*

"The application of that rule will vary with the quality and nature of the defendant's activity, but it is essential in each case that there be some act by which the defendant purposefully avails itself of the privilege of conducting activities within the forum State, thus invoking the benefits and protections of its laws."

Hanson v. Denkla, 357 U.S. 235, 253 (1958).

forge a digital signature *(electronic commerce)*

"[E]ither: (a) To create a digital signature without the authorization of the rightful holder of the private key; or (b) To create a digital signature verifiable by a certificate listing as subscriber a person who either: (i) Does not exist; or (ii) Does not hold the private key corresponding to the public key listed in the certificate."

Wash. Rev. Code § 19.34.020(13).

FORTRAN *(software)*

Acronym for "Formula Translation."

Lotus Dev. Corp. v. Paperback Software Int'l, 740 F. Supp. 37, 44 (D. Mass. 1990).

"The FORmula TRANslation programming language, originally developed in the late 1950's for engineering and scientific programming. It is still the most widely used language for these types of programs."

U.S. Copyright Office, *Compendium of Copyright Office Practices* II, §326 (1984).

Fourth Amendment *(Constitution)*

Related issues. "Government efforts to control encryption thus may well implicate not only the First Amendment rights or cryptographers intent on pushing the boundaries of their science, but also the constitutional rights of each of us as potential recipients of encryption's bounty. Viewed from this perspective, the government's efforts to retard progress in cryptography may implicate the Fourth Amendment, as well as the right to speak anonymously, the right against compelled speech, and the right to informational privacy."

Bernstein v. United States Dept. of Justice, 176 F.3d 1132, 1146 (9th Cir. 1999) (citations omitted).

FPS *(hardware)*
Acronym for "Frames Per Second." A measure of the number of individual digital images displayed on a computer screen or motion picture screen in one second.

fractional high-capacity access *(telecommunications)*
A telecommunications service which provides users with unlimited use of a single, high-bandwidth transmission channel at a price reflecting actual usage. *See also* **fractional T1.**

fractional T1 *(telecommunications)*
A dedicated transmission connection, which is a subset of T1. *See also* **fractional high-capacity access.**

frame *(video)*
A single, complete video picture stored on tape or disk or displayed on a computer screen.

(Internet)
A function that permits a computer screen to be divided into two or more simultaneously viewed web pages, each of which has full web page functionality.

Annotation. A feature of Internet browsers that allows a viewer's screen to be divided into two or more simultaneously viewed web pages. Each web page displayed on the screen has full web page functionality, including the ability to hyperlink to other pages. If a hyperlink to another web page is executed from a framed web page, the new page can be loaded into the same framed area of the screen or in one of the other framed areas. This option of changing one section of the screen by executing a hyperlink in another section of the screen can be very useful for indices and other navigational tools. A frame may also be used to position a static web page configured without hyperlinks. Such a configuration is sometimes used for logos or advertisements that remain in position notwithstanding changes to other sections of the screen.

The ability of frames to present a seamless or near-seamless compilation of web pages, however, is not without its potential dangers. If any of the individual web pages included in a set of framed web pages were to include a hyperlink to a third party's web page, the combination of pages displayed from time to time could present an unintended result. For example, if a framed web page with an athletic shoe manufacturer's logo across the top of the screen has hyperlinks to a third party's web page, the framed web page could potentially display an unaffiliated web page with photographs of famous sports figures who are sponsored by competing shoe manufacturers across the bottom of the screen. Such a page could prompt complaints from the shoe manufacturers, the web page owner, the pictured athletes, or, perhaps, consumers.

An additional complication may arise because the display area for a web page in a frame is smaller than a standard full-page display. As a result, the framed web page may not display all of its information. For example, a disclaimer or an advertisement located near the bottom of a web page may be missing when the web page is viewed in a frame. A web page developer's complex and careful positioning of graphics and text within the confines of a single page display may lose its effectiveness when viewed in an area that is 70% of that size.

Unlike a standard web page hyperlink, in which the primary web page is completely removed from the user's screen prior to the display of the hyperlinked web page, the use of frames can cause a third party's web page to be displayed simultaneously with other pages, arguably creating a derivative work from the third party's web page. Particular combinations of web pages also could create the false impression of an affiliation, endorsement, or sponsorship.

The situations mentioned above are only likely to occur in the event that a framed web page includes an "external" hyperlink to a third party's web page. The contents of a third party's web page, including its hyperlinks, are subject to change at any time without notice; thus, the potential combinations of pages that may be displayed in a framed web page with an external hyperlink cannot be controlled or predicted.

Frames are a very useful tool and can fill many important roles in web page development. The use of frames may be one of the easiest ways to create a simple, clean approach to navigating through a complex web site.

Nonetheless, when creating a web page using frames, caution should be exercised to avoid creating external hyperlinks. (jrb)

See also **framing.**

frame rate *(hardware)*

The speed at which individual frames are displayed on a computer screen.

framing *(Internet)*

"[R]efers to the process whereby one Web site can be visited while remaining in a previous Web site."

> *Digital Equip. Corp. v. Altavista Technology, Inc.,* 960 F. Supp. 456, 461 n.12 (D. Mass. 1997).

See also **frame; in-line linking.**

fraud *(criminal law; tort)*

Generally defined as a false statement of fact, made with the knowledge of its falsity, or made recklessly, without belief in its truth, with the intention that it be acted upon by the other party to his or her detriment.

Related issues. "Remedies for material misrepresentation or fraud include all remedies available under this Article for non-fraudulent breach."

> U.C.C. § 2-721 (1979).

See also **consumer fraud.**

fraud in the inducement *(contract)*

The use of false or misleading statements to induce a party to enter into an agreement. Generally, fraudulent inducement renders a contract voidable at the option of the defrauded party.

Related issues. "Fraud in the inducement should negate the provisions of a written contract at the behest of an injured plaintiff."

> *AccuSys., Inc. v. Honeywell Information Sys., Inc.,* 580 F. Supp. 474, 482 (S.D.N.Y. 1984).

"Sperry cannot shield itself with the language of a contract when [the plaintiff's] allegations are that the contract itself was induced through fraud."

> *Invacare Corp. v. Sperry Rand Corp.,* 612 F. Supp. 448, 454 (N.D. Ohio. 1984).

fraudulent database *(criminal law)*

"A computerized database application listing ESN and MIN combinations not assigned to a bona fide customer or subscriber."

> *United States v. Brady,* 820 F. Supp. 1346, 1353 n.15 (D. Utah 1993).

free ride *(software)*
Using the software copyrighted by a third party without licensing or paying the license fee for its use.

> *See, e.g., Triad Sys. Corp. v. Southeastern Express Co.,* 64 F.3d 1330, 1337 (9th Cir. 1995).

freedom of speech *(Constitution)*
"Congress shall make no law . . . abridging the freedom of speech."

> U. S. Const. amend I.

Annotation. "The Internet is a far more speech-enhancing medium than print, the village green, or the mails."

> *American Civil Liberties Union v. Reno,* 929 F. Supp. 824, 882 (E.D. Pa. 1996), *aff'd, Reno v. American Civil Liberties Union,* 521 U.S. 844 (1997).

"Cutting through the acronyms and *argot* that littered the hearing testimony, the Internet may fairly be regarded as a never-ending worldwide conversation. The Government may not, through the CDA, interrupt that conversation. As the most participatory form of mass speech yet developed, the Internet deserves the highest protection from governmental intrusion. True it is that many find some of the speech on the Internet to be offensive, and amid the din of cyberspace many hear discordant voices that they regard as indecent. The absence of governmental regulation of Internet content has unquestionably produced a kind of chaos, but as one of plaintiffs' experts put it with such resonance at the hearing:

'What achieved success was the very chaos that the Internet is. The strength of the Internet is that chaos.'

"Just as the strength of the Internet is chaos, so the strength of our liberty depends upon the chaos and cacophony of the unfettered speech the First Amendment protects."

> *American Civil Liberties Union v. Reno,* 929 F. Supp. 824, 883 (E.D. Pa. 1996) (emphasis in original), *aff'd, Reno v. American Civil Liberties Union,* 521 U.S. 844 (1997).

Related issues. ". . . Internet users have no way to determine the characteristics of their audience. . . . In fact, in online communications through newsgroups, mailing lists, chat rooms, and the Web, the user has no way to determine with certainty that any particular person has accessed the user's speech. . . . A speaker thus has no way of knowing the location of the recipient of his or her communication."

> *American Library Ass'n v. Pataki,* 969 F. Supp. 160, 167 (S.D.N.Y. 1997).

"[V]irtually all Internet speech is . . . available everywhere."
> *Cyberspace, Comm., Inc. v. Engler,* 55 F. Supp. 2d 737, 740-44 (E.D. Mich. 1999).

See also **First Amendment.**

free-nets *(Internet)*

"[C]ommunity networks to provide citizens with a local link to the Internet (and to provide local-oriented content and discussion groups)."
> *American Civil Liberties Union v. Reno,* 929 F. Supp. 824, 833 (E.D. Pa. 1996), *aff'd, Reno v. American Civil Liberties Union,* 521 U.S. 844 (1997).

Annotation. "Individuals typically can access free-nets at little or no cost via modem connection or by using computers available in community buildings. Free-nets are often operated by a local library, educational institution, or non-profit community group."
> *American Civil Liberties Union v. Reno,* 929 F. Supp. 824, 833 (E.D. Pa. 1996), *aff'd, Reno v. American Civil Liberties Union,* 521 U.S. 844 (1997).

free-riding *(criminal; telecommunications)*

"Use of a cellular telephone which has been programmed to avoid or defeat access or billing to an individual customer's account, e.g., by 'tumbling' the ESN and/or MIN."
> *United States v. Brady,* 820 F. Supp. 1346, 1348 n.7 (D. Utah 1993).

See also **ESN; MIN; tumbling.**

freeware *(software)*

Computer software that is either copyrighted or in the public domain and is freely distributed to potential users with no expectation of payment for its use.

ftp *(Internet)*

Also "FTP." Acronym for "File Transfer Protocol." A standard protocol for transferring files from one computer to another. Utilized by users to download files.

"A simple method [of information retrieval] uses 'ftp' (or file transfer protocol) to list the names of computer files available on a remote computer, and to transfer one or more of those files to an individual's local computer."
> *American Civil Liberties Union v. Reno,* 929 F. Supp. 824, 835 (E.D. Pa. 1996), *aff'd, Reno v. American Civil Liberties Union,* 521 U.S. 844 (1997).

Related issues. "Some types of Web client software also permit users to gain access to resources available on FTP and gopher sites."
> *Shea v. Reno,* 930 F. Supp. 916, 929 (S.D.N.Y. 1996).

"[A]n FTP server can be configured to verify a password against a list of passwords issued to users maintaining an account on the server before permitting access to certain files."
> *Shea v. Reno,* 930 F. Supp. 916, 942 n.17 (S.D.N.Y. 1996).

See also **data transfer protocol.**

full motion video *(hardware; multimedia)*
See **FMV.**

fully qualified domain name *(Internet)*
"In its most generic form, a fully qualified domain name consists of three elements. . . . [T]he three elements are hostname . . . a domain name . . . and a top level domain. . . ."
> *Intermatic, Inc. v. Toeppen,* 947 F. Supp. 1227, 1231 (N.D. Ill. 1996).

See also **domain name.**

function key *(hardware)*
A specific key on a terminal keyboard that causes a predefined process or activity to be requested of the system whenever the key is depressed.

functional *(trade dress)*
"A product is functional if it is essential to the use or purpose of the article or if it affects the cost or quality of the article."
> *Inwood Labs, Inc. v. Ives Labs., Inc.,* 456 U.S. 844, 851 n.10 (1982).

"[A] design is legally functional . . . if it is one of a limited number of equally efficient options available to competitors and free competition would be unduly hindered by according the design trademark protection."
> *Two Pesos, Inc. v. Taco Cabana, Inc.,* 505 U.S. 763, 775 (1992).

Related issues. "[A]n interesting question, unnecessary to reach here, whether computer input formats and output reports involving highly technical data are so inherently functional as not to be protectable."
> *Engineering Dynamics, Inc. v. Structural Software, Inc.,* 26 F.3d 1335, 1350 n.16 (5th Cir. 1994), *mod'd on other grounds,* 46 F.3d 408 (5th Cir. 1995).

See also **functionality; trade dress infringement.**

functionality

(free speech; software)

"The First Amendment is concerned with expression, and we reject the notion that the admixture of functionality necessarily puts expression beyond the protections of the Constitution."

> *Bernstein v. United States Dept. of Justice*, 176 F.3d 1132, 1142 (9th Cir. 1999).

(trade dress)

"The Ninth Circuit test for functionality looks at a product's trade dress as a whole, considering (1) whether a particular design yields a utilitarian advantage; (2) whether alternative designs are available in order to avoid hindering competition; and (3) whether the design achieves economics in manufacture or use.

Moreover, functional features are those that 'constitute the actual benefit that the consumer wishes to purchase, as distinguished from an assurance that a particular entity made, sponsored, or endorsed a product.' Although some of a product's individual features may be functional, the combination of these features may, when analyzed as a whole, be nonfunctional if it services to distinguish the product from rival products rather than being necessary to the product's use."

> *Interactive Networks, Inc. v. NTN Comm., Inc.*, 875 F. Supp. 1398, 1406 (N.D. Cal. 1995).

Related issues. (software) "[T]he functionalities of a software product are not provided by the mere presence of code on a computer's hard drive. For software code to provide any functionalities at all the code must be loaded into the computer's dynamic memory and executed. To uninstall a software program or to remove a set of functionalities from a software program, it is not necessary to delete all of the software code that is executed in the course of providing those functionalities. It is sufficient to delete and/or modify enough of the program so as to prevent the code in question from being executed."

> *United States v. Microsoft Corp.*, 65 F. Supp. 2d 1, 46 (D.D.C. 1999) (Finding of Fact 184).

See also **functional; trade dress infringement.**

FYI *(technology)*

Acronym for "For Your Information." A type of file containing answers to commonly asked questions about the Internet.

gallium arsenide (GaAs) *(manufacturing)*

A compound semiconductor material that allows transistors and integrated circuits to operate much more rapidly than similar devices made of silicon. Much more difficult and hence more expensive to manufacture than silicon.

Galoob *(copyright)*

Citation. Lewis Galoob Toys, Inc. v. Nintendo of Am., Inc., 780 F. Supp. 1283 (N.D. Cal. 1991).

Annotation. "In *Galoob*, we considered audiovisual displays created using a device called the Game Genie, which was sold for use with the Nintendo Entertainment System. The Game Genie allowed players to alter individual features of a game, such as a character's strength or speed, by selectively 'blocking the value for a single data byte sent by the game cartridge to the [Nintendo console] and replacing it with a new value.' Players chose which data value to replace by entering a code; over a billion different codes were possible. The Game Genie was dumb; it functioned only as a window into the computer program, allowing players to temporarily modify individual aspects of the game.

"Nintendo sued, claiming that when the Game Genie modified the game system's audiovisual display, it created an infringing derivative work. We rejected this claim because '[a] derivative work must incorporate a protected work in some concrete or permanent form.' The audiovisual displays generated by combining the Nintendo System with the Game Genie were not incorporated in any permanent form; when the game was over, they were gone. Of course, they could be reconstructed, but only if the next player chose to reenter the same codes."

Micro Star v. FormGen, Inc., 154 F.3d 1107, 1111 (9th Cir. 1998).

game *(copyright)*

Refers to video games.

Related issues. "Copyright protection does not extend to games as such." *Atari, Inc. v. North American Philips Consumer Elecs. Corp.,* 672 F.2d 607, 615 (7th Cir.), *cert. denied,* 459 U.S. 880 (1982).

game engine *(video game)*
"[T]he heart of the computer program; in some sense, it is the program. It tells the computer when to read data, save and load games, play sounds and project images onto the screen."
Micro Star v. FormGen, Inc., 154 F.3d 1107, 1110 (9th Cir. 1998).

gamer *(video game)*
A dedicated, and generally highly skilled, video game player.

garbage *(technology)*
Slang term for information that cannot be read or understood by the user. Most frequently, it is the result of a communications problem. *See also* **gibberish; GIGO; line noise.**

gate array *(hardware)*
A type of semicustom integrated circuit composed of a matrix of logic gates (switches) substituting for collections of gates on separate integrated circuits or other logic circuits.

gateway *(Internet; technology)*
A device that connects two or more networks using different protocols.

gateway technology *(Internet; technology)*
"Such technology requires Internet users to enter information about themselves—perhaps an adult identification number or a credit card number—before they can access certain areas of cyberspace . . . much like a bouncer checks a person's driver's license before admitting him to a nightclub."
Reno v. American Civil Liberties Union, 521 U.S. 844, 890 (1997) (O'Connor, J., concurring in part, dissenting in part) (citations omitted).

GATT *(contract; government)*
Acronym for "General Agreement on Tariffs and Trade." An international trade agreement dating back to 1948 under which member states agree to a set of rules to govern international trade in goods and services. Generally GATT is intended to reduce tariffs and open new markets to a country's products and services.

general jurisdiction *(jurisdiction)*

". . . exists when a defendant is domiciled in the forum state or his activities are 'substantial' or 'continuous and systematic.' *Helicopteros Nacionales de Colombia S.A. v. Hall,* 466 U.S. 408, 414-16 (1984)."

> *Panavision Int'l, L.P. v. Toeppen,* 141 F.3d 1316, 1320 (9th Cir. 1998)

" . . . arises when a defendant's contacts with the forum state are so "continuous and systematic," defendant may be subject to suit for causes of action entirely distinct from the in-state activities."

> *Coastal Video Comm. Corp. v. Staywell Corp.,* 59 F. Supp. 2d 562, 565 (E.D. Va. 1999) (citations omitted).

"To hold that the possibility of ordering products from a website establishes general jurisdiction would effectively hold that any corporation with such a website is subject to general jurisdiction in every state. The court is not willing to take such a step."

> *LaSalle Nat'l Bank v. Vitro,* 85 F. Supp. 2d 857, 862 (N.D. Ill. 2000).

Annotation. ". . . permits a court to exercise personal jurisdiction over a non-resident defendant for non-forum related activities when the defendant has engaged in 'systematic and continuous' activities in the forum state.

> *Zippo Mfg. Co. v. Zippo Dot Com, Inc.,* 952 F. Supp. 1119, 1122 (W.D. Pa. 1997).

general purpose computer *(technology)*

". . . is designed to perform operations under many different programs."

> *Gottschalk v. Benson,* 409 U.S. 63, 65 (1972).

See also **computer.**

generation *(technology)*

Refers to the time period during which a particular type of technology is dominant.

Annotation. "The computer industry, which is little more than 25 years old, has witnessed the introduction of three (and possibly four) 'generations' of equipment, each generation representing a major technological advance. The first computers, introduced in 1952, were built with vacuum tubes. The second generation, introduced in 1958, utilized transistor technology. In 1964 IBM introduced the third generation with the System 360 family of computers, employing integrated circuits and other advances. In 1970 IBM introduced an improved third (or possibly fourth) generation, the System 370 line. Because the electronic components of second and third generation equipment are virtually indestructible, the life of this equipment is a function of price and technological obsolescence rather than wear from usage."

> *Greyhound Computer Corp. v. IBM Corp.,* 559 F.2d 488, 491 (9th Cir. 1977).

generic *(trademark)*

A common descriptive name of the goods or services with which the term is used.

Annotation. "[T]he Lanham Act recognizes that a mark may become generic for a portion of the goods or services for which it is registered, causing the owner to lose trademark protection against use of the mark in connection with such goods."

> *Lockheed Martin Corp. v. Network Solutions, Inc.,* 985 F. Supp. 949, 963 (C.D. Cal. 1997).

generic mark *(trademark)*

". . . identifies a class of product or service, regardless of source."

> *America Online, Inc. v. AT&T Corp.,* 64 F. Supp. 2d 549, 560 (E.D. Va. 1999) (citation omitted).

"When a common word or phrase is used as a mark for its ordinary meaning, . . ."

> *America Online, Inc. v. AT&T Corp.,* 64 F. Supp. 2d 549, 565 (E.D. Va. 1999).

". . . is simply the name of the good or product itself and as such cannot ever receive trademark protection."

> *Washington Speakers Bureau, Inc. v. Leading Authorities, Inc.,* 33 F. Supp. 2d 488, 494 (E.D. Va. 1999).

". . . conveys information with respect to the nature or class of an article."

> *Washington Speakers Bureau, Inc. v. Leading Authorities, Inc.,* 33 F. Supp. 2d 488, 495 (E.D. Va. 1999) (citation omitted).

Annotation. "If a term is generic, then regardless of whether one particular company or individual has succeeded in having the public think of that company/individual when they think of the term, the term nonetheless describes a genus, when the purpose of trademarks is to describe the species."

> *America Online, Inc. v. AT&T Corp.,* 64 F. Supp. 2d 549, 565 (E.D. Va. 1999).

"[A]n abbreviation of a generic name that continues to convey to consumers the original generic connotation of the unabbreviated name is also generic."

> *America Online, Inc. v. AT&T Corp.,* 64 F. Supp. 2d 549, 566 (E.D. Va. 1999).

"While acronyms or initials can be entitled to protection if they are descriptive . . . if the initials have become so generally understood as being substantially synonymous with the words they represent, they are not protectible."

> *America Online, Inc. v. AT&T Corp.,* 64 F. Supp. 2d 549, 566 (E.D. Va. 1999).

". . . never qualify for the protections of the Lanham Act; are not registrable; and a registered mark can be canceled at any time upon a finding that the mark is, or has become, generic."

> *America Online, Inc. v. AT&T Corp.,* 64 F. Supp. 2d 549, 560-61 (E.D. Va. 1999).

". . . receive no trademark protection because 'no matter how much money and effort the user of a generic term has poured into promoting the sale of its merchandise and what success it has achieved in securing public identification, it cannot deprive competing manufacturers of the product of the right to call an article by its name.'"

> *Washington Speakers Bureau, Inc. v. Leading Authorities, Inc.,* 33 F. Supp. 2d 488, 495 (E.D. Va. 1999).

". . . cannot receive trademark protection because 'generic' and 'trademark' are mutually exclusive terms. Trademarks are used to distinguish a producer's goods and services from those of his competitors, while generic terms denote the product and the service itself, rather than the source, so they are in no way distinctive of the goods and services to which they are applied."

> *America Online, Inc. v. AT&T Corp.,* 64 F. Supp. 2d 549, 561 (E.D. Va. 1999) (citations omitted).

"[W]hen a common English word is used as a mark for its ordinary meaning, it cannot be appropriated for exclusive use because the mark is generic."

> *America Online, Inc. v. AT&T Corp.,* 64 F. Supp. 2d 549, 561 (E.D. Va. 1999).

"To determine whether the primary significance of a mark is generic, the Court should consider the following: (1) competitors' use of the mark, (2) plaintiff's use of the mark, (3) dictionary definitions, (4) media usage, (5) testimony of persons in the trade, and (6) consumer surveys."

> *America Online, Inc. v. AT&T Corp.,* 64 F. Supp. 2d 549, 563-64 (E.D. Va. 1999).

Related issues. "[G]eneric marks with secondary meaning are still not entitled to protection."

> *America Online, Inc. v. AT&T Corp.,* 64 F. Supp. 2d 549, 565 (E.D. Va. 1999).

"The conclusion is that IM stands for 'instant message' (as AOL admits), and because the primary significance of 'instant message' is to stand for an 'instant message,' the term IM reflects the genus, not the species."
> *America Online, Inc. v. AT&T Corp.,* 64 F. Supp. 2d 549, 566 (E.D. Va. 1999).

"Further, even if a producer or provider has achieved secondary meaning in its generic mark through promotion and advertising, the generic mark is still not entitled to protection because to allow protection would 'deprive competing manufacturers of the product of the right to call an article by its name.' "
> *America Online, Inc. v. AT&T Corp.,* 64 F. Supp. 2d 549, 561 (E.D. Va. 1999) (citation omitted).

"The existence of synonyms for a term does not mean the term is not generic. There may be more than one term which the consuming public understands as designating a category of goods."
> *America Online, Inc. v. AT&T Corp.,* 64 F. Supp. 2d 549, 561 (E.D. Va. 1999) (citation omitted).

generic term(s) *(trademark)*

". . . are those used by the public to refer generally to the product rather than a particular brand of the product."
> *Brookfield Comm., Inc. v. West Coast Entertainment Corp.,* 174 F.3d 1036, 1058 n.19 (9th Cir. 1999).

"[A] term is generic when it describes the genus of which the product belongs to the species."
> *America Online, Inc. v. AT&T Corp.,* 64 F. Supp. 2d 549, 563 (E.D. Va. 1999).

generic top-level domains *(Internet)*

Abbreviated as "gTLDs." *See* **top-level domain.**

geographic mark(s) *(Internet)*

". . . are generally understood to constitute descriptive marks when they indicate the geographic source of the service or product."
> *Washington Speakers Bureau, Inc. v. Leading Authorities, Inc.,* 33 F. Supp. 2d 488, 495 (E.D. Va. 1999).

gibberish *(general)*

"[T]he printout just produces 'gibberish' of two types. The source code 'gibberish' is understandable to engineers *if* sufficient commentary is provided. The object code 'gibberish' is understandable to no one but the computer. Courts have trouble enough reading contractual and statutory language and the undersigned judge has had to take on faith the foregoing gibberish-analysis presented by expert witnesses. As far as the court is concerned, one of the piles of gibberish looks pretty much like the other pile."

> *In re Bedford Corp.,* 62 Bankr. 555, 567 n.8 (D.N.H. 1986) (emphasis in original).

GIF *(technology)*

Acronym for "Graphics Interchange Format." Compressed image data format created by CompuServe to speed the downloading of images. Unisys claims a patent for the GIF technology.

giga *(technology)*

Prefix meaning billion, e.g., "gigaflops" means "one billion floating point operations per second" and "gigabits" means "one billion bits."

gigabyte *(technology)*

Abbreviated as "GB."

A unit of data equaling one billion bytes (1,073,741,824) or 1,000 megabytes.

"1024 kilobytes."

> *Universal City Studios, Inc. v. Reimerdes,* 111 F. Supp. 2d 294, 306 (S.D.N.Y. 2000) (footnote omitted).

GIGO *(technology)*

"Garbage In, Garbage Out."

> *Neal v. United States,* 402 F. Supp. 678, 680 (D.N.J. 1975).

See also **garbage.**

GII *(Internet)*

Acronym for "Global Information Infrastructure."

"The [Clinton] Administration's concept of the Global Information Infrastructure (GII) includes wired and wireless networks; information appliances such as computers, set-top boxes, video phones, and personal digital assistants; all of the information, applications and services accessible over these networks; and the skills required to build, design and use these information and communications technologies."

> The White House, *A Framework for Global Electronic Commerce* 1 n.1 (July 1, 1997).

gimbaled *(hardware)*

"[I]n the disk drive industry 'the term "gimbaled" . . . means a suspension system . . . that allows the head to pitch and roll.'"
    Tandon Corp. v. U.S. Int'l Trade Comm'n, 831 F.2d 1017, 1020 n.2 (Int'l Trade Comm'n 1987).

give notice *(contract)*

"[T]o take such steps as may be reasonably required to inform the other person in the ordinary course, whether or not the other person actually comes to know of it."
    UCITA § 102(a)(49).

glass master *(hardware)*

See one-off; worm.

Global Information Infrastructure *(Internet)*

Abbreviated as "GII." *See* **GII.**

gmc *(manufacturing)*

Acronym for "Gold Master Candidate." A CD-ROM that is pressed toward the end of the beta testing phase, and tested further to determine whether it qualifies as a gold master. *See also* **gold master.**

GO TO *(software)*

" 'GO TO 40' tells the computer to skip intervening steps and go to the step at line 40."
    Apple Computer, Inc. v. Franklin Computer Corp., 714 F.2d 1240, 1243 (3d Cir. 1983), *cert. dism.,* 464 U.S. 1033 (1984).

gold master *(manufacturing)*

Also called "golden master." The final version of an interactive CD-ROM, which is sent to the manufacturer at the end of the beta testing phase.

good faith *(contract)*

"[H]onesty in fact in the conduct or transaction concerned."
    U.C.C. § 1-201(19).

"[I]n the case of a *merchant* means honesty in fact and the observance of reasonable commercial standards of fair dealing in the trade."
    U.C.C. § 2-103(1)(b) (emphasis in original).

"[H]onesty in fact and the observance of reasonable commercial standards of fair dealing."
    UCITA §102(a)(32).

goods *(contract)*

"[A]ll things (including specially manufactured goods) which are movable at the time of identification to the contract for sale."

U.C.C. § 2-105(1).

"[A]ll things that are movable at the time relevant to the computer information transaction. The term includes the unborn young of animals, growing crops, and other identified things to be severed from realty which are covered by [Section 2-107 of the Uniform Commercial Code]. The term does not include computer information, money, the subject matter of foreign exchange transactions, documents, letters of credit, letter-of-credit rights, instruments, investment property, accounts, chattel paper, deposit accounts, or general intangibles."

UCITA § 102(a)(33).

Annotation. "Although the ideas or concepts involved in the custom designed software remained [the seller's] intellectual property, [the buyer] was purchasing the product of those concepts. That product required effort to produce, but it was a product nevertheless and, though intangible, is more readily characterized as 'goods' than 'services.'"

Triangle Underwriters, Inc. v. Honeywell, Inc., 457 F. Supp. 765, 769 (E.D.N.Y. 1978), *mod'd on other grounds,* 604 F.2d 737 (2d Cir. 1979).

"That a computer program may be copyrightable as intellectual property does not alter the fact that once in the form of a floppy disc or other medium, the program is tangible, moveable and available in the marketplace. The fact that some programs may be tailored for specific purposes need not alter their status as 'goods' because the Code definition includes 'specially manufactured goods.'"

* * *

"Applying the U.C.C. to computer software transactions offers substantial benefits to litigants and the courts. The Code offers a uniform body of law on a wide range of questions likely to arise in computer software disputes: implied warranties, consequential damages, disclaimers of liability, the statute of limitations, to name a few.

"The importance of software to the commercial world and the advantages to be gained by the uniformity inherent in the U.C.C. are strong policy arguments favoring inclusion. The contrary arguments are not persuasive, and we hold that software is a 'good' within the definition in the Code."

Advent Sys. Ltd. v. Unisys Corp., 925 F.2d 670, 675, 676 (3d Cir. 1991).

gopher *(Internet)*

"A gopher server presents information in a set of menus, enabling a user who gains access to the server to select a series of increasingly narrow menu items

305

before locating a desired file that can be displayed on or copied to the user's computer. A content provider who maintains a gopher server ordinarily has no way of knowing who will gain access to the information made available."
Shea v. Reno, 930 F. Supp. 916, 928-29 (S.D.N.Y. 1996) (citations omitted). "Another approach [to information retrieval] uses a program and format named 'gopher' to guide an individual's search through the resources available on a remote computer."
American Civil Liberties Union v. Reno, 929 F. Supp. 824, 835-36 (E.D. Pa. 1996), *aff'd, Reno v. American Civil Liberties Union,* 521 U.S. 844 (1997).

Related issues. "Some types of Web client software also permit users to gain access to resources available on FTP and gopher sites."
Shea v. Reno, 930 F. Supp. 916, 929 (S.D.N.Y. 1996) (citations omitted).

"To . . . access a gopher server, the user must search for or know the address of a particular server."
Shea v. Reno, 930 F. Supp. 916, 930 (S.D.N.Y. 1996).

"A content provider who makes files available on . . . a gopher . . . has no way of knowing the identity of other participants who will have access to those servers."
Shea v. Reno, 930 F. Supp. 916, 941 (S.D.N.Y. 1996).

.gov *(Internet)*
"A [top-level] domain reserved for government entities."
Intermatic, Inc. v. Toeppen, 947 F. Supp. 1227, 1231 (N.D. Ill. 1996).

graphic work *(copyright)*
See **pictorial, graphic, and sculptural works.**

graphical user interface *(copyright; technology)*
The visual display appearing on a computer screen that facilitates a person's use of that computer system.

Related issues. "[C]opyright does not protect the purely utilitarian or functional aspects of Apple's graphical user interface because those aspects are constrained by such limitations as the hardware, ergonomics, and issues of 'user friendliness.'"
Apple Computer, Inc. v. Microsoft Corp., 35 F.3d 1435, 1444 (9th Cir. 1995).
See **GUI.**

gray-market good *(business)*
"[A] foreign-manufactured good, bearing a valid United States trademark, that is imported without the consent of the United States trademark holder."
K-Mart Corp. v. Cartier, Inc., 486 U.S. 281, 285 (1989).

Green Paper *(copyright)*

A preliminary draft report prepared by the Working Group on Intellectual Property of the Information Infrastructure Task Force and released on July 7, 1994, entitled "Information Infrastructure Task Force, Working Group on Intellectual Property Rights, Intellectual Property and the National Information Infrastructure: A Preliminary Draft of the Report of the Working Group on Intellectual Property Rights" (July 1994). *See also* **IITF; White Paper.**

greenlight *(business)*

To grant approval for a interactive project to proceed, at least to the next stage of development.

greenlight document *(business)*

The materials prepared by the developer to justify getting a greenlight for the project, usually including some or all of following: the complete design document, marketing research results, focus group reports, pro forma sales projections, and profitability analysis.

gross revenues *(contract)*

All revenues received from distribution of products or services without deductions. *See also* **net revenues.**

groupware *(software)*

Software that permits communications, coordination, and collaboration between multiple users. *See also* **collaborative software.**

guest book *(Internet)*

A feature that allows visitors to a site to leave identifying information. Although only a small percentage of visitors actually provide such information, what is provided can be valuable in developing e-mail lists or determining the interests of visitors.

GUI *(technology)*

Acronym for "Graphical User Interface"; pronounced "gooey." Provides a symbolic representation (called icons) for the various computer programs, data files, and other items stored on the computer disk drive(s).

hacker(s) *(criminal)*

"[A]n individual who accesses another's computer system without authority."
Steve Jackson Games, Inc. v. U.S. Secret Service, 4 Computer Cas. (CCH)
¶ 46,817, at 65,028, 65,029 n.2 (W.D. Tex. 1993).

"The term 'hackers' has also been understood to encompass both those
who obtain unauthorized access to computer systems and those who simply
enjoy using computers and experimenting with their capabilities as 'innocent' hobbyists."
United States v. Riggs, 739 F. Supp. 414, 423 (N.D. Ill. 1990).

hacker software *(criminal; software)*

Annotation. "The Internet is a source for numerous varieties of hacker software, some of which are issued in the guise of network administrator tools,
freely available for downloading. Some of these 'tools' can be surreptitiously
attached to innocent-sounding files and, upon execution, embed themselves
in your computer system. These innocent programs can be games, utilities,
applications, etc. Although some of these tools have legitimate purposes, people with malicious intent can also use these programs for their own goals."
Office of the Comptroller of the Currency, Infrastructure Threats from
Cyber-Terrorists 4 (Mar. 19, 1999).

handle *(Internet)*

A pseudonymous user name.

"Many usernames are pseudonyms . . . which provide users with a distinct
online identity and preserve anonymity."
American Library Association v. Pataki, 969 F. Supp. 160, 165 (S.D.N.Y. 1997).

handshake protocol *(hardware)*

". . . governs the content, order, and timing of the digital signals transmitted between the sending and receiving machines."
Secure Servs. Technology, Inc. v. Time & Space Processing, Inc., 722 F. Supp.
1354, 1357 (E.D. Va. 1989).
See generally **protocol.**

handwriting measurements *(electronic commerce)*

"[T]he metrics of the shapes, speeds and/or other distinguishing features of a signature as the person writes it by hand with a pen or stylus on a flat surface."

> Cal. Code of Regs., tit. 2, div. 7, ch. 10, § 22003(b)(1)(A).

harassment *(criminal)*

Intentionally or knowingly engaging in a regular course of conduct designed to scare or annoy another.

hard copy *(general)*

Computer output printed on paper.

hard disk *(hardware)*

"[A] peripheral, customized option, which is available and purchased for storage capacity beyond that which is provided through the floppy disks."

> *Gross v. Systems Eng'g Corp.,* 36 U.C.C. Rep. Serv. 42, 45 (E.D. Pa. 1983).

hardware *(hardware)*

"The term applied to the computer equipment—the processor unit, the storage devices, input devices, printers, etc. Hardware is differentiated from 'software' and 'firmware.'"

> U.S. Copyright Office, *Compendium of Copyright Office Practices* II, § 326 (1984).

". . . includes the central processing unit ('CPU'), which contains the electronic circuits that control the computer and perform the arithmetic and logical functions, the internal memory of the computer ('random access memory' or 'RAM'), input devices such as a keyboard and mouse, output devices such as a display screen and printer, and storage devices such as hard and floppy disk drives."

> *Lotus Dev. Corp. v. Paperback Software Int'l,* 740 F. Supp. 37, 43 (D. Mass. 1990).

". . . refers to a computer system's physical elements."

> *Shea v. Reno,* 930 F. Supp. 916, 926 n.6 (S.D.N.Y. 1997). *Similarly United States v. Seidlitz,* 589 F.2d 152, 154 n.3 (4th Cir. 1978), *cert. denied,* 441 U.S. 922 (1979) ("the tangible machinery of the computer"); *Universal Computers (Systems) Ltd. v. Datamedia Corp.,* 653 F. Supp. 518, 520 n.2 (D.N.J. 1987) ("the physical components of a computer, the machine itself . . ."); *Infosystems Technology, Inc. v. Logical Software, Inc.,* 8 Computer L. Serv. Rep. 689, 697 (D. Md. 1985) ("the physical components of a computer"), *aff'd,* 835 F.2d 874 (4th Cir. 1987); *Synercom Technology, Inc. v. University Com-*

puting Co., 462 F. Supp. 1003, 1005 (N.D. Tex. 1978) ("the physical machinery"); *Computer Sciences Corp. v. Comm'r of Internal Revenue,* 63 T.C. 327, 329 (1974) ("the physical computer equipment"); *Honeywell, Inc. v. Lithonia Lightning, Inc.,* 317 F. Supp. 406, 408 (N.D. Ga. 1970) ("the naked, tangible parts of the machinery itself"); *Commerce Union Bank v. Tidwell,* 538 S.W.2d 405, 406 n.1 (1976) ("the tangible parts of the computer itself").

"[A]ny electronic or mechanical equipment used in association with data processing."

In re Graphics Tech. Corp., 222 U.S.P.Q. (BNA) 179, 180 n.2 (T.T.A.B. 1984).

"The hardware segment includes the manufacture of the machines themselves, their component parts, and related peripheral equipment."

EDS Fed. Corp. v. Ginsberg, 259 S.E.2d 618, 621 n.1 (W. Va. 1979).

"The data processing equipment or so-called 'hardware' comprising a data processing unit consists of a central processing unit or main frame and peripherals such as input and output terminals and memory storage devices."

Honeywell Information Sys. v. Maricopa County, 118 Ariz. 171, 575 P.2d 801, 808 (App. 1977).

"[T]he actual physical machinery, consists of discrete parts: a central processing unit, the electronic device which performs the basic logical and arithmetic operations; various devices for storing information, such as magnetic tape units, magnetic discs, and magnetic drums; and terminal devices, for the output and input of information. These parts, when physically interconnected, comprise a unique computer hardware configuration."

Response of Carolina, Inc. v. Leasco Response, Inc., 537 F.2d 1307, 1326 (5th Cir. 1976).

". . . consisted of a central processing unit (CPU) and various other devices, included magnetic drums for data storage, card readers, printers and display consoles. . . ."

Teamsters Sec. Fund v. Sperry Rand Corp., 6 Computer L. Serv. Rep. 951, 956 (N.D. Cal. 1977).

"[T]he computer, printer, collator and other equipment. . . ."

Triangle Underwriters, Inc. v. Honeywell, Inc., 457 F. Supp. 765, 767 (E.D.N.Y. 1978), *rev'd and remanded,* 604 F.2d 737, 739 (2d Cir. 1979).

"[T]he computer itself and its allied peripheral equipment such as printers, modems and so forth."

Northeast Datacom, Inc. v. City of Wallingford, 212 Conn. 639, 563 A.2d 688, 689 n.3 (1989).

"[T]he computer machinery, its electronic circuitry and peripheral items such as keyboards, readers, scanners and printers."
Advent Sys. Ltd. v. Unisys Corp., 925 F.2d 670, 674 (3d Cir. 1991).

"[The] tangible machinery of the computer."
United States v. Seidlitz, 589 F.2d 152, 154 (4th Cir. 1978).

[CANADA] "The physical components of a system or device as opposed to the procedures required for its operation."
Chequecheck Services Ltd. v. Ministry of Finance (1980), 24 B.C.L.R. 217 (B.C. S.C.), *rev'd,* [1982] 5 W.W.R. 340 (B.C. C.A.).

[CANADA] "[T]he machine itself with all its component parts."
Clarke Irwin & Co. v. Singer Co. of Can., Ont. Div. Ct., Keith J., Dec. 3, 1979, *summarized at* [1979] 3 A.C.W.S. 807.

[CANADA] "Hardware is the actual dealing in computers themselves or dealing in the rental by various businesses and organizations of computer time."
Digital Methods Ltd. v. Alphatext Ltd., Ont. H.C., Garrett J., June 30, 1978, *summarized at* [1978] 2 A.C.W.S. 376.

hardwired terminal *(hardware)*
A terminal directly connected to the central processing unit without going through telephone lines and modems.

hash function *(technology)*
". . . describes a function that transforms an input into a unique output of fixed (and usually smaller) size that is dependent on the input."
Bernstein v. United States Dept. of Justice, 176 F.3d 1132, 1135 n.1 (9th Cir. 1999).

Annotation. "For some purposes (e.g., error checking, digital signatures), it is desirable that it be impossible to derive the input data given only the hash function's output—this type of function is known as a 'one-way hash function.' Hash functions have many uses in cryptography and computer science, and numerous one-way hash functions are widely known."
Bernstein v. United States Dept. of Justice, 176 F.3d 1132, 1135 n.1 (9th Cir. 1999).
See also **one-way hash function.**

HDTV *(hardware)*
Acronym for "High Definition Television." A new television standard that will provide wide-screen, high-definition pictures and CD-quality sound.

head end *(telecommunications)*
The origination point of a network.

header
(technology)
1. Information placed at the beginning of a file, record, or document that precedes the main body of the file. 2. Text entered once by the user into a document, which is printed on every page of that document.

(Internet)
Information that appears at the top of an e-mail or newsgroup posting that contains information needed by the computers that route it from the sender to the recipient, including the message ID, date, and time.

head-mounted display *(hardware)*
Abbreviated as "HMD." A device that projects visual images to each eye and sound to each ear, giving the illusion of complete immersion in a simulated environment, and containing sensors to monitor the position of the user's head.

helper applications *(software)*
Computer programs that reside on the user's hard disk, and which assist the Web browser in handling different types of data, such as graphic formats (e.g., GIF, JPEG), video formats (e.g., MPEG), and audio formats (e.g., AU).

hexadecimal *(technology)*
"A base 16 numbering system used as a shorthand representation of a string of binary instructions."
    E.F. Johnson Co. v. Uniden Corp. of America, 623 F. Supp. 1485, 1488 (D. Minn. 1985).

Annotation. "Machine language may also be represented in hexadecimal form, . . . by the characters 0-9 and A-F, where 'A' represents 10, 'B' represents 11, and so on through 'F,' which represents 15. In hexadecimal machine language, only two rather than eight characters are required to allow for 256 unique combinations. . . . The computer is able to translate these hexadecimal instructions into binary form."
    Lotus Dev. Corp. v. Paperback Software Int'l, 740 F. Supp. 37, 43 (D. Mass. 1990).
See also **hexadecimal coding; hexadecimal notation.**

hexadecimal coding *(software)*

". . . in machine language uses letters and numbers."

> U.S. Copyright Office, *Compendium of Copyright Office Practices* II, at 300-16 (1984).

See also **hexadecimal; hexadecimal notation.**

hexadecimal notation *(technology)*

[CANADA] "Hexadecimal notation is based on a number system having a base 16. It is merely a shorthand way of writing the binary code. It is used because it uses less characters and is therefore less cumbersome than binary."

> *Apple Computer, Inc. v. Mackintosh Computers Ltd.* (1986), 28 D.L.R. (4th) 178 (Fed. T.D.).

[CANADA] "Instructions denoted by using a system in which 16 characters are used (in this case the numbers from 0 to 9 together with the letters from A to F)."

> *IBM Corp. v. Ordinateurs Spirales, Inc.* (1984), 2 C.I.P.R. 56 (Fed. T.D.).

See also **hexadecimal; hexadecimal coding.**

HFS *(technology)*

Acronym for "Hicrarchical File System." The file structure used by the Apple Macintosh computer system.

high-level language *(software)*

". . . , such as the commonly used BASIC and FORTRAN, uses English words and symbols, and is relatively easy to learn and understand (e.g., 'GO TO 40' tells the computer to skip intervening steps and go to the step at line 40). . . . Statements in high level language, . . . are referred to as written in source code."

> *Apple Computer, Inc. v. Franklin Computer Corp.,* 714 F.2d 1240, 1243 (3d Cir. 1983), *cert. dism.,* 464 U.S. 1033 (1984).

See also **assembly language; source code; source language(s); source program.**

high-performance computing and communications *(technology)*

Abbreviated as "HPCC."

"[A]dvanced computing, communications, and information technologies, including scientific workstations, supercomputer systems (including vector supercomputers and large scale parallel systems), high-capacity and high-speed networks, special purpose and experimental systems, and applications and systems software."

> High Performance Computing Act of 1991, 15 U.S.C. § 5503(3).

high resolution *(hardware)*

Abbreviated as "high-res." A type of video display with a large number of pixels per inch, resulting in a better picture.

high-resolution system *(hardware)*

An electronic video system capable of displaying roughly 1,000 lines along its vertical axis.

hit(s) *(advertising; Internet)*

A log entry on the web server that shows that an item was retrieved from a particular web page on that server. Depending on how a web site is created, a single access to a web page may generate multiple hits. The number of hits recorded for a web site provides a very rough estimate of the number of users who have accessed the web site.

"[A] match . . . ."

> *Niton Corp. v. Radiation Monitoring Devices, Inc.*, 27 F. Supp. 2d 102, 104 (D. Mass. 1998).

Annotation. "The more often a term appears in the metatags and in the text of the web page, the more likely it is that the web page will be 'hit' in a search for that keyword and the higher on the list of 'hits' the web page will appear."

> *Brookfield Comm., Inc. v. West Coast Entertainment Corp.*, 174 F.3d 1036, 1045 (9th Cir. 1999) (citation omitted).

The "hit" is now considered an outdated and not particularly useful measure of the traffic on a web site, since downloading a single web page may result in multiple hits. Today there are other measurements used for such purposes, such as page views.

See also **page view.**

H-matrix *(technology)*

"[A] series of ones and zeros arranged in rows and columns in a matrix format."

> *E.F. Johnson Co. v. Uniden Corp. of Am.*, 623 F. Supp. 1485, 1495 (D. Minn. 1985).

HMD *(multimedia; technology)*

Acronym for "Head-Mounted Display." *See* **head-mounted display.**

hold a private key *(electronic commerce)*

"[T]o be authorized to utilize a private key."

> Wash. Rev. Code § 19.34.020(14).

hold harmless *(contract)*

A contractual clause under which one party agrees to protect the other against liability for certain defined types of claims.

Sample clause. "Each party shall save the other harmless from and against and shall indemnify the other for any liability, loss, costs, expenses, or damages howsoever caused by reason of any injury (whether to body, property, or personal or business character or reputation) sustained by any person or to any person or to property by reason of any act, ne-glect, default, or omission of it or any of its agents, employees, or other representatives, and it shall pay all sums to be paid or discharged in case of an action or any such damages or injuries. Nothing herein is intended to nor shall it relieve either party from liability for its own act, omission, or negligence."

home page(s) *(Internet)*

"[D]ocuments which provide a set of links designed to represent the organization, and through links from the home page, guide the user directly or indirectly to information about or relevant to that organization."

American Civil Liberties Union v. Reno, 929 F. Supp. 824, 836 (E.D. Pa. 1996), *aff'd, Reno v. American Civil Liberties Union,* 521 U.S. 844 (1997).

"[T]he equivalent of individualized newsletters about the person or organization, which are available to everyone on the Web."

American Civil Liberties Union v. Reno, 929 F. Supp. 824, 837 (E.D. Pa. 1996), *aff'd, Reno v. American Civil Liberties Union,* 521 U.S. 844 (1997).

"[T]he first access point to the site."

United States v. Microsoft Corp., 65 F. Supp. 2d 1, 5 (D.D.C. 1999) (Finding of Fact 14).

Annotation. The home page is usually a hypertext document that presents an overview of the site and hyperlinks to the other pages comprising the site."

United States v. Microsoft Corp., 65 F. Supp. 2d 1, 5 (D.D.C. 1999) (Finding of Fact 14).

horizontal frequency rate *(hardware)*

"[T]he number of times the monitor generated a sweep from left to right (the vertical synchronization rate multiplied by the number of scan lines."

Princeton Graphics Operating L.P. v. NEC Home Elecs. (U.S.A.), Inc., 732 F. Supp. 1258, 1259 n.3 (S.D.N.Y. 1990).

horizontal synchronizing pulse(s) *(hardware)*
"[T]he pulses that direct the monitor to come back from right to left. . . ."
Princeton Graphics Operating L.P. v. NEC Home Elecs. (U.S.A.), Inc., 732 F. Supp. 1258, 1260 n.5 (S.D.N.Y. 1990).

host *(hardware; Internet)*
"A computer or device that is attached to the Internet. . . ."
Intermatic, Inc. v. Toeppen, 947 F. Supp;. 1227, 1230 (N.D. Ill. 1996).

Related issues. "[F]orty percent of all host computers are located outside the United States."
Shea v. Reno, 930 F. Supp. 916, 931 (S.D.N.Y. 1996).

hot link *(Internet)*
See hyperlink.

house mark *(trademark)*
"[A] mark that appears in conjunction with different 'product marks' or 'service marks' emanating from a single 'house' or company."
Digital Equipment Corp. v. Altavista Technology, Inc., 960 F. Supp. 456, 474 n.34 (D. Mass. 1997) (citation omitted).

HPCC *(technology)*
Acronym for "High-Performance Computing and Communications."
See **high-performance computing and communications.**

HTML *(Internet)*
Acronym for "Hypertext Mark-up Language."

"The Web utilizes a 'hypertext' formatting language called hypertext markup language (HTML), and programs that 'browse' the Web can display HTML documents containing text, images, sound, animation and moving video. Any HTML document can include links to other types of information or resources, so that while viewing an HTML document that, for example, describes resources available on the Internet, one can 'click' using a computer mouse on the description of the resource and be immediately connected to the resource itself. Such 'hyperlinks' allow information to be accessed and organized in very flexible ways, and allow people to locate and efficiently view related information even if the information is stored on numerous computers all around the world."
American Civil Liberties Union v. Reno, 929 F. Supp. 824, 836 (E.D. Pa. 1996), *aff'd, Reno v. American Civil Liberties Union,* 521 U.S. 844 (1997).

"[T]he standard Web formatting language."
Shea v. Reno, 930 F. Supp. 916, 929 (S.D.N.Y. 1996).

"[C]ommon information storage formats. . . ."
American Civil Liberties Union v. Reno, 929 F. Supp. 824, 837 (E.D. Pa. 1996), *aff'd, Reno v. American Civil Liberties Union,* 521 U.S. 844 (1997).

Annotation. "The ease of communication through the Internet is facilitated by the use of hypertext markup language (HTML) which allows for the creation of 'hyperlinks' or 'links.' HTML enables a user to jump from one source to another related source by clicking on the link."
American Civil Liberties Union v. Reno, 929 F. Supp. 824, 843 (E.D. Pa. 1996), *aff'd, Reno v. American Civil Liberties Union,* 521 U.S. 844 (1997).

http *(Internet)*

Acronym for "HyperText Transfer Protocol." An Internet communications standard (protocol) that permits access to web sites from a web browser and requests for information from the web pages on a server. The term "http" appears at the beginning of most web addresses and designates that the following alphanumeric character string is a web address.

Annotation. "Because Web servers are linked to the Internet through a common communications protocol, known as hypertext transfer protocol ('HTTP'), a user can move seamlessly between documents, regardless of [his/her] location; when a user viewing a document located on one server selects a link to a document located elsewhere, the browser will automatically contact the second server and display the document."
Shea v. Reno, 930 F. Supp. 916, 929 (S.D.N.Y. 1996).

"[A] common language for the exchange of Web documents."
American Civil Liberties Union v. Reno, 929 F. Supp. 824, 837 (E.D. Pa. 1996), *aff'd, Reno v. American Civil Liberties Union,* 521 U.S. 844 (1997).

human readable *(software)*

"All code is human readable. As source code is closer to human language than is object code, it tends to be comprehended more easily by humans than object code."
Universal City Studios, Inc. v. Reimerdes, 111 F. Supp. 2d 294, 306 (S.D.N.Y. 2000).

hung *(technology)*

When a computer unexpectedly stops functioning. *See also* **crash.**

hybrid *(technology)*

Also called "hybrid HFS-ISO disc." A CD-ROM that employs a dual media or multipurpose format, so it can be used on two or more different computer platforms.

hyperlink *(Internet)*

Also called "link" and "hot link."

"[A] link from one site on the Internet to a second site on the Internet. 'Clicking' on a designated space on the initial page which references the subsequent site by a picture, by some highlighted text or by some other indication will take a person viewing the initial web page to a second page. In addition to their use in indexes, hyperlinks are commonly placed on existing web pages, thus allowing Internet users to move from web page to web page at the click of a button, without having to type in URLs.

"Hyperlinks can be and commonly are established without reference to the domain name of the second site. . . . A hyperlink is not technically related to a domain name and therefore it can be identical to an existing domain name without conflicting with that domain name."

Intermatic, Inc. v. Toeppen, 947 F. Supp. 1227, 1232 (N.D. Ill. 1996).

"[H]ighlighted text or images that, when selected by the user, permit him to view another, related Web document."

Shea v. Reno, 930 F. Supp. 916, 929 (S.D.N.Y. 1996).

"[A]nnotated references. . . ."

United States v. Microsoft Corp., 65 F. Supp. 2d 1, 5 (D.D.C. 1999) (Finding of Fact 13).

Annotation. "'Clicking' on a designated space on the initial page which references the subsequent site by a picture, by some highlighted text or by some other indication will take a person viewing the initial web page to a second page. In addition to their use in indexes [sic], hyperlinks are commonly placed on existing web pages, thus allowing Internet users to move from web page to web page at the click of a button, without having to type in URLs."

Intermatic, Inc. v. Toeppen, 947 F. Supp. 1227, 1232 (N.D. Ill. 1996).

"Through a 'hyperlink,' a browser may connect to another web site by clicking on the specially highlighted text or images on the initial web site. After clicking on the highlighted text, the browser is then directly taken to that particular web site."

Blumenthal v. Drudge, 992 F. Supp. 44, 47 n.2 (D.D.C. 1998).

"Hyperlinks can be used as cross-references within a single document, between documents on the same site, or between documents on different sites."
> *United States v. Microsoft Corp.,* 65 F. Supp. 2d 1, 5 (D.D.C. 1999) (Finding of Fact 13).

See also **link(s).**

hypermedia *(multimedia)*

See **multimedia.**

hypertext *(Internet)*

Text or information that points (links) to other information. A method of information storage and retrieval where information is not stored linearly, but at different levels, so that the user can obtain increasingly detailed levels of information on specific issues, questions or words only when he/she requests it.

hypertext markup language *(Internet)*

"[T]he standard Web formatting language."
> *Shea v. Reno,* 930 F. Supp. 916, 929 (S.D.N.Y. 1996).

See also **HTML.**

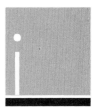

IAB *(advertising; organization)*
Acronym for "Internet Advertising Bureau."

A trade organization whose members are those involved in advertising on the Internet. Located at <http://www.iab.net>.

IAHC *(organization)*
Acronym for "International Ad Hoc Committee." A group formed by the Internet Assigned Numbers Authority to study and reform the administration and operation of the generic top-level domain system. The group issued its "Final Report" in February 1997. In April 1997, the IAHC issued a "Memorandum of Understanding on the Generic Top Level Domain ('gTLD') Name Space of the Internet Assigned Numbers Authority," which set forth a framework for the structure, policies, and procedures to govern the administration of seven new gTLDs. By November 1997, 179 entities had signed the Memorandum of Understanding. However, when the Clinton Administration announced its proposal to reform the domain name system in January 1998, the work of the IAHC was suspended.

IANA *(organization)*
See **Internet Assigned Numbers Authority.**

IBM *(business)*
Acronym for "International Business Machines Corporation."

". . . was incorporated on February 24, 1924. . . . Before its entry into the electronic data processing (EDP) industry, IBM manufactured punch card accounting machines and other products. In addition to its EDP business, IBM develops, manufactures, and markets other business machines, including copiers, dictating equipment, and electric typewriters. IBM has been deeply involved in the phenomenal growth of the electronic data processing industry since almost the beginning of the industry."
Telex Corp. v. IBM Corp., 367 F. Supp. 258, 270 (N.D. Okla. 1973), *aff'd in part, rev'd in part,* 510 F.2d 894 (10th Cir.), *cert. dism.* 423 U.S. 802 (1975).

"... is both a hardware and a software company. On the hardware side, IBM manufactures and licenses, among other things, Intel-compatible PCs. On the software side, IBM develops and sells, among other things, Intel-compatible PC operating systems and office productivity applications."

> *United States v. Microsoft Corp.*, 65 F. Supp. 2d 1, 29-30 (D.D.C. 1999) (Finding of Fact 115).

"[A] massive, multinational corporation which distributes, among other things, large business computers."

> *IBM Corp. v. Medlantic Healthcare Group*, 1 Computer Cas. (CCH) ¶ 46,032, at 60,914 (D.D.C. 1989).

"[T]he pacesetter and leader in the personal computer for business use arena."

> *Princeton Graphics Operating L.P. v. NEC Home Elecs. (U.S.A.), Inc.*, 732 F. Supp. 1258, 1259 (S.D.N.Y. 1990).

Annotation. "IBM is one of the largest industrial corporations in the world. It achieved technical leadership in the computer industry over other early entrants, such as Sperry Rand, in the mid-1950's and thereafter pioneered the development of many electronic data processing products. . . ."

> *California Computer Prods., Inc. v. IBM Corp.*, 613 F.2d 727, 731 (9th Cir. 1979).

IC *(hardware)*

Acronym for "Integrated Circuit."

"[A] collection of electronic elements which are interconnected to form an electronic circuit. These elements and interconnections are formed in or upon a substrate of semiconductor material."

> *National Semiconductor Corp. v. Linear Technology Corp.*, 703 F. Supp. 845, 846 (N.D. Cal. 1988).

See also **integrated circuit.**

ICANN *(Internet; organization)*

Acronym for "Internet Corporation for Assigned Names and Numbers." A nonprofit organization created to assume responsibility for IP address allocation, protocol parameter assignment, domain name system management, and root server system management.

Annotation. "In the fall of 1998, the Internet Corporation for Assigned Names and Numbers ('ICANN') was incorporated as a non-profit public benefit corporation in California, in order to assume the management of the DNS as contemplated in the White Paper. ICANN's bylaws state that it is to be aided by three supporting organizations, one of which is the Domain Name Supporting Organization ('DNSO'), the entity responsible for making policy recommendations to ICANN regarding the DNS, including, among other things, new TLDs. On November 25, 1998, ICANN and the Commerce Department entered into a Memorandum of Understanding, pursuant to which they agreed jointly to develop and test the mechanisms and procedures that should be in place in the new, privatized DNS. Specifically, ICANN and the Commerce Department agreed to collaborate on 'written technical procedures for operation of the primary root server including procedures that permit modifications, additions or deletions to the root zone file.'"

> *Name.Space, Inc. v. Network Solutions, Inc.*, 202 F.3d 573, 578-79 (2d Cir. 2000) (citations omitted).

"As of April 1999, Network Solutions, Inc. (NSI) the company previously responsible for registering domain names ending in '.com,' '.org,' and '.net' to owners, no longer holds a monopoly on this service. In April, the Internet Corporation for Assigned Names and Numbers (ICANN) announced five companies, including America Online, which will compete with NSI as domain name registrars for a two-month test period, after which period NSI will be required to open the registration system and its database of domain names to all registrars approved by ICANN."

> *Washington Speakers Bureau, Inc. v. Leading Authorities, Inc.,* 49 F. Supp. 2d 496, 498 n.2 (E.D. Va. 1999).

icon *(technology)*

A small symbol on the screen that stands for something, such as a command (e.g., open a file, cut text, delete a file), or an application (e.g., launch a word processing program).

idea *(copyright)*

Something that exists in the mind.

Annotation. "In no case does copyright protection for an original work of authorship extend to any idea, procedure, process, system, method of operation, concept, principle, or discovery, regardless of the form in which it is described, explained, illustrated, or embodied in such work."

> U.S. Copyright Act, 17 U.S.C. § 102(b).

"Some concern has been expressed lest copyright in computer programs should extend protection to the methodology or processes adopted by the programmer, rather than merely to the 'writing' expressing his ideas. Section 102(b) is intended, among other things, to make clear that the expression adopted by the programmer is the copyrightable element in a computer program, and that the actual processes or methods embodied in the program are not within the scope of the copyright law."

H.R. Rep No. 1476, 94th Cong., 2d Sess. 57 (1976).

"Section 102(b) . . . in no way enlarges or contracts the scope of copyright protection under the present law. Its purpose is to restate, in the context of the new single Federal system of copyright, that the basic dichotomy between expression and idea remains unchanged."

M. Kramer Mfg. Co. v. Andrews, 783 F.2d 421, 435 (4th Cir. 1986), *citing* H.R. Rep No. 1476, 94th Cong., 2d Sess. (1976).

"It is a fundamental principle of copyright law that a copyright does not protect an idea, but only the expression of the idea."

Computer Assocs. Int'l, Inc. v. Altai, Inc., 982 F.2d 693, 703 (2d Cir. 1992), *citing Baker v. Selden,* 101 U.S. 99 (1879) & *Mazer v. Stein,* 347 U.S. 201, 217 (1954).

"The author does not acquire exclusive rights to a literary work in its entirety. Under the Act, society is free to exploit facts, ideas, processes, or methods of operation in the copyrighted work."

Atari Games Corp. v. Nintendo of America, Inc., 975 F.2d 832, 842 (Fed. Cir. 1992).

"In order to enjoy a lawful monopoly over the idea or functional principle underlying the work, the creator must satisfy the more stringent standard imposed by patent law."

DSC Comm. Corp. v. DGI Technologies, Inc., 898 F. Supp. 1183, 1191 (N.D. Tex. 1995), *aff'd,* 81 F.3d 597 (5th Cir. 1996).

"[P]rogrammers are free to read copyrighted programs and use the ideas embodied in them in preparing their own works."

Apple Computer, Inc. v. Formula Int'l, Inc., 725 F.2d 521, 525 (9th Cir. 1984).

"The policy attempts to strike a balance between the dissemination of information for the promotion of learning, culture and development, and the protection of innovative works, thus creating an incentive for development."

Healthcare Affiliated Servs., Inc. v. Lippany, 701 F. Supp. 1142, 1150 (W.D. Pa. 1988). *Accord Whelan Assocs., Inc. v. Jaslow Dental Lab.,* 797 F.2d 1222, 1235 (3rd Cir. 1986); *Apple Computer, Inc. v. Franklin Computer Corp.,* 714 F.2d 1240, 1253 (3d Cir. 1983).

idea/expression dichotomy *(copyright)*
A judicially administered balancing test to determine whether something sought to be protected by copyright is protectable expression or an unprotectable idea.

"The primary objective of copyright is not to reward the labor of authors, but '[t]o promote the Progress of Science and useful Arts.' . . . To this end, copyright assures authors the right to their original expression, but encourages others to build freely upon the ideas and information conveyed by a work. This principle, known as the idea/expression or fact/expression dichotomy, applies to all works of authorship. . . . This result is neither unfair nor unfortunate. It is the means by which copyright advances the progress of science and art."
 Feist Publications, Inc. v. Rural Tel. Serv. Co., 499 U.S. 340, 348 (1991) (citations omitted).

Annotation. "Drawing the line between idea and expression is a tricky business. Judge Learned Hand noted that '[n]obody has ever been able to fix that boundary, and nobody ever can. . . .' Thirty years later his convictions remained firm. 'Obviously, no principle can be stated as to when an imitator has gone beyond copying the "idea," and has borrowed its "expression,"' Judge Hand concluded. 'Decisions must therefore inevitably be *ad hoc.*'"
 Computer Assocs. Int'l, Inc. v. Altai, Inc., 982 F.2d 693, 704 (2d Cir. 1992) (citations omitted; emphasis in original).

"A hypothetical, oversimplified example, may serve to illuminate the idea versus expression controversy. The familiar 'figure-H' pattern of an automobile stick is chosen arbitrarily by an auto manufacturer. Several different patterns may be imagined, some more convenient for the driver or easier to manufacture than others, but all representing possible configurations. The pattern chosen is arbitrary, but once chosen, it is the only pattern which will work in a particular model. The pattern (analogous to the computer 'format') may be expressed in several different ways: by a prose description in a driver's manual, through a diagram, photograph, or driver training film, or otherwise. Each of these expressions may presumably be protected through copyright. But the copyright protects copying of the particular expressions of the pattern, and does not prohibit another manufacturer from marketing a car using the same pattern. Use of the same pattern might be socially desirable, as it would reduce the retraining of drivers. Likewise, the second manufacturer is free to use its own prose descriptions, photographs, diagrams, or the like, so long as these materials take the form of original expressions of the copied idea. . . ."
 Synercom Technology, Inc. v. University Computing Co., 462 F. Supp. 1003, 1013 (N.D. Tex. 1978).

Related issues. "The copyright concepts of the idea/expression dichotomy and the fair use defense balance the important First Amendment rights with the constitutional authority for 'promot[ing] the progress of science and the useful arts.'. . ."

> *Religious Technology Ctr. v. Netcom On-line Comm. Servs., Inc.,* 907 F. Supp. 1361, 1377 (N.D. Cal. 1995).

"The Copyright Act of 1976 codifies this idea-expression dichotomy. 17 U.S.C. § 102(b)."

> *Atari, Inc. v. North American Philips Consumer Elecs. Corp.,* 672 F.2d 607, 615 (7th. Cir.), *cert. denied,* 459 U.S. 880 (1982).

"Summary judgment is particularly appropriate where the idea and expression are inseparable or where analytic dissection determines that all similarities arise from standard elements derived from a common idea."

> *Interactive Networks, Inc. v. NTN Comm., Inc.,* 875 F. Supp. 1398, 1403 (N.D. Cal. 1995) (citations omitted).

See also **abstractions test; fact/expression dichotomy; idea-expression distinction; idea/expression identity exception; merger doctrine.**

idea-expression distinction *(copyright)*

"CONTU concluded that the idea-expression distinction should be used to determine which aspects of computer programs are copyrightable."

> *Lotus Dev. Corp. v. Paperback Software Int'l,* 740 F. Supp. 37, 54 (D. Mass. 1990), *citing CONTU Final Report* 44 (1978).

See also **idea/expression dichotomy.**

idea/expression identity exception *(copyright)*

"The 'idea/expression identity' exception provides that copyrighted language may be copied without infringing when there is but a limited number of ways to express a given idea. This rule is the logical extension of the fundamental principle that copyright cannot protect ideas. In the computer context this means that when specific instructions, even though previously copyrighted, are the only and essential means of accomplishing a given task, their later use by another will not amount to an infringement.

* * *

"When other language is available, programmers are free to read copyrighted programs and use the ideas embodied in them in preparing their own works."

> *CONTU Final Report* 20 (1978), *quoted with approval in Apple Computer, Inc. v. Formula Int'l, Inc.,* 725 F.2d 521, 525 (9th Cir. 1984).

See also **idea/expression dichotomy; idea-expression distinction.**

idea-expression unity *(copyright)*
"[W]here idea and expression are indistinguishable, the copyright will protect against only identical copying."

> *Atari, Inc. v. North American Philips Consumer Elecs. Corp.*, 672 F.2d 607, 616 (7th Cir.), *cert. denied*, 459 U.S. 880 (1982).

See also **merger doctrine.**

IEEE *(organization)*
"An acronym for Institute for Electrical and Electronic Engineers."

> *National Semiconductor Corp. v. Linear Technology Corp.*, 703 F. Supp. 845, 847 (N.D. Cal. 1988) (emphasis added).

See **Institute for Electrical and Electronic Engineers.**

IESG *(organization)*
See **Internet Engineering Steering Group.**

IETF *(organization)*
Acronym for "Internet Engineering Task Force."
See **Internet Engineering Task Force.**

IFP *(contract)*
Acronym for "Invitation for Proposal." *IBM Corp. v. Florida Department of General Services*, Administrative Law Reports 548 (1979).

A document sent to vendors of computer products and/or services, setting forth the sender's requirements and inviting the vendors to submit a proposal (generally written) that describes how their products and/or services meet the requirements set forth in the document. *See also* **request for proposal.**

IITF *(organization)*
Acronym for "Information Infrastructure Task Force." *See* **Information Infrastructure Task Force.**

illegal character *(technology)*
A character that is not valid according to programming specifications.

IM *(Internet)*
Abbreviation for Instant Message.
"[T]he real-time chat component of the BUDDY LISTS® service. . . ."

> *America Online, Inc. v. AT&T Corp.*, 64 F. Supp. 2d 549, 553 (E.D. Va. 1999).

Related issues. "The conclusion is that IM stands for 'instant message' (as AOL admits), and because the primary significance of 'instant message' is to stand for an 'instant message,' the term IM reflects the genus, not the species."

> *America Online, Inc. v. AT&T Corp.,* 64 F. Supp. 2d 549, 566 (E.D. Va. 1999).

image *(technology)*

1. A graphical representation. 2. The file that results from premastering.

image identifier code(s) *(technology)*

"[T]he polarities in the horizontal and vertical synchronizing pulses."

> *Princeton Graphics Operating L.P. v. NEC Home Elecs. (U.S.A.), Inc.,* 732 F. Supp. 1258, 1260 n.5 (S.D.N.Y. 1990).

image processing *(technology)*

Manipulating an image by computer.

IMHO *(Internet)*

Abbreviation used in electronic messages for "In My Humble Opinion."

implied warranties *(contract)*

See implied warranty of fitness for a particular purpose; implied warranty of merchantability.

implied warranty of fitness for a particular purpose *(contract)*

"Where the seller at the time of contracting has reason to know any particular purpose for which the goods are required and the buyer is relying on the seller's skill or judgment to select or furnish suitable goods, there is unless excluded or modified . . . an implied warranty that the goods shall be fit for such purpose."

> U.C.C. § 2-315 (1979).

Annotation. "A manufacturer of computer software cannot ordinarily be expected to know whether its software will be fit for the particular use intended, but a retailer, having knowledge of the hardware with which the software will be used, can ordinarily be expected to know whether the software will be fit for the particular use intended, at least to the extent of its compatibility with the hardware."

> *Barazzotto v. Intelligent Sys., Inc.,* 1 Computer Cas. (CCH) ¶ 45,031, at 60,270, 60,271 (Ohio App. 1987).

"[W]hen the buyer before entering into contract has examined the goods or the sample or model as fully as he desired or has refused to examine the goods there is no implied warranty with regard to defects which an examination ought in the circumstances to have revealed to him."

U.C.C. § 2-316(3)(b) (1979).

implied warranty of merchantability *(contract)*

"Where the seller at the time of contracting has reason to know any particular purpose for which the goods are required and the buyer is relying on the seller's skill or judgment to select or furnish suitable goods, there is unless excluded or modified . . . an implied warranty that the goods shall be fit for such purpose."

U.C.C. § 2-315 (1979).

impoundment *(copyright)*

"At any time while an action under this title is pending, the court may order the impounding, on such terms as it may deem reasonable, of all copies . . . claimed to have been made or used in violation of the copyright owner's exclusive rights, and of all plates, molds, matrices, masters, tapes, film negatives, or other articles by means of which such copies . . . may be reproduced."

17 U.S.C. § 503(a).

Annotation. "[T]he statutory mandate is clear. 'All articles alleged to infringe the copyright' are to be impounded and 'all infringing copies . . .' are to be destroyed. Neither the statute nor the Supreme Court rules give the District Court any discretion to determine what to impound or what to destroy. The process Congress granted the aggrieved copyright proprietor is a summary one. . . . It is to impound *everything* the plaintiff alleges infringes his copyright. Rules 9 and 10 then provide that the defendant apply to the court for return of the seized articles if he shows that 'the articles seized are not infringing copies, records, plates, molds, matrices, or other means for making the copies alleged to infringe the copyright.' . . . If the articles seized are infringing copies or infringing means, the District Court has no discretion to return them."

Duchess Music Corp. v. Stern, 458 F.2d 1305, 1308 (9th Cir.), *cert. denied,* 409 U.S. 847 (1972) (emphasis in original).

impression *(advertising)*

Also called "ad impression" and "page impression."

An advertisement downloaded and seen by visitors to a web site.

improper means *(trade secret)*

"Improper means of acquiring another's trade secret . . . include theft, fraud, unauthorized interception of communications. . . . Independent discovery and analysis of publicly available products or information are not improper means of acquisition."

Restatement (Third) of Unfair Competition § 43 (1995).

"[T]heft, bribery, misrepresentation, breach or inducement of breach of a duty to maintain secrecy, or espionage through electronic or other means."

Minn. Stat. § 325C.01, subd. 2.

"[E]spionage, theft, bribery, misrepresentation and breach or inducement of a breach of duty to maintain secrecy."

Wis. Stat. § 134.90(1)(a).

"A complete catalogue of improper means is not possible. In general they are means which fall below the generally accepted standards of commercial morality and reasonable conduct."

Alcatel USA, Inc. v. DGI Technologies, Inc., 166 F.3d 772, 785 (5th Cir. 1999), *citing E.I. duPont deNemours & Co. v. Christopher,* 431 F.2d 1012 (5th Cir. 1970), *cert. denied,* 400 U.S. 1024 (1971).

See also **proper means; reverse engineering; trade secret.**

in commerce *(trademark)*

When a trademark or trade name is used in commercial transactions between states or between the United States and a foreign government.

Annotation. "Because Internet communications transmit instantaneously on a worldwide basis there is little question that the 'in commerce' requirement would be met in a typical Internet message, be it trademark infringement or false advertising."

Intermatic, Inc. v. Toeppen, 947 F. Supp. 1227, 1239 (N.D. Ill. 1996), *quoting* 1 Gilson, *Trademark Protection and Practice* § 5.11[2], at 5-234 (1996).

"The Supreme Court has held that the in commerce requirement should be construed liberally because the Lanham Act 'confers broad jurisdictional powers upon the courts of the United States.' "

Intermatic, Inc. v. Toeppen, 947 F. Supp. 1227, 1239-40 (N.D. Ill. 1996) (citation omitted).

See also **Commerce Clause.**

in sync(h) *(technology)*

See **synchronization.**

in the clear *(technology)*
A digital work in unencrypyted form. *See also* **plaintext.**

incidental *(copyright)*
". . . means related to and relatively minor by comparison."
17 U.S.C. § 1001(5)(C)(ii).

incidental damages *(contract)*
"[I]nclude expenses reasonably incurred in inspection, receipt, transportation and care and custody of goods rightfully rejected, any commercially reasonable charges, expenses or commissions in connection with effecting cover and any other reasonable expense incident to the delay or other breach."
U.C.C. § 2-715(1) (1979).

" . . . resulting from breach of contract:
(A) means compensation for any commercially reasonable charges, expenses, or commissions reasonably incurred by an aggrieved party with respect to:
(i) inspection, receipt, transmission, transportation, care, or custody of identified copies or information that is the subject of the breach;
(ii) stopping delivery, shipment, or transmission;
(iii) effecting cover or retransfer of copies or information after the breach;
(iv) other efforts after the breach to minimize or avoid loss resulting from the breach; and
(v) matters otherwise incident to the breach; and
(B) does not include consequential damages or direct damages."
UCITA § 102(a)(34).

incompatible *(technology)*
The inability of hardware and software to work together. Today, most software prepared for one platform will not run correctly on other platforms.

incorporate by reference *(electronic commerce)*
"[T]o make one message a part of another message by identifying the message to be incorporated and expressing the intention that it be incorporated."
Wash. Rev. Code § 19.34.020(15).

indecency *(criminal)*
"The definition of indecency, like the definition of obscenity, is not a rigid formula. Rather, it confers a large degree of autonomy to individual com-

munities to set the bounds for decency for themselves. This is as it should be, since this flexibility recognizes that ours is a country with diverse cultural and historical roots."

American Civil Liberties Union v. Reno, 929 F. Supp. 824, 871 (E.D. Pa. 1996) (citations omitted), *aff'd, Reno v. American Civil Liberties Union,* 521 U.S. 844 (1997).

Annotation. "Although no court of appeals has ever to my knowledge upheld a vagueness challenge to the meaning of 'indecency,' several recent cases have grappled with the elusive meaning of that word in the context of cable television and 'dial-a-porn.'"

American Civil Liberties Union v. Reno, 929 F. Supp. 824, 868 (E.D. Pa. 1996), *aff'd, Reno v. American Civil Liberties Union,* 521 U.S. 844 (1997).

"Sexual expression which is indecent but is not obscene is protected by the First Amendment."

American Civil Liberties Union v. Johnson, 194 F.3d 1149, 1156 (10th Cir. 1999) (citation omitted).

indemnification *(contract)*

The obligation of one party to pay the expenses and damages incurred by another.

Sample clause. "Upon prompt notice, in writing, from Customer or Customer's customer that an action has been commenced against Customer or Customer's customer based on a claim that the Software, or any component thereof, infringes any copyright, trademark, trade secret or United States patent, SoftCo shall defend or settle such action at its own expense and shall indemnify and hold harmless and pay any costs or damages finally awarded against Customer or Customer's customer including all expenses and legal fees (including Customer's) associated therewith. SoftCo shall have sole control of the defense of such action and all negotiations for its compromise or settlement. In the event that the Software becomes, or in the opinion of SoftCo is likely to become, subject to a claim of infringement of any copyright, trademark, trade secret or United States patents, Customer or Customer's customer shall permit SoftCo, at SoftCo's option and expense, to either:

(a) Procure, for the Customer and its customers, the right to continue using the Software; or

(b) Replace or modify the Software so that it becomes non-infringing, provided that the Software, as modified, is functionally equivalent to the Software purchased pursuant to this Agreement, or conforms to Customer's or its customers' reasonable satisfaction; or

(c)   If neither (a) nor (b) is reasonably available to SoftCo, SoftCo shall refund an amount equal to Customer's purchase of the infringing Software.

SoftCo shall have no obligation or liability to Customer or its customers with respect to any copyright, trademark, trade secret or patent infringement, or claim thereof, based on the use of the Software sold by SoftCo to Customer or Customer's customer in combination with other machines or devices, other than for a purpose or in a manner for which it was intended, or for Software which has been altered or modified.

The foregoing states the entire liability and obligation of SoftCo to Customer or Customer's customers with respect to infringement of any copyright, trademark, trade secret or patent by the Software, or any component thereof, and is Customer and its customers' exclusive remedy as to SoftCo."

independent contractor *(business; contract)*

One who works for another under contract, but retains control over the means, method, and manner of performing the work.

Sample clause. "Neither party is, and will not hold itself out as a, representative, agent, servant or employee of the other party for any purpose, except as may be provided from time to time by other written instruments signed by both parties. This Agreement creates no relationship of joint venture, partnership, limited partnership, or agency between the parties, and the parties hereby acknowledge that no other facts or relations exist that would create any such relationship between them. Neither party has any right or authority to assume or to create any obligation or responsibility on behalf of the other party except as may from time to time be provided by written instrument signed by both parties."

independent service organization *(business)*

See ISO.

independent software vendor(s) *(business)*

Abbreviated as "ISV(s)."

United States v. Microsoft Corp., 65 F. Supp. 2d 1, 9 (D.D.C. 1999) (Finding of Fact 28).

industrial automation software *(software)*

" . . . used by factory equipment operators to monitor, adjust, and control a variety of factory floor equipment from a single computer that graphically displays the necessary gauges and status indicators. Such software is operative only in computers that have been properly connected to the factory equipment by means of a device known as a 'programmable controller,' which allows for the interaction between the factory equipment and the computer."

Farmington Cas. Co. v. Cyberlogic Technologies, Inc., 996 F. Supp. 2d 695, 697 (E.D. Mich. 1998).

inevitable disclosure *(trade secret)*

See also non-competition.

Annotation. "It is also possible to establish irreparable harm based on the inevitable disclosure of trade secrets, particularly where the movant competes directly with the prospective employer and the transient employee possesses highly confidential or technical knowledge concerning manufacturing processes, marketing strategies, or the like."

Earthweb, Inc. v. Schlack, 71 F. Supp. 2d 299, 309 (S.D.N.Y. 1999).

"[I]n cases that do not involve the actual theft of trade secrets, the court is essentially asked to bind the employee to an implied-in-fact restrictive covenant based on a finding of inevitable disclosure. This runs counter to New York's strong public policy against such agreements and circumvents the strict judicial scrutiny they have traditionally applied."

Earthweb, Inc. v. Schlack, 71 F. Supp. 2d 299, 310 (S.D.N.Y. 1999).

"Thus, in its purest form, the inevitable disclosure doctrine treads an exceedingly narrow path through judicially disfavored territory. Absence evidence of actual misappropriation by an employee, the doctrine should be applied in only the rarest of cases. Factors to be considered in weighing the appropriateness of granting injunctive relief are whether: (1) the employers in question are direct competitors providing the same or very similar products or services; (2) the employee's new position is nearly identical to his old one, such that he could not reasonably be expected to fulfill his new job responsibilities without utilizing the trade secrets of his former employer; and (3) the trade secrets at issue are highly valuable to both employers. Other case-specific factors such as the nature of the industry and trade secrets should be considered as well."

Earthweb, Inc. v. Schlack, 71 F. Supp. 2d 299, 310 (S.D.N.Y. 1999).

Related issues. "While the inevitable disclosure doctrine may serve a salutary purpose of protecting a company's investment in its trade secrets, its application is fraught with hazards. Among these risks is the imperceptible shift in bargaining power that necessarily occurs upon the commencement of an employment relationship marked by the execution of a confidentiality agreement. When that relationship eventually ends, the parties' confidentiality agreement may be wielded as a restrictive covenant, depending on how the employer views the new job its former employee has accepted. This can be a powerful weapon in the hands of an employer; the risk of litigation alone may have a chilling effect on the employee. Such constraints should be the product of open negotiations."

Earthweb, Inc. v. Schlack, 71 F. Supp. 2d 299, 310 (S.D.N.Y. 1999).

"Another drawback to the doctrine is that courts are left without a frame of reference because there is no express non-compete agreement to test for reasonableness. Instead, courts must grapple with a decidedly more nebulous standard of 'inevitability,' The absence of specific guideposts staked-out in a writing will only spawn such litigation, especially as the Internet becomes a primary medium for ideas and commerce. Clearly, a written agreement that contains a non-compete clause is the best way of promoting predictability during the employment relationship and afterwards."

Earthweb, Inc. v. Schlack, 71 F. Supp. 2d 299, 311 (S.D.N.Y. 1999).

inflection points *(economics)*

"[E]vents, in which categories are redefined and leaders are superseded in the process. . . ."

United States v. Microsoft Corp., 65 F. Supp. 2d 1, 17 (D.D.C. 1999) (Finding of Fact 59).

Annotation. "The software industry in general is characterized by dynamic, vigorous competition. In many cases, one of the early entrants into a new software category quickly captures a lion's share of the sales, while other products in the category are either driven out altogether or relegated to niche positions. What eventually displaces the leader is often not competition from another product within the same software category, but rather a technological advance that renders the boundaries defining the category obsolete."

United States v. Microsoft Corp., 65 F. Supp. 2d 1, 17 (D.D.C. 1999) (Finding of Fact 59).

"The exponential growth of the Internet represents an inflection point born of complementary technological advances in the computer and telecommunications industries."

United States v. Microsoft Corp., 65 F. Supp. 2d 1, 17 (D.D.C. 1999) (Finding of Fact 60).

information *(contract)*

"[D]ata, text, images, sounds, mask works, or computer programs, including collections and compilations of them."

UCITA § 102(a)(35).

information appliance *(technology)*
"[A] hand-held computer, a 'smart' wireless telephone, a television set-top box, or a game console. . . ."
United States v. Microsoft Corp., 65 F. Supp. 2d 1, 7 (D.D.C. 1999) (Finding of Fact 22).

Annotation. "[W]hile some consumers may decide to make do with one or more information appliances in place of an Intel-compatible PC system, the number of these consumers will, for the foreseeable future, remain small in comparison to the number of consumers deciding that they still need an Intel-compatible PC system. One reason for this is the fact that no single type of information appliance, nor even all types in the aggregate, provides all of the features that most consumers have come to rely on in their PC systems and in the applications that run on them. Thus, most of those who buy information appliances will do so in addition to, rather than instead of, buying an Intel-compatible PC system.
United States v. Microsoft Corp., 65 F. Supp. 2d 1, 7 (D.D.C. 1999) (Finding of Fact 23).

information content provider *(Internet)*
"[A]ny person or entity that is responsible, in whole or in part, for the creation or development of information provided through the Internet or any other interactive computer service."
Communications Decency Act, 47 U.S.C. § 230(e)(3).
See also **content provider.**

Information Infrastructure Task Force *(organization)*
Abbreviated as "IITF." A federal interagency task force created by President Clinton in February 1993 to articulate and implement the Administration's vision for the National Information Infrastructure (NII). *See* **NII.**

information privacy *(tort)*
Aspects of privacy law that involve the right of individuals online to determine when, how, and to what extent they choose to share personal information about themselves with others.

information processing system *(contract)*
"[A]n electronic system for creating, generating, sending, receiving, storing, displaying, or processing information."
UCITA § 102(a)(36).

information publishing service *(Internet)*
"Provision to any unaffiliated person of any information (a) which the publisher has (or has caused to be) authored, originated, gathered, collected, produced, compiled, edited, categorized, or indexed; or (b) in which the publisher has a direct or indirect financial or proprietary interest."
> *United States v. American Tel. &Tel. Co.,* 552 F. Supp. 131, 180 n.206 (D.D.C. 1982), *aff'd sub nom. Maryland v. United States,* 460 U.S. 1001 (1983).

information security *(copyright)*
"[A]ctivities carried out in order to identify and address the vulnerabilities of a government computer, computer system, or computer network."
> 17 U.S.C. § 1202(d).

information service(s) *(Internet)*
"The offering of a capability for generating, acquiring, storing, transforming, processing, retrieving, using or making available information which may be conveyed via telecommunications."
> *United States v. American Tel. &Tel. Co.,* 552 F. Supp. 131, 179 (D.D.C. 1982), *aff'd sub nom. Maryland v. United States,* 460 U.S. 1001 (1983).

"The offering of a capability for generating, acquiring, storing, transforming, processing, retrieving, using or making available information via telecommunications, and includes electronic publishing, but does not include any use of any such capability for the management, control, or operation of a telecommunications system or the management of a telecommunications service."
> 47 U.S.C. § 153(20).

information superhighway *(Internet)*
A broadband, two-way, publicly accessible network providing information services in the areas of education, entertainment, and business. It combines elements of online services, the Internet, and interactive television.

information technology *(technology)*
"[A]ny equipment, or interconnected system(s) or subsystem(s) of equipment, that is used in the automatic acquisition, storage, manipulation, management, movement, control, display, switching, interchange, transmission, or reception of data or information by the agency."
> Federal Acquisition Regulations 2.101 (1999).

Information Technology Association of America *(organization)*
See ITAA.

informational content *(contract)*
"[I]nformation that is intended to be communicated to or perceived by an individual in the ordinary use of the information, or the equivalent of that information."
UCITA § 102(a)(37).

informational rights *(contract)*
"[I]nclude all rights in information created under laws governing patents, copyrights, mask works, trade secrets, trademarks, publicity rights, or any other law that gives a person, independently of contract, a right to control or preclude another person's use of or access to the information on the basis of the rights holder's interest in the information."
UCITA § 102(a)(38).

infotainment *(multimedia)*
A concatenation of the words "**info**rmation" and "enter**tainment**." Refers to a species of interactive media works that incorporates both informational materials and entertainment techniques, which is supposed to facilitate learning.

infrastructure *(business)*
The computer and communication hardware, software, databases, people, and policies supporting the enterprise's information management functions. (wsr)

infringement *(copyright; patent; trademark)*
See copyright infringement; patent infringement; trademark infringement.

infringement by authorization *(copyright)*
"Although infringement by authorization is a form of direct infringement, this does not change the proper focus of our inquiry; a party cannot authorize another party to infringe a copyright unless the authorized conduct would itself be unlawful."
Lewis Galoob Toys, Inc. v. Nintendo of America, Inc., 964 F.2d 965, 970 (9th Cir. 1992).

infringing conduct *(copyright)*
". . . is the unpermitted exercise of a right of the copyright owner."
Bateman v. Mnemonic, Inc., 79 F.3d 1532, 1542 n.23 (11th Cir. 1995).

infringing semiconductor chip product *(mask work)*

"[A] semiconductor chip product which is made, imported, or distributed in violation of the exclusive rights of the owner of a mask work under this chapter."

17 U.S.C. § 901(a)(9).

Annotation. "Although the Semiconductor Chip Protection Act does not use the word 'copy' to describe infringement, the parallel language reflects the incorporation of the well-explicated copyright principle of substantial similarity into the Semiconductor Chip Protection Act."

Brooktree Corp. v. Advanced Micro Devices, Inc., 977 F.2d 1555, 1564 (Fed. Cir. 1992).

initial interest confusion *(trademark)*

"[T]he use of another's trademark in a manner calculated 'to capture initial consumer attention, even though no actual sale is finally completed as a result of the confusion.' . . ."

Brookfield Comm., Inc. v. West Coast Entertainment Corp., 174 F.3d 1036, 1063 (9th Cir. 1999) (citation omitted).

initial public offering *(business)*

See IPO.

initialize *(technology)*

A procedure done when first using a system or new storage disk. Initializing sets a computer's counters, switches, and addresses to a starting value, and formats a disk surface so that it can accept data for storage.

injunction *(procedure)*

"Every order granting an injunction and every restraining order shall set forth the reasons for its issuance; shall be specific in terms; shall describe in reasonable detail, and not be referenced to the complaint or other document, the act or acts sought to be restrained. . . ."

Fed. R. Civ. Proc. 65(d).

injunctive relief

(copyright)
"Any court having jurisdiction of a civil action arising under this title may . . . grant temporary and final injunctions on such terms as it may deem reasonable to prevent or restrain infringement of a copyright."

17 U.S.C. § 502(a).

(trade secret)

"[I]n order to be entitled to injunctive relief against any employee for misappropriation of trade secrets, the employer bears the burden of demonstrating the following factors: (1) that there is a trade secret or secret process of manufacture; (2) that it is of value to the employer and important in the conduct of its business; (3) that by reason of discovery or ownership the employer has the right to use an enjoyment [sic] of the secret; and (4) that the secret was communicated to the employee while he was employed in a position of trust and confidence, under such circumstances as to make it inequitable and unjust for him to disclose it to others, or to make use of it himself, to the prejudice of the employer."

> *Healthcare Affiliated Servs., Inc. v. Lippany,* 701 F. Supp. 1142, 1150 (W.D. Pa. 1988) (Pennsylania law).

See also **permanent injunction; preliminary injunction.**

injury *(criminal)*

"[A]ny alteration, deletion, damage, or destruction of a computer system, computer network, computer program, or data caused by the access."

> Cal. Penal C. § 502.

in-line linking *(Internet)*

A link within a web page that causes content from another web site to be automatically loaded onto the web page. To the user, the content from the other web site appears to be part of the web page. *See also* **framing.**

innocent purchaser *(mask work)*

"[A] person who purchases a semiconductor chip product in good faith and without having notice of protection with respect to the semiconductor chip product; . . ."

> 17 U.S.C. § 901(a)(7).

input *(technology)*

"[T]he entering of data into storage."

> *Telex Corp. v. IBM Corp.,* 367 F. Supp. 258, 274 (N.D. Okla. 1973), *aff'd in part, rev'd in part,* 510 F.2d 894 (10th Cir.), *cert. dism.,* 423 U.S. 802 (1975).

"The function of Input is to get instructions and data, prepared in some computer-readable form, into the computer."

> *Computer Sys. of Am. v. Western Reserve Life Assur. Co.,* 19 Mass. App. 430, 431 n.2 (1985).

See also **inputting.**

input buffering *(software)*
"[A] software feature that permits faster data entry."
> *A.I. Root Co. v. Computer Dynamics, Inc.,* 615 F. Supp. 727, 729 (N.D. Ohio 1985).

input device(s) *(technology)*
". . . convert data from an 'ordinary' language form (i.e., English and numbers) to 'machine' language or electronic signals which are then understandable to a computer."
> *Telex Corp. v. IBM Corp.,* 367 F. Supp. 258, 274 (N.D. Okla. 1973), *aff'd in part, rev'd in part,* 510 F.2d 894 (10th Cir.), *cert. dism.,* 423 U.S. 802 (1975).

". . . such as a keyboard and mouse. . . ."
> *Lotus Dev. Corp. v. Paperback Software Int'l,* 740 F. Supp. 37, 43 (D. Mass. 1990).

See also **input/output devices.**

input document *(technology)*
"[A] document, usually a form, printed or handwritten, which is designed to be read by a machine for input to a computer. Thus, it is a form which is scanned or scannable by an optical reader."
> *Moore Bus. Forms, Inc. v. National Computer Sys., Inc.,* 211 U.S.P.Q. (BNA) 909, 912 (T.T.A.B. 1981).

input format *(technology)*
"In using a program one must have a format for input so that the input of data and the instruction to the computer are compatible with its program."
> *Synercom Technology, Inc. v. University Computing Co.,* 462 F. Supp. 1003, 1005 (N.D. Tex. 1978).

input/output devices *(technology)*
". . . include teletype machines, typewriter terminals, television-like cathode ray tubes, displays which use cathode ray tubes, card punches and punched card readers, magnetic tape drives and magnetic disk drives."
> *Telex Corp. v. IBM Corp.,* 367 F. Supp. 258, 274 (N.D. Okla. 1973), *aff'd in part, rev'd in part,* 510 F.2d 894 (10th Cir.), *cert. dism.,* 423 U.S. 802 (1975).

See also **input devices; output devices.**

inputting *(technology)*
"[T]he placement of a program into a computer. . . ."
> *Micro-Sparc, Inc. v. Amtype Corp.,* 592 F. Supp. 33, 35 (D. Mass. 1984).

Related issues. "Inputting a computer program entails the preparation of a copy."

Micro-Sparc, Inc. v. Amtype Corp., 592 F. Supp. 33, 35 (D. Mass. 1984), quoting *CONTU Final Report* 31 ("[T]he placement of a work into a computer is the preparation of a copy . . .").

See also **input.**

INS *(unfair competition)*

Citation: *International News Service v. Associated Press,* 248 U.S. 215 (1918).

Annotation. This case involved two wire services, the Associated Press ("AP") and International News Service ("INS"), that transmitted news stories by wire to member newspapers. INS lifted factual stories from AP bulletins and sent them by wire to INS papers. INS would also take factual stories from East Coast AP papers and wire them to INS papers on the West Coast that had yet to publish because of time differentials. The Supreme Court held that INS's conduct was a common-law misappropriation of AP's property.

[The] defendant in appropriating [news stories] and selling it as its own [was] endeavoring to reap where it has not sewn. . . . Stripped of all disguises, the process amounts to an unauthorized interference with the normal operating of complainant's business at the point where the profit is to be reaped. *Id.* at 239-40.

This case established the "hot news" misappropriation doctrine, under which someone who takes uncopyrighted (and uncopyrightable) facts could be enjoined under a misappropriation theory. Based on legislative history of the 1976 amendments, it is generally agreed that a "hot news" INS-like claim survived preemption. H.R. No. 94-1476 at 132 (1976).

This doctrine, while confirmed, was substantially restricted by the Second Circuit Court of Appeals in *National Basketball Ass'n v. Motorola, Inc.,* 105 F.3d 841 (2d Cir. 1997). *See* STATS.

installed [user] base *(business)*

The number of a particular platform actually in the hands of users/consumers.

instant message *(Internet)*

Abbreviated as "IM." *See* **IM.**

Institute for Electrical and Electronic Engineers *(organization)*

Abbreviated as "IEEE" or "I-triple-E."

"[A] professional organization of several hundred thousand engineers in the electronic industry."

National Semiconductor Corp. v. Linear Technology Corp., 703 F. Supp. 845, 847 (N.D. Cal. 1988).

instruction set *(hardware; software)*

". . . is a phrase standard in the microprocessor industry meaning the source code used by the customer to program the microprocessor to his liking."

Motorola, Inc. v. Hitachi, Ltd., 750 F. Supp. 1319, 1326-27 (W.D. Tex. 1990).

insurance *(contract)*

"[A] contract whereby one undertakes to indemnify another against loss, damage or liability arising from a contingent or unknown event."

Cal. Ins. Code § 22.

Sample clause. "Licensor shall, through the term of this Agreement and for a period of no less than one (1) year following termination or expiration of this Agreement, maintain insurance obtained from a reputable carrier with a Best's rating of 'A' or better in the amounts and for the purposes set forth in this Section _____.

(a) *General Liability.* Licensor will carry general liability insurance, which will include but not be limited to products liability coverage, covering any and all claims, demands and causes of action for personal injury or property damage arising out of or purporting to arise out of any defects in or failure to perform by the Licensed Products and any physical or intangible materiel used in connection therewith in a minimum amount of $2,000,000 combined annually and $1,000,000 for each occurrence for personal injury and property damage.

(b) *Producer's Error and Omissions.* Licensor will carry errors and omissions insurance, which will include but not be limited to indemnification, for claims arising out of: (i) infringement of copyright, patent, or trademark, whether under statutory or common law; (ii) invasion or infringement of or interference with the right of privacy or publicity, whether under common law or statutory law; or (iii) libel or slander. The amount of coverage under such insurance shall be a minimum of $1,000,000 for each occurrence."

insurance services transaction *(contract)*

"[A]n agreement between an insurer and an insured which provides for, or a transaction that is, or entails access to, use, transfer, clearance, settlement, or processing of:

(A) an insurance policy, contract, or certificate; or

(B) a right to payment under an insurance policy, contract, or certificate."

UCITA § 102(a)(39).

INTA *(organization)*

Acronym for "International Trademark Association." An international association of trademark owners and associated professionals dedicated to promoting the rule of trademarks worldwide. Located at <www.inta.org>.

integrated application program(s) *(software)*

"Programs [which] can perform several different kinds of tasks. . . ."
Lotus Dev. Corp. v. Paperback Software Int'l, 740 F. Supp. 37, 43 (D. Mass. 1990).
See also application program(s); application software.

integrated circuit *(hardware)*

Abbreviated as "IC." A complete electronic circuit composed of interconnected diodes and transistors and fabricated on a single semiconductor substrate, usually silicon. Also called a "computer chip."

"[C]ombine the various components making up an electronic circuit into a single chip, which is now about 1/8 inch square."
Telex Corp. v. IBM Corp., 367 F. Supp. 258, 275 (N.D. Okla. 1973), *aff'd in part, rev'd in part,* 510 F.2d 894 (10th Cir.), *cert. dism.,* 423 U.S. 802 (1975).

"The integrated circuit inscribed on a chip is an electro-mechanical pattern that determines a sequence of electrical events that occur within a chip only when the chip is performing."
Apple Computer, Inc. v. Franklin Computer Corp., 545 F. Supp. 812, 813 n.1 (E.D. Pa. 1982), *rev'd,* 714 F.2d 1240 (3d Cir. 1983), *cert. dism.,* 464 U.S. 1033 (1984).
See also IC; semiconductor; semiconductor product.

integrated system *(hardware; software)*

"A system able to interchange programs and run as a single system."
Management Sys. Assocs., Inc. v. McDonnell Douglas Corp., 762 F.2d 1161, 1181 (4th Cir. 1985).

integration clause *(contract)*

"A writing intended by the parties as a final expression of [the parties'] agreement with respect to such terms as are included therein may not be contradicted by evidence of any prior agreement or of a contemporaneous oral agreement. . . ."
U.C.C. § 2-202.

"Terms with respect to which the confirmatory memoranda of the parties agree or which are otherwise set forth in writing intended by the parties as a final expression of their agreement with respect to such terms as are included therein may not be contradicted by evidence of any prior agreement or of a contemporaneous oral agreement but may be explained or supplemented—(a) by course of dealing or usage of trade . . . or by course of performance . . . ; and, (b) by evidence of consistent additional terms unless the court finds the writing to have been intended also as a complete and exclusive statement of the terms of the agreement."

U.C.C. § 2-202.

Annotation. "The presence of an integration clause 'strongly supports a conclusion that the parties' agreement was fully integrated. . . .' Here, the absence of such a clause further supports the conclusion that the purchase order was not the complete agreement between the parties."

M.A. Mortenson Co., Inc. v. Timberline Software Corp., 998 P.2d 305, 311 (Wash. 2000) (citations omitted), *aff'g* 93 Wash. App. 819, 970 P.2d 803 (1999).

Sample clause. "This Agreement, including the Exhibits attached hereto, constitutes the entire agreement between Licensee and SoftCo concerning the subject matter hereof and supersedes all prior and contemporaneous agreements between the parties. This Agreement may be amended only by an instrument in writing which expressly refers to this Agreement and specifically states that it is intended to amend it. Neither party is relying upon any warranties, representations, or inducements not set forth herein."

See also Invacare Corp. v. Sperry Rand Corp., 612 F. Supp. 448, 452 (N.D. Ohio. 1984).

integration testing *(business)*
Testing to determine that the related information system components perform to specification.

Intel-compatible PC *(hardware; software)*
"[O]ne designed to function with Intel's 80x86/Pentium families of microprocessors or with compatible microprocessors manufactured by Intel or by other firms."

United States v. Microsoft Corp., 65 F. Supp. 2d 1, 4 (D.D.C. 1999) (Finding of Fact 3).

Intel-compatible PC operating system *(software)*
An operating system designed to run on Intel-compatible computer systems.

Annotation. "Currently there are no products, nor are there likely to be any in the near future, that a significant percentage of consumers world-wide could substitute for Intel-compatible PC operating systems without incurring substantial costs. Furthermore, no firm that does not currently market

Intel-compatible PC operating systems could start doing so in a way that would, within a reasonably short period of time, present a significant percentage of consumers with a viable alternative to existing Intel-compatible PC operating systems."

> *United States v. Microsoft Corp.*, 65 F. Supp. 2d 1, 5 (D.D.C. 1999) (Finding of Fact 18).

"Since only Intel-compatible PC operating systems will work with Intel-compatible PCs, a consumer cannot opt for a non-Intel-compatible PC operating system without obtaining a non-Intel-compatible PC. Thus, for consumers who already own an Intel-compatible PC system, the cost of switching to a non-Intel compatible PC operating system includes the price of not only a new operating system, but also a new PC and new peripheral devices. It also includes the effort of learning to use the new system, the cost of acquiring a new set of compatible applications, and the work of replacing files and documents that were associated with the old applications."

> *United States v. Microsoft Corp.*, 65 F. Supp. 2d 1, 6 (D.D.C. 1999) (Finding of Fact 20).

Related issues. "[S]igns do not indicate large demand for a new Intel-compatible PC operating system. To the contrary, they indicate that the demand for a new Intel-compatible PC operating system would be severely constrained by an intractable "chicken-and-egg" problem: The overwhelming majority of consumers will only use a PC operating system for which there already exists a large and varied set of high-quality, full-featured applications, and for which it seems relatively certain that new types of applications and new versions of existing applications will continue to be marketed at pace with those written for other operating systems. Unfortunately for firms whose products do not fit that bill, the porting of applications from one operating system to another is a costly process. Consequently, software developers generally write applications first, and often exclusively, for the operating system that is already used by a dominant share of all PC users. Users do not want to invest in an operating system until it is clear that the system will support generations of applications that will meet their needs, and developers do not want to invest in writing or quickly porting applications for an operating system until it is clear that there will be a sizeable and stable market for it. What is more, consumers who already use one Intel-compatible PC operating system are even less likely than first-time buyers to choose a newcomer to the field, for switching to a new system would require these users to scrap the investment they have made in applications, training, and certain hardware."

> *United States v. Microsoft Corp.*, 65 F. Supp. 2d 1, 9 (D.D.C. 1999) (Finding of Fact 30).

intellectual property *(law)*

A general term that describes inventions or other discoveries that have been registered with government authorities for sale or use by their owner. Such terms as patent, trademark, copyright or unfair competition fall within the category of intellectual property.

intelligent agent *(technology)*

See **agent.**

intelligent modem *(telecommunications)*

" 'Intelligent modem' describes a type of modem that possesses added or enhanced features as compared to a standard modem. The term 'intelligent' is commonly used in the data processing and data communications field in an adjectival sense to describe an advanced-type modem having sophisticated features and to distinguish said products from standard 'dumb' modems with the advanced features."

Hayes Microcomputer Prods., Inc. v. Business Computer Corp., 219 U.S.P.Q. (BNA) 634 (T.T.A.B. 1983).

See also **modem.**

interactive *(Internet; multimedia)*

A computer system that allows the user to type in a command and see an immediate response and/or to communicate with other end users on either a real-time basis or a store-and-forward basis.

interactive advertising *(advertising; business)*

A type of advertising in which the user chooses and interacts with the advertisement, instead of being a passive recipient.

interactive computer graphics *(technology)*

Graphic-based images that allow for user interaction.

Annotation. ". . . permits a creator to use another's images as the 'grist' for computer-assisted manipulation in the production of further works. Creators using this technology cannot only generate images of a nature that have never existed in reality; they can also take images from existing photographs or films, 'map' them into a computer memory, and bring them back to life in totally new settings, with new movement and dialog."

Office of Technology Assessment, *Intellectual Property in an Age of Electronics and Information* 70 (Apr. 1986).

interactive communications *(Internet)*

"Chat rooms, e-mail, and newsgroups are interactive forms of communication, providing the user with the opportunity both to speak and to listen."
American Civil Liberties Union v. Reno, 929 F. Supp. 824, 843 (E.D. Pa. 1996), *aff'd, Reno v. American Civil Liberties Union,* 521 U.S. 844 (1997).

interactive computer service *(Internet)*

"[A]ny information service, system, or access software provider that provides or enables computer access by multiple users to a computer server, including specifically a service or system that provides access to the Internet and such systems operated or services offered by libraries or educational institutions."
47 U.S.C. § 230(e)(2).

". . . encompasses the means of making 'content' available to multiple users both on the vast web of linked networks popularly known as 'the Internet' and on other information systems (such as electronic bulletin boards maintained by educational institutions or nonprofit organizations) not physically linked to the Internet."
Shea v. Reno, 930 F. Supp. 916, 925 (S.D.N.Y. 1996) (citation omitted).

"The phrase serves as a reasonable shorthand for the category of individuals targeted by the CDA—persons who send or display Internet content."
Shea v. Reno, 930 F. Supp. 916, 927 n.5 (S.D.N.Y. 1996).

Annotation. "The range of tools and forums available for users of interactive computer services is astounding: with access to the web of computer networks known as the Internet, a scholar can connect to a distant computer and make use of its capabilities; a researcher can peruse the card catalogs of libraries across the globe; users around the world can debate politics, sports, music, and literature. However trivial some of their uses might seem, emerging media technologies quite simply offer an unprecedented number of individual citizens an opportunity to speak and to be heard—at very little cost—by audiences around the world. In that sense, we are encountering a communication medium unlike any we have ever known."
Shea v. Reno, 930 F. Supp. 916, 922 (S.D.N.Y. 1996).

Related issues. "[I]n the CDA, Congress sought to target 'interactive' computer systems through which a listener or viewer, by definition, has the power to become a speaker. The relative ease of speaker entry and the relative parity among speakers accounts for the unprecedented and virtually unlimited opportunities for political discourse, cultural development, and intellectual activity that Congress found to characterize emerging communication technologies."

Shea v. Reno, 930 F. Supp. 916, 930 (S.D.N.Y. 1996).

Interactive Digital Software Association *(organization)*
Abbreviated as "IDSA."

". . . is a non-profit trade association of United States publishers of entertainment software. IDSA has many members who both sell their software in retail outlets and make their entertainment software available to the public on the Internet for demonstration, purchase, and play."

American Library Ass'n v. Pataki, 969 F. Supp. 160, 162 (S.D.N.Y. 1997).
Related issue. Located at <www.idsa.com>.

interactive fiction *(multimedia)*
"[A] computer-mediated form of storytelling/writing that permits the user of a program to 'co-author' a story by making choices about details of the plot as the story unfolds on the computer."

Office of Technology Assessment, *Intellectual Property in an Age of Electronics and Information* 70 (Apr. 1986).

interactive service *(Internet)*
"[O]ne that enables a member of the public to receive, on request, a transmission of a particular sound recording chosen by or on behalf of the recipient."

17 U.S.C. § 114(j)(4).

interactive television *(technology)*
A broadcast service or program that permits or requires active participation by the viewer.

interactivity *(multimedia)*
The flow of information between the computer and the user, which can be used to control the direction, pace, and content of the interactive multimedia work.

intercept *(criminal; telecommunications)*
"[T]he aural or other acquisition of the contents of any wire, electronic, or oral communication through the use of any electronic, mechanical, or other device."

18 U.S.C. § 2510(4).

Annotation. "Congress' use of the word 'transfer' in the definition of 'electronic communication,' and its omission in that definition of the phrase 'any electronic storage of such communication' (part of the definition of 'wire communication') reflects that Congress did not intend for 'intercept' to apply to 'electronic communications' when those communications are in 'electronic storage.'

* * *

"[T]he ECPA's legislative history makes it crystal clear that Congress did not intend to change the definition of 'intercept' as it existed at the time of the amendment."

> *Steve Jackson Games, Inc. v. United States Secret Serv.,* 36 F.3d 457, 462 (5th Cir. 1994).

"Wire and electronic communications are subject to different treatment under the Wiretap Act. The Act's exclusionary rule, 18 U.S.C. s 2515, applies to the interception of wire communications, including such communications in electronic storage, see 18 U.S.C. s 2510(1), but not to the interception of electronic communications. See 18 U.S.C. s 2518(10)(a). . . ."

> *Steve Jackson Games, Inc. v. United States Secret Serv.,* 36 F.3d 457, 461 n.6 (5th Cir. 1994).

Related issues. "[C]ongress did not intend for 'intercept' to apply to 'electronic communication' when those communications are in 'electronic storage.'"

> *Steve Jackson Games, Inc. v. United States Secret Serv.,* 36 F.3d 457, 462 (5th Cir. 1994).

interconnect system *(technology)*

". . . links a private branch exchange (called 'PBX system') of a business with a telephone utility company."

> *Lakefield Tel. Co. v. Northern Telecom, Inc.,* 696 F. Supp. 413, 415 (E.D. Wis. 1988).

interested copyright party *(copyright)*

". . . is—

(A) the owner of the exclusive right under section 106(1) of this title to reproduce a sound recording of a musical work that has been embodied in a digital musical recording or analog musical recording lawfully made under this title that has been distributed;

(B) the legal or beneficial owner of, or the person that controls, the right to reproduce in a digital musical recording or analog musical recording a musical work that has been embodied in a digital musical recording or analog musical recording lawfully made under this title that has been distributed;

(C) a featured recording artist who performs on a sound recording that has been distributed; or

(D) any association or other organization—

(i) representing persons specified in subparagraphs (A), (B), or (C), or

(ii) engaging in licensing rights in musical works to music users on behalf of writers and publishers."

17 U.S.C. § 1001(7).

interface *(technology)*

"[A] shared boundary which enables transfer of information in accord with a prescribed format, sequence, timing and encoding. An interface may refer to either hardware or software or a combination of both."

ILC Peripherals Leasing Corp. v. IBM Corp., 458 F. Supp. 423, 437 (N.D. Cal. 1978), *aff'd per curiam sub nom. Memorex Corp. v. IBM Corp.,* 636 F.2d 1188 (9th Cir. 1980), *cert. denied,* 452 U.S. 972 (1981).

"[A] shared boundary between electronic data processing machines, or more accurately between the channels or physical pathways connecting those machines, through which data or programs may be transmitted, received, stored or processed."

Telex Corp. v. IBM Corp., 367 F. Supp. 258, 270 (N.D. Okla. 1973), *aff'd in part, rev'd in part,* 510 F.2d 894 (10th Cir.), *cert. dism.,* 423 U.S. 802 (1975).

interface information *(technology)*

"This information essentially describes what a program does, but not how it does it. It is rather like giving the specifications for all the holes and plugs on the back of a stereo amplifier so that you can put compatible stereo components together. Interface information gives the same sort of specifications."

IBM Corp. v. Fujitsu Ltd., Copyright L. Rep. (CCH) ¶ 20,517, at 11,392, 11,400 (Am. Arb. Ass'n 1988).

Annotation. "In order for an application program to run on an operating system, the program must be able to request and utilize services provided by the operating system. This is accomplished via interfaces between the application program and the operating system. To use a simplified analogy, the application program must contain 'plugs' that will fit properly into all relevant 'sockets' offered by the operating system to allow the application to run.

* * *

"If an operating system's interfaces have been clearly defined, then relatively little information beyond that defined by one vendor as its products' customer interface specifications may be needed to independently develop a compatible operating system that allows customers to run existing application programs written for the original operating system. However, if such interfaces have not been clearly defined, then it may be the case that application programs have used more information, possibly including information relating to the internal design of the operating system, in order to request and utilize services offered by the operating system. As a result, application programs may fail to operate on a compatible operating system that provides only intended customer interfaces. Therefore, when interfaces have not been clearly defined in the operating system, additional interface information may be necessary to independently develop an operating system that meets the primary requirements of application program compatibility."

> *IBM Corp. v. Fujitsu Ltd.,* Copyright L. Rep. (CCH) ¶ 20,517, at 11,392, 11,400 (Am. Arb. Ass'n 1988).

interface standards *(technology)*

". . . set out criteria for evaluating whether or not a given program can be considered to clearly differentiate programming service interfaces from other information about the program."

> *IBM Corp. v. Fujitsu Ltd.,* Copyright L. Rep. (CCH) ¶ 20,517, at 11,392, 11,401 (Am. Arb. Ass'n 1988).

interference proceedings *(patent)*

Administrative proceedings to determine priority in the Patent and Trademark Office.

interlace *(hardware)*

Hardware process for displaying video images by displaying alternate scan lines in sequence.

intermediate copying *(copyright)*

The copying of a work during the process of analysis or reverse engineering.

Related issues. "[I]ntermediate copying falls squarely within the category of acts prohibited by the [Copyright] Act."

> *DSC Comm. Corp. v. DGI Technologies, Inc.,* 898 F. Supp. 1183, 1186 (N.D. Tex. 1995), *aff'd,* 81 F.3d 597 (5th Cir. 1996).; *Sega Enters. Ltd. v. Accolade, Inc.,* 977 F.2d 1510, 1518 (9th Cir. 1992).

"When the nature of a work requires intermediate copying to understand the ideas and processes in a copyrighted work, that nature supports a fair use for intermediate copying."

> *Atari Games Corp. v. Nintendo of America, Inc.,* 975 F.2d 832, 843 (Fed. Cir. 1992).

International Ad Hoc Committee *(organization)*
Abbreviated as "IAHC." *See* **IAHC.**

International News Service v. Associated Press *(unfair competition)*
See **INS.**

International Telecommunication Union *(organization)*
Abbreviated as "ITU." *See* **ITU.**

International Trademark Association *(organization)*
Abbreviated as "INTA." *See* **INTA.**

Internet *(Internet)*
"[A]n international network of interconnected computers. It is the out-growth of what began in 1969 as a military program called 'ARPANET,' which was designed to enable computers operated by the military, defense contractors, and universities conducting defense-related research to communicate with one another by redundant channels even if some portions of the network were damaged in a war. While the ARPANET no longer exists, it provided an example for the development of a number of civilian networks that, eventually linking with each other, now enable tens of millions of people to communicate with one another and to access vast amounts of information from around the world."
Reno v. American Civil Liberties Union, 521 U.S. 844, 849-50 (1997).

"The Internet is not a physical or tangible entity, but rather a giant network which interconnects innumerable smaller groups of linked computer networks. It is thus a network of networks. . . . Many networks . . . are connected to other networks, which are in turn connected to other networks in a manner which permits each computer in any network to communicate with computers on any other network in the system. This global Web of linked networks and computers is referred to as the Internet."
American Civil Liberties Union v. Reno, 929 F. Supp. 824, 830-31 (E.D. Pa. 1996), *aff'd, Reno v. American Civil Liberties Union,* 521 U.S. 844 (1997).

"[A] unique and wholly new medium of worldwide human communication."
American Civil Liberties Union v. Reno, 929 F. Supp. 824, 844 (E.D. Pa. 1996), *aff'd, Reno v. American Civil Liberties Union,* 521 U.S. 844 (1997).

" . . . is not a physical or tangible entity, but rather a giant network which interconnects innumerable smaller groups of linked computer networks. It is thus a network of networks."
Jews for Jesus v. Brodsky, 993 F. Supp. 282, 287 n.2 (D.N.J. 1998).

"[T]he world's largest computer network (a network consisting of two or more computers linked together to share electronic mail and files). The Internet is actually a network of thousands of independent networks, containing several million 'host' computers that provide information services. An estimated 25 million individuals have some form of Internet access, and this audience is doubling each year. The Internet is a cooperative venture, owned by no one, but regulated by several volunteer agencies."

> *MTV Networks, Inc. v. Curry*, 867 F. Supp. 202, 203 n.1 (S.D.N.Y. 1994) (citations omitted).

"[A] worldwide network of computers that enables various individuals and organizations to share information. The Internet allows computer users to access millions of web sites and web pages."

> *Panavision Int'l, L.P. v. Toeppen*, 141 F.3d 1316, 1318 (9th Cir. 1998).

"[A]n international 'super-network' connecting millions of individual computer networks and computers. The Internet is not a single entity. It is a highly diffuse and complex system over which no entity has authority or control."

> *Lockheed Martin Corp. v. Network Solutions, Inc.*, 985 F. Supp. 949, 951 (C.D. Cal. 1997).

"[A] vast and expanding network of computers and other devices linked together by various telecommunications media, enabling all the computers and other devices on the Internet to exchange and share data.

"The Internet provides information about a myriad of corporations and products, as well as educational, research and entertainment information and services. An estimated 30 million people worldwide use the Internet with 100 million predicted to be on the 'net' in a matter of years."

> *Intermatic, Inc. v. Toeppen*, 947 F. Supp. 1227, 1230 (N.D. Ill. 1996).

"[T]he world's largest computer network, often described as a 'network of networks.' The Internet is decentralized in that there is no central hub through which messages or information must be routed, and no central governing body."

> *United States v. Baker*, 890 F. Supp. 1375, 1379 n.1 (E.D. Mich. 1995). *See also CompuServe Corp. v. Patterson*, 89 F.2d 1257, 1271 n.2 (6th Cir. 1996); *United States v. Baker*, 890 F. Supp. 1375, 1379 n.1 (E.D. Mich. 1995).

"[T]he international computer network of both Federal and non-Federal interoperable packet switched data networks."

> Communications Decency Act, 47 U.S.C. § 230(e)(1).

"[A] global electronic network, consisting of smaller, interconnected networks, which allows millions of computers to exchange information over telephone wires, dedicated data cables, and wireless links."

> *United States v. Microsoft Corp.*, 65 F. Supp. 2d 1, 4 (D.D.C. 1999) (Finding of Fact 11).

"[A] global network of interconnected computers which allows individuals and organizations around the world to communicate and to share information with one another."

> *Brookfield Comm., Inc. v. West Coast Entertainment Corp.*, 174 F.3d 1036, 1044 (9th Cir. 1999).

Annotation. "The Internet may well be the premier technological innovation of the present age."

> *American Library Association v. Pataki*, 969 F. Supp. 160, 161 (S.D.N.Y. 1997).

"The nature of the Internet is such that it is very difficult, if not impossible, to determine its size at a given moment. It is indisputable, however, that the Internet has experienced extraordinary growth in recent years. In 1981, fewer than 300 computers were linked to the Internet, and by 1989, the number stood at fewer than 90,000 computers. By 1993, over 1,000,000 computers were linked. Today, over 9,400,000 host computers worldwide, of which approximately 60 percent located within the United States, are estimated to be linked to the Internet. This count does not include the personal computers people use to access the Internet using modems. In all, reasonable estimates are that as many as 40 million people around the world can and do access the enormously flexible communication Internet medium. That figure is expected to grow to 200 million Internet users by the year 1999.

"Some of the computers and computer networks that make up the Internet are owned by governmental and public institutions, some are owned by non-profit organizations, and some are privately owned. The resulting whole is a decentralized, global medium of communications—or 'cyberspace'—that links people, institutions, corporations, and governments around the world. The Internet is an international system. This communications medium allows any of the literally tens of millions of people with access to the Internet to exchange information. These communications can occur almost instantaneously, and can be directed either to specific individuals, to a broader group of people interested in a particular subject, or to the world as a whole.

"The Internet had its origins in 1969 as an experimental project of the Advanced Research Project Agency ('ARPA'), and was called ARPANET.

This network linked computers and computer networks owned by the military, defense contractors, and university laboratories conducting defense-related research. The network later allowed researchers across the country to access directly and to use extremely powerful supercomputers located at a few key universities and laboratories. As it evolved far beyond its research origins in the United States to encompass universities, corporations, and people around the world, the ARPANET came to be called the 'DARPA Internet,' and finally just the 'Internet.'

"From its inception, the network was designed to be a decentralized, self-maintaining series of redundant links between computers and computer networks, capable of rapidly transmitting communications without direct human involvement or control, and with the automatic ability to re-route communications if one or more individual links were damaged or otherwise unavailable. Among other goals, this redundant system of linked computers was designed to allow vital research and communications to continue even if portions of the network were damaged, say, in a war.

"To achieve this resilient nationwide (and ultimately global) communications medium, the ARPANET encouraged the creation of multiple links to and from each computer (or computer network) on the network. Thus, a computer located in Washington, D.C., might be linked (usually using dedicated telephone lines) to other computers in neighboring states or on the Eastern seaboard. Each of those computers could in turn be linked to other computers, which themselves would be linked to other computers.

"A communication sent over this redundant series of linked computers could travel any of a number of routes to its destination. Thus, a message sent from a computer in Washington, D.C., to a computer in Palo Alto, California, might first be sent to a computer in Philadelphia, and then be forwarded to a computer in Pittsburgh, and then to Chicago, Denver, and Salt Lake City, before finally reaching Palo Alto. If the message could not travel along that path (because of military attack, simple technical malfunction, or other reason), the message would automatically (without human intervention or even knowledge) be re-routed, perhaps, from Washington, D.C. to Richmond, and then to Atlanta, New Orleans, Dallas, Albuquerque, Los Angeles, and finally to Palo Alto. This type of transmission, and re-routing, would likely occur in a matter of seconds.

* * *

"No single entity—academic, corporate, governmental, or non-profit—administers the Internet. It exists and functions as a result of the fact that hundreds of thousands of separate operators of computers and computer networks independently decided to use common data transfer protocols to exchange communications and information with other computers (which in turn exchange communications and information with still other computers). There is no centralized storage location, control point, or communications channel for the Internet, and it would not be technically feasible for a single entity to control all of the information conveyed on the Internet."

American Civil Liberties Union v. Reno, 929 F. Supp. 824, 831-32 (E.D. Pa. 1996), *aff'd, Reno v. American Civil Liberties Union,* 521 U.S. 844 (1997) (paragraph numbers omitted).

"Although 'the Internet' now formally describes a collection of more than 50,000 networks linking some nine million host computers in ninety countries, it has existed for nearly three decades on a much smaller scale. What we now refer to as the Internet grew out of an experimental project of the Department of Defense's Advanced Research Projects Administration ('ARPA') designed to provide researchers with direct access to supercomputers at a few key laboratories and to facilitate the reliable transmission of vital communications. ARPA supplied funds to link computers operated by the military, defense contractors, and universities conducting defense-related research through dedicated phone lines, creating a 'network' known as ARPANet.

* * *

"As faster networks developed, most network traffic shifted away from ARPANet, which formally ceased operations in 1990. What we know as 'the Internet' today is the series of linked, overlapping networks that gradually supplanted ARPANet. Because the Internet links together independent networks that merely use the same data transfer protocols, it cannot be said that any single entity or group of entities controls, or can control, the consent made publicly available on the Internet or limits, or can limit, the ability of others to access public content. Rather, the resources available to one with Internet access are located on individual computers around the world.

"It is estimated that as many as forty million individuals have access to the information and tools of the Internet, and that figure is expected to grow to 200 million by the year 1999. Access to the Internet can take any one of several forms. First, many educational institutions, businesses, libraries, and individual communities maintain a computer network linked directly to the Internet and issue account numbers and passwords enabling users to gain access to the network directly or by modem. Second, 'Internet service providers,' generally commercial entities charging a monthly fee, offer modem access to computers or networks linked directly to the Internet. Third, national commercial 'on-line services'—such as America Online, CompuServe, Prodigy, and Microsoft Network—allow subscribers to gain access to the Internet while providing extensive content within their own proprietary networks. Finally, organizations and businesses can offer access to electronic bulletin-board systems—which, like national on-line services, provide certain proprietary content; some bulletin-board systems in turn offer users links to the Internet."

Shea v. Reno, 930 F. Supp. 916, 925-26 (S.D.N.Y. 1996) (citations omitted).

"For our purposes, there are two loose and overlapping categories of Internet use. First, an individual who has secured access to the Internet can correspond or exchange views with one or many other Internet users. Second, a user can locate and retrieve information available on other computers."

Shea v. Reno, 930 F. Supp. 916, 926 (S.D.N.Y. 1996).

"The range of tools and forums available for users of interactive computer services is astounding: with access to the web of computer networks known as the Internet, a scholar can connect to a distant computer and make use of its capabilities; a researcher can peruse the card catalogs of libraries across the globe; users around the world can debate politics, sports, music, and literature. However trivial some of their uses might seem, emerging media technologies quite simply offer an unprecedented number of individual citizens an opportunity to speak and to be heard-at very little cost-by audiences around the world. In that sense, we are encountering a communication medium unlike any we have ever known."

Shea v. Reno, 930 F. Supp. 916, 922 (S.D.N.Y. 1996).

"It enables people to communicate with one another with unprecedented speed and efficiency and is rapidly revolutionizing how people share and receive information. As Congress recognized in the Communications Decency Act of 1996, 'the rapidly developing array of Internet and other interactive computer services . . . represent[s] an extraordinary advance in the availability of educational and information resources to our citizens.' 47 U.S.C. 230(a)(1)."

Blumenthal v. Drudge, 992 F. Supp. 44, 48 (D.D.C. 1998).

"Once one has access to the Internet, there [is] a wide variety of different methods of communication and information exchange over the network. These many methods of communication and information retrieval are constantly evolving and are therefore difficult to categorize concisely. The most common methods of communications on the Internet (as well as within the major online services) can be roughly grouped into six categories:

(1) one-to-one messaging (such as 'e-mail'),

(2) one-to-many messaging (such as 'listserv'),

(3) distributed message databases (such as 'USENET newsgroups'),

(4) real time communication (such as 'Internet Relay Chat'),

(5) real time remote computer utilization (such as 'telnet'), and

(6) remote information retrieval (such as 'ftp,' 'gopher,' and the 'World Wide Web').

Most of these methods of communication can be used to transmit text, data, computer programs, sound, visual images (i.e., pictures), and moving video images."

American Civil Liberties Union v. Reno, 929 F. Supp. 824, 834 (E.D. Pa. 1996), *aff'd, Reno v. American Civil Liberties Union,* 521 U.S. 844 (1997).

"As the growth in Internet use and the wide availability of tools and resources to those with access to the Internet suggest, the Internet presents extremely low entry barriers to those who wish to convey Internet content or gain access to it. In particular, a user wishing to communicate through e-mail, newsgroups, or Internet Relay Chat need only have access to a computer with appropriate software and a connection to the Internet, usually available for a low monthly fee. The user then in a sense becomes a public 'speaker,' able to convey content, at relatively low cost, to users around the world to whom it may be of interest. Those who possess more sophisticated equipment and greater technical expertise can make content available on the Internet for retrieval by others (known or unknown) by running a server supporting anonymous FTP, a gopher server, or a Web server. Yet content providers need not necessarily run their own servers or have the programming expertise to construct their own sites; they can lease space on a Webserver from another or create a 'home page' through an on-line commercial service.

"The ease of entry of many speakers sets interactive computer systems apart from any other more traditional communications medium that Congress has attempted to regulate in the past. With one-way media such as radio and television broadcasting or cable programming, a user is merely a listener or viewer; in the CDA, Congress sought to target 'interactive' computer systems through which a listener or viewer, by definition, has the power to become a speaker. The relative ease of speaker entry and the relative parity among speakers accounts for the unprecedented and virtually unlimited opportunities for political discourse, cultural development, and intellectual activity that Congress found to characterize emerging communication technologies.

"In seeking to describe the range of tools and opportunities for Internet users to 'speak,' we recognize that the categories we delineate are far from clean and the technology is far from static. Indeed, by all indications, the way that we conceptualize various media that we have traditionally viewed as distinct—such as cable television, telephones, and computer networks—will change dramatically as these media 'converge' into common forms of communication."

Shea v. Reno, 930 F. Supp. 916, 929-30 (S.D.N.Y. 1996).

"The Internet is more than a means of communications; it also serves as a conduit for transporting digitized goods, including software, data, music, graphics, and videos which can be downloaded from the provider's site to the Internet user's computer."

American Library Association v. Pataki, 969 F. Supp. 160, 173 (S.D.N.Y. 1997).

Related issues. "The commercial use of the Internet tests the limits of these traditional, territorial-based concepts even further.

"The Internet has no boundaries. To paraphrase Gertrude Stein, as far as the Internet is concerned, not only is there perhaps 'no there there,' the 'there' is everywhere where there is Internet access. When business is transacted over a computer network via a Web-site accessed by a computer in Massachusetts, it takes place as much in Massachusetts, literally or figuratively, as it does anywhere.

* * *

"The change is significant. Physical boundaries typically have framed legal boundaries, in effect creating signposts that warn that we will be required after crossing to abide by different rules. To impose traditional territorial concepts on the commercial uses of the Internet has dramatic implications, opening the Web user up to inconsistent regulations throughout fifty states, indeed, throughout the globe. It also raises the possibility of dramatically chilling what may well be 'the most participatory marketplace of mass speech that this country—and indeed the world—has yet seen.' As a result courts have been, and should be, cautious in applying traditional concepts."

Digital Equip. Corp. v. Altavista Technology, Inc., 960 F. Supp. 456, 462 (D. Mass. 1997).

"[N]ot a physical or tangible entity, but rather a giant network which interconnects innumerable smaller groups of linked computer networks."

American Civil Liberties Union v. Reno, 929 F. Supp. 824, 830 (E.D. Pa. 1996), *aff'd, Reno v. American Civil Liberties Union,* 521 U.S. 844 (1997).

"[It is] no exaggeration to conclude that the content on the Internet is as diverse as human thought."

American Civil Liberties Union v. Reno, 929 F. Supp. 824, 842 (E.D. Pa. 1996), *aff'd, Reno v. American Civil Liberties Union,* 521 U.S. 844 (1997).

"In many respects, unconventional messages compete equally with the speech of mainstream speakers in the marketplace of ideas that is the Internet, certainly more than in most other media."

American Civil Liberties Union v. Reno, 31 F. Supp. 2d 473, 476 (E.D. Pa. 1999).

"Cutting through the acronyms and *argot* that littered the hearing testimony, the Internet may fairly be regarded as a never-ending worldwide conversation. The Government may not, through the CDA, interrupt that conversation. As the most participatory form of mass speech yet developed, the Internet deserves the highest protection from governmental intrusion. True it is that many find some of the speech on the Internet to be offensive, and amid the din of cyberspace many hear discordant voices that they regard as indecent. The absence of governmental regulation of Internet content has unquestionably produced a kind of chaos, but as one of plaintiffs' experts put it with such resonance at the hearing:

'What achieved success was the very chaos that the Internet is. The strength of the Internet is that chaos.'

"Just as the strength of the Internet is chaos, so the strength of our liberty depends upon the chaos and cacophony of the unfettered speech the First Amendment protects."

American Civil Liberties Union v. Reno, 929 F. Supp. 824, 883 (E.D. Pa. 1996), *aff'd, Reno v. American Civil Liberties Union,* 521 U.S. 844 (1997).

"The Internet is not exclusively, or even primarily, a means of commercial communication. Many commercial entities maintain Web sites to inform potential consumers about their goods and services, or to solicit purchases, but many other Web sites exist solely for the dissemination of non-commercial information. The other forms of Internet communication—e-mail, bulletin boards, newsgroups, and chat rooms—frequently have non-commercial goals."

American Civil Liberties Union v. Reno, 929 F. Supp. 824, 842 (E.D. Pa. 1996), *aff'd, Reno v. American Civil Liberties Union,* 521 U.S. 844 (1997).

"[T]he Internet is one of those areas of commerce that must be marked off as a national preserve to protect users from inconsistent legislation that taken to its most extreme, could paralyze development of the Internet altogether.

* * *

"There is no compelling reason to find that local legal officials must take a 'hands off' approach just because a crook or a con artist is technologically sophisticated enough to sell on the Internet. Invocation of 'the Internet' is not the equivalent to a cry of 'sanctuary' upon a criminal's entry into

a medieval church. It should be sufficient that the laws sought to be applied, even if they might tangentially implicate interstate commerce, are 'media neutral' and otherwise pass constitutional muster."
> *American Library Association v. Pataki,* 969 F. Supp. 160, 169 (S.D.N.Y. 1997).

"Unlike use of the mail, the internet, with its electronic mail, is a tremendously more efficient, quicker, and vast means of reaching a global audience. By simply setting up and posting information at a website in the form of an advertisement or solicitation, one has done everything necessary to reach the global internet audience."
> *Maritz, Inc. v. Cybergold, Inc.,* 947 F. Supp. 1328, 1332 (E.D. Mo. 1996).

"[D]istinctions in how Internet content is transmitted affect the degree of control that providers of content have over who will be able to gain access to their communications."
> *Shea v. Reno,* 930 F. Supp. 916, 926-27 (S.D.N.Y. 1996).

"[W]ith the exception of e-mail, no content appears on a user's screen without the user having first taken some affirmative step. One wishing to read articles posted to a newsgroup must connect to a Usenet server and select the relevant group. To retrieve a file through anonymous PTP or access a gopher server, the user must search for or know the address of a particular server. To gain access to content on the World Wide Web, a user must know the URL of a relevant site or type a keyword into one of several available search engines."
> *Shea v. Reno,* 930 F. Supp. 916, 930-31 (S.D.N.Y. 1996).

"The Internet links PCs by means of servers, which run specialized operating systems and applications designed for servicing a network environment."
> *United States v. Microsoft Corp.,* 65 F. Supp. 2d 1, 4-5 (D.D.C. 1999) (Finding of Fact 11).

"[T]he Internet has become both a major inducement for consumers to buy PCs for the first time and a major occupier of the time and attention of current PC users."
> *United States v. Microsoft Corp.,* 65 F. Supp. 2d 1, 20 (D.D.C. 1999) (Finding of Fact 70).

"[W]e observe that the lightning speed development of the Internet poses challenges for the common-law adjudicative process — a process which, ideally while grounded in the past, governs the present and offers direction for the future based on understandings of current circumstances. Mindful of the often unforeseeable impact of rapid technological change, we are wary of making legal pronouncements based on highly fluid circumstances, which almost certainly will give way to tomorrow's new realities."

> *Name.Space, Inc. v. Network Solutions, Inc.,* 202 F.3d 573, 584 (2d Cir. 2000).

"[O]ne of the most fluid, rapidly developing, and virtually daily changing areas of commerce that the law has had to focus upon and endeavor to apply established principles to."

> *ImOn, Inc. v. ImaginOn, Inc.,* 90 F. Supp. 2d 345, 350 (S.D.N.Y. 2000).

"The exponential growth of the Internet represents an inflection point born of complementary technological advances in the computer and telecommunications industries. The rise of the Internet in turn has fueled the growth of server-based computing, middleware, and open-source software development."

> *United States v. Microsoft Corp.,* 65 F. Supp. 2d 1, 17 (D.D.C. 1999) (Finding of Fact 60).

"The unique nature of the Internet highlights the likelihood that a single actor might be subject to haphazard, uncoordinated, and even outright inconsistent regulation by states that the actor never intended to reach and possibly was unaware were being accessed. Typically, states' jurisdictional limits are related to geography; geography, however, is a virtually meaningless construct on the Internet."

> *American Libraries Ass'n v. Pataki,* 969 F. Supp. 160, 164-67 (S.D.N.Y. 1997).

"Until recently, the Internet was of little use for the distribution of music because the average music computer file was simply too big: the digital information on a single compact disc of music required hundreds of computer floppy discs to store, and downloading even a single song from the Internet took hours. However, various compression algorithms (which make an audio file 'smaller' by limiting the audio bandwidth) now allow digital audio files to be transferred more quickly and stored more efficiently."

> *Recording Indus. Ass'n of America v. Diamond Multimedia Sys., Inc.,* 180 F.3d 1072, 1073-74 (9th Cir. 1999).

Internet access provider(s) *(Internet)*
Abbreviated as "IAP(s)."

> *United States v. Microsoft Corp.,* 65 F. Supp. 2d 1, 5 (D.D.C. 1999) (Finding of Fact 15).

Annotation. "PCs typically connect to the Internet through the services of Internet access providers ('IAPs'), which generally charge subscription fees to their customers in the United States. There are two types of IAPs. Online services ('OLSs') such as America Online ('AOL'), Prodigy, and the Microsoft Network ('MSN') offer, in addition to Internet access, various services and an array of proprietary content. Internet service providers ('ISPs') such as MindSpring and Netcom, on the other hand, offer few services apart from Internet access and relatively little of their own content."

> *United States v. Microsoft Corp.*, 65 F. Supp. 2d 1, 5 (D.D.C. 1999) (Finding of Fact 15).

Internet Architecture Board *(organization)*

The organization that oversees development of Internet standards and protocols, and acts as a liaison between the Internet Society (ISOC) and other standards bodies. Located at <www.iab.org/iab>.

Internet Assigned Numbers Authority *(Internet; organization)*

Abbreviated as "IANA."

"Initially, the Internet Assigned Numbers Authority retained responsibility for both Internet Protocol number allocation and domain name registration. In 1991 and 1992, NSF, an independent agency of the federal government, assumed responsibility for coordinating and funding the management of the nonmilitary portion of the Internet infrastructure.

"In March 1992, NSF solicited competitive proposals to provide a variety of infrastructure services, including domain name registration services. NSF issued the solicitation pursuant to the National Science Found. Act of 1950, 42 U.S.C. §§1861-1887, as amended, and the Federal Grant and Cooperative Agreement Act, 31 U.S.C. §§6301-6308. In December 1992, after an independent review of the proposals responsive to the solicitation, NSF selected the bid from, and entered into a cooperative agreement with, Network Solutions, Inc., a private company."

> *Thomas v. Network Solutions, Inc.*, 176 F.3d 500, 504 (D.C. Cir. 1999) (footnotes omitted).

"The Internet Assigned Numbers Authority (IANA) is responsible for the overall coordination and management of the Domain Name System (DNS), and especially the delegation of portions of the name space called top-level domains. . . . Applications for new top-level domains (for example, country code domains) are handled . . . with consultation with the IANA."

> *Name.Space, Inc. v. Network Solutions, Inc.*, 202 F.3d 573, 583 (2d Cir. 2000).

Internet content provider(s) *(Internet)*

Abbreviated as "ICP(s)."

"[I]ndividuals and organizations that have established a presence, or 'site,' on the Web by publishing a collection of Web pages."

United States v. Microsoft Corp., 65 F. Supp. 2d 1, 5 (D.D.C. 1999) (Finding of Fact 13).

Internet Corporation for Assigned Names and Numbers *(Internet; organization)*

See **ICANN.**

Internet domain name *(criminal)*

"[A] global unique, hierarchical reference to an Internet host or service, assigned through centralized Internet naming authorities, comprising a series of character strings separated by periods, with the rightmost character string specifying the top of the hierarchy."

Cal. Penal C. § 502.

See also **domain name; domain address.**

Internet Engineering Steering Group *(Internet; organization)*

Abbreviated as "IESG." The organization that acts as the operational management arm of the Internet Engineering Task Force. Located at <www.ietf.org/iesg.html>.

Internet Engineering Task Force *(Internet; organization)*

Abbreviated as "IETF."

"The group primarily responsible for Internet technical standards. . . ."

American Civil Liberties Union v. Reno, 929 F. Supp. 824, 842 n.16 (E.D. Pa. 1996), *aff'd, Reno v. American Civil Liberties Union,* 521 U.S. 844 (1997).

Related issue. Located at <www.ietf.org>.

Internet Explorer *(Internet; software)*

"Microsoft introduced its browser, called Internet Explorer, in July 1995."

United States v. Microsoft Corp., 65 F. Supp. 2d 1, 5 (D.D.C. 1999) (Finding of Fact 17).

See also **web browser.**

Internet host *(Internet)*

See **host.**

Internet protocol *(Internet)*

Abbreviated as "IP."

"A numbering system [which] gives each individual computer or network a unique numerical address on the Internet. The 'Internet Protocol number,' also known as the IP number,' consists of four groups of digits separated by periods, such as '192.215.247.50.'"

> *Lockheed Martin Corp. v. Network Solutions, Inc.,* 985 F. Supp. 949, 952 (C.D. Cal. 1997).

"The various protocols that allow such communications to take place are known as Internet protocols ('IP'), and each entity connected to the Internet is assigned one or more unique numeric addresses, known as IP numbers or IP addresses."

> *Name.Space, Inc. v. Network Solutions, Inc.,* 202 F.3d 573, 576 (2d Cir. 2000).

See also communications protocol(s); Internet protocol address.

Internet protocol address *(Internet)*

Also called "IP address" and "IP number." A unique set of numbers that indicates the exact connection between a particular computer and the network on the Internet. They are 32-bit addresses that consist of four octets, expressed as four numbers between 0 and 255, separated by periods (e.g., 198.41.0.52). Every Internet site is assigned a unique IP address. Because these numbers can be difficult for users to remember, most Internet sites also have a "domain name." The Internet, however, depends on the numerical address, so domain names must be translated by a computer called a name server into their corresponding IP addresses. *See also* **IP address; IP number.**

". . . an Internet location. . . ."

> *Avery Dennison Corp. v. Sumpton,* 189 F.3d 868, 872 (9th Cir. 1999).

" . . . consists of four numbers, each between 0 and 255, separated by periods. The first number signifies the computer's geographic region; the second number a specific Internet Service Provider; the third a specific group of computers; and the fourth a specific computer within that group."

> *Thomas v. Network Solutions, Inc.,* 176 F.3d 500, 502 n.1 (D.C. Cir. 1999) (citations omitted).

Annotation. "Because an Internet protocol address is a string of integer numbers separated by periods, for example, <129.137.84.101>, for ease of recall and use a user relies on a 'domain-name combination' to reach a given web site."

> *Avery Dennison Corp. v. Sumpton,* 189 F.3d 868, 872 (9th Cir. 1999).

Related issues. "The registrar of Internet domain names, Network Solutions, Inc., maintains a database of registrations and translates entered domain-name combinations into Internet protocol addresses."
Avery Dennison Corp. v. Sumpton, 189 F.3d 868, 872 (9th Cir. 1999).

Internet protocol number *(Internet)*

"Before using a domain name to locate an Internet computer site in 'cyberspace,' a computer must match the domain name to the domain name's Internet Protocol number. The match information is stored on various Internet-connected computers around the world known as domain name servers. The computer attempts to find the match information by sending out an address query. The goal of the address query is to find the particular domain name server containing the match information the user seeks.

"When ordered to translate an unknown domain name into an Internet Protocol number, a computer will ask its Internet Service Provider's server if it knows the domain name and corresponding Internet Protocol number. If that server lacks the information, it will pass the query to a 'root server,' also called a 'root zone' file, the authoritative and highest level of the domain name system database. The root zone file directs the query to the proper top-level domain zone file, which contains the domain names in a given domain and their corresponding Internet Protocol numbers. In the case of someone searching for the 'bettyandnicks.com' home page, the root zone file sends the query to the top-level domain zone file with information about '.com' domain names. The '.com' zone file then refers the query to a second-level domain name file with all the second-level domain names under '.com.' This is where the 'bettyandnicks.com' query ends: the second-level domain name file has the information matching the domain name to its associated Internet Protocol number. With the Internet Protocol number, the user's computer can connect the user to the requested Internet site. The 'bettyandnicks.com' home page will appear, just as if the user had typed in the Internet Protocol number instead of the domain name."
Thomas v. Network Solutions, Inc., 176 F.3d 500, 503-04 (D.C. Cir. 1999) (citations and footnotes omitted).

"For the domain name system to function, each domain name must be unique and correspond to a unique Internet Protocol number. A new user who wishes to have an Internet site with a domain name address first obtains an Internet Protocol number (e.g., 1.23.456.7). The user then registers a domain name and it becomes linked with that Internet Protocol number."
Thomas v. Network Solutions, Inc., 176 F.3d 500, 503 (D.C. Cir. 1999) (citations omitted).

Internet Relay Chat *(Internet)*
Abbreviated as "IRC."

". . . 'chat' software. . . ."
> *Shea v. Reno,* 930 F. Supp. 916, 928 (S.D.N.Y. 1996).

"[B]ecause of the technology of Internet relay chat, it would need to make this determination [the legality of the words used] *before* it organized the chat room, since it could not prescreen the discussion among the participants. Thus, it would need to predict, in advance, what the participants were likely to say. The participants would need to make a similar determination, unaided (I expect) by First Amendment lawyers."
> *American Civil Liberties Union v. Reno,* 929 F. Supp. 824, 872 n.12 (E.D. Pa. 1996) (emphasis in original), *aff'd, Reno v. American Civil Liberties Union,* 521 U.S. 844 (1997).

See also **IRC.**

Internet service provider *(business; Internet)*
Abbreviated as "ISP." Also called "service provider."

"[G]enerally commercial entities charging a monthly fee, offer modem access to computers or networks linked directly to the Internet."
> *Shea v. Reno,* 930 F. Supp. 916, 926 (S.D.N.Y. 1996).

"[P]rovide the host computers and connections necessary for communications on the Internet."
> *Lockheed Martin Corp. v. Network Solutions, Inc.,* 985 F. Supp. 949, 958 (C.D. Cal. 1997).

". . . typically offer modem telephone access to a computer or computer network linked to the Internet. Many such providers . . . are commercial entities offering Internet access for a monthly or hourly fee. Some Internet service providers, however, are non-profit organizations that offer free or very low cost access to the Internet."
> *American Civil Liberties Union v. Reno,* 929 F. Supp. 824, 833 (E.D. Pa. 1996), *aff'd, Reno v. American Civil Liberties Union,* 521 U.S. 844 (1997).

". . . generally commercial entities charging a monthly fee, offer modem access to computers or networks linked directly to the Internet."
> *Shea v. Reno,* 930 F. Supp. 916, 926 (S.D.N.Y. 1996).

Annotation. "Domain name service can be operated by the domain name holder or obtained from any entity with the proper computer equipment, including hundreds of Internet service providers."
> *Intermatic, Inc. v. Toeppen,* 947 F. Supp. 1227, 1231 (N.D. Ill. 1996).

". . . such as MindSpring and Netcom . . . offer few services apart from Internet access and relatively little of their own content."

United States v. Microsoft Corp., 65 F. Supp. 2d 1, 5 (D.D.C. 1999) (Finding of Fact 15).

Internet Society *(organization)*

Abbreviated as "ISOC." An international organization founded in 1992, which is dedicated to the expansion, development, and availability of the Internet. Located at <www.isoc.org>.

Internet taxation *(electronic commerce)*

"Any taxation of Internet sales should follow these principles:

• It should neither distort nor hinder commerce. No tax system should discriminate among types of commerce, nor should it create incentives that will change the nature or location of transactions.

• The system should be simple and transparent. It should be capable of capturing the overwhelming majority of appropriate revenues, be easy to implement, and minimize burdensome record keeping and costs for all parties.

• The system should be able to accommodate tax systems used by the United States and our international partners today.

"Wherever feasible, we should look to existing taxation concepts and principles to achieve these goals.

"Any such taxation system will have to accomplish these goals in the context of the Internet's special characteristics—the potential anonymity of buyer and seller, the capacity for multiple small transactions, and the difficulty of associating online activities with physically defined locations."

The White House, *A Framework for Global Electronic Commerce* 7 (July 1, 1997).

Internet telephony *(Internet; telecommunications)*

Voice transmission over the Internet; a subset of IP telephony. *See* **IP telephony.**

Internet 2 *(technology)*

Also referred to as "Internet II." A new global computer network being developing by a consortium of universities to permit enhanced video, audio, and data transfers.

Internet use *(Internet)*

"[T]here are two loose and overlapping categories of Internet use. First, an individual who has secured access to the Internet can correspond or exchange views with one or many other Internet users. Second, a user can locate and retrieve information available on other computers."

Shea v. Reno, 930 F. Supp. 916, 926 (S.D.N.Y. 1996).

InterNIC *(Internet)*

"[A] naming organization, not a regulator of content. InterNIC and two other European organizations maintain a master list of domain names to ensure that no duplication occurs. Creators of Web sites must register their domain name with InterNIC, and the agency will instruct the creator to choose another name if the new Web site has the name of an already-existing site. InterNIC has no control over content on a site after registration."

American Civil Liberties Union v. Reno, 929 F. Supp. 824, 848 n.20 (E.D. Pa. 1996), *aff'd, Reno v. American Civil Liberties Union,* 521 U.S. 844 (1997).

"The uniqueness of Internet addresses is ensured by the registration services of the Internet Network Information Center ('Internic'), a collaborative project established by the National Science Foundation."

MTV Networks, Inc. v. Curry, 867 F. Supp. 202, 203-04 n.2 (S.D.N.Y. 1994).

interoperability *(DMCA)*

"Defendants claim to fall under Section 1201(f) of the statute [DMCA], which provides in substance that one may circumvent, or develop and employ technological means to circumvent, access control measures in order to achieve interoperability with another computer program provided that doing so does not infringe another's copyright and, in addition, that one may make information acquired through such efforts 'available to others, if the person [in question] . . . provides such information solely for the purpose of enabling interoperability of an independently created computer program with other programs, and to the extent that doing so does not constitute infringement. . . .' They contend that DeCSS is necessary to achieve interoperability between computers running the Linux operating system and DVDs and that this exception therefore is satisfied.

"This contention fails.

"First, Section 1201(f)(3) permits information acquired through reverse engineering to be made available to others only by the person who acquired the information. But these defendants did not do any reverse engineering. They simply took DeCSS off someone else's web site and posted it on their own.

"Defendants would be in no stronger position even if they had authored DeCSS. The right to make the information available extends only to dissemination 'solely for the purpose' of achieving interoperability as defined in the statute. It does not apply to public dissemination of means of circumvention, as the legislative history confirms. These defendants, however, did not post DeCSS 'solely' to achieve interoperability with Linux or anything else.

". . . Accordingly, the reverse engineering exception to the DMCA has no application here."

> *Universal City Studios, Inc. v. Reimerdes,* 111 F. Supp. 2d 294, 319-20 (S.D.N.Y. 2000) (footnotes omitted).

(technology)

"[T]he ability of two or more components of a system or network to interact with each other in a meaningful way. . . ."

> U.S. General Accounting Office, *Information Superhighway: An Overview of Technology Changes* 31 (Jan. 1995).

"[T]he ability of one TEMPEST facsimile machine to send to and receive documents from another TEMPEST machine."

> *Secure Servs. Technology, Inc. v. Time & Space Processing, Inc.,* 722 F. Supp. 1354, 1357 n.4 (E.D. Va. 1989).

"[T]he ability of computer programs to exchange information, and of such programs mutually to use the information which has been exchanged."

> 17 U.S.C. § 1201(f)(4).

Annotation. "Interoperability—the ability of two or more components of a system or network to interact with each other in a meaningful way—is a key goal of the information superhighway. However, full interoperability among the thousands of networks, communications devices, and services that will comprise the information superhighway will be difficult to achieve. To do so, governments, industry, and standards-setting organizations must agree on well-defined international standards for rapidly advancing communications technologies, while manufacturers and service providers need to provide products and services conforming to these standards."

> U.S. General Accounting Office, *Information Superhighway: An Overview of Technology Changes* 31 (Jan. 1995).

See also **multi-vendor interoperability.**

interpolation *(technology)*

The process of calculated possible values of information from adjacent information. This process is used on compressed image sequences, where not every image is maintained by the compression algorithm, but only the basic information necessary to reconstruct a semblance of the original image.

interpreter *(software)*

"[A] computer program in the same general class as 'assembler' and 'compiler.' All three translate or change a programmer's source code into the object code that the computer uses."

> U.S. Copyright Office, *Compendium of Copyright Office Practices* II, § 326 (1984).

See also **interpreter program.**

interpreter program *(software)*

"[A] simultaneous translator that works in conjunction with the application program every time the application program is run, carrying out the instructions of the program one step at a time."

> *Lotus Dev. Corp. v. Paperback Software Int'l,* 740 F. Supp. 37, 44 (D. Mass. 1990).

[CANADA] "A program that enables a user to communicate with the computer in a high level language."

> *Apple Computer, Inc. v. Mackintosh Computers Ltd.* (1986), 28 D.L.R. (4th) 178 (Fed. T.D.).

See also **interpreter.**

intranet(s) *(technology)*

A private computer network within an organization, generally based on standard Internet protocols, which usually is protected from the general Internet by a firewall.

Annotation. Intranets are private networks that serve single companies or enterprises. Rather than use the Internet, an intranet usually keeps data on a server computer that is part of company's private local area network for access only by persons who have access to that network; in most cases an intranet cannot be reached from the Internet. An intranet will frequently include features common to the Internet such as e-mail, web sites, and FTP file transfers. (jrb)

intrinsic test *(copyright)*

"[T]he trier of fact must determine if the 'total concept and feel' of the expressive elements of both works are substantially similar."

> *Interactive Networks, Inc. v. NTN Comm., Inc.,* 875 F. Supp. 1398, 1404 (N.D. Cal. 1995).

invasion of privacy *(tort)*

Wrongful intrusion into the private activities of a person, the unauthorized disclosure of private facts or the casting of a person in a false light.

inventor *(patent)*

". . . carries an implication which excludes the results of only ordinary skill. . . ."

> *M. Kramer Mfg. Co. v. Andrews,* 783 F.2d 421, 438 (4th Cir. 1986), *quoting Bleistein v. Donaldson Lithographing Co.,* 188 U.S. 239, 250 (1903).

inventory

(advertising)
The number of ads available on a given web site. Inventory is determined by totaling the number of ads on a page, the number of pages with ads on them, and the number of page requests at a specific site.

(Year 2000)
The process of determining the components that comprise the organization's systems portfolio. The inventory should include all applications, databases, files, and related system components that will require inspection to locate date data and related date computations. (wsr)

inverse H-matrix *(technology)*
"An H-Matrix in which the rows of the matrix have been interchanged."
E.F. Johnson Co. v. Uniden Corp. of Am., 623 F. Supp. 1485, 1495 (D. Minn. 1985).

invisible GIF *(technology)*
See web bug.

invitation for bid *(contract)*
See invitation to bid.

invitation to bid *(contract)*
"Generally, in the field of government procurement, there are two types of competitive procurement: the Invitation For Bid or Invitation To Bid ('IFB') process and the Request for Proposal ('RFP') process. The difference between the two methods is the extent to which the vendor is given latitude to exercise judgment. An IFB is rigid while an RFP is flexible. Typically, an IFB identifies the solution to a problem while an RFP identifies a problem and requests a proposed solution."
IBM Corp. v. Florida Dep't of Gen. Servs., Administrative Law Reports 548, 7 Computer L. Serv. Rep. 495, 509 (1979).

I/O *(technology)*
Acronym for "Input/Output." The equipment such as a keyboard (input) or printer (output) used to communicate with a system. Every information transfer is an output from one device and an input into another.

ion implantation *(manufacturing)*
A semiconductor manufacturing process in which the silicon is bombarded with high-voltage ions in order to implant them in specific locations and

provide the appropriate electronic characteristics. Ion implantation is a more precise alternative to diffusion.

IP *(Internet)*

Acronym for "Internet protocol."

See **communications protocol(s); Internet protocol; Internet protocol address; IP address.**

IP address *(Internet)*

"The IP address is comprised of four groups of numbers separated by decimals."

> *Intermatic, Inc. v. Toeppen,* 947 F. Supp. 1227, 1230 (N.D. Ill. 1996).

"An IP address is a string of four sets of numbers, separated by periods, such as '98.37.241.30,' and every host or computer on the Internet is assigned such a numerical IP address."

> *Name.Space, Inc. v. Network Solutions, Inc.,* 202 F.3d 573, 576 (2d Cir. 2000).

Annotation. "Each host computer providing Internet services ('site') has a unique Internet address. Users seeking to exchange digital information (electronic mail ('email'), computer programs, images, music) with a particular Internet host require the host's address in order to establish a connection. Hosts actually possess two fungible addresses: a numeric 'IP' address such as 123.456.123.12, and an alphanumeric 'domain name' such as microsoft.com, with greater mnemonic potential."

> *MTV Networks, Inc. v. Curry,* 867 F. Supp. 202, 203 n.2 (S.D.N.Y. 1994).
> *See also Intermatic, Inc. v. Toeppen,* 947 F. Supp. 1227, 1230 (N.D. Ill. 1996).

Related issues. "In the early stages of the Internet's development, IP addresses were assigned and maintained by the late Dr. Jon Postel, whose work was eventually conducted under the auspices of a private entity known as the Internet Assigned Numbers Authority ('IANA'). Due at least in part to the difficulty of remembering numeric IP addresses, Dr. Postel and his colleagues also administered the assignment of alphanumeric names to each host computer on the Internet. A file containing the mappings of these host names to the corresponding IP addresses was updated and maintained on each host computer.

"However, as the Internet continued to grow in size and complexity, this horizontal system became increasingly unwieldy. By the mid-1980s, the time and resources necessary to update the files on each host computer, and the desire for greater local structure and control over host names, inter alia, suggested that a different system was necessary. Therefore, the Internet community developed a new DNS for mapping host names onto IP addresses."

Name.Space, Inc. v. Network Solutions, Inc., 202 F.3d 573, 576 (2d Cir. 2000) (citations omitted).

See also **Internet protocol address; IP number.**

IP number *(Internet)*

"A numbering system called the 'Internet Protocol' gives each individual computer or network a unique numerical address on the Internet. The 'Internet Protocol number,' also known as the 'IP number,' consists of four groups of digits separated by periods, such as '192.215.247.50.'"

Lockheed Martin Corp. v. Network Solutions, Inc., 985 F. Supp. 949, 952 (C.D. Cal. 1997).

See also **IP address; Internet protocol address.**

IP telecommunications *(telecommunications)*

The transmission of packets over IP-based, packet-switched networks.

IP telephony *(telecommunications)*

The transmission of voice over IP-based, packet-switched networks.

IPO *(business)*

Acronym for "Initial Public Offering." The first offering of a company's stock to the general public.

IRC *(Internet)*

Acronym for "Internet Relay Chat."

". . . allows two or more to type messages to each other that almost immediately appear on the others' computer screens. IRC is analogous to a telephone party line, using a computer and keyboard rather than a telephone. With IRC, however, at any one time there are thousands of different party lines available, in which collectively tens of thousands of users are engaging in conversations on a huge range of subjects. Moreover, one can create a new party line to discuss a different topic at any time. Some IRC conversations are 'moderated' or include 'channel operators.'"

American Civil Liberties Union v. Reno, 929 F. Supp. 824, 835 (E.D. Pa. 1996), *aff'd, Reno v. American Civil Liberties Union*, 521 U.S. 844 (1997).

Related issues. "Individual participants in an Internet Relay Chat discussion know other participants only by the names they choose upon entering the discussion; users can participate anonymously by using a pseudonym."

Shea v. Reno, 930 F. Supp. 916, 941 (S.D.N.Y. 1996).

"[A] user who joins an IRC discussion channel cannot determine the identity of other participants, beyond viewing a list of names."

> *Shea v. Reno,* 930 F. Supp. 916, 942 (S.D.N.Y. 1996).

See also **Internet Relay Chat.**

irreparable harm *(copyright)*

A showing of a reasonable likelihood of success on the merits raises a presumption of irreparable harm."

> *Triad Sys. Corp. v. Southeastern Express Co.,* 64 F.3d 1330, 1335 (9th Cir. 1995).

Related issues. "[A] defendant cannot, by asserting the adequacy of money damages, rebut the presumption of irreparable harm that flows from a showing of likelihood of success on the merits . . . ."

> *Cadence Design Sys., Inc. v. Avant! Corp.,* 125 F.3d 824, 827 (9th Cir. 1997).

"In the Fifth Circuit there is no presumption of irreparable harm in copyright infringement cases, and thus in the Fifth Circuit, a copyright defendant can prevail by showing the adequacy of money damages. The Fifth Circuit is the only court of appeals that does not apply the presumption of irreparable harm."

> *Cadence Design Sys., Inc. v. Avant! Corp.,* 125 F.3d 824, 827 n.4 (9th Cir. 1997).

See also **irreparable injury.**

irreparable injury *(copyright; trademark; First Amendment)*

Injury that cannot be remedied by damages.

Related issues

(copyright)

"[P]roving irreparable injury is generally not required in copyright litigation. Irreparable injury is presumed for the purposes of a preliminary injunction motion once the moving party has established a case of copyright infringement."

> *E.F. Johnson Co. v. Uniden Corp. of America,* 623 F. Supp. 1485, 1491 (D. Minn. 1985).

(copyright/trademark)

"In copyright and trademark cases, irreparable injury is presumed upon a showing of likelihood of success."

> *Playboy Enters., Inc. v. Welles,* 47 U.S.P.Q.2d (BNA) 1186, 1189 (S.D. Cal. 1998).

(First Amendment)
"The loss of First Amendment freedoms, for even minimal periods of time, unquestionably constitutes irreparable injury."
   Shea v. Reno, 930 F. Supp. 916, 935 (S.D.N.Y. 1996) (citation omitted).
See also **irreparable harm.**

ISDN *(hardware)*
Acronym for "Integrated Services Digital Network." A digital network interface standard established by the CCITT to replace the current analog telephone networks. A basic ISDN line provides a 16-kbps signaling channel and two 64-kbps digital transmission channels used to provide switched circuit connections. It allows digitized voice and data to be sent over existing telephone lines at high speed.

ISO

(business)
Acronym for "Independent Service Organization." An organization that provides servicing for another company's hardware/computer systems.

(organization)
Acronym for " International Organization for Standardization." The ISO is a nongovernmental, worldwide federation of national standards bodies from some 130 countries established in 1947. It promotes standardization and related activities worldwide to facilitate the international exchange of goods and services, and cooperation in the areas of intellectual, scientific, technological and economic activity. ISO works for international agreements, which are then published as international standards.

ISOC *(organization)*
Acronym for the "Internet Society." *See* **Internet Society.**

ISP *(business; Internet)*
Acronym for "Internet Service Provider."

"An entity that provides its customers the ability to obtain online information through the Internet. ISPs purchase analog and digital lines from local exchange carriers to connect to their dial-in subscribers. Under the typical arrangement, an ISP customer dials a seven digit number to reach the ISP server in the same local calling area. The ISP, in turn, combines computer processing, information storage, protocol conversion, and routing with transmission to enable users to access Internet content and services."

> *In re* Implementation of the Local Competition Provisions in the Telecommunications Act of 1996: Inter-Carrier Compensation for ISP-Bound Traffic, 14 F.C.C.R. 3689, ¶ 4 (Feb. 26, 1999).

See also **Internet service provider.**

ISSCC *(organization)*

Acronym for "International Solid State Circuits Conference."

> *National Semiconductor Corp. v. Linear Technology Corp.,* 703 F. Supp. 845, 847 (N.D. Cal. 1988).

issue a certificate *(electronic commerce)*

"[T]he acts of a certification authority in creating a certificate and notifying the subscriber listed in the certificate of the contents of the certificate."

> Wash. Rev. Code § 19.34.020(16).

ITAA *(organization)*

Acronym for "Information Technology Association of America." A membership organization of companies involved in information technology. Located at <www.itaa.org>.

iterative approach *(copyright)*

". . . requires proof (1) that the defendant 'used' the copyrighted work in preparing the alleged copy, which may be established by proof of access and similarity sufficient to reasonably infer use of the copyrighted work; and (2) that the defendant's work is an iterative reproduction, that is, one produced by iterative or exact duplication of substantial portions of the copyrighted work."

> *E.F. Johnson Co. v. Uniden Corp. of America,* 623 F. Supp. 1485, 1492 (D. Minn. 1985).

Annotation. "Under the iterative approach, . . . the factfinder's focus shifts from the hypothetical ordinary observer's impressions of the 'total concept and feel' of the copyrighted and allegedly infringing works to an analysis of the 'quantitative and qualitative evidence of similarities' as gauged by the Court's evaluation of expert testimony. The fiction of the lay observer is thus abandoned in favor of an analysis of similarities and differences in the copyrighted and allegedly offending computer program."

> *E.F. Johnson Co. v. Uniden Corp. of America,* 623 F. Supp. 1485, 1493 (D. Minn. 1985).

See also **infringement; iterative reproduction; ordinary observer test; substantial similarity.**

iterative reproduction *(copyright)*

"[O]ne produced by iterative or exact duplication of substantial portions of the copyrighted work."

> *E.F. Johnson Co. v. Uniden Corp. of America,* 623 F. Supp. 1485, 1493 (D. Minn. 1985).

See also **iterative approach.**

ITU *(organization)*

Acronym for "International Telecommunication Union." An international organization within which governments and the private sector coordinate global telecom networks and services. Located at <www.itu.int>.

jaggies *(technology)*
The jagged edges that appear along curved or diagonal lines on a computer screen, which are caused by aliasing. *See also* **aliasing.**

Java® *(software)*
"[A] computer programming language Sun developed to enable the writing of programs that work on any computer operating system."
Sun Microsys., Inc. v. Microsoft Corp., 188 F.3d 1115, 1117 (9th Cir. 1999).

"Sun had created Java so that programmers could write a single program that would work on any operating system."
Sun Microsys., Inc. v. Microsoft Corp., 188 F.3d 1115, 1118 (9th Cir. 1999).

Annotation. ". . . refers to four interlocking elements. First, there is a Java programming language with which developers can write applications. Second, there is a set of programs written in Java that expose APIs on which developers writing in Java can rely. These programs are called the 'Java class libraries.' The third element is the Java compiler, which translates the code written by the developer into Java 'bytecode.' Finally, there are programs called 'Java virtual machines,' or 'JVMs,' which translate Java bytecode into instructions comprehensible to the underlying operating system. If the Java class libraries and a JVM are present on a PC system, the system is said to carry a 'Java runtime environment.'"
United States v. Microsoft Corp., 65 F. Supp. 2d 1, 20 (D.D.C. 1999) (Finding of Fact 73).

"The inventors of Java at Sun Microsystems intended the technology to enable applications written in the Java language to run on a variety of platforms with minimal porting. A program written in Java and relying only on APIs exposed by the Java class libraries will run on any PC system containing a JVM that has itself been ported to the resident operating system. Therefore, Java developers need to port their applications only to the extent that those applications rely directly on the APIs exposed by a particular operating system. The more an application written in Java relies on

APIs exposed by the Java class libraries, the less work its developer will need to do to port the application to different operating systems. The easier it is for developers to port their applications to different operating systems, the more applications will be written for operating systems other than Windows. To date, the Java class libraries do not expose enough APIs to support the development of full-featured applications that will run well on multiple operating systems without the need for porting; however, they do allow relatively simple, network-centric applications to be written cross-platform. It is Sun's ultimate ambition to expand the class libraries to such an extent that many full-featured, end-user-oriented applications will be written cross-platform. The closer Sun gets to this goal of "write once, run anywhere," the more the applications barrier to entry will erode."

United States v. Microsoft Corp., 65 F. Supp. 2d 1, 20 (D.D.C. 1999) (Finding of Fact 74).

Java class libraries *(software)*

"[A] set of programs written in Java that expose APIs on which developers writing in Java can rely."

United States v. Microsoft Corp., 65 F. Supp. 2d 1, 20 (D.D.C. 1999) (Finding of Fact 73).

Java compiler *(software)*

"[T]ranslates the code written by the developer into Java 'bytecode.'"

United States v. Microsoft Corp., 65 F. Supp. 2d 1, 20 (D.D.C. 1999) (Finding of Fact 73).

Java virtual machine(s) *(software)*

Abbreviated as "JVM(s)."

"[P]rograms . . . which translate Java bytecode into instructions comprehensible to the underlying operating system."

United States v. Microsoft Corp., 65 F. Supp. 2d 1, 20 (D.D.C. 1999) (Finding of Fact 73).

jewel box *(multimedia)*

The hinged plastic (polystyrene) case that is widely used to store and distribute compact discs and CD-ROMs.

Joint Photographic Experts Group *(organization)*

Abbreviated as "JPEG." *See* **JPEG.**

joint venture *(business)*

"A joint venture is a 'special combination of two or more persons where in some specific venture a profit is jointly sought without any actual partnership or corporate designation.'"

> *MTV Networks, Inc. v. Curry,* 867 F. Supp. 202, 206 (S.D.N.Y. 1994) (citation omitted).

". . . is often used to describe a venture, other than one engaged in naked per se violations (like a price fixing cartel), that represents a collaborative effort between companies—who may or may not be competitors—to achieve a particular end (e.g., joint research and development, production of an individual product, or efficient joint purchasing)."

> *Addamax Corp. v. Open Software Found., Inc.,* 152 F.3d 48, 50 n.2 (1st Cir. 1998).

joint work *(copyright)*

"[A] work prepared by two or more authors with the intention that their contributions be merged into inseparable or interdependent parts of a unitary whole."

> U.S. Copyright Act, 17 U.S.C. § 101.

Annotation. "[A] person who merely describes to an author what the commissioned work should do or look like is not a joint author for purposes of the Copyright Act. . . . To be a joint author, one must supply more than mere direction or ideas; one must 'translate[] an idea into a fixed, tangible expression entitled to copyright protection.' . . . The supplier of an idea is no more an 'author' of a program than is the supplier of the disk on which the program is stored."

> *S.O.S., Inc. v. Payday, Inc.,* 886 F.2d 1081, 1087 (9th Cir. 1989).

Related issues. "In a world where there are many authors of one work . . . a law based on the concepts of originality and authorship may become too unwieldy to administer."

> Office of Technology Assessment, *Intellectual Property Rights in an Age of Electronics and Information* 6 (1986).

joystick *(hardware)*

"[A] handheld control."

> *Midway Mfg. Co. v. Strohon,* 564 F. Supp. 741, 743 (N.D. Ill. 1983).

JPEG *(technology)*

Acronym for "Joint Photographic Experts Group." A standard method used for 15-to-1 still image compression.

Jughead *(Internet)*

"[A]n aptly named tool for searching menus on only a single server."
  Shea v. Reno, 930 F. Supp. 916, 928 n.9 (S.D.N.Y. 1996).

jump cite *(copyright)*

"[C]itations that show the page location of the particular text in West's printed version of the opinions."
  Matthew Bender & Co. v. West Publ'g Co., 158 F.3d 693, 695 (2d Cir. 1998), *cert. denied*, 522 U.S. 3732 (1999).

junk e-mail *(Internet)*

See spam.

jurisdiction *(jurisdiction)*

The capacity of a court or other tribunal to interpret and apply a specific rule of law; generally limited by both territory and subject matter.

Annotation. "The unique nature of the Internet highlights the likelihood that a single actor might be subject to haphazard, uncoordinated, and even outright inconsistent regulation by states that the actor never intended to reach and possibly was unaware were being accessed. Typically, states' jurisdictional limits are related to geography; geography, however, is a virtually meaningless construct on the Internet."
  American Library Ass'n v. Pataki, 969 F. Supp. 160, 169 (S.D.N.Y. 1997).

"As technological progress has increased the flow of commerce between the States, the need for jurisdiction has undergone a similar increase."
  Hanson v. Denckla, 357 U.S. 235, 250-51 (1958).

"[I]t is an inescapable fact of modern commercial life that a substantial amount of commercial business is transacted solely by mail or wire communications across state lines, thus obviating the need for physical presence within a State in which business is conducted."
  Burger King Corp. v. Rudzewicz, 471 U.S. 462, 475 (1985).

"The Internet makes it possible to conduct business throughout the world entirely from a desktop. With this global revolution looming on the horizon, the development of the law concerning the permissible scope of personal jurisdiction based on Internet use is in its infant stages. The cases are scant."
  Zippo Mfg. Co. v. Zippo Dot Com, Inc., 952 F. Supp. 1119, 1123-24 (W.D. Pa. 1997).

"Through the use of computers, corporations can now transact business and communicate with individuals in several states simultaneously. Unlike communication by mail or telephone, messages sent through computers are available to the recipient and anyone else who may be watching. Thus, while modern technology has made nationwide commercial transactions simpler and more feasible, even for small businesses, it must broaden correspondingly the permissible scope of jurisdiction exercisable by the courts."

California Software, Inc. v. Reliability Research, Inc., 631 F. Supp. 1356, 1363 (C.D. Cal. 1986).

"The unique nature of the Internet highlights the likelihood that a single actor might be subject to haphazard, uncoordinated, and even outright inconsistent regulation by states that the actor never intended to reach and possibly was unaware were being accessed. Typically, states' jurisdictional limits are related to geography; geography, however, is a virtually meaningless construct on the Internet."

American Libraries Ass'n v. Pataki, 969 F. Supp. 160, 164-67 (S.D.N.Y. 1997).

"[C]ourts addressing the effect of a company's Internet presence on personal jurisdiction are in agreement that 'the likelihood that personal jurisdiction can be constitutionally exercised is directly proportional to the nature and quality of commercial activity that an entity conducts over the Internet.'"

Atlantech Distrib., Inc. v. Credit Gen. Ins. Co., 30 F. Supp. 2d 534, 536-37 (D. Md. 1998).

"It is unreasonable that by utilizing a New Jersey server, defendants should have foreseen being haled into a New Jersey federal court."

Amberson Holdings LLC v. Westside Story Newspaper, 110 F. Supp. 2d 332, 337 (D.N.J. 2000).

Related issues. "We are mindful that the Internet is a communication medium that lacks historical parallel in the potential extent of its reach and that regulation across jurisdictions may implicate fundamental first amendment concerns. It will undoubtedly take some time to determine the precise balance between the rights of those who use the Internet to disseminate information and the powers of the jurisdictions in which receiving computers are located to regulate for the general welfare."

State v. Granite Gate Resorts, Inc., 568 N.W.2d 715, 718 (Minn. App. 1997), *aff'd per curiam,* 576 N.W.2d 747 (Minn. 1998).

"[V]irtually all Internet speech is . . . available everywhere."
  Cyberspace, Comm., Inc. v. Engler, 55 F. Supp. 2d 737, 740-44 (E.D. Mich. 1999).

See **burden; general jurisdiction; personal jurisdiction; reasonableness; relatedness; specific jurisdiction; subject matter.**

justify *(technology)*

To control the position of the characters on a given page so that the text is aligned at both the left and right margins.

K *(technology)*

From the Greek word *kilo,* which means thousand. Represents a unit of memory measurement generally used when referring to storage capacity. One K capacity can store 1,024 characters (letters, numbers, and/or symbols).

". . . represents the potential amount of memory stored in the DRAM. Each kilobyte, or K, constitutes 1,024 units of memory."

Texas Instruments, Inc. v. International Trade Comm'n, 871 F.2d 1054, 1058 (Fed. Cir. 1989). *See also Universal City Studios, Inc. v. Reimerdes,* 111 F. Supp. 2d 294, 306 (S.D.N.Y. 2000) (footnote omitted).

See also **kilobyte.**

KBPS *(technology)*

Acronym for "Kilobytes Per Second." Also "Kbps." A measure of transmission speed of digital information.

kernel *(software)*

The "heart" of the operating system. The kernel controls task synchronization, scheduling, communication, and memory allocation activities.

key *(technology)*

"[A] unique sequence of letters, numbers, or combination of both that is used to encrypt and decrypt messages."

U.S. General Accounting Office, *Information Superhighway: An Overview of Technology Changes* 21 n.11 (Jan. 1995).

See also **decryption; encryption.**

key bit length *(technology)*

See **key length.**

key escrow *(encryption; software)*

A system for safeguarding keys or other information required to decrypt ciphertext.

key frames *(entertainment)*
In computer-based animation systems, the critical images that the animator creates. The computer then creates the images that come between key frames, giving a full-rendered animation.

key length *(technology)*
The number of bits contained in an encryption key; it determines the strength of the encryption algorithm.

key management *(technology)*
Procedures established to maintain the confidentiality of the private encryption keys used in an encryption product.

key padding *(encryption; software)*
The practice of allowing only 40 bits to be used in the generation of keys in an algorithm which is longer than 40 bits in order to gain export approval of an encryption product.

key pair *(electronic commerce; technology)*
"[A] private key and its corresponding public key in an asymmetric cryptosystem. The keys have the property that the public key can verify a digital signature that the private key creates."
Cal. Code of Regs., tit. 2, div. 7, ch. 10, § 22003(a)(1)(F).

"[A] private key and its corresponding public key in an asymmetric cryptosystem, keys which have the property that the public key can verify a digital signature that the private key creates."
Wash. Rev. Code § 19.34.020(17).

key recovery *(encryption; software)*
Also called data recovery.

Product features or system attributes which allow a user to gain access to keys or other information required to decrypt ciphertext after satisfaction of certain pre-established criteria.

key recovery agent *(encryption; software)*
Abbreviated as "KRA."

An organization which meets specified criteria of suitability and trustworthiness and implements security policies to assure the confidentiality of all keys and data escrowed.

Annotation. Under the U.S. Export Administration Regulations (15 C.F.R. § 742), the use of a key recovery agent (KRA) is required in order to qualify for a KMI license exception, which allows export of 56-bit or greater recoverable encryption products. A KRA is obligated to respond promptly to government agencies, acting under appropriate legal authority, with requests for keys and/or other information required to decrypt ciphertext and keep accurate and confidential records of all such activity.

keyboard(s) *(hardware)*

"[T]hese are the portion of the computer video terminal and other computer hardware which the operator uses to enter data and control computer functions. These are similar in appearance to a typewriter keyboard."

IRS Letter Ruling 8721016, Feb. 17, 1987.

keypunching *(technology)*

"[Translating] customers' data into codes which a computer can read, by punching holes in a particular order on keypunch cards or by inserting magnetic bits in a particular arrangement on magnetic tapes."

Janesville Data Center, Inc. v. Wisconsin Dept. of Revenue, 84 Wis. 2d 341, 342, 267 N.W.2d 656 (1978).

keystroke *(technology)*

A single depression of a key on the keyboard.

keyword(s) *(Internet)*

Annotation. "When a keyword is entered, the search engine processes it through a self-created index of web sites to generate a (sometimes long) list relating to the entered keyword. Each search engine uses its own algorithm to arrange indexed materials in sequence, so the list of web sites that any particular set of keywords will bring up may differ depending on the search engine used. . . . Search engines look for keywords in places such as domain names, actual text on the web page, and metatags."

Brookfield Comm., Inc. v. West Coast Entertainment Corp., 174 F.3d 1036, 1045 (9th Cir. 1999) (citations omitted).

See **search term(s).**

keyword advertising *(Internet)*

An advertisement on a web site that is keyed to the words typed in by a user. *See also* **search term(s).**

keyword metatag(s) *(Internet)*
". . . at least in theory, contain keywords relating to the contents of the web site."

> *Brookfield Comm., Inc. v. West Coast Entertainment Corp.,* 174 F.3d 1036, 1045 (9th Cir. 1999) (citation omitted).

See also **metatag(s).**

kill *(software)*
The term used to instruct the computer to stop a process.

kill file *(technology)*
Also called a "bozo filter." A file that can be set up to screen certain messages automatically (by name, keyword, subject, etc.) and reject them.

killer app *(software)*
A software application that establishes and dominates, at least in the early days of its distribution, a new market category.

kilo *(technology)*
A prefix meaning 1,024.

kilobyte *(technology)*
"1024 bytes."

> *Lotus Dev. Corp. v. Paperback Software Int'l,* 740 F. Supp. 37, 43 (D. Mass. 1990). *See also* Universal City Studios, Inc. v. Reimerdes, 111 F. Supp. 2d 294, 306 (S.D.N.Y. 2000) (footnote omitted).

See also **K.**

knowbot *(technology)*
Abbreviation for "**know**ledge ro**bot**." A computer program that performs functions automatically for a user, such as searching a network for specific types of information.

know-how *(trade secret)*
"[F]actual knowledge not capable of precise, separate description, but which, when used in an accumulated form, after being acquired as a result of trial and error, gives to the one acquiring it an ability to produce something that he otherwise would not have known how to produce with the same accuracy or precision found necessary for commercial success."

> *Mycalex Corp. of America v. Pemco Corp.,* 64 F. Supp. 420, 425 (D. Md. 1946).

[CANADA] "Practical knowledge of how to do something."
> *Beecham Group Ltd. v. Bristol Labs. Int'l S.A.*, [1978] R.P.C. 521 (H.L.).

See also **trade secret.**

knowledge (contract)

"A person 'knows' or has 'knowledge' of a fact when he has actual knowledge of it. 'Discover' or 'learn' or a word or phrase of similar import refers to knowledge rather than to reason to know. The time and circumstances under which a notice or notification may cease to be effective are not determined by this Act."
> U.C.C. § 1-201(25).

"[W]ith respect to a fact, means actual knowledge of the fact."
> UCITA § 102(a)(40).

(trademark)

"NSI's limited rule as a registrar of domain names coupled with the inherent uncertainty in defining the scope of intellectual property rights in a trademark militates against finding that NSI knew or had reason to know of potentially infringing uses of others."
> *Lockheed Martin Corp. v. Network Solutions, Inc.,* 985 F. Supp. 949, 951 (C.D. Cal. 1997).

knowledge management *(business)*

The process of creating, sharing and leveraging knowledge within an organization to achieve increased efficiency and/or profitability.

label *(Internet)*

"[A] string of characters, such as '-L18' (for 'not less than 18 years')—[embedded] into the address or name of a particular site so as to clearly identify the site as unsuitable for minors."

Shea v. Reno, 930 F. Supp. 916, 932-33 (S.D.N.Y. 1996).

See also **tagging.**

LAN *(hardware)*

Acronym for "Local Area Network." *See* **local area network;** *see also* **computer network; network.**

language(s) *(software)*

"In the computer field, the term generally means programming language used by a programmer for writing a computer program. This program usually must be translated or changed (assembled, compiled, interpreted) into object code before the computer can execute the program."

U.S. Copyright Office, *Compendium of Copyright Office Practices* II, § 326 (1984).

"There are three levels of computer language in which computer programs may be written. High level language, such as the commonly used BASIC or FORTRAN, uses English words and symbols, and is relatively easy to learn and understand (e.g., 'GO TO 40' tells the computer to skip intervening steps and go to the step at line 40). A somewhat lower level language is assembly language, which consists of alphanumeric labels (e.g., 'ADC' means 'add with carry'). Statements in high level language, and apparently also statements in assembly language, are referred to as written in 'source code.' The third, or lowest level computer language, is machine language, a binary language using two symbols, 0 and 1, to indicate an open or closed switch (e.g., '01101001' means, to the Apple, add two numbers and save the result). Statements in machine language are referred to as written in 'object code.'"

Apple Computer, Inc. v. Franklin Computer Corp., 714 F.2d 1240, 1243 (3d Cir. 1983), *cert. dism.* 464 U.S. 1033 (1984).

"Thus, the word 'languages,' as used in this operation is a collection of programs that individually allow a user to develop programs of his own in a language something like English, but which is susceptible to translation into such computer language as NEWBASIC, XTRAN, and QED."

> *Com-Share, Inc. v. Computer Complex, Inc.,* 338 F. Supp. 1229, 1230 (E.D. Mich. 1971), *aff'd,* 458 F.2d 1341 (6th Cir. 1972).

Lanham Act *(trademark)*

"[A] comprehensive trademark protection statute enacted in 1946."

> *America Online, Inc. v. AT&T Corp.,* 64 F. Supp. 2d 549, 559 (E.D. Va. 1999).

"Any person who, in connection with any goods or services . . . uses in commerce any word, term, name, symbol, or device, or any combination thereof, or any false designation of origin, false or misleading description of fact, or false or misleading representation of fact, which—

(A) is likely to cause confusion, or to cause mistake, or to deceive as to the affiliation, connection, or association of such person with another person, or as to the origin, sponsorship, or approval of his or her goods, services, or commercial activities by another person . . . shall be liable in a civil action by any person who believes that he or she is or is likely to be damaged by such act."

> 15 U.S.C. § 1125(a)(1).

Annotation. "The Lanham Act is designed to make actionable the misleading use of marks in interstate commerce and to protect those engaged in interstate commerce from unfair competition."

> *America Online, Inc. v. IMS,* 24 F. Supp. 2d 548, 551 (E.D. Va. 1998).

"A violation of the Lanham Act is tortious in nature."

> *Maritz, Inc. v. Cybergold, Inc.,* 947 F. Supp. 1328, 1331 (E.D. Mo. 1996).

"The purpose of the Lanham Act is to allow those who place their goods and services into the marketplace to distinguish such goods and services from those of their competitors."

> *America Online, Inc. v. AT&T Corp.,* 64 F. Supp. 2d 549, 559 (E.D. Va. 1999).

See also **false designation of origin.**

laptop computer *(technology)*

"[A] 'portable' computer with a built-in video display."

> *Princeton Graphics Operating L.P. v. NEC Home Elecs. (U.S.A.), Inc.,* 732 F. Supp. 1258, 1262 n.9 (S.D.N.Y. 1990).

laser disc *(hardware)*

[AUSTRALIA] ". . . is used in the electronics field to describe both video and audio discs, where both the recording and the reading process is performed by lasers. The words 'laser discs' are used in the trade as a generic term for video or compact or digital discs, the latter descriptions indicating the more specific functions of a laser-recorded and read disk.

In re Application by Pioneer Kabushiki Kaisha (1985), 5 I.P.R. 285 (Austrl. Pat. Off.).

laser printer *(hardware)*

Computer printer that prints one page at a time. The printed output is of high letter quality, but more expensive to produce than a dot matrix printout.

Lasercomb *(copyright)*

Citation: *Lasercomb America, Inc. v. Reynolds,* 911 F.2d 970, 976 (4th Cir. 1990).

Annotation. "In *Lasercomb America, Inc. v. Reynolds,* the Fourth Circuit explained that, whereas 'copyright law [seeks] to increase the store of human knowledge and arts by rewarding . . . authors with the exclusive rights to their works for a limited time . . . , the granted monopoly power does not extend to property not covered by the . . . copyright.' "

Alcatel USA, Inc. v. DGI Technologies, Inc., 166 F.3d 772, 793 (5th Cir. 1999) (citations omitted).

See also **copyright misuse doctrine.**

LATA *(telecommunications)*

Acronym for "Local Access and Transport Area." Geographic service areas defined in the AT&T Modified Final Judgment. Generally the BOCs and GTE are limited to providing local service within a given LATA. BOCs are generally not permitted to provide long-distance services between LATAs. There are approximately 200 LATAs in the United States.

late payment *(contract)*

A contractually required payment that is not made on or before the time stipulated in the agreement.

Sample clause. "If Licensee fails to pay any fees or royalties when due and payable, Licensee agrees that Licensor will have the right to invoice and Licensee will pay a late payment charge of 1-1/2 percent per month, but not in excess of the lawful maximum, on any past due balance."

latency *(hardware)*
The time period from when a user requests information stored on a rotating storage medium, such as a hard disk, until the rotating storage medium moves into position so the requested information can begin to be read.

launch *(business)*
The release of an interactive product in the retail channel.

(software)
The loading and execution of a computer program in a computer.

layout design *(hardware)*
[INTERNATIONAL] "[T]he three-dimensional disposition, however expressed, of the elements, at least one of which is an active element, and of some or all of the interconnections of an integrated circuit, or such a three-dimensional disposition prepared for an integrated circuit intended for manufacture."
    WIPO, *Treaty on Intellectual Property in Respect of Integrated Circuits.*
See also **mask works; topography.**

LCD *(hardware)*
Acronym for "Liquid Crystal Display." A type of display technology using polarizing filters and liquid-crystal cells to produce the image rather than phosphors illuminated by electron beams. This type of display is used for watches, clocks, laptop computers, and other consumer electronic devices that require low power consumption displays.

LCS *(technology)*
Acronym for "Large Core Storage."
    Telex Corp. v. IBM Corp., 367 F. Supp. 258, 274 (N.D. Okla. 1973), *aff'd in part, rev'd in part,* 510 F.2d 894 (10th Cir.), *cert. dism.,* 423 U.S. 802 (1975).
See also **core; computer memory; magnetic memory core; main memory; memory; memory plane.**

leading zero *(technology)*
A zero used as a fill character. It is entered to the left of the first digit of a numeric value. *See also* **zero fill.**

leap year *(general; Year 2000)*
Any year divisible by four is a leap year, unless it is divisible by 100, but not 400.

leased line *(telecommunications)*

A dedicated telephone line between two computers, or between a computer and a network or Internet service provider.

left justify *(technology)*

To control the position of characters on a page so that the left margin is regular.

legacy systems *(Year 2000)*

Application systems typically developed 10 to 35 years ago for mainframes and/or mini-computers. These systems were designed and developed (1) when memory and disk space were available in limited quantities for each system/application, (2) when memory and disk space were prohibitively expensive, and (3) before the creation and industry acceptance of key software engineering tools and techniques that make software more maintainable and less error prone.

letter of intent *(contract)*

See deal memo.

libel *(tort)*

A false and malicious written statement that defames an individual.

Related issues. "Web-sites are modern analogs of national publications; potentially innumerable 'copies' can be (and are) regularly 'distributed' wherever there is access to the World-Wide Web."

Digital Equipment Corp. v. Altavista Technology, Inc., 960 F. Supp. 456, 470 (D. Mass. 1997).

license *(contract)*

An agreement by the owner of property that permits a person or legal entity to exploit that property in a manner that it could otherwise not legally do.

"[A] contract that authorizes access to, or use, distribution, performance, modification, or reproduction of, information or informational rights, but expressly limits the access or uses authorized or expressly grants fewer than all rights in the information, whether or not the transferee has title to a licensed copy. The term includes an access contract, a lease of a computer program, and a consignment of a copy. The term does not include a reservation or creation of a security interest to the extent the interest is governed by [Article 9 of the Uniform Commercial Code]."

UCITA § 102(a)(41).

Annotation. (contract; copyright)

"The enforcement of a copyright license raises issues that lie at the intersection of copyright and contract law, an area of law that is not yet well developed."

    Sun Microsys., Inc. v. Microsoft Corp., 188 F.3d 1115, 1112 (9th Cir. 1999).

(copyright)
"Plainly, a party who purchases copies of software from the copyright owner can hold a license under a copyright while still being an 'owner' of a copy of the copyrighted software for purposes of section 117."

    DSC Comm. Corp. v. Pulse Comm., Inc., 170 F.3d 1354, 1360 (Fed. Cir. 1999).

"The fundamental purpose of this or any license agreement is to prevent the unauthorized exploitation of the product involved."

    S&H Computer Sys., Inc. v. SAS Inst., Inc., 568 F. Supp. 416, 421 (M.D. Tenn. 1983).

Related issues. "Licensing software instead of transferring ownership is common throughout the telecommunications and the software industry for the specific purpose . . . of protecting one's investment in research and development from piracy. A prohibition against copying or allowing a third party to copy licensed software is common [in] the software industry, for the same reasons."

    DSC Comm. Corp. v. DGT Telecommunications, Inc., 898 F. Supp. 1193, 1192 (N.D. Tex. 1995), *aff'd*, 81 F.3d 597 (5th Cir. 1996).

"If an analogy is to be made, licensing agreements are more similar to leases than to sales of property because of the limited nature of the interest conveyed."

    Lubrizol Enters., Inc. v. Richmond Metal Finishers, Inc., 756 F.2d 1043, 1046 n.[*] (4th Cir. 1985).

"A license is a lease for the use of . . . goods despite the terms expressed therein of a 'license to use' . . . 'proprietary' software for the payment of a one-time perpetual license fee. . . ."

    Communications Groups, Inc. v. Warner Comm., Inc., 138 Misc. 2d 80, 527 N.Y.S.2d 341, 344 (N.Y.C. Civ. Ct. 1988).

"'[C]opyright owner who grants a nonexclusive license to use his copyrighted material waives his right to sue the licensee for copyright infringement' and can sue only for breach of contract."

    Graham v. James, 144 F.3d 229, 236 (2d Cir. 1998).

"It is an affirmative defense to copyright infringement that the alleged infringer has received a license from the owner."

    Michaels v. Internet Entertainment Group, Inc., 5 F. Supp. 2d 823, 831 (C.D. Cal. 1998).

"A pure license agreement . . . does not involve transfer of title, and so is not a sale for Article 2 purposes."

> *Berthold Types Ltd. v. Abode Sys., Inc.*, 101 F. Supp. 2d 697, 698 (E.D. Ill. 2000).

"Because the predominant feature of the [license agreement] was a transfer of intellectual property rights, the agreement is not subject to Article 2 of the U.C.C."

> *Architectronics, Inc. v. Control Sys., Inc.*, 935 F. Supp. 425, 432 (S.D.N.Y. 1996).

"The[] numerous restrictions imposed by Adobe indicate a license rather than a sale because they undeniably interfere with the reseller's ability to further distribute the software."

> *Adobe Sys., Inc. v. One Stop Micro*, 84 F. Supp. 2d 1086, 1091 (N.D. Cal. 2000).

"The industry uses terms such as 'purchase,' 'sell,' buy,' . . . because they are convenient and familiar, but the industry is aware that all software . . . is distributed under license."

> *Adobe Sys., Inc. v. One Stop Micro*, 84 F. Supp. 2d 1086, 1091 (N.D. Cal. 2000).

licensed certification authority *(electronic commerce)*

"[A] certification authority to whom a license has been issued by the secretary and whose license is in effect."

> Wash. Rev. Code § 19.34.020(18).

licensee *(contract)*

One who receives a license.

"[A] person entitled by agreement to acquire or exercise rights in, or to have access to or use of, computer information under an agreement to which this [Act] applies. A licensor is not a licensee with respect to rights reserved to it under the agreement."

> UCITA § 102(a)(42).

licensor *(contract)*

One who grants a license.

"[A] person obligated by agreement to transfer or create rights in, or to give access to or use of, computer information or informational rights in it under an agreement to which this [Act] applies. Between the provider of access and a provider of the informational content to be accessed, the provider of content is the licensor. In an exchange of information or informational rights, each party is a licensor with respect to the information, informational rights, or access it gives."

> UCITA § 102(a)(43).

likelihood of confusion *(trademark)*
"Although the Ninth Circuit has yet to apply the likelihood of confusion analysis in the Internet context, a district court applying Ninth Circuit law based its finding of likelihood of confusion on (1) the virtual identity of marks, (2) the relatedness of plaintiff's and defendant's goods, and (3) the simultaneous use of the Web as a marketing channel."
> *Brookfield Comm., Inc. v. West Coast Entertainment Corp.*, 174 F.3d 1036, 1054 n.16 (9th Cir. 1999), *citing Comp Examiner Agency, Inc. v. Juris, Inc.*, No. 96-0213, 1996 WL 376600, at *1 (C.D. Cal. Apr. 26, 1996).

"This court has enumerated eight factors that are to be considered to determine whether a likelihood of confusion exists. The eight factors are: (1) the strength of the plaintiff's mark; (2) the relatedness of the goods or services; (3) the similarity of the marks; (4) evidence of actual confusion; (5) the marketing channels used; (6) the likely degree of purchaser care; (7) the defendant's intent in selecting the mark; and (8) the likelihood of the expansion of the product lines."
> *Data Concepts, Inc. v. Digital Consulting, Inc.*, 150 F.3d. 620, 624 (6th Cir. 1998).

"The core element of trademark infringement is the likelihood of confusion, i.e., whether the similarity of the mark is likely to confuse customers about the source of the product."
> *Brookfield Comm., Inc. v. West Coast Entertainment Corp.*, 174 F.3d 1036, 1053 (9th Cir. 1999) (citations omitted).

Annotation. "[A]bsolute identity is not necessary for infringement; all that is necessary is enough similarity between the marks to confuse consumers. In determining whether there is a likelihood of confusion between two marks, courts consider a number of factors, including '(a) the strength or distinctiveness of the mark; (b) the similarity of the two marks; (c) the similarity of the goods/services the marks identify; (d) the similarity of the facilities the two parties use in their businesses; (e) the similarity of the advertising used by the two parties; (f) the defendant's intent; (g) [evidence of] actual confusion.' Certain factors may not be relevant in some cases, and the factors may not deserve equal emphasis in each case."
> *Washington Speakers Bureau, Inc. v. Leading Authorities, Inc.*, 33 F. Supp. 2d 488, 497 (E.D. Va. 1999).

"The likelihood of confusion is a factual issue that turns on the particular circumstances of each case."
> *Washington Speakers Bureau, Inc. v. Leading Authorities, Inc.*, 33 F. Supp. 2d 488, 497 (E.D. Va. 1999) (citations omitted).

"We cannot think of more persuasive evidence that there is no *likelihood* of confusion between these two marks than the fact that they have been simultaneously used for five years without causing any consumers to be confused as to who makes what."

> *Brookfield Comm., Inc. v. West Coast Entertainment Corp.,* 174 F.3d 1036, 1050 (9th Cir. 1999) (emphasis in original).

Related issues. "[A] mixed question of law and fact."

> *Data Concepts, Inc. v. Digital Consulting, Inc.,* 150 F.3d. 620, 624 (6th Cir. 1998).

See also **trademark infringement.**

likelihood of success *(copyright)*

"A showing of a reasonable likelihood of success on the merits raises a presumption of irreparable harm."

> *Triad Sys. Corp. v. Southeastern Express Co.,* 64 F.3d 1330, 1335 (9th Cir. 1995).

(trademark)

"[C]onfusion, if not on the part of bulletin board users, is inevitable on the part of third parties who may see the copied games after they enter the stream of commerce."

> *Sega Enters. Ltd. v. MAPHIA,* 857 F. Supp. 679, 688 (N.D. Cal. 1994).

limitation of liability *(contract)*

A contractual provision that limits the potential liability of a party, or for particular types of claims, or the amount for which a party will be responsible.

Related issues. "The language of this section is clear and unambiguous, with the effect of limiting Sperry's liability for incidental and consequential damages arising out of the failure of the Univac System 80. However, for two reasons, the provisions are not a basis for summary judgment. . . .

"Primarily . . . Sperry cannot shield itself with the language of a contract when [the plaintiff's] allegations are that the contract itself was induced through fraud. Furthermore, [plaintiff] alleges that the Univac System 80, even as augmented, entirely failed of its essential purpose. It is axiomatic therefore, that [plaintiff] alleges the contract failed of its essential purpose. Under certain circumstances, when a contract, including its damage limitation provision, entirely fails of its essential purpose and the product in question cannot be remedied through the means provided in the contract, the Court will disregard the contract, thereby allowing traditional damages."

> *Invacare Corp. v. Sperry Rand Corp.,* 612 F. Supp. 448, 454 (N.D. Ohio. 1984).

Sample clause. "EVEN IF BUYER'S EXCLUSIVE REMEDY FAILS OF ITS ESSENTIAL PURPOSE, LICENSOR'S ENTIRE LIABILITY SHALL IN NO EVENT EXCEED THE LICENSE FEE PAID FOR THIS LICENSE. UNDER NO CIRCUMSTANCES SHALL LICENSOR BE LIABLE FOR GENERAL, CONSEQUENTIAL, INCIDENTAL OR SPECIAL DAMAGES ARISING FROM THIS AGREEMENT OR ANY ACTS OR OMISSIONS OF LICENSOR."
See also Invacare Corp. v. Sperry Rand Corp., 612 F. Supp. 448, 454 (N.D. Ohio. 1984).

limitations, statute of *(contract)*

See statute of limitations.

line *(technology)*

A single printed horizontal series of text characters. This usually includes all of the characters entered between carriage returns.

line noise *(telecommunications)*

Electronic interference on telephone lines due to storms, long distances, heavy simultaneous use, poor equipment, etc. The terminal may receive extraneous signals that it interprets as actual commands. As a result, garbage appears on the computer screen. *See also* **garbage.**

line of code *(software; Year 2000)*

A single computer program command, declaration, or instruction. Program size is often measured in lines of code.

line printer *(hardware)*

A high-speed printer that prints an entire line at one time instead of one character at a time.

linear programming *(software)*

[UNITED KINGDOM] ". . . means the control of digital data-processing machines to find solutions of sets of simultaneous linear equations or inequalities, or mixtures of both."
In re Slee & Harris' Application, [1966] R.P.C. 194.

link(s) *(Internet)*

"[H]ighlighted text or images that, when selected by the user, permit him to view another, related Web document."
Shea v. Reno, 930 F. Supp. 916, 929 (S.D.N.Y. 1996).

"[S]hort sections of text or image which refer to another document. Typically the linked text is blue or underlined when displayed, and when selected by the user, the referenced document is automatically displayed, wherever in the world it actually is stored. Links for example are used to lead from overview documents to more detailed documents, from tables of contents to particular pages, but also as cross-references, footnotes, and new forms of information structure. . . . Links may also take the user from the original Web site to another Web site on another computer connected to the Internet. These links from one computer to another, from one document to another across the Internet, are what unify the Web into a single body of knowledge, and what makes the Web unique. The Web was designed with a maximum target time to follow a link of one tenth of a second."

> *American Civil Liberties Union v. Reno,* 929 F. Supp. 824, 836 (E.D. Pa. 1996), *aff'd, Reno v. American Civil Liberties Union,* 521 U.S. 844 (1997).

"[A]n image or short section of text referring to another document on the Web."

> *Lockheed Martin Corp. v. Network Solutions, Inc.,* 985 F. Supp. 949, 952 (C.D. Cal. 1997) (citation omitted).

Annotation. "A user interested in accessing the referenced document selects the link, causing the document to be displayed automatically, along with a new set of links that the user may follow.

"While the linked structure of the Web is well-suited to allow users to browse among many sites following whatever links happen to draw their interest, it is poorly suited for [sic] user—who wants to find a single Web site directly."

> *Lockheed Martin Corp. v. Network Solutions, Inc.,* 985 F. Supp. 949, 952 (C.D. Cal. 1997) (citation omitted).

"Links may also take the user from the original Web site to another Web site on another computer connected to the Internet. These links from one computer to another, from one document to another across the Internet, are what unify the Web into a single body of knowledge, and what makes the Web unique."

> *American Civil Liberties Union v. Reno,* 929 F. Supp. 824, 836-37 (E.D. Pa. 1996), *aff'd, Reno v. American Civil Liberties Union,* 521 U.S. 844 (1997).

"The ease of communication through the Internet is facilitated by the use of hypertext markup language (HTML) which allows for the creation of 'hyperlinks' or 'links.' HTML enables a user to jump from one source to another related source by clicking on the link. A link might take the user from Web site to Web site, or to other files within a particular Web site."

> *American Civil Liberties Union v. Reno,* 929 F. Supp. 824, 843 (E.D. Pa. 1996), *aff'd, Reno v. American Civil Liberties Union,* 521 U.S. 844 (1997).

Related issues. "In addition to allowing access to the extensive content available *within* each online service, the [commercial online] services also allow subscribers to link to the much larger resources of the Internet. Full access to the online service (including access to the Internet) can be obtained for modest monthly or hourly fees."

> *American Civil Liberties Union v. Reno,* 929 F. Supp. 824, 833 (E.D. Pa. 1996), *aff'd, Reno v. American Civil Liberties Union,* 521 U.S. 844 (1997).

See also **hyperlink.**

Linux *(software)*

"[A]n 'open source' operating system that was created, and is continuously updated, by a global network of software developers who contribute their labor for free."

> *United States v. Microsoft Corp.,* 65 F. Supp. 2d 1, 14 (D.D.C. 1999) (Finding of Fact 50).

Annotation. "Although Linux has between ten and fifteen million users, the majority of them use the operating system to run servers, not PCs. Several ISVs have announced their development of (or plans to develop) Linux versions of their applications. To date, though, legions of ISVs have not followed the lead of these first movers. Similarly, consumers have by and large shown little inclination to abandon Windows, with its reliable developer support, in favor of an operating system whose future in the PC realm is unclear."

> *United States v. Microsoft Corp.,* 65 F. Supp. 2d 1, 14 (D.D.C. 1999) (Finding of Fact 50).

"Linux, which was and continues to be developed through the open source model of software development, also is an operating system. It can be run on a PC as an alternative to Windows, although the extent to which it is so used is limited. Linux is more widely used on servers."

> *Universal City Studios, Inc. v. Reimerdes,* 111 F. Supp. 2d 294, 305 (S.D.N.Y. 2000) (footnotes omitted).

See also **operating system.**

liquid crystal display *(hardware)*

See **LCD.**

liquidated damages *(contract)*

A contractual provision under which the parties agree to a stipulated amount of damages to be paid by a party for a breach of that agreement.

Sample clause. "If [Party #1] breaches the foregoing obligation [describe obligation], [Party #1] shall pay to [Party #2] as liquidated damages the sum of [amount]. The parties agree that the amount stated as liquidated damages is reasonable under the circumstances existing at the time that this agreement was executed."

list server *(Internet)*

A computer program that distributes e-mail, processes subscription requests, archives old messages, and creates digests for a specific mail list. Two common list servers are LISTSERV and Majordomo. *See also* **listserv.**

listing fee *(business)*

The amount a mail order catalog charges to have a title included in the catalog.

listserv *(Internet)*

"Once a mailing list is established, it is typically maintained using a 'mail exploder'—a program such as 'listserv' running on the server on which the list resides—that automatically (i.e., without human intervention) responds to a user's request to be added to or removed from the list of subscribers and retransmits messages posted by a subscriber to others on the mailing list."
    Shea v. Reno, 930 F. Supp. 916, 927 (S.D.N.Y. 1996).

"[A]utomatic mailing list services . . . that allow communications about particular subjects of interest to a group of people."
    American Civil Liberties Union v. Reno, 929 F. Supp. 824, 834 (E.D. Pa. 1996), *aff'd, Reno v. American Civil Liberties Union,* 521 U.S. 844 (1997).

Annotation. "The Internet also contains automatic mailing list services (such as 'listservs'), [also referred to by witnesses as 'mail exploders'] that allow communications about particular subjects of interest to a group of people. For example, people can subscribe to a 'listserv' mailing list on a particular topic of interest to them. The subscriber can submit messages on the topic to the listserv that are forwarded (via e-mail), either automatically or through a human moderator overseeing the listserv, to anyone who has subscribed to the mailing list. A recipient of such a message can reply to the message and have the reply also distributed to everyone on the mailing list. This service provides the capability to keep abreast of developments or events in a particular subject area. Most listserv-type mailing lists automatically forward all incoming messages to all mailing list subscribers.

There are thousands of such mailing list services on the Internet, collectively with hundreds of thousands of subscribers. Users of 'open' listservs typically can add or remove their names from the mailing list automatically, with no direct human involvement. Listservs may also be 'closed,' i.e., only allowing for one's acceptance into the listserv by a human moderator."

> *American Civil Liberties Union v. Reno,* 929 F. Supp. 824, 834 (E.D. Pa. 1996), *aff'd, Reno v. American Civil Liberties Union,* 521 U.S. 844 (1997).

literal element *(copyright)*
"It is now well settled that the literal elements of computer programs, i.e., their source and object codes, are the subject of copyright protection."

> *Computer Assocs. Int'l, Inc. v. Altai, Inc.,* 982 F.2d 693, 702 (2d Cir. 1992).

literal infringement *(patent)*
". . . requires that the accused device embody every element of the claim as properly interpreted. If the claim describes a combination of functions, and each function is performed by a means described in the specification or an equivalent of such means, then literal infringement holds."

> *Texas Instruments, Inc. v. United States Int'l Trade Comm'n,* 805 F.2d 1558, 1562 (Fed. Cir. 1986).

literary works *(copyright)*
"[W]orks, other than audiovisual works, expressed in words, numbers, or other verbal or numerical symbols or indicia, regardless of the nature of the material objects, such as books, periodicals, manuscripts, phonorecords, film, tapes, disks, or cards, in which they are embodied."

> U.S. Copyright Act, 17 U.S.C. § 101.

"The term . . . does not connote any criterion of literary merit or qualitative value: it includes catalogs, directories, and similar factual, reference, or instructional works and compilations of data. It also includes computer data bases and computer programs to the extent that they incorporate authorship in the programmer's expression of ideas, as distinguished from the ideas themselves."

> H.R. Rep. No. 94-1476, 94th Cong., 2d Sess. 54 (1976). *See also* S. Rep. No. 94-473, 94th Cong., 1st Sess. 50-51 (1975).

Related issues. "While computer programs are not specifically listed as part of the above statutory definition, the legislative history leaves no doubt that Congress intended them to be considered literary works."

> *Computer Assocs. Int'l, Inc. v. Altai, Inc.,* 982 F.2d 693, 702 (2d Cir. 1992), *citing* H.R. Rep. No. 1476, 94th Cong., 2d Sess. 54.

lithography *(manufacturing)*

A semiconductor manufacturing process in which the desired circuit pattern is projected onto a resist coating that covers the silicon wafer. When the resist is developed, somewhat like an ordinary photograph, portions of the resist can be selectively removed by use of a solvent, thus exposing parts of the wafer for etching and diffusion.

load *(technology)*

To enter data into memory.

loading *(hardware)*

". . . entails a transfer of the software program from a storage device such as a hard disk or floppy disk into the random access memory ('RAM') of the computer."

> *Advanced Computer Serv. v. MAI Sys. Corp.,* 845 F. Supp. 356, 360 (E.D. Va. 1994).

Related issues (copyright). "The act of loading a program from a medium of storage into a computer's memory constitutes a copy of the program."

> *Vault Corp. v. Quaid Software, Ltd.,* 847 F.2d 255, 260 (5th Cir. 1988), *rev'g* 655 F. Supp. 750, 758 (E.D. La. 1987).

loan *(copyright)*

Allowing a party to borrow the property of another, generally for a stipulated period of time and for a stipulated amount of money.

Annotation. "Among the exclusive rights given to the owner of a copyrighted work is the right to distribute copies of the work by lending. . . . Therefore, [defendant's] loaning of [plaintiff's] software, if established, would constitute a violation of the Copyright Act."

> *MAI Sys. Corp. v. Peak Computer, Inc.,* 991 F.2d 511, 519 (9th Cir. 1993), *cert. dism.,* 510 U.S. 1033 (1994).

local area network *(technology)*

Abbreviated as "LAN." A computer network that connects computers within a relatively small geographic area. The most common forms of LANs are Ethernet and token ring.

localization *(business)*

The process of changing a product or service to meet the requirements of a particular market. Localization normally involves translation into the local language, but it also can involve changes to account for cultural differences, as well as porting to the most popular platform(s) in that market.

lockout *(multimedia)*
A place in a video game or other multimedia work where control of the game is taken away from the user.

log in *(technology)*
Also called "log on." The procedure by which a user begins a session at the terminal. The user identifies himself or herself to the computer system for authorized access to his or her specific information base and programs.

log off *(technology)*
To instruct the computer to terminate a session.

log on *(technology)*
See **log in.**

logic *(hardware)*
". . . performs the arithmetic and logical operations."
> *Computer Sys. of Am. v. Western Reserve Life Assur. Co.,* 19 Mass. App. 430, 431 n.2 (1985).

"[T]he name given to a particular type of board which enables the equipment to perform predetermined functions. Chips, boards, and logic are all installed inside other units (personal computers, terminals, or control units)."
> IRS Letter Ruling 8721016, Feb. 17, 1987.

logic bomb *(software)*
"[A] desirable program which performs some useful function such as logic, but which contains a parasite or viral infection within its logic which is undetectable upon casual review. . . . [M]ore properly called a 'time bomb' or 'logic bomb.'"
> *State v. Corcoran,* 5 Computer Cas (CCH) ¶ 47,108, at 66,617 n.1 (Wis. App. 1994).

"A program routine that destroys data; for example, it may reformat the hard disk or randomly insert garbage into data files."
> Office of the Comptroller of the Currency, Infrastructure Threats from Cyber-Terrorists 3 (Mar. 19, 1999).

Annotation. "A logic bomb may be brought into a personal computer by downloading a public-domain program that has been tampered with. Once executed, it does its damage right away, whereas a virus keeps on destroying."
Office of the Comptroller of the Currency, Infrastructure Threats from Cyber-Terrorists 3 (Mar. 19, 1999).
See also **time bomb; Trojan horse.**

logic circuit *(hardware)*
A type of integrated circuit that performs certain logical or mathematical functions and often provides connections between other major parts of electronic equipment.

logic trunked radio system *(technology)*
"[O]ne consisting of mobile radio units, typically installed in a motor vehicle such as taxis, police cars, delivery trucks, etc., and 'repeaters,' base stations which receive and transmit signals to and from the mobile radio units."
E.F. Johnson Co. v. Uniden Corp. of America, 623 F. Supp. 1485, 1487 (D. Minn. 1985).

LOI *(business)*
Acronym for "Letter Of Intent." *See* **deal memo.**

LOL *(Internet)*
Abbreviation in electronic messages for "Laughing Out Loud."

long-arm statute *(jurisdiction)*
A state statute that defines the circumstances under which a court within that state can exercise personal jurisdiction over nonresidents of that state.

"California's long-arm statute permits a court to exercise personal jurisdiction over a defendant to the extent permitted by the Due Process Clause of the Constitution."
Panavision Int'l, L.P. v. Toeppen, 141 F.3d 1316, 1320 (9th Cir. 1998).

lossless compression *(technology)*
Compression methodology that retains all of the visual precision of the original image. Compression ratios for lossless compression are significantly lower than for lossy compression, since large amounts of information must be retained.

lossy compression *(technology)*

Compression methodology that sacrifices visual precision of the image for storage efficiency (between 10:1 and 50:1 for still images, and 50:1 to 200:1 for video images).

lurk *(Internet)*

To read articles or messages in a newsgroup without posting any messages or replies.

machine code *(software)*
See binary code; machine language; object code.

machine language *(software)*
"[T] he 'lowest'-level computer programming language . . . which is a binary language written in 'bits' (*BI*nary digi*TS*)."
> *Lotus Dev. Corp. v. Paperback Software Int'l,* 740 F. Supp. 37, 43 (D. Mass. 1990).

"[T]he instructions the machine actually executes."
> U.S. Copyright Office, *Compendium of Copyright Office Practices* II, § 326 (1984).

"The third, or lowest level computer language, is machine language, a binary language using two symbols, 0 and 1, to indicate an open or closed switch (e.g., '01101001' means, to the Apple, add two numbers and save the result). Statements in machine language are referred to as written in 'object code.'"
> *Apple Computer, Inc. v. Franklin Computer Corp.,* 714 F.2d 1240, 1243 (3d Cir. 1983), *cert. dism.,* 464 U.S. 1033.

"[A] series of numbers, letters of the alphabet, or special characters that are used to represent bit [(binary digit)] patterns which can be recognized by the computer and cause specific operations to take place."
> *Comptroller of the Treasury v. Equitable Trust Co.,* 464 A.2d 248, 250 (Md. 1983).

See also binary code; object code.

macro(s) *(software)*
"[A] single instruction that initiates a sequence of operations or module interactions within the program."
> *Computer Assocs. Int'l, Inc. v. Altai, Inc.,* 982 F.2d 693, 698 (2d Cir. 1992).

magnetic memory core *(hardware)*
"These devices, which range in size from 18 to 80 mils (thousandths of an inch), are used in the manufacture of electronic computers. The magnetic

memory core is the device which essentially performs the function of storing information. This is accomplished by passing electrical signals or impulses through specific combinations of the wires upon which the cores have been connected. The electrical signal magnetizes the selected core."
Sperry Rand Corp. v. Pentronix, Inc., 311 F. Supp. 910, 911 (E.D. Pa. 1970).
See also core; computer memory; main memory; memory plane.

magnetic tape *(hardware)*

A large volume data storage medium for computers. While a disk rotates like a phonograph and allows the tone arm (head) to access any portion of the surface very quickly, the tape method is much slower (and less expensive). Tape is a sequential access process in that information is recorded in parallel tracks that run the entire length of the tape. It must be moved forward or backward across the head, which takes much longer. *See also* tape, magnetic.

Magnuson-Moss Warranty Act *(contract)*

Citation: 15 U.S.C. §§ 1-2312.

Annotation. This legislation is the major federal consumer protection law. The Act, which is primarily administered by the Federal Trade Commission (FTC), prescribes comprehensive federal standards for written warranties and service contracts on and in connection with consumer products manufactured on or after July 4, 1975.

The Act seeks to meet four basic goals: (1) to promote consumer understanding of warranties; (2) to protect consumers who buy consumer products that are covered by written warranties; (3) to provide viable warranty enforcement on behalf of consumers; and (4) to stimulate manufacturers to produce more reliable products. To do so, the Act establishes minimum standards for various types of written warranties and service contracts, requires that consumers be given detailed warranty information before and after purchasing consumer products, and provides judicial, administrative, and informal warranty enforcement mechanisms.

The Act, however, does not require a manufacturer or seller to issue a warranty. Moreover, the FTC is not authorized to prescribe warranty duration. Instead, the Act applies to written warranties and service contracts that have been voluntarily provided in connection with consumer products.

It covers any "tangible property which is distributed in commerce and which is normally used for personal, family or household purposes." 15 U.S.C. § 2301(1). The law focuses on disclosure requirements relating to written warranties.

MAI v. Peak *(copyright)*
Citation: *MAI Systems Corp. v. Peak Computer, Inc.*, 991 F.2d 511 (9th Cir. 1993), *cert. dism.*, 510 U.S. 1033 (1994).

Annotation. This was a claim of copyright infringement by MAI against Peak, a third-party maintenance organization that had been hired by several MAI customers to maintain their systems. In doing so, Peak loaded MAI's operating system software and diagnostics software into the customer's computer. MAI claimed that the software license agreement specifically limited the rights of the customer to allow only the customer, and not a third party, to load the licensed software into the computer. Peak claimed that merely loading the software into the computer was not a copyright infringement.

The court held that (i) copying occurs when a computer program is loaded into the random access memory (RAM) of a computer; and (ii) the third-party maintenance organization violated the plaintiff's copyright in its software by loading the software into RAM and using it as part of its software maintenance services.

The Digital Millennium Copyright Act of 1998 legislatively overruled this decision, permitting third-party maintenance organizations to load a customer's software into the computer for maintenance purposes. *See also* **DMCA.**

mail exploder *(Internet)*
"Once a mailing list is established, it is typically maintained using a 'mail exploder'—a program such as 'listserv' running on the server on which the list resides—that automatically (i.e., without human intervention) responds to a user's request to be added to or removed from the list of subscribers and retransmits messages posted by a subscriber to others on the mailing list.

* * *

"An individual sending a message that will be retransmitted by a mail exploder program has no way of knowing the e-mail addresses of other subscribers."
Shea v. Reno, 930 F. Supp. 916, 927 (S.D.N.Y. 1996) (citations omitted).

"[A]utomatic mailing list services . . . that allow communications about particular subjects of interest to a group of people."
American Civil Liberties Union v. Reno, 929 F. Supp. 824, 839 (E.D. Pa. 1996), *aff'd, Reno v. American Civil Liberties Union*, 521 U.S. 844 (1997).

"[A] sort of e-mail group. Subscribers can send messages to a common e-mail address, which then forwards the message to the group's other subscribers."
Reno v. American Civil Liberties Union, 521 U.S. 844, 851 (1997).

Related issues. "[A]n individual sending a message that will be retransmitted by a mail exploder program has no way of knowing the identity of other subscribers (even if he knows the e-mail address of each subscriber)."

Shea v. Reno, 930 F. Supp. 916, 927 (S.D.N.Y. 1996).

See also **listserv.**

mail fraud *(criminal)*

A criminal act that involves the use of the U.S. mails to commit fraud.

Annotation. "A scheme to defraud is the defining concept of the mail and wire fraud statutes. Because of the conjunctive use of the word 'or' in the statutory phrase 'any scheme or artifice to defraud, or for obtaining money or property by false or fraudulent pretenses, representations, or promises,' the federal courts (encouraged by prosecutors) have essentially bifurcated mail and wire fraud into two separate offenses; the first, the devising of a scheme to defraud, the second, the devising of a scheme to obtain money or property by false pretenses. While the latter crime comports with common law notions of fraud, '[t]he phrase, "a scheme to defraud"' came to prohibit a plan, that is, to forbid a state of mind, rather than physical conduct."

United States v. LaMacchia, 871 F. Supp. 535, 541 (D. Mass. 1994) (citations omitted).

" 'Mail fraud . . . has been expanded to the point that a fiduciary, agent, or employee commits an offense when, through a material deception or a failure to disclose, a beneficiary, principal or employer suffers even an intangible, constructed detriment.'

* * *

"[M]ail and wire fraud statutes do not require that a defendant be shown to have sought to personally profit from the scheme to defraud."

United States v. LaMacchia, 871 F. Supp. 535, 541 (D. Mass. 1994) (citations omitted).

mail list *(Internet)*

See **mailing list.**

mailer *(Internet; software)*

"Using any one of dozens of available 'mailers'—client software capable of reading and writing e-mail—a user is able to address and transmit a message to one or more specific individuals."

Shea v. Reno, 930 F. Supp. 916, 927 (S.D.N.Y. 1996).

mailbox *(Internet)*

A location in a computer system in which electronic mail (e-mail) for a particular recipient is stored.

mailing list *(Internet)*

A list of recipient's e-mail addresses to which a user can automatically send mail. *See also* **closed mailing list; moderated mailing list.**

maillist *(Internet)*

See **mailing list.**

main memory *(hardware)*

"[T]he storage from which data are transferred to the processor and to which data are returned in their processed form."

Telex Corp. v. IBM Corp., 367 F. Supp. 258, 274 (N.D. Okla. 1973), *aff'd in part, rev'd in part,* 510 F.2d 894 (10th Cir.), *cert. dism.,* 423 U.S. 802 (1975).

See also **core; computer memory; magnetic memory core; memory; memory plane.**

mainframe *(hardware; software)*

A multiuser computer system characterized by large storage capacity and much peripheral support.

maintaining *(software)*

". . . is defined as the engaging in any act, including, without limitation, service, repair, or upkeep in any manner whatsoever, that involves as part of such act, or as a preliminary or subsequent step to such act, the use, directly or indirectly, of [t]he [s]oftware, including, without limitation, MAI's operating system, diagnostic, utility, and other software; . . ."

MAI Sys. Corp. v. Peak Computer, Inc., 991 F.2d 511, 515 (9th Cir. 1993) (quoting the district court's injunction).

maintenance *(software)*

"[F]ix latent bugs, adapt the program, or incur other so-called 'life cycle' costs. . . ."

Whelan Assocs., Inc. v. Jaslow Dental Lab., Inc., 797 F.2d 1222, 1231 n.21 (3d Cir. 1986).

majors *(business)*

The largest and most powerful entities in a particular industry.

make-good *(advertising)*
Impressions provided by a web site owner to make up for the failure to provide a specified number of impressions during a specific time period.

manual *(general)*
Generally, a written document containing information on the design, implementation and/or proper usage of computer hardware or software.

Related issues (copyright). "Verbatim copying of a computer manual is inferential evidence of pirating of the underlying software."
E.F. Johnson Co. v. Uniden Corp. of America, 623 F. Supp. 1485, 1497 (D. Minn. 1985).

manual trace *(telecommunications)*
"[A] physical tracing of the telephone circuitry backward through the various switching points from the equipment which receives the call."
United States v. Seidlitz, 589 F.2d 152, 154 n.7 (4th Cir. 1978).

manufacture *(copyright)*
"[T]o produce or assemble a product in the United States."
17 U.S.C. § 1001(8).

manufacturer *(copyright)*
"[A] person who manufactures."
17 U.S.C. § 1001(8).

MAP file(s) *(video game)*
"So-called because the files all end with the extension '.MAP'. Also, no doubt, because they contain the layout for the various levels."
Micro Star v. FormGen, Inc., 154 F.3d 1107, 1110 n.2 (9th Cir. 1998).

Annotation. "In order to create the audiovisual display for a particular level, the game engine invokes the MAP file that corresponds to that level. Each MAP file contains a series of instructions that tell the game engine (and, through it, the computer) what to put where. For instance, the MAP file might say scuba gear goes at the bottom of the screen. The game engine then goes to the source art library, finds the image of the scuba gear, and puts it in just the right place on the screen. The MAP file describes the level in painstaking detail, but it does not actually contain any of the copyrighted art itself; everything that appears on the screen actually comes from the art library. Think of the game's audiovisual display as a paint-by-numbers kit. The MAP file might tell you to put blue paint in section number 565, but it doesn't contain any blue paint itself; the blue paint comes from your palette, which is the low-tech analog of the art library, while you play the role of the game engine. When the player selects one of the N/I levels, the game engine references the N/I MAP files, but still uses the D/N-3D art library to generate the images that make up that level."

Micro Star v. FormGen, Inc., 154 F.3d 1107, 1110 (9th Cir. 1998) (footnote omitted).

market research *(business)*

Collection and analysis of demographic and other information concerning the potential market for a multimedia product.

market share *(antitrust)*

"Courts have long used market share as a principal indicator of market power and as an indication that a monopolizer has a dangerous probability of success. Generally, market share of more than fifty percent is adequate to establish a 'dangerous probability of success.'"

Advanced Computer Servs. v. MAI Sys. Corp., 845 F. Supp. 356, 369 (E.D. Va. 1994).

marquee value *(entertainment)*

The value that the name and reputation of a celebrity has in attracting buyers to an interactive media product or service.

mask *(hardware)*

The master pattern (usually made of quartz or glass) containing the circuit image that is used like a photographic negative in lithography to define the areas for etching in the resist.

mask works *(hardware)*

"[A] series of related images, however fixed or encoded, (1) having or representing the pre-determined three-dimensional pattern of metallic, insulating, or semiconductor material or removed from the layers of a semiconductor chip product; (2) in which series the relation of the images to one another is that each image has the pattern of the surface of one form of the semi-conductor chip product."

U.S. Copyright Act, 17 U.S.C. § 101. *See also* 17 U.S.C. § 901(a)(2).

Annotation. "The patent system alone was deemed not to provide the desired scope of protection of mask works. Although electronic circuitry and electronic components are within the statutory subject matter of patentable invention . . . and some original circuitry may be patentable if it also meets the requirements of the Patent Act . . . Congress sought more expeditious protection against copying of original circuit layouts, whether or not they met the criteria of patentable inventions."

> *Brooktree Corp. v. Advanced Micro Devices, Inc.,* 977 F.2d 1555, 1562-63 (Fed. Cir. 1992).

See also **layout design; topography.**

mass-market license *(contract)*

"[A]standard form used in a mass-market transaction."

> UCITA § 102(a)(44).

mass-market transaction *(contract)*

"[A] transaction that is:

(A) a consumer contract; or

(B) any other transaction with an end-user licensee if:

(i) the transaction is for information or informational rights directed to the general public as a whole, including consumers, under substantially the same terms for the same information;

(ii) the licensee acquires the information or informational rights in a retail transaction under terms and in a quantity consistent with an ordinary transaction in a retail market; and

(iii) the transaction is not:

(I) a contract for redistribution or for public performance or public display of a copyrighted work;

(II) a transaction in which the information is customized or otherwise specially prepared by the licensor for the licensee, other than minor customization using a capability of the information intended for that purpose;

(III) a site license; or

(IV) an access contract.

> UCITA § 102(a)(45).

master recording license *(entertainment)*

A license permitting the reproduction and distribution of a specific performance of a musical composition.

mastering *(manufacturing; multimedia)*

The step in a CD-ROM manufacturing process where data is converted into a stamping pattern used in replicating the actual CD-ROM.

mastering fee *(business; manufacturing)*

The fee charged by a manufacturer to create a master from which the actual CD-ROMs will be produced.

material objects *(copyright)*

"[T]he [Copyright] Act does not require absolute permanence for the creation of a copy. Rather, the Act requires only that the representation created in RAM be a 'material object' that is 'sufficiently permanent or stable to permit it to be perceived, reproduced, or otherwise communicated for a period of more than transitory duration.' . . . This language supports a reading of the Act that recognizes that electrical impulses of a program in RAM are material objects, which, although themselves imperceptible to the ordinary observer, can be perceived by persons with the aid of a computer."

Advanced Computer Servs., Inc. v. MAI Sys. Corp., 845 F. Supp. 356, 363 (E.D. Va. 1994).

Related issues. "This language supports a reading of the Act that recognizes that electrical impulses of a program in RAM are material objects, which, although themselves imperceptible to the ordinary observer, can be perceived by persons with the aid of a computer."

Advanced Computer Servs., Inc. v. MAI Sys. Corp., 845 F. Supp. 356, 363 (E.D. Va. 1994).

"Transfer of ownership of any material object, including the copy or phonorecord in which the work is first fixed, does not of itself convey any rights in the copyrighted work embodied in the object; nor, in the absence of an agreement, does transfer of ownership of a copyright or of any exclusive rights under a copyright convey property rights in any material object."

17 U.S.C. § 202.

mathematical algorithm *(technology)*

A step-by-step mathematical procedure used to solve a given problem.

Annotation. "Unpatentable mathematical algorithms are identifiable by showing they are merely abstract ideas constituting disembodied concepts or truths that are not 'useful.' From a practical standpoint, this means that to be patentable an algorithm must be applied in a 'useful' way."

State Street Bank & Trust Co. v. Signature Financial Group, Inc., 149 F.3d 1368, 1373 (Fed. Cir. 1998).

"[M]athematical algorithms are not patentable subject matter to the extent that they are merely abstract ideas."

State Street Bank & Trust, Co. v. Signature Financial Group, Inc., 149 F.3d 1368, 1373 (Fed. Cir. 1998).

"Unpatentable mathematical algorithms are identifiable by showing they are merely abstract ideas constituting disembodied concepts or truths that are not 'useful.' From a practical standpoint, this means that to be patentable an algorithm must be applied in a 'useful' way."

> *State Street Bank & Trust, Co. v. Signature Financial Group, Inc.*, 149 F.3d 1368, 1373 (Fed. Cir. 1998).

See also **algorithm.**

Mbone *(Internet; technology)*
A service using the Internet backbone to distribute live video over the network.

MBPS *(technology)*
Acronym for "Million Bits Per Second." Also "Mbps."

MDF *(business)*
Acronym for "Market Development Funds."

A fee paid to a retailer to defray some of the retailer's marketing costs. Usually the MDF payment is not earmarked for marketing related to the particular product, but is used by the retailer for any marketing it chooses.

mean time between failures *(technology)*
Abbreviated as "MTBF."

"Several exhibits proffered by Renfro contained references to performance goals set by NCR for the Century 100 in terms of a failure rate stated as mean time between equipment failures (MTBF). MTBF data are regarded as 'an indication of reliability.'"

> *Renfro Hosiery Mills Co. v. National Cash Register Co.*, 552 F.2d 1061, 1066 (4th Cir. 1977).

"means for" claim *(patent)*
"An element in a claim for a combination may be expressed as a means or step for performing a specified function without the recital of structure, material, or acts in support thereof, and such claim shall be construed to cover the corresponding structure, material, or acts described in the specification and equivalents thereof."

> 35 U.S.C. § 112.

See also **claim(s); means plus function claim.**

means plus function claim *(patent)*
"Each claim component, recited as a 'means' plus its function, is to be read, of course, pursuant to §112, ¶ 6, as inclusive of the 'equivalents' of

the structures disclosed in the written description portion of the specification."

> *State Street Bank & Trust, Co. v. Signature Financial Group, Inc.*, 149 F.3d 1368, 1372 (Fed. Cir. 1998).

See also claim(s); **"means for" claim.**

mechanical license *(copyright)*

The license required to manufacture and distribute the physical media containing the recording of a musical composition. Mechanical rights for most musical compositions can be obtained from The Harry Fox Agency, New York, NY.

medium-scale integration *(hardware)*

"[T]o produce multiple circuits on a chip."

> *Telex Corp. v. IBM Corp.*, 367 F. Supp. 258, 275 (N.D. Okla. 1973), *aff'd in part, rev'd in part*, 510 F.2d 894 (10th Cir.), *cert. dism.*, 423 U.S. 802 (1975).

mega *(technology)*

Prefix meaning million; e.g., "megaflops" means "millions of floating point operations per second" and "megabytes" means "million characters of storage."

megabyte *(technology)*

Abbreviated as "MB." 1,048,576 bytes of data.

"1024 kilobytes . . . ."

> *Universal City Studios, Inc. v. Reimerdes*, 111 F. Supp. 2d 294, 306 (S.D.N.Y. 2000) (footnote omitted).

Annotation. "[M]illions of combinations of bits of information. . . ."

> *Telex Corp. v. IBM Corp.*, 367 F. Supp. 258, 267 (N.D. Okla. 1973), *aff'd in part, rev'd in part*, 510 F.2d 894 (10th Cir.), *cert. dism.*, 423 U.S. 802 (1975).

memory *(hardware)*

Refers to a computer's capability to store information. Memory capacity was originally measured in kilobytes or K, and is now generally measured in megabytes.

Annotation. "Storage capacity . . . measured in millions of combinations of bits of information (megabytes). . . ."

> *Telex Corp. v. IBM Corp.*, 367 F. Supp. 258, 267 (N.D. Okla. 1973), *aff'd in part, rev'd in part*, 510 F.2d 894 (10th Cir.), *cert. dism.*, 423 U.S. 802 (1975).

memory device *(hardware)*

An electronic component that stores binary data. Categorized according to accessibility (random or serial), size, speed, and whether it is a device that can be written to or read only. Also categorized by storage media—that is, tape, disk, or semiconductor.

memory stack *(hardware)*

See memory plane.

menu *(software)*

A list of programs or applications that are easily available for selection by the user. *See also* menu command hierarchy.

menu command hierarchy *(software)*

A method of organizing commands, so that each command entry is a parent and/or child of another command entry. It is similar to a traditional outline structure, where subheadings are organized under main headings and sub-subheadings are organized under subheadings, etc.

menu program *(software)*

[SOUTH AFRICA] "[O]ne which displays on a computer screen a selection of options, each representing a specific function and a separate program, from which the user may choose a program."

Northern Off. Micro Computers Ltd. v. Rosenstein [1982], Fleet St. Rep. 124 (Supreme Ct. S. Africa).

merchandising rights *(business; entertainment)*

The right to manufacture and to sell or otherwise dispose of any unique and original object or thing first fully described in literary material written by a writer.

merchant *(contract)*

". . . means a person who deals in goods of the kind or otherwise by his occupation holds himself out as having knowledge or skill peculiar to the practices or goods involved in the transaction or to whom such knowledge or skill may be attributed by his employment of an agent or broker or other intermediary who by his occupation holds himself out as having such knowledge or skill."

U.C.C. § 2-104(1).

"[A] person:

(A) that deals in information or informational rights of the kind involved in the transaction;

(B) that by the person's occupation holds itself out as having knowledge or skill peculiar to the relevant aspect of the business practices or information involved in the transaction; or

(C) to which the knowledge or skill peculiar to the practices or information involved in the transaction may be attributed by the person's employment of an agent or broker or other intermediary that by its occupation holds itself out as having the knowledge or skill."

UCITA § 102(a)(46).

merge *(copyright)*

See merger doctrine.

merger doctrine *(copyright)*

"The doctrine's underlying principle is that '[w]hen there is essentially only one way to express an idea, the idea and its expression are inseparable and copyright is no bar to copying that expression.'"

Computer Assocs. Int'l, Inc. v. Altai, Inc., 982 F.2d 693, 708 (2d Cir. 1992).

"[W]hen an idea and a particular expression of that idea are so inseparable that protecting the expression would necessarily confer a monopoly on the idea because only a limited number of ways exist to express the idea, the court will not find substantial similarity absent virtually identical copying."

Interactive Networks, Inc. v. NTN Comm., Inc., 875 F. Supp. 1398, 1403 (N.D. Cal. 1995).

"[I]deas, as such, are not copyrightable and, as a corollary, necessary expressions incident to an idea 'merge' with that idea and also are not copyrightable."

Digital Com. Assocs., Inc. v. Softklone Distr. Corp., 659 F. Supp. 449, 457 (N.D. Ga. 1987).

Annotation. "CONTU recognized the applicability of the merger doctrine to computer programs. In its report to Congress it stated that:

'[C]opyrighted language may be copied without infringing when there is but a limited number of ways to express a given idea. . . . In the computer context, this means that when specific instructions, even though previously copyrighted, are the only and essential means of accomplishing a given task, their later use by another will not amount to infringement.'

"CONTU Report, at 29. While this statement directly concerns only the application of merger to program code, that is, the textual aspect of the program, it reasonably suggests that the doctrine fits comfortably within the general context of computer programs."

> *Computer Assocs. Int'l, Inc. v. Altai, Inc.,* 982 F.2d 693, 707 (2d Cir. 1992).

"[S]imilarity of expression . . . which necessarily results from the fact that the common idea is only capable of expression in more or less stereotyped form will preclude a finding of actionable similarity."

> *Atari, Inc. v. North American Philips Consumer Elecs. Corp.,* 672 F. Supp. 607, 616 (7th. Cir.), *cert. denied,* 459 U.S. 880 (1982).

"In the computer context, this means that when specific instructions, even though previously copyrighted, are the only and essential means of accomplishing a given task, their later use by another will not amount to an infringement."

> *CONTU Final Report* 20 (1978).

Related issues. "Ninth Circuit cases . . . appear uniformly to treat the 'merger' issue as a question of whether or not there is infringement rather than copyrightability."

> *NEC Corp. v. Intel Corp.,* 10 U.S.P.Q.2d (BNA) 1177, 1179 (N.D. Cal. 1989).

See also efficiency; idea/expression dichotomy; idea-expression unity.

message *(electronic commerce)*

"[A] digital representation of information intended to serve as a written communication with a public entity."

> Cal. Code of Regulations, tit. 2, div. 7, ch. 10, § 22000(a)(2).

"[A] digital representation of information."

> Wash. Rev. Code § 19.34.020(19).

meta description *(Internet)*

"[W]ords that identify an Internet site . . . ."

> *Niton Corp. v. Radiation Monitoring Devices, Inc.,* 27 F. Supp. 2d 102, 104 (D. Mass. 1998).

meta keywords *(Internet)*

"[K]eywords that are listed by the web page creator when creating a web site."

> *Niton Corp. v. Radiation Monitoring Devices, Inc.,* 27 F. Supp. 2d 102, 104 (D. Mass. 1998).

metallization *(manufacturing)*

A semiconductor manufacturing process in which a layer of metal, such as aluminum, is placed on the wafer to connect the transistors and diodes within an integrated circuit.

metal-oxide semiconductor *(hardware)*
Also abbreviated as "MOS." One of the two families of silicon transistors and integrated circuits; the other is bipolar. MOS is simpler to fabricate and hence is often used in manufacturing large, dense integrated circuits. It is also slower to fabricate than bipolar and sensitive to radiation, which limits its military applications.

metatags *(Internet)*
Also spelled "meta tags."

". . . are HTML code not visible to Web users but used by search engines in determining which sites correspond to the keywords entered by a Web user."
Brookfield Comm., Inc. v. West Coast Entertainment Corp., 174 F.3d 1036, 1061 n.23 (9th Cir. 1999).

". . . are HTML code intended to describe the contents of a web site."
Brookfield Comm., Inc. v. West Coast Entertainment Corp., 174 F.3d 1036, 1045 (9th Cir. 1999) (citation omitted).

"The meta tags are not visible to the websurfer although some search engines rely on these tags to help websurfers find certain websites. Much like the subject index of a card catalog, the meta tags give the websurfer using a search engine a clearer indication of the content of a website. The use of the term Playboy is not an infringement because it references not only her identity as a Playboy 'Playmate of the Year 1981,' but it may also reference the legitimate editorial uses of the term Playboy contained in the text of defendant's website . . . the court finds that defendant has not infringed on defendant's trademarks by using them in her website meta tags."
Playboy Enters., Inc. v. Welles, 7 F. Supp. 2d 1098, 1104 (S.D. Cal. 1998).

Annotation. "There are different types of metatags, but those of principal concern to us are the 'description' and 'keyword' metatags. The description metatags are intended to describe the web site; the keyword metatags, at least in theory, contain keywords relating to the contents of the web site. The more often a term appears in the metatags and in the text of the web page, the more likely it is that the web page will be 'hit' in a search for that keyword and the higher on the list of 'hits' the web page will appear."
Brookfield Comm., Inc. v. West Coast Entertainment Corp., 174 F.3d 1036, 1045 (9th Cir. 1999) (citation omitted).

Related issues. "Because we agree that the traditional eight-factor test is not well-suited for analyzing the metatags issue, we do not attempt to fit our discussion into one of the *Sleekcraft* factors."

> *Brookfield Comm., Inc. v. West Coast Entertainment Corp.,* 174 F.3d 1036, 1063 n.24 (9th Cir. 1999).

See also **description metatags; keyword metatags.**

metered use *(business)*

The method of charging for access and/or use of digital information. Charges can be based upon access time, processing time, output, or any combination of these.

method *(patent)*

"In conformance with the standards of patent law, title 35 provides protection for the process or method performed by a computer in accordance with a program. Thus, patent and copyright laws protect distinct aspects of a computer program."

> *Atari Games Corp. v. Nintendo of America, Inc.,* 975 F.2d 832, 839 (Fed. Cir. 1992), *citing Arrhythmia Research Technology v. Corazonix Corp.,* 958 F.2d 1053 (Fed. Cir. 1992).

method of operation *(copyright)*

The manner in which something is done.

Annotation. "In no case does copyright protection for an original work of authorship extend to any idea, procedure, process, system, method of operation, concept, principle, or discovery, regardless of the form in which it is described, explained, illustrated, or embodied in such work."

> U.S. Copyright Act, 17 U.S.C. § 102(b).

"Some concern has been expressed lest copyright in computer programs should extend protection to the methodology or processes adopted by the programmer, rather than merely to the 'writing' expressing his ideas. Section 102(b) is intended, among other things, to make clear that the expression adopted by the programmer is the copyrightable element in a computer program, and that the actual processes or methods embodied in the program are not within the scope of the copyright law."

> H.R. Rep No. 1476, 94th Cong., 2d Sess. 57 (1976).

"Where a portion of the computer program constitutes an unprotectable method of operation or process, it is not an expressive part of the work. It is particularly important to exclude methods of operation and processes from the scope of copyright in computer programs because much of the contents of computer programs is patentable. Were we to permit an author to claim copyright protection for those elements of the work that should be the province of patent law, we would be undermining the competitive principles that are fundamental to the patent system."

Bateman v. Mnemonics, Inc., 875 F. Supp. 1398, 1541 n.21 (11th Cir. 1995).

"Franklin argues that an operating system is either a 'process,' 'system,' or 'method of operation' and hence uncopyrightable. Franklin correctly notes that underlying section 102(b) and many of the statements for which *Baker v. Selden* is cited is the distinction which must be made between property subject to patent law, which protects discoveries, and that subject to copyright law, which protects the writings describing such discoveries. However, Franklin's argument misapplies that distinction in this case. Apple does not seek to copyright the method which instructs the computer to perform its operating functions but only the instructions themselves. . . .

"Since it is only the instructions which are protected, a 'process' is no more involved because the instructions in an operating system program may be used to activate the operation of the computer than it would be if instructions were written in ordinary English in a manual which described the necessary steps to activate an intricate complicated machine."

Apple Computer, Inc. v. Franklin Computer Corp., 714 F.2d 1240, 1250-51 (3d Cir.), *cert. denied,* 464 U.S. 1033 (1984).

See also **work of authorship.**

metrics *(software)*
A means by which software engineers measure and predict aspects of processes, resources, and products that are relevant to the software engineering activity. (wsr)

MFJ *(telecommunications)*
Acronym for "Modified Final Judgment."

micro *(technology)*
Prefix for 1/1,000,000th.

microchip *(technology)*
A very small computer chip.

Related issues (criminal). "The House Committee's reference to microchips as 'components' of counterfeit access devices appears to arise in the context of credit cards as access devices.[10]"

[n.10] " 'As the credit industry and other parts of our society enlarges its capacity in the use of computer technology, for example, in the use of 'smart cards' *which contain microchips* and are themselves a form of 'passive' computer, there is every indication that the criminal element is enlarging its capacity in this area.' H.R. Rep. No. 894, at 4, 1984 U.S. Code Cong. & Admin. News at 3690 (emphasis added)."

> *United States v. Brady*, 820 F. Supp. 1346, 1350 & n.10 (D. Utah 1993).

microcode

(technology)
A computer program embedded in a computer chip that directs the operation of that chip.

(copyright)
"As such, it comes squarely within the definition of a 'computer program,' which Congress added to the Copyright Act of 1976. . . ."

> *NEC Corp. v. Intel Corp.,* 10 U.S.P.Q.2d (BNA) 1177 (N.D. Cal. 1989).

(patent)

Related issues. Microcode has been held patentable. *See In re Bradley,* 600 F.2d 807 (C.C.P.A. 1979), *aff'd by an equally divided court sub nom. Diamond v. Diehr,* 450 U.S. 381 (1981).

(software)
". . . consists of a series of instructions that tell a microprocessor which of its thousands of transistors to actuate in order to perform the tasks directed by the macroinstruction set."

> *NEC Corp. v. Intel Corp.,* 10 U.S.P.Q.2d (BNA) 1177 (N.D. Cal. 1989).

". . . is a set of encoded instructions . . . that controls the fine details of the execution of one or more primitive functions of a computer. Microcode serves as a substitute for certain elements of the hardware circuitry that had previously controlled that function."

> *Lotus Dev. Corp. v. Paperback Software Int'l,* 740 F. Supp. 37, 43 (D. Mass. 1990), *quoting* Paula Samuelson, "CONTU Revisited: The Case Against Copyright Protection for Computer Programs in Machine-Readable Form," 1984 *Duke L.J.* 663, 677.

microcomputer *(hardware)*
A small but complete computer system, including CPU, memory, input/output interfaces, and power supply.

microdisk *(hardware)*

Also spelled "microdisc." Tested or untested magnetically coated polyester disks with a steel hub encased in a hard plastic jacket used to record and store encoded digital computer information for access by a 3.5-inch floppy disk drive. Microdisks include single-sided, double-sided, and high-density formats.

microfazers *(hardware)*

"[P]rint buffers and storage devices. They permit a machine to receive and store information faster than a printer can print the information. The microfazers that taxpayer plans to treat as mass assets are those designed to be used with mini or personal computers."

IRS Letter Ruling 8721016, Feb. 17, 1987.

micron *(technology)*

A micrometer, or one-millionth of a meter.

microprocessor *(hardware)*

"A miniature computer placed on a single microchip which is capable of performing arithmetic, logic, and control functions."

E.F. Johnson Co. v. Uniden Corp. of Am., 623 F. Supp. 1485, 1488 (D. Minn. 1985).

Microsoft *(organization)*

". . . Microsoft Corporation is organized under the laws of the State of Washington, and its headquarters are situated in Redmond, Washington. Since its inception, Microsoft has focused primarily on developing software and licensing it to various purchasers. . . . Microsoft is the leading supplier of operating systems for PCs. The company transacts business in all fifty of the United States and in most countries around the world."

United States v. Microsoft Corp., 65 F. Supp. 2d 1, 4 (D.D.C. 1999) (Findings of Fact 5, 9). See also Microsoft Corp. v. BEC Computer Co., 818 F.2d 1313, 1315 (C.D. Cal. 1992) ("Microsoft is in the business of developing and marketing computer software programs for use on personal computers").

Related issues. "While Microsoft may not be able to stave off all potential paradigm shifts through innovation, it can thwart some and delay others by improving its own products to the greater satisfaction of consumers."

United States v. Microsoft Corp., 65 F. Supp. 2d 1, 18 (D.D.C. 1999) (Finding of Fact 61).

middleware *(software)*

"[S]oftware [that] relies on the interfaces provided by the underlying operating system while simultaneously exposing its own APIs to developers."
> *United States v. Microsoft Corp.*, 65 F. Supp. 2d 1, 9 (D.D.C. 1999) (Finding of Fact 28).

Related issues. "Even if middleware deployed enough APIs to support full-featured applications, it would not function on a computer without an operating system to perform tasks such as managing hardware resources and controlling peripheral devices. But to the extent the array of applications relying solely on middleware comes to satisfy all of a user's needs, the user will not care whether there exists a large number of other applications that are directly compatible with the underlying operating system. Thus, the growth of middleware-based applications could lower the costs to users of choosing a non-Intel-compatible PC operating system like the Mac OS. It remains to be seen, though, whether there will ever be a sustained stream of full-featured applications written solely to middleware APIs."
> *United States v. Microsoft Corp.*, 65 F. Supp. 2d 1, 9 (D.D.C. 1999) (Finding of Fact 29).

MIDI *(technology)*

Acronym for "Musical Instrument Digital Interface." An international standard hardware interface for the computer control of musical instruments and other devices.

migration *(business)*

The effort to move the information processing capabilities from one platform to another, usually a radically different, and hopefully newer environment. For example, a move from a predominantly mainframe-based system to a client/server could be viewed as migration. (wsr)

milestone(s) *(business)*

Specific points in the development process where the developer has completed identifiable portions of the interactive media title. Milestones are usually tied to payments of specified portions of the development fee.

Miller *(obscenity)*

Citation: Miller v. California, 413 U.S. 15 (1973).

In *Miller,* the U.S. Supreme Court enunciated what is the current test for determining whether content is obscene and outside the protection of the First Amendment right of free speech:

"(a) whether the average person, applying contemporary community standards would find that the work, taken as a whole, appeals to the prurient interest; (b) whether the work depicts or describes, in a patently offensive way, sexual conduct specifically defined by the applicable state law; and (c) whether the work, taken as a whole, lacks serious literary, artistic, political, or scientific value." *Id.* at 24 (internal quotation marks and citations omitted).

milli *(technology)*
A prefix meaning one-thousandth.

mil(s) *(technology)*
"[T]housandths of an inch. . . ."
    Sperry Rand Corp. v. Pentronix, Inc. 311 F. Supp. 910, 911 (E.D. Pa. 1970).

MIME *(Internet)*
Acronym for "Multipurpose Internet Mail Extension." An extension to the Internet that provides information to a web server about the types of data the particular web browser can handle (e.g., text only), which results in only those types of data being sent back to the user. These extensions permit non-text data to be sent over the Internet. They are used for coding of attached documents.

MIN *(telecommunications)*
Acronym for "Mobile Identification Number."

"[A] ten-digit numerical telephone number (area code + seven-digit telephone number) assigned to each cellular telephone customer, usually identical to the customer's home telephone number."
    United States v. Brady, 820 F. Supp. 1346, 1348 n.3 (D. Utah 1993).

minicomputer *(hardware)*
A midrange computer that is larger than a microcomputer. Generally, a 16- or 32-bit computer with limited memory addressability.

minimum contact(s) *(jurisdiction)*
"Due process is satisfied where the defendant has enough 'minimum contacts' with the forum state such that requiring him to defend his interests there would not 'offend traditional notions of fair play and substantial justice.' Furthermore, the minimum contacts with the state must be such that the defendant could 'reasonably anticipate being haled into court there.' 'It is essential in each case that there be some act by which the defendant purposefully avails itself of the privilege of conducting activities

within the forum state, thus invoking the benefits and protection of its laws.'"

> *Coastal Video Comm. Corp. v. Staywell Corp.*, 59 F. Supp. 2d 562, 565 (E.D. Va. 1999) (citations omitted).

"The 'minimum contacts' aspect of the analysis can be established through 'contacts that give rise to "specific" personal jurisdiction or those that give rise to "general" personal jurisdiction.' Specific jurisdiction exists when the nonresident defendant's contacts with the forum state arise from, or are directly related to, the cause of action. General jurisdiction exists when a defendant's contacts with the forum state are unrelated to the cause of action but are "continuous and systematic."

> *Mink v. AAAA Dev. LLC*, 190 F.3d 333, 336 (5th Cir. 1999) (citations omitted).

"A court must consider five factors in determining whether a defendant has established minimum contacts with the forum state: (1) the quantity of the defendant's contacts; (2) the nature and quality of the defendant's contacts; (3) the connection between the cause of action and the defendant's contacts; (4) the state's interest in providing a forum; and (5) the convenience of the parties."

> *State v. Granite Gate Resorts, Inc.*, 568 N.W.2d 715, 718 (Minn. App. 1997), *aff'd per curiam*, 576 N.W.2d 747 (Minn. 1998).

"The 'Constitutional touchstone' of the minimum contacts analysis is embodied in the first prong, 'whether the defendant purposefully established' contacts with the forum state."

> *Zippo Mfg. Co. v. Zippo Dot Com, Inc.*, 952 F. Supp. 1119, 1123 (W.D. Pa. 1997).

Annotation. "Whether sufficient minimum contacts to obtain personal jurisdiction over a defendant can be established solely through the use of computers and telecommunications is a new issue under due process jurisprudence. Courts addressing the issue have recognized that such communications via computer are of a different nature."

> *Maritz, Inc. v. Cybergold, Inc.*, 947 F. Supp. 1328, 1334 (E.D. Mo. 1996).

"Through the use of computers, corporations can now transact business and communicate with individuals in several states simultaneously. Unlike communication by mail or telephone, message [sic] sent through computers are available to the recipient and anyone else who may be watching. Thus, while modern technology has made nationwide commercial transactions simpler and more feasible, even for small businesses, it must broaden correspondingly the permissible scope of jurisdiction exercisable by the courts."

> *California Software, Inc. v. Reliability Research, Inc.,* 631 F. Supp. 1356, 1363 (C.D. Cal. 1986).

"[T]he use of electronic mail and the telephone by a party in another state may establish sufficient minimum contacts with California to support personal jurisdiction. . . . Much has happened in the role that electronic communications plays in business transactions since [an earlier case] was decided more than 20 years ago. The speed and ease of such communications has increased the number of transactions that are consummated without either party leaving the office. There is no reason why the requisite minimum contacts cannot be electronic."

> *Hall v. La Ronde,* 56 Cal. App. 4th 1342, 1344 (1997).

See also **due process; foreseeability; personal jurisdiction.**

MIPS *(hardware)*

Acronym for "Millions of Instructions Per Second."

"[O]ne MIPS is the capacity to handle one million instructions per second."

> *Zayre Corp. v. Computer Sys. of America, Inc.,* 224 Mass. App. 559, 565 (1987).

mirror site *(Internet)*

An exact copy of a web site that usually resides on a separate server, uses a separate communications line and has a separate Internet address. It is used to provide redundancy and to provide faster access to popular web sites.

Annotation. As the number of people using the Internet continues to grow, many popular World Wide Web sites and FTP sites have become very congested. The number of visitors at these popular sites can overburden the processing power of the server computer and the capacity of the server's communication link to the Internet, causing a slow or unreliable connection. One solution to the congestion problem is to create a "mirror site." A mirror site is an exact copy of the original site that can reside on a separate server, use a separate communications line, and use a separate internet address or URL.

A mirror site raises many licensing issues. Even if establishing a mirror site of your own World Wide Web site, careful attention should be paid to the licenses for content on the original site. In most cases, server side software programs (operating systems, WWW server software, FTP server software, and server side helper programs) are licensed for use on a single computer, and a separate copy of the programs must be licensed for the mirror site. Further, if third-party content is included on the original site, its license terms must also be analyzed to determine if placement and use of the content on a mirror site is permissible.

Some World Wide Web site operators and Internet service providers create mirror sites of popular Internet destinations in order to provide faster, more reliable access for their users. In many cases, permission is obtained, but it is often neglected in the interest of providing speed and convenience. In addition to the obvious copyright and trademark issues, establishing an unauthorized mirror site can divert viewers of the original site's content from being counted as "hits" to the original site. Since the value of a World Wide Web site is largely dependent upon the number of hits that are recorded by the server, an unauthorized mirror site can easily dilute the value of the site. Also, if an original site is frequently updated, it is likely that an mirror site will not reflect the latest version of the content on the original site. This delay can adversely affect the developer of the original site by keeping an old or outdated page in circulation after it has been removed from or changed on the original site.

It may be possible to determine if a site has been mirrored by using an Internet search engine, such as Digital Electronic Corporation's Alta Vista, to search for unique words or combinations of words in the pages on the original site. The results of the search may yield URLs other than the original site that lead to the mirrored page.

Both the law and technology are seeking ways to deal with the ease of copying and distributing a third party's digital content. While imitation may indicate flattery, imitation without permission may be more likely to elicit a demand to cease and desist than to elicit gratitude. (jrb)

misappropriation

(trade secret)
"Improper acquisition, disclosure, or use of a 'trade secret.'"
Minn. Stat. § 325C.01.

"(1) Acquisition of a trade secret of another by a person who knows or has reason to know that the trade secret was acquired by improper means; or

(2) disclosure or use of a trade secret of another without express or implied consent by a person who:

(A) Used improper means to acquire knowledge of the trade secret; or

(B) At the time of disclosure or use, knew or had reason to know that his or her knowledge of the trade secret was:

(i) Derived from or through a person who had utilized improper means to acquire it; (ii) Acquired under circumstances giving rise to a duty to maintain its secrecy or limit its use; or (iii) Derived from or through a person who owed a duty to the person seeking relief to maintain its secrecy or limit it use; or

(C) Before a material change of his or her position knew or had reason to know that it was a trade secret and that knowledge of it had been acquired by accident or by mistake."

Cal. Civ. Code § 3426.1(b).

(unfair competition)
" 'Misappropriation' is not necessarily synonymous with copyright infringement, and thus a cause of action labeled 'misappropriation' is not preempted if it is in fact based neither on a right within the general scope of copyright as specified by section 106 nor on a right equivalent thereto. For example, state law should have the flexibility to afford a remedy (under traditional principles of equity) against a consistent pattern of unauthorized appropriation by a competitor of the facts (i.e., not the literary expression) constituting 'hot' news, whether in the traditional mold of [INS], or in the newer form of data updates from scientific, business, or financial data bases."

National Basketball Ass'n v. Motorola, Inc., 105 F.2d 841, 850 (2d Cir. 1997).

(trade secret)
. . . is established by showing: "(a) a trade secret existed; (b) the trade secret was acquired through a breach of a confidential relationship or discovered by improper means; and (c) use of the trade secret without authorization from the plaintiff."

Alcatel USA, Inc. v. DGI Technologies, Inc., 166 F.3d 772, 784 (5th Cir. 1999) (Texas law) (citation omitted).

Annotation (*unfair competition*)
"In contrast to federal copyright law, which focuses on the value of creativity, state misappropriation law is specifically designed to protect the *labor*—the so-called 'sweat equity'— that goes into creating a work."

Alcatel USA, Inc. v. DGI Technologies, Inc., 166 F.3d 772, 788 (5th Cir. 1999) (citations omitted) (emphasis in original).

Related issues *(trade secret).* "The UTSA definition of 'misappropriation' has been clarified by case law which establishes that the right to *announce* a new affiliation, even to trade secret clients of a former employer, is basic to an individual's right to engage in fair competition, and that the right to compete fairly and the right to announce a new business affiliation have survived the enactment of the UTSA. . . . However, misappropriation occurs if information from a customer database is used to *solicit* customers."

> *MAI Sys. Corp. v. Peak Computer, Inc.,* 991 F.2d 511, 521 (9th Cir. 1993) (citations omitted; emphasis in original), *cert. dism.,* 510 U.S. 1033 (1994).

"The misappropriation of a trade secret is an intentional tort, but it is not the law that the fact that a tort is intentional automatically authorizes the award of punitive damages. If it did, the Uniform Trade Secrets Act would not limit punitive damages to cases in which the violation of the Act is willful or malicious. When an award of punitive damages requires that the defendant have committed an aggravated form of the wrongful act sought to be punished, a defendant who commits the barebones tort is not liable for such damages."

> *Micro Data Base Sys., Inc. v. Dharma Sys., Inc.,* 148 F.3d 649, 654 (7th Cir. 1998) (citations omitted).

"Consequential damages, as long as they are reasonably foreseeable, are the norm in tort cases, and the misappropriation of a trade secret is a tort; we are just surprised not to have found any case in which consequential damages were awarded for such a misappropriation."

> *Micro Data Base Sys., Inc. v. Dharma Sys., Inc.,* 148 F.3d 649, 658 (7th Cir. 1998) (citation omitted).

"[S]tate law claims that rely on the misappropriation branch of unfair competition are preempted."

> *Warner Bros. v. American Broadcasting Cos.,* 720 F.2d 231, 247 (2d Cir. 1980).

mission-critical *(business)*
A computer system or software that is supporting a core business activity or process.

MITI *(organization)*
Acronym for the Japanese "Ministry of International Trade and Industry."

MMF *(business)*
An acronym for "Make Money Fast." A generic term for any illegal schemes promoted online that promise that the user can earn a great deal of money quickly with little or no work.

mnemonic *(software)*
See mnemonic code.

mnemonic code *(software)*

"Symbols used in programming to assist the human memory, e.g., an abbreviation such as 'MPY' for 'multiply.'"

U.S. Copyright Office, *Compendium of Copyright Office Practices* II, § 326 (1984).

mobile identification number *(telecommunications)*

See MIN.

modem *(hardware)*

Acronym for "**mo**dulation/**dem**odulation."

"[A]n acronym for 'modulation and demodulation.' Modems, when connected to telephone lines, allow computers to send and receive information to and from each other."

Western Elec. Co. v. Milgo Elec. Corp., 568 F.2d 1203, 1205 (5th Cir. 1978).

". . . (a contraction of 'modulator' and 'demodulator') is a device that translates digital information into a signal for transmission over a telephone line ('modulation') and translates a signal received over a telephone line into digital information ('demodulation')."

Shea v. Reno, 930 F. Supp. 916, 926 n.4 (S.D.N.Y. 1996).

". . . allows a terminal or computer to attach to a communication line. The modem performs the translation necessary to send and receive information over telephone lines. Some modems are contained in small boxes, but to save space, more and more are installed in racks or built into computers."

IRS Letter Ruling 8721016, Feb. 17, 1987.

"[A] contraction of 'Modulator/demodulator'. . . [which] refers to a device which modulates, or changes, the electrical characteristics of data signals before they are placed on the telephone line, and demodulates the signals at the receiving end, to change back into a form recognizable to computer equipment. . . ."

Racal-Vadic, Inc. v. Universal Data Sys., 207 U.S.P.Q. (BNA) 902, 906 (N.D. Ala. 1980).

"Modems, widely used in the data processing and data communications fields, provide a communication link between a signal generator, such as a computer terminal which generates discreet voltage levels to represent data, and a telephone distribution network. The modem modulates the discreet voltage level signal to produce a signal which can be transmitted over a telephone line. An identical or similar modem at the receiving end of the telephone line demodulates the signal to produce a discreet voltage level form signal which is compatible with a data receiver."

Hayes Microcomputer Prods., Inc. v. Business Computer Corp., 219 U.S.P.Q. (BNA) 634 (T.T.A.B. 1983).

Related issues. "Many home computers today have modems with a rated capacity of 56 kilobits per second."

Universal City Studios, Inc. v. Reimerdes, 111 F. Supp. 2d 294, 314 (S.D.N.Y. 2000) (footnote omitted).

See also **intelligent modem.**

moderated mailing list *(Internet)*

"Mailing lists (both open and closed) may also be 'moderated': all messages posted to the list are forwarded to a moderator, who approves certain messages and retransmits them to subscribers."

Shea v. Reno, 930 F. Supp. 916, 927 (S.D.N.Y. 1996).

See also **moderated newsgroup; Usenet.**

moderated newsgroup *(Internet)*

". . . all messages to the newsgroup are forwarded to one person who can screen them for relevance to the topics under discussion."

American Civil Liberties Union v. Reno, 929 F. Supp. 824, 835 (E.D. Pa. 1996), *aff'd, Reno v. American Civil Liberties Union,* 521 U.S. 844 (1997).

"Some Usenet newsgroups are moderated; messages to the newsgroup are forwarded to an individual who selects those appropriate for distribution."

Shea v. Reno, 930 F. Supp. 916, 928 (S.D.N.Y. 1996).

Related issues. "It is clear from the testimony that moderated newsgroups are the exception and unmoderated newsgroups are the rule."

American Civil Liberties Union v. Reno, 929 F. Supp. 824, 835 n.10 (E.D. Pa. 1996), *aff'd, Reno v. American Civil Liberties Union,* 521 U.S. 844 (1997).

See also **moderated mailing list; newsgroup; Usenet.**

moderator *(Internet)*

A person who moderates a newsgroup.

modification

(contract)

Sample clause. "No amendment, change or modification to this Agreement shall be effective or enforceable unless it is in writing and executed by [an officer or director of] each party to this Agreement."

(copyright)
See **enhancement.**

module *(software)*

"A series or group of related instructions within a computer program, analogous to a chapter of a book."

> U.S. Copyright Office, *Compendium of Copyright Office Practices* II, § 326 (1984).

monetary relief *(copyright)*

"[D]amages, costs, attorneys' fees, and any other form of monetary payment."

> 17 U.S.C. § 512(k)(2).

monitor

(hardware)
A computer display screen.

(technology)
To follow someone's movements on a computer system or network.

monopolization *(antitrust)*

"A finding of monopolization in violation of 2 of the Sherman Act is based upon three elements: (1) specific intent to monopolize the relevant market; (2) predatory or anticompetitive acts in furtherance of intent; and (3) dangerous probability of success."

> *Advanced Computer Servs. v. MAI Sys. Corp.,* 845 F. Supp. 356, 369 (E.D. Va. 1994).

"[T]he plaintiff must first establish the relevant product market. DGI disputes the district court's conclusion that it failed to prove that the 'capacity enhancement and expansion products' market for DSC-manufactured switches is the relevant market for antitrust purposes."

> *Alcatel USA, Inc. v. DGI Technologies, Inc.,* 166 F.3d 772, 781 (5th Cir. 1999) (citation omitted).

monopoly *(antitrust)*

"[T]he electronic data processing industry . . . which appears unique in monopoly context by reason of its youth and apparent dynamics, but which by the same token in this ultramodern setting may be unprecedented also because of increased inducements for, and vulnerability to, sophisticated submarket control on the one hand, and massive industrial espionage on the other."

> *Telex Corp. v. IBM Corp.,* 367 F. Supp. 258, 267 (N.D. Okla. 1973), *aff'd in part, rev'd in part,* 510 F.2d 894 (10th Cir.), *cert. dism.,* 423 U.S. 802 (1975).

"'. . . under §2 of the Sherman Act has two elements: (1) the possession of monopoly power in the relevant market and (2) the willful acquisition or maintenance of that power as distinguished from growth or development as a consequence of a superior product, business acumen, or historic accident.'"

Alcatel USA, Inc. v. DGI Technologies, Inc., 166 F.3d 772, 781 (5th Cir. 1999)

MOO *(Internet)*

Acronym for "Mud, Object Oriented." A type of text-based, multi-user, role-playing environment. *See also* **mud(s).**

moral rights *(copyright)*

"Independently of the author's economic rights, and even after the transfer of said rights, the author shall have the right to claim authorship of the work and to object to any distortion, mutilation, or other modification of, or other derogatory action in relation to, the said work, which would be prejudicial to his honor or reputation."

Berne Convention, art. 6bis.

morphing *(multimedia)*

Derived from the term "metamorphosis." Refers to the process of gradually changing one visual image to another or merging two or more images into a single image.

MOS *(hardware)*

Acronym for "Metal-Oxide Semiconductor." *See* **metal-oxide semiconductor.**

Mosaic *(Internet; software)*

The first Internet browser software program, which allows users to browse the World Wide Web.

most favored nation *(contract)*

A contract clause in which a seller agrees to give the buyer the best terms it makes available to any other buyer.

Sample clause. "All of the benefits and terms granted by licensor herein are at least as favorable as the benefits and terms granted by licensor to any previous licensee of the content described in this Agreement. Should licensor enter into any subsequent agreement with any other licensee, [during the term of this Agreement,] which provides for benefits or terms more favorable than those contained in this Agreement, then this Agreement shall be deemed to be modified to provide licensee with those more favorable benefits and terms.

"Licensor shall notify licensee promptly of the existence of such more favorable benefits and terms and licensee shall have the right to receive the more favorable benefits and terms immediately. If requested in writing by the licensee, licensor shall amend this Agreement to contain the more favorable terms and conditions."

motherboard *(hardware)*

"[A] large flat circuit board. . . . Mounted on this board, forming the electronic circuitry which is the operating center of the computer, are a number of small integrated circuits or chips."

Apple Computer, Inc. v. Franklin Computer Corp., 545 F. Supp. 812, 813 (E.D. Pa. 1982), *rev'd,* 714 F.2d 1240 (3d Cir. 1983), *cert. dism.,* 464 U.S. 1033 (1984).

"[G]enerally considered to be populated circuit boards that compose the main board of the processing unit of a personal computer and other automated processing machines."

135 Cong. Rec. E1696 (May 16, 1989).

Motion Picture Experts Group *(organization)*

See MPEG.

motion pictures *(copyright)*

"[A]udiovisual works consisting of a series of related images which, when shown in succession, impart an impression of motion, together with accompanying sounds, if any."

U.S. Copyright Act, 17 U.S.C. § 101.

MPC *(technology)*

Acronym for "Multimedia Personal Computer." A computer standard built around Microsoft's Windows software, which designates a minimum hardware and software configuration for which interactive media titles should be written. A second, upgraded standard—MPC2—has been introduced to reflect improved technology.

MPEG *(organization; technology)*

Acronym for "Motion Picture Experts Group." This group is developing standards for video compression. The MPEG-1 standard, already in use, permits 100-1 compression and allows VHS quality video (640 x 480 pixels and 30 frames per second) on a CD-ROM. A new, more advanced MPEG-2 compression standard is being developed.

MP3 *(technology)*

Acronym for "MPEG-1 Audio Layer **3**."

Recording Indus. Ass'n of America v. Diamond Multimedia Sys., Inc., 180 F.3d 1072, 1074 (9th Cir. 1999).

"[T]he most popular digital audio compression algorithm in use on the Internet, and the compression it provides makes an audio file 'smaller' by a factor of twelve to one without significantly reducing sound quality."

Recording Indus. Ass'n of America v. Diamond Multimedia Sys., Inc., 180 F.3d 1072, 1074 (9th Cir. 1999).

"[T]echnology [that] . . . permits rapid and efficient conversion of compact disc recordings ('CDs') to computer files easily accessed over the Internet."

UMG Recordings, Inc. v. MP3.com, Inc., 92 F. Supp. 2d 349, 350 (S.D.N.Y. 2000).

Annotation. "MP3's popularity is due in large part to the fact that it is a standard, non-proprietary compression algorithm freely available for use by anyone, unlike various proprietary (and copyright-secure) competitor algorithms. Coupled with the use of cable modems, compression algorithms like MP3 may soon allow an hour of music to be downloaded from the Internet to a personal computer in just a few minutes."

Recording Indus. Ass'n of America v. Diamond Multimedia Sys., Inc., 180 F.3d 1072, 1074 (9th Cir. 1999).

Related issues. "By most accounts, the predominant use of MP3 is the trafficking in illicit audio recordings, presumably because MP3 files do not contain codes identifying whether the compressed audio material is copyright protected."

Recording Indus. Ass'n of America v. Diamond Multimedia Sys., Inc., 180 F.3d 1072, 1074 (9th Cir. 1999).

See also **compression algorithm(s).**

MS-DOS *(software)*

Early PC operating system developed by Microsoft Corporation.

Annotation. "In 1981, Microsoft released the first version of its Microsoft Disk Operating System, commonly known as 'MS-DOS.' The system had a character-based user interface that required the user to type specific instructions at a command prompt in order to perform tasks such as launching applications and copying files. When the International Business Machines Corporation ('IBM') selected MS-DOS for pre-installation on its first generation of PCs, Microsoft's product became the predominant operating system sold for Intel-compatible PCs."

> *United States v. Microsoft Corp.,* 65 F. Supp. 2d 1, 4 (D.D.C. 1999) (Finding of Fact 6). *See also Microsoft Corp. v. BEC Computer Co.,* 818 F. Supp. 1313, 1315 (C.D. Cal. 1991) ("MS-DOS is a computer operating system developed and marketed by Microsoft, which is currently used on seventy million personal computers worldwide").

MTBF *(technology)*

Acronym for "Mean Time Between Failures." *See* **mean time between failures.**

MUD(s) *(multimedia)*

Acronym for "Multi-User Dungeons."

> *American Civil Liberties Union v. Reno,* 929 F. Supp. 824, 845 (E.D. Pa. 1996), *aff'd, Reno v. American Civil Liberties Union,* 521 U.S. 844 (1997). *See also American Library Ass'n v. Pataki,* 969 F. Supp. 160, 161 n.1 (S.D.N.Y. 1997).

A type of text-based adventure game.

multimedia *(multimedia)*

Works that integrate text, graphics, still images, sounds, music, animation, and/or video and with which the user can interact using a data input device.

multiplexer(s) *(telecommunications)*

". . . consolidate signals of several lines into one line and vice versa. The purpose is to save telephone lines. For example, sixteen lines can be consolidated into one line. Multiplexers can be used to send signals inhouse or over long distances. Many of taxpayer's multiplexers are installed on racks."

> IRS Letter Ruling 8721016, Feb. 17, 1987.

multiplexing *(telecommunications)*

"In a multiplexing scheme, the franchisee would not have his own hardware facility. Instead, the incoming telephone lines from the terminals would be input into a device known as a multiplexer, which would combine these lines into a single signal. This signal would then be sent out over a telephone line to a distant hardware facility, where it would then be broken down into the individual signals corresponding to each terminal, and processed by the computer hardware. Output from the computer to the terminals would be handled in the reverse manner."

> *Response of Carolina, Inc. v. Leasco Response, Inc.,* 537 F.2d 1307, 1328 (5th Cir. 1976).

multiprocessing *(technology)*

"[I]n which in their own peculiar language machines communicate with one another. . . ."

> *Telex Corp. v. IBM Corp.,* 367 F. Supp. 258, 267 (N.D. Okla. 1973), *aff'd in part, rev'd in part,* 510 F.2d 894 (10th Cir.), *cert. dism.,* 423 U.S. 802 (1975).

multiprogrammed format *(technology)*

"[O]ne in which the computer is capable of executing more than one program, and thus perform more than one application at the same time, without the need to reprogram the computer for each task it must perform."

> *In re Bradley,* 600 F.2d 807, 808 (C.C.P.A. 1979), *aff'd by an equally divided court sub nom. Diamond v. Bradley,* 450 U.S. 381 (1981).

See also **multiprogramming.**

multiprogramming *(technology)*

"[D]oing two or more jobs at the same time."

> *ILC Peripheral Leasing Corp. v. IBM Corp.,* 448 F. Supp. 228 (N.D. Cal. 1978), *aff'd per curiam, sub nom. Memorex Corp. v. IBM Corp.,* 636 F.2d 1188 (9th Cir. 1980), *cert. denied,* 452 U.S. 972 (1981).

See also **multiprogrammed format.**

multi-user system *(technology)*

A multi-user system allows more than one user to be signed on at the same time.

multi-vendor interoperability *(technology)*

"An ability to communicate between [different vendors'] systems, and, to a reasonable degree, share data between [these] systems."

> *IBM Corp. v. Fujitsu Ltd.,* Copyright L. Rep. (CCH) ¶ 20,517, at 11,392, 11,400 (Am. Arb. Ass'n 1988).

See also **interoperability.**

MUSE(s) *(Internet)*

Acronym for "Multi-User Simulation Environment."

> *American Civil Liberties Union v. Reno,* 929 F. Supp. 824, 845 (E.D. Pa. 1996), *aff'd, Reno v. American Civil Liberties Union,* 521 U.S. 844 (1997).

A type of text-based adventure game environment.

music pirate(s) *(copyright; entertainment)*

". . . use digital recording technology to make and to distribute near perfect copies of commercially prepared recordings for which they have not licensed the copyrights."

Recording Indus. Ass'n of America v. Diamond Multimedia Sys., Inc., 180 F.3d 1072, 1073 (9th Cir. 1999).

Related issues. "Various pirate websites offer free downloads of copyright material, and a single pirate site on the Internet may contain thousands of pirated audio computer files."

Recording Indus. Ass'n of America v. Diamond Multimedia Sys., Inc., 180 F.3d 1072, 1074 (9th Cir. 1999).

music publisher *(copyright)*

"[A] person that is authorized to license the reproduction of a particular musical work in a sound recording."

17 U.S.C. § 1001(9).

name server *(technology)*
Also called "domain name server." A computer system used by the Internet to translate (or "resolve") domain names into their corresponding IP addresses.

nano *(technology)*
A prefix meaning one-billionth.

nano-second *(technology)*
Also written as "nanosecond."
"billionths of seconds."
> *Telex Corp. v. IBM Corp.,* 367 F. Supp. 258, 267 (N.D. Okla. 1973), *aff'd in part, rev'd in part,* 510 F.2d 894 (10th Cir.), *cert. dism.,* 423 U.S. 802 (1975).

narrowcasting *(Internet; telecommunications)*
The opposite of "broadcasting." Refers to cable and other systems with numerous channels, each of which provides content aimed at more specialized audiences.

National Commission on New Technological Uses of Copyright Works *(copyright)*
See CONTU.

National Information Infrastructure *(technology)*
Abbreviated as "NII." A seamless web of communications networks, computers, databases, and consumer electronics that will make a vast amount of information available to end users.
> *See The National Information Infrastructure: Agenda for Action,* 58 Fed. Reg. 49,025 (Sept. 21, 1993).

National Science Foundation *(organization)*
Abbreviated as "NSF." An independent U.S. government agency that sponsors, funds, and fosters research and development in science and engineering. The NSF became involved in wide area networking in the mid-

1980s and founded NSFNET, a network connecting academic and research institutions. NSFNET was later connected to the Advanced Research Projects Agency Network (ARPANET), and eventually developed into the Internet. The NSF has gradually withdrawn from its responsibilities with the Internet. Located at <http://www.nsf.gov>.

National Telecommunications and Information Agency *(organization)*
Abbreviated as "NTIA." The executive branch agency principally responsible for developing and articulating domestic and international telecommunications policies. Located at <http://www.ntia.doc.gov>.

navigate *(Internet)*
"[S]earching for, communicating with, and retrieving information from various web sites."
> *Brookfield Comm., Inc. v. West Coast Entertainment Corp.,* 174 F.3d 1036, 1044 (9th Cir. 1999).

navigation *(Internet)*
The process of moving between web sites and moving from page to page within a web site. Navigation can be aided by the use of search engines, hyperlinks, and other aids.

Annotation. "Navigating the Web is relatively straightforward. A user may either type the address of a known page or enter one or more keywords into a commercial 'search engine' in an effort to locate sites on a subject of interest. A particular Web page may contain the information sought by the 'surfer,' or, through its links, it may be an avenue to other documents located anywhere on the Internet. Users generally explore a given Web page, or move to another, by clicking a computer 'mouse' on one of the page's icons or links. Access to most Web pages is freely available, but some allow access only to those who have purchased the right from a commercial provider. The Web is thus comparable, from the readers' viewpoint, to both a vast library including millions of readily available and indexed publications and a sprawling mall offering goods and services."
> *Reno v. American Civil Liberties Union,* 521 U.S. 844, 852-53 (1997).

Navigator *(Internet; software)*
"[T]he first widely-popular graphical browser distributed for profit . . . was brought to market by the Netscape Communications Corporation in December 1994.
> *United States v. Microsoft Corp.,* 65 F. Supp. 2d 1, 5 (D.D.C. 1999) (Finding of Fact 17).

Related issues. "As soon as Netscape released Navigator on December 15, 1994, the product began to enjoy dramatic acceptance by the public; shortly after its release, consumers were already using Navigator far more than any other browser product."

> *United States v. Microsoft Corp.,* 65 F. Supp. 2d 1, 20 (D.D.C. 1999) (Finding of Fact 72).

See also **Web browser.**

NBA *(copyright; misappropriation)*
    See STATS.

NC *(technology)*
    1. Acronym for "Network Computer." *See* **network computer. 2.** Acronym for "Numerical Control." *See White Consol. Indus., Inc. v. Vega Servo-Control, Inc.,* 214 U.S.P.Q. (BNA) 796, 799 n.4 (S.D. Mich. 1982), *aff'd,* 218 U.S.P.Q. (BNA) 961 (Fed. Cir. 1983).

negligence *(tort)*
    ". . . is the lack of ordinary care. It is a failure to exercise that degree of care which a reasonably prudent person would have exercised under the same or similar circumstances."

> *Invacare Corp. v. Sperry Rand Corp.,* 612 F. Supp. 448, 453 (N.D. Ohio. 1984), *citing* W. Prosser, *Law of Torts* 143-45 (4th ed. 1971).

"Unless he represents that he has a greater or less skill or knowledge, one who undertakes to render services in the practice of a profession or trade is required to exercise the skill and knowledge normally possessed by members of that profession or trade in good standing in similar communities."

> Restatement (Second) of Torts § 299A (1965), cited approvingly in *Invacare Corp. v. Sperry Rand Corp.,* 612 F. Supp. 448, 453 (N.D. Ohio. 1984).

.net *(Internet)*
    "[The top-level domain] reserved to networks."

> *Intermatic, Inc. v. Toeppen,* 947 F. Supp. 1227, 1231 (N.D. Ill. 1996).

'net *(Internet)*
    Abbreviation for "Internet." *See* **Internet.**

net lease *(business)*
    "The lessees were responsible for all fees and taxes incurred in connection with the equipment (including income taxes payable by the lessor), and were required to keep the equipment insured at their expense. The lessees

were also required to maintain the equipment at their expense and to keep in force an IBM maintenance agreement . . . with respect to the equipment. . . . The lessor was not responsible to the lessees for the consequences of defects in, damage to, or loss or destruction of the equipment. In the event of repairable damage to the equipment, the lessees were required to repair it at their own expense. In the event of damage beyond repair, the lessees were required, in one case, to replace the equipment, and in two others to pay the lessor a casualty loss value (which was specified in schedules to the leases as a percentage of equipment cost, such percentage declining slightly each month), and in the fourth case to pay the greater of the casualty loss value (which was specified as a lump-sum dollar value that declines each month) or the full replacement cost."

Estate of Thomas, 84 U.S.T.C. Rep. 412, 424 (1985).

net revenues *(business)*

Gross revenues minus certain specified deductibles, such as returns, credits, cost of goods, and marketing costs.

Annotation. In agreements for the payment of royalties based on "net" revenues, it is very important to understand what deductions are permitted from gross revenues before the royalty calculation is made. To the extent each deductible item is to be determined objectively, there are fewer problems than when a deductible item is to be determined subjectively by the payor.

Sample clause. "For purposes of this paragraph, 'Net Revenues' shall be defined as all money received by [Commissioning Party] relating to the Title, less returns and credits against sales, cost of goods and a reasonable reserve for future returns."

NETCOM *(business)*

Abbreviation for "Netcom On-Line Communication Services, Inc." An Internet service provider that was a defendant in an important case concerning copyright infringement brought by the Religious Technology Center.

See *Religious Tech. Ctr. v. Netcom On-Line Comm. Servs., Inc.*, 907 F. Supp. 1361 (N.D. Cal. 1995).

netiquette *(Internet)*

Abbreviation for "Internet etiquette."

"[T]he informal rules and customs that have developed on the Internet. . . ."

Religious Tech. Ctr. v. Netcom On-Line Comm. Servs., Inc., 907 F. Supp. 1361, 1375 (N.D. Cal. 1995).

netizen *(Internet)*
Concatenation of "**network citizen**." A citizen (i.e., user) of the Internet.

Netscape Navigator *(software)*
A browser developed by a company of the same name, which was originally based on the Mosaic program developed at the National Center for Super-computing Applications ("NCSA"). The browser is now known as the "Net-scape Navigator." In 1998, Netscape was acquired by America Online, Inc.

network *(technology)*
"[A] linked group of computers.
> *American Civil Liberties Union v. Reno,* 929 F. Supp. 824, 830 (E.D. Pa. 1996), *aff'd, Reno v. American Civil Liberties Union,* 521 U.S. 844 (1997).

Annotation. "Many networks . . . are connected to other networks, which are in turn connected to other networks to communicate with computers on any other network in the system. This global Web of linked networks and computers is referred to as the Internet."
> *American Civil Liberties Union v. Reno,* 929 F. Supp. 824, 830 (E.D. Pa. 1996), *aff'd, Reno v. American Civil Liberties Union,* 521 U.S. 844 (1997).

See **computer network; LAN; network system.**

network access points *(Internet; technology; telecommunications)*
Abbreviated as "NAP." The places where the Internet backbone networks interconnect with each other.

network computer *(technology)*
Abbreviated as "NC." A low-priced, stripped down personal computer that acts primarily as a terminal for accessing the Internet. Most of the processing power, storage, and other capabilities are maintained by server computers with which network computers communicate. *See also* **thin client computer.** *See also* **network computer system.**

network computer system *(hardware; software)*
Also called a "thin client."

". . . typically contains central processing components with basic capabilities, certain key peripheral devices (such as a monitor, a keyboard, and a mouse), an operating system, and a browser. The system contains no mass storage, however, and it processes little if any data locally. Instead, the system receives processed data and software as needed from a server across a network."
> *United States v. Microsoft Corp.,* 65 F. Supp. 2d 1, 7 (D.D.C. 1999) (Finding of Fact 24).

Annotation. "Network computers can run applications residing on a designated server. . . . Moreover, a network computer system typically can run
applications residing on other servers, so long as those applications are
accessible through Web sites. The ability to run server-based applications is
not exclusive to network computer systems, however. Generally speaking,
any PC system equipped with a browser and an Internet connection is
capable of accessing applications hosted through Web sites."

> *United States v. Microsoft Corp.,* 65 F. Supp. 2d 1, 7 (D.D.C. 1999) (Finding
> of Fact 24).

"Since the network computing model relies heavily on the processing
power and memory of servers, the requirements for the user's hardware
(and thus the price of that hardware) are low relative to those of an Intel-
compatible PC system."

> *United States v. Microsoft Corp.,* 65 F. Supp. 2d 1, 7 (D.D.C. 1999) (Finding
> of Fact 24).

Related issues. "Only a few firms currently market network computer systems, and the systems have yet to attract substantial consumer demand. In
part, this is because PC systems, which can store and process data locally as
well as communicate with a server, have decreased so much in price as to call
into question the value proposition of buying a network computer system. . . .
Another reason for the limited demand for network computer systems is
the fact that few consumers are in a position to turn from PC systems to
network computer systems without making substantial sacrifices; for the
network computing option exhibits significant shortcomings for current
PC owners and first-time buyers alike. The problems of latency, congestion, asynchrony, and insecurity across a communications network, and
contention for limited processing and memory resources at the remote
server, can all result in a substantial derogation of computing performance.
Moreover, the owner of a network computer is required to enter into long-
term dependency upon the owner of a remote server in order to obtain
functionality that would reside within his control if he owned a PC system.
If network computing becomes a viable alternative to PC-based computing, it will be because innovation by the proponents of the network computing model overcomes these problems. . . ."

> *United States v. Microsoft Corp.,* 65 F. Supp. 2d 1, 8 (D.D.C. 1999) (Finding
> of Fact 26).

See also **network computer.**

network connection *(technology; telecommunications)*
The point at which a host computer is connected to a network.

network element *(telecommunications)*

"[A] facility or equipment used in the provision of a telecommunications service. Such term also includes features, functions, and capabilities that are provided by means of such facility or equipment, including subscriber numbers, databases, signaling systems, and information sufficient for billing and collection or used in the transmission, routing, or other provision of a telecommunications service."

47 U.S.C. § 153(29).

network license *(contract)*

A software license that permits the use of the software by anyone connected to a specified computer network.

network service provider *(business)*

Abbreviated as "NSP." The owner of a telephone, cable, or computer network that provides access for a fee. *See also* **Internet service provider.**

Network Solutions, Inc. *(business; Internet)*

Abbreviated as "NSI."

"[A] publicly traded corporation with its principal place of business in Herndon, Virginia. Under a contract with the National Science Foundation, NSI is the exclusive registrar of most Internet domain names."

Lockheed Martin Corp. v. Network Solutions, Inc., 985 F. Supp. 949, 951 (C.D. Cal. 1997).

"The registrar of Internet domain names . . . maintains a database of registrations and translates entered domain-name combinations into Internet protocol addresses."

Avery Dennison Corp. v. Sumpton, 189 F.3d 868, 872 (9th Cir. 1999).

Annotation. "The contract [with NSF] authorizes NSI to charge $100 for an initial two-year registration and $50 annually starting the third year. NSI registers approximately 100,000 Internet domain names per month. Registration applications are made via e-mail and in more than 90% of registrations no human intervention takes place. On average, a new registration occurs approximately once every 20 seconds.

"NSI performs two functions in the domain name system. First, it screens domain name applications against its registry to prevent repeated registrations of the same name. Second, it maintains a directory linking domain names with the IP numbers of domain name servers. The domain name servers, which are outside of NSI's control, connect domain names with Internet resources such as Web sites and e-mail systems.

"NSI does not make an independent determination of an applicant's right to use a domain name. Nor does NSI assign domain names; users may choose any available second-level domain name.

Lockheed Martin Corp. v. Network Solutions, Inc., 985 F. Supp. 949, 953 (C.D. Cal. 1997).

"Initially, the Internet Assigned Numbers Authority retained responsibility for both Internet Protocol number allocation and domain name registration. In 1991 and 1992, NSF, an independent agency of the federal government, assumed responsibility for coordinating and funding the management of the nonmilitary portion of the Internet infrastructure.

"In March 1992, NSF solicited competitive proposals to provide a variety of infrastructure services, including domain name registration services. NSF issued the solicitation pursuant to the National Science Found. Act of 1950, 42 U.S.C. §§1861-1887, as amended, and the Federal Grant and Cooperative Agreement Act, 31 U.S.C. §§6301-6308. In December 1992, after an independent review of the proposals responsive to the solicitation, NSF selected the bid from, and entered into a cooperative agreement with, Network Solutions, Inc., a private company."

Thomas v. Network Solutions, Inc., 176 F.3d 500, 504 (D.C. Cir. 1999) (footnotes omitted).

"[O]n the terms of the cooperative agreement, which took effect January 1, 1993, and, as amended, runs through September 30, 2000, at the latest, Network Solutions became the exclusive registry and exclusive registrar for the '.com,' '.org,' '.net,' and '.edu' top-level domains. As a registry, Network Solutions maintains a top-level domain's zone files, the directory databases listing domain names and their Internet Protocol numbers. As registrar, Network Solutions acts as go-between for domain-name holders and the registry, providing various services, including the registration of domain names on a first-come, first-served basis. The company also currently maintains the 'A' root server."

Thomas v. Network Solutions, Inc., 176 F.3d 500, 504-05 (D.C. Cir. 1999).

"NSI registers names on a first-come, first-served basis for a $100 registration fee. NSI does not make a determination about a registrant's right to use a domain name. However, NSI does require an applicant to represent and warrant as an express condition of registering a domain name that (1) the applicant's statements are true and the applicant has the right to use the requested domain name; (2) the 'use or registration of the domain name . . . does not interfere with or infringe the rights of any third party in any jurisdiction with respect to trademark, service mark, trade name, company name or any other intellectual property right'; and (3) the applicant is not seeking to use the domain name for any unlawful purpose, including unfair competition."

Panavision Int'l LP v. Toeppen, 141 F.3d 1316, 1319 (9th Cir. 1998).

"As of April 1999, Network Solutions, Inc. (NSI), the company previously responsible for registering domain names ending in '.com,' '.org,' and '.net' to owners, no longer holds a monopoly on this service. In April, the Internet Corporation for Assigned Names and Numbers (CANN) announced five companies, including America Online, which will compete with NSI as domain name registrars for a two-month test period, after which period NSI will be required to open the registration system and its database of domain names to all registrars approved by ICANN."

Washington Speakers Bureau, Inc. v. Leading Authorities, Inc., 49 F. Supp. 2d 496, 498 n.2 (E.D. Va. 1999).

Related issues. "[T]he court concludes that NSI's limited role as a registrar of domain names coupled with the inherent uncertainty in defining the scope of intellectual property rights in a trademark militates against finding that NSI knew or had reason to know of potentially infringing uses by others. Furthermore, contributory infringement doctrine does not impose upon NSI an affirmative duty to seek out potentially infringing uses of domain names by registrants."

Lockheed Martin Corp. v. Network Solutions, Inc., 985 F. Supp. 949, 951 (C.D. Cal. 1997).

". . . NSI has not made a commercial use of domain names as trademarks, and therefore cannot satisfy the commercial use element of dilution under 15 U.S.C. § 1125(c)."

Lockheed Martin Corp. v. Network Solutions, Inc., 985 F. Supp. 949, 951 (C.D. Cal. 1997).

"NSI's limited role as a registrar of domain names coupled with the inherent uncertainty in defining the scope of intellectual property rights in a trademark militates against finding that NSI knew or had reason to know of potentially infringing uses of others."

Lockheed Martin Corp. v. Network Solutions, Inc., 985 F. Supp. 949, 951 (C.D. Cal. 1997).

See also **NSI Domain Name Policy.**

network system *(telecommunications)*
[NEW ZEALAND] "This is a telecommunications network comprising terminals, terminal controllers, lines and modems (which convert digital

information so it can be carried by Telecom's voice grade lines) linked via a communications computer to the main computer."

> *Databank Systems Ltd. v. Commissioner of Inland Revenue* [1987], N.Z.L.R. 312 (H.C. Wellington).

See also **LAN; computer network.**

network worm *(criminal; software)*

"[A] program that scans a system or an entire network for available, unused space in which to run. Worms tend to tie up all computing resources in a system or on a network and effectively shut it down."

> Office of the Comptroller of the Currency, Infrastructure Threats from Cyber-Terrorists 2 (Mar. 19, 1999).

See also **worm.**

Newbie *(Internet)*

A new Internet user.

newsgroup(s) *(Internet)*

"[A]n electronic discussion group, serving as a bulletin board for users to post universally accessible messages, and to read and reply to those from others."

> *Religious Tech. Ctr. v. F.A.C.T.Net, Inc.,* 901 F. Supp. 1519, 1524 n.4 (D. Colo. 1995).

". . . thousands of discussion groups, arranged by subject matter. . . ."

> *Shea v. Reno,* 930 F. Supp. 916, 927 (S.D.N.Y. 1996).

Annotation. ". . . serve groups of regular participants, but these postings may be read by others as well. There are thousands of such groups, each serving to foster an exchange of information or opinion on a particular topic running the gamut from, say, the music of Wagner to Balkan politics to AIDS prevention to the Chicago Bulls. About 100,000 new messages are posted every day. In most newsgroups, postings are automatically purged at regular intervals."

> *Reno v. American Civil Liberties Union,* 521 U.S. 844, 851 (1997).

"There are newsgroups on more than fifteen thousand different subjects. In 1994, approximately 70,000 messages were posted to newsgroups each day, and those messages were distributed to the approximately 190,000 computers or computer networks that participate in the USENET newsgroup system. Once the messages reach the approximately 190,000 receiving computers or computer networks, they are available to individual users of those computers or computer networks. Collectively, almost 100,000 new messages (or 'articles') are posted to newsgroups each day."

> *American Civil Liberties Union v. Reno,* 929 F. Supp. 824, 835 (E.D. Pa. 1996), *aff'd, Reno v. American Civil Liberties Union,* 521 U.S. 844 (1997).

Related issues. "[O]ne person can reach many other users through bulletin board services, newsgroups and numerous other Internet-based means of communication."

> *Lockheed Martin Corp. v. Network Solutions, Inc.,* 985 F. Supp. 949, 951 (C.D. Cal. 1997).

"One wishing to read articles posted to a newsgroup must connect to a Usenet server and select the relevant group."

> *Shea v. Reno,* 930 F. Supp. 916, 930 (S.D.N.Y. 1996).

See also **bulletin board; computer bulletin board; moderated newsgroup; unmoderated newsgroup.**

newsreader *(Internet)*

"Once a message reaches a particular Usenet site, it is temporarily stored there so that individual users—running client software, known as a 'news-reader,' capable of sorting articles according to header information identifying the newsgroup to which the article was posted—can review and respond to the message."

> *Shea v. Reno,* 930 F. Supp. 916, 928 (S.D.N.Y. 1996).

See also **newsgroups; Usenet.**

NIC

(business)
Acronym for "Networked Information Center." The office that handles information for a computer network.

(hardware)
Acronym for "Network Interface Card." A card that plugs into a computer and permits the computer to operate on a specific computer network, such as ISA, PCI, and PCMCIA cards.

NII *(government; Internet)*
Acronym for "National Information Infrastructure."

"[A] seamless web of communications networks, computers, databases, and consumer electronics that will put vast amounts of information at users' fingertips."

> National Infrastructure Task Force, U.S. Dep't of Commerce, *The National Information Infrastructure: Agenda for Action,* 58 Fed. Reg. 49,025 (1993).

1980 Amendments to Copyright Act *(copyright)*
See Copyright Act 1980 Amendments.

NNTP *(Internet)*
Acronym for "Network News Transfer Protocol." The communications protocol used by Usenet newsgroups for subscribing, posting, and reading messages.

node *(telecommunications)*
A single unit within a communications network, used as a junction or connection point. It can be a terminal or a complete computer.

noise *(technology)*
Meaningless information in an analog or digital signal.

non-disclosure *(contract; trade secret)*
Can refer either to an agreement or a clause within an agreement that sets forth the obligations of one or more parties regarding the maintenance and/or disclosure of confidential information of the other party(ies).

"A trade secret is simply a piece of information the value of which to the creator of the information depends on its not being generally known. It is not a property right in the sense that a patent is, for it is perfectly lawful for a competitor to buy a product embodying a trade secret and unmask the secret by reverse engineering of the product. Only if the competitor (or anyone else for that matter) discovers the secret by breaking a contract or engaging in other unlawful or improper conduct can the individual or firm whose secret it was obtain a remedy.

"The significance of breach of contract in this connection is that a commercial secret rarely has value if it is known only to one person. Others must be let in on the secret and the remaining secrecy preserved by contracts forbidding disclosure to still others who might exploit it commercially to the harm of the secret holder."
Micro Data Base Sys., Inc. v. Dharma Sys., Inc., 148 F.3d 649, 657 (7th Cir. 1998).

Sample clause. "In the performance of this Agreement or in contemplation thereof, each party and its employees and agents may have access to private or confidential information owned or controlled by the other party relating to equipment, apparatus, programs, software, plans, drawings, specifications and other data (hereinafter 'Information'), and the Information may contain proprietary details and disclosures. All Information supplied by one party to the other which is clearly marked 'Proprietary,' or which is Licensed Software, or which is derived therefrom (collectively, 'Proprietary Information') shall remain the exclusive property of the party supplying same. The receiving party shall use a reasonable degree of care, which in any event shall not be less than the same degree of care which the receiving party uses to protect its own proprietary and confidential information, to keep, and have its employees and agents keep, confidential any and all Proprietary Information. In keeping therewith, the recipient shall not copy or publish or disclose the Proprietary Information to others, or authorize its employees, or agents or anyone else to copy, publish or disclose it to others, without the disclosing party's written approval, nor shall the receiving party make use of the Proprietary Information except for the purposes of executing its obligations hereunder, and shall return the Proprietary Information to the disclosing party at its request. These nondisclosure obligations will not apply to Proprietary Information which: (a) becomes generally known to the public by publication or by any means other than a breach of duty on the part of the recipient hereunder; (b) is information previously known to the recipient; (c) is information independently developed by or for the recipient; or (d) is information released by the owning party without restriction or released pursuant to a judicial or governmental decree."

nonexclusive license *(contract)*

"[A] license that does not preclude the licensor from transferring to other licensees the same information, informational rights, or contractual rights within the same scope. The term includes a consignment of a copy."
UCITA § 102(a)(47).

Related issues. "[A] non-exclusive license [to a copyrighted work] may be transferred without a written contract. The contract to transfer a non-exclusive license may be oral; and where evidence is lacking to prove the contract's existence, it may be inferred from the conduct of the parties."
Michaels v. Internet Entertainment Group, Inc., 5 F. Supp. 2d 823, 831 (C.D. Cal. 1998).

non-literal elements *(copyright)*

Elements of a copyrightable work other than the textual elements.

Related issues. "As a general matter, and to varying degrees, copyright protection extends beyond a literary work's strictly textual form to its non-literal components."
Computer Assocs. Int'l, Inc. v. Altai, Inc., 982 F.2d 693, 701 (2d Cir. 1992).
See also **non-literal infringement; nonliteral similarity; non-literal structures.**

non-literal infringement *(copyright)*
Infringement of the non-literal expression of a copyrightable work.

Related issues. "[A] party can prove non-literal infringement by showing access to the copyrighted work along with 'substantial similarity.'"
Interactive Networks, Inc. v. NTN Comm., Inc., 875 F. Supp. 1398, 1402-03 (N. Cal. 1995).
See also non-literal elements; nonliteral similarity; non-literal structures.

nonliteral similarity *(copyright)*
". . . can be thought of as paraphrasing or copying the essence or structure of a work just short of literal copying. Both literal and nonliteral similarity may warrant a finding of copyright infringement, although we note that the application of these theories becomes more difficult as cases assume an increasing technological complexity."
Bateman v. Mnemonic, Inc., 79 F.3d 1532, 1543-44 n.25 (11th Cir. 1995).
See also non-literal elements; non-literal infringement; non-literal structures.

non-literal structures *(copyright)*
Structural elements of a copyrightable work other than the text.

Related issues. "[I]f the non-literal structures of literary works are protected by copyright; and if computer programs are literary works, as we are told by the legislature; then the non-literal structures of computer programs are protected by copyright."
Computer Assocs. Int'l, Inc. v. Altai, Inc., 982 F.2d 693, 702 (2d Cir. 1992).
See also non-literal elements; non-literal infringement; nonliteral similarity.

nonobviousness *(patent)*
"A patent may not be obtained though the invention is not identically disclosed or described as set forth in section 102 of this title, if the differences between the subject matter sought to be patented and the prior art are such that the subject matter as a whole would have been obvious at the time the invention was made to a person having ordinary skill in the art to which said subject matter pertains. Patentability shall not be negatived by the manner in which the invention is made."
35 U.S.C. §103.

non-proprietary node
An Internet access point available to the public.

non-recoverable encryption *(encryption; software)*
An encryption product that does not permit access to the key or other information by which ciphertext can be decrypted, except for the user's knowledge of the key.

notice *(contract)*
" . . . of a fact means knowledge of the fact, receipt of notification of the fact, or reason to know the fact exists."
UCITA § 102(a)(48).

notify
"[T]o take such steps as may be reasonably required to inform the other person in the ordinary course, whether or not the other person actually comes to know of it."
UCITA § 102(a)(49).

(electronic commerce)
"[T]o communicate a fact to another person in a manner reasonably likely under the circumstances to impart knowledge of the information to the other person."
Wash. Rev. Code § 19.34.020(20).

novation *(contract)*
"[W]here a party to [a] contract expressly agrees to accept the responsibility of the other party's assignee in the stead and place of that assignor."
Smith v. Wrene, 199 Neb. 753, 760, 261 N.W.2d 620, 625 (1978).

Sample clause. "None of the duties prescribed by this Agreement, either express or implied, are subject to novation unless such novation is expressly agreed to in writing by each party to this Agreement."

novelty *(trade secret)*
"An overwhelming majority of authorities on the subject ruled that novelty and uniqueness are not a requirement for trade secret protection."
Structural Dynamics Res. Corp. v. Engineering Mechanics Res. Corp., 401 F. Supp. 1102, 1117 (E.D. Mich. 1975).

"[No trade secret protection, where] [a]ll of the individual features [of the business system] are either sufficiently obvious that anyone entering the reminder letter business would be likely to incorporate them into his system, or easily duplicated by anyone with legitimate, publicly available knowledge of Computer Care's business."

Computer Care v. Service Sys. Enters., Inc., 982 F.2d 1063, 1075 (7th Cir. 1992).

See also **invention** (trade secret); **originality** (trade secret).

NSF *(organization)*

Acronym for "National Science Foundation." *See* **National Science Foundation.**

"In 1987, the NSF awarded grants to IBM, MCI, and Merit to develop the NSFNET, a national high-speed network based on Internet protocols. The NSFNET, the largest of the governmental networks, provided the 'backbone' to connect other networks serving more than 4,000 research and educational institutions throughout the country. In 1992, Congress gave the NSF statutory authority to allow commercial activity on the NSFNET. *See id.* This facilitated connections between NSFNET and newly forming commercial network service providers, paving the way for today's Internet."

Thomas v. Network Solutions, Inc., 176 F.3d 500, 504 n.5 (D.C. Cir. 1999) (citations omitted).

NSI *(organization)*

Acronym for "Network Solutions, Inc." *See* **Network Solutions, Inc.**

NSI Domain Name Policy *(Internet)*

"In 1995, NSI responded to the problem of conflicting claims to domain names by instituting a domain name dispute policy. Under the current policy, in effect since September 9, 1996, NSI requires applicants to represent and warrant that their use of a particular domain name does not interfere with the intellectual property rights of third parties. Under the policy, if a trademark holder presents NSI with a United States Patent and Trademark Office registration of a trademark identical to a currently registered domain name, NSI will require the domain name holder to prove that it has a pre-existing right to use the name. If the domain name holder fails to do so, NSI will cancel the registration. NSI's policy has been criticized as favoring trademark owners over domain name holders, and favoring owners of federally registered marks over owners of non-registered marks, because owners of federally registered marks can invoke NSI's policy to effectively enjoin the use of identical domain names without having to make any showing of infringement or dilution. If a trademark holder and domain name registrant take their dispute to court, NSI will deposit the domain name in the registry of the court. This process maintains the status quo; the domain name remains active while in the registry of the court."

Lockheed Martin Corp. v. Network Solutions, Inc., 985 F. Supp. 949, 953 (C.D. Cal. 1997) (citations omitted).

See also **Network Solutions, Inc.**

NTIA *(organization)*

Acronym for "National Telecommunications and Information Agency." *See* **National Telecommunications and Information Agency.**

NTSC *(hardware)*

Acronym for "National Television Systems Committee" of the Electronics Industry Association. The standard format for commercial color television broadcasting and reception in North America, Japan, and parts of South America. The NTSC format has 525 scan lines and 30 frames per second.

numerical control *(technology)*

". . . involves automatically moving a machine tool under the control of a prerecorded part program for precisely cutting a particular workpiece or part."

White Consol. Indus., Inc. v. Vega Servo-Control, Inc., 214 U.S.P.Q. (BNA) 796, 799 (S.D. Mich. 1982), *aff'd,* 218 U.S.P.Q. (BNA) 961 (Fed. Cir. 1983).

object code *(software)*

"[T]he version of a program in which the source code language is converted or translated into the machine language of the computer with which it is to be used."

> *CONTU Final Report* 21 n.109 (1978), *quoted in Williams Elecs., Inc. v. Artic Int'l, Inc.,* 685 F.2d 870, 876 n.7 (3d Cir. 1982).

"[A] program written in machine language that can be executed directly by the computer's CPU without need for translation."

> *Lotus Dev. Corp. v. Paperback Software Int'l,* 740 F. Supp. 37, 44 (D. Mass. 1990).

"[A] translation of the source code language into the machine language of the computer (e.g., binary coding using zeros and ones or hexadecimal coding using letters and numbers or octal coding using zero to seven) that the computer executes. Only instructions expressed in object code can be used 'directly' by the computer. Thus the source code is converted into electrical impulses to carry out the tasks set forth in the source code. The binary code of machine code (or object code) is virtually unintelligible to programmers."

> *CONTU Final Report* 54 n.109 (1978).

"[T]he representation of the program in machine language (e.g., using binary coding zeros and ones or hexadecimal coding using letters and numbers or octal code using 0 and 7) which the computer executes."

> U.S. Copyright Office, *Compendium II of Copyright Office Practices* § 321.02, *quoted in Manufacturing Technology, Inc. v. Cams, Inc.,* 706 F. Supp. 984, 991 n.10 (D. Conn. 1989).

"In order to operate a computer, source code must be translated into computer readable form, or 'object code.' Object code uses only two symbols, 0 and 1, in combinations which represent the alphanumeric characters of the source code."

> *Sega Enters. Ltd. v. Accolade, Inc.,* 977 F.2d 1510, 1514 n.2 (1992).

"[A] binary code, simply a concatenation of '0's and '1's. In every program, it is the object code, not the source code, that directs the computer to perform its functions. The object code is therefore the final instruction to the computer."

> *Whelan Assocs., Inc. v. Jaslow Dental Lab., Inc.,* 797 F.2d 1222, 1230-31 (3d Cir. 1986).

"Computer program expressed as sequence of ones and zeros, readable only by machines."

> *E.F. Johnson Co. v. Uniden Corp. of Am.,* 623 F. Supp. 1485, 1488 (D. Minn. 1985).

"[S]tatement[s] in machine language are referred to as written in 'object code.'

> *Apple Computer, Inc. v. Franklin Computer Corp.,* 714 F.2d 1240, 1243 (3d Cir. 1983), *cert. dism.,* 464 U.S. 1033 (1984).

"[M]achine language useable by the machine."

> *Apple Computer, Inc. v. Formula Int'l, Inc.,* 562 F. Supp. 775, 778 (C.D. Cal. 1983), *aff'd,* 725 F.2d 521 (9th Cir. 1984).

"A program is . . . translated into computer-readable language called object code (binary machine language)."

> *Pearl Sys., Inc. v. Competition Elecs., Inc.,* 8 U.S.P.Q.2d (BNA) 1520, 1520 n.1 (S.D. Fla. 1988).

"[T]he engineer's instructions translated into a language that only the computer hardware can 'read' to become a functioning machine. It is an essential part of the machine in that sense."

> *In re Bedford Computer Corp.,* 62 Bankr. 555, 562 n.6 (D.N.H. 1986).

"Computers operate by sensing the presence or absence of these electrical charges at each cycle of their operation. The presence or absence of such charge is represented by a '1' or a '0' respectively, in written program representations called object code. . . . Computers understand only these pulses."

> *Jostens, Inc. v. National Computer Sys., Inc.,* 318 N.W.2d 691, 695 n.3 (Minn. 1982).

"Computers do not act directly on such source code instructions, however. Instead, the source code must be transformed, within the machine, into a proportionately enormous series of binary, 'machine readable,' 'object code' instructions: the presence or absence of an electrical charge, which may be represented by the values '1' or '0,' at each cycle of a computer's operation is what ultimately directs the computer's activity."

> *Midway Mfg. Co. v. Strohon,* 564 F. Supp. 741, 750 (N.D. Ill. 1983).

"[T]he basic set of instructions that the computer actually executes, and consists of a series of numbers."

> *Dynamic Solutions, Inc. v. Planning & Control, Inc.*, 646 F. Supp. 1329, 1332 n.2 (S.D.N.Y. 1986).

"The 'object code' version is in machine readable language and is unintelligible to humans."

> *Rav Com., Inc. v. Phillip Bros., Inc.*, 1988 Copr. L. Dec. ¶ 26,263, 3d ¶ (S.D.N.Y. 1988).

"[T]he software program used to operate the computer."

> *Hudson v. Good Rush Messenger Services, Inc.*, CCH Copr. L. Serv. ¶ 26,089 (S.D.N.Y. 1987).

"The computer readable form, which operates on a binary system . . . ."

> *Cadence Design Sys., Inc. v. Avant! Corp.*, 125 F.3d 824, 825 n.2 (9th Cir. 1997).

[CANADA] "[T]he program in its electrical code form."

> *Apple Computer, Inc. v. Mackintosh Computers Ltd.* (1986), 28 D.L.R. (4th) 178 (Fed. T.D.).

Annotation. "Software engineers generally do not create software in object code — the series of binary digits (1's and 0's)—which tells a computer what to do because it would be enormously difficult, cumbersome and time-consuming. Instead, software engineers use high-level computer programming languages such as 'C' or 'Basic' to create source code as a shorthand method for telling the computer to perform a desired function."

> *Bernstein v. United States Dept. of Justice*, 176 F.3d 1132, 1147-48 (9th Cir. 1999) (Nelson, T.G., dissenting).

Related issues. "Once a programmer has access to the source code of a program, he is able to determine the construction of the program and write his own version. For this reason, source code programs are typically compiled (translated) into and sold as object code or machine language, which is not discernible to even an expert programmer, but which is readily usable by the computer."

> *United States v. Brown*, 925 F.2d 1301, 1303 n.4 (10th Cir. 1991).

"We express no opinion regarding whether object code manifests a 'close enough nexus to expression' to warrant application of the prior restraints doctrine."

> *Bernstein v. United States Dept. of Justice*, 176 F.3d 1132, 1141 n.15 (9th Cir. 1999).

"Object code often is directly executable by the computer into which it is entered. It sometimes contains instructions, however, that are readable only by computers containing a particular processor, such as a Pentium processor, or a specific operating system such as Microsoft Windows. In such instances, a computer lacking the specific processor or operating system can execute the object code only if it has an emulator program that simulates the necessary processor or operating system or if the code first is run through a translator program that converts it into object code readable by that computer."

> *Universal City Studios, Inc. v. Reimerdes*, 111 F. Supp. 2d 294, 306 n.18 (S.D.N.Y. 2000) (footnotes omitted).

"The distinction between source and object code is not as crystal clear as first appears. Depending upon the programming language, source code may contain many 1's and 0's and look a lot like object code or may contain many instructions derived from spoken human language. Programming languages the source code for which approaches object code are referred to as low level source code while those that are more similar to spoken language are referred to as high level source code."

> *Universal City Studios, Inc. v. Reimerdes*, 111 F. Supp. 2d 294, 306 (S.D.N.Y. 2000).

See also **binary code; machine language; object program.**

object program *(software)*

"[A] program written in machine language that can be executed directly by the computer's CPU without need for translation."

> *Lotus Dev. Corp. v. Paperback Software Int'l,* 740 F. Supp. 37, 44 (D. Mass. 1990).

"[A] conversion of the machine language into a device commanding a series of electrical impulses. Object programs, which enter into the mechanical process itself, cannot be read without the aid of special equipment and cannot be understood by even the most highly trained programmers."

> *Data Cash Sys., Inc. v. JS&A Group, Inc.,* 480 F. Supp. 1063, 1065 (N.D. Ill. 1979), *aff'd,* 628 F.2d 1038, 1040 (7th Cir. 1980).

"[A] program readable by a computer."

> *Management Technologies, Inc. v. Manufacturers Hanover Trust Co.,* 1 Computer L. Cas. (CCH) ¶ 46,040, at 60,955, 60,956 (N.Y. Supreme Ct. 1989).

See also **binary code; machine language; object code.**

obscenity *(criminal)*

Material which, to the average person, applying contemporary community standards, and taken as a whole: (i) predominantly appeals to prurient interests; (ii) lacks serious literary, artistic, political, or scientific value; and (iii) depicts or describes nudity, sex, or excretion in a patently offensive way.

Annotation. "The Government could also completely ban obscenity and child pornography from the Internet. No Internet speaker has a right to engage in these forms of speech, and no Internet listener has a right to receive them. Child pornography and obscenity have 'no constitutional protection, and the government may ban [them] outright in certain media, or in all.'"

> *American Civil Liberties Union v. Reno,* 929 F. Supp. 824, 865 (E.D. Pa. 1996), *aff'd, Reno v. American Civil Liberties Union,* 521 U.S. 844 (1997) (citation omitted).

See also **child pornography; pornography.**

obsolete *(technology)*
". . . refers to the lessee's technical or functional requirements; the equipment, or some part of it (becoming) technologically outmoded or no longer capable of handling the lessee's day-to-day business needs."

> *Computer Sys. of Am. v. Western Reserve Life Assur. Co. of Ohio,* 475 N.E.2d 745, 19 Mass. App. 430, 435 (1985).

OCO *(software)*
Acronym for "Object Code Only."

> *IBM Corp. v. Fujitsu Ltd.,* Copyright L. Rep. (CCH) ¶ 20,513, at 11,392, 11,400 n.21 (Am. Arb. Ass'n 1988).

OCR *(technology)*
Acronym for "Optical Character Recognition." A device for scanning text and images into digital computer files.

octal coding *(software)*
"Machine code that uses zero to seven."

> U.S. Copyright Office, *Compendium of Copyright Office Practices* II, at 300-16 (1984).

OECD *(organization)*
Acronym for "Organization for Economic Cooperation and Development."

"The Organization for Economic Cooperation and Development (OECD), whose membership consists of twenty-four industrialized countries, including the United States, Canada, most Western European countries, and Japan. . . ."

> Department of Commerce, *Inquiry on Privacy Issues Relating to Private Sector Use of Telecommunications-Related Personal Information,* 59 Fed. Reg. 6841, 6848 (Feb. 11, 1994).

Annotation. "The OECD has been active since the 1970s in considering the impact of computers and telecommunications technologies on the international flow of data. In 1978, it instructed a 'Group of Experts' to develop a set of basic guidelines to govern transborder data flow and the privacy of personal data. The Group of Experts adopted 'Guidelines on the Protection of Privacy and Transborders Data Flows,' in 1980.

* * *

"The OECD guidelines include the following eight principles:

• There should be limits on the collection of personal data, and it should be obtained fairly and lawfully and, where appropriate, with the data subject's consent.

• Personal data should be accurate, complete, current, and relevant to the purposes for which it is obtained.

• Personal data should be used for legitimate, specified purposes and the data subject should be notified of any changes in those purposes.

• Personal data should not be used for purposes other than those for which it was originally intended, except with the consent of the data subject or legal authorization.

• Personal data should be protected by reasonable security safeguards.

• There should be a policy of openness about practices and policies related to the collection and use of personal data.

• Individuals should have the ability to examine and correct data relating to them upon request.

• Organizations should have a data controller who is responsible for complying with the above principles."

> Department of Commerce, *Inquiry on Privacy Issues Relating to Private Sector Use of Telecommunications-Related Personal Information,* 59 Fed. Reg. 6841, 6848-49 & n.58 (Feb. 11, 1994).

Related issues. The OECD web site is located at <http://www.oecd.org>.

OEM *(business)*

Acronym for "Original Equipment Manufacturer." More recently, many companies replace the term with "Value Added Reseller," or VAR. Also refers to the practice of bundling.

"[A] company which purchases hardware . . . and systems software . . . from a vendor and adds value, in the form of applications software or other components, and then resells both the hardware and software at a markup to end users. An OEM is thus a type of middleman in the computer business."

> *Accusystems, Inc. v. Honeywell Information Sys., Inc.,* 580 F. Supp. 474, 476 n.2 (S.D.N.Y. 1984).

"[A]n intermediate purchaser who purchases Data General's equipment for resale after incorporating the equipment into a system which includes substantial hardware and/or software developed or manufactured by the purchaser and which represents a significant enhancement transformation of the equipment purchased from Data General, both as to value and function."

> Data Gen. Marketing Practices, 1980-1 Trade Cas. (CCH) ¶ 63,045, at 77,198 n.4 (1979).

Related issues. "An OEM typically installs a copy of Windows onto one of its PCs before selling the package to a consumer under a single price."

> *United States v. Microsoft Corp.,* 65 F. Supp. 2d 1, 4 (D.D.C. 1999) (Finding of Fact 10).

"OEMs are the most important direct customers for operating systems for Intel-compatible PCs."

> *United States v. Microsoft Corp.,* 65 F. Supp. 2d 1, 15 (D.D.C. 1999) (Finding of Fact 54).

See also **bundling; original equipment manufacturer(s); VAR.**

off-line data processing system *(technology)*

". . . exists where data is entered by means of punch cards or computer tapes rather than directly by a computer terminal."

> *Liberty Fin. Management Corp. v. Beneficial Data Processing Corp.,* 670 S.W.2d 40, 45 (Mo. App. 1984).

OLS *(Internet)*

Acronym for "Online Services." *See* **Online service(s).**

". . . such as America Online ('AOL'), Prodigy, and the Microsoft Network ('MSN') offer, in addition to Internet access, various services and an array of proprietary content."

> *United States v. Microsoft Corp.,* 65 F. Supp. 2d 1, 5 (D.D.C. 1999) (Finding of Fact 15).

1-by-1 GIF *(technology)*

See **web bug.**

one-call system *(telecommunications)*

"[A] communications system established for the purpose of providing one telephone number (that of a 'one-call center') for excavators and the general public to call to give notification of their plans to excavate, tunnel, or demolish structures at a particular site where underground utilities might exist. The one-call center processes the notification information and disseminates it to the system's participating members who might be affected by the work, so that they can take steps to avoid damages to the underground utilities."

Benard v. Hoff, 2 Computer L. Cas. (CCH) ¶ 46,247, at 61,928, 61,929 (D. Md. 1989).

one-off *(multimedia)*

Also called glass master or worm. A writable CD-ROM disc containing the actual file images for a multimedia product, and which plays on a CD-ROM drive. *See also* **glass master; worm.**

one-to-many messaging *(Internet)*

"The Internet also contains automatic mailing list services (such as 'listservs'), [also referred to by witnesses as 'mail exploders'] that allow communications about particular subjects of interest to a group of people. For example, people can subscribe to a 'listserv' mailing list on a particular topic of interest to them. The subscriber can submit messages on the topic to the listserv that are forwarded (via e-mail), either automatically or through a human moderator overseeing the listserv, to anyone who has subscribed to the mailing list. A recipient of such a message can reply to the message and have the reply also distributed to everyone on the mailing list. This service provides the capability to keep abreast of developments or events in a particular subject area. Most listserv-type mailing lists automatically forward all incoming messages to all mailing list subscribers. There are thousands of such mailing list services on the Internet, collectively with hundreds of thousands of subscribers. Users of 'open' listservs typically can add or remove their names from the mailing list automatically, with no direct human involvement. Listservs may also be 'closed,' i.e., only allowing for one's acceptance into the listserv by a human moderator."

American Civil Liberties Union v. Reno, 929 F. Supp. 824, 834 (E.D. Pa. 1996), aff'd, Reno v. American Civil Liberties Union, 521 U.S. 844 (1997).

one-to-one messaging *(Internet)*

"One method of communication on the Internet is via electronic mail, or 'e-mail,' comparable in principle to sending a first class letter. One can address and transmit a message to one or more other people. E-mail on the Internet is not routed through a central control point, and can take many and varying paths to the recipients. Unlike postal mail, simple e-mail generally is not "sealed" or secure, and can be accessed or viewed on intermediate computers between the sender and recipient (unless the message is encrypted)."

> *American Civil Liberties Union v. Reno,* 929 F. Supp. 824, 834 (E.D. Pa. 1996), *aff'd, Reno v. American Civil Liberties Union,* 521 U.S. 844 (1997).

See also **e-mail.**

one-way hash function *(technology)*

"[W]here it is desirable that it be impossible to derive the input data given only the hash function's output. . . ."

> *Bernstein v. United States Dept. of Justice,* 176 F.3d 1132, 1135 n.1 (9th Cir. 1999).

See also **hash function.**

on-line *(Internet)*

"(1) Pertaining to a user's ability to interact with a computer, (2) Pertaining to a user's access to computer via terminal, (3) Pertaining to the operation of a functional unit that is under the continual control of a computer. The term 'on line' is also used to describe a user's access to a computer via a terminal."

> *In re TBG, Inc.,* 229 U.S.P.Q. (BNA) 759, 759 n.1 (T.T.A.B. 1986).

"[C]apable of being displayed and 'accessed' by increasingly common interactive computer services."

> *Shea v. Reno,* 930 F. Supp. 916, 925 (S.D.N.Y. 1996).

online data processing *(technology)*

". . . refers to a system by which one communicates directly with the computer and obtains immediate responses from the computer via computer terminals, provided that one's communications are in a format that the computer is programmed to understand."

> *Liberty Fin. Management Corp. v. Beneficial Data Processing Corp.,* 670 S.W.2d 40, 45 (Mo. App. 1984).

". . . requires the use of computer terminals at the thrift institution's teller windows connected via telephone lines to a main computer located on the premises of a data processing service center. As each depositor's transaction is processed through the institution's teller terminal, the data is transmitted electronically to the main computer, where the particular customer's account information is stored in the computer's memory bank. The computer up-dates the account information and then instantaneously transmits the data back to the teller's window terminal. The entire process normally occurs within one or two seconds."

> *ADAPSO v. FHLB of Cincinnati,* 421 F. Supp. 384, 387 n.3 (S.D. Ohio 1976).

online database search *(technology)*
"[E]ach execution of a command by a subscriber that requests information to be located or retrieved from a file."
> *Meites v. City of Chicago,* 1 Computer Cas. (CCH) ¶ 46,115, at 61,314, 61,316 (Ill. App. 1989).

online service(s) *(Internet)*
Abbreviated as "OLS."
> *United States v. Microsoft Corp.,* 65 F. Supp. 2d 1, 5 (D.D.C. 1999) (Finding of Fact 15).

Services, such as e-mail, chat rooms, search engines, etc., provided over a proprietary network, like America Online.

Annotation. "These online services offer nationwide computer networks (so that subscribers can dial-in to a local telephone number), and the services provide extensive and well organized content within their own proprietary computer networks. In addition to allowing access to the extensive content available within each online service, the services also allow subscribers to link to the much larger resources of the Internet. Full access to the online service (including access to the Internet) can be obtained for modest monthly or hourly fees. The major commercial online services have almost twelve million individual subscribers across the United States."
> *American Civil Liberties Union v. Reno,* 929 F. Supp. 824, 833 (E.D. Pa. 1996), *aff'd, Reno v. American Civil Liberties Union,* 521 U.S. 844 (1997).

". . . allows subscribers to gain access to the Internet while providing extensive content within their own proprietary networks."
> *Shea v. Reno,* 930 F. Supp. 916, 926 (S.D.N.Y. 1996).

See also **commercial on-line services.**
See **OLS.**

online service provider *(Internet)*
Abbreviated as "OSP."

"[C]ompanies and nongovernmental institutions such as libraries and schools that provide access to the Internet and other online services, and groups that create content that is delivered over these networks."
> The White House, *A Framework for Global Electronic Commerce* 1 n.1 (July 1, 1997).

open architecture *(hardware)*
". . . meant that IBM did not endeavor to keep secret its codes, programs, or internal workings of its computers. . . . IBM published these specifica-

tions so that third-party vendors would be encouraged to make products and/or software that would be compatible with the IBM-PC computer."

Princeton Graphics Operating L.P. v. NEC Home Elecs. (U.S.A.), Inc., 732 F. Supp. 1258, 1260 n.4 (S.D.N.Y. 1990).

Open Software Foundation *(organization)*

"[I]n May 1988, a number of important computer manufacturers—including defendants Hewlett-Packard and Digital Equipment Corp.—formed the Open Software Foundation as a non-profit joint research and development venture. OSF registered under the National Cooperative Research Act of 1984, 15 U.S.C. § 4301, although that status has no direct importance for the issues before us. At least one of OSF's professed objectives was to develop an alternative Unix operating system, denominated OSF-1, as a competitor to the Unix system being developed jointly by AT&T and Sun Microsystems."

Addamax Corp. v. Open Software Found., Inc., 152 F.3d 48, 50 (1st Cir. 1998).

open source *(software)*

"[A] software development model by which the source code to a computer program is made available publicly under a license that gives users the right to modify and redistribute the program. The program develops through this process of modification and redistribution and through a process by which users download sections of code from a web site, modify that code, upload it to the same web site, and merge the modified sections into the original code."

Universal City Studios, Inc. v. Reimerdes, 111 F. Supp. 2d 294, 305 n.6 (S.D.N.Y. 2000) (footnotes omitted).

Annotation. Since application developers working under an open-source model are not looking to recoup their investment and make a profit by selling copies of their finished products, they are free from the imperative that compels proprietary developers to concentrate their efforts on Windows. . . . Fortunately for Microsoft . . . there are only so many developers in the world willing to devote their talents to writing, testing, and debugging software pro bono publico. A small corps may be willing to concentrate its efforts on popular applications, such as browsers and office productivity applications, that are of value to most users. It is unlikely, though, that a sufficient number of open-source developers will commit to developing and continually updating the large variety of applications that an operating system would need to attract in order to present a significant number of users with a viable alternative to Windows."

United States v. Microsoft Corp., 65 F. Supp. 2d 1, 14-15 (D.D.C. 1999) (Finding of Fact 51).

operating program(s) *(software)*
"[G]enerally internal to the computer and is designed only to facilitate the operating of the application program."
> *Apple Computer, Inc. v. Franklin Computer Corp.,* 545 F. Supp. 812, 814 (E.D. Pa. 1982), *rev'd,* 714 F.2d 1240 (3d Cir. 1983), *cert. dism.,* 464 U.S. 1033 (1984).

See also operating system; operating system program(s); operational program(s).

operating system *(software)*
Abbreviated as "OS."

"[A] complex computer program written in the basic machine language. In one aspect, the operating system is an interpreter, accepting instructions written in a more sophisticated language, and translating those instructions into the basic machine language instructions comprehendible by the computer hardware. In another aspect, the operating system acts as a controller, coordinating the activities of the various pieces of hardware with each other. Because of this latter task, the operating system is unique to the specific hardware configuration."
> *Response of Carolina, Inc. v. Leasco Response, Inc.,* 537 F.2d 1307, 1326 (5th Cir. 1976).

". . . provides the basic instructions for the operation of a computer in any practical application. . . . [It] essentially serves as the liaison between the applications software and hardware."
> *In re Data Gen. Corp. Antitrust Litigation,* 490 F. Supp. 1089, 1098 (N.D. Cal. 1980).

"[A] set of computer programs which guide and control the basic function of a computer."
> *Innovation Data Processing, Inc. v. IBM Corp.,* 585 F. Supp. 1470, 1472 (D.N.J. 1984).

"[T]he brain of the computer. It determines the computer's capability to store memory, operate peripheral items such as view terminals, and do other basic operating chores. The operating system itself is in the form of a disc or tape, and is loaded into a computer to start its operation."
> *Hubco Data Prods. Corp. v. Management Assistance, Inc.,* 219 U.S.P.Q. (BNA) 450, 451 (D. Idaho 1983).

"[A]n organized collection of software used to assist and in part to control the operations of a computer. . . . Operating systems generally manage the internal functions of the computer, and facilitate use of applications software (e.g., accounts receivable and payroll programs). . . . They co-ordinate the reading and writing of data between the internal memory and the external devices (e.g., disc drives, keyboard, printer), perform basic housekeeping functions for the computer system, and prepare the computer to execute applications programs. . . . Operating system programs for mainframe computers are extremely large and complex, involving hundreds of thousands (and in some cases millions) of lines of code."

IBM Corp. v. Fujitsu Ltd., Copyright L. Rep. (CCH) ¶ 20,517, at 11,392, 11,393 n.1 (Am. Arb. Ass'n 1988) (citations omitted).

"[A] term which is used to describe a certain type of program. In essence, it is characterized by a program that controls other programs.

"There is apparently beyond that statement no general agreement as to what software programs should be made, or described to be a part of an operating system, although we can identify which programs have, in fact, been made part of an operating system.

"The size of the operating system can vary greatly, depending on the number of programming functions included. This control function contained in the operating system is critical to the efficient function of the computer."

United Software Corp. v. Sperry Rand Corp., 5 Computer L. Serv. Rep. 1492, 1496 (E.D. Pa. 1974).

"[P]rograms that control the basic functions of the computer hardware, such as the efficient utilization of memory and the starting and stopping of application programs."

Lotus Dev. Corp. v. Paperback Software Int'l, 740 F. Supp. 37, 43 (D. Mass. 1990).

"[A] software program that controls the allocation and use of computer resources (such as central processing unit time, main memory space, disk space, and input/output channels)."

United States v. Microsoft Corp., 65 F. Supp. 2d 1, 3-4 (D.D.C. 1999) (Finding of Fact 2).

Annotation. "An operating system that consists of a variety of separate operating programs is in a sense a part of the machine; it provides the functioning system that allows the user to progress in an orderly fashion as he moves through the physical process of keying information into a computer. The operating system instructs the machine how to use this information and receives the solutions to the problems posed. Once in the machine, either permanently implanted as a ROM or entered from a floppy disk, an operating system is very nearly 'transparent'; the user is not aware of the work and order of the work it is processing."

Apple Computer, Inc. v. Franklin Computer Corp., 545 F. Supp. 812, 814 (E.D. Pa. 1982), *rev'd,* 714 F.2d 1240 (3d Cir. 1983), *cert. dism.*, 464 U.S. 1033 (1984).

"The operating system also supports the functions of software programs, called 'applications,' that perform specific user-oriented tasks. The operating system supports the functions of applications by exposing interfaces, called 'application programming interfaces,' or 'APIs.' These are synapses at which the developer of an application can connect to invoke pre-fabricated blocks of code in the operating system. These blocks of code in turn perform crucial tasks, such as displaying text on the computer screen. Because it supports applications while interacting more closely with the PC system's hardware, the operating system is said to serve as a 'platform.'"

United States v. Microsoft Corp., 65 F. Supp. 2d 1, 4 (D.D.C. 1999) (Finding of Fact 2).

Related issues. "An operating system designed to run on an Intel-compatible PC will not function on a non-Intel-compatible PC, nor will an operating system designed for a non-Intel-compatible PC function on an Intel-compatible one."

United States v. Microsoft Corp., 65 F. Supp. 2d 1, 4 (D.D.C. 1999) (Finding of Fact 4).

"Consumer interest in a PC operating system derives primarily from the ability of that system to run applications. The consumer wants an operating system that runs not only types of applications that he knows he will want to use, but also those types in which he might develop an interest later. Also, the consumer knows that if he chooses an operating system with enough demand to support multiple applications in each product category, he will be less likely to find himself straitened later by having to use an application whose features disappoint him. Finally, the average user knows that, generally speaking, applications improve through successive versions. He thus wants an operating system for which successive generations of his favorite applications will be released—promptly at that."

United States v. Microsoft Corp., 65 F. Supp. 2d 1, 11 (D.D.C. 1999) (Finding of Fact 37).

See also **operating program(s); operating system program(s); operational program(s); operations system software.**

operating system program(s) *(software)*

". . . generally manage the internal functions of the computer or facilitate use of application programs."

Apple Computer, Inc. v. Franklin Computer Corp., 714 F.2d 1240, 1243 (3d Cir. 1983), *cert. dism.*, 464 U.S. 1033 (1984).

". . . such as DOS, XENIX, and OS/2—are programs that control the basic functions of the computer hardware, such as the efficient utilization of memory and the starting and stopping of application programs."

Lotus Dev. Corp. v. Paperback Software Int'l, 740 F. Supp. 37, 43 (D. Mass. 1990).

[CANADA] "Operating system programs are designed primarily to facilitate the operation of application programs and perform tasks common to any application program, such as reading and writing data to a disc. Without them, each application program would need to duplicate their functions."

Apple Computer, Inc. v. Computermat, Inc. (1983), 1 C.I.P.R. 1 (Ont. H.C.); *Apple Computer, Inc. v. Mackintosh Computers Ltd.* (1985), 3 C.I.P.R. 133 (Fed. T.D.).

See also operating program(s); operating system; operating system software; operational program(s); operations system software.

operating system software *(software)*

"[A] computer program designed solely to help someone else program or use a computer."

Computer Sciences Corp. v. Commissioner of Internal Revenue, 63 T.C. 327, 329 (1974).

". . . is necessary for a computer to function because it provides the interface between the equipment and the operator."

Graphic Sales, Inc. v. Sperry Univac Div., Sperry Corp., 824 F.2d 576, 578 n.1 (7th Cir. 1987).

"[A] set of computer programs that guide and control the basic function of a computer. It also provides the necessary link between the computer equipment 'hardware' and the various application programs 'software,' designed to perform specific functions, such as accounting, word processing and payroll."

A.I. Root Co. v. Computer Dynamics, Inc., 615 F. Supp. 727, 729 n.5 (N.D. Ohio 1985).

"[O]perating systems software, which brings the system alive and "tames" it for the user to utilize. . . ."

Jostens, Inc. v. National Computer Sys., Inc., 8 Computer L. Serv. Rep. 146, 149 (Minn. Cty. Ct. 1981).

[CANADA] "This is the basic set of instructions to the computer on how it is to operate. These instructions describe how the computer is to deal with all its tasks but not with any particular task."

> *Continental Comm. Sys. Corp. (Telecheque Can.) v. R.,* [1982] 5 W.W.R. 340 (B.C. C.A).

See also operating program(s); operating system; operating system program(s); operational program(s); operations system software.

operational program(s) *(software)*

". . . controls the hardware and actually makes the machine run; it is fundamental and necessary to the functioning of the computer hardware itself."

> *Commerce Union Bank v. Tidwell,* 538 S.W.2d 405, 406 (Tenn. 1976).

"Every computer has a 'background' program running at all times. This background program, called by many names but usually referred to as 'monitor,' 'operating system,' or 'executive system,' does exactly what its name says it should do: it monitors and directs everything that is going on in the computer. It allocates space for data on disk (and it remembers where it put it), it tells the memory to get data from the disk, and it decides where there is room in memory for these data; it mingles in everything from getting the user 'signed on' to getting him 'signed off' the computer, [and] it is the universal 'policeman' of the system. Everything that goes on inside the computer, at any time, is guided by the monitor. Needless to say, the monitor is usually the largest and most complicated program that is running; it is certainly the most important, for without it even the most sophisticated computer is only a bunch of wires, transistors, and metal that is totally inadequate to solve any problems. Operational software includes compilers, which translate input symbolic codes into machine [instructions] and can replace certain items of input with series of instructions called subroutines; sorts, which place items of data in order, and utility routines, which perform tasks useful for the efficient operation of the machine, such as copying one magnetic tape from another."

> *Comptroller of the Treasury v. Equitable Trust Co.,* 464 A.2d 248, 250 n.2 (Md. 1983).

". . . controls the hardware and actually makes the machine operate. It is fundamental and necessary to the functioning of the hardware."

> *First National Bank of Springfield v. Department of Revenue,* 421 N.E.2d 175, 176 (Ill. 1981) (Tax).

". . . control the basic internal operation of the computer."

> *Alabama v. Central Computer Servs., Inc.,* 349 So.2d 1156, 1157 (Ala. App. 1977).

"... the basic functions of the computer."

> *Honeywell Information Systems v. Maricopa County,* 118 Ariz. 171, 575 P.2d 801, 808 (App. 1977).

See also operating program(s); operating system; operating system program(s); operating system software; operations system software.

operations system software *(software)*

"... usually considered an integral part of the hardware provided by the manufacturer and consists of the basic programming necessary to enable the machine to be operated, i.e. to be applied by further programming to the task to be performed."

> *Jostens, Inc. v. National Computer, Systems, Inc.,* 318 N.W.2d 691, 695 n.3 (Minn. 1982).

See also operating program(s); operating system; operating system program(s); operating system software; operational program(s).

operative personnel *(electronic commerce)*

"[O]ne or more natural persons acting as a certification authority or its agent, or in the employment of, or under contract with, a certification authority, and who have: (a) Managerial or policy making responsibilities for the certification authority; or (b) Duties directly involving the issuance of certificates, creation of private keys, or administration of a certification authority's computing facilities."

> Wash. Rev. Code § 19.34.020(21).

OPM *(business)*

Acronym for "Other People's Money."

OPS *(hardware)*

Acronym for "Operations Per Second." A general measurement of computer performance.

opt-in *(Internet; privacy)*

A user affirmatively agrees (i) to allow a web site to use personal information about him or her or (ii) to allow a web site to send the user e-mail. *See also* privacy; privacy policy.

opt-out *(Internet; privacy)*

A web site may communicate with or use personal information about a user unless the user specifically direct it not to do so. *See also* privacy; privacy policy.

optical reader *(hardware)*

Also called "optical scanner."

"[A] scanner, an electronic device, which senses the presence or absence of marks on input paper as the sheet is mechanically transported through the scanner. It is essentially a device that reads data from a printed or handwritten sheet and translates the data into machine-readable language."

> *Moore Bus. Forms, Inc. v. National Computer Sys., Inc.,* 211 U.S.P.Q. (BNA) 909, 912 (T.T.A.B. 1981).

optical scanner *(hardware)*

See OCR; optical reader.

option *(contract)*

A contractual arrangement, or deal, in which a payment is made toward the purchase of a literary, musical, or other type of creative property, and secures the rights to exploit the property for a given period of time (usually six months to a year).

oral communication *(criminal)*

"[A]ny oral communication uttered by a person exhibiting an expectation that such communication is not subject to interception under circumstances justifying such expectation, but such term does not include any electronic communication. . . ."

> 18 U.S.C. § 2510(2).

See also electronic communication.

ordinary observer test *(copyright)*

"[W]hether the work is recognizable by an ordinary observer as having been taken from the copyrighted source."

> *E.F. Johnson Co. v. Uniden Corp. of America,* 623 F. Supp. 1485, 1492-93 (D. Minn. 1982) (citations omitted).

Annotation. "The ordinary observer test has proven 'one of the most difficult questions in copyright law, and one which is the least susceptible of helpful generalizations.' Under any formulation it is clear that '[s]light differences will not serve as a defense, and that there is substantial similarity where enough "material of substance and value" has been taken so that an ordinary observer would recognize that there is "borrowing" from the original.' The copying need not be slavishly detailed, so long as the accused work has captured the 'total concept and feel' of copyrighted work.

* * *

"Because a copyrighted computer program is stored on a computer chip or disc well-hidden from public view, application of the ordinary observer test in a computer software context has proven problematic. The absence of an easily perceived general aura or feel emanating from a silicon chip has led some commentators to suggest an 'iterative' approach to substantial similarity."

> *E.F. Johnson Co. v. Uniden Corp. of America,* 623 F. Supp. 1485, 1492-93 (D. Minn. 1982) (citations omitted).

See also **infringement; iterative approach; substantial similarity.**

.org *(Internet)*

The top-level domain designated for entities that do not fit under any of the other top-level domains.

original equipment manufacturer(s) *(business; organizations)*

Abbreviated as "OEM(s)."

"[M]anufacturers of PCs. . . ."

> *United States v. Microsoft Corp.,* 65 F. Supp. 2d 1, 4 (D.D.C. 1999) (Finding of Fact 10).

See also **OEM.**

original work of authorship *(copyright)*

See **work of authorship.**

originality *(copyright)*

"The test of originality is a 'modest' one, requiring only a 'faint trace' of originality. . . . [O]riginality sufficient for copyright protection exists if the 'author' has introduced any element of novelty as contrasted with the material previously known to him."

> *E.F. Johnson Co. v. Uniden Corp. of America,* 623 F. Supp. 1485, 1498 (D. Minn. 1985) (citations omitted).

Annotation. "There is no definition of 'originality' . . . in the Act. The legislative history, however, demonstrates that Congress purposely omitted any such definition because it accepted the standards as 'established [for originality] by the courts under the present copyright law [i.e., the Act of 1909],' though it did explain in that connection that '[t]his standard [did] not include requirements of novelty, ingenuity, or esthetic intention to enlarge the standard of copyright protection to require them.'"

> *M. Kramer Mfg. Co. v. Andrews,* 783 F.2d 421, 434 (4th Cir. 1986) (citations omitted).

"For a work to qualify for copyright protection, it must be original. And originality, as the term is used in copyright, requires both 'independent creation' and 'a modicum of creativity.' The requisite level of creativity is extremely low. Nevertheless, without some creative spark—'no matter how crude, humble or obvious'—the labor that goes into independently creating (as opposed to simply reproducing) a work is insufficient to bring that work within the scope of copyright."

> *Alcatel USA, Inc. v. DGI Technologies, Inc.,* 166 F.3d 772, 787 (5th Cir. 1999) (citations omitted).

"The grant to the author of the special privilege of a copyright carries out a public policy adopted by the Constitution and laws of the United States, 'to promote the Progress of Science and useful arts, by securing for limited Times to [Authors] . . . the exclusive Right . . .' to their 'original' works. United States Constitution, Art. I, §8, cl. 8, 17 U.S.C. §102. But the public policy which includes original works within the granted monopoly excludes from it all that is not embraced in the original expression."

> *Alcatel USA, Inc. v. DGI Technologies, Inc.,* 166 F.3d 772, 793 (5th Cir. 1999) (citations omitted).

Related issues. "The vast majority of works make the grade quite easily, as they possess some creative spark."

> *Feist Publications, Inc. v. Rural Tel. Serv. Co.,* 499 U.S. 340, 345 (1991).

"The mere fact that a work is copyrighted does not mean that every element of the work may be protected. Originality remains the *sine qua non* of copyright; accordingly, copyright protection may extend only to those components of a work that are original to the author."

> *Feist Publications, Inc. v. Rural Tel. Serv. Co.,* 499 U.S. 340, 348 (1991).

"A compiler may settle upon a selection or arrangement that others have used; novelty is not required. Originality requires only that the author make the selection and arrangement independently (i.e., without copying that selection or arrangement from another work), and that it display some minimum level of creativity."

> *Feist Publications, Inc. v. Rural Tel. Serv. Co.,* 499 U.S. 340, 358 (1991).

"[If] the work is unprotected by federal law because of a lack of originality, then its use is neither unfair nor unjustified."

> *Financial Infor., Inc. v. Moody's Investors Serv., Inc.,* 808 F.2d 204, 208 (2d Cir. 1986).

"[W]hile original expression is necessary for copyright protection, we do not think that it is alone sufficient. Courts must still inquire whether original expression falls within one of the categories foreclosed from copyright protection by § 102(b), such as being a 'method of operation.'"

> *Lotus Dev. Corp. v. Borland Int'l, Inc.,* 49 F.3d 807, 818 (1st Cir. 1995), *aff'd by an equally divided court,* 516 U.S. 233 (1996).

"The fact that an arrangement of data responds *logically* to the needs of the market for which the compilation was prepared does not negate originality. To the contrary, the use of logic to solve the problems of how best to present the information being compiled is independent creation."

> *CCC Infor. Servs., Inc. v. Maclean Hunter Market Rpts., Inc.,* 44 F.3d 61, 67 (2d Cir. 1994) (emphasis in original).

OS *(software)*

Acronym for "Operating System." *See* **operating program(s); operating system; operating system program(s); operating system software; operational program(s); operations system software.**

OSI *(hardware)*

Acronym for "Open Systems Interconnection."

> *IBM Corp. v. Fujitsu Ltd.,* Copyright L. Rep. (CCH) ¶ 20,517 (Am. Arb. Ass'n 1988).

OSP *(Internet)*

Acronym for "Online Service Provider." *See* **online service provider.**

OS/2 Warp *(software)*

An Intel-compatible operating system introduced by IBM.

Annotation. "In late 1994, IBM introduced its Intel-compatible OS/2 Warp operating system and spent tens of millions of dollars in an effort to attract ISVs to develop applications for OS/2 and in an attempt to reverse-engineer, or 'clone,' part of the Windows API set. Despite these efforts, IBM could obtain neither significant market share nor ISV support for OS/2 Warp. Thus, although at its peak OS/2 ran approximately 2,500 applications and had 10% of the market for Intel-compatible PC operating systems, IBM ultimately determined that the applications barrier prevented effective competition against Windows 95. For that reason, in 1996 IBM stopped trying to convince ISVs to write for OS/2 Warp.

> *United States v. Microsoft Corp.,* 65 F. Supp. 2d 1, 13 (D.D.C. 1999) (Finding of Fact 46).

OTA *(organization)*

Acronym for "U.S. Office of Technology Assessment."

OTP *(organization)*

Acronym for "U.S. Office of Telecommunication Policy."

output *(technology)*

". . . disgorges the requisite information in accordance with instructions."
Computer Sys. of Am. v. Western Reserve Life Assur. Co., 19 Mass. App. 430, 431 n.2 (1985).

"Input is the entering of data into storage. The input devices convert data from an 'ordinary' language form (i.e., English and numbers) to 'machine' language or electronic signals which are then understandable to a computer. Output is the opposite."
Telex Corp. v. IBM Corp., 367 F. Supp. 258, 274 (N.D. Okla. 1973), *aff'd in part, rev'd in part,* 510 F.2d 894 (10th Cir.), *cert. dism.,* 423 U.S. 802 (1975).

output devices *(hardware)*

". . . convert the 'machine' language or electronic signals to the output form desired, such as printed or typed in humanly understandable language on paper, recorded on magnetic tape or magnetic disk, punched as a hole in a punched card, or displayed on a television-like screen. Output devices can also be used to open or close a valve, or to transfer electrical impulses to another computer system."
Telex Corp. v. IBM Corp., 367 F. Supp. 258, 274 (N.D. Okla. 1973), *aff'd in part, rev'd in part,* 510 F.2d 894 (10th Cir.), *cert. dism.,* 423 U.S. 802 (1975).

". . . such as a display screen and printer. . . ."
Lotus Dev. Corp. v. Paperback Software Int'l, 740 F. Supp. 37, 43 (D. Mass. 1990).

See also **input/output devices.**

outsourcing *(business)*

Hiring another company to provide data processing services that an organization might otherwise have performed itself, e.g., software development.

overbreadth *(Constitution)*

"The doctrine of overbreadth recognizes that an unconstitutional restriction of freedom of expression may deter parties not before the court from engaging in protected speech and thereby escape judicial review."
Shea v. Reno, 930 F. Supp. 916, 939 (S.D.N.Y. 1996).

overlapping window system *(technology)*

See **window.**

owner *(copyright)*

"Since [plaintiff] licensed its software, the [defendant's] customers do not qualify as 'owners' of the software and are not eligible for protection under § 117."

> *MAI Sys. Corp. v. Peak Computer, Inc.,* 991 F.2d 511, 518 (9th Cir. 1993), *cert. dism.,* 510 U.S. 1033 (1994).

Annotation. "Only the 'owner of a copy of a computer program' may take advantage of the privileges set out in section 117. An owner is one who purchases a disk, diskette, or other medium in which a program is stored. A person who does not own a copy of the plaintiff's computer program may not take advantage of a section 117 defense. The licensee who acquires possession but not ownership of a disk copy of a licensed program is not entitled to exercise these privileges. There must be a transfer of title, as provided for under applicable State law, for the privilege to obtain.

"This requirement of ownership in section 117 is a change in the statutory language from the CONTU recommendation. CONTU would have allowed a rightful possessor of a copy of a program to perform or authorize the acts permitted by the section. There appears to be no legislative history on the reasons for this change; however, those who were involved in the congressional hearing on the 1980 amendments say that the change reflects concerns of the Justice Department relating to antitrust considerations."

> Office of Technology Assessment, *Finding a Balance: Computer Software, Intellectual Property, and the Challenge of Technological Change* 67-68 (May 1992).

See also **Section 117 limitations.**

ownership

(contract)

"It is true that the transfer of rights to the . . . software in each of the agreements did not take the form of a lease, and that the transfer in each case was in exchange for a single payment and was for a term that was either unlimited or nearly so. One commentator has argued that when a copy of a software program is transferred for a single payment and for an unlimited term, the transferee should be considered an 'owner' of the copy of the software program regardless of other restrictions on his use of the software. That view has not been accepted by other courts, however, and we think it overly simplistic. The concept of ownership of a copy entails a variety of rights and interests. The fact that the right of possession is perpetual, or that the possessor's rights were obtained through a single payment, is certainly relevant to whether the possessor is an owner, but those factors are not necessarily dispositive if the possessor's right to use the software is heavily encumbered by other restrictions that are inconsistent with the status of owner."

> *DSC Comm. Corp. v. Pulse Comm., Inc.*, 170 F.3d 1354, 1362 (Fed. Cir. 1999).

(copyright)
"Unfortunately, ownership is an imprecise concept, and the Copyright Act does not define the term. Nor is there much useful guidance to be obtained from either the legislative history of the statute or the cases that have construed it. The National Commission on New Technological Uses of Copyrighted Works ('CONTU') was created by Congress to recommend changes in the Copyright Act to accommodate advances in computer technology. In its final report, CONTU proposed a version of section 117 that is identical to the one that was ultimately enacted, except for a single change. The proposed CONTU version provided that 'it is not an infringement for the *rightful possessor* of a copy of a computer program to make or authorize the making of another copy or adaptation of that program . . . .' Congress, however, substituted the words 'owner of a copy' in place of the words 'rightful possessor of a copy.' The legislative history does not explain the reason for the change, . . . but it is clear from the fact of the substitution of the term 'owner' for 'rightful possessor' that Congress must have meant to require more than 'rightful possession' to trigger the section 117 defense."

> *DSC Comm. Corp. v. Pulse Comm., Inc.*, 170 F.3d 1354, 1360 (Fed. Cir. 1999) (citations omitted).

"Plainly, a party who purchases copies of software from the copyright owner can hold a license under a copyright while still being an 'owner' of a copy of the copyrighted software for purposes of section 117."

> *DSC Comm. Corp. v. Pulse Comm., Inc.*, 170 F.3d 1354, 1360 (Fed. Cir. 1999).

"Ownership of a copyright, or of any of the exclusive rights under a copyright, is distinct from ownership of any material object in which the work is embodied."

> U.S. Copyright Act, 17 U.S.C. § 202.

Annotation (copyright). "Unfortunately, ownership is an imprecise concept, and the Copyright Act does not define the term. Nor is there much useful guidance to be obtained from either the legislative history of the statute or the cases that have construed it."

> *DSC Comm. Corp. v. Pulse Comm., Inc.*, 170 F.3d 1354, 1360 (Fed. Cir. 1999).

The plaintiff in a copyright infringement action normally bears the burden of proving ownership of a valid copyright. In order to meet this burden, the plaintiff must show that the work is original and that the applicable statutory formalities were followed.

Montgomery v. Noga, 168 F.3d 1282, 1289 (11th Cir. 1999).

Related issues (copyright). "Transfer of ownership of any material object, including the copy . . . in which the work is first fixed, does not of itself convey any rights in the copyrighted work embodied in the object; nor, in the absence of an agreement, does transfer of ownership of a copyright or of any exclusive rights under a copyright convey property rights in any material object."

U.S. Copyright Act, 17 U.S.C. § 202.

"The ownership and control of information and the means of disseminating it are emerging as national and international policy issues. Concerns about the impact on individual freedom posed by the control of the flow of information are at the forefront of public debate. The adequacy of the legal structure to cope with the pace and rate of technological change frequently has been called into question."

CONTU Final Report 3 (1978) (citations omitted).

"A copyright owner holds the right to create sequels."

Micro Star v. FormGen, Inc., 154 F.3d 1107, 1112 (9th Cir. 1998).

"Registration certificates are prima facie evidence that the plaintiff owns a valid copyright."

17 U.S.C. § 410(c).

PAC-MAN *(video game)*
"[A]n electronic arcade maze-chase game."
Atari, Inc. v. North American Philips Consumer Elecs. Corp., 672 F.2d 607, 610
(7th Cir.), *cert. denied,* 459 U.S. 880 (1982).

package *(business; software)*
A group of functions offered as one unit.

packet *(technology; telecommunications)*
The standard unit of data with appended information on source, destination, etc., that is sent over the Internet or other packet switching network.
A message sent over the Internet is broken into individual packets, which
may take different routes to the destination, and are reassembled at the
destination in the correct sequence.

packet switching *(telecommunications)*
"Transmission is effected by breaking up whatever information is to be sent
in small 'packets' that are individually routed. Routing is done by computers that are connected to the Internet. A single transmission of, e.g., a
twenty-page document, might be accomplished with several dozen packets,
each of which might travel a different path through the network. Computers at the sending end are responsible for creating the packets; at the receiving end, computers re-assemble the packets back into a single document."
I. Trotter Hardy, *Project Looking Forward: Sketching the Future of Copyright in
a Networked World* 12 (May 1998).

Annotation. "The Internet uses 'packet switching' communication protocols
that allow individual messages to be subdivided into smaller "packets" that are
then sent independently to the destination, and are then automatically reassembled by the receiving computer. While all packets of a given message
often travel along the same path to the destination, if computers along the
route become overloaded, then packets can be re-routed to less loaded computers."
American Civil Liberties Union v. Reno, 929 F. Supp. 824, 832 (E.D. Pa.
1996), *aff'd, Reno v. American Civil Liberties Union,* 521 U.S. 844 (1997).

"Programs on the linked computers implemented a technical scheme known as 'packet-switching,' through which a message from one computer to another would be subdivided into smaller, separately addressed pieces of data, known as 'packets,' sent independently to the message's destination and reassembled upon arrival."
   Shea v. Reno, 930 F. Supp. 916, 926 (S.D.N.Y. 1996).
   See also **circuit switching.**

padding *(technology)*
   Characters used to fill a field or block. If data takes up less space than its designated unit of storage, the remainder of the space must be filled with some padding character, such as a blank.

page *(Internet)*
   See **web page(s).**

page break *(technology)*
   The location within a document where one page ends and a new page begins.

page impression(s) *(technology)*
   The number of times a page is displayed from a site to a user.

page view *(Internet)*
   A web page that is downloaded and viewed by a user.

pagination *(technology)*
   The layout of a document. It is the format such as the number of lines per inch, number of characters per inch, spacing between characters, etc.

PAL *(broadcasting)*
   Acronym for "Phase Alternation Line." The standard for color television broadcasting and reception in Australia, most of Western Europe (except France), and parts of South America. Televisions meeting this standard have 625 scan lines and 25 frames per second.

PAL technology *(technology)*
   ". . . is used to save space on a circuit board and to conserve power."
   Bateman v. Mnemonics, Inc., 79 F.3d 1532, 1538 n.14 (11th Cir. 1996).

palming off *(trademark)*

"[A]n intentional effort to induce retailers to substitute his product for other products requested by consumers. . . ."
> *M. Kramer Mfg. Co. v. Andrews,* 783 F.2d 421, 449 (4th Cir. 1986).

Panavision *(Internet; trademark)*

Citation: *Panavision Int'l, L.P. v. Toeppen,* 945 F. Supp. 1296 (C.D. Cal. 1996), *aff'd,* 141 F.3d 1316 (9th Cir. 1998).

Court held that a lower court had properly found that it had jurisdiction over the defendant, who was a "cyber pirate," and had registered a famous trademark as a domain name, then attempted to sell the domain name back to the trademark owner.

paper trail *(mask work)*

Annotation. "[R]everse engineering generally produces a 'paper trail' recording the engineer's efforts to understand the original chip and to design a different version after reverse engineering. . . . [T]he 'paper trail' was expected to document efforts in 'analyzing, or evaluating the concepts or techniques embodied in the mask work or the circuitry, logic flow or organization of components used in the mask work,' as the effort required would be reflected in the documents."
> *Brooktree Corp. v. Advanced Micro Devices, Inc.,* 977 F.2d 1555, 1566-67 (Fed. Cir. 1992).

"The statute does not reflect an intent to excuse copying, as a matter of law, if the copier had first tried and failed to do the job without copying. The paper trail is evidence of independent effort, but it is not conclusive or incontrovertible proof of either originality or the absence of copying."
> *Brooktree Corp. v. Advanced Micro Devices, Inc.,* 977 F.2d 1555, 1570 (Fed. Cir. 1992).

parallel citation(s) *(copyright)*

"[I]dentifying the volume and first page numbers on which a particular case appears . . . ."
> *Matthew Bender & Co. v. West Publ'g Co.,* 158 F.3d 693, 700 (2d Cir. 1998), *cert. denied,* 522 U.S. 3732 (1999).

parallel processor *(hardware)*

A computer design using more than one processor simultaneously.

parameter *(software)*

Any item of information that defines the limits of a program when it is run. Parameters are variables that can be defined by the user.

parameter list *(software)*

"A parameter list . . . is 'the information sent to and received from the subroutine.' The term 'parameter list' refers to the form in which information is passed between modules (e.g. for accounts receivable, the designated time frame and particular customer identifying number) and the information's actual content (e.g. 8/91–7/92; customer No. 3). With respect to form, interacting modules must share similar parameter lists so that they are capable of exchanging information."

> *Computer Assocs. Int'l, Inc. v. Altai, Inc.,* 982 F.2d 693, 697-98 (2d Cir. 1992) (citations omitted).

parental control software *(software)*

"Systems have been developed to help parents control the material that may be available on a home computer with Internet access. A system may either limit a computer's access to an approved list of sources that have been identified as containing no adult material, it may block designated inappropriate sites, or it may attempt to block messages containing identifiable objectionable features. 'Although parental control software currently can screen for certain suggestive words or for known sexually explicit sites, it cannot now screen for sexually explicit images.' Nevertheless, the evidence indicates that 'a reasonably effective method by which parents can prevent their children from accessing sexually explicit and other material which parents may believe is inappropriate for their children will soon be available.'"

> *Reno v. American Civil Liberties Union,* 521 U.S. 844, 854-55 (1997), *quoting American Civil Liberties Union v. Reno,* 929 F. Supp. 830, 844 (3d Cir. 1996) (citations omitted).

Paris Convention *(trademark)*

Abbreviation for the "Paris Convention for the Protection of Intellectual Property."

party *(contract)*

"[A] person that engages in a transaction or makes an agreement under this [Act]."

> UCITA § 102(a)(50).

password *(technology)*

A string of characters entered by the user during login that verifies the identity of the user to the system, thus permitting access to specific files.

password guessing *(criminal)*

"[A] program . . . whereby various combinations of letters are tried out in rapid sequence in the hope that one will be an authorized user's password, which is entered to permit whatever level of activity that user is authorized to perform."

United States v. Morris, 928 F.2d 504, 506 (2d Cir. 1991).

patch *(software)*

"Segments of program code (individual statements or routines) added to the body of a completed computer program to enhance or amend the program."

U.S. Copyright Office, *Compendium of Copyright Office Practices* II, § 326 (1984).

patching *(software)*

See patch.

patent *(patent; software)*

A form of intellectual property protection authorized by the U.S. Constitution (art. I, § 8, cl. 8), and provided by federal law. See Title 35, United States Code.

Annotation. "[P]atent and copyright law protect distinct aspects of a computer program. Title 35 protects the process or method performed by a computer program; title 17 protects the expression of that process or method. While title 35 protects any novel, nonobvious, and useful process, title 17 can protect a multitude of expressions that implement that process. If the patentable process is embodied inextricably in the line-by-line instructions of the computer program, however, then the process merges with the expression and precludes copyright protection."

Atari Games Corp. v. Nintendo of America, Inc., 975 F.2d 832, 839-40 (Fed. Cir. 1992) (citations omitted).

Related issues. "[I]t is an old observation that the training of Anglo-American judges ill fits them to discharge the duties cast upon them by patent legislation."

Marconi Wireless Telegraph v. United States, 320 U.S. 1, 60 (1943) (Frankfurter, J.).

patent claim(s) *(patent)*

See also claim(s).

"Each claim component, recited as a 'means' plus its function, is to be read, of course, pursuant to §112, ¶ 6, as inclusive of the 'equivalents' of the structures disclosed in the written description portion of the specification."
State Street Bank & Trust, Co. v. Signature Financial Group, Inc., 149 F.3d 1368, 1372 (Fed. Cir. 1998).

patent clause *(patent)*

"Congress shall have the Power to promote the Progress of Science and useful Arts, by securing for limited Times to Authors and Inventors the exclusive Right to their respective Writings and Discoveries."
U.S. Const., art. I, sec. 8.

Annotation. "[This] limited grant is a means by which an important public purpose may be achieved. It is intended to motivate the creative activity of authors and inventors by the provision of a special reward, and to allow the public access to the products of their genius after the limited period of exclusive control has expired."
Sony Corp. of America v. Universal City Studios, Inc., 464 U.S. 417, 429 (1984).

patent infringement *(patent)*

"[W]hoever without authority makes, uses or sells any patented invention, within the United States during the term of the patent therefor, infringes the patent."
35 U.S.C. § 271(a).

Annotation. "Analysis of patent infringement entails two inquiries: determination of the scope of the claims, as a matter of law; and the factual finding of whether properly construed claims encompass the accused structure."
Texas Instruments, Inc. v. United States Int'l Trade Comm'n, 805 F.2d 1558, 1562 (Fed. Cir. 1986).

Related issues. "[T]he Patent Act expressly brands anyone who 'actively induces infringement of a patent' as an infringer, 35 U.S.C. § 271(b), and further imposes liability on certain individuals labeled 'contributory' infringers. § 271(c)."
Sony Corp. v. Universal City Studios, Inc., 464 U.S. 417, 434-35 (1984).

"Whoever actively induces infringement of a patent shall be liable as an infringer."
35 U.S.C. § 271(b).

patent validity *(patent)*

"A patent shall be presumed valid. Each claim of a patent (whether independent, dependent, or multiple dependent form) shall be presumed valid independently of the validity of other claims; dependent or multiple dependent claims shall be presumed valid even though dependent upon an invalid claim. The burden of establishing invalidity of a patent or any claim thereof shall rest on the party asserting such invalidity."

35 U.S.C. § 282.

patentable subject matter *(patent)*

[A]nything under the sun that is made by man."

Diamond v. Chakrabarty, 447 U.S. 303, 309 (1980); *In re Alappat,* 33 F.3d 1526, 1542 (Fed. Cir. 1994).

path *(technology)*

The route taken to locate a file on a computer system.

pathname *(technology)*

The name of a file or directory that specifies where it belongs in the directory system.

PC *(technology)*

Acronym for "Personal Computer." This term generally is used to refer to IBM and IBM-compatible computers operating with the MS-DOS, PC-DOS, or Windows operating systems.

See also **personal computer; personal computer system.**

PC-DOS *(software)*

"A CP/M-like operating system for the IBM Personal Computer, developed by IBM and Microsoft."

In re Digital Research Inc., 4 U.S.P.Q. (BNA) 2d 1242, ___ (T.T.A.B. 1987).

PCM *(technology)*

Acronym for "Plug-Compatible Manufacturer."

Telex Corp. v. IBM Corp., 367 F. Supp. 258, 272 (N.D. Okla. 1973), *aff'd in part, rev'd in part,* 510 F.2d 894 (10th Cir.), *cert. dism.,* 423 U.S. 802 (1975).

See also **plug-compatible; plug-compatible peripheral device; plug-compatible product.**

PCS *(technology)*

Acronym for "Personal Communications Services."

"[A] new type of service designed to support hand-held personal voice and data communications terminals."

U.S. General Accounting Office, *Information Superhighway: An Overview of Technology Changes* 55 (Jan. 1995).

PDA *(technology)*

Acronym for "Personal Data Assistant." A handheld computing device that allows a user to organize personal information. Most PDAs provide for pen-based input and data synchronization with a computer.

peer-to-peer *(business)*

See P2P.

peering agreements *(contract; Internet)*

"Gentlemen's agreements" between Internet service providers or backbone providers, which allow users of one provider to send communications over the other provider's network at no cost.

Annotation. While these agreements were not a problem in the early days of the Internet when virtually all ISPs were approximately the same size, as time went on, and many new, smaller ISPs entered the market, some of the larger Internet backbone providers did not believe that these agreements were appropriate, since they were subsidizing the telecommunications costs of the smaller ISPs. In the spring of 1997, Uunet Technologies, Inc. created a furor by indicating that it would no longer honor peering agreements with small ISPs, and would charge them for access to their networks. Such a course, if adopted generally, would have driven many of the smaller ISPs out of business and could have balkanized the Internet—creating situations where users of some ISPs could not get access to certain web sites on ISPs with which they had no peering agreement.

perform *(copyright)*

"To 'perform' a work means to recite, render, play, dance, or act it, either directly or by means of any device or process or, in the case of a motion picture or other audiovisual work, to show its images in any sequence or to make the sounds accompanying it audible."

U.S. Copyright Act, 17 U.S.C. § 101.

periodical *(Internet)*

A publication that appears at regular intervals.

Related issues. "Posting a message to the sports bulletin board is a random communication of computerized messages analogous to posting a written notice on a public bulletin board, not a publication that appears at regular intervals."

It's in the Cards, Inc. v. Fuschetto, 193 Wis.2d 429, 436, 535 N.W.2d 11, 14 (1995).

peripheral *(hardware)*

See peripheral devices; peripheral equipment; peripheral products.

peripheral devices *(hardware)*

"[Devices] connected with the central processing unit and which perform various special functions in the data processing system. These include information storage components like magnetic tape drives [and] magnetic disk drives . . . ; terminal devices such as printers; memory units, which are specialized storage units, and other similar types of peripheral components."

> *Telex Corp. v. IBM Corp.,* 510 F.2d 894, 899 (10th Cir.), *cert. dism.,* 423 U.S. 802 (1975).

See also peripheral equipment; peripheral products.

peripheral equipment *(hardware)*

". . . includes means for storing information, such as disk and tape drives, and input and output devices, such as printers and terminals."

> *Greyhound Computer Corp. v. IBM Corp.,* 559 F.2d 488, 492 (9th Cir. 1977).

". . . such as disks, tapes, printers, and terminals, which [are] connected to the central processing unit ('CPU') to enable the data processing system to perform particular functions."

> *California Computer Prods., Inc. v. IBM Corp.,* 613 F.2d 727, 731 (9th Cir. 1979).

See also peripheral devices; peripheral products.

peripheral products *(hardware)*

"[D]evices, including disk drives, disk drive control units, and communications control units, that are outside the central processing unit."

> *ILC Peripherals Leasing Corp. v. IBM Corp.,* 458 F. Supp. 423, 437 (N.D. Cal. 1978).

See also peripheral devices; peripheral equipment.

permanent injunction *(copyright)*

"As a general rule, a permanent injunction will be granted when liability has been established and there is a threat of continuing violations. . . . However, § 502(a) of the Copyright Act authorizes the court to 'grant temporary and final injunctions on such terms as it may deem reasonable *to prevent or restrain infringement of a copyright.*'"

> *MAI Sys. Corp. v. Peak Computer, Inc.,* 991 F.2d 511, 519 (9th Cir. 1993) (citations omitted; emphasis in original).

permission

(hardware)
Level of access to a computer system. *See also* **file access permission.**

(entertainment)
See **clearance.**

person

(contract)
"[A]n individual, corporation, business trust, estate, trust, partnership, limited liability company, association, joint venture, governmental subdivision, instrumentality, or agency, public corporation, or any other legal or commercial entity."
UCITA § 102(a)(51).

(electronic commerce)
"[A] human being or an organization capable of signing a document, either legally or as a matter of fact."
Wash. Rev. Code § 19.34.020(22).

personal computer *(hardware; software)*
Abbreviated as "PC."

"[A] digital information processing device designed for use by one person at a time."
United States v. Microsoft Corp., 65 F. Supp. 2d 1, 3 (D.D.C. 1999) (Finding of Fact 1).

Annotation. "A typical PC consists of central processing components (e.g., a microprocessor and main memory) and mass data storage (such as a hard disk). A typical PC system consists of a PC, certain peripheral input/output devices (including a monitor, a keyboard, a mouse, and a printer), and an operating system. PC systems, which include desktop and laptop models, can be distinguished from more powerful, more expensive computer systems known as 'servers,' which are designed to provide data, services, and functionality through a digital network to multiple users."
United States v. Microsoft Corp., 65 F. Supp. 2d 1, 3 (D.D.C. 1999) (Finding of Fact 1).
See also **PC; personal computer system.**

personal computer system *(technology)*
Abbreviated as "PC."

". . . consists of hardware and software. The hardware includes the central processing unit ('CPU'), which contains the electronic circuits that control the computer and perform the arithmetic and logical functions, the internal memory of the computer ('random access memory,' or 'RAM'), input devices such as a keyboard and mouse, output devices such as a display screen and printer, and storage devices such as hard and floppy disk drives. The software includes one or more computer programs, usually stored magnetically on hard or floppy disks, along with such items as instruction manuals and 'templates,' which are pieces of plastic that fit around the function keys on the keyboard, identifying the specific functions or commands that can be invoked by those keys."

Lotus Dev. Corp. v. Paperback Software Int'l, 740 F. Supp. 37, 43 (D. Mass. 1990).

See also **PC; personal computer.**

personal information *(privacy)*

Any recorded information about an identifiable individual, such as a person's religion, age, financial transactions, medical history, address, or blood type.

personal jurisdiction *(jurisdiction)*

For a court to adjudicate a dispute involving a particular defendant, the court must find that the defendant has sufficient contacts with the jurisdiction to permit the court to adjudicate the claim.

Annotation. Courts addressing the issue of whether personal jurisdiction can be constitutionally exercised over a defendant look to the "nature and quality of commercial activity that an entity conducts over the Internet." *Zippo Mfg. Co. v. Zippo Dot Com, Inc.,* 952 F. Supp. 1119, 1124 (W.D. Pa. 1997). The *Zippo* decision categorized Internet use into a spectrum of three areas. At one end of the spectrum are situations in which a defendant clearly does business over the Internet by entering into contracts with residents of other states that "involve the knowing and repeated transmission of computer files over the Internet . . . ." *Zippo,* 952 F. Supp. at 1124. In this situation, personal jurisdiction is proper. *See id. (citing CompuServe, Inc. v. Patterson,* 89 F.3d 1257 (6th Cir. 1996)). At the other end of the spectrum are situations in which a defendant merely establishes a passive website that does nothing more than advertise on the Internet. With passive websites, personal jurisdiction is not appropriate. *See id. (citing Bensusan Restaurant Corp., v. King,* 937 F. Supp. 295 (S.D.N.Y. 1996), *aff'd,* 126 F.3d 25 (2d Cir. 1997)). In the middle of the spectrum are situations in which a defendant has a website that allows a user to exchange information

with a host computer. In this middle ground, "the exercise of jurisdiction is determined by the level of interactivity and commercial nature of the exchange of information that occurs on the Website." *Id. (citing Maritz, Inc. v. Cybergold, Inc.*, 947 F. Supp. 1328 (E.D. Mo. 1996)).
   Mink v. AAAA Dev. LLC, 190 F.3d 333, 336 (5th Cir. 1999).

"The [I]nternet, a new and rapidly developing means of mass communications and information exchange, raises different questions regarding the scope of the court's personal jurisdiction in the context of due process jurisprudence."
   Maritz, Inc. v. Cybergold, Inc., 947 F. Supp. 1328, 1332 (E.D. Mo. 1996).

"We are mindful that the Internet is a communication medium that lacks historical parallel in the potential extent of its reach and that regulation across jurisdictions may implicate fundamental First Amendment concerns. It will undoubtedly take some time to determine the precise balance between the rights of those who use the Internet to disseminate information and the powers of the jurisdiction in which receiving computers are located to regulate for the general welfare."
   State v. Granite Gate Resorts, Inc., 568 N.W.2d 715, 718 (Minn. App. 1997), *aff'd per curiam,* 576 N.W.2d 747 (Minn. 1998).

"Personal jurisdiction may be founded on either general or specific jurisdiction."
   Panavision Int'l, L.P. v. Toeppen, 141 F.3d 1316, 1320 (9th Cir. 1998).

"The Constitutional limitations on the exercise of personal jurisdiction differs depending upon whether a court seeks to exercise personal or specific jurisdiction over a non-resident defendant. General jurisdiction permits a court to exercise personal jurisdiction over a non-resident defendant for non-forum related activities when the defendant has engaged in 'systematic and continuous' activities in the forum state. In the absence of general jurisdiction, specific jurisdiction permits a court to exercise personal jurisdiction over a non-resident defendant for forum-related activities where the 'relationship between the defendant and the forum falls within the "minimum contacts" framework' of *International Shoe Co. v. Washington,* 326 U.S. 310, 66 S. Ct. 154, 90 L. Ed. 140 (1945) and its progeny."
   Zippo Mfg. Co. v. Zippo Dot Com, Inc., 952 F. Supp. 1119, 1122 (W.D. Pa. 1997) (citations omitted).

"Whether the Court can exercise personal jurisdiction over a defendant requires a two-part inquiry. The Court first examines whether personal jurisdiction exists under Missouri's long-arm statute. Next, the Court must determine whether the exercise of personal jurisdiction is consistent with due process."

Maritz, Inc. v. Cybergold, Inc., 947 F. Supp. 1328, 1329 (E.D. Mo. 1996) (citation omitted).

"To determine whether personal jurisdiction exists over a defendant, federal courts apply the law of the forum state, subject to the limits of the Due Process Clause of the Fourteenth Amendment."

CompuServe, Inc. v. Patterson, 89 F.3d 1257, 1262 (6th Cir. 1996)

"Traditionally, in order to exercise personal jurisdiction over an out-of-state defendant, a court must determine whether the defendant has sufficient minimum contacts with the jurisdiction in which the court sits such that maintenance of a suit does not offend 'traditional notions of fair play and substantial justice.' *International Shoe Co. v. Washington,* 326 U.S. 310, 316, 90 L. Ed. 95, 66 S. Ct. 154 (1945)."

Blumenthal v. Drudge, 992 F. Supp. 44, 57 (D.D.C. 1998).

"In order to find 'minimum contacts,' a non-resident defendant must meet the following requirements:

"First, the claim underlying the litigation must directly arise out of, or relate to, the defendant's forum state activities. Second, the defendant's in-state contacts must represent a purposeful availment of the privilege of conducting activities in the forum state, thereby invoking the benefits and protections of that state's laws and making the defendant's involuntary presence before the state's courts foreseeable. Third, the exercise of jurisdiction must, in light of the gestalt factors, be reasonable. These three tests have been called relatedness, purposeful availment, and reasonableness."

Digital Equipment Corp. v. Altavista Technology, Inc., 960 F. Supp. 456, 468 (D. Mass. 1997) (citations omitted).

"With this global revolution looming on the horizon, the development of the law concerning the permissible scope of personal jurisdiction based on Internet use is in its infant stages. The cases are scant."

Zippo Mfg. Co. v. Zippo Dot Com, Inc., 952 F. Supp. 1119, 1123 (W.D. Pa. 1997).

"[A]lthough Internet transactions might appear to pose novel jurisdictional issues, traditional jurisdictional standards have proved to be sufficient to resolve all civil Internet jurisdictional issues raised to date, refuting the view of '[s]ome commentators [who] believed a new body of jurisprudence is needed to address' questions of personal jurisdiction and the Internet."

People v. Lipsitz, 663 N.Y.S.2d 468, 475 (Sup. Ct. N.Y. Cty. 1997).

"The legal questions surrounding the exercise of personal jurisdiction in 'cyberspace' are relatively new, and different courts have reached different conclusions as to how far their jurisdiction extends in cases involving the Internet. Generally, the debate over jurisdiction in cyberspace has revolved around two issues: [p]assive web sites versus interactive web sites, and whether a defendant's Internet-related contacts with the forum combined with other non-Internet related contracts are sufficient to establish at course of conduct.

* * *

"Under the analysis adopted by these courts, the exercise of personal jurisdiction is contingent upon the web site involving more than just the maintenance of a home page; it must also allow browsers to interact directly with the web site on some level. In addition, there must also be some other non-Internet related contacts between the defendant and the forum state in order for the court to exercise personal jurisdiction."

Blumenthal v. Drudge, 992 F. Supp. 44, 54-55 (D.D.C. 1998).

"The likelihood that personal jurisdiction can be constitutionally exercised is directly proportionate to the nature and quality of commercial activity that an entity conducts over the Internet. . . . At one end of the spectrum are situations where a defendant clearly does business over the Internet. If the defendant enters into contracts with residents of a foreign jurisdiction that involve the knowing and repeated transmission of computer files over the Internet, personal jurisdiction is proper. At the opposite end are situations where a defendant has simply posted information on an Internet Web site which is accessible to users in foreign jurisdiction. A passive Web site that does little more than make information available to those who are interested in it is not grounds for the exercise [of] personal jurisdiction. The middle ground is occupied by interactive Web sites where a user can exchange information with the host computer. In these cases, the exercise of jurisdiction is determined by examining the level of interactivity and commercial nature of the exchange of information that occurs on the Web site.

Zippo Mfg. Co. v. Zippo Dot Com, Inc., 952 F. Supp. 1119, 1124 (W.D. Pa. 1997)

"The first jurisdictional consideration is whether the litigation target has established a physical presence or a sufficiently close equivalent in the jurisdiction. Such a physical presence is not established, for example, by merely maintaining an Internet site accessible by an individual in a given jurisdiction. . . . '[A] finding of personal jurisdiction in New York based on an Internet web site would mean that there would be nationwide (indeed, worldwide) personal jurisdiction over anyone and everyone who establishes an Internet web site. Such nationwide jurisdiction is not consistent with traditional personal jurisdiction case law nor acceptable to the

Court as a matter of policy.' . . . However, where a person or business conducts a business within the forum state by being a subscriber to a local Internet service provider and selling a product through that provider, jurisdiction is proper. . . .

"The second jurisdictional consideration is of the acts done by the litigation 'target' within the jurisdiction, which must provide sufficient 'minimum contracts' with the forum to meet the constitutional jurisdiction test enunciated in *International Shoe Co. v. Washington,* 326 U.S. 310, 316˚ (1945). Traditionally, advertising alone is not sufficient presence within a forum to support jurisdiction. The mailing of a letter or making a telephone call to a forum resident, if that act is done outside a jurisdiction, however, does not alone support jurisdiction in a forum. . . . Here, again, these actions were done within this jurisdiction.

"In summary, for Internet consumer fraud claims, the Internet medium is essentially irrelevant, for the focus is primarily upon the location of the messenger and whether the messenger delivered what was purchased. In some cases, it might be necessary to analyze the location of certain other business operations, such as the site used or the place orders were received."

People v. Lipsitz, 663 N.Y.S.2d 468, 473-74 (Sup. Ct. N.Y. Cty. 1997) (citations omitted).

"The Supreme Court has noted, on more than one occasion, the confluence of the 'increasing nationalization of commerce' and 'modern transportation and communication,' and the resulting relaxation of the limits that the Due Process Clause imposes on courts' jurisdiction. Simply stated, there is less perceived need today for the federal constitution to protect defendants from 'inconvenient litigation,' because all but the most remote forums are easily accessible for the pursuit of both business and litigation. The Court has also, however, reminded us that the due process rights of a defendant should be the courts' primary concern where personal jurisdiction is at issue.

"The Internet represents perhaps the latest and greatest manifestation of these historical, globe-shrinking trends. It enables anyone with the right equipment and knowledge . . . to operate an international business cheaply, and from a desktop. That business operator, however, remains entitled to the protection of the Due Process Clause, which mandates that potential defendants be able 'to structure their primary conduct with some minimum assurance as to where the conduct will and will not render them liable to suit.'"

CompuServe, Inc. v. Patterson, 89 F.3d 1257, 1262 (6th Cir. 1996) (citations omitted)

"On the one hand, it troubles me to force corporations that do business over the Internet, precisely because it is cost-effective, to now factor in the potential costs of defending against litigation in each and every state; anticipating these costs could make the maintenance of a Web-based business more expensive. On the other hand, it is also troublesome to allow those who conduct business on the Web to insulate themselves against jurisdiction in every state, except in the state (if any) where they are physically located.

"Massachusetts has an interest in protecting its citizens from confusion, and its corporations from trademark infringement. It has a further interest in alerting its citizens who maintain Web-sites for business purposes that there is a chance that they may be haled into court in any state where their Web-site potentially causes harm or transacts business. On the whole, this factor leans toward this Court's assertion of jurisdiction over [defendant]."

Digital Equipment Corp. v. Altavista Technology, Inc., 960 F. Supp. 456, 471 (D. Mass. 1997).

"Personal jurisdiction clearly exists, for example, when Internet activity involves business over the Internet, including on-line contracts with residents of a foreign jurisdiction or substantial interactivity of a commercial nature with the Web site."

Barrett v. Catacombs Press, 44 F. Supp. 2d 717, 724 (E.D. Pa. 1999).

"In one line of cases, courts have declined to exercise jurisdiction on the basis that the Web site is passive where the site merely provides information to those who seek it. . . . Another line of cases has rejected the holding that advertisement Web sites are merely passive. . . . The weight of the case law, however, seems to favor the analysis that requires something more than a Web site that acts as a worldwide advertisement to trigger personal jurisdiction."

Barrett v. Catacombs Press, 44 F. Supp. 2d 717, 725 (E.D. Pa. 1999).

"In the Internet context, courts are divided as to whether personal jurisdiction should be exercised where the defendant merely maintains a Web site without any contract to sell goods or any active solicitation. While some courts have held that such 'passive' Web sites are insufficient to trigger jurisdiction, . . . , others have held that a Web site advertisement in and of itself is sufficient to confer jurisdiction, . . . Not only does the weight of the authority favor the rationale that a 'passive' Web site is insufficient to trigger jurisdiction, but we believe that such decisions comport with the traditional concept of personal jurisdiction where merely fortuitous contact is insufficient."

Barrett v. Catacombs Press, 44 F. Supp. 2d 717, 727 (E.D. Pa. 1999) (citations omitted).

"We agree with the Plaintiff that posting of messages to listserves [sic] and USENET discussion groups technically differs from the maintenance of a "passive" Web page because messages are actively disseminated to those who participate in such groups. However, for jurisdictional purposes, we find that these contacts are akin to a 'passive' Web site and insufficient to trigger this court's jurisdiction."

Barrett v. Catacombs Press, 44 F. Supp. 2d 717, 728 (E.D. Pa. 1999).

"The analogy of a listserve [sic] or USENET discussion group to a 'passive' Web site comports with the limited case law on the relationship between Internet activity and personal jurisdiction. Unlike distributors of magazines or other materials who can affirmatively decide not to sell or distribute to certain forums, after posting to a listserve or USENET discussion group on the Internet, the option of bypassing certain regions is not available."

Barrett v. Catacombs Press, 44 F. Supp. 2d 717, 728 (E.D. Pa. 1999).

"Because the web enables easy world-wide access, allowing computer interaction via the web to supply sufficient contacts to establish [general[jurisdiction would eviscerate the personal jurisdiction requirement as it currently exists."

McDonough v. Fallon McElligott, Inc., 40 U.S.P.Q.2d (BNA) 1826 (S.D. Cal. 1996).

"[P]ersonal jurisdiction surely cannot be based solely on the ability of District residents to access the defendants' websites, for this does not by itself show any persistent course of conduct by the defendants in the District."

GTE New Media Servs., Inc. v. Bellsouth Corp., 199 F.3d 1343, 1349-50 (D.C. Cir. 2000).

"Although [defendant's] website provides information about the company, customer service, and technical support, a substantial portion of the site is dedicated to allowing the consumer to purchase [defendant's] products online. [Defendant's] online sales constitutes conducting business over the Internet, and therefore . . . asserting personal jurisdiction comports with due process."

Stomp v. NeatO, LLC, 61 F. Supp. 2d 1074, 1078 (C.D. Cal. 1999).

"A federal court sitting in diversity may exercise personal jurisdiction over a nonresident defendant if (1) the long-arm statute of the forum state confers personal jurisdiction over that defendant; and (2) exercise of such jurisdiction by the forum state is consistent with due process under the United States Constitution."

Mink v. AAAA Dev. LLC, 190 F.3d 333, 335 (5th Cir. 1999).

"The Due Process Clause of the Fourteenth Amendment permits the exercise of personal jurisdiction over a nonresident defendant when (1) that defendant has purposefully availed himself of the benefits and protections of the forum state by establishing 'minimum contacts' with the forum state; and (2) the exercise of jurisdiction over that defendant does not offend 'traditional notions of fair play and substantial justice.'"

Mink v. AAAA Dev. LLC, 190 F.3d 333, 336 (5th Cir. 1999).

Related issues. "We agree that simply registering someone else's trademark as a domain name and posting a web site on the Internet is not sufficient to subject a party domiciled in one state to jurisdiction in another. . . . [T]here must be 'something more' to demonstrate that the defendant directed his activity toward the forum state."

Panavision Int'l, Inc. v. Toeppen, 141 F.3d 1316, 1322 (9th Cir. 1998).

"The Internet makes it possible to conduct business throughout the world entirely from a desktop. With this global revolution looming on the horizon, the development of the law concerning the permissible scope of personal jurisdiction based on Internet use is in its infant stages. The cases are scant. Nevertheless, our review of the available cases and materials reveals that the likelihood that personal jurisdiction can be constitutionally exercised is directly proportionate to the nature and quality of commercial activity that an entity conducts over the Internet. If the defendant enters into contracts with residents of a foreign jurisdiction that involve the knowing and repeated transmission of computer files over the Internet, personal jurisdiction is proper. At the opposite end are situations where a defendant has simply posted information on an Internet Web site which is accessible to users in foreign jurisdictions. A passive Web site that does little more than make information available to those who are interested in it is not grounds for the exercise of personal jurisdiction. The middle ground is occupied by interactive Web sites where a user can exchange information with the host computer. In these cases, the exercise of jurisdiction is determined by examining the level of interactivity and commercial nature of the exchange of information that occurs on the Web site."

Zippo Mfg. Co. v. Zippo Dot Com, Inc., 952 F. Supp. 1119, 1124 (W.D. Pa. 1997) (citations omitted).

See also **burden; effects doctrine; general jurisdiction; minimum contact(s); purposeful availment; reasonableness; relatedness; specific jurisdiction.**

personal newspaper *(Internet)*

"[S]ervices [which] allow a user to specify what sort of news, weather, sports, and the like that the user has an interest in. These organizations will then gather, on a daily or other specified basis, just the news and information that the user has indicated, for delivery to that specific user. Other users get their own, tailored information."

> I. Trotter Hardy, *Project Looking Forward: Sketching the Future of Copyright in a Networked World* 94 (May 1998).

PGA *(hardware)*

Acronym for "Professional Graphic Array."

> Princeton Graphics Operating L.P. v. NEC Home Elecs. (U.S.A.), Inc., 732 F. Supp. 1258, 1259 n.3 (S.D.N.Y. 1990).

See **professional graphic array.**

PGP *(technology)*

Acronym for "Pretty Good Privacy." *See* **Pretty Good Privacy.**

phonorecords *(copyright)*

"[M]aterial objects in which sounds, other than those accompanying a motion picture or other audiovisual work, are fixed by any method now known or later developed, and from which the sounds can be perceived, reproduced, or otherwise communicated, either directly or with the aid of a machine or device. The term 'phonorecords' includes the material object in which the sounds are first fixed."

> U.S. Copyright Act, 17 U.S.C. § 101.

PICS *(organization; technology)*

Acronym for "Platform for Internet Content Selection."

"The Platform for Internet Content Selection (PICS) project is designed to facilitate user-based zoning by encouraging Internet speakers to rate the content of their speech using codes recognized by all screening programs."

> *Reno v. American Civil Liberties Union,* 521 U.S. 844, 890-91 (1997)
> (O'Connor, J., concurring in part, dissenting in part).

Annotation. "PICS will provide the ability for third parties, as well as individual content providers, to rate content on the Internet in a variety of ways. When fully implemented, PICS-compatible World Wide Web browsers, Usenet News Group readers, and other Internet applications, will provide parents the ability to choose from a variety of rating services, or a combination of services."

> *American Civil Liberties Union v. Reno,* 929 F. Supp. 824, 838 (E.D. Pa. 1996), *aff'd, Reno v. American Civil Liberties Union,* 521 U.S. 844 (1997).

"Platform for Internet Content Selection ('PICS') to develop technical standards for attaching electronic ratings to Internet addresses. When the system is fully implemented, PICS-compatible client software (including browsers, newsgroup readers, and mail readers); Internet service providers; and commercial on-line services will be able to detect PICS tags and block content based on how a parent has configured the software. PICS will thus enable parents to design from an array of categories blocking criteria that suit the parents' values or needs. The PICS program envisages both rating by content providers and rating by third parties. The vast majority of Internet sites currently remain unrated."

Shea v. Reno, 930 F. Supp. 916, 932 (S.D.N.Y. 1996).

pictorial, graphic, and sculptural works *(copyright)*

"[I]include two-dimensional and three-dimensional works of fine, graphic, and applied art, photographs, prints and art reproductions, maps, globes, charts, diagrams, models, and technical drawings, including architectural plans. Such works shall include works of artistic craftsmanship insofar as their form but not their mechanical or utilitarian aspects are concerned; the design of a useful article, as defined in this section, shall be considered a pictorial, graphic, or sculptural work only if, and only to the extent that, such design incorporates pictorial, graphic, or sculptural features that can be identified separately from, and are capable of existing independently of, the utilitarian aspects of the article."

U.S. Copyright Act, 17 U.S.C. §101.

pilot project *(Year 2000)*

A small, controllable compliance project. The purpose of the pilot project is to learn about the process and apply that learning to subsequent, larger applications. During the pilot project, the organization can expect to learn how well the Year 2000 committee (or team) works together. They need to use the pilot project to learn what obstacles were encountered while converting the application, and how much time, cost, and other resources were required to bring the application into compliance. (wsr)

PIN *(technology)*

Acronym for "Personal Identification Number."

[NEW ZEALAND] "Personal Identification Number."

Databank Systems Ltd. v. Commissioner of Inland Revenue [1987], N.Z.L.R. 312 (H.C. Wellington).

piracy *(copyright)*

> *Annotation.* "RIAA asserts that Internet distribution of serial digital copies of pirated copyrighted material will discourage the purchase of legitimate recordings, and predicts that losses to digital Internet piracy will soon surpass the $300 million that is allegedly lost annually to other more traditional forms of piracy."
>
> > *Recording Indus. Ass'n of America v. Diamond Multimedia Sys., Inc.,* 180 F.3d 1072, 1074 (9th Cir. 1999).

> "Whether or not piracy causes such financial harm is a subject of dispute. Critics of the industry's piracy loss figures have noted that a willingness to download illicit files for free does not necessarily correlate to lost sales, for the simple reason that persons willing to accept an item for free often will not purchase the same item, even if no longer freely available. Critics further note that the price of commercially available recordings already reflects the existence of copying and the benefits and harms such copying causes; thus, they contend, the current price of recordings offsets, at least in part, the losses incurred by the industry from home taping and piracy."
>
> > *Recording Indus. Ass'n of America v. Diamond Multimedia Sys., Inc.,* 180 F.3d 1072, 1074 n.1 (9th Cir. 1999) (citations omitted).

> "In contrast to piracy, the Internet also supports a burgeoning traffic in legitimate audio computer files. Independent and wholly Internet record labels routinely sell and provide free samples of their artists' work online, while many unsigned artists distribute their own material from their own websites."
>
> > *Recording Indus. Ass'n of America v. Diamond Multimedia Sys., Inc.,* 180 F.3d 1072, 1074 (9th Cir. 1999).

> *See also* **music pirate(s).**

pirate(s)

> *See* **music pirate(s).**

pirated copy *(copyright; criminal)*

> "[A]n unauthorized copy of a performance already commercially released."
>
> > *Dowling v. United States,* 473 U.S. 207 (1985).

pitch *(technology)*

> "Movement [of disk heads] about the X [axis]."
>
> > *Tandon Corp. v. U.S. Int'l Trade Comm'n,* 831 F.2d 1017, 1020 n.3 (Fed. Cir. 1987).

pixel *(technology)*

Acronym for "pic[x]ture element." The smallest controllable unit on a display screen.

pixel pusher *(general)*

A computer artist.

pixelation *(technology)*

A video distortion problem caused by digitization or compression technology, where the individual pixels are replaced with blocks of pixels, giving a blocky look to the picture.

place and route *(software)*

"[S]oftware . . . used to design integrated circuits, i.e., computer chips. The software is designed to place the thousands (sometimes, millions) of tiny transistors that comprise the chip and 'route' (or, connect) the transistors to other transistors."

Cadence Design Sys., Inc. v. Avant! Corp., 125 F.3d 824, 825 n.1 (9th Cir. 1997).

plaintext *(technology)*

Also called "clear text." A message before it is encrypted or after it is decrypted, in plain English or another language. *See also* **in the clear.**

plasma display *(hardware)*

A type of flat-panel video display.

platform *(technology)*

A format or system on which software can be run. Examples of platforms are the IBM-PC and Apple Macintosh computers. Today, versions of software must be specially prepared for each platform, since many existing platforms are incompatible with one another.

Platform for Internet Content Selection *(organization)*

See PICS.

Platform for Privacy Protection Project *(organization)*

See P3P.

play mode *(video game)*

"[T]he audiovisual effects displayed during the actual play of the game, when the game symbols move and interact on the screen and the player controls the movement of one of the symbols (e.g., a spaceship)."

> *Williams Elec., Inc. v. Artic Int'l, Inc.,* 685 F.2d 870, 872 n.3 (3d Cir. 1982).

". . . refers to the audio-visual display seen and heard by a person playing the game."

> *Stern Elecs., Inc. v. Kaufman,* 669 F.2d 852, 854 n.2 (2d Cir. 1982).

"[A]fter the quarter has been deposited in the machine."

> *Midway Mfg. Co. v. Strohon,* 564 F. Supp. 741, 743 (N.D. Ill. 1983).

plug-compatible *(hardware)*

"[M]agnetic tape drives which were functionally equivalent to IBM magnetic tape drives and which could be 'plugged' into . . . IBM central processing units."

> *Telex Corp. v. IBM Corp.,* 367 F. Supp. 258, 272 (N.D. Okla. 1973), *aff'd in part, rev'd in part,* 510 F.2d 894 (10th Cir.), *cert. dism.,* 423 U.S. 802 (1975).

See also compatibility; plug-compatible peripheral device; plug-compatible product.

plug-compatible manufacturer *(manufacturing)*

Abbreviated as "PCM." *See* compatibility; PCM; plug-compatible; plug-compatible peripheral device; plug-compatible product.

plug-compatible peripheral device *(hardware)*

"What is meant is that a producer of a complete electronic processing unit manufactures . . . the central processing unit and peripheral components which are geared to use on that central processing unit. Many manufacturers produce peripheral components primarily for attachment to central processing units of a particular manufacturer and so, therefore, the plug compatible peripheral device refers to a component which is functionally equivalent to the manufacturer's peripheral device and can be readily plugged into that central processing unit."

> *Telex Corp. v. IBM Corp.,* 510 F.2d 894, 899 (10th Cir.), *cert. dism.,* 423 U.S. 802 (1975).

See also compatibility; peripheral devices; peripheral equipment; peripheral products; plug-compatible; plug-compatible product.

plug-compatible product *(hardware)*

"[A] device which can be used in place of another device without substantial electronic, mechanical or programming modifications and without significant change in operation of the computer system."

> *ILC Peripherals Leasing Corp. v. IBM Corp.*, 458 F. Supp. 423, 428 (N.D. Cal. 1978).

See also **compatibility; plug-compatible; plug-compatible peripheral device.**

plug-in *(Internet; software)*

A small program that improves the capabilities of a web browser in a specific way. Generally, plug-ins can be downloaded directly from a web site and self-installed to be usable from the web browser.

point of presence *(Internet; telecommunications)*

Abbreviated "POP."

A specific location within a Local Access Transport Area where a connection to the Internet terminates and/or originates its service.

point of purchase *(business)*

See **POP.**

point of sale *(business)*

[NEW ZEALAND] "These transactions, often referred to as EFT-POS (Electronic Funds Transfer—Point of Sale) transactions, are similar to ATM transactions in that they are card initiated. They are used solely for sale transactions so that each transaction results in a debit to the customer's account and a credit to the merchant's account. The authorization procedure is the same for ATM's."

> *Databank Sys. Ltd. v. Commissioner of Inland Revenue* [1987], N.Z.L.R. 312, (H.C. Wellington).

See also **EFT-POS; POP.**

point-to-multipoint *(telecommunications)*

A type of communications where a single source delivers information to many recipients. One example of this is broadcast television.

point-to-point *(telecommunications)*

A type of communications where two users are directly connected. One example of this is a regular telephone connection.

pointer *(Internet; technology)*

See **hyperlink; link(s).**

POP

(business)

Acronym for "Point **of** Purchase." A display at the retailer to promote one or more products.

(Internet)

Acronym for "Point **of** Presence." A location from which a user can connect to a network, often by dial-up phone lines.

pornographer *(criminal)*

"[F]or-profit purveyors of sexually explicit, 'adult' material. . . ."
> *American Civil Liberties Union v. Reno,* 929 F. Supp. 824, 866 (E.D. Pa. 1996), *aff'd, Reno v. American Civil Liberties Union,* 521 U.S. 844 (1997).

See also **obscenity.**

pornography *(criminal)*

"[S]exually explicit, 'adult' material. . . ."
> *American Civil Liberties Union v. Reno,* 929 F. Supp. 824, 866 (E.D. Pa. 1996), *aff'd, Reno v. American Civil Liberties Union,* 521 U.S. 844 (1997).

Annotation. "Apart from hardcore and child pornography, however, the word 'pornography' does not have a fixed legal meaning."
> *American Civil Liberties Union v. Reno,* 929 F. Supp. 824, 866 (E.D. Pa. 1996), *aff'd, Reno v. American Civil Liberties Union,* 521 U.S. 844 (1997).

See also **obscenity.**

port

(Internet)

A number that is part of a URL, appearing after a colon (:), right after the domain name.

(technology)

To transfer a computer program or database from one computer platform to another or to convert a computer program from one operating system to another. Porting often requires the translation of a computer program into a different computer language or a different version of the same computer language.

The I/O (input/output) connection of a computer. A port is where a connecting cable plugs into the CPU case.

"[O]utlets for direct network connections. . . ."

> *American Civil Liberties Union v. Reno,* 929 F. Supp. 824, 832 (E.D. Pa. 1996), *aff'd, Reno v. American Civil Liberties Union,* 521 U.S. 844 (1997).

Annotation. *(software)* "An application that is written for one PC operating system will operate on another PC operating system only if it is ported to that system, and porting applications is both time-consuming and expensive. Therefore, application developers tend to write first to the operating system with the most users—Windows. Developers might then port their applications to other operating systems, but only to the extent that the marginal added sales justify the cost of porting. In order to recover that cost, ISVs that do go to the effort of porting frequently set the price of ported applications considerably higher than that of the original versions written for Windows."

> *United States v. Microsoft Corp.,* 65 F. Supp. 2d 1, 11 (D.D.C. 1999) (Finding of Fact 38).

portable *(software)*

"[I]t [a software program] could be transported to and executed on computers other than the . . . equipment for which the [original software] was designed."

> *SAS Inst., Inc. v. S&H Computer Sys., Inc.,* 605 F. Supp. 816, 819 (M.D. Tenn. 1985).

portal *(Internet)*

"Web sites, which aggregate Web content and provide services such as search engines, E-mail, and travel reservation systems. . . ."

> *United States v. Microsoft Corp.,* 65 F. Supp. 2d 1, 8 (D.D.C. 1999) (Finding of Fact 27).

Annotation. ". . . could begin to host full lines of the server-based, personal-productivity applications that have begun to appear in small numbers on the Web. If so, increasing numbers of computer users equipped with Web browsers and IAP connections could begin to conduct a significant portion of their computing through these portals."

> *United States v. Microsoft Corp.,* 65 F. Supp. 2d 1, 8 (D.D.C. 1999) (Finding of Fact 27).

portfolio *(business)*

Refers to the inventory—preferably automated—of software applications in use by an organization, grouped by business area. A company's portfolio may also include some unused applications.

POS *(business)*
Acronym for "Point of Sale." *See* **point of sale.**

positive feedback loop *(economics)*
"[S]elf-reinforcing cycle. . . ."
> *United States v. Microsoft Corp.,* 65 F. Supp. 2d 1, 11 (D.D.C. 1999) (Finding of Fact 39).

Related issues. "The main reason that demand for Windows experiences positive network effects, however, is that the size of Windows' installed base impels ISVs to write applications first and foremost to Windows, thereby ensuring a large body of applications from which consumers can choose. The large body of applications thus reinforces demand for Windows, augmenting Microsoft's dominant position and thereby perpetuating ISV incentives to write applications principally for Windows."
> *United States v. Microsoft Corp.,* 65 F. Supp. 2d 1, 11 (D.D.C. 1999) (Finding of Fact 39).

positive network effect *(economics)*
". . . is a phenomenon by which the attractiveness of a product increases with the number of people using it."
> *United States v. Microsoft Corp.,* 65 F. Supp. 2d 1, 11 (D.D.C. 1999) (Finding of Fact 38).

positive roamer verification *(telecommunications)*
See **PRV.**

post *(Internet)*
1. *(noun)* A message displayed on a newsgroup for others to read.
2. *(verb)* To send a message to a specific location, such as a newsgroup.

posting *(Internet)*
Placing a message on the Internet for others to read.

Annotation. "Any Internet user can communicate by posting a message to one of the thousands of newsgroups and bulletin boards or by engaging in an on-line 'chat,' and thereby reach an audience worldwide that shares an interest in a particular topic."
> *American Civil Liberties Union v. Reno,* 929 F. Supp. 824, 843 (E.D. Pa. 1996), *aff'd, Reno v. American Civil Liberties Union,* 521 U.S. 844 (1997).

Related issues. "Once a provider posts its content on the Internet, it is available to all other Internet users worldwide. Similarly, once a user posts a message to a newsgroup or bulletin board, that message becomes available to all subscribers to that newsgroup or bulletin board.

* * *

"Once a provider posts its content on the Internet, it cannot prevent that content from entering any community."
American Civil Liberties Union v. Reno, 929 F. Supp. 824, 844 (3d Cir. 1996), *aff'd, Reno v. American Civil Liberties Union,* 521 U.S. 844 (1997).

"Posting a message to the sports bulletin board is a random communication of computerized messages analogous to posting a written notice on a public bulletin board, not a publication that appears at regular intervals."
It's in the Cards, Inc. v. Fuschetto, 193 Wis.2d 429, 436, 535 N.W.2d 11, 14 (1995).

"We agree that simply registering someone else's trademark as a domain name and posting a web site on the Internet is not sufficient to subject a party domiciled in one state to jurisdiction in another. . . . [T]here must be 'something more' to demonstrate that the defendant directed his activity toward the forum state."
Panavision Int'l, Inc. v. Toeppen, 141 F.3d 1316, 1322 (9th Cir. 1998).

post-production *(entertainment; multimedia)*
The phase following production of an interactive title or video game, including quality assurance, focus testing, and marketing.

Postscript *(technology)*
A method of drawing alphanumeric characters by describing the shape of the character as a series of lines and curves.

POTS *(telecommunications)*
Acronym for "Plain Old Telephone Service." Refers to traditional voice telephone communications. *See also* **PSTN.**

PPP *(Internet; telecommunications)*
Acronym for "Point-to-Point Protocol." The communications protocol that permits a computer to communicate with the Internet.

PPU *(hardware)*
Acronym for "Picture Processing Unit." A hardware chip that processes video images.

PPV *(entertainment; telecommunications)*
Acronym for "Pay Per View."

practice statement *(electronic commerce)*
"[D]ocumentation of the practices, procedures and controls employed by a Certification Authority."
Cal. Code of Regs., tit. 2, div. 7, ch. 10, § 22003(a)(1)(G).

preemption *(copyright)*
Also called "copyright preemption"; "federal preemption."
"(a) On and after January 1, 1978, all legal or equitable rights that are equivalent to any of the exclusive rights within the general scope of copyright as specified by section 106 in works of authorship that are fixed in a tangible medium of expression and come within the subject matter of copyright as specified by sections 102 and 103, whether created before or after that date and whether published or unpublished, are governed exclusively by this title. Thereafter, no person is entitled to any such right or equivalent right in any such work under the common law or statutes of any State.
"(b) Nothing in this title annuls or limits any rights or remedies under the common law or statutes of any State with respect to—(1) subject matter that does not come within the subject matter of copyright as specified by sections 102 and 103, including works of authorship not fixed in any tangible medium of expression; or (2) any cause of action arising from undertakings commenced before January 1, 1978; (3) activities violating legal or equitable rights that are not equivalent to any of the exclusive rights within the general scope of copyright as specified by section 106; or (4) State and local landmarks, historic preservation, zoning, or building codes, relating to architectural works protected under section 102(a)(8).

* * *

"(e) The scope of Federal preemption under this section is not affected by the adherence of the United States to the Berne Convention or the satisfaction of obligations of the United States thereunder."
17 U.S.C. § 301.

Annotation. "Congress carefully designed the statutory framework of federal copyright preemption. In order to insure that the enforcement of these rights remains solely within the federal domain, section 301(a) of the Copyright Act expressly preempts

'all legal or equitable rights that are equivalent to any of the exclusive rights within the general scope of copyright as specified by section 106 in works of authorship that are fixed in a tangible medium of expression and come within the subject matter of copyright as specified by sections 102 and 103. . . .'

"17 U.S.C. § 301(a). This sweeping displacement of state law is, however, limited by section 301(b), which provides, in relevant part, that

'[n]othing in this title annuls or limits any rights or remedies under the common law or statutes of any State with respect to . . . activities violating legal or equitable rights that are equivalent to any of the exclusive rights within the general scope of copyright as specified by section 106. . . .'

"17 U.S.C. § 301(b)(3)."

Computer Assocs. Int'l, Inc. v. Altai, Inc., 982 F.2d 693, 716 (2d Cir. 1992).

"The Copyright Act set forth a two-part test for determining whether a state law claim is preempted. First, the work on which the state law claim is based must be within the subject matter of copyright, i.e., the state law claim must arise from rights in a work of authorship fixed in a tangible medium of expression. Second, the state law claim must assert rights that are equivalent to the exclusive rights specified by Section 106 of the Act, i.e., the right to prohibit reproduction, creation of derivative works, performance, distribution, or display of a work.

"In order to apply the second prong, courts focus on whether the state claim has an 'extra element' that differentiates if from the rights protected by federal law."

Michaels v. Internet Entertainment Group, Inc., 5 F. Supp. 2d 823, 836-37 (C.D. Cal. 1998) (citations omitted).

"But are rights created by contract 'equivalent to any of the exclusive rights within the general scope of copyright'? Three courts of appeals have answered 'no.' The district court disagreed with these decisions, but we think them sound."

ProCD, Inc. v. Zeidenberg, 86 F.3d 1447, 1454 (7th Cir. 1996).

"[S]tate law claims that rely on the misappropriation branch of unfair competition are preempted."

Warner Bros. v. American Broadcasting Cos., 720 F.2d 231, 247 (2d Cir. 1980).

Related issues. "Copyrightable material often contains uncopyrightable elements within it, but Section 301 preemption bars state law misappropriation claims with respect to uncopyrightable as well as copyrightable elements."

   National Basketball Ass'n v. Motorola, Inc., 105 F.2d 841, 850 (2d Cir. 1997).

"[If] the work is unprotected by federal law because of a lack of originality, then its use is neither unfair nor unjustified."

   Financial Infor., Inc. v. Moody's Investors Serv., Inc., 808 F.2d 204, 208 (2d Cir. 1986).

"Two computer programs may be sufficiently dissimilar on the level of expression to defeat liability for copyright infringement, but they may be sufficiently similar on a more abstract or ideational level to establish liability for trade secret protection."

   Comprehensive Technologies Int'l, Inc. v. Software Artisans, Inc., 3 F.3d 730, 736 nn. 6-7 (4th Cir. 1993).

See also **extra element.**

prejudgment interest *(contract)*

". . . is awarded in contract cases to compensate the claimant for the loss of income the money owed would have earned if payment had not been delayed."

   AGS Computers v. Bear, Stearns & Co., 581 A.2d 508, 509-10, 244, N.J. Super. 1, 4 (1990).

preliminary injunction

(First Amendment)

"In a case in which the injury alleged is a threat to First Amendment interests, the finding of irreparable injury is often tied to the likelihood of success on the merits."

   American Civil Liberties Union v. Reno, 929 F. Supp. 824, 851 (E.D. Pa. 1996), *aff'd, Reno v. American Civil Liberties Union,* 521 U.S. 844 (1997).

(procedure)

"To obtain a preliminary injunction, plaintiffs must establish that they are likely to prevail on the merits and that they will suffer irreparable harm if injunctive relief is not granted. We also must consider whether the potential harm to the defendant from issuance of a temporary restraining order outweighs possible harm to the plaintiffs if such relief is denied, and whether the granting of injunctive relief is in the public interest."

   American Civil Liberties Union v. Reno, 929 F. Supp. 824, 851 (E.D. Pa. 1996), *aff'd, Reno v. American Civil Liberties Union,* 521 U.S. 844 (1997).

"To prevail on a request for preliminary injunction, the plaintiff must demonstrate 1) a substantial likelihood of success on the merits; 2) irreparable harm or injury absent an injunction; 3) less harm or injury to the other parties involved; and 4) the service of the public interest.

> *McVeigh v. Cohen,* 983 F. Supp. 215, 218 (D.D.C. 1998).

(trademark)
"To be entitled to a preliminary injunction, a party must show either (1) a combination of probable success on the merits and a possibility of irreparable harm, or (2) the existence of serious questions on the merits and the balance of hardships weighing heavily in its favor. These are not two distinct tests, but ends of a continuum in which the required showing of harm 'varies inversely with the required showing of meritoriousness.'"

> *Playboy Enters., Inc. v. Welles,* 47 U.S.P.Q.2d (BNA) 1186, 1988 (S.D. Cal. 1998) (citations omitted).

"A plaintiff is entitled to a preliminary injunction in a trademark case when he demonstrates either (1) a combination of probable success on the merits and the possibility of irreparable injury; or (2) the existence of serious questions going to the merits and that the balance of hardships tips sharply in his favor."

> *Brookfield Comm., Inc. v. West Coast Entertainment Corp.,* 174 F.3d 1036, 1046 (9th Cir. 1999) (citation omitted).

Annotation *(copyright).* The test for a preliminary injunction varies among the federal circuit courts of appeal. In the Ninth Circuit, for example, the plaintiff "must show a likelihood of success on the merits of its copyright infringement action and the possibility of irreparable injury." *See, e.g., Apple Computer, Inc. v. Formula Int'l, Inc.,* 725 F.2d 521, 523 (9th Cir. 1984).

"A plaintiff seeking preliminary injunctive relief must demonstrate 'either a likelihood of success on the merits and the possibility of irreparable injury[] or that serious questions going to the merits were raised and the balance of hardships tips sharply in its favor.'"

> *Cadence Design Sys., Inc. v. Avant! Corp.,* 125 F.3d 824, 826 (9th Cir. 1997), quoting *Sega Enters. Ltd. v. Accolade, Inc.,* 977 F.2d 1510, 1517 (9th Cir. 1992).

While in the Fifth Circuit, the plaintiff "must satisfy four stringent criteria: (a) that they are substantially likely to succeed on the merits of their claims, (b) that the Court's failure to issue the injunction poses a substantial threat of irreparable injury, (c) that the threatened injury outweighs any damage that the injunction's issuance might cause to the opposing party, and (d) that the injunction's issuance will not undermine the public interest."

> *DSC Comm. Corp. v. DGI Technologies, Inc.,* 898 F. Supp. 1183, 1187 (N.D. Tex. 1995), *aff'd,* 81 F.3d 597 (5th Cir. 1996).

Related issues *(copyright)* "A district court's preliminary injunction order will be reversed only if the district court abused its discretion or based its decision on an erroneous legal standard or on clearly erroneous findings of fact."

> *Cadence Design Sys., Inc. v. Avant! Corp.,* 125 F.3d 824, 826 (9th Cir. 1997); *Triad Sys. Corp. v. Southeastern Express Co.,* 64 F.3d 1330, 1334 (9th Cir. 1995).

"We further note that if the defendant is using copyrighted material owned by the plaintiff and a court awards damages instead of enjoining such use, the court has, in essence, made the plaintiff an involuntary licensor of its copyrighted material. The defendant can then use the copyrighted material to compete with the plaintiff."

> *Cadence Design Sys., Inc. v. Avant! Corp.,* 125 F.3d 824, 828 n.8 (9th Cir. 1997).

"In this circuit, as well as in other circuits, a defendant who knowingly infringes another's copyright 'cannot complain of the harm that will befall it when properly forced to desist from its infringing activities.'"

> *Cadence Design Sys., Inc. v. Avant! Corp.,* 125 F.3d 824, 829 (9th Cir. 1997).

"[A] defendant cannot, by asserting the adequacy of money damages, rebut the presumption of irreparable harm that flows from a showing of likelihood of success on the merits . . . ."

> *Cadence Design Sys., Inc. v. Avant! Corp.,* 125 F.3d 824, 827 (9th Cir. 1997).

"In the Fifth Circuit there is no presumption of irreparable harm in copyright infringement cases, and thus in the Fifth Circuit, a copyright defendant can prevail by showing the adequacy of money damages. The Fifth Circuit is the only court of appeals that does not apply the presumption of irreparable harm."

> *Cadence Design Sys., Inc. v. Avant! Corp.,* 125 F.3d 824, 827 n.4 (9th Cir. 1997).

premastering *(multimedia)*
One step in the CD-ROM manufacturing process in which the individual files of a CD-ROM are combined into a single file.

pre-production *(multimedia)*
The phase preceding actual production of the multimedia title, when the developer is licensing content, creating the design, hiring the team, and obtaining the financing.

present value *(contract)*

"[T]he value, as of a date certain, of one or more sums payable in the future or one or more performances due in the future, discounted to a date certain. The discount is determined by the interest rate specified by the parties in their agreement unless that rate was manifestly unreasonable when the transaction was entered into. Otherwise, the discount is determined by a commercially reasonable rate that takes into account the circumstances of each case when the transaction was entered into."

U.C.C. 2B-102(a)(36) (proposed).

Pretty Good Privacy *(technology)*

Abbreviated as "PGP."

"[A] public key cryptographic system developed by Philip Zimmerman."

U.S. General Accounting Office, *Information Superhighway: An Overview of Technology Changes* 21 n.13 (Jan. 1995).

price protection *(contract)*

An agreement between a seller and buyer, whereby (i) in the case of a price increase, the buyer will be able to continue purchasing the product at the lower price for a period of time after the price increase, and (ii) in the case of a price decrease, the seller will give the buyer a credit or rebate for the difference in price between the old price and the new price for all of the stock the buyer has on hand that was purchased at the higher price.

prima facie case

(copyright)

"To establish a prima facie case of copyright infringement, Plaintiffs must prove (1) ownership of a valid copyright in the infringed work; and (2) 'copying' by the Defendants."

Sega Enters. Ltd. v. MAPHIA, 857 F. Supp. 679, 686 (N.D. Cal. 1994).

(trademark)

"A certificate of registration of a mark upon the principal register provided by this chapter shall be prima facie evidence of the validity of the registered mark and of the registration of the mark, of the registrant's ownership of the mark, and of the registrant's exclusive right to use the registered mark in commerce on or in connection with the goods or services specified in the certificate, subject to any conditions or limitations stated in the certificate."

15 U.S.C. § 1057(b).

"A prima facie case for trademark infringement under the Lanham Act is established by a showing that (1) the mark is owned by or associated with a particular plaintiff and (2) that the Defendants' use of the mark is likely to cause confusion or mistake among the public."

> *Sega Enters. Ltd. v. MAPHIA,* 857 F. Supp. 679, 686 (N.D. Cal. 1994).

(unfair competition)
"To prevail on its unfair competition claims under the Lanham Act, [plaintiff] must . . . establish that the public is likely to be deceived or confused by the similarity of the marks."

> *Sega Enters. Ltd. v. MAPHIA,* 857 F. Supp. 679, 686 (N.D. Cal. 1994).

See also **prima facie evidence.**

prima facie evidence

(copyright)
"Although a timely obtained certificate of registration constitutes prima facie evidence of the validity of the claim of copyright, this presumption is rebuttable."

> *Bateman v. Mnemonics, Inc.,* 79 F.3d 1532, 1541 n.20 (11th Cir. 1995).

"[A] certificate of copyright registration constitutes prima facie evidence of copyrightability and shifts the burden of proof to the defendant to show why the copyright is not valid."

> *DSC Comm. Corp. v. DGI Technologies, Inc.,* 898 F. Supp. 1183, 1187 (N.D. Tex. 1995), *aff'd,* 81 F.3d 597 (5th Cir. 1996).

(trademark)
"[Plaintiff's] registration of the mark on the Principal Register in the Patent and Trademark Office constitutes prima facie evidence of the validity of the registered mark and of [plaintiff's] exclusive right to use the mark on the goods and services specified in the registration."

> *Brookfield Comm., Inc. v. West Coast Entertainment Corp.,* 174 F.3d 1036, 1047 (9th Cir. 1999) (citation omitted).

Annotation. *(trademark)* "[Defendant] can rebut this presumption by showing that it used the mark in commerce first, since a fundamental tenet of trademark law is that ownership of an inherently distinctive mark . . . is governed by priority of use."

> *Brookfield Comm., Inc. v. West Coast Entertainment Corp.,* 174 F.3d 1036, 1047 (9th Cir. 1999).

See also **prima facie case.**

printed circuit board *(technology)*

"Chips are mounted onto printed circuit boards (usually referred to as 'boards'). Logic is the name given to a particular type of board which enables the equipment to perform predetermined functions. Chips, boards, and logic are all installed inside other units (personal computers, terminals, or control units)."

IRS Letter Ruling 8721016, Feb. 17, 1987.

[CANADA] "[A] sheet of fiberglass or epoxy onto which a thin layer of metal has been applied, then etched away to form traces. Electronic components can then be attached to the board with molten solder, and they can exchange electronic signals via the etched traces on the board."

Apple Computer, Inc. v. Mackintosh Computers Ltd. (1986), 28 D.L.R. (4th) 178 (Fed. T.D.).

printer *(hardware)*

". . . perform an output function. Like a typewriter terminal, a printer converts electrical signals into printed characters and numbers."

Telex Corp. v. IBM Corp., 367 F. Supp. 258, 274 (N.D. Okla. 1973), *aff'd in part, rev'd in part,* 510 F.2d 894 (10th Cir.), *cert. dism.,* 423 U.S. 802 (1975).

See also **character printer; daisy wheel; dot matrix printer; laser printer; line printer.**

printout *(technology)*

"A visually perceptible printed copy. Is used variously to mean a listing of the computer instructions that form the program or the product resulting from the operation of the computer program."

U.S. Copyright Office, *Compendium of Copyright Office Practices* II, § 326 (1984).

prior art *(patent)*

"A person shall be entitled to a patent unless—

(a) the invention was known or used by others in this country, or patented or described in a printed publication in this or a foreign country, before the invention thereof by the applicant for patent, or

(b) the invention was patented or described in a printed publication in this or a foreign country or in public use or on sale in this country, more than one year prior to the date of the application for patent in the United States; or

* * *

"(f) he did not himself invent the subject matter sought to be patented, or

(g) before the applicant's invention thereof the invention was made in this country by another who had not abandoned, suppressed, or concealed it. In determining priority of invention there shall be considered not only the respective dates of conception and reduction to practice of the invention, but also the reasonable diligence of one who was first to conceive and last to reduce to practice, from a time prior to conception by the other."

35 U.S.C. § 102.

prior restraint *(constitutional)*

Annotation. "It is axiomatic that 'prior restraints on speech and publication are the most serious and least tolerable infringement on First Amendment rights.' *Nebraska Press Ass'n v. Stuart,* 427 U.S. 539, 559 (1976). Indeed, the Supreme Court has opined that 'it is the chief purpose of the [First Amendment] guaranty to prevent previous restraints upon publication.' *Near v. Minnesota,* 283 U.S. 697, 713 (1931). Accordingly, '[a]ny prior restraint on expression comes . . . with a "heavy presumption" against its constitutional validity.' At the same time, the Supreme Court has cautioned that '[t]he phrase "prior restraint" is not a self-wielding sword. Nor can it serve as a talismanic test.' We accordingly turn from '[t]he generalization that prior restraint is particularly obnoxious' to a 'more particularistic analysis.'"

Bernstein v. United States Dept. of Justice, 176 F.3d 1132, 1138 (9th Cir. 1999) (citations omitted).

"The Supreme Court has treated licensing schemes that act as prior restraints on speech with suspicion because such restraints run the twin risks of encouraging self-censorship and concealing illegitimate abuses of censorial power. As a result, 'even if the government may constitutionally impose content-neutral prohibitions on a particular manner of speech, it may not condition that speech on obtaining a license or permit from a government official in that official's boundless discretion.'"

Bernstein v. United States Dept. of Justice, 176 F.3d 1132, 1139 (9th Cir. 1999) (citations omitted).

"In *Freedman v. Maryland,* [380 U.S. 51], the Supreme Court set out three factors for determining the validity of license schemes that impose a prior restraint on speech: (1) any restraint must be for a specified brief period of time; (2) there must be expeditious judicial review; and (3) the censor must bear the burden of going to court to suppress the speech in question and must bear the burden of proof."

> *Bernstein v. United States Dept. of Justice,* 176 F.3d 1132, 1144 (9th Cir. 1999) (citation omitted).

"[W]e conclude that encryption software, in its source code form and as employed by those in the field of cryptography, must be viewed as expressive for First Amendment purposes, and thus is entitled to the protections of the prior restraint doctrine."

> *Bernstein v. United States Dept. of Justice,* 176 F.3d 1132, 1145 (9th Cir. 1999) (footnote omitted).

"We express no opinion regarding whether *object* code manifests a 'close enough nexus to expression' to warrant application of the prior restraints doctrine."

> *Bernstein v. United States Dept. of Justice,* 176 F.3d 1132, 1141 n.15 (9th Cir. 1999) (emphasis in original).

"We emphasize the narrowness of our First Amendment holding. We do not hold that all software is expressive. Much of it surely is not."

> *Bernstein v. United States Dept. of Justice,* 176 F.3d 1132, 1145 (9th Cir. 1999).

Related issues. "The fact that computers will soon be able to respond directly to spoken commands, for example, should not confer on this government the unfettered power to impose prior restraints on speech in an effort to control its 'functional' aspects."

> *Bernstein v. United States Dept. of Justice,* 176 F.3d 1132, 1142 (9th Cir. 1999).

See also **First Amendment.**

privacy *(tort)*

"[T]he right to be left alone."

> Samuel D. Warren & Louis D. Brandeis, "The Right of Privacy," 4 HARV. L. REV. 193, 205 (1890).

"[T]he right to be left alone [is] the most comprehensive of rights, and the right most valued by civilized men."

> *Olmstead v. United States,* 277 U.S. 438, 478 (1928) (Brandeis, J., dissenting).

Annotation. "There is no single privacy law in the United States[;] rather, U.S. privacy law is a patchwork of constitutional, statutory, regulatory, and common law protections. While the Supreme Court has held that the Fourth Amendment restricts the ability of government to collect information from places in which an individual has a reasonable expectation of privacy, there is no constitutional right to be free from analogous intrusions by private parties. Tort law limits intrusive collection of private information, penalizes unwarranted disclosure of erroneous information about individuals. A number of statutes, at both the federal and state level, protect individuals from governmental misuse of personal information, while other statutes adopt 'fair information principles' for private sector record keepers in specific industries.

"In 1974, Congress established the Privacy Protection Study Commission to undertake a broad study of whether privacy rights were being adequately protected in the emerging information society. In its final report, issued in 1977, the Commission concluded that federal privacy laws should advance three concurrent policy goals—

• To minimize intrusiveness by creating a proper balance between what an individual is expected to divulge to a record-keeping organization and what he or she seeks in return;

• To maximize fairness by opening up record-keeping operations in ways that will minimize the extent to which recorded information about an individual is itself a source of unfairness in any decision about him or her; and

• To create legitimate, enforceable expectations of confidentiality by creating and defining obligations with respect to the uses and disclosures that will be made of recorded information about an individual.

"Today, more than fifteen years later, there have been further advances in telecommunications and information technology. Given the proliferation of computerized data collection and the prospect of converging technologies—computers, telephones, and mass media—it is time to reconsider what privacy means in developing electronic communities."

Department of Commerce, *Inquiry on Privacy Issues Relating to Private Sector Use of Telecommunications-Related Personal Information,* 59 Fed. Reg. 6841, 6843 (Feb. 11, 1994) (footnotes omitted).

Related issues. "In these days of 'big brother,' where through technology and otherwise the privacy interests of individuals from all walks of life are being ignored or marginalized, it is imperative that statutes explicitly protecting these rights be strictly observed."

McVeigh v. Cohen, 983 F. Supp. 215, 220 (D.D.C. 1998).

"[U]nlike transmissions by cordless telephone, or calls made to a telephone with six extensions, or telephone calls which may be answered by anyone at the other end of the line, there is virtually no risk that appellant's computer transmissions would be received by anyone other than the intended recipients. . . . In the modern age of communications, society must recognize that such expectations of privacy are reasonable."

United States v. Maxwell, 42 M.J. 568 (U.S. Air Force Crim. App. 1995), *aff'd in relevant part,* 45 M.J. 406 (U.S. Air Force App. 1996).

"In this increasingly electronic age, we are all required in our everyday lives to rely on modern technology to communicate with one another. This reliance on electronic communication, however, has brought with it a dramatic diminution in our ability to communicate privately. Cellular phones are subject to monitoring, email is easily intercepted, and transactions over the internet are often less than secure. Something as commonplace as furnishing our credit card number, social security number, or bank account number puts each of us at risk. Moreover, when we employ electronic methods of communication, we often leave electronic 'fingerprints' behind, fingerprints that can be traced back to us. Whether we are surveilled by our government, by criminals, or by our neighbors, it is fair to say that never has our ability to shield our affairs from prying eyes been at such a low ebb. The availability and use of secure encryption may offer an opportunity to reclaim some portion of the privacy we have lost. Government efforts to control encryption thus may well implicate not only the First Amendment rights or cryptographers intent on pushing the boundaries of their science, but also the constitutional rights of each of us as potential recipients of encryption's bounty. Viewed from this perspective, the government's efforts to retard progress in cryptography may implicate the Fourth Amendment, as well as the right to speak anonymously, the right against compelled speech, and the right to informational privacy."

Bernstein v. United States Dept. of Justice, 176 F.3d 1132, 1145-46 (9th Cir. 1999) (citations omitted).

"The Legislature further finds and declares that protection of the integrity of all types and forms of lawfully created computers, computer systems, and computer data is vital to the protection of the privacy of individuals. . . ."

Cal. Penal C. § 502(a).

"Development of photocopying machines, electronic computers and other sophisticated instruments have accelerated the ability of government to intrude into areas which a person normally chooses to exclude from prying eyes and inquisitive minds. Consequently, judicial interpretations of the reach of the constitutional protection of individual privacy must keep pace with the perils created by these new devices."

United States v. Miller, 425 U.S. 435, 451-52 (1976).

"[Defendant] may well have forfeited his right to privacy to any email transmissions that were downloaded to the computer by another subscriber or removed by a private individual from the on-line service."

United States v. Maxwell, 42 M.J. 568 (U.S. Air Force Crim. App. 1995), *aff'd in relevant part,* 45 M.J. 406 (U.S. Air Force App. 1996).

"The fact that an unauthorized 'hacker' might intercept an e-mail message does not diminish the legitimate expectation of privacy in any way."

United States v. Maxwell, 45 M.J. 406, 418 (U.S. Air Force Crim. App. 1995).

"One who gives publicly to a matter concerning the private life of another is subject to liability to the other for invasion of privacy, if the information is of a kind that

    (a) would be highly offensive to a reasonable person, and

    (b) is not legitimate concern to the public."

Restatement (Second) of Torts § 652D (1997).

"The Electronic Communications Privacy Act of 1986 (the 'Electronic Communications Act') provides a system of privacy protections for electronic communications (i.e., email messages), as well as procedures for government access to the communications and related records. In general, when the Government seeks to obtain information from a provider of electronic communication or remote computing services, the Government must demonstrate specific and articulable facts showing that there are reasonable grounds to believe that the requested information is relevant and material to an ongoing criminal investigation. The procedures required differ depending on whether the Government seeks to discover the contents of electronic communications or merely records related to them (i.e., personal information of subscribers, user activity logs, billing records and so on). Most notably, when the Government seeks only the related information, notice is not required to be given to the affected customer or subscriber. Any provider of electronic communication or remote computing services that discloses information in accordance with section 2703 is shielded from liability for any cause of action relating to the disclosure."

In re Application of the United States of America for an order pursuant to 18 U.S.C. 2703(d), 8 Computer Cas. (CCH) ¶ 47,897 (D. Mass. 1999) (citations omitted).

"[T]he government's efforts to regulate and control the spread of knowledge relating to encryption may implicate more than the First Amendment rights of cryptographers. In this increasingly electronic age, we are all required in our everyday lives to rely on modern technology to communicate with one another. This reliance on electronic communication, however, has brought with it a dramatic diminution in our ability to communicate privately. Cellular phones are subject to monitoring, email is easily intercepted, and transactions over the internet are often less than secure. Something as commonplace as furnishing our credit card number, social security number, or bank account number puts each of us at risk. Moreover, when we employ electronic methods of communication, we often leave electronic 'fingerprints' behind, fingerprints that can be traced back to us. Whether we are surveilled by our government, by criminals, or by our neighbors, it is fair to say that never has our ability to shield our affairs from prying eyes been at such a low ebb. The availability and use of secure encryption may offer an opportunity to reclaim some portion of the privacy we have lost. Government efforts to control encryption thus may well implicate not only the First Amendment rights of cryptographers intent on pushing the boundaries of their science, but also the constitutional rights of each of us as potential recipients of encryption's bounty. Viewed from this perspective, the government's efforts to retard progress in cryptography may implicate the Fourth Amendment, as well as the right to speak anonymously, . . . While we leave for another day the resolution of these difficult issues, it is important to point out that Bernstein's is a suit not merely concerning a small group of scientists laboring in an esoteric field, but also touches on the public interest broadly defined."

> *Bernstein v. United States Dept. of Justice*, 176 F.3d 1132, 1145-46 (9th Cir. 1999) (citations omitted).

privacy policy *(privacy)*

A statement on a web site that sets forth the types of personal information collected by the site, and how it will be used. *See also* **opt-in; opt-out.**

private key *(electronic commerce)*

"[T]he key of a key pair used to create a digital signature."

> Cal. Code of Regs., tit. 2, div. 7, ch. 10, § 22003(a)(1)(H); Wash. Rev. Code § 19.34.020(23).

private key encryption *(technology)*

A type of encryption in which both the sender and the recipient of a message use a single, common key for both encryption and decryption of the message.

Pro-CD *(contract; copyright)*

Citation: *Pro-CD, Inc. v. Zeidenberg*, 86 F.3d 1447 (7th Cir.), *rev'g* 908 F. Supp. 640 (W.D. Wis. 1996).

"*ProCD* was in part an application of the extra-element test. Having held the misappropriation claims to be preempted, Judge Easterbrook went on to hold that the plaintiffs could bring a state law contract claim. The court held that the defendants were bound by the software's shrink-wrap licenses as a matter of contract law and that the private contract rights were not preempted because they were not equivalent to the exclusive rights granted by copyright law. In other words, the contract right claims were not preempted because the general scope requirement was not met."

National Basketball Ass'n v. Motorola, Inc., 105 F.3d 841, 850 (2d Cir. 1997).

process

(copyright)

"In no case does copyright protection for an original work of authorship extend to any idea, procedure, process, system, method of operation, concept, principle, or discovery, regardless of the form in which it is described, explained, illustrated, or embodied in such work."

U.S. Copyright Act, 17 U.S.C. § 102(b).

(patent)

"In conformance with the standards of patent law, title 35 provides protection for the process or method performed by a computer in accordance with a program. Thus, patent and copyright laws protect distinct aspects of a computer program."

Atari Games Corp. v. Nintendo of America, Inc., 975 F.2d 832, 839 (Fed. Cir. 1992), *citing Arrhythmia Research Technology v. Corazonix Corp.*, 958 F.2d 1053 (Fed. Cir. 1992).

Annotation (copyright). "Some concern has been expressed lest copyright in computer programs should extend protection to the methodology or processes adopted by the programmer, rather than merely to the 'writing' expressing his ideas. Section 102(b) is intended, among other things, to make clear that the expression adopted by the programmer is the copyrightable element in a computer program, and that the actual processes or methods embodied in the program are not within the scope of the copyright law."

H.R. Rep No. 1476, 94th Cong., 2d Sess. 57 (1976).

"Franklin argues that an operating system is either a 'process,' 'system,' or 'method of operation' and hence uncopyrightable. Franklin correctly notes that underlying section 102(b) and many of the statements for which *Baker v. Selden* is cited is the distinction which must be made between property subject to patent law, which protects discoveries, and that subject to copyright law, which protects the writings describing such discoveries. However, Franklin's argument misapplies that distinction in this case. Apple does not seek to copyright the method which instructs the computer to perform its operating functions but only the instructions themselves. . . .

"Since it is only the instructions which are protected, a 'process' is no more involved because the instructions in an operating system program may be used to activate the operation of the computer than it would be if instructions were written in ordinary English in a manual which described the necessary steps to activate an intricate complicated machine."

Apple Computer, Inc. v. Franklin Computer Corp., 714 F.2d 1240, 1250-51 (3d Cir.), *cert. denied,* 464 U.S. 1033 (1984).

"Where a portion of the computer program constitutes an unprotectable method of operation or process, it is not an expressive part of the work. It is particularly important to exclude methods of operation and processes from the scope of copyright in computer programs because much of the contents of computer programs is patentable. Were we to permit an author to claim copyright protection for those elements of the work that should be the province of patent law, we would be undermining the competitive principles that are fundamental to the patent system."

Bateman v. Mnemonics, Inc., 875 F. Supp. 1398, 1541 n.21 (11th Cir. 1995).

processing function *(hardware; software)*

"[T]he computation or performance of logical operations. These logical operations involve additions, subtractions, and comparisons. The logic is composed of simple steps done rapidly to achieve the ultimate results."

Telex Corp. v. IBM Corp., 367 F. Supp. 258, 274 (N.D. Okla. 1973), *aff'd in part, rev'd in part,* 510 F.2d 894 (10th Cir.), *cert. dism.,* 423 U.S. 802 (1975).

produce *(criminal)*

". . . includes design, alter, authenticate, duplicate, or assemble. . . ."

18 U.S.C. § 1029(e)(4).

production *(business)*

The system environment in which an organization performs its routine environment information processing activities.

professional graphic array *(hardware)*

"IBM video standard. . . ."

Princeton Graphics Operating L.P. v. NEC Home Elecs. (U.S.A.), Inc., 732 F. Supp. 1258, 1259 n.3 (S.D.N.Y. 1990).

See also **PGA.**

program(s) *(software)*

"[A] set of statements or instructions to be used directly or indirectly in a computer in order to bring about a certain result."

U.S. Copyright Act, 17 U.S.C. § 101, *quoted in E.F. Johnson Co. v. Uniden Corp. of America,* 623 F. Supp. 1485, 1488 (D. Minn. 1985).

"A list of instructions, one line at a time, each of which causes the computer to take a specific action. . . . In the industry, computer programs are referred to as 'software,' which term encompasses systems programs and application programs."

Computer Sciences Corp. v. Commissioner of Internal Revenue, 63 T.C. 327, 329 (1974).

". . . tells the hardware items which task to perform."

In re Data Gen. Corp. Antitrust Litig., 490 F. Supp. 1089, 1098 (N.D. Cal. 1980).

"A set of 'predetermined instructions.' "

Comptroller of the Treasury v. Equitable Trust Co., 464 A.2d 248, 250 (Md. 1983).

"[S]equences of instructions which tell the various devices what to do. Programs are also referred to as software."

Telex Corp. v. IBM Corp., 367 F. Supp. 258, 274 (N.D. Okla. 1973), *aff'd in part, rev'd in part,* 510 F.2d 894 (10th Cir.), *cert. dism.,* 423 U.S. 802 (1975).

"[C]odes prepared by a programmer that instruct the computer to perform certain functions."

Advent Sys. Ltd. v. Unisys Corp., 925 F.2d 670, 674 (3d Cir. 1991).

Related issues. "Large programs are created by 'knitting' together many such routines in layers, where the lower layers are used to provide fundamental functionality relied upon by higher, more focused layers. Some preliminary aspects of this 'knitting' are performed by the software developer. The user who launches a program, however, is ultimately responsible for causing routines to be loaded into memory and executed together to produce the program's overall functionality."

United States v. Microsoft Corp., 65 F. Supp. 2d 1, 41 (D.D.C. 1999) (Finding of Fact 162).

See also **computer program; computer software; program listing; software.**

program flow control instructions *(software)*

[CANADA] "These instructions alter the content of the program counter (a 16 bit location holding the address of the next instruction to be executed) and hence affect normal sequential execution of instructions into memory, for example, 'branch, jump to subroutine,' etc."

> *Apple Computer, Inc. v. Mackintosh Computers Ltd.* (1986), 28 D.L.R. (4th) 178 (Fed. T.D.).

program listing *(software)*

[SOUTH AFRICA] "The set of instructions which constitute the program or suite of programs."

> *Northern Off. Micro Computers Ltd. v. Rosenstein* [1982], F.S.R. 124 (Supreme Ct. S. Africa).

See also **program(s)**.

programmed routine *(software)*

See **routine**.

programmer(s) *(software)*

One who writes a computer program.

Annotation. "During the early period of computing, 'programmers' ordinarily wrote programs exclusively in machine language. Today, object code is rarely written directly by computer programmers. Rather, modern programmers typically write computer programs in a 'higher'-level programming language. These programs are called source programs, or source code."

> *Lotus Dev. Corp. v. Paperback Software Int'l*, 740 F. Supp. 37, 44 (D. Mass. 1990).

programming *(software)*

". . . to translate the narrative, which is in the English language, into computer language."

> *Pezzillo v. General Tel. & Elec. Information Sys., Inc.,* 414 F. Supp. 1257, 1259 (M.D. Tenn. 1976).

programming language *(software)*

"Some highly skilled human beings can reduce data and instructions to strings of 1's and 0's and thus program computers to perform complex tasks by inputting commands and data in that form. But it would be inconvenient, inefficient and, for most people, probably impossible to do so. In consequence, computer science has developed programming languages. These languages, like other written languages, employ symbols and syntax to convey meaning. The text of programs written in these languages is referred to as source code. And whether directly or through the medium of another program, the sets of instructions written in programming languages—the source code—ultimately are translated into machine 'readable' strings of 1's and 0's, known in the computer world as object code, which typically are executable by the computer."

> *Universal City Studios, Inc. v. Reimerdes*, 111 F. Supp. 2d 294, 306 (S.D.N.Y. 2000) (footnotes omitted).

See also **computer program; computer software; programs(s) program listing; software.**

[JAPAN] "[L]etters and other symbols as well as their systems for use as means of expressing a program."

> Japanese Copyright Law, Law No. 48 of 1970, art. 10(3)(1).

projected reality *(technology)*

A virtual reality system in which the user enters a virtual environment, but remains in the real world.

PROM *(hardware)*

"Anagram for 'Programmable Read-Only Memory.'"

> *E.F. Johnson Co. v. Uniden Corp. of America*, 623 F. Supp. 1485, 1488 (D. Minn. 1985) (emphasis added).

"A programmable ROM."

> U.S. Copyright Office, *Compendium of Copyright Office Practices* II, § 326 (1984).

"A PROM . . . can be plugged into a programming device at any remote location and one can actually program in the software there."

> *Bateman v. Mnemonics, Inc.*, 79 F.3d 1532, 1537 n.7 (11th Cir. 1995).

"A microchip-mounted program from which a computer may read instructions. Nonerasable."

> *E.F. Johnson v. Uniden Corp.*, 623 F. Supp. 1485, 1488 (D. Minn. 1985).

"[M]emory storage devices . . . an acronym for 'programmable read only memory.'"

> *Stern Elecs., Inc. v. Kaufman*, 669 F.2d 852, 854 n.1 (2d Cir. 1982).

"[A] ROM into which information can be imprinted (programmed) after manufacture; once the information is programmed in a PROM, it cannot be changed simply by writing in a new program."

> *Stern Elecs., Inc. v. Kaufman*, 669 F.2d 852, 854 n.1 (2d Cir. 1982).

"[A] 'ROM' memory which may be programmed in the field by the customer."

> *Intel Corp. v. Radiation, Inc.*, 184 U.S.P.Q. (BNA) 54, 55 (T.T.A.B. 1974).

Related issues. "[A] 'PROM' memory has the advantage over a 'ROM' device in that it enables the customer, that is, the user of the memory, to insert the desired program at his facilities."

Intel Corp. v. Radiation, Inc., 184 U.S.P.Q. (BNA) 54, 55 (T.T.A.B. 1974).

See also **ROM.**

prompt *(technology)*

The signal from the computer that it is waiting for user input.

proof of identification *(electronic commerce)*

"[T]he document or documents presented to a Certification Authority to establish the identity of a subscriber."

Cal. Code of Regs., tit. 2, div. 7, ch. 10, § 22003(a)(1)(I).

See also **Certification Authority.**

proper means *(trade secret)*

"Proper means include

(1) Discovery by independent invention;

(2) Discovery by 'reverse engineering,' that is, by starting with the known product and working backwards to find the method by which it was developed. The acquisition of the known product must[,] of course, also be by a fair and honest means, such as purchase of the item on the open market for reverse engineering to be lawful;

(3) Discovery under a license from the owner of the trade secret;

(4) Observation of the item in public use or on public display;

(5) Obtaining the trade secret from published literature."

Comment (a), La. Rev. Stat. 51:1431, *quoted in Vault Corp. v. Quaid Software, Ltd.,* 655 F. Supp. 750, 761 (E.D. La. 1987).

See also **improper means; reverse engineering; trade secret.**

proprietary viewer *(software)*

"[A] computer program that keeps a digital object always under its control."

I. Trotter Hardy, *Project Looking Forward: Sketching the Future of Copyright in a Networked World* 14 (1998).

See also **digital object.**

protected computer *(criminal)*

"[A] computer—

(A) exclusively for the use of a financial institution or the United States Government, or, in the case of a computer not exclusively for such use,

used by or for a financial institution or the United States Government and the conduct constituting the offense affects that use by or for the financial institution or the Government; or
(B) which is used in interstate or foreign commerce or communication; . . ."
 18 U.S.C. § 1030(e)(2).
See also **computer (criminal).**

protection device *(hardware)*

"[A] piece of hardware that must be affixed to a computer in order to operate the Bid Analysis software; the program will not operate without the device. Mortenson received one protection device for each copy of software it ordered."
 M.A. Mortenson Co., Inc. v. Timberline Software Corp., 998 P.2d 305, 308 n.4 (Wash. 2000), *aff'g* 93 Wash. App. 819, 970 P.2d 803 (1999).

protocol *(technology)*

"[A] series of procedures and conventions that govern communications between a computer and various terminals linked to that computer. Put another way, the protocol tells the computer 'how' as opposed to 'what' to communicate."
 Telerate Sys., Inc. v. Caro, 689 F. Supp. 221, 224 (S.D.N.Y. 1988).

"Protocol refers to the procedure followed in sending and receiving control data."
 IRS Letter Ruling 8721016, Feb. 17, 1987.

Annotation. "No single entity—academic, corporate, governmental, or non-profit—administers the Internet. It exists and functions as a result of the fact that hundreds of thousands of separate operators of computers and computer networks independently decided to use common data transfer protocols to exchange communications and information with other computers (which in turn exchange communications and information with still other computers)."
 American Civil Liberties Union v. Reno, 929 F. Supp. 824, 832 (E.D. Pa. 1996), *aff'd, Reno v. American Civil Liberties Union,* 521 U.S. 844 (1997).

". . . permit the information to become part of a single body of knowledge accessible by all Web visitors."
 American Library Ass'n v. Pataki, 969 F. Supp. 160, 166 (S.D.N.Y. 1997).
See also **handshake protocol.**

protocol analyzer *(hardware)*
"[Machine that] slows down the transmission so that the protocol signals can be analyzed."

> *Secure Servs. Technology, Inc. v. Time & Space Processing, Inc.,* 722 F. Supp. 1354, 1358 n.11 (E.D. Va. 1989).

prototype *(technology)*
"The first full-scale model of a new type of design of furniture, machinery, or vehicle."

> *Fargo Mach. & Tool Co. v. Kearney & Trecker Corp.,* 428 F. Supp. 364, 377 (E.D. Mich. 1977).

PRV *(telecommunications)*
Acronym for "Positive Roamer Verification."

"[A] computer-based system used to verify valid cellular telephone ESN/MIN combinations assigned to authorized customers on any participating system. If the PRV identifies a particular combination as valid, the local cellular telephone system will permit telephone calls to be placed using that combination. If the combination is not identified as valid, the local system will deny service to a telephone using that combination."

> *United States v. Brady,* 820 F. Supp. 1346, 1353 n.15 (D. Utah 1993).

pseudonym *(Internet)*
A fictitious name or identity used by an author.

Related issues. "Individual participants in an Internet Relay Chat discussion know other participants only by the names they choose upon entering the discussion; users can participate anonymously by using a pseudonym."

> *Shea v. Reno,* 930 F. Supp. 916, 941 (S.D.N.Y. 1996).

pseudonymous work *(copyright)*
"[A] work on the copies or phonorecords of which the author is identified under a fictitious name."

> U.S. Copyright Act, 17 U.S.C. §101.

PSTN *(telecommunications)*
Acronym for "Public Switched Telephone Network." The traditional telephone system. *See also* POTS.

P3P *(organization)*
Acronym for "Platform for Privacy Protection Project."

A worldwide industry and academic initiative to protect consumer privacy online. It intends to provide technology companies with guidelines to design their products for protecting consumer privacy and to work together.

PTO *(government; organization)*
Acronym for "U.S. Patent and Trademark Office." Located at <www.uspto.gov>.

PTP *(business)*
See **P2P.**

P2P *(business)*
Acronym for "Peer-to-Peer."

A type of business/web site/technology that facilitates communications and transactions directly between end users/consumers. An example is Napster, whose technology allows end users to locate and exchange music with other end users directly. Another example is instant messaging, which allows end users to send messages in real time.

PTT *(telecommunications)*
Acronym for "Postal, Telegraph and Telephone Authority."

public

Related issues (criminal). "[T]here is no case law interpreting the word 'public' as used in the ECPA."
Andersen Consulting LLP v. UOP, 991 F. Supp. 2d 1041, 1042 n.1 (N.D. Ill. 1998).

public display *(copyright)*

Annotation. "Distribution of the Tape on the Internet . . . would also interfere with the plaintiff's public display rights, which include the right to display 'individual images of a motion picture.' 17 U.S.C. § 106(5). Therefore, the display of still images from the Tape on the Internet would also conflict with rights conferred exclusively on the plaintiffs by the Copyright Act."
Michaels v. Internet Entertainment Group, Inc., 5 F. Supp. 2d 823, 830-31 (C.D. Cal. 1998).

public domain

(copyright)

An often misunderstood term. Generally, it means that the material is not protected by copyright law. However, much material that is in the "public domain" in the United States may still be protected by copyright elsewhere in the world.

"Such material is free for the taking and cannot be appropriated by a single author even though it is included in a copyrighted work. We see no reason to make an exception to this rule for elements of a computer program that have entered the public domain by virtue of freely accessible program exchanges and the like."
Computer Assocs. Int'l, Inc. v. Altai, Inc., 982 F.2d 693, 710 (2d Cir. 1992).

(trade secret)
See **disclosure; trade secret.**

public key *(electronic commerce)*

"[T]he key of a key pair used to verify a digital signature."
Cal. Code of Regs., tit. 2, div. 7, ch. 10, § 22003(a)(1)(J); Wash. Rev. Code § 19.34.020(24).

public key block *(encryption)*

See **public key.**

public key cipher *(technology)*

"A special class of asymmetric cipher in which the encrypting key is public but the decrypting key is kept secret."
U.S. Congress, Office of Technology Assessment, *Defending Secrets, Sharing Data: New Locks and Keys for Electronic Information* 61 (Oct. 1987).

public key cryptography *(electronic commerce)*

A type of cryptographic system with two keys—one key known by the general public, and a second key known only to an individual user.

Related issues. "The technology known as Public Key Cryptography is an acceptable technology for use by public entities in California, provided that the digital signature is created consistent with the provisions in Section 22003(a)1-5."
Cal. Code of Regs., tit. 2, div. 7, ch. 10, § 22003(a).
See also **private key; public key.**

public key encryption *(technology)*

A type of encryption in which there are two keys, a public key that is made available to everyone and a private key that is known only to the sender of a message. The public and private keys are a unique pair, which work together. The public key can be used to encrypt data that only the corresponding private key can decrypt. Alternatively, the public key can be used to decrypt data, but only if it was encrypted with the corresponding private key. The public key technology can be used to authenticate that the sender is who he claims to be and that the message has not been altered in transmission. *See also* **public key cipher.**

public key/private key encryption

Also called "asymmetric key encryption."
See **asymmetric key encryption.**

public performance *(copyright)*

See **publicly.**

public performance license *(contract)*

A license that permits the public performance of a musical composition.

publication *(copyright)*

"[T]he distribution of copies or phonorecords of a work to the public by sale or other transfer of ownership, or by rental, lease, or lending. The offering to distribute copies or phonorecords to a group of persons for purposes of further distribution, public performance, or public display, constitutes publication. A public performance or display of a work does not of itself constitute publication."

U.S. Copyright Act, 17 U.S.C. §101.

publication right *(contract)*

The right to publish a work in one or more media, as specified by contract.

publicity *(contract)*

A property right of a celebrity to control the exploitation of his or her persona.

Sample clause. "Producer is hereby granted the right to photograph or otherwise reproduce in connection with [work] all or any part of your acts, poses, plays, and appearances of every kind and nature made or done by you in connection with the Performances and/or your services hereunder; and all instrumental, musical, or other sound effects produced by you in connection with the Performances and/or your services hereunder; to re-produce, re-record, and transmit the same in connection with the [work] in conjunction with such acts, poses, plays, and appearances, and perpetually and throughout the world to exhibit, transmit, reproduce, distribute, broadcast and exploit, and license or permit others to exhibit, transmit, reproduce, distribute, broadcast, and exploit, any or all of such photographs, reproductions, and recordations in connection with all or any portion of the [work] or the advertising or exploitation thereof, in and by all media and means whatsoever.

"Producer shall have the right throughout the world to use and display, and to license or permit others to use and display, your name and likeness for advertising or publicizing the Performance in conjunction with the [work] provided, however, that Producer shall not have the right to utilize your name, voice, or likeness in connection with any so-called 'commercial tie-ups.' Without limiting the generality of the foregoing, Producer shall have the right to use your name and likeness in the [work] and issued in connection with the advertising and exploitation thereof."

publicly *(copyright)*

"To perform or display a work 'publicly' means—

(1) to perform or display it at a place open to the public or at any place where a substantial number of persons outside of a normal circle of a family and its social acquaintances is gathered; or

(2) to transmit or otherwise communicate a performance or display of the work to a place specified by clause (1) or to the public, by means of any device or process, whether the members of the public capable of receiving the performance or display receive it in the same place or in separate places and at the same time or at different times."

U.S. Copyright Act, 17 U.S.C. §101.

publish

(electronic commerce)
"[T]o record or file in a repository."

Wash. Rev. Code § 19.34.020(25).

(Internet)
"When information is made available, it is said to be 'published' on the Web."

American Civil Liberties Union v. Reno, 929 F. Supp. 824, 837 (E.D. Pa. 1996), *aff'd, Reno v. American Civil Liberties Union,* 521 U.S. 844 (1997).

See also **web publishing.**

Annotation (Internet). "Any person or organization with a computer connected to the Internet can 'publish' information. Publishers include government agencies, educational institutions, commercial entities, advocacy groups, and individuals. Publishers may either make their material available to the entire pool of Internet users, or confine access to a selected group, such as those willing to pay for the privilege."
American Civil Liberties Union v. Reno, 521 U.S. 844, 853 (1997), *aff'g Reno v. American Civil Liberties Union,* 929 F. Supp. 824 (E.D. Pa. 1996).

"Information to be published on the Web must also be formatted according to the result of the Web standards."
American Civil Liberties Union v. Reno, 929 F. Supp. 824, 837 (E.D. Pa. 1996), *aff'd, Reno v. American Civil Liberties Union,* 521 U.S. 844 (1997).

"[T]he open nature of the Web makes it easy for publishers to reach their intended audiences without having to know in advance what kind of computer each potential reader has, and what kind of software they will be using."
American Civil Liberties Union v. Reno, 929 F. Supp. 824, 838 (3d Cir. 1996), *aff'd, Reno v. American Civil Liberties Union,* 521 U.S. 844 (1997).

published informational content *(contract)*

"[I]nformational content prepared for or made available to recipients generally, or to a class of recipients, in substantially the same form. The term does not include informational content that is:
(A) customized for a particular recipient by one or more individuals acting as or on behalf of the licensor, using judgment or expertise; or
(B) provided in a special relationship of reliance between the provider and the recipient."
UCITA § 102(a)(52).

publisher *(business)*

One who acquires the rights to distribute an interactive media product or service from an outside developer. A publisher usually provides for marketing and sales, customer service, upgrades, and other services.

Related issues. "No provider or user of an interactive computer service shall be treated as the publisher or speaker of any information provided by another information content provider."
47 U.S.C. § 230(e)(1).

pull *(Internet)*

Technology that permits a user to request specific information or types of information from a database or web site.

Annotation. "With 'pull' technology, every command that requests information is initiated by a user sitting in front of a PC at that time."
I. Trotter Hardy, *Project Looking Forward: Sketching the Future of Copyright in a Networked World* 92-93 (May 1998).

punitive damages
(contract)
"An award not reduced by the benefit received by the plaintiff would be too large to be compensatory, and so it would be punitive, and punitive damages are rarely, and in New Hampshire never, awarded in contract cases; and so a victim of a breach of contract who wants to keep the contract breaker's money above and beyond the amount necessary to compensate for the breach may be said to be 'unjustly enriched,' entitling the contract breaker to restitution."
Micro Data Base Sys., Inc. v. Dharma Sys., Inc., 148 F.3d 649, 656 (7th Cir. 1998).

(trade secrets)
"Punitive damages may be awarded only if a statute authorizes their award. But there is such a statute here—the Uniform Trade Secrets Act, which both New Hampshire and Indiana have adopted, and which authorizes punitive damages for the willful and malicious appropriation of a trade secret."
Micro Data Base Sys., Inc. v. Dharma Sys., Inc., 148 F.3d 649, 653 (7th Cir. 1998).

"The misappropriation of a trade secret is an intentional tort, but it is not the law that the fact that a tort is intentional automatically authorizes the award of punitive damages. If it did, the Uniform Trade Secrets Act would not limit punitive damages to cases in which the violation of the Act is willful or malicious. When an award of punitive damages requires that the defendant have committed an aggravated form of the wrongful act sought to be punished, a defendant who commits the barebones tort is not liable for such damages."
Micro Data Base Sys., Inc. v. Dharma Sys., Inc., 148 F.3d 649, 654 (7th Cir. 1998) (citations omitted).

purchase *(contract)*
"[I]ncludes taking by sale, discount, negotiation, mortgage, pledge, lien, issue or re-issue, gift or any other voluntary transaction creating an interest in property."
U.C.C. § 1-201(32).

purchaser *(contract)*
". . . means a *person* who takes by *purchase.*"
U.C.C. § 1-201(33) (emphasis in original).

purposeful availment *(jurisdiction)*

"The Internet as well as toll-free numbers are designed to communicate with people and their businesses in every state. Advertisement on the Internet can reach as many as 10,000 Internet users within Connecticut alone. Further, once posted on the Internet, unlike television and radio advertising, the advertisement is available continuously to any Internet user. [Defendant,] therefore, purposely availed itself of the privilege of doing business within Connecticut."

Inset Sys., Inc. v. Instruction Set, Inc., 937 F. Supp. 161, 165 (D. Conn. 1996).

"[T]he question of whether a defendant has purposefully availed itself of the privilege of doing business in the forum state is 'the sine qua non for in personam jurisdiction.' The 'purposeful availment' requirement is satisfied when the defendant's contacts with the forum state 'proximately result from actions by the defendant himself that create a "substantial connection" with the forum State,' and when the defendant's conduct and connection with the forum are such that he 'should reasonably anticipate being haled into court there.' Courts require purposeful availment to insure that 'random,' 'fortuitous,' or 'attenuated' contacts do not cause a defendant to be haled into a jurisdiction. This requirement does not, however, mean that a defendant must be physically present in the forum state. . . . 'So long as a commercial actor's efforts are "purposefully directed" toward residents of another State, we have consistently rejected the notion that an absence of physical contacts can defeat personal jurisdiction there.' Further, . . . 'Physical presence of an agent is not necessary . . . for the transaction of business in a state. The soliciting of insurance by mail, the transmission of radio broadcasts into a state, and the sending of magazines and newspapers into a state to be sold there by independent contractors are all accomplished without the physical presence of an agent; yet all have been held to constitute the transaction of business in a state."

CompuServe, Inc. v. Patterson, 89 F.3d 1257, 1263 (6th Cir. 1996).

"[T]he purposeful availment test focuses on the deliberateness of the defendant's contacts. The contacts with the forum state must be voluntary—not based on the unilateral actions of another party or a third person. And they must be foreseeable; the defendant's contacts must be such that he should reasonably be able to anticipate 'being haled into court' in the forum state."

Digital Equipment Corp. v. Altavista Technology, Inc., 960 F. Supp. 456, 468 (D. Mass. 1997) (citations omitted).

Related issues. "The purposeful availment requirement ensures that a non-resident defendant will not be haled into court based upon 'random, fortuitous or attenuated' contacts with the forum state."

Panavision Int'l, Inc. v. Toeppen, 141 F.3d 1316, 1320 (9th Cir. 1998) (citation omitted).

See also **personal jurisdiction; specific jurisdiction.**

push *(Internet)*

Technology that permits specific information or types of information to be automatically delivered to a user.

Annotation. "With 'push' technology, the user commands a computer program to set up a schedule for information requests. After that, the computer makes the requests in accordance with the user's chosen schedule: hourly, daily, etc."

I. Trotter Hardy, *Project Looking Forward: Sketching the Future of Copyright in a Networked World* 93 (May 1998).

QB1 *(video game)*

"[A]n interactive game played in conjunction with televised football games, which was first used in sports bars and restaurants."
Interactive Networks, Inc. v. NTN Comm., Inc., 875 F. Supp. 1398, 1401 (N.D. Cal. 1995).

qualified right to payment *(electronic commerce)*

"[A]n award of damages against a licensed certification authority by a court having jurisdiction over the certification authority in a civil action for violation of this chapter."
Wash. Rev. Code § 19.34.020(26).

quality assurance *(technology)*

Also called "quality control." All the planned and systematic actions necessary to provide adequate confidence that a product or service will satisfy given requirements for quality.

quality control *(technology)*

See **quality assurance**.

query *(technology)*

A search request submitted to a search engine.

Quicktime® *(software)*

An Apple Macintosh system extension for time-based data (i.e., data that can be stored as samples taken over time), which includes audio, video, and animation. Also available for MPC-compatible computers (Quicktime® for Windows).

quiet enjoyment *(contract)*

The right of someone with an interest in property to be able to enjoy the use of that property without interference by the property's owner.

Sample clauses
(hardware)
"The buyer [lessee] shall, [during the term of this lease and any renewals,] be entitled to the use of the hardware transferred pursuant to this Agreement without any disturbance, interference, interruption, lawsuit, or claim concerning title to or the right to use the hardware, subject only to its obligation to make payment as required by this Agreement. Seller [Lessor] shall not create or be a party to any such disturbance, interference, interruption, lawsuit, or claim, and shall, in good faith, defend any such lawsuit or claim. In the event that buyer [lessee] suffers any damage as a result of any such disturbance, interference, interruption, lawsuit, or claim, seller [lessor] shall compensate buyer [lessee] for all such damages subject to buyer's [lessee's] duty, in good faith, to mitigate such damages."

(software)
"The licensee shall, during the term of this license [and any renewals], be entitled to the use of the software licensed pursuant to this Agreement without any disturbance, interference, interruption, lawsuit, or claim concerning title to or the right to use the software, subject only to its obligation to make payment as required by this Agreement. Licensor shall not create or be a party to any such disturbance, interference, interruption, lawsuit, or claim, and shall, in good faith, defend any such lawsuit or claim. In the event that licensee suffers any damage as a result of any such disturbance, interference, interruption, lawsuit, or claim, licensor shall compensate licensee for all such damages subject to licensee's duty, in good faith, to mitigate such damages."

rack jobber *(business)*
A distributor who guarantees a retailer a certain dollar sales figure per linear foot of shelf space, and performs stocking and restocking functions.

RAM *(hardware)*
Acronym for "Random Access Memory."
> *Apple Computer, Inc. v. Formula Int'l, Inc.,* 594 F. Supp. 617, 622 (C.D. Cal. 1984). *See also Intel Corp. v. Radiation, Inc.,* 184 U.S.P.Q. (BNA) 54, 55 (T.T.A.B. 1974).

"Computer storage device in which words may be 'written' (stored) or 'read' (recovered) in any order at random. Conventional internal memory."
> U.S. Copyright Office, Compendium of Copyright Office Practices II, §326 (1984).

"[A] chip on which volatile internal memory is stored which is erased when the computer's power is turned off."
> *Apple Computer, Inc. v. Franklin Computer Corp.,* 714 F.2d 1240, 743 n.3 (3d Cir. 1983), *cert. dism.,* 464 U.S. 1033 (1984).

"Some chips store information only as long as the machine is on; these are Random Access Memory chips (RAMs). When the power is turned off, the information stored in these chips is lost."
> *Apple Computer, Inc. v. Franklin Computer Corp.,* 545 F. Supp. 812 (E.D. Pa. 1982), *rev'd,* 714 F.2d 1240 (3d Cir. 1983), *cert. dism.,* 104 S. Ct. 890 (1984).

"[M]emory device in which stored information can be changed simply by writing in new information that replaces old information."
> *Stern Elecs., Inc. v. Kaufman,* 669 F.2d 852, 854 n.1 (2d Cir. 1982).

"[T]he internal memory of the computer. . . ."
> *Lotus Dev. Corp. v. Paperback Software Int'l,* 740 F. Supp. 37, 43 (D. Mass. 1990).

RBOC *(telecommunications)*

Abbreviation for "Regional Bell Operating Company(ies)."

DSC Comm. Corp. v. Pulse Comm., Inc., 170 F.3d 1354, 1357 (Fed. Cir. 1999).

"AT&T was required to divest itself of its twenty-two local exchange subsidiaries, which became known as the Bell Operating Companies or 'BOCs.' The BOCs were then grouped into seven 'regional Operating Companies' or 'RBOCs.'"

SBC Comm., Inc. v. Federal Comm. Comm'n, 154 F.3d 226, 230 (5th Cir. 1998).

RDMS *(software)*

Acronym for "Relational Database Management System."

Micro Data Base Sys., Inc. v. Dharma Sys., Inc., 148 F.3d 649, 651 (7th Cir. 1998).

read *(hardware; software)*

An instruction to a computer to retrieve data from a storage device or other source. Just like reading a book, the content remains in its original place.

read-only memory *(hardware)*

See firmware; ROM.

RealNetworks *(organization)*

"[T]he leader, in terms of usage share, in software that supports the 'streaming' of audio and video content from the Web."

United States v. Microsoft Corp., 65 F. Supp. 2d 1, 29 (D.D.C. 1999) (Finding of Fact 111).

real time *(technology)*

". . . means that the processing of the input to the system (of which the computer is a part) obtains a result occurring almost simultaneously with the event generating the data."

White Consol. Indus., Inc. v. Vega Servo-Control, Inc., 214 U.S.P.Q. (BNA) 796 (S.D. Mich. 1982), *aff'd*, 218 U.S.P.Q. (BNA) 961 (Fed. Cir. 1983).

Related issues. "The reference to 'real time' really has nothing to do with 'time' as such. It simply means the . . . systems . . . were able to display 'the whole page' being worked on as it would actually appear in print, without distracting computer signals and commands."

In re Bedford Corp., 62 Bankr. 555, 557 n.1 (D.N.H. 1986).

real-time communication *(Internet)*

"In addition to transmitting messages that can be later read or accessed, individuals on the Internet can engage in an immediate dialog, in 'real time,' with other people on the Internet."

> *American Civil Liberties Union v. Reno*, 929 F. Supp. 824, 835 (E.D. Pa. 1996), *aff'd, Reno v. American Civil Liberties Union*, 521 U.S. 844 (1997).

Annotation. "In its simplest forms, 'talk' allows one-to-one communications and 'Internet Relay Chat' (or IRC) allows two or more to type messages to each other that almost immediately appear on the others' computer screens. IRC is analogous to a telephone party line, using a computer and keyboard rather than a telephone. With IRC, however, at any one time there are thousands of different party lines available, in which collectively tens of thousands of users are engaging in conversations on a huge range of subjects. Moreover, one can create a new party line to discuss a different topic at any time. Some IRC conversations are 'moderated' or include 'channel operators.'"

> *American Civil Liberties Union v. Reno*, 929 F. Supp. 824, 835 (E.D. Pa. 1996), *aff'd, Reno v. American Civil Liberties Union*, 521 U.S. 844 (1997).

reason to know *(contract)*

"[T]hat a person has knowledge of a fact or that, from all the facts and circumstances known to the person without investigation, the person should know that a fact exists."

> U.C.C. 2B-102(a)(38) (proposed).

reasonable precautions *(trade secret)*

"[T]rade secrets also do not survive when the alleged owner fails to take 'reasonable precautions' to keep the information secret."

> *Advanced Computer Servs., Inc. v. MAI Sys. Corp.*, 845 F. Supp. 356, 370 (E.D. Va. 1994).

reasonableness *(jurisdiction)*

"Satisfying the purposeful availment tests does not end the due process inquiry. Jurisdiction must still comport with 'traditional notions of "fair play and substantial justice."' The First Circuit enumerated the following five 'gestalt factors' to be used to determine the fairness and reasonableness of asserting personal jurisdiction:

"(1) the defendant's burden of appearing, (2) the forum state's interest in adjudicating the dispute, (3) the plaintiff's interest in obtaining convenient and effective relief, (4) the judicial system's interest in obtaining the most effective resolution of the controversy, and (5) the common interests of all sovereigns in promoting substantive social policies.

"While 'the gestalt factors may tip the constitutional balance,' in this case they serve to buttress the constitutionality of this Court's assertion of jurisdiction. Moreover, 'a strong showing of reasonableness may serve to fortify a more marginal showing of relatedness and purposefulness.'"

Digital Equipment Corp. v. Altavista Technology, Inc., 960 F. Supp. 456, 470 (D. Mass. 1997).

receipt *(contract)*
"(A) with respect to a copy, taking delivery; or

(B) with respect to a notice:

(i) coming to a person's attention; or

(ii) being delivered to and available at a location or system designated by agreement for that purpose or, in the absence of an agreed location or system:

(I) being delivered at the person's residence, or the person's place of business through which the contract was made, or at any other place held out by the person as a place for receipt of communications of the kind; or

(II) in the case of an electronic notice, coming into existence in an information processing system or at an address in that system in a form capable of being processed by or perceived from a system of that type by a recipient, if the recipient uses, or otherwise has designated or holds out, that place or system for receipt of notices of the kind to be given and the sender does not know that the notice cannot be accessed from that place."

UCITA § 102(a)(53).

receive *(contract)*
"[T]o take receipt.

UCITA § 102(a)(54).

recipient *(electronic commerce)*
"[A] person who has received a certificate and a digital signature verifiable with reference to a public key listed in the certificate and is in a position to rely on it."

Wash. Rev. Code § 19.34.020(27).

reciprocal compensation *(telecommunications)*
"An arrangement between two carriers . . . in which each of the two carriers receives compensation from the other carrier for the transport and termina-

tion on each carrier's network facilities of local telecommunications traffic that originates on the network facilities of the other carrier."
47 C.F.R. § 51.701(3).

recognized repository *(electronic commerce)*
"[A] repository recognized by the secretary under [this Act]."
Wash. Rev. Code § 19.34.020(28).

recommended reliance limit *(electronic commerce)*
"[T]he monetary amount recommended for reliance on a certificate under [this Act]."
Wash. Rev. Code § 19.34.020(29).

record
(contract)
"[I]nformation that is inscribed on a tangible medium or that is stored in an electronic or other medium and is retrievable in perceivable form."
UCITA § 102(a)(55).

(technology)
". . . data in a file which relates to a particular subject."
Dickerman Assocs., Inc. v. Tiverton Bottled Gas Co., 594 F. Supp. 30, 34 n.2 (D. Mass. 1984).

Recording Industry Association of America *(organization)*
See RIAA.

recoverable encryption *(encryption; software)*
An encryption product that allows access to the key required to decrypt ciphertext.

Recreational Software Advisory Council *(organization)*
Abbreviated as "RSAC."

"[A] non-profit corporation which developed rating systems for video games. . . ."
American Civil Liberties Union v. Reno, 929 F. Supp. 830, 841 (3d Cir. 1996), *aff'd, Reno v. American Civil Liberties Union,* 521 U.S. 844 (1997).

redhibition *(contract)*
"[T]he avoidance of a sale on account of some vice or defect in the thing sold, which renders it either absolutely useless, or its use so inconvenient

and imperfect, that it must be supposed that the buyer would not have purchased it, had he known of the vice."

La. Civ. Code, art. 2520.

Regional Bell Operating Company *(telecommunications)*

Abbreviated as "RBOC."

DSC Comm. Corp. v. Pulse Comm., Inc., 170 F.3d 1354, 1357 (Fed. Cir. 1999).

regional network *(telecommunications)*

"[S]maller networks in a given region of the country. . . . A regional network with no further connections to other networks could only provide services such as e-mail and Web browsing directly within its own area. Regional networks therefore contract with a backbone network to be connected to, and thereby have access to, any place on the Internet that that backbone network reaches. This is the means by which the backbone companies earn revenue from the installation of the backbone."

I. Trotter Hardy, *Project Looking Forward: Sketching the Future of Copyright in a Networked World* 48 (May 1998).

registrar *(Internet)*

An intermediary between a domain name registry and someone who wishes to obtain a unique domain name for its web site. For example, a firm could employ the services of a registrar, to help the firm choose the registry best suited to its demands and register the client's domain name and IP number with the chosen registry.

registration

(copyright)

"Registration certificates are prima facie evidence that the plaintiff owns a valid copyright."

17 U.S.C. § 410(c).

Annotation. (trademark) "[Plaintiff's] registration of the mark on the Principal Register in the Patent and Trademark Office constitutes prima facie evidence of the validity of the registered mark and of [plaintiff's] exclusive right to use the mark on the goods and services specified in the registration. . . ."

Brookfield Comm., Inc. v. West Coast Entertainment Corp., 174 F.3d 1036, 1047 (9th Cir. 1999).

"[Defendant] can rebut this presumption by showing that it used the mark in commerce first, since a fundamental tenet of trademark law is that ownership of an inherently distinctive mark . . . is governed by priority of use."

> *Brookfield Comm., Inc. v. West Coast Entertainment Corp.*, 174 F.3d 1036, 1047 (9th Cir. 1999).

registration certificate(s) *(copyright)*

"Registration certificates are prima facie evidence that the plaintiff owns a valid copyright."

> 17 U.S.C. § 410(c).

"Presentation of the certificates shifts the burden to the defendants to overcome the presumption of validity."

> *Michaels v. Internet Entertainment Group, Inc.*, 5 F. Supp. 2d 823, 830 (C.D. Cal. 1998).

registry *(Internet)*

A entity responsible for delegating Internet addresses (such as IP numbers and domain names), and keeping a record of those addresses and the information associated with their owners. Examples of domain name registries include Network Solution's InterNIC operation (.com, .net, and .org) and the ISO 3166 country code registries (e.g., .fr, .de, .uk, .us).

regression testing *(technology)*

Selective retesting to detect faults introduced during modification of a system.

rejection *(contract)*

"[I]f the goods or tender of delivery fails in any respect to conform to the contract, the buyer may . . . reject the whole . . . or accept any commercial unit or units and reject the rest."

> U.C.C. § 2-601 (1979).

"Under the UCC, goods are deemed accepted if the buyer (or, we think it clear though we cannot find any case, its delegate) fails, after having had a reasonable amount of time in which to inspect them, to communicate its rejection to the seller. This is a commonsensical rule. The seller is entitled to know where he stands, so that he can cure any defects in the goods. In addition, the rule saves on paperwork by allowing silence to count as acceptance. And it also discourages buyers who after receiving the goods decide they don't want them after all from trying to get out of their contract by making phony claims of nonconforming tender, perhaps when it is too late to verify the claims."

> *Micro Data Base Sys., Inc. v. Dharma Sys., Inc.*, 148 F.3d 649, 655 (7th Cir. 1998).

relatedness *(jurisdiction)*

"As an initial matter, 'we know . . . that the [relatedness] requirement focuses on the nexus between the defendant's contacts and the plaintiff's cause of action.' . . . [T]he requirement serves two purposes: First, relatedness is the 'divining rod that separates specific jurisdiction cases from general jurisdiction cases.' Second, it ensures that 'the element of causation remains in the forefront of the due process investigation.'"

> *Digital Equipment Corp. v. Altavista Technology, Inc.*, 960 F. Supp. 456, 468 (D. Mass. 1997) (citations omitted).

relay chat *(Internet)*

See chat; Internet Relay Chat.

release *(contract)*

"[A]n agreement by a party not to object to, or exercise any rights or pursue any remedies to limit, the use of information or informational rights which agreement does not require an affirmative act by the party to enable or support the other party's use of the information or informational rights. The term includes a waiver of informational rights."

> UCITA § 102(a)(56).

relevant market *(antitrust)*

"In determining whether there is monopoly power to control prices or exclude competitors in any part or line of commerce, the court is required to consider the relevant market or markets within which such determination can be made."

> *Telex Corp. v. IBM Corp.*, 367 F. Supp. 258, 276 (N.D. Okla. 1973), *aff'd in part, rev'd in part*, 510 F.2d 894 (10th Cir.), *cert. dism.*, 423 U.S. 802 (1975).

See also relevant product market.

relevant product market *(antitrust)*

"The reality of the marketplace must serve as the lodestar."

> *Alcatel USA, Inc. v. DGI Technologies, Inc.*, 166 F.3d 772, 781 (5th Cir. 1999) (citation omitted).

See also relevant market.

reliability *(technology)*

"[T]he probability that a system will not fail over a given period of time and under specified conditions. It is based on the combined reliability of all of the components that make up a system, their interconnections, and the environment in which the system operates."

> U.S. General Accounting Office, *Information Superhighway: An Overview of Technology Changes* 35 (Jan. 1995).

Religious Technology Center *(organization)*

See RTC.

remailer *(Internet)*

See anonymous remailer.

remedy *(contract)*

". . . means any remedial right to which an aggrieved party is entitled with or without resort to a tribunal."

> U.C.C. § 1-201(34).

See also repair or replacement.

remote data processing *(technology)*

". . . differs from conventional batch-data processing primarily because the customer has electronic or like connections with a remote data center, so that records do not have to be physically transmitted."

> *Kaplan v. Burroughs Corp.*, 426 F. Supp. 1328, 1330 (N.D. Cal. 1977).

remote file access *(technology)*

"Use of high-speed channel-to-channel data transfer interfaces."

> *IBM Corp. v. Fujitsu Ltd.*, Copyright L. Rep. (CCH) ¶ 20,517 (Am. Arb. Ass'n 1988).

remote information retrieval *(Internet)*

"[T]he search for and retrieval of information located on remote computers."

> *American Civil Liberties Union v. Reno*, 929 F. Supp. 824, 835 (E.D. Pa. 1996), *aff'd, Reno v. American Civil Liberties Union*, 521 U.S. 844 (1997).

See also ftp; gopher; World Wide Web.

removal services *(telecommunications)*

"[t]he business of removing that old switching equipment (and other obsolete telephone equipment). . . ."

> *Nynex Corp. v. Discon, Inc.*, 525 U.S. 128, 131 (1998).

remove *(Internet)*

To delete your e-mail address from the subscription list of a newsgroup. *See also* **unsubscribe.**

rendering *(technology)*

The process of drawing visual images on a computer display screen.

Reno v. ACLU *(First Amendment; Internet)*

Citation: Reno v. American Civil Liberties Union, 521 U.S. 844, 117 S. Ct. 2329 (1997), *aff'g American Civil Liberties Union v. Reno,* 929 F. Supp. 824 (3d Cir. 1996).

"The Court in Reno held that two provisions of the CDA were facially overbroad. The first imposed liability on anyone who:

> (B) by means of a telecommunications device knowingly—
> (i) makes, creates, or solicits, and
> (ii) initiates the transmission of, any . . . communication which is obscene or indecent, knowing that the recipient of the communication is under 18 years of age. . . .

47 U.S.C. §223(a). The second imposed liability on anyone who knowingly:

> (A) uses an interactive computer service to send to a specific person or persons under 18 years of age, or
> (B) uses any interactive computer service to display in a manner available to a person under 18 years of age, any . . . communication that, in context, depicts or describes, in terms patently offensive as measured by contemporary community standards, sexual or excretory activities or organs. . . .

47 U.S.C. §223 (d). The CDA contained two defenses virtually identical to two of the defenses provided in section 30-37-3.2(A). One defense addressed those who take 'good faith, reasonable, effective, and appropriate actions' to restrict access by minors to the prohibited communications. §223(e)(5)(A). The other defense addressed those who restrict access to the prohibited communications 'by requiring use of a verified credit card, debit account, adult access code, or adult personal identification number.' §223(e)(5)(B).

"Plaintiffs in *Reno* challenged the CDA as facially overbroad in violation of the First Amendment and vague in violation of the Fifth Amendment. The Court held the statute was overbroad and vague in violation of the First Amendment without separately reaching Fifth Amendment vagueness. The Court reached that conclusion by considering both the particular language and structure of the CDA, as well as the nature and function of the Internet. It held that 'the vague contours of the coverage of the statute' cause it to 'unquestionably silence [ ] some speakers whose messages would be entitled to constitutional protection.'

"This is particularly troublesome because the CDA is a 'content-based regulation of speech' which imposes criminal liability.

"Significantly, in rejecting the government's argument that the CDA does not prohibit protected adult communication, the Court rejected the government's 'incorrect factual premise that prohibiting a transmission whenever it is known that one of its recipients is a minor would not interfere with adult-to-adult communication.' That factual premise is incorrect when the communication medium is the Internet because '[g]iven the size of the potential audience for most messages, . . . the sender must be charged with knowing that one or more minors will likely view it.' Moreover, it would be prohibitively expensive to require Internet users, many of whom are non-commercial entities, to verify the age of those to whom communications are sent.

"Given its vagueness and breadth, the Court concluded that the CDA was not narrowly tailored to achieve the goal of protecting minors, in view of the fact that:

> possible alternatives [exist] such as requiring that indecent material be 'tagged' in a way that facilitates parental control of material coming into their homes, making exceptions for messages with artistic or educational value, providing some tolerance for parental choice, and regulating some portions of the Internet—such as commercial web sites—differently than others, such as chat rooms.

"The Court also rejected the government's narrowing interpretation of the CDA, which attempted to limit the CDA's scope by focusing on the 'plain meaning' of the Act's 'knowledge' and 'specific person' requirements. The government argued that, properly and narrowly construed, the CDA prohibited 'the dissemination of indecent messages only to persons known to be under 18.' The Court rejected this interpretation, stating that it 'ignores the fact that most Internet fora—including chat rooms, newsgroups, mail exploders, and the Web—are open to all comers. The Government's assertion that the knowledge requirement somehow protects the communications of adults is therefore untenable. Even the strongest reading of the 'specific person' requirement of §223(d) cannot save the statute.'

"Finally, the Court rejected the contention that the CDA's defenses salvage the Act. The Court first held that the defense requiring 'good faith, reasonable, effective, and appropriate actions,' . . . to prevent access by minors is 'illusory' because current technology does not permit *effective* prevention of access. With respect to the defense of requiring use of a verified credit card or adult identification number, the Court observed that commercial providers of sexually explicit material already employ such techniques, but there is no proof that they actually work, and it is not economically feasible for non-commercial speakers to employ such techniques. Thus, the Government has 'failed to prove that the proffered defense[s] would significantly reduce the heavy burden on adult speech produced by the prohibition on offensive displays.' The Court accordingly concluded that the CDA 'threatens to torch a large segment of the Internet community.'"

> *American Civil Liberties Union v. Johnson,* 194 F.3d 1149, 1156-58 (10th Cir. 1999) (citations omitted) (emphasis in original).

See also **Communications Decency Act.**

repair or replacement *(contract)*

"The remedy of repair and replacement offers the seller an opportunity to cure defects and to minimize its liability exposure . . . and provides the buyer with goods which conform to the contract within a reasonable period of time."

> *Ritchie Enters. v. Honeywell Bull, Inc.,* 730 F. Supp. 1041, 1048 (D. Kan. 1990).

Annotation. "Such agreements are common in commercial transactions between businessmen acting at arm's length; and . . . there is nothing unconscionable about them."

> *W.R. Weaver Co. v. Burroughs Corp.,* 580 S.W.2d 76, 82 (Tex. Civ. App. 1979).

"The limited remedy of repair and a consequential damage exclusion are two distinct ways of attempting to limit recovery for breach of warranty. . . . The Code, moreover, tests each by a different standard. The former survives unless it fails of its essential purpose, while the latter is valid unless it is unconscionable. We therefore see no reason to hold, as a general proposition, that the failure of the limited remedy provided in the contract, without more, invalidates a wholly distinct term in the agreement excluding consequential damages. The two are not mutually exclusive."

> *Chatlos Sys., Inc. v. National Cash Register Co.,* 635 F.2d 1081, 1086 (3d Cir. 1980), *cert. dism.,* 457 U.S. 1112 (1982) (citations and footnote omitted).

Related issues. "To be effective the repair remedy must be provided within a reasonable time after discovery of the defect."

> *Chatlos Sys., Inc. v. National Cash Register Co.,* 625 F.2d 1081, 1085 (3d Cir. 1980), *cert. dism.,* 457 U.S. 1112 (1982).

repeaters *(technology)*

"[B]ase stations which receive and transmit signals to and from the mobile radio units."

> *E.F. Johnson Co. v. Uniden Corp. of America,* 623 F. Supp. 1485, 1487 (D. Minn. 1985).

"[A]re analogous to radio station transmitters."

> *E.F. Johnson Co. v. Uniden Corp. of America,* 623 F. Supp. 1485, 1489 (D. Minn. 1985).

replevin *(contract)*

"[A] procedure in the nature of a provisional remedy, is ancillary to an action for recovery of a chattel. [A]n order of replevin is appropriate if plaintiff shows a present right to possession of the chattel. [T]he issue is strictly whether plaintiff or defendant has the superior possessory right."

> *Honeywell Information Sys., Inc. v. Demographic Systems, Inc.,* 396 F. Supp. 273, 275 (S.D.N.Y. 1975) (citations omitted).

replication *(manufacturing)*

The step in the CD-ROM manufacturing process where the CD-ROMs are pressed from a master.

reply *(Internet)*

To post a response to an e-mail or message on a newsgroup.

repository *(electronic commerce)*

"[A] system for storing and retrieving certificates and other information relevant to digital signatures."

> Wash. Rev. Code § 19.34.020(30).

representative *(contract)*

"[I]ncludes an agent, an officer of a corporation or association, and a trustee, executor or administrator of an estate, or any other person empowered to act for another."

> U.C.C. § 1-201(35).

republisher *(business; multimedia)*

A foreign company that assists in the localization of a multimedia product, designs the packaging, manufactures the title from a gold master, and provides marketing and sales services in its territory.

repurpose *(multimedia)*

Also called "reuse." Adopting existing content, such as text, still images or moving images for use in an interactive media product or service.

request for proposal *(contract)*

See IFP; RFP.

reservation of rights *(contract)*

A contractual provison under which one party reserves certain rights in the subject matter of the agreement to itself.

Sample clause. "All rights in the Work not specifically granted to Licensee, now or hereafter known, developed or in existence and whether or not competitive with the rights granted herein, are reserved to the Licensor in all forms of media throughout the world for the Licensor's use or disposition at his sole discretion, without obligation to the Liccnsee."

resolve *(Internet)*

The process of translating the alphanumeric domain name into a unique, numerical IP address required by the Internet network.

response time *(technology)*

"The time between the last keystroke made by the operator and the first listing displayed on the CRT."
> *Hawaiian Tel. Co. v. Microform Data Sys., Inc.,* 829 F.2d 919, 920 n.1 (9th Cir. 1987).

". . . is the amount of time between entry of a command into the system and the appearance on the screen of the requested output."
> *USM Corp. v. Arthur D. Little, Inc.* 546 N.E.2d 888, 890 n.4, 28 Mass. App. 108, 112 n.4 (1989).

". . . is directly related to, and primarily determined by, the number of disk accesses that must be accomplished to satisfy the requirements of the command given by the operator. . . ."
> *USM Corp. v. Arthur D. Little, Inc.* 546 N.E.2d 888, 890-91 n.5, 28 Mass. App. 108, 112 n.5 (1989).

restitution *(contract)*

"An award not reduced by the benefit received by the plaintiff would be too large to be compensatory, and so it would be punitive, and punitive damages are rarely, and in New Hampshire never, awarded in contract cases; and so a victim of a breach of contract who wants to keep the contract breaker's money above and beyond the amount necessary to compensate for the breach may be said to be 'unjustly enriched,' entitling the contract breaker to restitution."

Micro Data Base Sys., Inc. v. Dharma Sys., Inc., 148 F.3d 649, 656 (7th Cir. 1998).

retail channel *(business)*

"[D]istributors, wholesalers, retailers, retail chains, and corporate purchasing personnel. . . ."

Princeton Graphics Operating L.P. v. NEC Home Elecs. (U.S.A.), Inc., 732 F. Supp. 1258, 1260 (S.D.N.Y. 1990).

return

(contract)

"[W]ith respect to a record containing contractual terms that were rejected, refers only to the computer information and means:

(A) in the case of a licensee that rejects a record regarding a single information product transferred for a single contract fee, a right to reimbursement of the contract fee paid from the person to which it was paid or from another person that offers to reimburse that fee, on:

(i) submission of proof of purchase; and

(ii) proper redelivery of the computer information and all copies within a reasonable time after initial delivery of the information to the licensee;

(B) in the case of a licensee that rejects a record regarding an information product provided as part of multiple information products integrated into and transferred as a bundled whole but retaining their separate identity:

(i) a right to reimbursement of any portion of the aggregate contract fee identified by the licensor in the initial transaction as charged to the licensee for all bundled information products which was actually paid, on:

(I) rejection of the record before or during the initial use of the bundled product;

(II) proper redelivery of all computer information products in the bundled whole and all copies of them within a reasonable time after initial delivery of the information to the licensee; and

(III) submission of proof of purchase; or

(ii) a right to reimbursement of any separate contract fee identified by the licensor in the initial transaction as charged to the licensee for the separate information product to which the rejected record applies, on:

(I) submission of proof of purchase; and

(II) proper redelivery of that computer information product and all copies within a reasonable time after initial delivery of the information to the licensee; or

(C) in the case of a licensor that rejects a record proposed by the licensee, a right to proper redelivery of the computer information and all copies from the licensee, to stop delivery or access to the information by the licensee, and to reimbursement from the licensee of amounts paid by the licensor with respect to the rejected record, on reimbursement to the licensee of contract fees that it paid with respect to the rejected record, subject to recoupment and setoff."

UCITA § 102(a)(57).

(technology)
The "RETURN" key is used to enter input to the system. It is like a carriage return key on a typewriter because it signifies the end of a line and causes the cursor to move down.

reuse *(entertainment; multimedia)*
See **repurpose.**

reverse engineering
(copyright)
"Notwithstanding the provisions of subsection (a)(1)(A), a person who has lawfully obtained the right to use a copy of a computer program may circumvent a technological measure that effectively controls access to a particular portion of that program for the sole purpose of identifying and analyzing those elements of the program that are necessary to achieve interoperability of an independently created computer program with other programs, and that have not previously been readily available to the person engaging in the circumvention, to the extent any such acts of identification and analysis do not constitute infringement under this title [17 U.S.C. §1 *et seq.*].

17 U.S.C. § 1201(f)(1).

(mask work)
"Notwithstanding the provisions of section 905, it is not an infringement of the exclusive rights of the owner of a mask work for—

(1) a person to reproduce the mask work solely for the purpose of teaching, analyzing, or evaluating the concepts or techniques embodied in the mask work or the circuitry, logic flow, or organization of the components used in the mask work; or

(2) a person who performs the analysis or evaluation described in paragraph (1) to incorporate the results of such conduct in an original mask work which is made to be distributed."

17 U.S.C. § 906(a).

(trade secret)
"[A]nalyzing unpatented products and then duplicating their functionality. . . ."

Alcatel USA, Inc. v. DGI Technologies, Inc., 166 F.3d 772, 778 (5th Cir. 1999).

"[I]t is perfectly lawful for a competitor to buy a product embodying a trade secret and unmask the secret by reverse engineering of the product. Only if the competitor (or anyone else for that matter) discovers the secret by breaking a contract or engaging in other unlawful or improper conduct can the individual or firm whose secret it was obtain a remedy."

Micro Data Base Sys., Inc. v. Dharma Sys., Inc., 148 F.3d 649, 657 (7th Cir. 1998).

"[T]he process of starting with the known product and working backwards to divine the process which aided in its development or manufacture."

Kewanee Oil Co. v. Bicron Corp., 470 U.S. 470, 476 (1974).

"[T]he process of starting with a finished product and working backwards to analyze how the product operates or how it was made."

Secure Servs. Technology, Inc. v. Time & Space Processing, Inc., 722 F. Supp. 1354, 1361 n.16 (E.D. Va. 1989).

"The process by which a person takes a legitimately acquired item, disassembles it to learn its component parts, and from that process determines how the product is manufactured."

Motorola, Inc. v. Computer Displays Int'l, Inc., 739 F.2d 1149, 1152 n.4 (7th Cir. 1984).

"It involves starting with a known product and working backwards to discover the process by which it was developed and manufactured; in the context of the semiconductor industry, it includes the purchase of several computer chips of a competitor, stripping layers, photographing the circuitry of each layer through a microscope, dissecting the chip to discover the actual layout design and then drawing inferences about the technical process used to make the device."

People v. Gopal, 171 Cal. App. 3d 524, 533, 217 Cal. Rptr. 487, 492 (1985).

"[S]tarting with the known product and working backwards to find the method by which it was developed. The acquisition of the known product must[,] of course, also be by a fair and honest means, such as purchase of the item on the open market for reverse engineering to be lawful. . . ."

Comment (a), La. Rev. Stat. 51:1431, *quoted in Vault Corp. v. Quaid Software, Ltd.,* 655 F. Supp. 750, 761 (E.D. La. 1987).

"[A]ny process by which computer software is converted from one form to another form which is more readily understandable to human beings, including without limitation, any decoding or decrypting of any computer program which has been encoded or encrypted in any manner."

Vault Corp. v. Quaid Software Ltd., 655 F.2d 750 (E.D. La. 1987), *aff'd,* 847 F.2d 255, 269 (5th Cir. 1988) (*quoting* La. Rev. Stat. 51:1962 (3)—invalidated by the court).

"[S]imply buying a device . . . , taking it apart, and building a similar one. . . ."

California Computer Prods., Inc. v. IBM Corp., 613 F.2d 727, 731 (9th Cir. 1979).

Annotation

(copyright)

"Once a programmer has access to the source code of a program, he is able to determine the construction of the program and write his own version. For this reason, source code programs are typically compiled (translated) into and sold as object code or machine language, which is not discernible to even an expert programmer, but which is readily usable by the computer."

United States v. Brown, 925 F.2d 1301, 1303 n.4 (10th Cir. 1991).

(mask works)

"The statute thus provides that one engaged in reverse engineering shall not be liable for infringement when the end product is itself original. In performing reverse engineering a person may disassemble, study, and analyze an existing chip in order to understand it. This knowledge may be used to create an original chip having a different design layout, but which performs the same or equivalent function as the existing chip, without penalty or prohibition. Congress was told by industry representatives that reverse engineering was an accepted and fair practice and leads to improved chips having 'form, fit, and function' compatibility with the existing chip, thereby serving competition while advancing the state of technology.

>   *Brooktree Corp. v. Advanced Micro Devices, Inc.,* 977 F.2d 1555, 1565 (Fed. Cir. 1992).

Related issues. "An author cannot acquire patent-like protection by putting an idea, process, or method of operation in an unintelligible format and asserting copyright infringement against those who try to understand that idea, process, or method of operation."

>   *Atari Games Corp. v. Nintendo of America, Inc.,* 975 F.2d 832, 842 (Fed. Cir. 1992).

"When the nature of a work requires intermediate copying to understand the ideas and processes in a copyrighted work, that nature supports a fair use for intermediate copying. Thus, reverse engineering object code to discern the unprotectable ideas in a computer program is a fair use."

>   *Atari Games Corp. v. Nintendo of America, Inc.,* 975 F.2d 832, 843 (Fed. Cir. 1992).

"Allowing a computer programmer to hide his ideas, processes and concepts in copyrighted object code defeats the fundamental purpose of the Copyright Act to encourage the creation of original works by protecting the creator's expression while leaving the ideas, facts, and functional concepts in the free marketplace to be built upon by others."

>   *DSC Comm. Corp. v. DGI Technologies, Inc.,* 898 F. Supp. 1183, 1191 (N.D. Tex. 1995), *aff'd,* 81 F.3d 597 (5th Cir. 1996).

"[A]lthough there has been some uncertainty as to whether reverse engineering constitutes copyright infringement, the one federal circuit court that has squarely addressed the issue has concluded that reverse engineering may be a fair use. *See Sega Enters. Ltd. v. Accolade, Inc.,* 977 F.2d 1510, 1527-28 (9th Cir. 1992) (holding that 'where disassembly is the only way to gain access to the ideas and functional elements embodied in a copyrighted computer program and where there is a legitimate reason for seeking such access, disassembly is a fair use of the copyrighted work, as a matter of law'). Another federal circuit court has addressed the issue, although its highly unusual factual posture seems to limit its precedential value. *See Atari Games Corp. v. Nintendo of America, Inc.,* 975 F.2d 832, 843 (Fed. Cir. 1992) (concluding that 'reverse engineering object code to discern the unprotectable ideas in a computer program is a fair use,' although denying the defendant's fair use claim, based on the fact that it was wrongfully in possession of the source code)."

Bateman v. Mnemonics, Inc., 79 F.3d 1532, 1539-40 n.18 (11th Cir. 1995).

"The Semiconductor Chip Protection Act of 1984 permits, in some limited circumstances, reverse engineering to reproduce a mask work. 17 U.S.C. § 906."

Atari Games Corp. v. Nintendo of America, Inc., 975 F.2d 832, 842 n.5 (Fed. Cir. 1992).

See also **disassembly; proper means; trade secret.**

reverse passing off *(tort)*

"We recognize that in false designation of origin claims of the 'reverse passing off' variety, the defendant often has merely removed the plaintiff's mark from a product, added its own mark, and sold the product without altering it in any other way. . . . [T]he doctrine of reverse passing off is applicable in situations where a defendant resells another person's product that has been only 'slightly modified.'"

Montgomery v. Noga, 168 F.3d 1282, 1299 n.27 (11th Cir. 1999).

reverse video *(multimedia)*

A command that will change the screen setup so that text that was black on a light background will be displayed as white on a dark background, or vice versa.

revocation *(contract)*

"(1) The buyer may revoke his acceptance of a lot or commercial unit whose non-conformity substantially impairs its value to him if he has accepted it

(a) on the reasonable assumption that its non-conformity would be cured and it has not been seasonally cured, or

(b) without discovery of such non-conformity if his acceptance was reasonably induced either by the difficulty of discovery before acceptance or by the seller's assurances."

U.C.C. § 2-608(1) (1979).

revoke a certificate *(electronic commerce)*

"[T]o make a certificate ineffective permanently from a specified time forward. Revocation is effected by notation or inclusion in a set of revoked certificates, and does not imply that a revoked certificate is destroyed or made illegible."

Wash. Rev. Code § 19.34.020(31).

RFCs *(Internet)*

Acronym for "Request For Comments."

> *Name.Space, Inc. v. Network Solutions, Inc.*, 202 F.3d 573 577 n.4 (2d Cir. 2000).

"[M]emoranda addressing the various protocols that facilitate the functioning of the Internet."

> *Name.Space, Inc. v. Network Solutions, Inc.*, 202 F.3d 573 577 n.4 (2d Cir. 2000).

Annotation. "The Internet community developed RFCs as a mechanism for the generation of consensus on various engineering, technical and other protocols in the early days of the Internet's history. RFCs, which were previously edited by the late Dr. Jon Postel, are openly and freely available on the Internet and periodically amended and updated. Anyone may comment on the standards and protocols proposed or articulated in RFCs."

> *Name.Space, Inc. v. Network Solutions, Inc.*, 202 F.3d 573 577-78 n.4 (2d Cir. 2000).

RFP *(contract)*

Acronym for "Request For Proposal."

> *IBM Corp. v. Florida Dep't of Gen. Servs.*, Admin. L. Rep. 548, 7 Computer L. Serv. Rep. 495, 509 (1979).

"Generally, in the field of government procurement, there are two types of competitive procurement: the Invitation For Bid or Invitation To Bid ('IFB') process and the Request for Proposal ('RFP') process. The difference between the two methods is the extent to which the vendor is given latitude to exercise judgment. An IFB is rigid while an RFP is flexible. Typically, an IFB identifies the solution to a problem while an RFP identifies a problem and requests a proposed solution."

> *IBM Corp. v. Florida Dep't of Gen. Servs.*, Administrative Law Reports 548, 7 Computer L. Serv. Rep. 495, 509 (1979).

See also **IFP.**

RIAA *(organization)*

Acronym for "Recording Industry Association of America."

". . . represents the roughly half-dozen major record companies (and the artists on their labels) that control approximately ninety percent of the distribution of recorded music in the United States."

> *Recording Indus. Ass'n of America v. Diamond Multimedia Sys., Inc.*, 180 F.3d 1072, 1074 (9th Cir. 1999).

right of distribution *(copyright)*

See distribution, right of.

right of first refusal *(contract)*

A contractual provision that gives one party to the agreement the right to priority in negotiating with the other party for some right, such as a license.

Sample clause. "Right of First Refusal. For the purpose of this Agreement, 'right of first refusal' shall mean that LICENSOR shall first negotiate with LICENSEE in good faith on the terms and conditions which LICENSOR is prepared to accept for such license. If after _____ (___)business days of negotiation, LICENSOR and LICENSEE have not reached an agreement on such terms and conditions, LICENSOR shall be free to contact third parties to negotiate an agreement with them for the license."

right of last refusal *(contract)*

A contractual provision that gives one party to the agreement the right to match the terms the other party is willing to accept from a third party for some right, such as a license.

Sample clause. "Right of Last Refusal. For the purpose of this Agreement, 'right of last refusal' shall mean that prior to entering into any agreement with a third party on a transaction which LICENSEE has previously de-clined to enter into, LICENSOR shall first submit to LICENSEE the terms and conditions which LICENSOR is prepared to accept from such third party, and LICENSEE shall have the right, within _____ (___) business days after receipt of such terms and conditions, to notify LICENSOR that LICENSEE elects to enter into an agreement with LI-CENSOR on those identical terms and conditions, in which event LICENSOR shall enter into an agreement with LICENSEE on such terms and conditions. If LICENSEE does not, within _____ (___) business days, notify LICENSOR that it wishes to enter into such an agree-ment on such terms and conditions, LICENSOR shall be free to enter into an agreement with the third party on such terms and conditions."

rightfully hold a private key *(electronic commerce)*

"[T]he authority to utilize a private key: (a) That the holder or the holder's agents have not disclosed to a person in violation of [this Act] and (b) That the holder has not obtained through theft, deceit, eavesdropping, or other unlawful means."

Wash. Rev. Code § 19.34.020(32).

Rio *(hardware)*

"[A] small device (roughly the size of an audio cassette) with headphones that allows a user to download MP3 audio files from a computer and listen to them anywhere."

Recording Indus. Ass'n of America v. Diamond Multimedia Sys., Inc., 180 F.3d 1072, 1073 (9th Cir. 1999).

Annotation. "Prior to the invention of devices like the Rio, MP3 users had little option other than to listen to their downloaded digital audio files through headphones or speakers at their computers, playing them from their hard drives. The Rio renders these files portable. More precisely, once an audio file has been downloaded onto a computer hard drive from the Internet or some other source (such as a compact disc player or digital audio tape machine), separate computer software provided with the Rio . . . allows the user further to download the file to the Rio itself via a parallel port cable that plugs the Rio into the computer."

Recording Indus. Ass'n of America v. Diamond Multimedia Sys., Inc., 180 F.3d 1072, 1074-75 (9th Cir. 1999).

ripping *(technology)*

Copying music from a compact disc to a computer hard drive using software, often with compression of the digital file to a fraction of its original size. The most popular format for ripping music is MP3.

risk assessment *(business)*

A continuous process performed during all phases of system development to provide an estimate of the damage, loss, or harm that could result from a failure to successfully develop individual system components.

risk management *(business)*

A management approach designed to reduce risks inherent to system development.

roamer *(telecommunications)*

"A cellular telephone user who is a customer of a system in a market outside of the local cellular telephone system who accesses the local system while present in the area."

United States v. Brady, 820 F. Supp. 1346, 1353 n.14 (D. Utah 1993).

robot *(technology)*

A general-purpose system, with a great degree of autonomy, through which a computer senses its environment, plans and decides its actions, and performs mechanical manipulations and data handling, sometimes doing tasks normally done by humans.

role-playing *(Internet)*

A type of computer or online game in which the players assume the identities of specified entities within the game.

Annotation. "Role playing and adopting assumed identities is common in on-line communities."

United States v. Baker, 890 F. Supp. 1375, 1386 n.17 (E.D. Mich. 1995).

roll *(hardware)*

"Movement [of disk heads] about the . . . Y [axis]."

Tandon Corp. v. U.S. Int'l Trade Comm'n, 831 F.2d 1017, 1020 n.3 (Fed. Cir. 1987).

ROM *(hardware)*

Acronym for "Read Only Memory."

"A computer device containing a program or data permanently stored when the unit was made. In theory, it can apply to either internal memory or large-volume, external data storage. Today, it is applied to the former. Programs stored in ROM cannot be changed easily and they execute faster."

U.S. Copyright Office, *Compendium of Copyright Office Practices* II, § 326 (1984).

"A ROM normally is preprogrammed at the factory and cannot be programmed by an individual in the field."

Bateman v. Mnemonics, Inc., 79 F.3d 1532, 1537 n.7 (11th Cir. 1995).

"[A] memory device in which information is permanently stored. This device is distinguishable from a RAM (Random-Access Memory) in that in a RAM the stored information may be continuously changed even as the device is in operation. In a ROM memory a fixed pattern of signals or program is placed within the device by the manufacturer and not the customer. This is sometimes referred to as mask programmed."

Intel Corp. v. Radiation, Inc., 184 U.S.P.Q. (BNA) 54, 55 (T.T.A.B. 1974).

"[A]n internal permanent memory device consisting of a semi-conductor 'chip' which is incorporated into the circuitry of the computer. A program in object code is embedded on a ROM before it is incorporated in the computer. Information stored on a ROM can only be read, not erased or rewritten."

> *Apple Computer, Inc. v. Franklin Computer Corp.*, 714 F.2d 1240, 1243 (3d Cir. 1983), *cert. dism.*, 464 U.S. 1033 (1984).

"ROM is an acronym for Read Only Memory. A ROM is a photochemically imprinted silicon chip which stores information in the form of minute 'bits.' Bits are simply on-and-off switches. The pattern, sequence and frequency with which these switches are activated gives instructions to the machine and causes it to function in its various modes. The entire pattern imprinted on a ROM makes up what is generically called a computer program."

> *Apple Computer, Inc. v. Formula Int'l, Inc.*, 526 F. Supp. 775, 778 (C.D. Cal. 1983), *aff'd*, 725 F.2d 521 (9th Cir. 1984).

"[T]iny computer 'chips' containing thousands of data locations which store the instructions and data of a computer program."

> *Williams Elecs., Inc. v. Artic Int'l, Inc.*, 685 F.2d 870, 872 (3d Cir. 1982).

"[A] silicon chip that has been chemically imprinted with tiny switches, an assembly language 'one' becoming a connection and a 'zero' becoming the absence of a connection."

> *Data Cash Systems, Inc. v. JS&A Group, Inc.*, 628 F.2d 1038, 1040 (7th Cir. 1980).

"The ROM silicon chip is only one medium of several in which the object code version of a computer program may be stored."

> *Midway Mfg. Co. v. Strohon*, 564 F. Supp. 741, 750 (N.D. Ill. 1983).

"The stored information in a ROM cannot be changed; it is imprinted into the ROM when the device is manufactured."

> *Stern Elecs., Inc. v. Kaufman*, 669 F.2d 852, 854 n.1 (2d Cir. 1982).

[CANADA] "Read-Only Memory."

> *IBM Corp. v. Ordinateurs Spirales, Inc.* (1984), 2 C.I.P.R. 56 (Fed. T.D.);
> *Apple Computer, Inc. v. Mackintosh Computers Ltd.* (1986), 28 D.L.R. (4th) 178 (Fed. T.D.).

[CANADA] "ROM chips are permanent storage devices designed to plug into printed circuit boards within computers. The devices are generic in the sense that they are manufactured in a raw state. The raw state includes circuitry within the chip, known as decoders, designed to locate areas of memory storage therein and deliver the contents thereof to the microprocessor. ROM's, by their very name (Read-Only Memories), are specialized chips designed to act as storage media for programs or data. They are permanent in the sense that any programs and data encoded therein reside therein whether or not power is turned on or off. The programs and data contained therein are readable by computers, and the contents thereof can be displayed or printed in various languages by a computer."

Apple Computer, Inc. v. Mackintosh Computers Ltd. (1986), 28 D.L.R. (4th) 178 (Fed. T.D.).

[CANADA] "[I]s a type of memory that is permanently structured, through having been permanently etched with electric circuits, to carry a particular program, which can subsequently be read (by way of contrast with RAM or Random-Access Memory, which is erased when the power is turned off). ROM circuits consist of interconnected transistors built in and of the silicon. Their pattern cannot be discerned by the human eye except with the aid of an electron microscope."

Apple Computer, Inc. v. Mackintosh Computers Ltd. (1986), 28 D.L.R. (4th) 178 (Fed. T.D.).

[CANADA] "ROMS are customized chips."

Apple Computer, Inc. v. 115778 Can., Inc. (1988), 23 C.P.R. (3d) 22 (Fed. T.D.).

[ISRAEL] "ROM is nothing other than a means of storage of spiritual fruit and labour of the artist who wrote the software, by means of which the work can be executed and used. The ROM is, in fact, a memory unit that facilitates the reading of the software, while serving for storage, and forms the expression of the software that was written on the paper, and enables the creator of the software to express it by means of a machine that is called a 'computer.' The ROM is identical to the status of a sheet of paper upon which the program is written, only that instead of inscribing it on a sheet of paper with pen and ink, it is assembled within the ROM; because it is inscribed therein in a new form of writing, our minds, apparently, find difficulty in grasping the concept."

Apple Computer, Inc. v. New-Com Technologies Ltd. (1986), 8 I.P.R. 353 (Israel Dist. Ct. Tel Aviv).

root

(technology)

In a file directory, the highest segment in the hierarchy. The symbol for the root directory in Windows is a slash (/). All full pathnames begin with a slash to indicate that they start at the root directory. *See also* **directory; file system; pathname.**

(Internet)

The top of the Domain Name System hierarchy. Often referred to as the "dot."

root server *(technology)*

A computer system with the software and database required to locate name servers with data on specific top level domains. The root server for the .com, .net, and .edu domains is currently maintained by Network Solutions, Inc. Other root servers are located in the U.S., the U.K., Sweden, and Japan.

Annotation. "There are 13 root servers, named A through M, which together contain authoritative domain name databases. Information that a domain name is associated with a certain Internet Protocol number goes on the A root server. Servers B through M download new domain name registration and Internet Protocol number information on a voluntary and daily basis from the A root server. In this way, no matter which root server a user's computer utilizes to commence an address inquiry, the query can be completed successfully."

Thomas v. Network Solutions, Inc., 176 F.3d 500, 504 n.4 (D.C. Cir. 1999) (citations omitted).

"When ordered to translate an unknown domain name into an Internet Protocol number, a computer will ask its Internet Service Provider's server if it knows the domain name and corresponding Internet Protocol number. If that server lacks the information, it will pass the query to a 'root server,' also called a 'root zone' file, the authoritative and highest level of the domain name system database. The root zone file directs the query to the proper top-level domain zone file, which contains the domain names in a given domain and their corresponding Internet Protocol numbers. In the case of someone searching for the 'bettyandnicks.com' home page, the root zone file sends the query to the top-level domain zone file with information about '.com' domain names. The '.com' zone file then refers the query to a second-level domain name file with all the second-level domain names under '.com.' This is where the 'bettyandnicks.com' query ends: the second-level domain name file has the information matching the domain name to its associated Internet Protocol number. With the Internet Protocol number, the user's computer can connect the user to the requested Internet site. The 'bettyandnicks.com' home page will appear, just as if the user had typed in the Internet Protocol number instead of the domain name."

> *Thomas v. Network Solutions, Inc.*, 176 F.3d 500, 503-04 (D.C. Cir. 1999) (citations and footnotes omitted).

root zone file *(Internet)*

" . . . directs the query to the proper top-level domain zone file, which contains the domain names in a given domain and their corresponding Internet Protocol numbers."

> *Thomas v. Network Solutions, Inc.*, 176 F.3d 500, 503 (D.C. Cir. 1999) (citations and footnotes omitted).

Annotation. "In the case of someone searching for the 'bettyandnicks.com' home page, the root zone file sends the query to the top-level domain zone file with information about '.com' domain names. The '.com' zone file then refers the query to a second-level domain name file with all the second-level domain names under '.com.'"

> *Thomas v. Network Solutions, Inc.*, 176 F.3d 500, 503-04 (D.C. Cir. 1999) (citations and footnotes omitted).

"The process of converting domain names into IP numbers begins with the 'root zone file,' which is the highest level of the domain name system and contains the databases enabling an Internet address query to be routed to its proper destination. The master root zone server of the DNS contains the authoritative root zone file, from which the other 12 duplicate root zone servers download new domain name information on a daily basis. The root zone file serves the function of directing an address query to the proper TLD zone file, which contains information regarding the location of the numerous gTLDs and ccTLDs. The TLD zone file in turn directs the address query to SLD zone files, which contain listings of all SLDs and corresponding IP numbers under the TLD in question. The SLD zone files then direct the query to lower level portions of the DNS, until the address query is fully resolved."

> *Name.Space, Inc. v. Network Solutions, Inc.*, 202 F.3d 573, 577 (2d Cir. 2000).

Related issues. "NSI currently maintains the master root zone server, and was the sole registrar for new domain names under the .com, .org, .net, .edu and .gov gTLDs when this action was first commenced in the district court. NSI has performed these functions since 1993, pursuant to Cooperative Agreement No. NCR-9218742 (the 'Cooperative Agreement'), awarded by NSF through a competitive process pursuant to the National Science Found. Act, 42 U.S.C. §1861 et seq., and the Federal Grant and Cooperative Agreement Act, 31 U.S.C. §6301 et seq. Article 3 of the Co-operative Agreement states that NSI shall provide domain name registration services in accordance with RFC 1174."

Name.Space, Inc. v. Network Solutions, Inc., 202 F.3d 573, 577 (2d Cir. 2000) (citations omitted).

rotoscoping *(entertainment; multimedia)*

The process of creating each video frame individually. Often used to refer to the process of filming a live actor moving in a designated manner, then creating an animated character with the same movements by tracing the live actors movements frame by frame.

router *(hardware)*

"[A] switching computer which looks at each incoming packet to see where that packet should be routed next."

I. Trotter Hardy, *Project Looking Forward: Sketching the Future of Copyright in a Networked World* 49 (May 1998).

routine *(software)*

"A series or group of instructions usually contained within a main program analogous to a paragraph within textual work."

U.S. Copyright Office, *Compendium of Copyright Office Practices* II, § 326 (1984).

"[A] program or set of instructions with a beginning and a defined end, which can be invoked at its beginning and will always return to its end after performing a given function between those two points. An example is a square root routine which will calculate the square root of a number when it is started and will produce the answer when it returns at its end."

Jostens, Inc. v. National Computer Sys., Inc., 318 N.W.2d 691, 702 n.8 (Minn. 1982).

royalties *(contract)*

Payments made in exchange for a grant of certain rights, such as a copyright license.

Sample clause. "All advances against royalties shall be recouped by [Commissioning Party] from first dollar revenues. [Commissioning Party] shall pay Developer the following royalty rates on sales of the Product:

___ % of Net Revenues on sales in the retail channel

___ % of Net Revenues on OEM sales

___ % of Net Revenues on direct sales

For purposes of this paragraph, 'Net Revenues' shall be defined as all money received by [Commissioning Party] relating to the Title, less returns and credits against sales, cost of goods, and a reasonable reserve for future returns."

RPM *(technology)*

Acronym for "Revolutions Per Minute." A measure of speed of a rotating storage medium, such as a CD-ROM.

RSA *(technology)*

Acronym for "Rivest-Shamir-Adelman."

"[A] public key algorithm used for both encryption and authentication; it was invented in 1977 by Ron Rivest, Adi Shamir and Leonard Adelman."
    U.S. General Accounting Office, *Information Superhighway: An Overview of Technology Changes* 19 n.5 (Jan. 1995).

RSAC *(organization)*

See **Recreational Software Advisory Council.**

RTC *(organization)*

Acronym for "Religious Technology Center."

The Church of Scientology has charged RTC with securing the sacred texts and policing any breaches in security or unauthorized disclosures that may occur. RTC has enacted a comprehensive protection plan that includes locked vaults, numerous guards, key cards, and signed nondisclosure statements by all church members. RTC has also been aggressive in tracking down suspected offenders and pursuing legal remedies against them.
    Cases in which RTC has been involved include *Religious Technology Ctr. v. Netcom On-line Com. Servs., Inc.,* 907 F. Supp. 1361 (N.D. Cal. 1995); *Religious Technology Ctr. v. F.A.C.T.Net, Inc.,* 901 F. Supp. 1519 (D. Colo. 1995).

RTM *(manufacturing)*

Acronym for "Release To Manufacturing." This is the point in the development process when the product has been fully tested and is ready for manufacturing.

rule of doubt *(copyright)*

"[The Copyright Office] will register a claim even though there is a reasonable doubt about the ultimate action which might be taken under the same circumstances by an appropriate court with respect to whether (1) the material deposited for registration constitutes copyrightable subject matter or (2) the other legal and formal requirements of the statute have been met."

U.S. Copyright Office *Compendium of Copyright Office Practices* II, § 602.05 (1984).

Annotation. "The Copyright Office will issue a certificate of registration, even when an applicant for registration of a computer program containing trade secrets is not willing to submit source code and submits object code instead. When it issues such a registration, it does so under the 'rule of doubt' procedure. The 'rule of doubt' is more accurately described as the rule of 'the benefit of the doubt' (in favor of the copyright applicant). If the application is otherwise proper, the Copyright Office will issue such a registration, which makes it clear that no determination has been made concerning the existence of copyrightable authorship. The Copyright Office issues its registration on this limited basis because of its belief that object code is 'basically unintelligible' to its examiners, so that they cannot make a definitive determination of its copyrightability. In order to receive such a rule of doubt registration, the applicant must submit a letter stating that the program does contain original authorship.

"While there is no clear law delineating how the rule of doubt registration affects the status of the registered work in litigation, it is likely that such a registration would not be accorded the same weight as a conventional registration. The Copyright Office has recognized that in making this kind of registration, the burden is placed on the courts to make a determination about the existence of copyrightable subject authorship. This additional burden is especially important in the case of requests to the court for preliminary relief in the form of temporary restraining orders and preliminary injunctions."

Office of Technology Assessment, *Finding a Balance: Computer Software, Intellectual Property, and the Challenge of Technological Change* 66 (May 1992) (citations omitted).

Rule 11 sanctions *(general)*

Citation: Fed. R. Civ. Proc. 11.

"Rule 11. Signing of Pleadings, Motions, and Other Papers; Representations to Court; Sanctions

(a) Signature.

Every pleading, written motion, and other paper shall be signed by at least one attorney of record in the attorney's individual name, or, if the party is not represented by an attorney, shall be signed by the party. Each paper shall state the signer's address and telephone number, if any. Except when otherwise specifically provided by rule or statute, pleadings need not be verified or accompanied by affidavit. An unsigned paper shall be stricken unless omission of the signature is corrected promptly after being called to the attention of attorney or party.

(b) Representations to Court.

By presenting to the court (whether by signing, filing, submitting, or later advocating) a pleading, written motion, or other paper, an attorney or unrepresented party is certifying that to the best of the person's knowledge, information, and belief, formed after an inquiry reasonable under the circumstances,—

(1) it is not being presented for any improper purpose, such as to harass or to cause unnecessary delay or needless increase in the cost of litigation;

(2) the claims, defenses, and other legal contentions therein are warranted by existing law or by a nonfrivolous argument for the extension, modification, or reversal of existing law or the establishment of new law;

(3) the allegations and other factual contentions have evidentiary support or, if specifically so identified, are likely to have evidentiary support after a reasonable opportunity for further investigation or discovery; and

(4) the denials of factual contentions are warranted on the evidence or, if specifically so identified, are reasonably based on a lack of information or belief.

(c) Sanctions.

If, after notice and a reasonable opportunity to respond, the court determines that subdivision (b) has been violated, the court may, subject to the conditions stated below, impose an appropriate sanction upon the attorneys, law firms, or parties that have violated subdivision (b) or are responsible for the violation.

(1) How Initiated.

(A) By Motion. A motion for sanctions under this rule shall be made separately from other motions or requests and shall describe the specific conduct alleged to violate subdivision (b). It shall be served as provided in Rule 5, but shall not be filed with or presented to the court unless, within 21 days after service of the motion (or such other period as the court may prescribe), the challenged paper, claim, defense, contention, allegation, or denial is not withdrawn or appropriately corrected. If warranted, the court may award to the party prevailing on the motion the reasonable expenses and attorney's fees incurred in presenting or opposing the motion. Absent exceptional circumstances, a law firm shall be held jointly responsible for violations committed by its partners, associates, and employees.

(B) On Court's Initiative. On its own initiative, the court may enter an order describing the specific conduct that appears to violate subdivision (b) and directing an attorney, law firm, or party to show cause why it has not violated subdivision (b) with respect thereto.

(2) Nature of Sanction; Limitations. A sanction imposed for violation of this rule shall be limited to what is sufficient to deter repetition of such conduct or comparable conduct by others similarly situated. Subject to the limitations in subparagraphs (A) and (B), the sanction may consist of, or include, directives of a nonmonetary nature, an order to pay a penalty into court, or, if imposed on motion and warranted for effective deterrence, an order directing payment to the movant of some or all of the reasonable attorneys' fees and other expenses incurred as a direct result of the violation.

(A) Monetary sanctions may not be awarded against a represented party for a violation of subdivision (b)(2).

(B) Monetary sanctions may not be awarded on the court's initiative unless the court issues its order to show cause before a voluntary dismissal or settlement of the claims made by or against the party which is, or whose attorneys are, to be sanctioned.

(3) Order. When imposing sanctions, the court shall describe the conduct determined to constitute a violation of this rule and explain the basis for the sanction imposed.

(d) Inapplicability to Discovery.

Subdivisions (a) through (c) of this rule do not apply to disclosures and discovery requests, responses, objections, and motions that are subject to the provisions of *Rules 26 through 37.*"

running *(software)*

When a program is being executed it is said to be running. The system can be said to be running when it is "up" ("operating" or "on line").

running parallel *(hardware; software)*

"This means using both the old and new equipment at the same time."

Wang Labs., Inc. v. Docktor Pet Centers, Inc., 1981 Mass. App. Ct. Adv. Sh. 1332, 1335 n.2 (1981); *Renfro Hosiery Mills Co. v. National Cash Register Co.,* 552 F.2d 1061, 1064 (4th Cir. 1977).

Rural Telephone *(copyright)*

See **Feist.**

sale *(contract)*
"... consists in the passing of title from the seller to the buyer for a price."
U.C.C. § 2-106(1).

Related issues. "A 'sale' is defined as 'the passing of title from the seller to
the buyer for a price.' A pure license agreement ... does not involve transfer of title, and so is not a sale for Article 2 purposes."
Berthold Types Ltd. v. Abode Sys., Inc., 101 F. Supp. 2d 697, 698 (E.D. Ill.
2000).

sale of goods *(contract)*
"It is clear that the sale of a computer system consists not only of physical
goods, but of substantial services essential for producing the final product.
Nevertheless, most authorities agree that the sale of a computer system
involving both hardware and software is a sale of goods notwithstanding
the incidental service aspects of the sale; therefore, Article 2 of the Uniform
Commercial Code applies."
Dreier Co. v. Unitronix Corp., 218 N.J. Super. 260, 527 A.2d 875, 879
(1986).
See also **U.C.C.**

SAM *(hardware)*
Acronym for "Simultaneous-Access Memory."
Intel Corp. v. Radiation, Inc., 184 U.S.P.Q. (BNA) 54, 55 (T.T.A.B. 1974).

sampling *(copyright; technology)*
"[A]ctually physically copying the sounds from one recording to another."
Tin Pan Apple, Inc. v. Miller Brewing Co., 30 U.S.P.Q.2d (BNA) 1791, 1795
(S.D.N.Y. 1994).

Annotation. "[I]t is common ground that if defendants did sample
plaintiff's copyrighted sound recording, they infringed that copyright."
Tin Pan Apple, Inc. v. Miller Brewing Co., 30 U.S.P.Q.2d (BNA) 1791, 1795
(S.D.N.Y. 1994).
See also **digital sampling.**

sampling rate *(technology)*
The number of times within a given time period that audio is sampled. The higher the sampling rate, the more accurate the recorded sound, but the more storage space required.

scalability *(technology)*
The ability of a computer system to accommodate a significant growth in the size of the system without the need for substantial redesign.

scanning *(technology)*
1. Dividing an image into a series of pixels and assigning a series of numbers to the characteristics of that pixel (brightness, color, etc.), which can then be used to reconstruct the image. 2. A methodical search by hackers on computer servers for valid passwords or trapdoors.

scenes à faire *(copyright)*
"[I]ncidents, characters or settings which are as a practical matter indispensable, or at least standard, in the treatment of a given topic."
    Atari, Inc. v. North American Philips Consumer Elecs. Corp., 672 F.2d 607, 616 (7th Cir.), *cert. denied,* 459 U.S. 880 (1982).

Annotation. "[W]here 'it is virtually impossible to write about a particular historical era or fictional theme without employing certain "stock" or standard literary devices,' such expression is not copyrightable. . . . This is known as the *scenes à faire* doctrine, and like 'merger,' it has its analogous application to computer programs.

"Professor Nimmer points out that 'in many instances it is virtually impossible to write a program to perform particular functions without employing standard techniques.' This is a result of the fact that a programmer's freedom of design choice is often circumscribed by extrinsic considerations such as (1) the mechanical specifications of the computer on which a particular program is intended to run; (2) compatibility requirements of other programs with which a program is designed to operate in conjunction; (3) computer manufacturers' design standards; (4) demands of the industry being serviced; and (5) widely accepted programming practices within the computer industry."
    Computer Assocs. Int'l, Inc. v. Altai, Inc., 982 F.2d 693, 709-10 (2d Cir. 1992) (citations omitted).

". . . are afforded no copyright protection because the subject matter represented can be expressed in no other way. . . ."
    Whelan Assocs., Inc. v. Jaslow Dental Lab., Inc., 797 F.2d 1222, 1236 (3d Cir. 1986).

"'. . . denies copyright protection to elements of expression that are 'as a practical matter, indispensable or at least standard in the industry.'"
Interactive Networks, Inc. v. NTN Comm., Inc., 875 F. Supp. 1398, 1403 (N.D. Cal. 1995) (citation omitted).

"Plaintiff may not claim copyright protection of an . . . expression that is, if not standard, then commonplace in the computer software industry."
Brown Bag Software v. Symantec Corp., 960 F.2d 1465, 1473 (9th Cir.), *cert. denied*, 506 U.S. 869 (1992).

Related issues. "Video games, as well as other genres such as quiz shows, commonly award points for successful actions by the player and subtract points for mistaken actions. Likewise, it is inherent in the nature of a predictive game that more points be awarded for successful actions that are statistically less likely to occur."
Interactive Networks, Inc. v. NTN Comm., Inc., 875 F. Supp. 1398, 1404 (N.D. Cal. 1995).

SCMS *(copyright; technology)*
Acronym for "Serial Copyright Management System."
See **Serial Copyright Management System.**

scope *(contract)*
"[W]ith respect to terms of a license, means:
(A) the licensed copies, information, or informational rights involved;
(B) the use or access authorized, prohibited, or controlled;
(C) the geographic area, market, or location; or
(D) the duration of the license."
UCITA § 102(a)(58).

scope creep *(business)*
A common phenomenon on development projects, where the original scope is allowed to expand and encompass functionality or areas not originally intended. This is a major cause of delayed projects and cost overruns.

scratchpad register *(hardware)*
"[A] plurality of multibit storage locations, usually located in the central processing unit (CPU) of a computer, used for temporary storage of program information, operands, and calculation results for use by the computer's arithmetic and logic unit, and other information of a temporary nature."
In re Bradley, 600 F.2d 807, 808 n.1 (C.C.P.A. 1979), *aff'd sub nom. Diamond v. Bradley*, 450 U.S. 381(1981).

screen *(hardware)*

An illuminated display surface, for example, the display surface of a CRT.

Related issues. "[I]t is well established that screen displays . . . warrant copyright protection as non-literal elements of the program."
> *O.P. Solutions, Inc. v. Intellectual Property Network, Ltd.*, 52 U.S.P.Q.2d (BNA) 1818 (2d Cir. 1999).

See also **cathode-ray tube; screen display(s).**

screen display(s) *(hardware)*

". . . are the products of a program and are not considered to be a literal element of a program. They fall 'under the copyright rubric of audiovisual works.'"
> *Bateman v. Mnemonic, Inc.*, 79 F.3d 1532, 1545 n.26 (11th Cir. 1995) (citation omitted).

Related issues. "[I]t is well established that screen displays . . . warrant copyright protection as non-literal elements of the program."
> *O.P. Solutions, Inc. v. Intellectual Property Network, Ltd.*, 52 U.S.P.Q.2d (BNA) 1818 (2d Cir. 1999).

See also **cathode-ray tube; screen.**

screen name *(Internet)*

A name, usually chosen by the user, that is used when the user is communicating online. It may be an abbreviation of the user's real name or a purely fictitious name. Users often have several screen names.

screening software *(software)*

Application software that blocks or screens web sites containing objectionable materials.

Related issues. "There is no way that a speaker can use current technology to know if a listener is using screening software."
> *American Civil Liberties Union v. Reno,* 929 F. Supp. 824, 848 (E.D. Pa. 1996), *aff'd, Reno v. American Civil Liberties Union,* 521 U.S. 844 (1997).

See **filtering software; PICS.**

scrolling *(software)*

Allows browsing through information at a terminal by providing a shifting display of a document.

SCSI *(hardware)*

Acronym for "Small Computer System Interconnect." A type of system that enables up to seven different devices to be connected to a single port of a computer in a daisy chain. SCSI is both a connection and a bus.

search

(software)

A program that can locate strings of characters or keywords in a data file.

(Internet)

The ability of a program, generally referred to as a "search engine," to locate a particular web site or web page containing strings of characters of keywords.

Annotation (Internet). "Users searching for a specific Web site have two options. First, if users know or can deduce the address of a Web site, they can type the address of a Web site, they can type the address into a browser and connect directly to the Web site as if dialing a telephone number, More often, users do not know the exact address and must rely on 'search engines' available on the Web to search for key words and phrases associated with the desired Web site. Because of the quantity of information on the Web, searches often yield thousands of possible Web sites."
   Lockheed Martin Corp. v. Network Solutions, Inc., 985 F. Supp. 949, 952 (C.D. Cal. 1997).

"Even if a broad search will, on occasion, retrieve unwanted materials, the user virtually always receives some warning of its content, significantly reducing the element of surprise or 'assault' involved in broadcasting."
   American Civil Liberties Union v. Reno, 929 F. Supp. 824, 852 (E.D. Pa. 1996), *aff'd, Reno v. American Civil Liberties Union,* 521 U.S. 844 (1997).
See also **search engine.**

search engine *(Internet; software)*

"[T]he software and database architecture that allows a user to search the World-Wide Web ('the Web')."
   Digital Equipment Corp. v. Altavista Technology, Inc., 960 F. Supp. 456, 459 n.2 (D. Mass. 1997).

"[S]ervices . . . which allow users to search for Web sites that contain certain categories of information, or to search for key words."
   American Civil Liberties Union v. Reno, 929 F. Supp. 824, 837 (E.D. Pa. 1996), *aff'd, Reno v. American Civil Liberties Union,* 521 U.S. 844 (1997).

Annotation. "If a computer user does not know a domain name, she can use an Internet 'search engine.' To do this, the user types in a key word search, and the search will locate all of the web sites containing the key word. Such key word searches can yield hundreds of web sites."
   Panavision Int'l, L.P. v. Toeppen, 141 F.3d 1316, 1319 (9th Cir. 1998).

"More often, users do not know the exact address and must rely on 'search engines' available on the Web to search for key words and phrases associated with the desired Web site. Because of the quantity of information on the Web, searches often yield thousands of possible Web sites."

Lockheed Martin Corp. v. Network Solutions, Inc., 985 F. Supp. 949, 952 (C.D. Cal. 1997).

"A number of 'search engines'—such as Yahoo, Magellan, Alta Vista, Web-Crawler, and Lycos—are available to help users navigate the World Wide Web. For example, the service Yahoo maintains a directory of documents available on various Web servers. A user can gain access to Yahoo's server and type a string of characters as a search request. Yahoo returns a list of documents whose entries in the Yahoo directory match the search string and organizes the list of documents by category. Search engines make use of software capable of automatically contacting various Web sites and extracting relevant information. Some search engines, such as Alta Vista, store the information in a database and return it in response to a user request. Others, such as Yahoo, employ a group of individuals to determine whether and how a site should be categorized in the Yahoo directory."

Shea v. Reno, 930 F. Supp. 916, 929 (S.D.N.Y. 1997) (citations omitted).

"[B]y typing a request into a search engine, a user can retrieve many different sources of content related to the search that the creators of the engine have collected."

American Civil Liberties Union v. Reno, 929 F. Supp. 824, 843 (E.D. Pa. 1996), *aff'd, Reno v. American Civil Liberties Union,* 521 U.S. 844 (1997).

". . . various indexes, commonly referred to as search engines. . . . These indexes will allow the user to enter a name or a word or a combination of words, much like a Lexis or WestLaw search, and will return the results of the search as a list of 'hyperlinks' to web pages that have information within or associated with the document comprising the page responding to the search."

Intermatic, Inc. v. Toeppen, 947 F. Supp. 1227, 1232 (N.D. Ill. 1996).

"A Web surfer's second option when he does not know the domain name is to utilize an Internet search engine, such as Yahoo, Altavista, or Lycos. . . . When a keyword is entered, the search engine processes it through a self-created index of web sites to generate a (sometimes long) list relating to the entered keyword. Each search engine uses its own algorithm to arrange indexed materials in sequence, so the list of web sites that any particular set of keywords will bring up may differ depending on the search engine used. . . . Search engines look for keywords in places such as domain names, actual text on the web page, and metatags."

Brookfield Comm., Inc. v. West Coast Entertainment Corp., 174 F.3d 1036, 1045 (9th Cir. 1999) (citations omitted).

Related issues. "[T]he inevitable imprecision of search engines—a broad search will almost always return some irrelevant results."
Shea v. Reno, 930 F. Supp. 916, 931 (S.D.N.Y. 1996).

"It is possible that a search engine can accidentally retrieve material of a sexual nature through an imprecise search. . . . Imprecise searches may also retrieve irrelevant material that is not of a sexual nature. The accidental retrieval of sexually explicit material is one manifestation of the larger phenomenon of irrelevant search results."
American Civil Liberties Union v. Reno, 929 F. Supp. 824, 844 (E.D. Pa. 1996), *aff'd, Reno v. American Civil Liberties Union,* 521 U.S. 844 (1997).

"Most of these services do not charge users for search requests and are sustained primarily by advertising revenues."
Shea v. Reno, 930 F. Supp. 916, 929 n.10 (S.D.N.Y. 1996).

"For many content providers on the Web, the ability to be found by these search engines is very important."
American Civil Liberties Union v. Reno, 929 F. Supp. 824, 837 (E.D. Pa. 1996), *aff'd, Reno v. American Civil Liberties Union,* 521 U.S. 844 (1997).

" . . . searches the 'META' keywords and identifies a match or a 'hit.'"
Niton Corp. v. Radiation Monitoring Devices, Inc., 27 F. Supp. 2d 102, 104 (D. Mass. 1998).

search service *(Internet)*

"[R]efers both to the search engine software and the way the search service appears to users. Search services are often used to find information or locate sites on the Web."
Digital Equipment Corp. v. Altavista Technology, Inc., 960 F. Supp. 456, 459 n.2 (D. Mass. 1997).
See also **search engine.**

search term(s) *(software)*

Also called "keyword(s)." A word or phrase submitted to a search program, describing what information a user is looking for.

seasonable *(contract)*

"[W]ith respect to an act, means taken within the time agreed or, if no time is agreed, within a reasonable time."
UCITA § 102(a)(59).

SECAM *(broadcasting; hardware)*

The television video format used in France and most of Eastern Europe.

second-level domain *(Internet)*

Abbreviated as "SLD." The next highest level of the hierarchy after the top-level domain. In a domain name, it is the alphanumeric string immediately to the left of the top-level domain, separated from it by a dot. Second-level domain names are often the name of the organization that owns the domain name, e.g., microsoft.com.

"[S]imply a term or series of terms (e.g., westcoastvideo). . . ."
Brookfield Comm., Inc. v. West Coast Entertainment Corp., 174 F.3d 1036, 1044 (9th Cir. 1999).

"[A]ny word not already reserved in combination with the TLD."
Avery Dennison Corp. v. Sumpton, 189 F.3d 868, 872 (9th Cir. 1999).

Related issues. "Second-level domain names, the name just to the left of '.com,' must be exclusive. Therefore, although two companies can have non-exclusive trademark rights in a name, only one company can have a second-level domain name that corresponds to its trademark. . . . In short, the exclusive quality of second-level domain names has set trademark owners against each other in the struggle to establish a commercial presence on the Internet, and has set businesses against domain name holders who seek to continue the traditional use of the Internet as a non-commercial medium of communication."
Lockheed Martin Corp. v. Network Solutions, Inc., 985 F. Supp. 949, 952-53 (C.D. Cal. 1997).

secondary meaning *(trademark)*

". . . is shown where 'if "in the minds of the public, the primary significance of a product feature or term is to identify the source of the product rather than the product itself."'"
America Online, Inc. v. AT&T Corp., 64 F. Supp. 2d 549, 560 (E.D. Va. 1999) (citations omitted). *See also Washington Speakers Bureau, Inc. v. Leading Authorities, Inc.,* 33 F. Supp. 2d 488, 494-95 (E.D. Va. 1999).

"A trade term acquires a secondary meaning when '[I]t means a single thing coming from a single source, and is well known in the community. . . . Put another way, the owner of a mark must establish that 'the primary significance of the term in the minds of the consuming public is not the product but the producer.' . . ."
Stratus Computer, Inc. v. NCR Corp., 2 U.S.P.Q.2d (BNA) 1375, 1376 (D. Mass. 1987) (citations omitted).

Annotation. "Plaintiff can establish secondary meaning through either direct or indirect proof, including proof of (1) its long and exclusive use of the mark; (2) the size and prominence of its enterprise; (3) the success of its promotional efforts; and (4) identification by the members of the appropriate 'consuming public.'"

Stratus Computer, Inc. v. NCR Corp., 2 U.S.P.Q.2d (BNA) 1375, 1376 (D. Mass. 1987).

"A variety of factors is relevant to the secondary meaning inquiry and it is important to note that no single factor or particular combination of factors is dispositive of the question. The relevant factors include '(1) advertising expenditures; (2) consumer studies linking the mark to a source; (3) sales success; (4) unsolicited media coverage of the product; (5) attempts to plagiarize the mark; and (6) the length and exclusivity of the mark's use.'"

Washington Speakers Bureau, Inc. v. Leading Authorities, Inc., 33 F. Supp. 2d 488, 496 (E.D. Va. 1999).

Section 43(a) of the Lanham Act *(trademarks)*

"To prevail under §43(a) of the Lanham Act, a plaintiff must show that it has 'a valid, protectible trademark and that the defendant's use of a colorable imitation of the trademark is likely to cause confusion among consumers.'"

Washington Speakers Bureau, Inc. v. Leading Authorities, Inc., 33 F. Supp. 2d 488, 493 (E.D. Va. 1999).

"Nevertheless, §43(a) of the Lanham Act 'generally has been construed to protect against trademark, service mark, and trade name infringement even though the mark or name has not been federally registered.'"

Washington Speakers Bureau, Inc. v. Leading Authorities, Inc., 33 F. Supp. 2d 488, 494 (E.D. Va. 1999).

Section 117 limitations *(copyright)*

"Notwithstanding the provisions of section 106, it is not an infringement for the owner of a copy of a computer program to make or authorize the making of another copy or adaptation of that computer program provided:

(1) that such a new copy or adaptation is created as an essential step in the utilization of the computer program in conjunction with a machine and that it is used in no other manner, or

(2) that such new copy or adaptation is for archival purposes only and that all archival copies are destroyed in the event that continued possession of the computer program should cease to be rightful.

Any exact copies prepared in accordance with the provisions of this section may be leased, sold, or otherwise transferred, along with the copy from which such copies were prepared, only as part of the lease, sale, or other transfer of all rights in the program. Adaptations so prepared may be transferred only with the authorization of the copyright owner."

U.S. Copyright Act, 17 U.S.C. § 117 (as amended in 1980).

Annotation. "The current § 117 was enacted by Congress in 1980, as part of the Computer Software Copyright Act. This Act adopted the recommendations contained in the *Final Report of the National Commission on the Net Technological Uses of Copyright Works* ('CONTU') (1978), H.R. Rep. No. 1307, 96th Cong., 2d Sess., pt. 1, at 23. The CONTU was established by Congress in 1974 to perform research and make recommendations concerning copyright protection for computer programs. The new § 117 reflects the CONTU's conclusion that: 'Because the placement of a work into a computer is the preparation of a copy, the law should provide that persons in rightful possession of copies of programs be able to use them freely without fear of exposure to copyright liability.' Final Report at 13."

MAI Sys. Corp. v. Peak Computer, Inc., 991 F.2d 511, 519 n.6 (9th Cir. 1993), *cert. dism.,* 510 U.S. 1033 (1994).

"But the Commission went on to stress the limited nature of the right to copy as granted in Section 117. It said that the right exists, only 'to the extent which will permit its use by that possessor.' And 'this permission would not be extended to other copies of the program.'"

Apple Computer, Inc. v. Formula Int'l, Inc., 594 F. Supp. 617, 621 (C.D. Cal. 1984).

"Prior to that amendment there has been some doubt whether a computer program was copyrightable under the Act of 1976 in view of the language of section 117 in that Act, which appeared to continue the status quo in copyright law for computer programs.

* * *

"We are of the opinion that the reason for finding that computer programs were copyrightable under the 1976 Act . . . are [sic] convincing. We agree that computer programs were copyrightable under the Act of 1976. Congress chose to make crystal clear by the Amendments of 1980 that fact. . . ."

M. Kramer Mfg. Co. v. Andrews, 783 F.2d 421, 432 n.9 (4th Cir. 1986),

"Unfortunately, ownership is an imprecise concept, and the Copyright Act does not define the term. Nor is there much useful guidance to be obtained from either the legislative history of the statute or the cases that have construed it. The National Commission on New Technological Uses of Copyrighted Works ('CONTU') was created by Congress to recommend changes in the Copyright Act to accommodate advances in computer technology. In its final report, CONTU proposed a version of section 117 that is identical to the one that was ultimately enacted, except for a single change. The proposed CONTU version provided that 'it is not an infringement for the *rightful possessor* of a copy of a computer program to make or authorize the making of another copy or adaptation of that program . . . .' Congress, however, substituted the words 'owner of a copy' in place of the words 'rightful possessor of a copy.' The legislative history does not explain the reason for the change, . . . but it is clear from the fact of the substitution of the term 'owner' for 'rightful possessor' that Congress must have meant to require more than 'rightful possession' to trigger the section 117 defense."

    DSC Comm. Corp. v. Pulse Comm., Inc., 170 F.3d 1354, 1360 (Fed. Cir. 1999) (citations omitted).

"As we have seen, section 117 limits the copyright owner's exclusive rights by allowing an owner of a copy of a computer program to reproduce or adapt the program if reproduction or adaptation is necessary for the program to be used in conjunction with a machine."

    DSC Comm. Corp. v. Pulse Comm., Inc., 170 F.3d 1354, 1361 (Fed. Cir. 1999).

Related issues. "Since [plaintiff] licensed its software, the [defendant's] customers do not qualify as 'owners' of the software and are not eligible for protection under § 117."

    MAI Sys. Corp. v. Peak Computer, Inc., 991 F.2d 511, 518 (9th Cir. 1993), *cert. dism.*, 510 U.S. 1033 (1994).

"Section 117 does not purport to protect a user who disassembles object code, converts it from assembly into source code, and makes printouts and photocopies of the refined source code version."

    Sega Enters. Ltd. v. Accolade, Inc., 977 F.2d 1510, 1520 (9th Cir. 1992).

See also **CONTU Final Report; owner.**

Section 301 *(copyright)*

"With a few exceptions, all causes of action falling within the scope of the Copyright Act are expressly preempted."

    Alcatel USA, Inc. v. DGI Technologies, Inc., 166 F.3d 772, 785 (5th Cir. 1999) (citation omitted).

Annotation. ". . . sets forth two conditions, both of which must be satisfied, for preemption of a right under state law to occur: First, the work in which the right is asserted must come within the *subject matter* of copyright as defined in section 102 and 103. Second, the right that the author seeks to protect must be equivalent to any of the exclusive rights within the general scope of copyright as specified by section 106.

* * *

"The second prong is more complex, however, requiring a comparison of the nature of the rights protected under federal copyright law with the nature of the state rights for which DSC seeks protection. If these rights are determined to be 'equivalent,' then the state law cause of action is preempted. We evaluate the equivalency of rights under what is commonly referred to as the 'extra element' test. According to this test, if the act or acts of DGI about which DSC complains would violate both misappropriation law and copyright law, then the state right is deemed 'equivalent to copyright.' If, however, one or more qualitatively different elements are required to constitute the state-created cause of action being asserted, then the right granted under state law does not lie 'within the general scope of copyright,' and preemption does not occur."

Alcatel USA, Inc. v. DGI Technologies, Inc., 166 F.3d 772, 785-86, 787 (5th Cir. 1999) (citations omitted) (emphasis in original).

secure *(technology; telecommunications)*

"[A] relative term that refers to how difficult and costly it is to gain unauthorized access to a communication. The more difficult and costly it is, the more secure a communication is."

I. Trotter Hardy, *Project Looking Forward: Sketching the Future of Copyright in a Networked World* 61 (May 1998).

Secure Electronic Transaction *(technology)*

See SET.

Secure HTTP *(Internet; technology)*

Abbreviated as "S-HTTP." This is a proposed set of extensions to the HTTP protocol to add security features.

secured facility regime *(technology)*

". . . provides an integrated and strictly monitored preventative approach to resolving disputes with respect to the use of one party's information in the other party's software development process."

IBM Corp. v. Fujitsu Ltd., Copyright L. Rep. (CCH) ¶ 20,517 (Am. Arb. Ass'n 1988).

security *(trade secret)*

"[T]he protection of information from discovery by outsiders."

Electro-Craft Corp. v. Controlled Motion, Inc., 332 N.W.2d 890, 902 (Minn. 1983).

security certificate *(Internet)*

Information used by the SSL protocol to establish a secure network connection. *See* SSL.

security software *(software)*

"[A] component that can be used with the operating system to restrict outside access to sensitive information and to restrict a particular user to information consistent with that user's security classification."

Addamax Corp. v. Open Software Found., Inc., 152 F.3d 48, 49 (1st Cir. 1998).

security testing *(DMCA)*

"[A]ccessing a computer, computer system, or computer network solely for the purpose of good faith testing, investigating, or correcting, a security flaw or vulnerability, with the authorization of the owner or operator of such computer, computer system, or computer network."

17 U.S.C. § 1201(j).

"Defendants contended earlier that their actions should be considered exempt security testing under Section 1201(j) of the statute. This exception, however, is limited to 'assessing a computer, computer system, or computer network, solely for the purpose of good faith testing, investigating, or correcting [of a] security flaw or vulnerability, with the authorization of the owner or operator of such computer system or computer network.'

"The record does not indicate that DeCSS has anything to do with testing computers, computer systems, or computer networks. Certainly defendants sought, and plaintiffs' granted, no authorization for defendants' activities. This exception therefore has no bearing in this case."

Universal City Studios, Inc. v. Reimerdes, 111 F. Supp. 2d 294, 321 (S.D.N.Y. 2000) (footnotes omitted).

self-escrow *(encryption)*

A system in which the key recovery agent is internal to an end-user's organization. No third-party agents are necessary and the escrowed information is not deposited with the government.

self-help *(technology)*

When a person or entity acts on its own to resolve a dispute, rather than submitting the dispute to a court or other dispute resolution procedure.

Related issues. "[T]his court also notes that the implementation of techno-logical means of self-help, to the extent that reasonable measures are effective, is particularly appropriate in this type of situation [spamming] and should be exhausted before legal action is proper."

> *CompuServe, Inc. v. Cyber Promotions, Inc.,* 962 F. Supp. 1015, 1023 (S.D. Ohio 1997).

sell in *(business)*

The amount of product (usually in units) that has been sold into the distribution channel.

sell sheets *(business)*

Printed promotional materials (usually a single sheet) that describe a product.

sell through *(business)*

The amount of product (usually in units) that has actually been purchased by end users.

seller *(contract)*

"[A] person who sells or *contracts* to sell *goods.*"

> U.C.C. § 2-103(1)(d) (emphasis in original).

semiconductor *(hardware)*

A material that is neither a good insulator nor a good conductor. Usually silicon, germanium, or gallium arsenide, it is crafted to take advantage of the unusual properties of charge carriers or field effects derived from knowledge of solid state physics. The term has come to refer to all devices made of semiconducting material, including integrated circuits, transistors, and diodes.

"[O]ne of a class of materials (such as silicon) whose electrical conductivity falls between that of a conductor (metal) and that of an insulator."

> *Sperry Rand Corp. v. Rothlein,* 241 F. Supp. 549, 552 (D. Conn. 1964).

See also **integrated circuit; semiconductor chip product.**

semiconductor chip product *(mask work)*

". . . is the final or intermediate form of any product (a) having two or more layers of metallic, insulating, or semiconductor material, deposited or otherwise placed on, or etched away or otherwise removed from, a piece of semiconductor material in accordance with a pre-determined pattern; and (b) intended to perform electronic functions."

U.S. Copyright Act, 17 U.S.C. § 101.

"[T]he final or intermediate form of any product—

(A) having two or more layers of metallic, insulating, or semiconductor material, deposited or otherwise placed on, or etched away or otherwise removed from, a piece of semiconductor material in accordance with a predetermined pattern; and

(B) intended to perform electronic circuitry functions; . . .

17 U.S.C. § 901(a)(1).

[EUROPE] "The final or an intermediate form of any product: (i) consisting of a body of material which includes a layer of semiconducting material; and (ii) having one or more other layers composed of conducting, insulating or semiconducting material, the layers being arranged in accordance with a pre-determined three-dimensional pattern; and (iii) intended to perform, exclusively or together with other functions, an electronic function."

EEC Council Directive 87/54/EEC (OJ No. L.24, 27.1.87).

See also **integrated circuit; semiconductor.**

Semiconductor Chip Protection Act *(mask work)*
Citation: 17 U.S.C. §§ 901-14.

Annotation. "The Semiconductor Chip Protection Act . . . arose from concerns that existing intellectual property laws did not provide adequate protection of proprietary rights in semiconductor chips that had been designed to perform a particular function. The Act, enacted after extensive congressional consideration and hearings over several years, adopted relevant aspects of existing intellectual property law, but for the most part created a new law, specifically adapted to the protection of design layouts of semiconductor chips."

Brooktree Corp. v. Advanced Micro Devices, Inc., 977 F.2d 1555, 1561 (Fed. Cir. 1992).

"The Semiconductor Chip Protection Act was an innovative solution to this new problem of technology-based industry. While some copyright principles underlie the law, the Act was uniquely adapted to semiconductor mask works, in order to achieve appropriate protection for original designs while meeting the competitive needs of the industry and serving the public interest."

Brooktree Corp. v. Advanced Micro Devices, Inc., 977 F.2d 1555, 1563 (Fed. Cir. 1992).

semi-custom circuit *(hardware)*

An integrated circuit that has the initial phases of its fabrication standardized but allows the later stages to be tailored to suit the individual customer.

send *(contract)*

"[I]n connection with any writing or notice means to deposit in the mail or deliver for transmission by any other usual means of communication with postage or cost of transmission provided for and properly addressed and in the case of an instrument to an address specified thereon or otherwise agreed, or if there be none to any address reasonable under the circumstances. The receipt of any writing or notice within the time at which it would have arrived if properly sent has the effect of a proper sending."
    U.C.C. § 1-201(38).

"[M]eans, with any costs provided for and properly addressed or directed as reasonable under the circumstances or as otherwise agreed, to deposit a record in the mail or with a commercially reasonable carrier, to deliver a record for transmission to or re-creation in another location or information processing system, or to take the steps necessary to initiate transmission to or re-creation of a record in another location or information processing system. In addition, with respect to an electronic message, the message must be in a form capable of being processed by or perceived from a system of the type the recipient uses or otherwise has designated or held out as a place for the receipt of communications of the kind sent. Receipt within the time in which it would have arrived if properly sent, has the effect of a proper sending."
    UCITA § 102(a)(60).

send mail *(Internet; software)*

"[A] computer program that transfers and receives electronic mail on a computer."
    United States v. Morris, 928 F.2d 504, 506 (2d Cir. 1991).

senior enterprise management *(business)*

Typically refers to the top, or senior, management of an organization: CEO, COO, CFO, and heads of major departments including IS and/or subsidiaries. For public sector and nonprofit organizations, the hierarchical counterparts (e.g., CEO, COO, CFO, etc.) may be used.

senior user *(trademark)*

"The first to use a mark . . ."
    Brookfield Comm., Inc. v. West Coast Entertainment Corp., 174 F.3d 1036, 1047 (9th Cir. 1999).

Annotation. "The [senior user] . . . has the right to enjoin 'junior' users from using confusingly similar marks in the same industry and market or within the senior user's natural zone of expansion."

> *Brookfield Comm., Inc. v. West Coast Entertainment Corp.,* 174 F.3d 1036, 1047 (9th Cir. 1999).

separation of rights *(copyright; contract)*

Under current copyright law, the underlying rights to a copyrighted work can be separated, some retained by the author and others licensed or sold to others.

sequels *(copyright)*

"A copyright owner holds the right to create sequels."

> *Micro Star v. FormGen, Inc.,* 154 F.3d 1107, 1112 (9th Cir. 1998).

serial copying *(copyright)*

"[T]he duplication in a digital format of a copyrighted musical work or sound recording from a digital reproduction of a digital musical recording. The term 'digital reproduction of a digital musical recording' does not include a digital musical recording as distributed, by authority of the copyright owner, for ultimate sale to consumers."

> 17 U.S.C. § 1001(11).

Serial Copyright Management System *(copyright)*

Abbreviated as "SCMS."

". . . that sends, receives, and acts upon information about the generation and copyright status of the files that it plays."

> *Recording Indus. Ass'n of America v. Diamond Multimedia Sys., Inc.,* 180 F.3d 1072, 1075 (9th Cir. 1999).

Related issues. "[T]he Act seems designed to allow files to be 'laundered' by passage through a computer, because even a device with SCMS would be able to download MP3 files lacking SCMS codes from a computer hard drive, for the simple reason that there would be no codes to prevent the copying."

> *Recording Indus. Ass'n of America v. Diamond Multimedia Sys., Inc.,* 180 F.3d 1072, 1079 (9th Cir. 1999) (citations omitted; emphasis in original).

server

(business)

An Internet service provider. *See also* **Internet service provider.**

(hardware)

A storage device connected to a network that can deliver digital content, such as text, movies, music, and interactive content on demand. *See also* **web server.**

Related issues (hardware; software). "The Internet links PCs by means of servers, which run specialized operating systems and applications designed for servicing a network environment."

United States v. Microsoft Corp., 65 F. Supp. 2d 1, 4-5 (D.D.C. 1999) (Finding of Fact 11).

server software *(software)*

". . . provides information in response to requests by client software."

Shea v. Reno, 930 F. Supp. 916, 927 (S.D.N.Y. 1996).

service bureau *(business)*

"An organization that leases or sells computer time, manpower, or other computational support to the public."

Systems Dev. Corp. v. United States, 531 F.2d 529, 531 (Ct. Cl. 1976).

"[L]easing of time on in-house computers."

University Computing Co. v. Lykes-Youngstown Corp., 504 F.2d 518, 527 n.1 (5th Cir.), rehearing denied, 505 F.2d 1304 (5th Cir. 1974).

". . . owns or leases computer products and/or services and then performs data processing services for customers for a fee."

Telex Corp. v. IBM Corp., 367 F. Supp. 258, 273 (N.D. Okla. 1973), aff'd in part, rev'd in part, 510 F.2d 894 (10th Cir.), cert. dism., 423 U.S. 802 (1975).

"[A] company which uses its own computer system to process applications for customers who do not have computer systems."

Accusystems, Inc. v. Honeywell Information Sys., Inc., 580 F. Supp. 474, 476 n.1 (S.D.N.Y. 1984).

"[O]thers, who are sometimes referred to within the industry as 'software houses' or 'service bureaus,' provide mostly services such as computer programming, systems support, engineering services and classroom education."

Honeywell Information Sys. v. Maricopa County, 118 Ariz. 171, 575 P.2d 801, 808 (App. 1977).

[CANADA] "A computer facility maintained by someone else."

Mackenzie Patten & Co. v. British Olivetti Ltd. (1984), 48 M.L.R. 344 (Q.B.D.).

service contract *(contract)*

"A contract in writing to perform, over a fixed period of time or for a specified duration, services relating to the maintenance or repair (or both) of a consumer product."

15 U.S.C. § 2301(8).

service mark *(trademark)*

"[A]ny word, symbol, name or device or any combination thereof used to identify the source of commercial services and to distinguish the services from those of another provider."

15 U.S.C. § 1127.

Annotation. "[S]ince trademarks and service marks are source-identifying, their purpose is to answer the questions 'Who are you?' and 'Where do you come from?' "

America Online, Inc. v. AT&T Corp., 64 F. Supp. 2d 549, 559 (E.D. Va. 1999).

service provider *(copyright)*

"(A) As used in subsection (a), . . . means an entity offering the transmission, routing, or providing of connections for digital online communications, between or among points specified by a user, of material of the user's choosing, without modification to the content of the material as sent or received."

"(B) As used in this section, other than subsection (a), . . . means a provider of online services or network access, or the operator of facilities therefor, and includes an entity described in subparagraph (A)."

17 U.S.C. § 512(k)(1)(A)-(B).

SET *(technology)*

Acronym for "Secure Electronic Transaction." A protocol developed by Mastercard and Visa to permit secure use of credit cards over the Internet.

set-top box *(hardware)*

A hardware component that plugs directly into a television receiver and requires no independent computer system. Set-top boxes can be used for video games or accessing the Internet via cable modems or direct broadcast satellite systems.

set-up *(technology)*

Specifying the characteristics of the CRT, i.e., a blinking cursor or a steady light, printer hook-up or not, amount of space between tabs, etc.

severability *(contract)*

A contractual provision that permits unenforceable provisions to be deleted from the contract without affecting the remaining terms of the agreement.

Sample clause. "Should any clause, provision, or portion of this Agreement be ruled invalid, void, illegal, or otherwise unenforceable by any court, magistrate, referee, arbitrator, or by any other process or in any other proceeding, it shall be deemed to be stricken and the remainder of this Agreement shall continue to be in effect and fully enforceable."

sexually explicit *(Internet; obscenity)*

"Sexually explicit material on the Internet includes text, pictures, and chat and 'extends from the modestly titillating to the hardest-core.'"

Reno v. American Civil Liberties Union, 521 U.S. 844, 853 (1997), *quoting American Civil Liberties Union v. Reno,* 929 F. Supp. 830, 844 (E.D. Pa. 1996).

". . . is descriptive rather than legal and does not appear in the statutory provision at issue, but the Government employs it as a shorthand to describe Internet content depicting 'sexual or excretory activities or organs'— possibly though not necessarily in a patently offensive way. That is, the Government does not contend that all sexually explicit material is 'patently offensive' and therefore within the scope of the CDA, but claims that there is certainly content available on the Internet that is both sexually explicit and patently offensive."

Shea v. Reno, 930 F. Supp. 916, 930 (S.D.N.Y. 1996).

Related issues. "[S]exually explicit content is available on the Internet through almost any form of Internet communication. Yet there is no evidence that sexually explicit content constitutes a substantial—or even significant—portion of available Internet content. While it is difficult to ascertain with any certainty how many sexually explicit sites are accessible through the Internet, the president of a manufacturer of software designed to block access to sites containing sexually explicit material testified in the Philadelphia litigation that there are approximately 5,000 to 8,000 such sites, with the higher estimate reflecting the inclusion of multiple pages (each with a unique URL) attached to a single site. The record also suggests that there are at least thirty-seven million unique URLs. Accordingly, even if there were twice as many unique pages on the Internet containing sexually explicit materials as this undisputed testimony suggests, the percentage of Internet addresses providing sexually explicit content would be well less than one tenth of one percent of such addresses."

Shea v. Reno, 930 F. Supp. 916, 931 (S.D.N.Y. 1996).

SGML *(Internet)*

Acronym for "Standard Generic Markup Language." A standard language used worldwide that is independent of any particular hardware, making it fairly transportable to different systems.

shareware *(software)*

"[S]oftware that is copyrighted, and for which the author seeks payment, but whose reproduction is not limited by the author. Shareware computer programs are intended to be copied and circulated freely to others. Payment is rendered either on an 'honor system' or in order to gain additional features or capabilities."

I. Trotter Hardy, *Project Looking Forward: Sketching the Future of Copyright in a Networked World* 75 (May 1998).

"[S]oftware which a user is permitted to download and use for a trial period after which the user is asked to pay a fee to the author for continued use."

Zippo Mfg. Co. v. Zippo Dot Com, Inc., 952 F. Supp. 1119, 1124 n.6 (W.D. Pa. 1997) (citations omitted); *CompuServe, Inc. v. Patterson,* 89 F.3d 1257, 1260 (6th Cir. 1996).

"VPIC 2.9a and subsequent versions included a notice of Montgomery's copyright as well as information about how users that obtained VPIC from bulletin boards could register with Montgomery to avoid copyright infringement liability. Software that is marketed in this way is called 'shareware.'"

Montgomery v. Noga, 168 F.3d 1282, 1286-87 n.2 (11th Cir. 1999).

Annotation. "Shareware makes money only through the voluntary compliance of an 'end user' . . . who may or may not pay the creator's suggested licensing fee if she uses the software beyond a speciWed trial period."

CompuServe, Inc. v. Patterson, 89 F.3d 1257, 1260 (6th Cir. 1996).

shopping agent *(e-commerce)*

A program that will search web sites based on specific criteria/rules provided by the user and will either provide information to the user, or in more advanced configurations, will actually negotiate for and purchase the goods or services sought by the user.

See also **agent; bot; intelligent agent.**

shortened statute of limitations *(contract)*

A contractual provision that provides for a shorter time period in which to file a lawsuit arising from a breach of the agreement than is provided by statute.

Sample clauses. "No action concerning, related to, or arising out of this Agreement or any breach of or default under this Agreement, may be commenced more than _____ years [months] after the occurrence of any such breach or default."

"In the event that such breach or default was not discovered by the injured party at the time it occurred, no action may be commenced more than _____ years [months] after such breach or default could have been discovered by the injured party with the exercise of reasonable diligence, given the experience of the injured party."

See also **statute of limitations.**

shovelware *(software)*

A derogatory term for multimedia titles that repurpose content from other media without any effort to take advantage of the characteristics or capabilities of the multimedia platform, but simply to fill the disc.

shrinkwrap license *(contract)*

A preprinted, standard-form software license that is contained in the packaging with the software. The name evolved from the early practice of displaying the terms of the license through the plastic wrapping (shrinkwrap) used to seal the packaging.

"Vendors of computer software use plastic shrink-wrapping as a mechanism of attaching terms under which they purport to make their product available.

> *M.A. Mortenson Co., Inc. v. Timberline Software Corp.*, 998 P.2d 305, 317 n.1 (Wash. 2000) (Sanders, J., dissenting), *aff'g* 93 Wash. App. 819, 970 P.2d 803 (1999).

"In the mass market/consumer context, the shrinkwrap license provides an efficient way for the software vendor to dictate the terms of each sale. When a business purchases a specialized software program, it typically negotiates, with the vendor, its rights of use in the software. In the mass market setting, however, the negotiation of terms for each sale is clearly impractical."

> *M.A. Mortenson Co., Inc. v. Timberline Software Corp.*, 998 P.2d 305, 317 n.1 (Wash. 2000) (Sanders, J., dissenting), *aff'g* 93 Wash. App. 819, 970 P.2d 803 (1999).

Annotation. The enforceability of shrinkwrap licenses has been in doubt since their widespread introduction in the early 1980s in connection with mass-marketed personal computer software. In *Vault Corp. v. Quaid Software, Ltd.*, 847 F.2d 255 (5th Cir. 1988), the court held that a state statute validating the terms of a shrinkwrap license was preempted by federal copyright law. Two subsequent cases (*Arizona Retail Sys. v. Software Link, Inc.*,

831 F. Supp. 759 (D. Ariz. 1993) and *Step-Saver Data Sys., Inc. v. Wyse Technology*, 939 F.2d 91, 100-04 (3d Cir. 1991) held that shrinkwrap licenses were unenforceable, since the contract had been completed before the licensee was made aware of the initial terms. However, several recent cases have upheld the enforceability of shrinkwrap licenses. *See, e.g., Pro-CD, Inc. v. Zeidenberg*, 86 F.3d 1147 (7th Cir. 1996); *Hill v. Gateway 2000, Inc.*, 105 F.3d 1147 (7th Cir. 1997) *cert. denied*, 118 S. Ct. 47 (1997); *Brower v. Gateway 2000, Inc.*, 1998 WL 481066 N.Y.AD1Dept. (Aug. 13, 1998). *See also* **click-wrap license.**

S-HTTP *(electronic commerce)*
Acronym for "Secure **HTTP.**"

side scroller *(video game)*
A type of game where the background scenery unfolds across a two-dimensional space and the player can only go to the left or right (side to side), and not up or down.

signature *(electronic commerce)*
Digital code attached to a file or message that uniquely identifies the sender of the file or message. The digital equivalent of a handwritten signature.

signature digest *(electronic commerce)*
"[T]he resulting bit-string produced when a signature is tied to a document using signature dynamics.
Cal. Code of Regs., tit. 2, div. 7, ch. 10, § 22003(b)(1)(B).
See also **signature dynamics.**

signature dynamics *(electronic commerce)*
"[M]easuring the way a person writes his or her signature by hand on a flat surface and binding the measurements to a message through the use of cryptographic techniques."
Cal. Code of Regs., tit. 2, div. 7, ch. 10, § 22003(b)(1)(D).

signed *(contract)*
"[I]ncludes any symbol executed or adopted by a *party* with present intention to authenticate a *writing*."
U.C.C. § 1-201(39) (emphasis in original).

"[Any] symbol executed or adopted by a party with present intention to authenticate a writing."
U.C.C. § 1-201(39).

Related issues. "A telegram may be a sufficient signed writing if it identifies its sender by an authorized authentication. The authentication may be in code. . . ."
U.C.C. § 5-104(2).

signer *(electronic commerce)*
"[T]he person who signs a digitally signed communication with the use of an acceptable technology to uniquely link the message with the person sending it."
Cal. Code of Regulations, tit. 2, div. 7, ch. 10, § 22000(a)(5).

silicon *(hardware)*
A semiconducting material commonly used in semiconductor devices because it is so easy to work with.

single disc testing equipment *(hardware)*
"[A] machine designed for testing the quality of a single disc surface or the two surfaces of a single disc."
Pace Indus., Inc. v. Three Phoenix Co., 813 F.2d 234, 236 (9th Cir. 1987).

site(s) *(Internet)*
"[A]n Internet address that permits the exchange of information with a host computer."
Zippo Mfg. Co. v. Zippo Dot Com, Inc., 952 F. Supp. 1119, 1120 n.2 (W.D. Pa. 1997); *MTV Computers v. Curry,* 867 F. Supp. 202, 203 n.2 (S.D.N.Y. 1994).
See also **web site.**

site license *(contract)*
A software license that permits use of the software on any computer within a particular site, e.g., an office building.

SKU *(business)*
Acronym for "Stock Keeping Unit." Each product sold at retail has a unique SKU number to identify it.

skunk marks *(technology)*
"[C]ode marks printed in black ink, generally in squares or circles, on input documents to designate such items as the page of an exam booklet, the type of document, and similar items."
Moore Bus. Forms, Inc. v. National Computer Sys., Inc., 211 U.S.P.Q. (BNA) 909, 912 (T.T.A.B. 1981).
See also **input document.**

slander *(tort)*
A false and malicious oral statement that defames an individual.

SLD *(Internet)*
Acronym for "Second-Level Domain name."

Related issues. "Some specific 'vulgar' words and a few words that are prevented by federal statute from being used by private entities are not available as SLDs."
> *Avery Dennison Corp. v. Sumpton,* 189 F.3d 868, 872 (9th Cir. 1999).

See also **second-level domain name.**

Sleekcraft factors *(trademark)*

Related issues. "Because we agree that the traditional eight-factor test is not well-suited for analyzing the metatags issue, we do not attempt to fit our discussion into one of the *Sleekcraft* factors."
> *Brookfield Comm., Inc. v. West Coast Entertainment Corp.,* 174 F.3d 1036, 1062 n.24 (9th Cir. 1999).

SLIP *(technology)*
Acronym for "Single (Serial) Line Internet Protocol." A type of connection permitting a computer to communicate with the Internet.

smart card *(hardware)*
A plastic card similar in appearance to a credit card, which contains a microchip that stores encrypted digital information that designates cash. Smart cards are currently used with PCs, telephones, ATMs, and other devices containing card readers.

smiley *(Internet)*
See **emoticon.**

SMTP *(Internet)*
Acronym for "Simple Mail Transport Protocol." An Internet standard protocol for e-mail transfers between Internet servers.

SNA *(hardware)*
Acronym for IBM's "Systems Network Architecture."
> *IBM Corp. v. Fujitsu Ltd.,* Copyright L. Rep. (CCH) ¶ 20,517 (Am. Arb. Ass'n 1988).

SNI *(technology)*
Acronym for "SNA Network Interconnections."

". . . is simply a set of protocols that allows communications to flow across a boundary between two SNA networks."
> *IBM Corp. v. Fujitsu Ltd.,* Copyright L. Rep. (CCH) ¶ 20,517 (Am. Arb. Ass'n 1988).

SNI protocols *(technology)*
". . . allow communications to flow across a boundary between two SNA networks."
> *IBM Corp. v. Fujitsu Ltd.,* Copyright L. Rep. (CCH) ¶ 20,517 (Am. Arb. Ass'n 1988).

software *(software)*
"A set of computer programs, procedures, and possibly associated documentation concerned with the operation of a data processing system, e.g., compilers, library routines, manuals, circuit diagrams. Contrasts with hardware."
> U.S. Copyright Office, *Compendium of Copyright Office Practices* II, § 326 (1984).

". . . refers to the logic and directions loaded into the machine that cause it to do certain things on command."
> *United States v. Seidlitz,* 589 F.2d 152, 1554 n.3 (4th Cir. 1978).

"[A]ny set of binary instructions, codes, programs or routines used to cause a computer to perform a specific task or function."
> *Northeast Datacom, Inc. v. City of Wallingford,* 212 Conn. 639, 640 n.1, 563 A.2d 688, 689 n.1 (1989).

". . . includes one or more computer programs, usually stored magnetically on hard or floppy disks, along with such items as instruction manuals and 'templates,' which are pieces of plastic that fit around the function keys on the keyboard, identifying the specific functions or commands that can be invoked by those keys."
> *Lotus Dev. Corp. v. Paperback Software Int'l,* 740 F. Supp. 37, 43 (D. Mass. 1990).

". . . the combination of programs and procedures that serve as instructions to the computer. The term is often used in contrast with 'hardware,' which refers to a computer system's physical elements."
> *Shea v. Reno,* 930 F. Supp. 916, 927 n.6 (S.D.N.Y. 1997).

"[T]he logic and directions loaded into the machine that cause it to do certain things on command."

> *United States v. Seidlitz,* 589 F.2d 152, 154 n.3 (4th Cir. 1978), *cert. denied,* 441 U.S. 922 (1977).

"[A] term . . . used in the industry to describe computer programs."

> *Parker v. Flook,* 437 U.S. 584, 587 n.7 (1978).

"[I]nstructions or programs, recorded electronically either on magnetic tape or disk or contained in punched cards to be read into the central processing unit through peripheral devices."

> *Teamsters Security Fund v. Sperry Rand Corp.,* 6 Computer L. Serv. Rep. (Callaghan) 951, 956 (N. D. Cal. 1977).

"[R]efers to the programs and systems used by the hardware."

> *Universal Computers (Systems) Ltd. v. Datamedia Corp.,* 653 F. Supp. 518, 520 n.2 (D.N.J. 1987).

"(1) Computer programs, routines, programming languages and systems. (2) The collection of related utility, assembly, and other programs that are desirable for properly presenting a given machine to a user. (3) Detailed procedures to be followed, whether expressed as programs for a computer or as procedures for an operator or other person. (4) Documents, including hardware manuals and drawings, computer program listings and diagrams, etc."

> *In re Graphics Tech. Corp.,* 222 U.S.P.Q. (BNA) 179, 180 n.2 (T.T.A.B. 1984) (citation omitted).

"[C]onsists of programs that operate the computer system. Software can be divided into two categories: operating system software, and application software. Operating system software is necessary for a computer to function because it provides the interface between the equipment and the operator. Application software, in contrast, consists of programs designed to perform a specific task, such as balancing an account."

> *Graphic Sales, Inc. v. Sperry Univac Div., Sperry Corp.,* 824 F.2d 576, 578 n.1 (7th Cir. 1987).

"[D]enotes the information loaded into the machine and the directions given to the machine (usually by card or teleprompter) as to what it is to do and upon what command. 'Software' is also frequently used to include 'support,' that is, advice, assistance, counselling, and sometimes even expert engineering help furnished by the vendor in loading the machine for a certain program such as inventory control or preparation of payroll."

> *Honeywell, Inc. v. Lithonia Lighting, Inc.,* 317 F. Supp. 406, 408 (N.D. Ga. 1970).

"[A]ny of the written programs, flowcharts, etc., including general subroutines, that may be included in computer programs."

In re Graphics Tech. Corp., 222 U.S.P.Q. (BNA) 179, 180 n.2 (T.T.A.B. 1984) (citation omitted).

" '[T]he instructions that you give a computer that tell the computer what it is supposed to do when you want it to do it.' It includes memory tapes, punch cards and paper tapes programmed to instruct the computer what to do."

Law Research Serv., Inc. v. General Automation, Inc., 494 F.2d 202, 204 n.3 (2d Cir. 1974).

"[A] computer program encoded on punch cards, tapes, or discs or other media in machine-readable form and in written documents in human-readable form."

Kalil Bottling Co. v. Burroughs Corp., 127 Ariz. 278, 619 P.2d 1055 (App. 1980).

"[R]efers to the programs and controls that are used in the computer.

Com-Share, Inc. v. Computer Complex, Inc., 338 F. Supp. 1229, 1231 (E.D. Mich. 1971), *aff'd*, 458 F.2d 1341 (6th Cir. 1972).

"In the industry, the physical machinery is referred to as hardware and the instructional material as software."

Synercom Technology, Inc. v. University Computing Co., 462 F. Supp. 1003, 1005 (N.D. Tex. 1978).

"The type of package sold by UCC included programs, programming instructions and computer language listings. In the industry the generic name for these materials is 'software.'"

University Computing Co. v. Lykes-Youngstown Corp., 504 F.2d 518, 527 n.2 (5th Cir. 1974).

"[C]onsist of instructions recorded on punched cards, magnetic tapes, and magnetic discs. These devices instruct the computer as to what functions it will perform."

Alabama v. Central Computer Servs., Inc., 349 So.2d 1156, 1157 (Ala. Civ. App. 1977).

"Software is developed by a team of engineers who create a complex logical network of commands or instructions. Once the overall logic, or 'architecture' is developed, 'routines' are created for the completion of specific tasks, consisting of step-by-step instructions, or 'algorithms.' Finally, this logic is translated into computer language or 'source code' in order that it may be placed in the memory circuits of the computer itself."

Bell Telephone Laboratories, Inc. v. General Instrument Corp., 8 Computer L. Serv. Rep. 297, 299 (Pa. Common Pleas, June 30, 1983).

"[A] set of logical instructions designed to enable a computer to perform the computations, comparisons and sequential steps necessary to process and produce a certain desired output."

Chittenden Trust Co. v. King, No. 82-294 at pages 1-2 (Vt. Sup. Ct. 1983).

"[G]enerally refers to the instructions and directions which dictate or otherwise enable a computer to perform various functions."

Citizens & Southern Systems, Inc. v. South Carolina Tax Comm'n, 311 S.E.2d 717, 718 (S.C. 1984).

"[R]efers to information and directions loaded into the machine which dictate different functions for the machine to perform."

Commerce Union Bank v. Tidwell, 538 S.W.2d 405, 406 n.1 (1976).

"[R]efers to the information and directions which are programmed into the computer which direct the computer to perform the different functions that may be required. Computer software is also referred to as computer 'programs' and such programs are bought and sold, delivered and programmed into the computer through the use of magnetic tapes, discs, drums, punched cards, etc., with the usual method of delivery being magnetic tapes as in the instant case."

Citizens & Southern Sys., Inc. v. South Carolina Tax Comm'n, 8 Computer L. Serv. Rep. (Callaghan) 107, 108 (Common Pleas 1980).

"[B]roadly defined as instructional programs which are fed into a computer to tell it what to do."

Commerce Union Bank v. Tidwell, 7 Computer L. Serv. Rep. (Callaghan) 204 (Tenn. Chancery Ct. 1975), *rev'd,* 538 S.W.2d 405 (1976).

"[T]he program which instructs the computer on its function."

EDS Federal Corp. v. Ginsberg, 259 S.E.2d 618, 621 n.1 (W. Va. 1979).

"[T]he information loaded into the machine and the directions given to the machine (usually through the media of punch cards, discs or magnetic tapes) as to what it is to do and upon what command. Software also may include counseling and expert engineering assistance furnished by the seller of software, as well as flow charts and instructions manuals."

First National Bank of Springfield v. Department of Revenue, 421 N.E.2d 175, 176 (Ill. 1981); *Honeywell, Inc. v. Lithonia Lighting, Inc.,* 317 F. Supp. 406, 408 (N.D. Ga. 1970).

"[P]rofessional and technological services, such as classroom education, systems support engineering services, and computer programs (often collectively referred to as the computer 'software')."

> *Honeywell Information Sys. v. Maricopa County,* 118 Ariz. 171, 575 P.2d 801, 808 (App. 1977).

"[A] computer program encoded on punch cards, tapes or discs or other media in machine-readable form and in written documents in human-readable form."

> *Kalil Bottling Co. v. Burroughs Corp.,* 127 Ariz. 278, 619 P.2d 1055, 1056 (App. 1980).

"[E]verything that is not hardware. . . . Software generally comprises three classes of subject matter: computer program, data bases, and documentation. . . . All forms of computer programs are software."

> *Management Sys. Assocs., Inc. v. McDonnell Douglas Corp.,* 762 F.2d 1161, 1163 n.2 (4th Cir. 1985).

". . . denotes the information loaded into the computer and the directions given to the computer as to what to do and upon what command."

> *Nova Computing Services, Inc. v. Askew,* 6 Computer L. Serv. Rep. (Callaghan) 18, 21-22 (Fla. 1976).

"[T]he generic name for a computer program, or a group of computer programs. Computer programs are sequences of instructions to direct hardware to carry out specific operations. They establish in advance the operations that hardware is to go through in order to perform the desired functions. The set of instructions together solve a problem, and the creation of the coded instructions is a complex, logical task."

> *United Software Corp. v. Sperry Rand Corp.,* 5 Computer L. Serv. Rep. (Callaghan) 1492, 1495–96 (E.D. Pa. 1974).

". . . is a more elusive concept [than hardware]. Generally speaking, 'software' refers to the medium that stores input and output data as well as computer programs. The medium includes hard disks, floppy disks, and magnetic tapes."

> *Advent Sys. Ltd. v. Unisys Corp.,* 925 F.2d 670, 674 (3d Cir. 1991).

"[A]n entire set of programs and procedures, with appropriate documentation, which perform a series of functions on a computer."

> *Infosystems Technology, Inc. v. Logical Software, Inc.,* 8 Computer L. Serv. Rep. 689, 697 (D. Md. 1985).

"Although no single universally accepted definition of software exists, software is generally defined as a set of statements or instructions to be used directly or indirectly in a computer to perform a desired task or set of tasks. Software does not generally include procedures which are external to computer operations."

> Certain Computer Aided Software Engineering Products from Singapore, ITA Docket C-559-804, 54 Fed. Reg. 37013, Sept. 6, 1989.

"[A]ny set of binary instructions, codes, programs or routines used to cause a computer to perform a specific task or function."

> *Northeast Datacom, Inc. v. City of Wallingford,* 212 Conn. 639, 563 A.2d 688, 689 n.1 (1989).

[CANADA] ". . . may be very broadly defined as a collection of instructions of programs (such as assemblers, compilers, utility routines, application programs and operating systems) which are fed into a computer to tell it what to do."

> *Chequecheck Services Ltd. v. Ministry of Finance* (1980), 24 B.C.L.R. 217 (B.C. S.C.), *rev'd,* [1982] 5 W.W.R. 340 (B.C. C.A.).

[CANADA] "The collection of programs that can be used with a particular kind of computer, especially the general and routine ones not written for specific tasks and often supplied by the manufacturer."

> *Chequecheck Servs. Ltd. v. Ministry of Finance* (1980), 24 B.C.L.R. 217 (B.C. S.C.), *rev'd,* [1982] 5 W.W.R. 340 (B.C. C.A.).

Annotation. "When a program is transposed onto a medium compatible with the computer's needs, it becomes software."

> *Advent Sys. Ltd. v. Unisys Corp.,* 925 F.2d 670, 674 (3d Cir. 1991).

Related issues. "We emphasize the narrowness of our First Amendment holding. We do not hold that all software is expressive. Much of it surely is not. Nor need we resolve whether the challenged regulations constitute content-based restrictions, subject to the strictest constitutional scrutiny, or whether they are, instead, content-neutral restrictions meriting less exacting scrutiny. We hold merely that because the prepublication licensing regime challenged here applies directly to scientific expression, vests boundless discretion in government officials, and lacks adequate procedural safeguards, it constitutes an impermissible prior restraint on speech."

> *Bernstein v. United States Dept. of Justice,* 176 F.3d 1132, 1145 (9th Cir. 1999).

"[I]nsofar as the EAR regulations on encryption software were intended to slow the spread of secure encryption methods to foreign nations, the government is intentionally retarding the progress of the flourishing science of cryptography. To the extent the government's efforts are aimed at interdicting the flow of scientific ideas (whether expressed in source code or otherwise), as distinguished from encryption products, these efforts would appear to strike deep into the heartland of the First Amendment. In this regard, the EAR regulations are very different from content-neutral time, place and manner restrictions that may have an incidental effect on expression while aiming at secondary effects."

    Bernstein v. United States Dept. of Justice, 176 F.3d 1132, 1145 (9th Cir. 1999).

See also **computer program; computer software; object code; software package; software product; source code.**

software agent *(software)*

"[A] computer program designed to search regularly and automatically across the Internet to look for things such as information or products or services desired by its 'owner.' And perhaps even be able to execute contracts for the purchase of goods or services on behalf of its owner."

    I. Trotter Hardy, *Project Looking Forward: Sketching the Future of Copyright in a Networked World* 95-96 (May 1998).

See also **agent; electronic agent.**

software development *(software)*

Annotation. "Software development is characterized by substantial economies of scale. The fixed costs of producing software, including applications, is very high. By contrast, marginal costs are very low. Moreover, the costs of developing software are "sunk"—once expended to develop software, resources so devoted cannot be used for another purpose. The result of economies of scale and sunk costs is that application developers seek to sell as many copies of their applications as possible. An application that is written for one PC operating system will operate on another PC operating system only if it is ported to that system, and porting applications is both time-consuming and expensive. Therefore, application developers tend to write first to the operating system with the most users— Windows. Developers might then port their applications to other operating systems, but only to the extent that the marginal added sales justify the cost of porting. In order to recover that cost, ISVs that do go to the effort of porting frequently set the price of ported applications considerably higher than that of the original versions written for Windows."

    United States v. Microsoft Corp., 65 F. Supp. 2d 1, 11 (D.D.C. 1999) (Finding of Fact 38).

software house(s) *(business)*

". . . provide mostly services such as computer programming, systems support engineering services and classroom education."

> *Honeywell Information Sys. v. Maricopa County,* 118 Ariz. 171, 575 P.2d 801, 808 (App. 1977).

". . . prepare and market computer programs or instructions designed to cause the central processor and peripheral products to perform their required functions. Examples are instructions that will cause data from input devices to be transferred to storage devices, to be retrieved when needed, then processed in a usable form."

> *Telex Corp. v. IBM Corp.,* 367 F. Supp. 258, 273 (N.D. Okla. 1973), *aff'd in part, rev'd in part,* 510 F.2d 894 (10th Cir.), *cert. dism.,* 423 U.S. 802 (1975).

software license *(contract; software)*

Annotation. "It is true that the transfer of rights to the . . . software in each of the agreements did not take the form of a lease, and that the transfer in each case was in exchange for a single payment and was for a term that was either unlimited or nearly so. One commentator has argued that when a copy of a software program is transferred for a single payment and for an unlimited term, the transferee should be considered an 'owner' of the copy of the software program regardless of other restrictions on his use of the software. That view has not been accepted by other courts, however, and we think it overly simplistic. The concept of ownership of a copy entails a variety of rights and interests. The fact that the right of possession is perpetual, or that the possessor's rights were obtained through a single payment, is certainly relevant to whether the possessor is an owner, but those factors are not necessarily dispositive if the possessor's right to use the software is heavily encumbered by other restrictions that are inconsistent with the status of owner."

> *DSC Comm. Corp. v. Pulse Comm., Inc.,* 170 F.3d 1354, 1362 (Fed. Cir. 1999).

Related issues. "The license for one of Microsoft's operating system products prohibits the user from transferring the operating system to another machine, so there is no legal secondary market in Microsoft operating systems."

> *United States v. Microsoft Corp.,* 65 F. Supp. 2d 1, 16 (D.D.C. 1999) (Finding of Fact 57).

"This case illustrates how fast technology can outdistance the capacity of contract drafters to provide for the ramifications of a computer software licensing arrangement."

> *Sun Microsys., Inc. v. Microsoft Corp.*, 188 F.3d 1115, 1116-17 (9th Cir. 1999).

See also license.

software package *(software)*

". . . consist[s] of one or more pre-programmed routines or applications that go onto a computer as a sort of base program. As one witness testified, 'They are to a computer what a record is to a Victrola.'"

> *Honeywell, Inc. v. Lithonia Lighting, Inc.*, 317 F. Supp. 406, 411 (N.D. Ga. 1970).

See also computer program; object code; software; software product; source code.

software product *(software)*

"There exists in this area—and everyone seems to agree—what is called a software product. Generally, it is described as software, which can find general use by a number of users, as contrasted with a particular program for a particular entity."

> *United Software Corp. v. Sperry Rand Corp.*, 5 Computer L. Serv. Rep. (Callaghan) 1492, 1495-96 (E.D. Pa. 1974).

See also computer program; object code; software; software package; source code.

software protection *(copyright; patent)*

"[P]atent and copyright law protect distinct aspects of a computer program. Title 35 protects the process or method performed by a computer program; title 17 protects the expression of that process or method. While title 35 protects any novel, nonobvious, and useful process, title 17 can protect a multitude of expressions that implement that process. If the patentable process is embodied inextricably in the line-by-line instructions of the computer program, however, then the process merges with the expression and precludes copyright protection."

> *Atari Games Corp. v. Nintendo of America, Inc.*, 975 F.2d 832, 839-40 (Fed. Cir. 1992) (citations omitted).

software upgrade *(software)*

Related issues. "Unlike a 'pocket part' supplement to a book, a software upgrade need not consist only of new material. A service pack upgrade may install a combination of new software files and/or replacements for existing software files."

> *United States v. Microsoft Corp.*, 65 F. Supp. 2d 1, 47 (D.D.C. 1999) (Finding of Fact 188).

See also **upgrade.**

SOHO *(business)*
Abbreviation for "small office/home office."

solution provider *(Year 2000)*
A company that offers to take computer systems that have a Year 2000 problem and make them Year 2000 compliant.

solution vendor(s) *(Year 2000)*
Individuals or companies that provide tools and/or resources to assist organizations in their Year 2000 compliance efforts. The level of involvement of vendors can vary depending on the needs of the organization.

SONET *(telecommunications)*
Acronym for "Synchronous Optical Network."

sort *(software)*
1. *(noun)* A program to reorder data sequentially, usually in alphabetic or numeric order. 2. *(verb)* To segregate items into groups according to specified criteria, or to rearrange data, i.e., to sort by batch number.

sound bite *(technology)*
A small amount of sound contained in a sound file, often obtained by sampling.

sound board *(technology)*
An analog-to-digital converter that converts digital information into sound (analog signals). *See also* **sound card.**

sound card *(technology)*
A printed circuit board that permits the computer to produce sound. *See also* **sound board.**

sound recordings *(copyright)*
"[W]orks that result from the fixation of a series of musical, spoken, or other sounds, but not including the sounds accompanying a motion picture

or other audiovisual work, regardless of the nature of the material objects, such as disks, tapes, or other phonorecords, in which they are embodied."
U.S. Copyright Act, 17 U.S.C. §101.

soundex *(software)*

"[A]n algorithm that transcribes names into standard codes and clusters names that sound alike into the same codes and allows one to locate a name based on its sound, rather than its exact spelling."
Yellow Freight Sys., Inc. v. United States, 24 Ct. Cl. 804, 811 n.4 (1991).

source code *(software)*

"[T]he computer program code as the programmer originally writes it, using a particular programming language, generally written in a high-level language, such as BASIC, COBOL, or FORTRAN. A program in source code must be changed into object code before the computer can execute it."
U.S. Copyright Office, *Copyright Office Practices II* § 321.01, *quoted in Manufacturers Technology, Inc. v. CAMS, Inc.,* 706 F. Supp. 984, 991 n.10 (D. Conn. 1989).

"[A] computer program written in some programming language—such as FORTRAN (FORmula TRANslation), COBOL, (COmmon Business Oriented Language), Pascal, BASIC, or C—that uses complex symbolic names, along with complex rules of syntax."
Lotus Dev. Corp. v. Paperback Software Int'l, 740 F. Supp. 37, 44 (D. Mass. 1990).

"Computer programs are written in specialized alphanumeric languages, or 'source code.'"
Sega Enters. Ltd. v. Accolade, Inc., 977 F.2d 1510, 1514 n.2 (1992).

"[A] computer program written in any of several programming languages employed by computer programmers."
CONTU Final Report 21 n.109 (1978), *quoted in Williams Elecs., Inc. v. Artic Int'l, Inc.,* 685 F.2d 870, 876 n.7 (3d Cir. 1982).

"[T]he computer program code as the programmer writes it, using a particular programming language, generally a program written in high-level language, such as Basic, Cobol, or Fortran. A program in source code must be changed into object code before the computer can execute it. This change is accomplished by a separate program within the computer called an assembler or a compiler to enable the program to be run on a particular brand and model computer."
CONTU Final Report 53 (1978).

620

"Statements in high level language, and apparently also statements in assembly language, are referred to as written in 'source code.'"

Apple Computer, Inc. v. Franklin Computer Corp., 714 F.2d 1240, 1243 (3d Cir. 1983), *cert. dism.,* 464 U.S. 1033 (1984).

"[A] programming language, understandable to humans, in which a computer is given instructions."

United States v. Seidlitz, 589 F.2d 152, 154 n.6 (4th Cir. 1978), *cert. denied,* 441 U.S. 922 (1979).

"[T]he series of instructions to the computer for carrying out the various tasks which are performed by the program, expressed in a programming language which is easily comprehensible to appropriately trained human beings."

SAS Inst., Inc. v. S&H Computer Sys., Inc., 605 F. Supp. 816, 818 (M.D. Tenn. 1985).

"[T]he series of instructions to the computer for carrying out the various tasks which are performed by the program, expressed in a human-readable programming language. The source code serves two functions. First, it can be treated as comparable to text material, and in that respect can be printed out, read and studied, and loaded into a computer's memory, in much the same way as documents are loaded into word processing equipment. Second, the source code can be used to cause the computer to execute the program. To accomplish this, the source code is compiled. This involves an automatic process, performed by the computer under the control of a program called a compiler, which translates the source code into object code, which is very difficult to comprehend by human beings. The object code version of the program is then loaded into the computer's memory and causes the computer to carry out the program function."

SAS Inst., Inc. v. S&H Computer Sys., Inc., 605 F. Supp. 816 (M.D. Tenn. 1985).

"Disassembled object code, expressed in humanly-readable form with accompanying comments and labels."

E.F. Johnson Co. v. Uniden Corp. of America, 623 F. Supp. 1485, 1488 (D. Minn. 1985).

"[T]he original set of programming instructions drawn up by its creator. Because Source Code reveals the mechanics of the program, software is rarely distributed to users in this form."

Infosystems Tech., Inc. v. Logical Software, Inc., 1 Computer L. Cas. (CCH) ¶ 45,035, at 60,287 (4th Cir. 1987).

"[G]enerally regarded as the alphanumeric translation of the flowchart idea into the problem-oriented computer language, that is, Fortran, COBOL, or ALGOL, and may be punched on a deck of cards or imprinted on discs, tapes, or drums."

> *Paine, Webber, Jackson & Curtis, Inc. v. Merrill Lynch, Pierce, Fenner & Smith, Inc.,* 564 F. Supp. 1358, 1364 (D. Del. 1983).

"A program is written in human-readable computer languages called source code (e.g, FORTRAN, BASIC). . . ."

> *Pearl Sys., Inc. v. Competition Elecs., Inc.,* 8 U.S.P.Q.2d (BNA) 1520, 1520 n.1 (S.D. Fla. 1988).

"The graphic rendition or source code is itself copyrightable. If flow charts are used, they are reduced to source code by the programmer."

> *Apple Computer, Inc. v. Formula Int'l, Inc.,* 218 U.S.P.Q. (BNA) 47, 49 (C.D. Cal. 1983).

"[A] term of art, generally refers to that information recorded on paper and magnetic discs by Mr. Boles in the course of programming the computer and in this instance, retained in his possession, thus causing the dispute to arise."

> *Computer Billing Servs., Inc. v. Boles,* 8 Computer L. Serv. Rep. 245 n.1 (Tenn. App. Ct. 1982).

"[T]he . . . original set of instructions, expressed in a language that the engineers can read and deal with. Customers are almost never given the source code when they purchase a computer product. . . . The source code is the 'life blood' of any computer company and is rarely disclosed."

> *In re Bedford Computer Corp.,* 62 Bankr. 555, 562 n.6 (D.N.H. 1986).

"[I]nstructions prepared by a programmer (the author)."

> *Infosystems Technology, Inc. v. Logical Software, Inc.,* 8 Computer L. Serv. Rep. 689, 697 (D. Md. 1985).

". . . the text is translated into an 'object code' and then directs the computer to perform its functions."

> *Broderbund Software, Inc. v. Unison World, Inc.,* 648 F. Supp. 1127, 1130 (N.D. Cal. 1986).

"The programmer actually writes a series of instructions known as the 'source code.' Source codes may be written in a number of different computer languages; the languages involved in this case are known as 'FORTRAN' and 'Pascal.'"

> *Dynamic Solutions, Inc. v. Planning & Control, Inc.,* 646 F. Supp. 1329, 1332 n.2 (S.D.N.Y. 1986).

"[A] computer program used to create an object program, which, in turn, is a program readable by a computer."

> *Management Technologies, Inc. v. Manufacturers Hanover Trust Co.,* 1 Computer L. Cas. (CCH) ¶ 46,040, at 60,955, 60,956 (N.Y. Supreme Ct. 1989).

"[A]t least as understood by computer programs, refers to the text of a program written in a 'high-level' programming language, such as 'PASCAL' or 'C'."

> *Bernstein v. United States Dept. of Justice,* 176 F.3d 1132, 1140 (9th Cir. 1999).

". . . is the form of computer program written in a language that suitably trained programmers can read and understand."

> *Computer Assocs., Inc. v. American Fundware, Inc.,* 133 F.R.D. 166, 168 n.1 (D. Colo. 1990).

"[T]he language of words and symbols that resemble English."

> *ISC-Bunker Ramo Corp. v. Altech, Inc.,* 765 F. Supp. 1310, 1317 (N.D. Ill. 1990).

"'Source code,' at least as currently understood by computer programmers, refers to the text of a program written in a 'high-level' programming language, such as 'PASCAL' or 'C.' The distinguishing feature of source code is that it is meant to be read and understood by humans and that it can be used to express an idea or a method. A computer, in fact, can make no direct use of source code until it has been translated ('compiled') into a 'low-level' or 'machine' language, resulting in computer-executable 'object code.' That source code is meant for human eyes and understanding, however, does not mean that an untutored layperson can understand it. Because source code is destined for the maw of an automated, ruthlessly literal translator—the compiler—a programmer must follow stringent grammatical, syntactical, formatting, and punctuation conventions. As a result, only those trained in programming can easily understand source code."

> *Bernstein v. United States Dept. of Justice,* 176 F.3d 1132, 1140 (9th Cir. 1999) (footnote omitted).

"Computer programs . . . written in specialized languages (e.g., PASCAL, COBOL). . . . The source code, which humans can read, is then translated into a form that computers can 'read.'"

> *Cadence Design Sys., Inc. v. Avant! Corp.,* 125 F.3d 824, 825 n.2 (9th Cir. 1997).

Annotation "Although 'source code' has been defined far more broadly in some of the literature in the field, and in some of the expert testimony in this case, more commonly the term 'source code' refers to a computer program written in some programming language . . . that uses complex symbolic names, along with complex rules of syntax."

> *Lotus Dev. Corp. v. Paperback Software Int'l,* 740 F. Supp. 37, 44 (D. Mass. 1990).

"The distinguishing feature of source code is that it is meant to be read and understood by humans, and that it can be used to express an idea or a method. A computer, in fact, can make no direct use of source code until it has been translated ('compiled') into a 'low-level' or 'machine' language, resulting in computer executable 'object code.' That source code is meant for human eyes and understanding, however, does not mean that an untutored layperson can understand it. Because source code is destined for the maw of an automated, ruthlessly literal translator—the compiler—a programmer must follow stringent grammatical, syntactical, formatting, and punctuation conventions. As a result, only those trained in programming can easily understand source code."

> *Bernstein v. United States Dept. of Justice,* 176 F.3d 1132, 1140 (9th Cir. 1999).

"While source code, when properly prepared, can be easily compiled into object code by a user, ignoring the distinction between source and object code obscures the important fact that source code is not meant solely for the computer, but is rather written in a language intended also for human analysis and understanding."

> *Bernstein v. United States Dept. of Justice,* 176 F.3d 1132, 1142 (9th Cir. 1999).

"Programmers often write programs in source code, also called assembly language. This type of code contains mnemonic abbreviations for each step and can be read by expert programmers. Once a programmer has access to the source code of a program, he is able to determine the construction of the program and write his own version. For this reason, source code programs are typically compiled (translated) into and sold as object code or machine language, which is not discernible to even an expert programmer, but which is readily usable by the computer."

> *United States v. Brown,* 925 F.2d 1301, 1303 n.4 (10th Cir. 1991).

Related issues. "By utilizing source code, a cryptographer can express algorithmic ideas with precision and methodical rigor that is otherwise difficult to achieve. This has the added benefit of facilitating peer review—by compiling the source code, the cryptographer can create a working model subject to rigorous security tests."

> *Bernstein v. United States Dept. of Justice,* 176 F.3d 1132, 1141 (9th Cir. 1999).

"[W]e conclude that encryption software, in its source code form and as employed by those in the field of cryptography, must be viewed as expressive for First Amendment purposes, and thus is entitled to the protections of the prior restraint doctrine."

> *Bernstein v. United States Dept. of Justice,* 176 F.3d 1132, 1141 (9th Cir. 1999) (footnote omitted).

"The distinction between source and object code is not as crystal clear as first appears. Depending upon the programming language, source code may contain many 1's and 0's and look a lot like object code or may contain many instructions derived from spoken human language. Programming languages the source code for which approaches object code are referred to as low level source code while those that are more similar to spoken language are referred to as high level source code."

> *Universal City Studios, Inc. v. Reimerdes,* 111 F. Supp. 2d 294, 306 (S.D.N.Y. 2000).

See also **assembly language; high-level language; source language(s); source program.**

source code escrow *(contract)*

An arrangement under which a copy of the source code of a computer program is physically transferred to a third party to hold, and to release to the licensee or another entity upon the occurrence of one or more events, such as the licensor's bankruptcy.

Sample clause.

"a. *Initial Deposit.* Within thirty (30) business days of the Effective Date of this Agreement, Vendor shall deposit with Source Code Escrow Agent ('SEA') a complete copy of the Source Code of the Software as well as a complete copy of the current systems documentation ('Documentation') for the Software as they currently exist.

b. *Subsequent Deposit.* Within thirty (30) business days after the release to Licensee of any material update to the Software by Vendor under this Agreement, Vendor shall deposit with SEA a complete copy of the Source Code of the Software update as well as a complete copy of any updated systems documentation for the Software update (hereinafter referred to collectively as 'Source Code').

c. *Purpose of Deposit.* The deposit of the Source Code and the license thereof to Licensee pursuant to Section ____ hereof are intended to provide assurance to Licensee of access to, and the right of use of, the Source Code in the event that Vendor fails (or is rendered unable by an Impact Event) to provide the Support Services it may be obligated to render under this Agreement. SEA shall release copies of the Source Code deposited in escrow pursuant to this Agreement only in accordance with the terms of this Agreement. In each instance where SEA is authorized to release a copy of the Source Code to Licensee, SEA may either release a copy on hand (provided that at all times it shall retain at least one copy of the Source Code) or make a duplicate copy to be released to such Licensee.

d. *Triggering Event.* The escrow provisions of this Agreement shall be triggered by any of the following events:

(1) Vendor discontinues the Support Services required pursuant to this Agreement;

(2) Vendor ceases doing business; or

(3) Vendor declares bankruptcy, seeks protection under the bankruptcy act, or is forced into bankruptcy by its creditors, unless such bankruptcy proceedings are terminated within sixty (60) days of filing.

e. *Procedure.*

(1) *Notice.* If Licensee determines that a Triggering Event has occurred, it shall so notify Vendor in writing and describe such Triggering Event in reasonable detail.

(2) *Right to Cure.* For a period of thirty (30) days following its receipt of such notice ('Cure Period'), Vendor shall have the right to cure the Triggering Event. If the Triggering Event cured within such Cure Period, then such notice shall be of no effect, and this Agreement shall continue as if no notice had been sent. In the event that, at the conclusion of the Cure Period, Licensee reasonably determines that the Triggering Event has not been substantially cured, Licensee may so notify both Vendor and SEA in writing and demand that SEA release a copy of the Source Code to Licensee.

(3) *Dispute by Vendor.* If Vendor disputes Licensee's claim that the Triggering Event exists and has not been substantially cured following the expiration of the Cure Period, Vendor may so notify SEA and Licensee in writing within five (5) business days after receipt of Licensee's demand for release of the Source Code. Failure of Vendor to give timely notice of such an objection shall conclusively establish its consent to the release of the Source Code to Licensee, whereupon SEA shall release a copy of the Source Code to Licensee. If Vendor provides notice of its objection, the parties shall utilize the Dispute Resolution Process of Section __.

f. *License of Source Code.* In the event that a copy of the Source Code is released to Licensee, Licensee shall receive only a non-exclusive, non-transferable license from Vendor to use, modify, maintain, and update the Source Code as may be necessary to enable Licensee to exercise its rights under Section __. Licensee shall have no right to sell, license, disclose, or permit others access to the Source Code.

g. *Escrow Fees.* Licensee shall pay all fees of SEA at its prescribed rate.

h. *Exclusive Remedy.* The release of the Source Code, subject to the license restrictions of Section ___, shall be the sole and exclusive remedy for Licensee for the occurrence of a Triggering Event which is not cured during the Cure Period. Such occurrence shall not constitute a material breach of this Agreement and shall not permit termination under Section ___."

source language(s) *(software)*

". . . were invented to enable a person to communicate with the machine, to be able to write a program."

> *Jostens, Inc. v. National Computer Sys., Inc.,* 318 N.W.2d 691, 695 n.3 (Minn. 1982).

See also assembly language; high-level language; source code; source program(s).

source program(s) *(software)*

"[A] translation of the flow chart into computer programming language, such as FORTRAN or COBOL. Source programs may be punched on decks of cards or imprinted on discs, tapes or drums."

> *Data Cash Sys., Inc. v. JS&A Group, Inc.,* 480 F. Supp. 1063, 1065 (N.D. Ill. 1979).

". . . generally regarded as the alphanumeric translation of the flow chart idea into the problem-oriented computer language; that is, FORTRAN, COBOL, or ALGOL, and may be punched on a deck of cards or imprinted on discs, tapes or drums."

> *Paine, Webber, Jackson & Curtis, Inc. v. Merrill Lynch, Pierce, Fenner & Smith, Inc.,* 564 F. Supp. 1358, 1364 (D. Del. 1983).

See also assembly language; high-level language; source code; source language(s).

spaghetti code *(software)*

Unstructured, patched-together program logic that is hard to follow/trace— much like following a single strand of spaghetti in a fully mixed bowl. (wsr)

spam *(Internet)*

1. *(noun)* Unsolicited, commercial e-mail sent to numerous addressees or newsgroups.

"[U]nauthorized bulk e-mail advertisements. . . ."

> *America Online, Inc. v. IMS,* 24 F. Supp. 2d 548, 549 (E.D. Va. 1998).

2. *(verb)* To disseminate unsolicited commercial e-mail to a large number of recipients.

Annotation. Spam, as well as being a trademark of the Hormel Foods Corporation for deviled luncheon meat spread, is an Internet term that describes mass, unsolicited advertising or solicitations through e-mail, Usenet postings, or other online means. The term is believed to have derived from the Monty Python comedy sketch regarding a restaurant in which every item on the menu includes Spam. In the sketch, as a waitress recites the menu to a customer, "Spam" is repeated over and over. Similarly, a spam posting to a number of Usenet newsgroups may appear repeatedly to persons who subscribe to multiple newsgroups.

Although online advertising has become generally accepted on the Internet, spam is still considered a serious violation of Internet etiquette ("Netiquette"). Some of the best known examples of spamming have been conducted by Canter & Seigel of Arizona. In 1994, Canter and Seigel allegedly spammed almost 6,000 newsgroups with an advertisement for their services to assist persons in entering an immigration green card lottery. So many complaints were sent in response to the 1994 spamming that Canter & Seigel's Internet service provider's server crashed several times, and the provider terminated Canter & Seigel's service.

In some cases, spam recipients have organized and sent large quantities of reply e-mail messages to the spamming party. In other cases, individual recipients have created the same effect with programs that send repeated e-mails to the spamming party.

Notwithstanding the online community's unwelcome response to spam, the quantity of spamming has increased dramatically. America Online, for example, stated that it receives in excess of 700,000 messages per day directed to America Online subscribers from companies who specialize in spamming (often called "junk e-mail").

In response, America Online and some other online services have implemented filters to reject messages from certain Internet addresses or messages that meet other criteria of spam. (jrb)

Related issues. "The mere receipt of these lengthy e-mails was objectionable, for a recipient may be paying for units of Internet access time while reviewing messages and bulk e-mail is a burden on the finite capacity of receiving computers. . . ."

People v. Lipsitz, 663 N.Y.S.2d 468, 471 (Sup. Ct. N.Y. Cty. 1997).

spammer *(Internet)*
Someone who sends spam.

spamming *(Internet)*

The act of sending spam.

speaker *(Internet)*

One who is communicating by voice or text.

Annotation. "[T]he Internet provides an easy and inexpensive way for a speaker to reach a large audience, potentially of millions. The start-up and operating costs entailed by communication on the Internet are significantly lower than those associated with use of other forms of mass communications, such as television, radio, newspapers, and magazines. This enables operation of their own Web sites not only by large companies . . . but also be small, not-for-profit groups. . . ."

American Civil Liberties Union v. Reno, 929 F. Supp. 824, 843 (E.D. Pa. 1996), aff'd, Reno v. American Civil Liberties Union, 521 U.S. 844 (1997).

Related issues. "The user then in a sense becomes a public 'speaker,' able to convey content, at relatively low cost, to users around the world to whom it may be of interest."

Shea v. Reno, 930 F. Supp. 916, 929 (S.D.N.Y. 1996).

"[I]n the CDA, Congress sought to target 'interactive' computer systems through which a listener or viewer, by definition, has the power to become a speaker. The relative ease of speaker entry and the relative parity among speakers accounts for the unprecedented and virtually unlimited opportunities for political discourse, cultural development, and intellectual activity that Congress found to characterize emerging communication technologies."

Shea v. Reno, 930 F. Supp. 916, 930 (S.D.N.Y. 1996).

"[A] speaker posting a message to a newsgroup or to a list maintained by a mail exploder has no control over who will receive the message; . . ."

Shea v. Reno, 930 F. Supp. 916, 942 (S.D.N.Y. 1996).

"Because of the different forms of Internet communication, a user of the Internet may speak or listen interchangeably, blurring the distinction between 'speakers' and 'listeners' on the Internet. Chat rooms, e-mail, and newsgroups are interactive forms of communication, providing the user with the opportunity both to speak and to listen."

American Civil Liberties Union v. Reno, 929 F. Supp. 824, 843 (E.D. Pa. 1996), aff'd, Reno v. American Civil Liberties Union, 521 U.S. 844 (1997).

special usage dates *(software; Year 2000)*

These are dates, such as 1/1/99 and 9/9/99, that have been used by programmers to trigger special programming logic.

specific jurisdiction *(jurisdiction)*

"[T]he crucial federal constitutional inquiry is whether, given the facts of the case, the nonresident defendant has sufficient contacts with the forum state that the district court's exercise of jurisdiction would comport with 'traditional notions of fair play and substantial justice.' *International Shoe Co. v. Washington*, 326 U.S. 310, 316 (1945)."

> *CompuServe, Inc. v. Patterson*, 89 F.3d 1257, 1263 (6th Cir. 1996).

"We apply a three-part test to determine if a district court may exercise specific jurisdiction:

(1) The nonresident defendant must do some act or consummate some transaction with the forum or perform some act by which he purposely avails himself of the privilege of conducting activities in the forum, thereby invoking the benefits and protections of its laws; (2) the claim must be one which arises out of or results from the defendant's forum-related activities; and (3) exercise of jurisdiction must be reasonable."

> *Panavision Int'l, L.P. v. Toeppen*, 141 F.3d 1316, 1320 (9th Cir. 1998); *Zippo Mfg. Co. v. Zippo Dot Com, Inc.*, 952 F. Supp. 1119, 1122 (W.D. Pa. 1997). *See also CompuServe, Inc. v. Patterson*, 89 F.3d 1257, 1263 (6th Cir. 1996).

"In the absence of general jurisdiction, specific jurisdiction permits a court to exercise personal jurisdiction over a non-resident defendant for forum-related activities where the 'relationship between the defendant and the forum falls within the "minimum contacts" framework' of *International Shoe Co. v. Washington*, 326 U.S. 310, 66 S. Ct. 154, 90 L. Ed. 140 (1945) and its progeny."

> *Zippo Mfg. Co. v. Zippo Dot Com, Inc.*, 952 F. Supp. 1119, 1122 (W.D. Pa. 1997).

"Traditionally, when an entity intentionally reaches beyond its boundaries to conduct business with foreign residents, the exercise of specific jurisdiction is proper. Different results should not be reached simply because business is conducted over the Internet."

> *Zippo Mfg. Co. v. Zippo Dot Com, Inc.*, 952 F. Supp. 1119, 1124 (W.D. Pa. 1997) (citation omitted).

"The vast majority of Internet-based personal jurisdiction cases involve specific jurisdiction."

> *Coastal Video Comm. Corp. v. Staywell Corp.*, 59 F. Supp. 2d 562, 570 n.6 (E.D. Va. 1999) (citations omitted).

See also **purposeful availment.**

speech *(First Amendment)*
See **freedom of speech.**

spider *(Internet)*

Sometimes spelled "spyder." Automated software that searches the Internet to locate and index the content of web sites.

spif *(business)*

Acronym for "sales performance incentive fund." A rebate paid to a distributor or retailer for every unit of a product sold.

spoofing *(Internet)*

"[T]he practice of using a fictitious source. . . ."
> *People v. Lipsitz,* 663 N.Y.S.2d 468, 471 (Sup. Ct. N.Y. Cty. 1997).

spool *(software)*

Acronym for "simultaneous peripheral operations on line." Spooling stores transactions on a disk for eventual processing. Several reports or transactions can be processed simultaneously since output is temporarily diverted. Output to the printer is spooled so that if the printer is off when data is sent, it will be printed later when the printer is activated.

spreadsheet *(software)*

Refers to the electronic equivalent of a worksheet. It appears as a matrix of cells, each cell identified with a row and column number. It can be horizontally or vertically scrolled, using the cursor keys. Cells are filled with either numerical data or descriptions (i.e., labels) that refer to data. Equations are created by the user that tie data together. The total of one cell can be used as data for other cells so that calculations can ripple through the entire spreadsheet.

sprite *(hardware)*

". . . involves the use of a special technique for creating mobile graphic images on a computer screen that is appropriate for animation. An increase in sophistication of sprite techniques used in the computer program will increase the graphic quality of the game's animation."
> *Data East USA, Inc. v. Epyx, Inc.,* 862 F.2d 204, 209 n.5 (4th Cir. 1988).

SRAM *(hardware)*

Acronym for "Static Random Access Memory." A type of integrated circuit that has self-contained memory circuitry. Contrasts with dynamic random access memory. Categorized by speed and memory capacity.

SRP *(business)*

Acronym for "Suggested Retail Price."

SSL *(hardware)*

Acronym for "Secure Sockets Layer." A protocol designed by Netscape Communications to permit encrypted, authenticated communications across the Internet. The SSL protocol provides privacy, authentication, and message integrity.

SSO *(software)*

See **structure, sequence, and organization.**

stalking *(criminal)*

Willfully, maliciously, and repeatedly harassing another or making a credible threat, with the intent to place another in reasonable fear of death or great bodily harm.

stand-alone *(technology)*

The ability of a computer to do its work independently of other computers, as opposed to a terminal that must be connected to another machine. *See also* **dumb terminal.**

standard *(technology)*

A set of detailed technical guidelines used as a means of establishing uniformity in an area of hardware or software development.

Annotation. "Although the information itself may be in many different formats, and stored on computers which are not otherwise compatible, the basic Web standards provide a basic set of standards which allow communication and exchange of information. Despite the fact that many types of computers are used on the Web, and the fact that many of those machines are otherwise incompatible, those who 'publish' information on the Web are able to communicate with those who seek to access information with little difficulty because of those basic technical standards."

American Civil Liberties Union v. Reno, 929 F. Supp. 824, 838 (E.D. Pa. 1996), *aff'd, Reno v. American Civil Liberties Union,* 521 U.S. 844 (1997).

standard form *(contract)*

"[M]eans a record or a group of related records containing terms prepared for repeated use in transactions and so used in a transaction in which there was no negotiated change of terms by individuals except to set the price, quantity, method of payment, selection among standard options, or time or method of delivery."

UCITA § 102(a)(61).

Standard Generic Markup Language *(Internet; software)*
See SGML.

standard program *(software; taxation)*
". . . are produced for a general class of users. Unlike custom and feature programs, they are not created to meet the specific needs of an individual customer, nor are they tailored to any one customer's system or equipment. Rather, they are pre-written programs which may be transferable to other users, need little if any modification to be implemented by any user in the class, and may be run on any compatible line of microcomputers. In addition, little or no manufacturer assistance or training is necessary after installation."
> *Health Micro Data Sys., Inc. v. Wisconsin Dept. of Revenue,* 2 Guide to Computer L. (CCH) ¶ 60,056, at 80,228 (Tax. App. Comm. 1989).

standard technical measures *(copyright)*
"[T]echnical measures that are used by copyright owners to identify or protect copyrighted works and—
(A) have been developed pursuant to a broad consensus of copyright owners and service providers in an open, fair, voluntary, multi-industry standards process;
(B) are available to any person on reasonable and nondiscriminatory terms; and
(C) do not impose substantial costs on service providers or substantial burdens on their systems or networks."
> 17 U.S.C. § 512(i)(2).

star pagination *(copyright)*
"[A]n asterisk and citation or page number are inserted in the text of the judicial opinion to indicate when a page break occurs in a different version of the case."
> *Matthew Bender & Co. v. West Publ'g Co.,* 158 F.3d 693, 695 n.1 (2d Cir. 1998), *cert. denied,* 522 U.S. 3732 (1999).

state
(copyright)
". . . includes the District of Columbia and the Commonwealth of Puerto Rico, and any territories to which this title is made applicable by an Act of Congress."
> U.S. Copyright Law, 17 U.S.C. §101.

(criminal)

"[A]ny State of the United States, the District of Columbia, the Commonwealth of Puerto Rico, and any territory or possession of the United States."
18 U.S.C. § 2510(3).

". . . includes the District of Columbia, the Commonwealth of Puerto Rico, and any other commonwealth, possession or territory of the United States."
18 U.S.C. § 1030(e)(3).

state-of-the-art *(general)*
Current, up-to-date.

STATS *(copyright; unfair competition)*
Citation: National Basketball Ass'n v. Motorola, Inc. and Sports Team Analysis & Tracking Sys. Inc., 105 F.3d 841 (2d Cir. 1997), *rev'g* 931 F. Supp. 1124 (S.D.N.Y. 1996).

In this case, the court had to decide whether the "hot news" misappropriation doctrine would protect information on sports contests from being broadcast by third parties. The NBA had sued a paging news broadcaster (STATS) for broadcasting certain statistics on NBA basketball games to pager users who subscribed to the service. The lower court held that STATS had violated New York misappropriation law, which is based upon the earlier decision in *International News Service v. Associated Press,* 248 U.S. 215 (1918), holding that taking "hot news" violated state misappropriation law.

The court held that "the surviving 'hot-news' INS-like claim is limited to cases where: (i) a plaintiff generates or gathers information at a cost; (ii) the information is time-sensitive; (iii) a defendant's use of the information constitutes free-riding on the plaintiff's efforts; (iv) the defendant is in direct competition with a product or service offered by the plaintiffs; and (v) the ability of other parties to free-ride on the efforts of the plaintiff or others would so reduce the incentive to produce the product or service that its existence or quality would be substantially threatened." 105 F.3d 841, 845 (2d Cir. 1997).

statute of frauds *(contract)*
"Except as otherwise provided in this section a contract for the sale of goods for the price of $500 or more is not enforceable by way of action or defense unless there is some writing sufficient to indicate that a contract for sale has been made between the parties and signed by the party against whom enforcement is sought or by his authorized agent or broker."
U.C.C. 2-201(1)(1979).

Related issues. "The reason for excepting exclusive requirements contracts from the strictures of the statute of frauds are [sic] strong. The purchasing party, perhaps unable to anticipate its precise needs, nevertheless wishes to have assurances of supply and fixed prices. The seller, on the other hand, finds an advantage in having a steady customer. Such arrangements have commercial value. To deny enforceability through a rigid reading of the quantity term in the statute of frauds would run contrary to the basic thrust of the Code—to conform the law to business reality and practices." *Advent Sys. Ltd. v. Unisys Corp.,* 925 F.2d 670, 678 (3d Cir. 1991).

statute of limitations *(contract)*

A state or federal law that provides a time period within which a lawsuit for a breach of that law must be filed.

Annotation. The primary purpose of a statute of limitations is to force a party to exercise a right of action it might have within a reasonable period of time, so that the opposing party will have a fair opportunity to defend itself. The purpose of the statutes is to suppress fraudulent and stale claims, which might otherwise be brought after evidence has been lost and the facts of the case obscured by the passage of time. *Am. Jur. 2d Limitation of Actions* § 17 (1970).

Statutes of limitations are primarily designed to assure fairness to defendants. Such statutes "promote justice by preventing surprises through revival of claims that have been allowed to slumber until evidence has been lost, memories have faded, and witnesses have disappeared." *Burnett v. New York Cent. R.R.,* 380 U.S. 424, 428 (1965).

Normally, an action for breach of contract must be brought within the period specified by the statute of limitations of the state whose laws are to be applied. *See* 51 *Am. Jur. 2d Limitation of Actions* § 92 (1970). The limitation period generally begins to run "when the breach occurs, regardless of the aggrieved party's lack of knowledge of the breach."

Related issues. "Considering that Sperry accepted the benefits of the many supplemental contracts, it cannot now assert that the only contracts that apply for the purposes of the statute of limitations, are those contracts entered into more than two years before the commencement of this action. Upon a review of the contract, the Court concludes that the contracts incorporate each other and are not independent agreements. Fairness dictates that the most appropriate time to commence the running of the period of limitations is the date of the final supplemental contract." *Invacare Corp. v. Sperry Rand Corp.,* 612 F. Supp. 448, 452 (N.D. Ohio. 1984).

statutory subject matter *(patent)*

"The question of whether a claim encompasses statutory subject matter should not focus on *which* of the four categories of subject matter a claim is directed to—process, machine, manufacture, or composition of matter—but rather on the essential characteristics of the subject matter, in particular, its practical utility."

* * *

"The first door which must be opened on the difficult path to patentability is §101. The person approaching that door is an inventor, whether his invention is patentable or not. Being an inventor or having an invention, however, is no guarantee of opening even the first door. What kind of an invention or discovery is it? In dealing with the question of kind, as distinguished from the qualitative conditions which make the invention patentable, § 101 is broad and general; its language is: 'any . . . process, machine, manufacture, or composition of matter, or any . . . improvement thereof.' Section 100(b) further expands 'process' to include 'art or method, and . . . a new use of a known process, machine, manufacture, composition of matter, or material.' If the invention, as the inventor defines it in his claims (pursuant to § 112, second paragraph), falls into any one of the named categories, he is allowed to pass through to the second door, which is § 102; 'novelty and loss of right to patent' is the sign on it. Notwithstanding the words 'new and useful' in § 101, the invention is not examined under that statute for novelty because that is not the statutory scheme of things or the long-established administrative practice."

> *State Street Bank & Trust, Co. v. Signature Financial Group, Inc.*, 149 F.3d 1368, 1375, 1372 n.2 (Fed. Cir. 1998) (citing *In re Bergy*, 596 F.2d 952, 960, 201 U.S.P.Q. (BNA) 352,360 (CCPA 1979) (citations omitted).

stickiness *(Internet)*

A characteristic of web sites relating to how long the average user is likely to spend at the site before moving to another site. Web sites try to maximize the time spent by each user through their design, content offerings, or both.

stock balancing *(business)*

A euphemism for sending back titles that are not selling. In some cases, stock is returned for credit or refund. In other cases, slow moving titles are exchanged for more successful titles.

storage *(hardware)*
". . . retains the data and instructions so entered, as well as the intermediate and final results of processing."
> *Computer Sys. of Am. v. Western Reserve Life Assur. Co.,* 19 Mass. App. 430, 431 n.2 (1985).

storage control unit *(hardware)*
"The function of the [IBM] 3880 storage control unit is to control the flow of information between a string of disk drives and a central processing unit."
> *Mukerji v. Commissioner,* 87 T.C. No. 61, C.C.H. Tax Court Dec., ¶ 43,469, at 3701(1986)

storage device(s) *(hardware)*
". . . such as hard and floppy disk drives. . . ."
> *Lotus Dev. Corp. v. Paperback Software Int'l,* 740 F. Supp. 37, 43 (D. Mass. 1990).

". . . store data for later access by the central processing unit (CPU)."
> *Allen-Myland, Inc. v. IBM Corp.,* 693 F. Supp. 262, 275 (E.D. Pa. 1988).

See **storage media.**

storage media *(hardware)*
"Digital files may be stored on several different kinds of storage media, some of which are readily transportable. Perhaps the most familiar of these are so-called floppy disks or 'floppies,' which now are 3 ½ inch magnetic disks upon which digital files may be recorded. For present purposes, however, we are concerned principally with two more recent developments, CD-ROMs and digital versatile disks, or DVDs."
> *Universal City Studios, Inc. v. Reimerdes,* 111 F. Supp. 2d 294, 307 (S.D.N.Y. 2000) (footnote omitted).

See **storage device(s).**

stored wire communications *(criminal)*
A wire communication stored in any computer storage device.

Related issue. "Stored wire communications are subject to different treatment than stored electronic communications. Generally, a search warrant, rather than a court order, is required to obtain access to the contents of a stored electronic communication. See 18 U.S.C. § 2703(a). But, compliance with the more stringent requirements of § 2518, including obtaining a court order, is necessary to obtain access to a stored wire communication, because § 2703 expressly applies only to stored *electronic* communications, and not stored *wire* communications."

> *Steve Jackson Games, Inc. v. United States Secret Serv.,* 36 F.3d 457, 462 n.7 (5th Cir. 1994) (emphasis in original).

See also **electronic storage; wire communication.**

strategic plan *(business)*

A long-term, high-level plan that identifies broad business goals and provides a road map for their achievement.

streaming *(Internet)*

A method of distributing files, particularly sound and/or video files, over the Internet, that permits the information to be viewed/heard as it arrives, instead of waiting for the entire file to download.

Annotation. Streaming is a method of data delivery and playback used on the World Wide Web. Prior to streaming, audio, video, and multimedia files that were included in World Wide Web pages were downloaded from the server computer as part of the web page and played by the client computer when the download was complete. For example, if a web page included a large video file, the client computer would download the entire file before playing it. The download process could take a very long time, which, of course, makes for a slow browsing experience.

Streaming technology permits sequential downloading of the essential parts of a media file necessary to begin playback, followed by a stream of the data to permit the file to continue to completion. In the case of the video file mentioned above, playback could begin shortly after beginning the download, and the playback could continue for so long as the download process continues. The use of streaming permits media delivery on the World Wide Web that simulates radio or television broadcasts. World Wide Web sites such as Macromedia's Shockzone <http://www.macromedia.com /shockzone>, Timecast <http://www.timecast.com>, and Music Net <http:// www.musicnet.com> provide a number of multimedia, music, and talk show venues from which to choose.

Almost all streaming technology formats require at least two components, special software to convert a standard video, audio, or multimedia computer file into a streaming format and special software at the client computer to permit playback of the formatted file. Some streaming technology formats also require special software for the server computer to deliver the streaming data.

Licensing schemes for streaming technology formats vary. Almost all streaming software companies distribute the client computer software necessary to play back streaming data (the "player" software) without charge. Some companies license the software required to create the streaming files for a fixed fee, and other companies license the software necessary to enable the server computers to deliver streaming data for a usage-based fee (based upon the number of simultaneous streams that the server may transmit to client computers).

Examples of streaming delivery systems are available at the World Wide Web sites of Progressive Networks <http://www.real.com>, Macromedia, Inc. <http://www.macromedia.com>, Vivo Software, Inc. <http://www.vivo.com>, and VDOnet Corporation <http://www.vdo.net>. (jrb)

street price *(business)*

The price at which a title is actually selling at retail. It is generally 20% to 25% less than the suggested retail price.

striking similarity *(copyright)*

Annotation. "In the absence of access, courts have required a showing of 'striking similarity' sufficient to 'preclude the possibility of independent creation.'"
 E.F. Johnson Co. v. Uniden Corp. of America, 623 F. Supp. 1485, 1492 n.5 (D. Minn. 1985) (citations omitted).

See also access **(copyright); substantial similarity.**

strong mark *(trademark)*

"A mark that has been registered and uncontested for five years, as Digital's was, is entitled to a presumption that it is a strong mark."
 Data Concepts, Inc. v. Digital Consulting, Inc., 150 F.3d. 620, 625 (6th Cir. 1998).

structure *(software)*

"The functions of the modules in a program together with each module's relationship to other modules constitute the 'structure' of the program. Additionally, the term structure may include the category of modules referred to as 'macros.'"
 Computer Assocs. Int'l, Inc. v. Altai, Inc., 982 F.2d 693, 698 (2d Cir. 1992).

"[A] program's structure includes its non-literal components such as general flow charts as well as the more specific organization of inter-modular relationships, parameter lists, and macros."
 Computer Assocs. Int'l, Inc. v. Altai, Inc., 982 F.2d 693, 702 (2d Cir. 1992).

Related issues. "In fashioning the structure, a programmer will normally attempt to maximize the program's speed, efficiency, as well as simplicity for user operation, while taking into consideration certain externalities such as the memory constraints of the computer upon which the program will be run."

> *Computer Assocs. Int'l, Inc. v. Altai, Inc.,* 982 F.2d 693, 698 (2d Cir. 1992).

structure, sequence, and organization *(software)*

Abbreviated as "SSO."

"The structure, sequence, and organization of a computer program consists of the manner in which the program operates, controls, and regulates the computer in receiving, assembling, calculating, retaining, correlating, and producing useful information."

> *Healthcare Affiliated Servs., Inc. v. Lippany,* 701 F. Supp. 1142, 1144 (W.D. Pa. 1988).

"We use the terms 'structure,' 'sequence,' and 'organization' interchangeably when referring to computer programs, and we intend them to be synonymous in this opinion."

> *Whelan Assocs., Inc. v. Jaslow Dental Lab., Inc.,* 797 F.2d 1222, 1224 n.1 (3d Cir. 1986).

subdirectory *(technology)*

A directory within or below another in the file system, i.e., a subchapter within a chapter.

subject matter *(patent)*

Patent protection is available for "any new and useful process, machine, manufacture, or composition of matter. . . ."

> 35 U.S.C. § 101.

Annotation. "The subject matter provisions of the patent law have been cast in broad terms to fulfill the constitutional and statutory goal of promoting 'the progress of sciences and the useful arts.' Congress employed broad language in drafting Section 101 precisely because such inventions are often unforeseeable."

> *Diamond v. Chakrabarty,* 447 U.S. 303, 309 (1980).

subroutine *(software)*

"[A] routine that can be part of another routine; analogous to a sentence within a paragraph of narrative text."

> U.S. Copyright Office, *Compendium of Copyright Office Practices* II, § 326 (1984).

"[B]asically a discrete part of a program with a readily identifiable task."
Pearl Sys., Inc. v. Competition Elecs., Inc., 8 U.S.P.Q.2d (BNA) 1520, 1521 n.2 (S.D. Fla. 1988).

See also **routine.**

subscribe *(Internet)*

"A user can also 'subscribe' to an electronic mailing list on a topic of interest; the user receives a copy of messages posted by other subscribers and, in turn, can post messages for forwarding to the full mailing list."
Shea v. Reno, 930 F. Supp. 916, 927 (S.D.N.Y. 1996).

subscriber

(electronic commerce)
"[A] person who:
    i. is the subject listed in a certificate;
    ii. accepts the certificate; and
    iii. holds a private key which corresponds to a public key listed in that certificate."
Cal. Code of Regs., tit. 2, div. 7, ch. 10, § 22003(a)(1)(K); Wash. Rev. Code § 19.34.020(34).

(Internet)
"Even if the user could obtain an e-mail address for each subscriber to a particular list, those addresses alone would provide no authoritative information about subscribers. There is no directory that identifies persons using a certain e-mail address. In addition, a user can avoid disclosing his true e-mail address by developing an e-mail 'alias' or by using an 'anonymous remailer'—a server that purges identifying information from a communication before forwarding it to its destination."
Shea v. Reno, 930 F. Supp. 916, 927 (S.D.N.Y. 1996).

substantial similarity

(copyright)
". . . does not require complete identity. Substantial similarity has been found in numerous instances where the similar material is quantitatively quite small, particularly if that material is qualitatively important."
In re Certain Personal Computers and Components Thereof, 224 U.S.P.Q. (BNA) 270, 281 (U.S. Int'l Trade Comm'n 1984), *cited in E.F. Johnson Co. v. Uniden Corp. of America,* 623 F. Supp. 1485, 1497 n.9 (D. Minn. 1985).

Annotation. (copyright) "Under the Ninth Circuit's two-step analysis of substantial similarity, the party claiming infringement must meet an 'extrinsic' test to determine whether the ideas found in the two works are substantially similar and an 'intrinsic' test to compare forms of expression."

> *Interactive Networks, Inc. v. NTN Comm., Inc.,* 875 F. Supp. 1398, 1403 (N.D. Cal. 1995).

"Similarity of ideas may be shown by comparing the objective details of the works: plot, theme, dialogue, mood, setting, characters, etc. Similarity of expression focuses on the response of the ordinary reasonable person, and considers the total concept and feel of the works."

> *Micro Star v. FormGen, Inc.,* 154 F.3d 1107, 1112 (9th Cir. 1998) (citing *Litchfield v. Spielberg,* 736 F.2d 1352, 1356 (9th Cir. 1984)) (citations omitted).

Related issues. "Generally, summary judgment is not favored on the issue of substantial similarity in copyright cases. Nevertheless, summary judgment is appropriate on the issue of substantial similarity if no reasonable jury could find that the works are substantially similar in protectible expression."

> *Interactive Networks, Inc. v. NTN Comm., Inc.,* 875 F. Supp. 1398, 1403 (N.D. Cal. 1995) (citations omitted).

(mask work)
"Although the Semiconductor Chip Protection Act does not use the word 'copy' to describe infringement, the parallel language reflects the incorporation of the well-explicated copyright principle of substantial similarity into the Semiconductor Chip Protection Act."

> *Brooktree Corp. v. Advanced Micro Devices, Inc.,* 977 F.2d 1555, 1564 (Fed. Cir. 1992).

See also **infringement; iterative approach; ordinary observer test; striking similarities.**

subsystems *(software)*
"[P]ackages that are themselves comprised of a number of programs or modules."

> *In re* Inslaw, 83 B.R. 89, 97-98 (Bkrtcy. D.C. 1988).

suggestive mark *(trademark)*
". . . is one that requires some measure of imagination to reach a conclusion regarding the nature of the products."

> *Maritz, Inc. v. Cybergold, Inc.,* 947 F. Supp. 1338, 1340 (E.D. Mo. 1996) (citation omitted).

" '. . . connote, without describing, some quality, ingredient, or characteristic of the product.' While these marks conjure up positive images, courts consider these marks suggestive because 'a person without actual knowledge would have difficulty in ascertaining the nature of the products that the marks represent.' Suggestive marks, too, are inherently distinctive and fully protected by the Lanham Act."

America Online, Inc. v. AT&T Corp., 64 F. Supp. 2d 549, 560 (E.D. Va. 1999) (citations omitted).

". . . connote, but do not describe, some quality, ingredient, or characteristic of the product, such as 'Coppertone' suntan lotion. These marks are not descriptive in that a person without actual knowledge of the product involved would not likely surmise what product a suggestive mark represents."

Washington Speakers Bureau, Inc. v. Leading Authorities, Inc., 33 F. Supp. 2d 488, 494-95 (E.D. Va. 1999).

". . . conveys an impression of a good but requires the exercise of some imagination and perception to reach a conclusion as to the product's nature."

Brookfield Comm., Inc. v. West Coast Entertainment Corp., 174 F.3d 1036, 1058 n.19 (9th Cir. 1999).

See also **trademark infringement.**

sui generis *(general)*

A Latin phrase used to describe any law that is "of its own kind or class."

sui generis software protection *(software)*

"To be frank, the exact contours of copyright protection for non-literal program structure are not completely clear. . . . Indeed, it may well be that the Copyright Act serves as a relatively weak barrier against public access to the theoretical interstices behind a program's source and object codes. This results from the hybrid nature of a computer program, which, while it is literary expression, is also a highly functional, utilitarian component in the larger process of computing.

"Generally, we think that copyright registration—with its indiscriminating availability—is not ideally suited to deal with the highly dynamic technology of computer science. Thus far, many of the decision in this area reflect the courts' attempt to fit the proverbial square peg in a round hole."

Computer Assocs. Int'l, Inc. v. Altai, Inc., 982 F.2d 693, 712 (2d Cir. 1992).

suitable guaranty *(electronic commerce)*

"[E]ither a surety bond executed by a surety authorized by the insurance commissioner to do business in this state, or an irrevocable letter of credit issued by a financial institution authorized to do business in this state, which, in either event, satisfies all of the following requirements: (a) It is issued payable to the secretary for the benefit of persons holding qualified rights of payment against the licensed certification authority named as the principal of the bond or customer of the letter of credit; (b) It is in an amount specified by rule by the secretary under RCW 19.34.030; (c) It states that it is issued for filing under this chapter; (d) It specifies a term of effectiveness extending at least as long as the term of the license to be issued to the certification authority; and (e) It is in a form prescribed or approved by rule by the secretary. A suitable guaranty may also provide that the total annual liability on the guaranty to all persons making claims based on it may not exceed the face amount of the guaranty."

Wash. Rev. Code § 19.34.020(35).

summary judgment *(procedure)*

"The purpose of summary judgment is to avoid a trial when there is no genuine factual issue and the moving party is entitled to judgment as a matter of law. Summary judgment is proper when 'the pleadings, depositions, answers to interrogatories, and admissions on file, together with affidavits, if any, show that there is no genuine issue as to any material fact and that the moving party is entitled to judgment as a matter of law.' Fed. R. Civ. P. 56(C). There is a 'genuine' issue of material fact only when there is sufficient evidence such that a reasonable juror could find for the party opposing the motion. Entry of summary judgment is mandated against a party if, after adequate time for discovery and upon motion, the party fails to make a showing sufficient to establish the existence of an element essential to that party's case, and on which that party will bear the burden of proof at trial."

Interactive Networks, Inc. v. NTN Comm., Inc., 875 F. Supp. 1398, 1401 (N.D. Cal. 1995) (citations omitted). *See also Lockheed Martin Corp. v. Network Solutions, Inc.,* 985 F. Supp. 949, 955 (C.D. Cal. 1977) (trademark).

"Summary judgment is particularly appropriate where the idea and expression are inseparable or where analytic dissection determines that all similarities arise from standard elements derived from a common idea."

Interactive Networks, Inc. v. NTN Comm., Inc., 875 F. Supp. 1398, 1403 (N.D. Cal. 1995) (citations omitted).

Related issues (copyright). See **substantial similarity.**

super user *(technology)*

A computer user with the ability to access any and all files, as well as to execute many privileged commands associated with system growth and maintenance, without regard to normal access privileges.

Super-Zap *(software)*

A software correction supplied by a vendor that bypasses the need for the vendor to provide a whole new version of a system or application, including the source code, to a user.

supplier *(contract)*

"[A]ny person engaged in the business of making a consumer product directly or indirectly available to consumers."

15 U.S.C. § 2301(4).

supporting documentation

(criminal)

". . . includes, but is not limited to, all information, in any form, pertaining to the design, construction, classification, implementation, use, or modification of a computer, computer system, computer network, computer program, or computer software, which information is not generally available to the public, and is necessary for the operation of a computer, computer system, computer network, computer program, or computer software."

Cal. Penal C. § 502.

See also documentation; supporting material.

supporting material *(general)*

[INTERNATIONAL] ". . . means any material, other than a computer program or a program description, created for aiding the understanding or application of a computer program, such as, for example, problem descriptions and user instructions."

WIPO, *Model Provisions on the Protection of Computer Software* (1978).

surfing *(Internet)*

Browsing the World Wide Web. Often, the user has no specific goal in mind, other than locating interesting information.

SurfWatch *(software)*

". . . is also designed to allow parents and other concerned users to filter unwanted material on the Internet."

American Civil Liberties Union v. Reno, 929 F. Supp. 830, 841 (3d Cir. 1996), *aff'd, Reno v. American Civil Liberties Union,* 521 U.S. 844 (1997).

suspend a certificate *(electronic commerce)*

"[T]o make a certificate ineffective temporarily for a specified time forward."

Wash. Rev. Code § 19.34.020(36).

sweat of the brow *(copyright)*

"The Supreme Court has disapproved the 'sweat of the brow' standard, explaining that its defect lies in the fact that the copyright laws were never intended to protect information merely for the reason that it may stem from effort or labor."

> *Bellsouth Advertising & Publ'g Corp. v. Donnelley Info. Publ'g, Inc.*, 933 F.2d 952, 957 (11th Cir. 1991).

See also **Feist.**

SWIFT *(organization)*

Acronym for "Society for Worldwide Inter-Bank Financial Telecommunications."

[NEW ZEALAND] "[C]onceived in 1973 to provide a secure method of payment instructions between major banks in different countries using a standard format for messages."

> *Databank Systems Ltd. v. Commissioner of Inland Revenue* [1987], N.Z.L.R. 312 (H.C. Wellington).

switch(es) *(hardware)*

". . . used to connect several units to a single source. For example, several personal computers can be hooked up to a single plotter (a plotter produces graphs). A switch is used to connect and disconnect each computer to the plotter so that only one computer can send signals to the plotter at one time. Without a switch, it would be necessary to physically connect and disconnect each computer each time it is used with the plotter. Switches are usually contained in small boxes (approximately 6″ × 6″ × 3″)."

> IRS Letter Ruling 8721016, Feb. 17, 1987.

[CANADA] ". . . appears in MacQuari's [sic] Dictionary, 1981, as a colloquial abbreviation for 'switchboard,' in turn defined as 'an arrangement of switches, plugs, and jacks mounted on a board or frame enabling an operator to make temporary connections between telephone users.' 'Switch,' of course, also has the meaning of 'a mechanical device that completes or breaks the path of the current or sends it over a different path.'"

> *In re Application by Mitel Corp.* (1985), 5 I.P.R. 260 (Austrl. Pat. Office).

symmetric bandwidth *(telecommunications)*

A transmission channel that provides both uploading and downloading capabilities at the same speed.

symmetric cipher *(technology)*

"An encryption method using one key, known to both the sender and receiver of a message, that is used both to encrypt and to decrypt a message."

U.S. Congress, Office of Technology Assessment, *Defending Secrets, Sharing Data: New Locks and Keys for Electronic Information* 176 (Oct. 1987).

symmetric key encryption *(technology)*

The type of encryption using a single key for both encryption and decryption. This form of encryption is inherently insecure, since the key must be transmitted to the recipient of encrypted data.

symmetrical compression *(technology)*

A compression methodology that takes the same amount of time to compress an image as it does to decompress the image.

synch right *(entertainment)*

See synchronization license.

synchronization *(technology)*

Making two or more video and/or audio elements operate in specific time relation to one another.

synchronization license *(contract)*

Also called "synch right." The license required to synchronize music with visual images.

syntax error *(technology)*

An invalid expression that is not understood by the operating system.

synthespians *(entertainment; multimedia)*

Contraction of the term "**syn**thetic **thespians**." Virtual actors.

sysop *(Internet; technology)*

Contraction of the term "**sys**tem **op**erator." A person in charge of a computer system. Usually the system operator controls who has access to and can use the system, determines what information can be stored and retrieved from the system, and has the right to read (and if necessary delete) data stored on the system.

system *(copyright)*

See method of operation.

system *(technology)*

". . . clearly includes the software which is an indispensable prerequisite to achieving the specified results. The policy letter also states that the purchase price is to be based on the 'installed value' of the system that expressly includes installation supervision, correlation, certification, initial systems engineering and cable. In particular, correlation and certification presuppose that the balance of the software is installed and operational in the system. The system cannot begin to function unless the software is in place."

> *Chelsea Indus., Inc. v. Accuray Leasing Corp.,* 8 Computer L. Serv. Rep. 374, 377 (D. Mass. 1984).

". . . consists of a NOVA CPU designed to perform a particular 'instruction set' or group of tasks, and a copyrighted NOVA operating system called RDOS containing the basic commands for operation of the system."

> *Digidyne Corp. v. Data General Corp.,* 734 F.2d 1336, 1338 (9th Cir. 1984).

See also **computer system; electronic data processing system.**

system base *(technology)*

"The system base of a computer is a fixed area in main memory which acts as the root for all information structures in the computer."

> *In re Bradley,* 600 F.2d 807, 808 (C.C.P.A. 1980), *aff'd sub nom. Diamond v. Bradley,* 450 U.S. 381 (1981).

system design *(technology)*

"This system included four functions of Catamore's operations: (1) an 'order entry system' for the analysis of incoming orders from customers (i.e., showing what end product items were required); (2) invoicing (i.e., showing what end product items have been shipped); (3) inventory control (i.e., showing what items are on hand); and (4) a bill of materials system (i.e., showing what components are required to fill incoming orders).

"The second stage of systems design, analogized by a Catamore witness to the reduction of an architect's concept of a house to the specifications given a draftsman for the purpose of preparing blueprints. Its parameters, however, do not seem to be the subject of widespread agreement.

"Pursuing the architect analogy, the instructions to men and machines who build the house; there, the writing, in machine language, of a multitude of explicit instructions to a machine to enable it, for example, to produce from appropriately organized data, a payroll. The process was described by Catamore's witness as starting with logical analysis, continuing with the writing of instructions, followed by a host of more explicit instructions ('coding'), and concluding with tests to identify and eliminate the inevitable human error encountered in writing instructions. The witness stated that a payroll program would probably require 20,000 explicit instructions, which might take a programmer a year, in the course of which he might initially write an erroneous instruction in every 200 or 250 instructions."

> *IBM Corp. v. Catamore Enters., Inc.,* 548 F.2d 1065, 1068 n.3–5 (1st Cir. 1976), *cert. denied,* 431 U.S. 960 (1977).

system engineering consultants *(business)*

". . . provide the customer with systems engineering and design services as well as services for the actual operation of the end-user's computer facilities."

> *Telex Corp. v. IBM Corp.,* 367 F. Supp. 258, 273 (N.D. Okla. 1973), *aff'd in part, rev'd in part,* 510 F.2d 894 (10th Cir.), *cert. dism.,* 423 U.S. 802 (1975).

system(s) integrator *(business)*

A contractor who teams up with different vendors to create a system and usually does not manufacture its own equipment.

system program(s) *(software)*

"[A] computer program designed solely to help someone else program or use a computer."

> *Computer Sciences Corp. v. Commissioner of Internal Revenue,* 63 T.C. 327, 329 (1974).

". . . activate and control the computer hardware to facilitate its use and to control the use and sharing of the basic resources of a computer system."

> *B.I. Moyle Assocs., Inc. v. Wisconsin Dept. of Revenue,* Guide to Computer Law (CCH) ¶60, 236, at 80,675 (Tax App. Comm. 1990).

See also system(s) **software.**

system(s) software *(software)*

Also called "system(s) program(s)."

"[A] computer program designed solely to help someone else program or use a computer."

> *Computer Sciences Corp. v. Commissioner of Internal Revenue,* 63 T.C. 327, 329 (1974).

"[A] computer program that controls the computer hardware and schedules the execution of its functions."

> *Apple Computer, Inc. v. Microsoft Corp.,* 759 F. Supp. 1444, 1447 (N.D. Cal. 1991).

[CANADA] "Describe the material pre-programmed by the manufacturer's representatives to suit the general use to be made of the computer by the operator and which help the computer to run more efficiently by taking care of 'housekeeping' chores such as queuing jobs for the printer, or locating a particular piece of stored information."

Clarke Irwin & Co. v. Singer Co. of Can., Ont. Div. Ct., Keith J., December 3, 1979, *summarized at* [1979] 3 A.C.W.S. 807.

See also **operating system program(s); system program.**

system(s) support engineering services *(business)*

"Systems support engineering services are provided by personnel who assist the computer user in the programming and usage of the data processing equipment."

Honeywell Information Systems v. Maricopa County, 118 Ariz. 171, 575 P.2d 801, 808 (App. 1977).

system testing *(business)*

Testing to determine that the results generated by the enterprise's information systems and their components are accurate and the systems perform to specification.

System/360 *(technology)*

"A series of mainframe computers and related products sharing a common architecture. First announced and marketed in 1964, the IBM System/360 revolutionized the data processing industry by providing users with the ability to install upward and downward compatible computer systems. For example, a user's application program designed to run on a particular central processing unit (such as an IBM Model 30) could, for the first time, run equally well on a more powerful processor (such as an IBM Model 40). The IBM System/360 and System/370, including mainframe computers and related products such as software operating systems, achieved widespread acceptance in the world marketplace. An enormous base of mainframe computer users have made extensive investments in applications programs developed to run in conjunction with IBM Operating System Software."

IBM Corp. v. Fujitsu Ltd., Copyright L. Rep. (CCH) ¶ 20,517 (Am. Arb. Ass'n 1988).

table-driven program *(software)*

"In a table-driven program . . . information or data used repeatedly by different parts of the program is segregated into tables rather than represented in ordinary lines of code. . . . The use of tables simplifies maintenance and modifications, and makes the program easier to understand." *Allen-Myland, Inc. v. IBM Corp.,* 746 F. Supp. 520, 533 n.9 (E.D. Pa. 1990).

tacking *(trademark)*

"The use of an earlier mark can be tacked onto the use of a subsequent mark only if the previously used mark is 'the legal equivalent of the mark in question or indistinguishable therefrom' such that consumers 'consider both as the same mark.' Furthermore, tacking should be permitted 'only in rare circumstances.'" *Data Concepts, Inc. v. Digital Consulting, Inc.,* 150 F.3d. 620, 623 (6th Cir. 1998) (citations omitted).

Annotation. "[O]ur sister circuits have explicitly recognized the ability of a trademark owner to claim priority in a mark based on the first use date of a similar, but technically distinct mark—but only in the exceptionally narrow instance where 'the previously used mark' is 'the legal equivalent of the mark in question or indistinguishable therefrom' such that consumers 'consider both as the same mark.' . . . This constructive use theory is known as 'tacking,' as the trademark holder essentially seeks to 'tack' his first use date in the earlier mark onto the subsequent mark." *Brookfield Comm., Inc. v. West Coast Entertainment Corp.,* 174 F.3d 1036, 1047-48 (9th Cir. 1999) (citation omitted).

"[T]acking should be allowed if two marks are so similar that consumers generally would regard them as essentially the same. Where such is the case, the new mark serves the same identificatory function as the old mark." *Brookfield Comm., Inc. v. West Coast Entertainment Corp.,* 174 F.3d 1036, 1048 (9th Cir. 1999).

"The standard for 'tacking,' however, is extremely strict: 'The marks must create the *same, continuing commercial impression,* and the later mark should not materially differ from or alter the character of the mark attempted to be tacked.'"

> *Brookfield Comm., Inc. v. West Coast Entertainment Corp.*, 174 F.3d 1036, 1048 (9th Cir. 1999) (citations omitted; emphasis in original).

tag *(Internet)*

"[A] string of characters, such as '-L18' (for 'not less than 18 years')—[embedded] into the address or name of a particular site so as to clearly identify the site as unsuitable for minors."

> *Shea v. Reno*, 930 F. Supp. 916, 932-33 (S.D.N.Y. 1996).

See also **tagging**.

tagging *(Internet)*

The process of placing a tag on a web site.

Annotation. " 'Tagging' would require content providers to label all of their 'indecent' or 'patently offensive' material by imbedding a string of characters, such as 'XXX,' in either the URL or HTML. If a user could install software on his or her computer to recognize the 'XXX' tag, the user could screen out any content with that tag."

> *American Civil Liberties Union v. Reno*, 929 F. Supp. 824, 847 (E.D. Pa. 1996), *aff'd, Reno v. American Civil Liberties Union*, 521 U.S. 844 (1997).

"All parties agree that tagging alone does nothing to prevent children from accessing potentially indecent material, because it depends upon the cooperation of third parties to block the material on which the tags are embedded."

> *American Civil Liberties Union v. Reno*, 929 F. Supp. 824, 856 (E.D. Pa. 1996), *aff'd, Reno v. American Civil Liberties Union*, 521 U.S. 844 (1997).

See also **tag**.

talk

(Internet)

". . . [a]llows one-to-one communications."

> *American Civil Liberties Union v. Reno*, 929 F. Supp. 824, 835 (E.D. Pa. 1996), *aff'd, Reno v. American Civil Liberties Union*, 521 U.S. 844 (1997).

See also **one-to-one messaging**.

(software)

"Using a program called 'Talk,' two users can exchange messages while they are both on line; a message typed on one user's computer will appear almost immediately on the receiver's screen."

> *Shea v. Reno*, 930 F. Supp. 916, 928 (S.D.N.Y. 1996).

tampering *(criminal)*

See computer tampering.

tangible personal property *(criminal)*

"[P]ersonal property which may be seen, weighed, measured, felt, or touched or which is in any other manner perceptible to the senses and includes tangible personal property which is used to convey computer software."

Neb. Rev. Stat. § 77-2702(18) (1986).

tape, magnetic *(hardware)*

"Large volume data storage medium for computers."

U.S. Copyright Office, *Compendium of Copyright Office Practices* II, § 326 (1984).

See also **magnetic tape.**

tarnishment *(trademark)*

". . . occurs when a famous mark is improperly associated with an inferior or offensive product or service."

Panavision Int'l, L.P. v. Toeppen, 141 F.3d 1316, 1326 n.7 (9th Cir. 1998).

tax clause *(contract)*

A contractual provision that indicates which party is responsible for paying any taxes assessed in connection with the transaction.

Sample clause. "DISTRIBUTOR agrees to pay and to hold harmless DEVELOPER on account of any taxes or other government charges (however denominated) imposed by the government within the Territory with respect to the execution or delivery of this Agreement, or any sales, licenses, or other transactions hereunder or any income earned or payments received by DEVELOPER hereunder. To the extent DISTRIBUTOR is required to withhold or pay such taxes on payments to DEVELOPER, DISTRIBUTOR will promptly thereafter furnish DEVELOPER with funds in the full amount of the sums withheld or paid."

TCP *(technology)*

Acronym for "Transmission Control Protocol." A set of rules used by host computers on the Internet for the transmission of information from one computer to another.

TCP/IP *(technology)*

Acronym for "Transmission Control Protocol/Internet Protocol." The set of rules that permit all computers connected to the Internet to communicate with each other. Web sites, e-mail, FTPs, and telnet all use TCP/IP.

tear-off menu *(technology)*

"[A] menu bar or window that may be repositioned at will to different locations on the display screen."

Apple Computer, Inc. v. Articulate Sys., Inc., 234 F.2d 14, 18 n.2 (Fed. Cir. 2000).

teasers *(Internet)*

"[F]ree sexually explicit images and animated graphic image files designed to entice a user to pay a fee to browse the whole site."

American Civil Liberties Union v. Reno, 31 F. Supp. 2d 473, 476 (E.D. Pa. 1999).

technological access control measures *(technology)*

See **DMCA.**

technology *(electronic commerce)*

"[T]he computer hardware and/or software-based method or process used to create digital signatures."

Cal. Code of Regulations, tit. 2, div. 7, ch. 10, § 22000(a)(6).

Technology Steering Committee *(Year 2000)*

A subcommittee of the board of directors, chosen to oversee the Year 2000 project, as well as to ensure that other technology projects and live production are carried out in an appropriate manner.

telecommunication(s) *(telecommunications)*

"[T]he transmission, between or among points specified by the user, of information of the user's choosing, without change in the form or content of the information as sent and received."

47 U.S.C. § 153(40).

". . . encompasses voice telephony and data services, including information access technology."

The White House, *A Framework for Global Electronic Commerce* 22 (July 1, 1997).

[CANADA] "[A]ny transmission, emission or reception of signs, signals, writing, images, sounds or intelligence of any nature by radio, visual, electronic or other electromagnetic system."

Criminal Code of Canada, R.S.C. 1985, c. C-46, s. 326(2).

[CANADA] "[C]ommunication at a distance (as by cable, radio, telegraph, or television)."

Intra Can. Telecommunications Ltd. v. C.P. Ltd. (1986), 8 C.P.R. (3d) 390 (T.M. Opp. Bd.), *rev'd,* Fed. T.D., Doc. Nos. T-650-86, T-651-86, Cullen J., Jan. 25, 1988 (unreported).

[CANADA] "[A]ny transmissions of signs, signals, writing, images or sounds or intelligence of any nature by wire, radio, visual, optical or other electromagnetic system."

Canadian Copyright Act, R.S.C. 1985, c. C-42, s. 2 [am. S.C. 1988, c. 65, s. 61].

telecommunication service *(telecommunications)*

The offering of telecommunications for a fee directly to the public, or to such classes of users as to be effectively available directly to the public, regardless of the facilities used.

47 U.S.C. § 153(46).

Telecommunications Act of 1996 *(defamation; Internet; obscenity; telecommunications)*

"The Telecommunications Act of 1996, Pub. L. 104-104, 110 Stat. 56, was an unusually important legislative enactment. As stated on the first of its 103 pages, its primary purpose was to reduce regulation and encourage 'the rapid deployment of new telecommunications technologies.' The major components of the statute have nothing to do with the Internet; they were designed to promote competition in the local telephone service market, the multichannel video market, and the market for over-the-air broadcasting. The Act includes seven Titles, six of which are the product of extensive committee hearings and the subject of discussion in Reports prepared by Committees of the Senate and the House of Representatives. By contrast, Title V—known as the 'Communications Decency Act of 1996' (CDA)—contains provisions that were either added in executive committee after the hearings were concluded or as amendments offered during floor debate on the legislation."

Reno v. American Civil Liberties Union, 521 U.S. 844, 857-58 (1997).

See also **Communications Decency Act.**

telecommunications system *(telecommunications)*
[CANADA] ". . . devices and techniques employed for the transmission of signs, signals, writings, images, sounds or data of any nature by wire, radio or other electromagnetic equipment."
> *Maltais v. R.* (1977), 33 C.C.C. (2d) 465 (S.C.C.).

[UNITED KINGDOM] "[A] system for conveying visual images, sounds, or other information via electronic means."
> U.K. Copyright, Designs, and Patents Act 1988, c. 48.

telephone patching *(telecommunications)*
"[A] procedure where a [vendor] employee instructed a [customer] employee by telephone how to correct the malfunctions in [software]."
> *RRX Indus., Inc. v. Lab-Con, Inc.,* 772 F.2d 543, 545 (9th Cir. 1985).

telephone switch *(telecommunications)*
". . . routes long distance telephone calls to their destinations."
> *Alcatel USA, Inc. v. DGI Technologies, Inc.,* 166 F.3d 772, 777 (5th Cir. 1999).

telephony *(telecommunications)*
Voice communications.

Teletext *(telecommunications)*
[AUSTRALIA] "Teletext was adopted in and has been used since 1976 by the CCITT as the provisional name for a new public text communication service proposed to be used initially and which, in addition to the existing telex services, would offer more sophisticated features combining certain office typewriter facilities (including editing functions) and transmission functions to communicate with remote stations via the public switched networks. The name 'Teletext' has been consistently and widely used in the telecommunications field to refer to the particular system of text communication."
> *In re Application by Siemens Aktiengesellschaft* (1983), 1 I.P.R. 1 (Austrl. Pat. Office).

telnet *(Internet; software)*
A computer program that permits a computer to log in to a remote computer.

Annotation. "Another method to use information on the Internet is to access and control remote computers in 'real time' using 'telnet.' For example, using telnet, a researcher at a university would be able to use the computing power of a supercomputer located at a different university. A student can use telnet to connect to a remote library to access the library's online card catalog program."

American Civil Liberties Union v. Reno, 929 F. Supp. 824, 835 (E.D. Pa. 1996), *aff'd, Reno v. American Civil Liberties Union,* 521 U.S. 844 (1997).

TEMPEST *(technology)*

". . . refers to the certification with the Industrial Tempest Program of the National Security Administration."

Secure Servs. Technology, Inc. v. Time & Space Processing, Inc., 722 F. Supp. 1354, 1357 n.3 (E.D. Va. 1989).

TEMPEST machines *(technology)*

"[M]achines especially equipped for the secure transmission and receipt of sensitive or classified documents. TEMPEST machines are sold to American and NATO agencies and to qualified private government contractors."

Secure Servs. Technology, Inc. v. Time & Space Processing, Inc., 722 F. Supp. 1354, 1357 (E.D. Va. 1989).

templates *(general)*

"[P]ieces of plastic that fit around the function keys on the keyboard, identifying the specific functions or commands that can be invoked by those keys."

Lotus Dev. Corp. v. Paperback Software Int'l, 740 F. Supp. 37, 43 (D. Mass. 1990).

tender of delivery *(contract)*

". . . must therefore be interpreted to include not only delivery of the hardware components, but the incidental, customized 'installation' of the software programs as well. Only when the reasonable vendee knows or should know that installation of the program bargained for is complete, has there been tender of delivery of the entire computer system. It may be that use of the programs with live data over a period of time is necessary before it is apparent that the software has or has not been completely installed."

Dreier Co. v. Unitronix Corp., 217 N.J. Super. 260, 527 A.2d 875, 881 (1986).

tera *(technology)*

Prefix meaning trillion (or a thousand billion), e.g., "terabytes" meaning "one trillion bytes of information."

term *(contract)*

"[T]hat portion of an agreement which relates to a particular matter."

U.C.C. § 1-201(42).

"[W]ith respect to an agreement, means that portion of the agreement which relates to a particular matter."
UCITA § 102(a)(63).

terminal *(hardware)*

A device that acts as the point of communication between user and computer. Usually a terminal is a video display unit with a keyboard attached. The terminal can be used as both an input and an output device. Information can be typed in using the keyboard, and results can be seen on the display screen.

terminate *(contract)*

See termination.

termination *(contract)*

". . . occurs when either party pursuant to a power created by agreement or law puts an end to the contract otherwise than for its breach. On 'termination' all obligations which are still executory on both sides are discharged but any right based on prior breach or performance survives."
U.C.C. § 2-106(3).

"[T]he ending of a contract by a party pursuant to a power created by agreement or law otherwise than because of breach of contract."
UCITA § 102(a)(64).

Sample clause. "Either party shall have the right to terminate this Agreement, prior to the expiration of the term (or any renewal term) hereof, upon the occurrence of any of the following events:
(a) Breach or default by the other of any of the terms, obligations, covenants, representations of warranties under this Agreement which is not waived in writing by the non-defaulting party. In such case, the non-defaulting party shall notify the other of such alleged breach or default and the other party shall have a period of thirty (30) days to cure the same; or
(b) If the other party is declared insolvent or bankrupt, or makes an assignment for the benefit of creditors, or a receiver is appointed or any proceeding is demanded by, for, or against the other under any provision of the Federal Bankruptcy Act or any amendment thereof."

terminator *(hardware)*

"[A] device housed in the tape drive which is designed to terminate the signal."
Datamatic, Inc. v. IBM Corp., 613 F. Supp. 715, 717 (D. La. 1985).

test *(technology)*

The process of exercising a product to identify differences between expected and actual behavior.

test bed *(technology)*

A set of hardware and software that mirrors the operating environment as closely as possible. The purpose of a test bed is to simulate a unique operating environment to test applications that have been made compliant. The testing occurs outside of the real system, thus protecting the data and the business in the event the newly fixed application contains bugs. (wsr)

test facility *(technology)*

A computer system isolated from the production environment, dedicated to the testing and validation of applications and system components.

text editor *(software)*

A computer program used to revise data or text. Text editing is often called "word processing" when document-oriented commands are included in the system.

thin client computer *(technology)*

A computer with limited processing power and storage; intended to be used as a terminal to access the Internet or other network, and which will download the software it needs to perform its functions from a network server. *See also* **network computer; network computer system.**

third-level domain *(Internet)*

In the domain name system, the level of the hierarchy below the second-level domains, being that portion of the domain name two segments to the left of the top-level domain. For example, in www.altavista.digital.com, the third level domain is "altavista."

thread *(Internet)*

A series of messages relating to a specific topic or posting on a newsgroup or mailing list.

threat(s) *(criminal)*

"Whoever transmits in interstate or foreign commerce any communication containing any threat to kidnap any person or any threat to injure the person of another, shall be fined under this title or imprisoned not more than five years, or both."

18 U.S.C. § 875(c).

"Because § 875(c) is a general intent crime, intent must be proved by 'objectively looking at the defendant's behavior in the totality of the circumstances,' rather than by 'probing the defendant's subjective state of mind.' . . . '[A] specific individual as a target of the threat need not be identified.' Even so, the threat must be aimed as some discrete, identifiable group. The threat need not be communicated to the person or group identified as its target. . . . Because prosecution under 18 U.S.C. § 875(c) involves punishment of pure speech, it necessarily implicates and is limited by the First Amendment. . . . [A] statute such as this one, which makes criminal a form of pure speech, must be interpreted with the commands of the First Amendment clearly in mind. What is a threat must be distinguished from what is constitutionally protected speech. . . . [T]o pass constitutional muster the government must initially prove 'a true "threat."' . . . Factors . . . bearing on whether a specific statement can be taken as a true threat include the context of the statement, including whether the statement has a political dimension; whether the statement was conditional; and the reaction of the listeners. Watts also makes clear that the question of whether a statement constitutes a true threat in light of the First Amendment is distinct from the question of the defendant's intent: 'whatever the "willfulness" requirement implies, the statute initially requires the Government to prove a true "threat."'

"The distinction between the two questions of whether a statement is a 'true threat' for the purposes of First Amendment limitation, and the intention of the statement's maker, is important but unfortunately often confused. The confusion results from too loose a use of the phrase 'true threat.' The purpose and effect of the *Watts* constitutionally-limited definition of the term 'threat' is to insure that only unequivocal, unconditional and specific expressions of intention immediately to inflict injury may be punished—only such threats, in short, as are of the same nature as those threats which are . . . 'properly punished every day under statutes prohibiting extortion, blackmail and assault without consideration of First Amendment issues.'

* * *

"So long as the threat on its face and in the circumstances in which it is made is so unequivocal, unconditional, immediate and specific as to the person threatened, as to convey a gravity of purpose and imminent prospect of execution, the statute may properly be applied. This clarification of the scope of 18 U.S.C. § 875(c) is, we trust, consistent with a rational approach to First Amendment construction which provides for governmental authority in instances of inchoate conduct, where a com-

munication has become 'so interlocked with violent conduct as to constitute for all practical purposes part of the [proscribed] action itself.'"
United States v. Baker, 890 F. Supp. 1375, 1380, 1381, 1382 (E.D. Mich. 1995) (citations omitted).

"[M]essages constituting 'shared fantasies fall short of . . . an unequivocal, unconditional, immediate and specific threat conveying an imminent prospect of execution and therefore are not 'true threats' unprotected by the First Amendment.

* * *

"The language of the statement must be considered as it would be interpreted by the foreseeable recipients of the communication containing it. Statements expressing musings, considerations of what it would be like to kidnap or injure someone, or desires to kidnap or injure someone, however unsavory, are not constitutionally actionable under § 875(c) absent some expression of an intent to commit the injury or kidnapping. In addition, while the statement need not identify a specific individual as its target, it must be sufficiently specific as to its potential target or targets to render the statement more than hypothetical."
United States v. Baker, 890 F. Supp. 1375, 1385, 1386 (E.D. Mich. 1995) (citations omitted).

"Baker is being prosecuted under 18 U.S.C. § 875(c) for his use of words, implicating fundamental First Amendment concerns. Baker's words were transmitted by means of the Internet, a relatively new communications medium that is itself currently the subject of much media attention. The Internet makes it possible with unprecedented ease to achieve world-wide distribution of material, like Baker's story, posted to its public areas. When used in such a fashion, the Internet may be likened to a newspaper with unlimited distribution and no locatable printing press—and with no supervising editorial control. But Baker's e-mail messages, on which the superseding indictment is based, were not publicly published but privately sent to Gonda. While new technology such as the Internet may complicate analysis and may sometimes require new or modified laws, it does not in this instance qualitatively change the analysis under the statute or under the First Amendment."
United States v. Baker, 890 F. Supp. 1375, 1390 (E.D. Mich. 1995) (citations omitted).

thumbnail *(technology)*
A very small still image, usually about the size of a thumbnail.

TIA *(Internet)*
Abbreviation in electronic messages for "Thanks In Advance."

tie *(antitrust)*
"A tie exists when a seller refuses to sell a product (the tying product) alone and insists that any buyer who wants it must also purchase another product (the tied product)."
> *Allen-Myland, Inc. v. International Business Machines Corp.,* 693 F. Supp. 262, 268 (E.D. Pa. 1988).

tiff *(technology)*
Acronym for "Tagged Image File Format." A data format for high-resolution scanned images accessible by many different computer systems.

time and materials contract *(contract)*
"[One which] provides for acquiring supplies or services on the basis of (1) direct labor hours at specified fixed hourly rates that include wages, overhead, general and administrative expenses, and profit and (2) materials at cost, including, if appropriate, material handling costs as part of material costs."
> Fed. Acquisition Regs. § 16.601.

time bomb *(software)*
"[A] desirable program which performs some useful function such as logic, but which contains a parasite or viral infection within its logic which is undetectable upon casual review. . . . [M]ore properly called a 'time bomb' or 'logic bomb.'"
> *State v. Corcoran,* 5 Computer Cas (CCH) ¶ 47,108, at 66,617 n.1 (Wis. App. 1994).

See also **logic bomb; Trojan horse.**

time stamp *(electronic commerce)*
"[E]ither: (a) To append or attach to a message, digital signature, or certificate a digitally signed notation indicating at least the date, time, and identity of the person appending or attaching the notation; or (b) The notation thus appended or attached."
> Wash. Rev. Code § 19.34.020(37).

time-sharing *(technology)*
A method of operating a computer so that computer access can be furnished to a number of customers, essentially simultaneously.
> *Derived from First Data Corp. v. State Tax Comm'n,* 5 Computer L. Serv. Rep. (Callaghan) 1231 (Mass. App. Tax. Bd. 1976).

"[A] system of using a computer whereby a user has a terminal of some capability, some small, some large, and the terminal is hooked to the computer via telephone lines at some remote distance, and this allows the user to access the computer through the telephone lines and through his terminal."

> *Greyhound Computer Corp. v. IBM Corp.*, 559 F.2d 488, 494 n.9 (9th Cir. 1977), *quoted approvingly in Meites v. City of Chicago,* 1 Computer L. Cas. (CCH) ¶ 46,115, at 61,314, 61,316 (Ill. App. 1989).

"This business and its mechanisms are so set up that different customers can use the computer system simultaneously from their places of business through the use of telephone facilities."

> *Com-Share, Inc. v. Computer Complex, Inc.,* 3 Computer L. Serv. Rep. (Callaghan) 462, 464 (E.D. Mich. 1971).

See also time-sharing company; time-sharing computer network; time-sharing system.

time-sharing company *(business)*

Also written as "timesharing company."

"[O]ne that installs a terminal facility in the customer's business location; the terminal is connected to the time-sharing company's computer system via telephone communication lines. The end-user can then timeshare the computer system by means of the remote terminal for a fee."

> *Telex Corp. v. IBM Corp.,* 367 F. Supp. 258, 273 (N.D. Okla. 1973), *aff'd in part, rev'd in part,* 510 F.2d 894 (10th Cir.), *cert. dism.,* 423 U.S. 802 (1975), *quoted approvingly in Meites v. City of Chicago,* 1 Computer L. Cas. (CCH) ¶ 46,115, at 61,314, 61,316 (Ill. App. 1989).

See also time-sharing; time-sharing computer network; timesharing system.

time-sharing computer network *(technology)*

". . . consists of a central computer, which stores programs and performs all calculations, and user terminals. Individual users access the central computer through telephone connections and terminals located in their own offices. Typically, users pay some monthly fee for access privileges plus an hourly rate for time actually spent utilizing the central computer."

> *Flip Mortgage Corp. v. McElhone,* 841 F.2d 531 (4th Cir. 1988), *quoted approvingly in Meites v. City of Chicago,* 1 Computer L. Cas. (CCH) ¶ 46,115, at 61,314, 61,316 (Ill. App. 1989).

See also time-sharing; time-sharing company; timesharing system.

timesharing system *(technology)*

"This means that users of the computer system, the customers of the franchisees, would not have to be located at the situs of the computer hardware in order to utilize its services. Rather, each customer would have its own computer terminal. In order to gain access to the computer, the customer would dial a telephone number assigned to a port, or input of the computer. The terminal would then be connected to the computer by use of the telephone line."

> *Response of Carolina, Inc. v. Leasco Response Inc.,* 537 F.2d 1307, 1328 (5th Cir. 1976).

See also time-sharing; time-sharing company; time-sharing computer network.

timing mark *(technology)*

See timing track.

timing track *(technology)*

"[A] column of rectangles along the vertical side of the input paper or form which signals the scanner to read an area that has been programmed to be read. The rectangles correspond to the rows of bubbles [the response positions]. Each rectangle is referred to as a timing mark."

> *Moore Bus. Forms, Inc. v. National Computer Sys., Inc.,* 211 U.S.P.Q. (BNA) 909, 912 (T.T.A.B. 1981).

See also input document.

title *(contract)*

Ownership.

Sample clause. "Title to the Programs shall not pass from Licensor to Licensee or its end users, and the Programs and any master copies thereof shall at all times remain the sole and exclusive property of Licensor. Licensee acknowledges that by virtue of the licenses under this Agreement, Licensee acquires only the right to use for its internal business purposes (including marketing and distribution) the original and permitted duplicate copies of the Programs as described in this Agreement. In addition, Licensee shall not reproduce, modify or translate all or any part of the Programs or prepare derivative works therefrom without the prior written consent of Licensor."

TLD *(Internet)*

See top-level domain.

Toeppen *(trademark; domain name)*
Citation: Panavision Int'l, L.P. v. Toeppen, 938 F. Supp. 616 (C.D. Cal. 1996); 945 F. Supp. 1296 (C.D. Cal. 1996), *aff'd,* 141 F.3d 1316 (9th Cir. 1998).

Dennis Toeppen registered a large number of domain names, most of which were famous trademarks, in the hope that he would later be able to sell these domain names to the trademark owners for a substantial profit. This was one of several lawsuits brought by trademark owners against Toeppen in an effort to get the domain names from him. In this case, the trial court ruled that it had jurisdiction over the defendant, who was a "cyber pirate," as a consequence of his efforts to obtain large payments from a California company for the domain name in issue. It also held that in registering the "panavision.com" domain name and then attempting to sell it back to the plaintiff, Toeppen had violated both the federal and California antidilution statutes. The Ninth Circuit referred to Toeppen as a "cyberpirate." A similar result was reached in *Intermatic, Inc. v. Toeppen,* 947 F. Supp. 1227 (N.D. Ill. 1996).
See also **cybersquatter; trademark infringement.**

tool vendor *(Year 2000)*
A generic term for a Year 2000 vendor that provides a specific software "tool" to automate a common function, such as scanning for date references in a particular platform or language. Tool vendors often do not provide a complete solution to the Year 2000 problem. However, their tools can greatly enhance the productivity of the team during key phases of the technical solution process (e.g., impact analysis).

top-level domain *(Internet)*
Abbreviated as "TLD." In the domain name system, the highest level of the hierarchy after the root. In a domain name, that portion of the domain name that appears farthest to the right. The TLD initially denoted the intended function of that portion of the domain space. For example, ".com" was established for commercial users, ".org" for not-for-profit organizations, and ".net" for network service providers. The registration and propagation of TLDs has been performed by Network Solutions, Inc. ("NSI") under a five-year cooperative agreement with the National Science Foundation that expired in March 1998. There are five worldwide top-level domains (.com, .org, .net, .edu, and .int), two U.S.-only top-level domains (.mil and .gov), and numerous country code top-level domains (e.g., .us for the United States, .au for Australia, etc.).

"The Internet is divided into several 'top level' domains: .edu for education; .org for organizations; .gov for government entities; .net for networks; and .com for 'commercial[,]' which functions as the catchall domain for Internet users."

> *Panavision Int'l, L.P. v. Toeppen,* 141 F.3d 1316, 1318 (9th Cir. 1998). *See also Intermatic, Inc. v. Toeppen,* 947 F. Supp. 1227, 1231 (N.D. Ill. 1996).

Annotation. "[M]any of which describe the nature of the enterprise. Top-level domains include '.com' (commercial), '.edu', (educational), '.org' (non-profit and miscellaneous organizations), '.gov' (government), '.net' (networking provider), and '.mil' (military).

> *Brookfield Comm., Inc. v. West Coast Entertainment Corp.,* 174 F.3d 1036, 1044 (9th Cir. 1999).

"The domain-name combination must include a top-level domain ('TLD'), which can be <.com>, <.net>, <.org>, <.gov> or <.edu>, among others, although some, like <.gov> and <.edu>, are reserved for specific purposes."

> *Avery Dennison Corp. v. Sumpton,* 189 F.3d 868, 872 (9th Cir. 1999).

"Not only are the current gTLDs not expressive speech, but . . . any entity may currently apply for domain names within the gTLDs .com, .net, and .org, and therefore they may not convey any information about a website at all."

> *Name.Space, Inc. v. Network Solutions, Inc.,* 202 F.3d 573, 587 (2d Cir. 2000).

"Currently, there are no restrictions on the types of organizations that may register for the .com, .org, and .net gTLDs, but some gTLDs, such as .gov and .mil, indicate the nature of the entities maintaining websites in that portion of the domain space."

> *Name.Space, Inc. v. Network Solutions, Inc.,* 202 F.3d 573, 577 n.2 (2d Cir. 2000).

"The two-letter ccTLDs are determined pursuant to a list updated and maintained by the International Standards Organization ('ISO'), ISO 3166-1. *See* IANA, Country Code Top-Level Domains (CCTLDs) (last modified Oct. 31, 1999), <http://www.iana.org/cctld.html>. The list of current ccTLDs is available on the website of the ISO 3166 Maintenance Agency, which also contains additional information on the administration and content of this ISO standard. *See* ISO 3166 Maintenance Agency (ISO1366/MA) (last modified Dec. 3,1999), <http://www.din.de/gremien /nas/nabd/iso3166ma/index.html>."

> *Name.Space, Inc. v. Network Solutions, Inc.,* 202 F.3d 573, 577 n.3 (2d Cir. 2000).

See also **generic domain.**

top-level server *(Internet; technology)*

The computer that matches the domain name with the IP address of a domain name server that directs the user to the computer hosting the web page.

Annotation. "Once a URL is entered into the browser, the corresponding IP address is looked up in a process facilitated by a 'top level server.' In other words, all queries for addresses are routed to certain computers, the so-called 'top level servers.' The top level server matches the domain name to the IP address of a domain name server capable of directing the inquiry to the computer hosting the web page."

    Intermatic, Inc. v. Toeppen, 947 F. Supp. 1227, 1231 (N.D. Ill. 1996).

topography *(hardware)*

[CANADA] ". . . means a series of related images, however fixed or encoded, which represents the three-dimensional pattern of the layers constituting a semiconductor integrated circuit; and in which series, each image has the pattern or part of the pattern of the surface of the semiconductor integrated circuit in its final or any intermediate form."

    Semiconductor Chip Protection in Canada, Proposals for Legislation, Consumer and Corporate Affairs Canada (1985).

[EUROPE] "A series of related images, however fixed or encoded: (i) representing the three-dimensional pattern of the layers of which a semiconductor product is composed; and (ii) in which series, each image has the pattern or part of the pattern of a surface of the semiconductor product at any stage of its manufacture."

    EEC Council Directive, 87/54/EEC (OJ No. L.24, 27.1.87).

[UNITED KINGDOM] "The design, however expressed, of any of the following: (a) the pattern fixed, or intended to be fixed in or upon a layer of a semiconductor product; (b) the pattern fixed, or intended to be fixed, in or upon a layer of material in the course of, and for the purpose of, the manufacture of a semiconductor product; (c) the arrangement of the layers of a semiconductor product in relation to one another."

    U.K. Semiconductor Products (Protection of Topography) Regulations 1987.

See also **layout design; mask works.**

tortious interference with prospective contract or business relationships *(tort)*

"To establish a claim for tortious interference with prospective contract or business relationships under Texas law, a plaintiff must show: '(1) a reasonable probability that the parties would have entered into a contractual relationship, (2) an intentional and malicious act by the defendant that prevented the relationship from occurring, with the purpose of harming the plaintiff, (3) the defendant lacked privilege or justification to do the act, and (4) actual harm or damage resulted from the defendant's interference.'"

> *Alcatel USA, Inc. v. DGI Technologies, Inc.*, 166 F.3d 772, 797 (5th Cir. 1999).

Total News *(copyright; trademark; unfair competition)*
Citation: *The Washington Post Co. v. Total News, Inc.*, 97 Civ. 1190 (PKL) (S.D.N.Y. Feb. 20, 1997).

The defendant, Total News, Inc., is a web site owner that provides a portal to various news services available on the Internet. Total News's site, at the time of the complaint, was designed to frame the plaintiffs' sites, that is, place them within a window surrounded ("framed") by Total News's own content and advertising, so that the plaintiffs' web sites appeared to be "on" Total News's web site. The complaint asserted a number of claims against Total News, including misappropriation, trademark dilution, trademark infringement, false designation of origin, tortious interference with contract (with plaintiffs' advertisers), and copyright infringement.

On June 1997, the case was settled without any judicial decisions on the legality of framing. The following are relevant portions of the settlement agreement:

"4. Plaintiffs agree that Defendants may link from the totalnews.com website or any other website to any Plaintiff's website, provided that:

(a) Defendants may link to Plaintiffs' websites only via hyperlinks consisting of the names of the linked sites in plain text, which may be highlighted;

(b) Defendants may not use on any website, as hyperlinks or in any other way, any of Plaintiffs' proprietary logos or other distinctive graphics, video or audio material, nor may Defendants otherwise link in any manner reasonably likely to: (i) imply affiliation with, endorsement or sponsorship by any Plaintiff; (ii) cause confusion, mistake or deception; (iii) dilute plaintiffs' marks; or (iv) otherwise violate state or federal law;

(c) Defendants' link must operate in a manner consistent with paragraph 2; and

(d) each Plaintiff's agreement to permit linking by Defendants remains revocable, on 15 business days' notice in accordance with paragraph 14 below, at each Plaintiff's sole discretion. . . ."

See also **copyright; framing; trademark dilution; trademark infringement; unfair competition.**

trade dress infringement *(trademark)*

". . . focuses on 'the total image of plaintiff's product, package and advertising and compare[s] this with the defendant's image.'"

> *M. Kramer Mfg. Co. v. Andrews,* 783 F.2d 421, 448 n.25 (4th Cir. 1986), *quoting* 1 J. McCarthy, Trademark and Unfair Competition § 8:1, at 282-83 (2d ed. 1984).

Annotation. "In the Ninth Circuit, the burden of proving nonfunctionality is on the party claiming trade dress infringement. However, whether trade dress is functional is a question of fact. Nevertheless, the party claiming trade dress infringement must make some showing of nonfunctional features or a nonfunctional arrangement in order to avoid summary judgment."

> *Interactive Networks, Inc. v. NTN Comm., Inc.,* 875 F. Supp. 1398, 1406 (N.D. Cal. 1995) (citation omitted).

"To enjoin a competitor's use of a particular trade dress, a plaintiff must show two things: that his own trade dress has acquired a secondary meaning and that there is a likelihood that the defendant's use of that trade dress will confuse the public."

> *M. Kramer Mfg. Co. v. Andrews,* 783 F.2d 421, 448-49 (4th Cir. 1986).

See also **functionality.**

trade secret *(trade secret)*

"[A]ny formula, pattern, device or compilation of information which is used in one's business, and which give him an opportunity to obtain an advantage over competitors who do not know or use it. . . . A substantial element of secrecy must exist, so that, except by use of improper means, there would be difficulties in acquiring the information. . . . Protection is not based on a policy of rewarding or otherwise encouraging the development of secret processes or devices. The protection is merely against breach of faith and reprehensible means of learning another's secret."

> Restatement (First) of Torts § 757, comment b.

"[I]nformation, including a formula, pattern, compilation, program, device, method, technique, or process, that:

(i) derives independent economic value, actual or potential, from not being generally known to, and not being readily ascertainable by proper means by, other persons who can obtain economic value from its disclosure or use, and

(ii) is the subject of efforts that are reasonable under the circumstances to maintain its secrecy."

> Minn. Stat. § 325.C.01, subd. 5; La. Rev. Stat. 51:1431(4).

"[I]nformation, including a formula, pattern, compilation, program, device, method, technique, or process, that:

(i) derives independent economic value, actual or potential, from not being generally known to the public or to other persons who can obtain economic value from its disclosure or use, and

(ii) is the subject of efforts that are reasonable under the circumstances to maintain its secrecy."

Cal. Civ. Code § 3426(1)(d).

"[A]ll forms and types of financial, business, scientific, technical, economic, or engineering information, including patterns, plans, compilations, program devices, formulas, designs, prototypes, methods, techniques, processes, procedures, programs, or codes, whether tangible or intangible, and whether or how stored, compiled, or memorialized physically, electronically, graphically, photographically, or in writing if:

(A) the owner thereof has taken reasonable measures to keep such information secret;

(B) the information derives independent economic value, actual or potential, from not being generally known to, and not being readily ascertainable through proper means by, the public. . . ."

18 U.S.C. § 1839(3).

"[In the] more common . . . approach . . . the secret must be taken by improper means for the taking to give rise to liability. . . . Trade secrecy . . . allows the victim . . . to obtain damages based on the competitive value of the information taken. The second conception of trade secrecy . . . is that 'trade secret' picks out a class of socially valuable information that the law should protect even against non-trespassory or other lawful conduct."

Rockwell Graphic Sales, Inc. v. DEV Indus., Inc., 925 F.2d 174, 178 (7th Cir. 1991) (citation omitted).

" . . . is simply a piece of information the value of which to the creator of the information depends on its not being generally known. It is not a property right in the sense that a patent is, for it is perfectly lawful for a competitor to buy a product embodying a trade secret and unmask the secret by reverse engineering of the product. Only if the competitor (or anyone else for that matter) discovers the secret by breaking a contract or engaging in other unlawful or improper conduct can the individual or firm whose secret it was obtain a remedy."

Micro Data Base Sys., Inc. v. Dharma Sys., Inc., 148 F.3d 649, 657 (7th Cir. 1998).

Related issues. "Precisely because trade secret doctrine protects the discovery of ideas, processes, and systems which are explicitly precluded from coverage under copyright law, courts and commentators alike consider it a necessary and integral part of the intellectual property protection extended to computer programs."

> *Computer Assocs. Int'l, Inc. v. Altai, Inc.,* 982 F.2d 693, 717 (2d Cir. 1992).

"We recognize that computer software can qualify for trade secret protection under the UTSA."

> *MAI Sys. Corp. v. Peak Computer, Inc.,* 991 F.2d 511, 522 (9th Cir. 1993), *cert. dism.,* 510 U.S. 1033 (1994).

"[A] plaintiff who seeks relief for misappropriation of trade secrets must identify the trade secrets and carry the burden of showing that they exist."

> *MAI Sys. Corp. v. Peak Computer, Inc.,* 991 F.2d 511, 522 (9th Cir. 1993), *cert. dism.,* 510 U.S. 1033 (1994).

"Trade secrets rights do not survive when otherwise protectible information is disclosed to others, such as customers or the general public, 'who are under no obligation to protect [its] confidentiality. . . .' Trade secrets also do not survive when the alleged owner fails to take 'reasonable precautions' to keep the information secret."

> *Advanced Computer Servs. v. MAI Sys. Corp.,* 845 F. Supp. 356, 370 (E.D. Va. 1994).

"In determining whether given information constitutes a trade secret, this Court is required to examine the following factors: the extent to which the information is known outside of the owner's business; the extent to which it is known by employees and other [sic] involved in the owner's business; the extent of measures taken by the owner to guard the secrecy of the information; the value of the information to the owner and to his competitors; the amount of effort or money expended by the owner in developing the information; and the ease or difficulty with which the information could be properly acquired or duplicated by others."

> *Healthcare Affiliated Servs., Inc. v. Lippany,* 701 F. Supp. 1142, 1154-55 (W.D. Pa. 1988) (Pennsylvania law). *Accord SI Handling Sys., Inc. v. Heisley,* 753 F.2d 1244, 1256 (3d Cir. 1985).

Related issues. "[T]here is no difficulty in finding the existence of a trade secret in the source or object codes to computer programs."

> *Avtec Sys., Inc. v. Peiffer,* 21 F.3d 568, 575, 30 U.S.P.Q.2d (BNA) 1365, 1370 (4th Cir. 1994).

"[M]atters which are generally known in the trade or readily ascertainable by those in the trade cannot be made secret by being so labeled in an agreement."

> *Sarkes Tarzian, Inc. v. Audio Devices, Inc.,* 166 F. Supp. 250, 265 (S.D. Cal. 1958), *aff'd,* 283 F.2d 695 (9th Cir. 1960), *cert. denied,* 365 U.S. 869 (1961) (footnote omitted).

"[T]he MIS communications interface, as a whole, is not readily ascertainable by proper means. Even assuming for the moment that the wiretap method of intercepting transmissions . . . is a proper means of obtaining the information, by their own testimony [defendants] devoted more than 2,000 man hours to this project. [The evidence shows that defendants] 'spent a considerable amount of effort' before they were able to decipher two of the non-standard control and function codes used in the [plaintiff's] MIS. On this record, I conclude that the alleged trade secrets are 'not readily ascertainable.'"

> *Technicon Data Sys. Corp. v. Curtis 1000, Inc.,* 224 U.S.P.Q. (BNA) 286, 289-90 (Del. Ch. 1984).

"Two computer programs may be sufficiently dissimilar on the level of expression to defeat liability for copyright infringement, but they may be sufficiently similar on s more abstract or ideational level to establish liability for trade secret protection."

> *Comprehensive Technologies Int'l, Inc. v. Software Artisans, Inc.,* 3 F.3d 730, 736 nn. 6-7 (4th Cir. 1993).

See also **disclosure; improper means; proper means; public domain; reverse engineering.**

trademark *(trademark)*

". . . includes: any word, name, symbol, or device, or any combination thereof—

(1) used by a person, or

(2) which a person has a bona fide intention to use in commerce and applies to register on the principal register established by this chapter, to identify and distinguish his or her goods, including a unique product, from those manufactured or sold by others to indicate the source of the goods, even if that source is unknown."

> 15 U.S.C. §1127.

Annotation. "In trademark law, the spectrum of categories into which any mark involving words may fall, 'in their ascending order of eligibility for protection . . . are: (1) generic, (2) descriptive, (3) suggestive, and (4) arbitrary and fanciful.' Generic marks are entitled to the least protection (if any), while arbitrary and fanciful marks, . . . and suggestive marks, . . . are entitled to the most protection against infringement."

   Digital Equipment Corp. v. Altavista Technology, Inc., 960 F. Supp. 456, 478 (D. Mass. 1997).

"[S]ince trademarks and service marks are source-identifying, their purpose is to answer the questions 'Who are you?' and 'Where do you come from?'"

   America Online, Inc. v. AT&T Corp., 64 F. Supp. 2d 549, 559 (E.D. Va. 1999).

". . . are used to distinguish a producer's goods and services from those of his competitors. . . ."

   America Online, Inc. v. AT&T Corp., 64 F. Supp. 2d 549, 561 (E.D. Va. 1999) (citations omitted).

"The purpose of a trademark is to help consumers identify the source, but a mark cannot serve a source-identifying function if the public has never seen the mark and thus is not meritorious of trademark protection until it is used in public in a manner that creates an association among consumers between the mark and the mark's owner."

   Brookfield Comm., Inc. v. West Coast Entertainment Corp., 174 F.3d 1036, 1051 (9th Cir. 1999).

Related issues. "In short, the exclusive quality of second-level domain names has set trademark owners against each other in the struggle to establish a commercial presence on the Internet, and has set businesses against domain name holders who seek to continue the traditional use of the Internet as a non-commercial medium of communication."

   Lockheed Martin Corp. v. Network Solutions, Inc., 985 F. Supp. 949, 952 (C.D. Cal. 1997).

"If the Internet were a technically ideal system for commercial exploitation, then every trademark owner would be able to have a domain name identical to its trademark. But the parts of the Internet that perform the critical addressing functions still operate on the 1960s and 1970s technologies that were adequate when the Internet's function was to facilitate academic and military research. Commerce has entered the Internet only recently. In response, the Internet's existing addressing systems will have to evolve to accommodate conflicts among holders of intellectual property rights, and conflicts between commercial and noncommercial users of the Internet. 'In the long run, the most appropriate technology to access Web sites and e-mail will be directories that point to the desired Internet address. Directory technology of the necessary scale and complexity is not yet available, but when it is developed it will relieve much of the pressure on domain names.' [Citation omitted.] No doubt trademark owners would like to make the Internet safe for their intellectual property rights by reordering the allocation of existing domain names so that each trademark owner automatically owned the domain name corresponding to the owner's mark. Creating an exact match between Internet addresses and trademarks will require overcoming the problem of concurrent uses of the same trademark in different classes of goods and geographic areas. Various solutions to this problem are being discussed, such as a graphically-based Internet directory that would allow the presentation of trademarks in conjunction with distinguishing logos, new top-level domains for each class of goods, or a new top-level domains for trademarks only. The solution to the current difficulties faced by trademark owners on the Internet lies in the sort of technical innovation, not in attempts to assert trademark rights over legitimate nontrademark uses of this important new means of communication."

> *Lockheed Martin Corp. v. Network Solutions, Inc.*, 985 F. Supp. 949, 967-68 (C.D. Cal. 1997).

"An owner's rights in a trademark do not remain stable over time. The scope of the owner's rights is subject to contraction if the trademark is abandoned or becomes generic for all or part of the goods or services identified. This dynamic nature of trademark rights increases their inherent uncertainty."

> *Lockheed Martin Corp. v. Network Solutions, Inc.*, 985 F. Supp. 949, 963 (C.D. Cal. 1997).

"[T]rademark law permits multiple parties to use and register the same mark for different classes of goods and services."

> *Lockheed Martin Corp. v. Network Solutions, Inc.*, 985 F. Supp. 949, 964 (C.D. Cal. 1997).

"Internet users may also have a free speech interest in noninfringing uses of domain names that are similar or identical to trademarks."

> *Lockheed Martin Corp. v. Network Solutions, Inc.*, 985 F. Supp. 949, 964 n.9 (C.D. Cal. Cal. 1997).

"Sometimes, a trademark is better known than the company itself, in which case a Web surfer may assume that the domain address will be '"trademark".com'."

> *Brookfield Comm., Inc. v. West Coast Entertainment Corp.*, 174 F.3d 1036, 1045 (9th Cir. 1999) (citation omitted).

"Nothing in trademark law requires that title to domain names that incorporate trademarks or portions of trademarks be provided to trademark holders. Instead, the law simply prevents others from making use of a company's trademarks in a manner likely to confuse the consuming public."

Washington Speakers Bureau, Inc. v. Leading Authorities, Inc., 49 F. Supp. 2d 496, 498 (E.D. Va. 1999).

"[Domain name] registration in no way trumps federal trademark law. Registration of a mark or name with NSI does not itself confer any federal trademark rights on the registrant."

Washington Speakers Bureau, Inc. v. Leading Authorities, Inc., 33 F. Supp. 2d 488, 491 n.3 (E.D. Va. 1999) (citation omitted).

"'The degree of protection a trademark receives "is directly related to the mark's distinctiveness.' Courts applying §43(a) have categorized marks as 'fanciful,' 'arbitrary,' 'suggestive,' 'descriptive,' or 'generic,' in descending order of strength. The stronger the mark, the greater the degree of protection afforded by law. But there are no bright line demarcations between these categories; they are, instead, 'like colors in a spectrum, [that] tend to blur at the edges and merge together, making it difficult to apply the appropriate label.'"

Washington Speakers Bureau, Inc. v. Leading Authorities, Inc., 33 F. Supp. 2d 488, 494 (E.D. Va. 1999) (citations).

"When a mark is shown to be fanciful, arbitrary, or suggestive, its distinctiveness is presumed without further showing."

Washington Speakers Bureau, Inc. v. Leading Authorities, Inc., 33 F. Supp. 2d 488, 494-95 (E.D. Va. 1999).

"When a domain name is used only to indicate an address on the Internet and not to identify the source of specific goods and services, the name is not functioning as a trademark."

Data Concepts, Inc. v. Digital Consulting, Inc., 150 F.3d. 620, 627 (6th Cir. 1998) (Merritt, J., concurring).

Sample clause. "Company will (i) conduct business in a manner that reflects favorably at all times on the good name, goodwill, and reputation of Licensor; (ii) not engage in deceptive, misleading, or unethical practices that are or might be detrimental to Licensor; (iii) not make any false or misleading representation with regard to Licensor or its Software; (iv) not publish or utilize or cooperate in the publication or utilization of any misleading or deceptive advertising material that relates in any way to Licensor or its Software; (v) not make any representation or warranty to anyone with respect to the specifications, features, or capabilities of Licensor's Software that are inconsistent with the literature distributed by Licensor, including all disclaimers contained in such literature; (vi) not make any warranty or representation to anyone that would give the recipient any claim or right of action against Licensor; and (vii) not engage in illegal or deceptive trade practices with respect to the Licensor Programs or its own hardware.

"Licensee acknowledges that Licensor. is the exclusive owner of the mark, and shall undertake no action that will interfere with or diminish Licensor's right, title or interest in the Mark. Licensee shall not alter or re-create the Mark in any manner, and will display the Mark only in conjunction with its own trademarks and trade name and only in a manner that does not suggest that the Mark is Licensee's mark or part of a composite mark. Licensee shall not use or advertise any other certification mark, trademark, or symbol which, in Licensor's opinion, may be confusingly similar to or an imitation of the Mark.

"Only Licensor shall have the right to complain to third parties concerning the Mark and to take any action to enforce or protect the Mark. However, Licensee shall notify Licensor promptly of any infringement, violation, or misuse of the Mark which comes to Licensee's attention and, when requested by Licensor, shall cooperate with Licensor in protecting the Mark."

See also **domain name; generic.**

trademark dilution *(trademark)*

See dilution; Federal Trademark Dilution Act.

trademark infringement *(trademark)*

"To prove infringement, a trademark owner must prove that the competing use of the mark is capable of generating a likelihood of confusion concerning the source of its product."

Stratus Computer, Inc. v. NCR Corp., 2 U.S.P.Q.2d (BNA) 1375, 1378 (D. Mass. 1981).

"To prevail on a trademark infringement claim under §1125 (for unregistered service marks), a plaintiff must both demonstrate '(1) that it has a valid and protectible [mark] and (2) that the defendant's use of the mark in question creates a likelihood of consumer confusion.'"

America Online, Inc. v. AT&T Corp., 64 F. Supp. 2d 549, 562 (E.D. Va. 1999) (citation omitted).

"As an essential element of a trademark infringement action, regardless of whether the trademark or trade name is registered or unregistered, a plaintiff must prove that a defendant's use of a particular name 'creates a likelihood of confusion, deception, or mistake among an appreciate number of ordinary buyers as to the source of or association' between the two marks.

* * *

"Factors pertinent to a finding of likelihood of confusion include: (1) the strength of the trademark; (2) the similarity between the plaintiff's and defendant's marks; (3) the competitive proximity of the parties' products; (4) the alleged infringer's intent to confuse the public; (5) evidence of any actual confusion; (6) the degree of care reasonably expected of the plaintiff's potential customers."

> *Maritz, Inc. v. Cybergold, Inc.,* 947 F. Supp. 1338, 1340 (E.D. Mo. 1996) (citation omitted).

Related issues. "The use of an identical or similar mark does not necessarily constitute infringement. In order to be infringing, such use must be in connection with goods or services that are competitive with, or at least related to, the goods or services for which the trademark has been registered or used in commerce. The use must also cause a likelihood of confusion as to origin or sponsorship. Whether a use is likely to cause confusion depends on numerous variables including the strength of the mark, the proximity of the goods, the similarity of the marks, evidence of actual confusion, marketing channels used, the type of goods and degree of care used by purchasers, the defendant's intent in selecting the mark, and the likelihood of expansion of product lines."

> *Lockheed Martin Corp. v. Network Solutions, Inc.,* 985 F. Supp. 949, 963 (C.D. Cal. 1997) (citation omitted).

See also **contributory infringement; Lanham Act.**

trades *(business)*

Periodicals that focus on a particular industry. In the entertainment industry, the trades include the *Hollywood Reporter* and *Daily Variety.* In the multimedia industry, the trades include *New Media* and *Wired.*

traffic

(criminal)

"[To] transfer, or otherwise dispose of, to another, or to obtain control of with intent to transfer or dispose of."

> 18 U.S.C. § 1029(e)(5).

(Internet)

The volume of Internet users that visit a specific web site, newsgroup, or other location online.

traffic in *(copyright)*

"[T]ransport, transfer, or otherwise dispose of, to another, as consideration for anything of value, or make or obtain control of with intent to transport, transfer, or dispose of.

17 U.S.C. § 1101(b).

trailer *(entertainment; multimedia)*

A short promotional videotape (or disc) used to create interest in an interactive product.

transaction code *(technology)*

"[A] randomly selected, alphanumeric sequence of characters that indicates to the computer what steps should be executed in a given situation or 'transaction' when the code is transmitted."

CMAX/Cleveland, Inc. v. UCR, Inc., 804 F. Supp. 337, 349 n.8 (M.D. Ga. 1992).

transaction costs *(business)*

Those expenditures that a proprietor must make to negotiate and execute a transaction agreement.

transactional certificate *(electronic commerce)*

"[A] valid certificate incorporating by reference one or more digital signatures."

Wash. Rev. Code § 19.34.020(38).

transfer *(contract)*

"(A) with respect to a contractual interest, includes an assignment of the contract, but does not include an agreement merely to perform a contractual obligation or to exercise contractual rights through a delegate or sublicensee; and

(B) with respect to computer information, includes a sale, license, or lease of a copy of the computer information and a license or assignment of informational rights in computer information."

UCITA § 102(a)(65).

See also **assignment.**

transfer of copyright ownership *(copyright)*

"[A]n assignment, mortgage, exclusive license, or any other conveyance, alienation, or hypothecation of a copyright or of any of the exclusive rights comprised in a copyright, whether or not it is limited in time or place of effect, but not including a nonexclusive license."

U.S. Copyright Act, 17 U.S.C. §101.

"A transfer of copyright ownership, other than by operation of law, is not valid unless an instrument of conveyance, or note or memorandum of the transfer, is in writing and signed by the owner of the rights conveyed or such owner's duly authorized agent."

U.S. Copyright Act, 17 U.S.C. § 204(a).

Related issues. "Transfer of ownership of any material object, including the copy or phonorecord in which the work is first fixed, does not of itself convey any rights in the copyrighted work embodied in the object; nor, in the absence of an agreement, does transfer of ownership of a copyright or of any exclusive rights under a copyright convey property rights in any material object."

17 U.S.C. § 202.

transfer rate *(technology)*

A measure of the rate at which digital information can be transferred from one place within a multimedia system to another.

transformative use *(copyright)*

A use of a copyrighted work that changes the work in some creative manner.

Annotation. "Although such transformative use is not absolutely necessary for a finding of fair use, . . . the goal of copyright, to promote science and useful arts, is generally furthered by the creation of transformative works. Such works thus lie at the heart of the fair use doctrine's guarantee of breathing space within the confines of copyright, . . . and the more transformative the new work, the less likely will be the significance of other factors, like commercialism, that may weigh against a finding of fair use."

Campbell v. Acuff-Rose Music, Inc., 510 U.S. 569, 579, 114 S. Ct. 1164, 1171 (1994).

See also **fair use.**

transformative work(s) *(copyright)*

" . . . have greater recourse to the fair use defense as they 'lie at the heart of the fair use doctrine's guarantee of breathing space within the confines of copyright . . . and the more transformative the new work, the less will be the significance of other factors, like commercialism, that may weigh against a finding of fair use.'"

Micro Star v. FormGen, Inc., 154 F.3d 1107, 1113 n.6 (9th Cir. 1998).

"[T]he more transformative the new work, the less will be the significance of other factors, like commercialism, that may weigh against a finding of fair use."

Campbell v. Acuff-Rose Music, 510 U.S. 569, 579 (1994).

transistor *(technology)*

"[A] semiconductor device with three electrodes called emitter, collector, and base region. It performs most of the functions of a vacuum tube with the added advantages of longer life, ruggedness, and small size. Its typical uses are as an amplifier and as an electrical switch."

Sperry Rand Corp. v. Rothlein, 241 F. Supp. 549, 552 (D. Conn. 1964).

transition *(multimedia)*

The portion of a game where the user is moving from one scene to another.

transitory duration *(copyright)*

" . . . is a relative term that must be interpreted and applied in context. This concept is particularly important in cases involving computer technology where speed and complexity of machines and software is rapidly advancing, and where the diversity of computer architecture and software design is expanding at an ever increasing rate."

Triad Sys. Corp. v. Southwestern Express Co., 31 U.S.P.Q.2d (BNA) 1239 (N.D. Cal. 1994).

translation *(copyright; software)*

"The conversion of a program from one higher-level language to another to facilitate use would fall within this right, as would the right to add features to the program that were not present at the time of rightful acquisition."

CONTU Final Report 13 (1978).

Related issues. "[I]t is as clear an infringement to translate a computer program from, for example, FORTRAN to ALGOL, as it is to translate a novel or play from English to French. In each case the substance of the expression (if one may speak in such contradictory language) is the same between original and copy, with only the external manifestation of the expression changing. Likewise, it would probably be a violation to take a detailed description of a particular problem solution, such as a flow chart or step-by-step set of prose instructions, written in human language, and program such a description in computer language."

Synercom Technology, Inc. v. University Computing Co., 462 F. Supp. 1003, 1013 (M.D. Tex. 1978).

"[I]t would be very difficult if not impossible to literally translate a program written in EDL to a program written in BASIC. The evidence makes clear that transferring or converting from one computer language to another is not comparable to translating a book written in English to French. At least, it would be a very inefficient method of copying of a program to attempt to work solely from the source code and literally translate it from EDL to BASIC."

Whelan Assocs., Inc. v. Jaslow Dental Labs., Inc., 225 U.S.P.Q. (BNA) 156, 166 (E.D. Pa. 1985).

Transmission Control Protocol/Internet Protocol *(technology)*
See TCP/IP.

transmission controller *(technology)*
". . . provides communication for a group of terminal devices. The controller provides message handling, screen formatting, and error handling functions."
IRS Letter Ruling 8721016, Feb. 17, 1987.

transmission program *(copyright)*
"[A] body of material that, as an aggregate, has been produced for the sole purpose of transmission to the public in sequence and as a unit."
U.S. Copyright Act, 17 U.S.C. §101.

transmit *(copyright)*
"To 'transmit' a performance or display is to communicate it by any device or process whereby images or sounds are received beyond the place from which they are sent."
U.S. Copyright Act, 17 U.S.C. §101.

transparent multi-vendor networking solution *(technology)*
"[A]ny-to-any connections such that the user remains unaware of what system it is physically connected to or what system its applications are running on."
IBM Corp. v. Fujitsu Ltd., Copyright L. Rep. (CCH) ¶ 20,517 (Am. Arb. Ass'n 1988).

trap and trace *(criminal)*
". . . means using a device that captures the incoming electronic or other impulses which identify the originating phone number of an instrument or device from which a wire or electronic communication was transmitted."
Office of the Comptroller of the Currency, Infrastructure Threats from Cyber-Terrorists 5 (Mar. 19, 1999).

trap door *(technology)*

"[A] hidden software or hardware mechanism that allows systems controls to be circumvented. Software developers often introduce trap doors in their code to enable them to reenter the system later and perform certain functions."

> U.S. General Accounting Office, *Information Superhighway: An Overview of Technology Changes* 27 n.19 (Jan. 1995).

trespass *(tort)*

"One is subject to liability to another for trespass, irrespective of whether he thereby causes harm to any legally protected interest of the other, if he intentionally

(a) enters land in the possession of the other, or causes a thing or a third person to do so, or

(b) remains on the land, or

(c) fails to remove from the land a thing which he is under a duty to remove."

> Rest. (Second) of Torts § 158 (1965).

Related issues. "To the extent that defendants' multitudinous electronic mailings demand the disk space and drain the processing power of plaintiff's computer equipment, those resources are not available to serve CompuServe subscribers. Therefore, the value of that equipment to CompuServe is diminished even though it is not physically damaged by defendants' conduct."

> *CompuServe, Inc. v. Cyber Promotions, Inc.,* 962 F. Supp. 1015, 1022 (S.D. Ohio 1997).

trespass to chattels *(tort)*

". . . occurs when one party intentionally uses or intermeddles with personal property in rightful possession of another without authorization."

> *America Online, Inc. v. IMS,* 24 F. Supp. 2d 548, 550 (E.D. Va. 1998), *citing* Restatement (Second) of Torts § 217(b). *See also CompuServe, Inc. v. Cyber Promotions, Inc.,* 962 F. Supp. 1015 (S.D. Ohio 1997).

". . . lies where an intentional interference with the possession of personal property has proximately caused injury."

> *Thrifty-Tel v. Bezenek,* 46 Cal. App. 4th 1559, 1566 (1996).

TRIPS *(general)*

Abbreviation for "Trade-Related Aspects of Intellectual Property Rights." Part of an agreement prepared by the World Intellectual Property Organization that addresses the international protection of intellectual property rights.

Trojan horse *(criminal; software)*

"[A] program that conceals malicious computer code. Typically, a Trojan horse masquerades as a useful program that users would want or need to execute. It performs, or appears to perform, as expected, but also does surreptitious harm."

> U.S. General Accounting Office, *Information Superhighway: An Overview of Technology Changes* 20 n.7 (Jan. 1995).

"[A] program that appears to perform a useful function, and sometimes does so quite well, but also includes an unadvertised feature, which is usually malicious in nature."

> Office of the Comptroller of the Currency, Infrastructure Threats from Cyber-Terrorists 2 (Mar. 19, 1999).

"[A] desirable program which performs some useful function such as logic, but which contains a parasite or viral infection within its logic which is undetectable upon casual review. . . . [M]ore properly called a 'time bomb' or 'logic bomb.'"

> *State v. Corcoran,* 5 Computer Cas (CCH) ¶ 47,108, at 66,617 n.1 (Wis. App. 1994).

true font *(technology)*

". . . in the actual type style that would be used."

> *In re Bedford Corp.,* 62 Bankr. 555, 557 n.1 (D.N.H. 1986).

trunk *(telecommunications)*

"Because the telephone industry has more users than it has circuits, it 'trunks' or pools circuits so that an open circuit can be automatically selected whenever a call is made. Not every owner of a telephone has a private 'line.' Rather, the system takes advantage of pauses in speech to create a single uninterrupted communications montage."

> *E.F. Johnson Co. v. Uniden Corp. of America,* 623 F. Supp. 1485, 1489 n.1 (D. Minn. 1985).

See also **trunking.**

trunk system *(telecommunications)*

See **trunk; trunking.**

trunking *(telecommunications)*

" '[T]runking' of frequency channels permits the system to afford all system users automatic access to all channels for maximum efficiency. Rather than assigning each user a discrete channel, the trunked system, through

the use of sophisticated computer software, patches together unutilized airwave 'spaces' to create an uninterrupted channel of communication."
> *E.F. Johnson Co. v. Uniden Corp. of America,* 623 F. Supp. 1485, 1489 (D. Minn. 1985).

trusted host(s) *(technology)*
"[A] feature, which permits a user with certain privileges on one computer to have equivalent privileges on another computer without using a password."
> *United States v. Morris,* 928 F.2d 504, 506 (2d Cir. 1991).

trustworthy system *(electronic commerce)*
"[C]omputer hardware and software that: (a) Are reasonably secure from intrusion and misuse; (b) Provide a reasonable level of availability, reliability, and correct operation; and (c) Are reasonably suited to performing their intended functions."
> Wash. Rev. Code § 19.34.020(39).

tumbling *(telecommunications)*
"[C]hanging either the ESN or the MIN (or both) programmed into a particular cellular telephone instrument, often using numbers chosen at random."
> *United States v. Brady,* 820 F. Supp. 1346, 1348 n.7 (D. Utah 1993).

See also **ESN; MIN; free-riding.**

turnaround *(business)*
The status of an interactive project when a publisher or other entity funding development decides not to continue and offers it to others for completion.

turnkey computer system *(technology)*
"[A] system sold as a package which is ready to function immediately."
> *Neilson Bus. Equip. Corp. v. Monteleone,* 524 A.2d 1172, 1174 (Del. 1987), cited in *USM Corp. v. Arthur D. Little, Inc.,* 28 Mass. App. 108, 546 N.E.2d 888, 893 n.9 (1989).

". . . is defined in the plaintiff's complaint as 'hardware and software in a complete package such that a purchaser could utilize it for his business as a working system without having to perform any additional programming or systems work.'"
> *Management Consultants, Ltd. v. Data General Corp.,* 8 Computer L. Serv. Rep. 66 (E.D. Va. 1980).

See also **turnkey system.**

turnkey system *(technology)*

"[S]oftware pre-prepared and the system ready for immediate functioning."
Triangle Underwriters, Inc. v. Honeywell, Inc., 457 F. Supp. 765, 767
(E.D.N.Y. 1978), *aff'd in part, rev'd in part,* 604 F.2d 737 (2d Cir. 1979).

"[A] system which is pre-prepared and can be virtually plugged right in and
ready to function immediately."
Triangle Underwriters, Inc. v. Honeywell, Inc., 604 F.2d 737, 740 n.3 (2d Cir.
1979).

"[I]ts system would be a 'turn-key' system (Count I), able to 'function
immediately in place of [Triangle's] present system' (Count II). Count III
alleges an oral contract to install a 'turnkey' system that would be capable
of operating within a relatively short period of time."
Triangle Underwriters, Inc. v. Honeywell, Inc., 604 F.2d 737, 741 (2d Cir.
1979).

"[O]ne which is fully operative when turned over to plaintiff."
Wm. C. Brown Co. v. General Automation, Inc., 8 Computer L. Serv. Rep. 19
(N.D. Iowa 1978).

". . . is intended to describe a self-sufficient system in which the purchaser
need only 'turn the key' to commence operation."
Diversified Graphics v. Groves, 868 F.2d 293, 297 (8th Cir. 1989).

"[A] system sold as a package which is ready to function immediately. The
hardware and software elements are combined into a single unit—the computer system—prior to sale."
Neilson Bus. Equip. Center, Inc. v. Monteleone, 524 A.2d 1172, 1174 (Del.
1987).

"[O]ne that is easily adapted for various uses, requiring a minimum
amount of reprogramming to be modified for a particular user. It can be
used almost straight 'off the shelf.'"
Computer Sys. Eng'g, Inc. v. Qantel Corp., 740 F.2d 59, 63 n.4 (1st Cir.
1984).

"Frequently, software is sold with the hardware as part of a 'turn-key' system, able to be turned on and function immediately in place at the
vendee's place of business."
Dreier Co. v. Unitronix Corp., 218 N.J. Super. 260, 267, 527 A.2d 875, 879
(1986).

"[T]he providing of an item of personal or real property which can be
made operational by the insertion of a key or other triggering device which

will cause the property involved to become usable and useful for the purposes for which it has been acquired."

> *In re* BKW Sys., Inc., 2 Computer Cas. (CCH) ¶ 46,263, at 62,011 (Bkrtcy. N.H. 1989).

See also **turnkey computer system.**

turnover *(business)*

A measure of how quickly inventory is being replaced. The higher the turnover, the better a product is selling.

turns *(business)*

See **turnover.**

2600 *(general)*

"The name '2600' was derived from the fact that hackers in the 1960's found that the transmission of a 2600 hertz tone over a long distance trunk connection gained access to 'operator mode' and allowed the user to explore aspects of the telephone system that were not otherwise accessible."

> *Universal City Studios, Inc. v. Reimerdes*, 111 F. Supp. 2d 294, 308 (S.D.N.Y. 2000).

twitch games *(video game)*

Video games that rely more on fast reflexes than on thinking.

tying arrangement *(antitrust)*

"[A]n agreement by a party to sell one product but only on the condition that the buyer also purchases a different (or tied) product, or at least agrees that he will not purchase that product from any other supplier."

> *United States v. IBM Corp.*, 163 F.3d 737, 738 n.1 (2d Cir. 1998) (citations omitted) (citing *Northern Pacific Ry. Co. v. United States*, 356 U.S. 1, 5-6 (1958)).

" . . . will violate section 1 of the Sherman Act if 'the seller has appreciable economic power in the tying product market and if the arrangement affects a substantial volume of commerce in the tied market.'"

> *United States v. IBM Corp.*, 163 F.3d 737, 738 n.1 (2d Cir. 1998) (citations omitted) (citing *Eastman Kodak Co. v. Image Technical Servs., Inc.*, 504 U.S. 451, 462 (1992)).

Annotation. "The evil of tying 'lies in the seller's exploitation of its control over the tying product to force the buyer into the purchase of the tied product.' The tied product market is thereby distorted. Four essential elements must be established to prove an illegal tying arrangement under either a *per se* or rule of reason theory. They are:

(1) The existence of two separate products;

(2) An agreement conditioning purchase of the tying product upon purchase of the tied product or upon agreement not to purchase;

(3) Seller's possession of sufficient economic power in tying product to restrain competition in tied product market; and

(4) A not insubstantial impact on interstate commerce."

Advanced Computer Serv. v. MAI Sys. Corp., 845 F. Supp. 356, 368 (E.D. Va. 1994), *cert. dism.,* 510 U.S. 1033 (1994).

See also **tie.**

typeface *(technology)*

"[A] set of letters, numbers, or other symbolic characters, whose forms are related by repeating design elements consistently applied in a notational system and are intended to be embodied in articles whose intrinsic utilitarian function is for use in composing text or other cognizable combinations of characters."

U.S. Library of Congress, Copyright Office, 53 Fed. Reg. 38110 (Sept. 18, 1988), *quoting* H.R. Rep. No. 1476, 94th Cong., 2d Sess. 55 (1976). *See also Eltra Corp. v. Ringer,* 579 F.2d 294, 296 n.2 (4th Cir. 1978).

See also **digital typefont; font.**

T1 *(telecommunications)*

A dedicated telecommunications line capable of transmitting at 1.54 Mbps.

T-3 *(telecommunications)*

A dedicated telecommunications line capable of transmitting at 44.7 Mbps, which permits full-screen, full-motion video.

U.C.C. *(contract)*
Abbreviation for "Uniform Commercial Code."

"Underlying purposes and policies of the Act are
    (a) to simplify, clarify and modernize the law governing commercial transactions;
    (b) to permit the continued expansion of commercial practices through custom, usage and agreement of the parties;
    (c) to make uniform the law among the various jurisdictions."
U.C.C. § 1-102.

Annotation. "Applying the U.C.C. to computer software transactions offers substantial benefits to litigants and the courts. The Code offers a uniform body of law on a wide ranger of questions likely to arise in computer software disputes: implied warranties, consequential damages, disclaimers of liability, the statute of limitations, to make a few. . . . The importance of software to the commercial world and the advantages to be gained by uniformity inherent in the U.C.C. are strong policy arguments favoring inclusion. The contrary arguments are not persuasive . . . ."
    Advent Systems, Inc. v. Unisys Corp., 925 F.2d 670, 676 (3d Cir. 1991).

Related issues. "A 'sale' is defined as 'the passing of title from the seller to the buyer for a price.' A pure license agreement . . . does not involve transfer of title, and so is not a sale for Article 2 purposes."
    Berthold Types Ltd. v. Abode Sys., Inc., 101 F. Supp. 2d 697, 698 (E.D. Ill. 2000).

"Because the predominant feature of the [agreement] was a transfer of intellectual property rights, the agreement is not subject to Article 2 of the U.C.C."
    Architectronics, Inc. v. Control Sys., Inc., 935 F. Supp. 425, 432 (S.D.N.Y. 1996).
See also **good(s)**.

U.C.C. applicability clause *(contract)*

In situations in which the applicability of the Uniform Commercial Code may be in doubt (e.g., when services may be more significant than the goods, or when the transaction is not a sale, but something else), the parties may include a clause indicating their intention to have the U.C.C. apply.

Sample clause. "Except to the extent that the provisions of this Agreement are inconsistent therewith, this Agreement shall be governed by the Uniform Commercial Code. To the extent that there are any services to be rendered in performance of the terms of this Agreement, such services shall be deemed 'goods' within the definition of such Code, except where deeming such services as 'goods' would be clearly unreasonable."

U.C.C. Article 2B *(contract)*

"Article 2B deals with transactions in information; it focuses on a subgroup of transactions in the 'copyright industries' associated with transactions involving software, on-line and internet commerce in information and licenses involving data, text, images and similar information. It excludes core licensing activities in many traditional fields of licensing including patent, motion picture, and broadcasting, but covers transactions in digital and related industries. In the digital economy, information industries are rapidly converging into a multi-faceted industry with common concerns. That converged industry exceeds in importance the goods manufacturing sector."

Aug. 1, 1998 Draft of U.C.C. Article 2B, Introduction, available at <http://www.law.uh.edu/ucc2b/080198/download.html>.

U.C.C. Article 4 *(contract)*

A uniform code developed primarily to deal with risks and responsibilities of the parties to wholesale wire transfers. However, Article 4 also covers electronic credit transfers.

UCITA *(contract)*

Acronym for "Uniform Computer Information Transactions Act."

"In 1999 the National Conference of Commissioners on Uniform State Laws promulgated the Uniform Computer Information Transactions Act (UCITA) to cover agreements to 'create, modify, transfer, or license computer information or informational rights in computer information.' The UCITA, formerly known as proposed U.C.C. Article 2B, was approved and recommended for enactment by the states in July 1999."

M.A. Mortenson Co., Inc. v. Timberline Software Corp., 998 P.2d 305, 310 n.6 (Wash. 2000), *aff'g* 93 Wash. App. 819, 970 P.2d 803 (1999).

UHF *(technology)*
Acronym for "Ultra High Frequency."

unauthorized access (to stored wire or electronic communications) *(criminal)*
"Except as provided in subsection (c) of this section whoever—
(1) intentionally accesses without authorization a facility through which an electronic communication service is provided; or
(2) intentionally exceeds an authorization to access that facility; and thereby obtains, alters, or prevents authorized access to a wire or electronic communication while it is in electronic storage in such system shall be punished. . . ."
18 U.S.C. § 2701(a).

unauthorized access device *(criminal)*
"[A]ny access device that is lost, stolen, expired, revoked, canceled, or obtained with intent to defraud. . . ."
18 U.S.C. § 1029(e)(3).
See also **access device.**

unauthorized signature *(contract)*
"[O]ne made without actual, implied, or apparent authority and includes a forgery."
U.C.C. § 1-201(43).

UNCITRAL *(organization)*
Acronym for "United Nations Commission on International Trade Law."

unclean hands *(copyright)*
"The doctrine of unclean hands is an equitable defense which provides that a party must have acted fairly and justly in its dealings with another in order to assert a cause of action against that party. A party is said to possess 'unclean hands' if it is guilty of conduct involving fraud or bad faith. If you find that either party acted in a fraudulent, underhanded, unfair or unjust manner then you may conclude that party had 'unclean hands.'"
Alcatel USA, Inc. v. DGI Technologies, Inc., 166 F.3d 772, 796 (5th Cir. 1999).

unconscionability *(contract)*
"If the court as a matter of law finds the contract or any clause of the contract to have been unconscionable at the time it was made, the court may refuse to enforce the contract, or it may enforce the remainder of the

contract without the unconscionable clause, or it may so limit the application of any unconscionable clause as to avoid any unconscionable result."
  U.C.C. § 2-302(1) (1979).

Annotation. "The basic test [for unconscionability] is whether, in the light of the general commercial background and the commercial needs of the particular trade or case, the clauses involved are so one-sided as to be unconscionable under the circumstances existing at the time of the making of the contract. . . . The principle is one of the prevention of oppression and unfair surprise and not of disturbance of allocation of risks because of superior bargaining power."
  U.C.C. § 2-302, comment 1 (1979) (citations omitted).

"Only such provisions of the standardized form which fail to comport with [the] reasonable expectations [of the parties] and which are unexpected and unconscionably unfair are held to be unenforceable."
  Hartland Computer Leasing Corp. v. Insurance Man, Inc., 770 S.W.2d 525, 527 (Mo. App. 1989).

"The principle is one of the prevention of oppression and unfair surprise . . . and not of disturbance of allocation of risks because of superior bargaining power."
  Harper Tax Servs., Inc. v. Quick Tax Ltd., 686 F. Supp. 106 (D. Md. 1988).

Related issues. "Consequential damages may be limited or excluded unless the limitation or exclusion is unconscionable. Limitations of consequential damages for injury to the person in the case of consumer goods is prima facie unconscionable but limitations of damage where the loss is commercial is not."
  U.C.C. § 2-719(3) (1979).

"That the agreement was an adhesion contract . . . does not lead to the conclusion that it was unconscionable: parties routinely purchase products without expecting to negotiate the terms of sale with the seller and there is 'nothing unusual' in this limitation of damages, it being common in these types of commercial agreements."
  Harper Tax Servs., Inc. v. Quick Tax Ltd., 686 F. Supp. 109, 112 (D. Md. 1988), *quoting Bakal v. Burroughs Corp.,* 74 Misc.2d 202, 205, 343 N.Y.S.2d 541 (1972).

unfair competition *(tort)*

"[A]ny unlawful, unfair or fraudulent business act or practice and unfair, untrue or misleading advertising. . . ."
  Cal. Bus & Prof. Code § 17200.

Annotation. "Unfair competition is almost universally regarded as a question of whether the defendant is passing off his goods or services as those of the plaintiff by virtue of substantial similarity between the two, leading to confusion on the part of potential customers."

> *Digital Equipment Corp. v. Altavista Technology, Inc.,* 960 F. Supp. 456, 476 n.40 (D. Mass. 1997) (citation omitted).

"Unfair competition, which 'bans "any form of commercial immorality." A cause of action for unfair competition requires unfairness and an unjustifiable attempt to profit from another's expenditure of time, labor and talent.'

* * *

"Unfair competition is an imprecisely defined cause of action in New York. There appear to be 'few limits on this evolving tort.' '[I]ts confines are marked only by the "conscience, justice and equity of common-law judges."'"

> *MTV Networks, Inc. v. Curry,* 867 F. Supp. 202, 207 (S.D.N.Y. 1994) (citations omitted).

Uniform Commercial Code *(contract)*
See U.C.C.; U.C.C. Article 2B.

Uniform Computer Information Transactions Act *(contract)*
Abbreviated as "UCITA." *See* UCITA.

Uniform Resource Locator *(Internet)*
See URL.

Uniform Trade Secrets Act *(trade secret)*
Abbreviated as "UTSA."

". . . codifies the basic principles of common law trade secret protection."

> *MAI Sys. Corp. v. Peak Computer, Inc.,* 991 F.2d 511, 5212 (9th Cir. 1993), *cert. dism.,* 510 U.S. 1033 (1994).

Related issues. "To establish a violation under the UTSA, it must be shown that a defendant has been unjustly enriched by the improper appropriation, use or disclosure of a 'trade secret.'"

> *MAI Sys. Corp. v. Peak Computer, Inc.,* 991 F.2d 511, 5212 (9th Cir. 1993), *cert. dism.,* 510 U.S. 1033 (1994).

See also trade secret.

unique visitor(s) *(Internet)*
The number of individuals who visit a web site within a specific time period.

unit testing *(technology)*
Testing to determine that individual program modules perform according to specification.

United Nations Convention on Contracts for the International Sale of Goods *(contract)*
An international convention that member states agreed will apply to contracts between members states, unless the parties opt out of the provisions of the Convention. The Convention was prepared by the United Nations Commission on International Trade Law (UNCITRAL).

Sample clause. "The parties agree that the rights and obligations under this Agreement shall not be governed by the U.N. Convention on Contracts for the International Sale of Goods, the application of which is expressly excluded, but shall be governed instead by the laws of the State of _____, excluding the application of its conflicts of laws rules."

United States *(copyright)*
"[W]hen used in a geographical sense, comprises the several States, the District of Columbia and the Commonwealth of Puerto Rico, and the organized territories under the jurisdiction of the United States Government."
U.S. Copyright Act, 17 U.S.C. § 101.

UNIX *(software)*
"[A] software program which controls the operation of computer hardware and the interaction of software applications on that hardware."
Infosystems Technology, Inc. v. Logical Software, Inc., 8 Computer L. Serv. Rep. 689, 697 (D. Md. 1985).

"[A] very popular operating system for larger computers."
Addamax Corp. v. Open Software Found., Inc., 152 F.3d 48, 49 (1st Cir. 1998).

Annotation. "In the late 1960s and early 1970s, AT&T developed UNIX, a computer operating system facilitating communications over the Internet. Once a user connects to UNIX, the UNIX system checks to see if the user has e-mail in an electronic mailbox when the user logs in, and every time a command is executed."
America Online, Inc. v. AT&T Corp., 64 F. Supp. 2d 549, 555 (E.D. Va. 1999).

unjust enrichment *(contract)*

"An award not reduced by the benefit received by the plaintiff would be too large to be compensatory, and so it would be punitive, and punitive damages are rarely, and in New Hampshire never, awarded in contract cases; and so a victim of a breach of contract who wants to keep the contract breaker's money above and beyond the amount necessary to compensate for the breach may be said to be "unjustly enriched," entitling the contract breaker to restitution."

> *Micro Data Base Sys., Inc. v. Dharma Sys., Inc.*, 148 F.3d 649, 656 (7th Cir. 1998).

unmatched call *(telecommunications)*

"A telephone call placed through a cellular telephone using an ESN/MIN combination not assigned to a bona fide customer or subscriber."

> *United States v. Brady*, 820 F. Supp. 1346, 1354 n.16 (D. Utah 1993).

unmoderated newsgroup *(Internet)*

"For unmoderated newsgroups, when an individual user with access to a USENET server posts a message to a newsgroup, the message is automatically forwarded to all adjacent USENET servers that furnish access to the newsgroup, and it is then propagated to the servers adjacent to those servers, etc."

> *American Civil Liberties Union v. Reno*, 929 F. Supp. 824, 835 (E.D. Pa. 1996), *aff'd, Reno v. American Civil Liberties Union*, 521 U.S. 844 (1997).

See also **newsgroup; Usenet.**

unsubscribe *(Internet)*

To remove one's name or e-mail address from a newsgroup or mailing list.

up *(technology)*

When the operating system is turned on and working. *See also* **up and running.**

up and running *(technology)*

"[T]he system is fully performing the functions for which it is intended."

> *Chatlos Sys., Inc. v. National Cash Register Corp.*, 479 F. Supp. 738, 741 n.2 (D.N.J. 1979), *aff'd in part, rev'd in part*, 635 F.2d 1081 (3d Cir. 1980), *cert. dism.*, 457 U.S. 1112 (1982).

upgrade *(hardware; software)*

A software or hardware modification that enhances the performance of the computer system or network.

Annotation. "Generally, the purpose of any upgrade . . . is to enhance the performance of the computer, often to increase the capabilities of a used computer to match the performance level of a newer model. Upgrades include model upgrades (MIPS upgrades), increases in the memory capacity (memory upgrades), and increases in the number of computer channels (channel upgrades)."

Allen-Myland, Inc. v. IBM Corp., 693 F. Supp. 262, 266-67 (E.D. Pa. 1988).

See also **software upgrade.**

upload *(Internet)*

The process of communicating digital information from one computer to another—usually from a personal computer to a large, centrally located computer.

uploading *(Internet)*

"[T]ransferring computer-stored data from one's own computer to a remote computer."

United States v. Riggs, 739 F. Supp. 414, 417 n.3 (N.D. Ill. 1990).

"Third parties, known as 'users,' of electronic bulletin boards can transfer information over telephone lines from their own computers to the storage media on the bulletin board. . . ."

Sega Enters. Ltd. v. MAPHIA, 857 F. Supp. 679, 683 (N.D. Cal. 1994).

upside *(business)*

The profit potential of a project.

URL *(Internet)*

Acronym for "Uniform Resource Locator."

Intermatic, Inc. v. Toeppen, 947 F. Supp. 1227, 1231 (N.D. Ill. 1996).

"[A]n address . . . identifying, among other things, the server on which it [a document] resides."

Shea v. Reno, 930 F. Supp. 916, 929 (S.D.N.Y. 1996).

"[T]he domain name of a host computer."

Digital Equipment Corp. v. Altavista Technology, Inc., 960 F. Supp. 456, 459 n.3 (D. Mass. 1997).

Annotation. "The first element of the URL is a transfer protocol (most commonly, 'http'—standing for hypertext transfer protocol). The remaining elements of this URL . . . are an alias for the fully qualified domain name of the host. . . ."

Intermatic, Inc. v. Toeppen, 947 F. Supp. 1227, 1231 (N.D. Ill. 1996).

The URL (pronounced as in "Duke of . . .") or U.R.L. indicates the protocol, name and location of a file on a computer network or a local computer.

An URL is different than an e-mail address. An e-mail address is a location to which you would send a message file in order to reach a particular addressee. An URL, on the other hand, is a reference to a particular file. If somebody were to ask you for your URL, he would not be asking how to contact you; rather, he would likely be asking for the location and name of your World Wide Web home page file.

An URL is generally made up of three parts. The first part of an URL is the protocol specifier. This is the section of an URL up to and including the first set of slash marks. Examples are "http://," which indicates Hyper-Text Transport Protocol, the standard for World Wide Web files; "ftp://," which indicates File Transfer Protocol, the standard for retrieving a file from a given host; or "file:///," which indicates a computer file of no particular protocol.

The second part of an URL is the domain at which the file resides. This may be an Internet domain such as "www.jrb.com," or it may be a disk drive designation on a local machine or network such as "c|/" or "d|/." The end of a domain section of an URL may also include numbers indicating a network port, such as "www.jrb.com:8181/."

The third part of an URL contains the path to a specific file. For example, the path "images/vacation/italy.html" indicates a file named "italy.html" located in the "vacation" subdirectory of the "images" directory of the server.

It should be noted that an URL will direct a user to a file with a particular protocol, location, and name on a particular server computer, but it does not assure a user that the named file at a particular location is the same file that earlier was at the same location. From time to time any file designated by an URL may be altered or replaced by a different file with the same name. Thus, searching for a specific version of a file by using its URL can sometimes be like searching for the perfect wave—the same location, at the same beach, can have different waves from day to day. It's no wonder that browsing the web is called "surfing."

Additional information regarding URLs can be found at <http://www.ncsa.uiuc.edu/demoweb/url-primer.html>. (jrb)

usage of trade *(contract)*

"[A]ny practice or method of dealing having such regularity of observance in a place, vocation or trade as to justify an expectation that it will be observed with respect to the transaction in question."

U.C.C. § 1-205.

"[A]ny practice or method of dealing that has such regularity of observance in a place, vocation, or trade as to justify an expectation that it will be observed with respect to the transaction in question."

UCITA § 102(a)(66).

Annotation. "[A] course of dealing between the parties and any usage of trade in a vocation or trade in which they are engaged or of which they are or should be aware give particular meaning to and supplement or qualify terms of an agreement."

U.C.C. § 1-205.

See also **course of dealing.**

use *(contract)*

"Initially, the Court finds nothing in the agreement itself to suggest any intent to deviate from the everyday meaning of the word 'use.' . . . [T]he common understanding of the term 'use' is 'the act or practice of employing something.' "

S&H Computer Sys., Inc. v. SAS Inst., Inc., 568 F. Supp. 416, 421 (M.D. Tenn. 1983) (citation omitted).

". . . is defined as including, without limitation, the acts of running, loading, or causing to be run or loaded, any MAI software from any magnetic storage or read-only memory device into the computer memory of the central processing unit of the computer system. . . ."

MAI Sys. Corp. v. Peak Computer, Inc., 991 F.2d 511, 515 (9th Cir. 1993) (quoting the district court's injunction), *cert. dism.,* 510 U.S. 1033 (1994).

use in commerce *(trademark)*

"[A] mark shall be deemed to be in use in commerce—

(1) on goods when—

   (A) it is placed in any manner on the goods or their containers or the displays associated therewith or on the tags or labels affixed thereto, or if the nature of the goods makes such placement impracticable, then on documents associated with the goods or their sale, and

   (B) the goods are sold or transported in commerce, and

(2) on services when it is used or displayed in the sale or advertising of services and the services are rendered in commerce, or the services are rendered in more than one State or in the United States and a foreign country and the person rendering the services is engaged in commerce in connection with the services."

15 U.S.C. § 1127.

Annotation. The bona fide use of a trademark or service mark in either interstate or foreign commerce in the ordinary course of trade. Nominal use made merely to reserve a right in a mark does not qualify. Use of the mark in advertising or promotional materials before the product or service is actually provided under the mark is not use in commerce. *See also* **commercial use.**

Related issues. "Registration with Network Solutions . . . does not in itself constitute 'use' for purposes of acquiring trademark priority."
> *Brookfield Comm., Inc. v. West Coast Entertainment Corp.,* 174 F.3d 1036, 1051 (9th Cir. 1999) (citation omitted).

useful article *(copyright)*

"[A]n article having an intrinsic utilitarian function that is not merely to portray the appearance of the article or to convey information. An article that is normally a part of a useful article is considered a 'useful article.'"
> U.S. Copyright Act, 17 U.S.C. § 101.

Annotation. "The design of a useful article is protectable under the copyright laws, 'only if, and only to the extent that, such design incorporates pictorial, graphic, or sculptural features that can be identified separately from, and are capable of existing independently of, the utilitarian aspects of the article.'"
> *E.F. Johnson Co. v. Uniden Corp. of America,* 623 F. Supp. 1485, 1498 (D. Minn. 1985), *citing* 17 U.S.C. § 101.

"Unpatentable mathematical algorithms are identifiable by showing they are merely abstract ideas constituting disembodied concepts or truths that are not 'useful.' From a practical standpoint, this means that to be patentable an algorithm must be applied in a 'useful' way."
> *State Street Bank & Trust, Co. v. Signature Financial Group, Inc.,* 149 F.3d 1368, 1373 (Fed. Cir. 1998).

Usenet *(Internet)*

"[A] worldwide community of electronic BBSs that is closely associated with the Internet and with the Internet community. The messages in Usenet are organized into thousands of topical groups, or 'Newsgroups.' . . . As a Usenet user, you read and contribute ('post') to your local Usenet site. Each Usenet site distributes its users' postings to other Usenet sites based on various implicit and explicit configuration settings, and in turn receives postings from other sites. Usenet traffic typically consists of as much as 30 to 50 Mbytes of messages per day. Usenet is read and contributed to on a daily basis by a total population of millions of people. . . . There is no specific network that is the Usenet. Usenet traffic flows over a wide range of networks, including the Internet and dial-up phone links."

> *Religious Tech. Ctr. v. Netcom On-Line Comm. Servs., Inc.,* 907 F. Supp. 1361, 1365 (N.D. Cal. 1995).

Annotation. "At the same time that ARPANET was maturing (it subsequently ceased to exist), similar networks developed to link universities, research facilities, businesses, and individuals around the world. These other formal or loose networks included BITNET, CSNET, FIDONET, and USENET. Eventually, each of these networks (many of which overlapped) were themselves linked together, allowing users of any computers linked to any one of the networks to transmit communications to users of computers on other networks. It is this series of linked networks (themselves linking computers and computer networks) that is today commonly known as the Internet."

> *American Civil Liberties Union v. Reno,* 929 F. Supp. 824, 832 (E.D. Pa. 1996), *aff'd, Reno v. American Civil Liberties Union,* 521 U.S. 844 (1997).

"Similar in function to listservs—but quite different in how communications are transmitted—are distributed message databases such as 'USENET newsgroups.' User-sponsored newsgroups are among the most popular and widespread applications of Internet services, and cover all imaginable topics of interest to users. Like listservs, newsgroups are open discussions and exchanges on particular topics. Users, however, need not subscribe to the discussion mailing list in advance, but can instead access the database at any time. Some USENET newsgroups are 'moderated' but most are open access. For the moderated newsgroups, all messages to the newsgroup are forwarded to one person who can screen them for relevance to the topics under discussion. USENET newsgroups are disseminated using ad hoc, peer to peer connections between approximately 200,000 computers (called USENET 'servers') around the world. For unmoderated newsgroups, when an individual user with access to a USENET server posts a message to a newsgroup, the message is automatically forwarded to all adjacent USENET servers that furnish access to the newsgroup, and it is then propagated to the servers adjacent to those servers, etc. The messages are temporarily stored on each receiving server, where they are available for review and response by individual users. The messages are automatically and periodically purged from each system after a time to make room for new messages. Responses to messages, like the original messages, are automatically distributed to all other computers receiving the newsgroup or forwarded to a moderator in the case of a moderated newsgroup. The dissemination of messages to

USENET servers around the world is an automated process that does not require direct human intervention or review."

American Civil Liberties Union v. Reno, 929 F. Supp. 824, 834-35 (E.D. Pa. 1996), *Reno v. American Civil Liberties Union, aff'd,* 521 U.S. 844 (1997).

"Internet users may also transmit or receive 'articles' posted daily to thousands of discussion groups, arranged by subject matter and known as 'newsgroups,' available through an electronic bulletin-board system known as 'Usenet.' When a user with access to a Usenet server—that is, a computer participating in the Usenet system—posts an article to a particular newsgroup, the server automatically forwards the article to adjacent Usenet servers, which in turn forward it to other servers, until the article is available on all Usenet sites that furnish access to the newsgroup in question. Once a message reaches a particular Usenet site, it is temporarily stored there so that individual users—running client software, known as a 'newsreader,' capable of sorting articles according to header information identifying the newsgroup to which the article was posted—can review and respond to the message."

Shea v. Reno, 930 F. Supp. 916, 927-28 (S.D.N.Y. 1996) (citations omitted).

Related issues. "Some Usenet newsgroups are moderated; messages to the newsgroup are forwarded to an individual who selects those appropriate for distribution. Because Usenet articles are distributed to (and made available on) multiple servers, one who posts an article to a newsgroup has no way of knowing who will choose to retrieve it, whether or not the newsgroup is moderated. There is no newsgroup equivalent of a 'closed' mailing list: access to a particular newsgroup can only be limited by restricting the number of servers participating in the newsgroup."

Shea v. Reno, 930 F. Supp. 916, 928 (S.D.N.Y. 1996).

"A content provider has no way of knowing who will have access to an article posted to a Usenet newsgroup."

Shea v. Reno, 930 F. Supp. 916, 941 (S.D.N.Y. 1996).

See also **bulletin board systems; newsgroups.**

Usenet server *(Internet)*

"[A] computer participating on the Usenet system. . . ."

Shea v. Reno, 930 F. Supp. 916, 927 (S.D.N.Y. 1996).

Related issues. "In order to ease transmission and for the convenience of Usenet users, Usenet servers maintain postings from newsgroups for a short period of time. . . . Once on Netcom's computers, messages are available to Netcom's customers and Usenet neighbors, who may then download the messages to their own computers. Netcom's local server makes available its postings to a group of Usenet servers, which do the same for other servers until all Usenet sites worldwide have obtained access to the postings, which takes a matter of hours."

> *Religious Technology Ctr. v. Netcom On-line Com. Servs., Inc.,* 907 F. Supp. 1361, 1367-68 (N.D. Cal. 1995).

user-based zoning *(Internet)*

". . . is also in its infancy. For it to be effective, (i) an agreed-upon code (or 'tag') would have to exist; (ii) screening software or browsers with screening capabilities would have to be able to recognize the 'tag'; and (iii) those programs would have to be widely available—and widely used—by Internet users. At present, none of these conditions is true. Screening software 'is not in wide use today' and 'only a handful of browsers have screening capabilities.' . . . There is, moreover, no agreed-upon 'tag' for those programs to recognize."

> *Reno v. American Civil Liberties Union,* 521 U.S. 844, 891 (1997) (O'Connor, J., concurring in part, dissenting in part) (citations omitted).

user friendly *(technology)*

Descriptive of both hardware and software that are designed to assist the user by being scaled to human dimensions (self-instructing, error-proof, easy to understand, etc.).

user interface *(technology)*

". . . also called 'look and feel' of the program, is generally the design of the video screen and the manner in which information is presented to the user."

> *Johnson Controls, Inc. v. Phoenix Control Sys., Inc.,* 886 F.2d 1173, 1175 (9th Cir. 1989).

"The whole Macintosh user interface includes both its graphic elements or visual displays and the mouse technology which enables the user to point on these graphic elements and command some computer operations."

> *Apple Computer, Inc. v. Microsoft Corp.,* 759 F. Supp. 1444, 1447 (N.D. Cal. 1991).

See also **end-user interface; look and feel.**

user name *(technology)*

The name used by a user in logging into a computer network.

utility *(patent)*

Annotation. "If the claimed subject matter is inoperable, the patent may indeed be invalid for failure to meet the utility requirement of §101 and the enablement requirement of §112."
> *Brooktree Corp. v. Advanced Micro Devices, Inc.,* 977 F.2d 1555, 1571 (Fed. Cir. 1992).

utility codes *(software)*
"... are often developed and stored in a 'subroutine library,' which can then be called upon in various programming contexts to perform necessary common functions."
> *Dynamic Solutions, Inc. v. Planning & Control, Inc.,* 646 F. Supp. 1328, 1332 n.2 (S.D.N.Y. 1986).

utility program *(software)*
A software program that helps programmers and users perform specific types of common jobs. A program that sorts names and addresses is a common utility program, as is copying data from one storage disk to another.

UTSA *(trade secret)*
See Uniform Trade Secrets Act.

UUCP *(Internet)*
Acronym for "UNIX-to-UNIX Copy Program." An early transfer protocol that permitted two UNIX-based computers to share data over a telephone line.

uudecode *(software)*
A computer program that reconstructs binary data that was uuencoded. *See* **uuencode.**

uuencode *(software)*
Acronym for "UNIX to UNIX Encod[e]ing." A method of converting binary files into ASCII format so they can be transmitted over the Internet by e-mail. *See* ASCII.

valid certificate *(electronic commerce)*
"[A] certificate that: (a) A licensed certification authority has issued;
(b) The subscriber listed in it has accepted; (c) Has not been revoked or
suspended; and (d) Has not expired. However, a transactional certificate is
a valid certificate only in relation to the digital signature incorporated in it
by reference."
Wash. Rev. Code § 19.34.020(40).

validation *(business)*
The process of evaluating a system or component during or at the end of
the development process to determine whether it satisfies specified requirements.

value added reseller *(business)*
Abbreviated as "VAR."

" . . . evaluates the needs of a particular group of potential computer users,
compares those needs with the available technology, and develops a pack-
age of hardware and software to satisfy those needs."
M.A. Mortenson Co., Inc. v. Timberline Software Corp., 998 P.2d 305, 312 n.8
(Wash. 2000), *aff'g* 93 Wash. App. 819, 970 P.2d 803 (1999).
See also **VAR.**

vaporware *(hardware; software)*
Computer software or other computer product announced long before its
availability. Usually done to convince users not to purchase a competitor's
product.

VAR *(business)*
Acronym for "Value Added Reseller." The class of resellers who purchase
computer components or computer systems, add value (usually applications software) and resell the enhanced system to retailers or end users. *See
also* **OEM.**

VCR *(hardware)*
Acronym for "Videocassette Recorder."

VDU *(hardware)*
Acronym for "Visual Display Unit." *See* **visual display unit.**

vendor *(business)*
A seller (or licensor) of computer hardware and/or software.

verification *(electronic commerce)*
"[T]he method by which a user types in his or her credit card number, and the Web site ensures that the credit card is valid before it allows the user to enter the site."
American Civil Liberties Union v. Reno, 929 F. Supp. 824, 846 n.19 (E.D. Pa. 1996), *aff'd, Reno v. American Civil Liberties Union,* 521 U.S. 844 (1997).

Annotation. "There is an alternative means to shield minors from sexually explicit content available uniquely to content providers on the World Wide Web: verification of a user's 'adulthood' before allowing him access to a site. A content provider operating a Web server can create and display an electronic form to retrieve information from a user visiting the Web site; after processing the information by using a program such as a Common Gateway Interface ('cgi') script, the server could grant or deny access to the site. Not all content providers who make material available on the Web, however, can use programs such as cgi scripts; for example, commercial on-line services such as America Online and CompuServe provide subscribers with the opportunity to post content by configuring their own Web pages but do not permit subscribers to use cgi scripts. For Web content providers who lack access to cgi scripts, there is no means of age verification.

"Although some Web providers can query the user of a site for a credit card number, the cost of verification is significant, ranging from sixty cents per transaction to more than a dollar per transaction. To take advantage of adult access code or adult identification code verification, a content provider would either have to establish and maintain a registration and verification system (or hire someone else to do so) and issue access codes to users after verifying their ages—or associate with one of several adult verification services, such as Adult Check, Adult Verification System, First Virtual, Validate, or VeriSign. Although neither of the Government's expert witnesses had any first-hand familiarity with adult verification services, advertising materials suggest that an adult can obtain an identification number from a particular service and access any site registered with the service.

. . . Although most verification services do not charge content providers to register their sites, at least one service does impose a fee on site owners registered with it."
Shea v. Reno, 930 F. Supp. 916, 933-34 (S.D.N.Y. 1996).

"Verification of a credit card number over the Internet is not now technically possible. . . . Although users can and do purchase products over the Internet by transmitting their credit card number, the seller must then process the transaction with Visa or Mastercard offline using telephone lines in the traditional way."
American Civil Liberties Union v. Reno, 929 F. Supp. 824, 846 (E.D. Pa. 1996), *aff'd, Reno v. American Civil Liberties Union,* 521 U.S. 844 (1997).

Related issues. "If a content provider cannot discern who receives his messages, there is no way for him to obtain verification of recipients' ages."
Shea v. Reno, 930 F. Supp. 916, 942 (S.D.N.Y. 1996).

verify a digital signature *(electronic commerce)*
"[I]n relation to a given digital signature, message, and public key, to determine accurately that: (a) The digital signature was created by the private key corresponding to the public key; and (b) The message has not been altered since its digital signature was created."
Wash. Rev. Code § 19.34.020(41).

Veronica *(Internet)*
Acronym for "Very Easy Rodent Oriented Net-wide Index to Computerized Archives."

"[A] . . . server . . . capable of searching menus on all gopher servers."
Shea v. Reno, 930 F. Supp. 916, 928 n.9 (S.D.N.Y. 1996).

vertical frequency *(hardware)*
"[T]he rate at which the entire monitor screen was redrawn one time."
Princeton Graphics Operating L.P. v. NEC Home Elecs. (U.S.A.), Inc., 732 F. Supp. 1258, 1259 n.3 (S.D.N.Y. 1990).
See also **vertical synchronization rate.**

vertical synchronization rate *(hardware)*
"[T]he rate at which the entire monitor screen was redrawn one time."
Princeton Graphics Operating L.P. v. NEC Home Elecs. (U.S.A.), Inc., 732 F. Supp. 1258, 1259 n.3 (S.D.N.Y. 1990).
See also **vertical frequency.**

vertical synchronizing pulse(s) *(hardware)*

"[T]he pulses that direct the monitor to come back . . . from the lower right to upper left."

> *Princeton Graphics Operating L.P. v. NEC Home Elecs. (U.S.A.), Inc.,* 732 F. Supp. 1258, 1260 n.5 (S.D.N.Y. 1990).

VGA *(hardware)*

Acronym for "Video Graphics Array."

> *Princeton Graphics Operating L.P. v. NEC Home Elecs. (U.S.A.), Inc.,* 732 F. Supp. 1258, 1259 (S.D.N.Y. 1990).

VGA compatible *(hardware)*

". . . may be used to describe the performance of a monochrome gas plasma display of a lap-top computer. . . ."

> *Princeton Graphics Operating L.P. v. NEC Home Elecs. (U.S.A.), Inc.,* 732 F. Supp. 1258, 1262 n.9 (S.D.N.Y. 1990).

VHF *(hardware; telecommunications)*

Acronym for "Very High Frequency."

vicarious infringement *(copyright)*

"A defendant is liable for vicarious liability for the actions of a primary infringer where the defendant (1) has the right and ability to control the infringer's acts and (2) receives a direct financial benefit from the infringement. . . . Unlike contributory infringement, knowledge is not an element of vicarious liability."

> *Religious Technology Ctr. v. Netcom On-line Com. Servs., Inc.,* 907 F. Supp. 1361, 1375 (N.D. Cal. 1995) (citations omitted).

Related issues. "[The court] is not convinced that Usenet servers are directly liable for causing a copy to be made, and absent evidence of knowledge and participation or control and direct profit, they will not be contributorily or vicariously liable."

> *Religious Technology Ctr. v. Netcom On-line Com. Servs., Inc.,* 907 F. Supp. 1361, 1377 (N.D. Cal. 1995).

See also copyright infringement; vicarious liability.

vicarious liability *(copyright)*

"The theory of vicarious liability in the context of intellectual property is alternatively called 'contributory infringement.'"

> *Telerate Sys., Inc. v. Caro,* 689 F. Supp. 221, 228 n.8 (S.D.N.Y. 1988).

See also copyright infringement; vicarious infringement.

victim expenditure *(criminal)*
"[A]ny expenditure reasonably and necessarily incurred by the owner or lessee to verify that a computer system, computer network, or data was or was not altered, deleted, damaged, or destroyed by the access."
Cal. Penal C. § 502.

video bookends *(video game)*
See bookends.

video bumpers *(video game)*
See bookends.

video compression *(technology)*
A process of removing unnecessary and redundant visual information to permit reduced storage and transmission of a video image.

video computer systems *(technology)*
Abbreviated as "VCS."

[AUSTRALIA] ". . . electronic units comprising a multi-circuit unit and auxiliary equipment."
Atari, Inc. v. Fairstar Elecs. Pty. Ltd. (1982), 1 I.P.R. 291 (Austrl. Fed. Ct.).

video display terminal *(hardware)*
Abbreviated at "VDT."

[CANADA] "[A] device for transmitting data and instructions to the central processing unit of a computer and for receiving and displaying the computer's output. The terminal consists of a keyboard, by which the user enters the information, and video monitor which displays both the user input and the computer output. Ordinarily, a reference manual for instruction and consultation on the use of the terminal is provided with such a unit."
Digital Equip. Corp. v. C. Itoh & Co. (Can.) Ltd. (1985), 6 C.P.R. (3d) 511 (Fed. T.D.).

video game(s) *(video game)*
"[C]omputers programmed to create on a television screen cartoons in which some of the action is controlled by the player."
Stern Elecs., Inc. v. Kaufman, 669 F.2d 852, 853 (2d Cir. 1981), *quoted approvingly in Red Baron-Franklin Parks, Inc. v. Taito Corp.,* 883 F. Supp. 275, 277 (4th Cir. 1989); *M. Kramer Mfg. Co. v. Andrews,* 783 F.2d 421 (4th Cir. 1986).

"[C]onsists of an electronic printed circuit board, a television monitor, a cabinet and a coin mechanism."
> *Red Baron-Franklin Parks, Inc. v. Taito Corp.*, 883 F. Supp. 275, 277 (4th Cir. 1989).

Related issues. ". . . are copyrightable as audiovisual works under the 1976 Copyright Act. . . ."
> *Midway Mfg. Co. v. Artic Int'l, Inc.*, 704 F.2d 1009, 1012 (7th Cir. 1983).

"It is also unquestionable that video games in general are entitled to copyright protections as audiovisual works."
> *Midway Mfg. Co. v. Bandai-America, Inc.*, 546 F. Supp. 125, 139 (D.N.J. 1982).

"While board games may never die, good video games are mortal."
> *Lewis Galoob Toys, Inc. v. Nintendo of America*, 780 F. Supp. 1283, 1295 (N.D. Cal. 1991), *aff'd*, 864 F.2d 965 (9th Cir. 1992).

See also **videogame unit.**

video game machine *(video game)*

". . . consists of a cabinet containing, inter alia, a cathode ray tube (CRT), a sound system, hand controls for the player, and electronic circuit boards. The electronic circuitry includes a microprocessor and memory devices, called ROMs (Read-Only Memory), which are tiny computer chips containing thousands of data locations which store the instructions and data of a computer program. The microprocessor executes the computer program to cause the game to operate."
> *Williams Elecs., Inc. v. Artic Int'l, Inc.*, 685 F.2d 870, 872 (3d Cir. 1982).

video graphics array *(technology)*

"[A] new 'video standard.' . . ."
> *Princeton Graphics Operating L.P. v. NEC Home Elecs. (U.S.A.), Inc.*, 732 F. Supp. 1258, 1259 (S.D.N.Y. 1990).

See also **VGA.**

video server *(technology)*

A specialized computer system that delivers high-speed "streams" of digital audio and video.

videogame unit *(video game)*

". . . consists of an electronic printed circuit board, a monitor, a cabinet, and, possibly, a coin mechanism. When the component parts are connected and an electric current, activated by the insertion of the proper coin, runs through the machinery, the game's audiovisual images appear on the video screen."

> *Red Baron-Franklin Park, Inc. v. Taito Corp.*, 883 F.2d 275, 279 (4th Cir. 1989).

See also **video game(s)**.

videotex *(technology)*
Also called "Videotex" and "videotext."

"[A] new and rapidly developing area of computer technology. It is similar to many home computers with a video display, except Videotex allows for two-way communication, over telephone or cable, with a large data base containing a wide variety of specialized information in both written and graphic form. The Videotex System contains two computers, a 'Frame Creation Terminal' (FCT) where graphic designers create frames of information which are sent over telephone lines to a central computer for storage. With a Customer Terminal (CT) an individual consumer can retrieve this information from the central computer and reconstruct it as a frame on his home television screen."

> *Bell Tel. Labs., Inc. v. General Instrument Corp.*, 8 Computer L. Serv. Rep. 297, 298 (Common Pleas 1983).

[AUSTRALIA] "[A] simple means of making information visually available by means of public or provided telephone lines. The information is displayed on a television or terminal screens."

> *Re Application by Int'l Computers Ltd.* (1985), 5 I.P.R. 263 (Austrl. Pat. Office).

virtual reality *(technology)*
A computer-created three-dimensional, multisensory environment that simulates reality when perceived by the user.

virus *(contract; software)*
"[A] migrating program . . . that attaches itself to the operating system of any computer it enters and can infect any other computer that uses files from the infected computer."

> *United States v. Morris*, 928 F.2d 504, 505 n.1 (2d Cir. 1991).

Sample clause. "The vendor further warrants that:
(1) 'neither the Software nor the media containing the Software contains any "back door," "time bomb," "Trojan horse," "worm," "drop dead device," "virus" or other software code designed to (i) permit access or use of the end user's computer system by a non-authorized party,

(ii) disable, damage or erase any software or data on the end user's system, or (iii) perform any other unauthorized action on the end user's system, and

(2) the Software does not contain preprogrammed preventative routines or similar devices which could prevent Epson or its customers from exercising any of the rights granted under this License Agreement, or from utilizing the Software for the purposes for which it was designed.'"

See also computer virus.

Visicalc *(software)*
"[T]he first interactive computerized spreadsheet."
> *SAPC, Inc. v. Lotus Dev. Corp.*, 921 F.2d 360, 361 (1st Cir. 1990).

visit *(Internet)*
To go to another's web site.

visitor *(Internet)*
One who goes to another's web site.

visual display *(technology)*
". . . necessarily is what the user sees on the screen. In the context of the Agreement it consists of or includes those features to which one would look to assess similarity for purposes of determining whether the copyright has been infringed."
> *Apple Computer, Inc. v. Microsoft Corp.*, 717 F. Supp. 1428, 1432 (N.D. Cal. 1989).

visual display unit *(hardware)*
Abbreviated as "VDU."

[CANADA] "[A] screen upon which the operator can call up stored information to be displayed."
> *Mackenzie Patten & Co. v. British Olivetti Ltd.* (1984), M.L.R. 344 (Q.B.D.).

voice-grade *(telecommunications)*
The quality of a regular copper telephone line.

voice recognition *(technology)*
"The fact that computers will soon be able to respond directly to spoken commands, for example, should not confer on this government the unfet-

tered power to impose prior restraints on speech in an effort to control its 'functional' aspects."

Bernstein v. United States Dept. of Justice, 176 F.3d 1132, 1142 (9th Cir. 1999).

volatile memory *(hardware)*

"[I]n contrast with ROM, the contents of which are semi-permanent."

Advanced Computer Servs., Inc. v. MAI Sys. Corp., 845 F. Supp. 356, 362 (E.D. Va. 1994).

vortex business *(business)*

This term refers to a new type of online business that provides a conduit through which sellers of specific types of products (e.g., office supplies) will be able to communicate directly with potential buyers of such products. The vortex business provides the forum for the exchange of information, allowing a buyer to compare quality, price, and other variables across a large number of suppliers, choosing the best combination of terms to fit its particular needs.

VRCs *(technology)*

[CANADA] "Visible Records Computers."

Mackenzie Patten & Co. v. British Olivetti Ltd. (1984), M.L.R. 344 (Q.B.D.).

wafer *(hardware)*

When most semiconducting material is purified, it comes out in sausage-like lengths between one and eight inches in diameter that are a single crystal, which are then sliced into wafers roughly one millimeter thick. The wafer is then used as the substrate for forming semiconductor devices.

WAIS *(Internet)*

Acronym for "Wide Area Information System." A system that allows users on a network to do keyword searches through the full text of various databases on the network, with the results ranked according to relevance.

walker *(video game)*

A type of video game in which the characters walk around the screen.

WAN *(technology)*

Acronym for "Wide Area Network." A computer network that connects computers over a large geographic area.

warrantor *(contract)*

"[A]ny supplier or other person who gives or offers to give a written warranty or who is or may be obligated under an implied warranty."

15 U.S.C. § 2301(5).

warranty disclaimer *(contract)*

"[I]f the final integrated written expression contains a clause disclaiming all express and implied warranties, any prior or contemporaneous oral express warranties are effectively excluded."

Ritchie Enters. v. Honeywell Bull, Inc., 730 F. Supp. 1041, 1047 (D. Kan. 1990).

Sample Warranty Disclaimer Clause. EXCEPT AS EXPRESSLY PROVIDED HEREIN, THERE ARE NO OTHER WARRANTIES, EXPRESS OR IMPLIED, INCLUDING, BUT NOT LIMITED TO, ANY IMPLIED WARRANTIES OF MERCHANTABILITY OR FITNESS FOR A PARTICULAR PURPOSE.

Sample Title Disclaimer Clause. [Seller] transfers only his right, title, and interest to the [describe goods] to [Buyer]. Since [Seller] is without knowledge as to what claims may or may not exist with respect to ownership of the goods, SELLER MAKES NO WARRANTY WHATEVER WITH RESPECT TO TITLE.

watermark *(technology)*
See digital watermark.

watermarking *(technology)*
A technique for embedding identifying information in a digital work by invisibly changing a small percentage of digital bits in the work.

WAV *(technology)*
Acronym for "**wav**eform audio" file format. A file format for sampled audio data.

web *(Internet)*
Abbreviation for "World Wide **Web**."

"[A] vast decentralized collection of documents containing text, visual images, and even audio clips. . . . The web is designed to be inherently accessible from every Internet site in the world."
> *Blumenthal v. Drudge,* 992 F. Supp. 44, 48 n.6 (D.D.C. 1998) (citation omitted).

" '[F]ast becoming the most well-known' way of using the Internet, consists of a series of displayed documents which can contain text, images, sound, animation, moving video, etc."
> *Digital Equip. Corp. v. Altavista Technology, Inc.,* 960 F. Supp. 456, 459 n.2 (D. Mass. 1997).

"[A] collection of information resources contained in documents located on individual computers around the world, [which] is the most widely used and fastest growing part of the Internet except perhaps for electronic mail ('e-mail')."
> *Brookfield Comm., Inc. v. West Coast Entertainment Corp.,* 174 F.3d 1036, 1044 (9th Cir. 1999).

". . . refers to the collection of sites available on the Internet."
> *Zippo Mfg. Co. v. Zippo Dot Com, Inc.,* 952 F. Supp. 1119, 1120 n.2 (W.D. Pa. 1997).

Annotation. "Documents available on the Web are not collected in any central location; rather, they are stored on servers a round the world running Web server software. To gain access to the content available on the Web, a user must have a Web 'browser'—client software, such as Netscape Navigator, Mosaic, or Internet Explorer, capable of displaying documents formatted in 'hypertext markup language' ('HTML'), the standard Web formatting language. Each document has an address, known as a Uniform Resource Locator ('URL'), identifying, among other things, the server on which it resides; most documents also contain 'links'—highlighted text or images that, when selected by the user, permit him to view another, related Web document. Because Web servers are linked to the Internet through a common communications protocol, known as hypertext transfer protocol ('HTTP'), a user can move seamlessly between documents, regardless of their location; when a user viewing a document located on one server selects a link to a document located elsewhere, the browser will automatically contact the second server and display the document. Some types of Web client software also permit users to gain access to resources available on FTP and gopher sites."

Shea v. Reno, 930 F. Supp. 916, 929 (S.D.N.Y. 1996) (citations omitted).

"[M]any laypeople erroneously believe that the Internet is co-extensive with the Web. The Web is really a publishing forum; it is comprised of millions of separate 'Web sites' that display content provided by particular persons or organizations."

American Library Ass'n v. Pataki, 969 F. Supp. 160, 166 (S.D.N.Y. 1997).

"The Web is thus comparable, from the readers' viewpoint, to both a vast library including millions of readily available and indexed publications and a sprawling mall offering goods and services."

Reno v. American Civil Liberties Union, 521 U.S. 844, 853 (1997).

"From the publishers' point of view, it constitutes a vast platform from which to address and hear from a world-wide audience of millions of readers, viewers, researchers, and buyers. Any person or organization with a computer connected to the Internet can 'publish' information. Publishers include government agencies, educational institutions, commercial entities, advocacy groups, and individuals. Publishers may either make their material available to the entire pool of Internet users, or confine access to a selected group, such as those willing to pay for the privilege."

Reno v. American Civil Liberties Union, 521 U.S. 844, 853 (1997).

"For commercial users, the Web is the most important part of the Internet. Unlike previous Internet-based communications formats, the Web is easy to use for people inexperienced with computers. Information on the Web can be presented on 'pages' of graphics and text that contain 'links' to other pages—either within the same set of data files ('Web site') or within data files located on other computer networks. Users access information on the Web using 'browser' programs. Browser programs process information from Web sites and display the information using graphics, text, sound and animation. Because of these capabilities, the Web has become a popular medium for advertising and for direct consumer access to goods and services. At the same time, the Web, like the rest of the Internet, is an important medium of non-commercial communications. The Web has made it easier for individuals and small organizations to publish information to the general public. Publication on the Web simply requires placing a formatted file on a host computer."

> *Lockheed Martin Corp. v. Network Solutions, Inc.,* 985 F. Supp. 949, 951 (C.D. Cal. 1997).

"[T]he Web is what is known as a distributed system. The Web was designed so that organizations with computers containing information can become part of the Web simply by attaching their computers to the Internet and running appropriate World Wide Web software. No single organization controls any membership in the Web, nor is there any centralized point from which individual Web sites or services can be blocked from the Web."

> *American Civil Liberties Union v. Reno,* 929 F. Supp. 830, 838 (3d Cir. 1996), *aff'd, Reno v. American Civil Liberties Union,* 521 U.S. 844 (1997).

"The World Wide Web has become so popular because of its open, distributed, and easy-to-use nature. Rather than requiring those who seek information to purchase new software or hardware, and to learn a new kind of system for each new database of information they seek to access, the Web environment makes it easy for users to jump from one set of information to another. By the same token, the open nature of the Web makes it easy for publishers to reach their intended audiences without having to know in advance what kind of computer each potential reader has, and what kind of software they will be using."

> *American Civil Liberties Union v. Reno,* 929 F. Supp. 830, 838 (3d Cir. 1996), *aff'd, Reno v. American Civil Liberties Union,* 521 U.S. 844 (1997).

Related issues. "With the Web becoming an important mechanism for commerce . . . companies are racing to stake out their place in cyberspace."

> *Brookfield Comm., Inc. v. West Coast Entertainment Corp.,* 174 F.3d 1036, 1044 (9th Cir. 1999).

See also **Internet; World Wide Web.**

web browser *(Internet)*

A computer program that facilitates the location of content on the Internet.

"[A] type of Web client that enables a user to select, retrieve, and perceive resources on the Web."

> *United States v. Microsoft Corp.*, 65 F. Supp. 2d 1, 5 (D.D.C. 1999) (Finding of Fact 16).

Annotation. "Web browsers feature access to various indexes, commonly referred to as search engines. These indexes will allow the user to enter a name or a word or a combination of words, much like a Lexis or WestLaw search, and will return the results of the search as a list of 'hyperlinks' to web pages that have information within or associated with the document comprising the page responding to the search."

> *Intermatic, Inc. v. Toeppen*, 947 F. Supp. 1227, 1232 (N.D. Ill. 1996).

"While the meaning of the term "Web browser" is not precise in all respects, there is a consensus in the software industry as to the functionalities that a Web browser offers a user. Specifically, a Web browser provides the ability for the end user to select, retrieve, and perceive resources on the Web. There is also a consensus in the software industry that these functionalities are distinct from the set of functionalities provided by an operating system."

> *United States v. Microsoft Corp.*, 65 F. Supp. 2d 1, 39 (D.D.C. 1999) (Finding of Fact 150).

"Using a Web browser, . . . a cyber 'surfer' may navigate the Web—searching for, communicating with, and retrieving information from various web sites. . . . Upon entering a domain name into [the] web browser, the corresponding web site will quickly appear on the computer screen."

> *Brookfield Comm., Inc. v. West Coast Entertainment Corp.*, 174 F.3d 1036, 1044 (9th Cir. 1999).

"In particular, Web browsers provide a way for a user to view hypertext documents and follow the hyperlinks that connect them, typically by moving the cursor over a link and depressing the mouse button."

> *United States v. Microsoft Corp.*, 65 F. Supp. 2d 1, 5 (D.D.C. 1999) (Finding of Fact 16).

"Although certain Web browsers provided graphical user interfaces as far back as 1993, the first widely-popular graphical browser distributed for profit, called Navigator, was brought to market by the Netscape Communications Corporation in December 1994. Microsoft introduced its browser, called Internet Explorer, in July 1995."

> *United States v. Microsoft Corp.*, 65 F. Supp. 2d 1, 5 (D.D.C. 1999) (Finding of Fact 16).

"The use of Web browsers to conduct Web transactions has grown at pace with the growth of the Web, reflecting the immense value that subsists in the digital information resources that have become available on the Web. Consumer demand for software functionality that facilitates Web transactions, and the response by browser vendors to that demand, creates a market for Web browsing functionality. Although Web browsers are now generally not licensed at a positive price, all Web transactions impose significant costs on consumers, and all browser vendors, including Microsoft, have significant economic interests in maximizing usage of the browsing functionality they control."

> *United States v. Microsoft Corp.,* 65 F. Supp. 2d 1, 49 (D.D.C. 1999) (Finding of Fact 201).

Related issues. "Most web browsers will show somewhere on the screen the domain name of the web page being shown and will automatically include the domain name in any printout of the web page."

> *Intermatic, Inc. v. Toeppen,* 947 F. Supp. 1227, 1231 (N.D. Ill. 1996).

See also **browser.**

web bug *(technology)*

A graphic (often 1 pixel × 1 pixel) on a web page or in an e-mail message that monitors who is reading the page/message and can provide the sender with useful marketing information on the reader, usually without the reader's knowledge or consent.

web client *(Internet; software)*

"[S]oftware that, when running on a computer connected to the Internet, sends information to and receives information from Web servers throughout the Internet."

> *United States v. Microsoft Corp.,* 65 F. Supp. 2d 1, 5 (D.D.C. 1999) (Finding of Fact 16).

Related issues. "Web clients and servers transfer data using a standard known as the Hypertext Transfer Protocol ('HTTP')."

> *United States v. Microsoft Corp.,* 65 F. Supp. 2d 1, 5 (D.D.C. 1999) (Finding of Fact 16).

web host *(Internet)*

A service provider that offers access to the World Wide Web. *See also* **Internet service provider.**

web page(s) *(Internet)*

"Information on the Web can be presented on 'pages' of graphics and text that contain 'links' to other pages—either within the same set of data files ('Web site') or within data files located on other computer networks."

> *Lockheed Martin Corp. v. Network Solutions, Inc.,* 985 F. Supp. 949, 951 (C.D. Cal. 1997).

"[A] computer data file on a host operating a web server within a given domain name."

> *Intermatic, Inc. v. Toeppen,* 947 F. Supp. 1227, 1231 (N.D. Ill. 1996).

"[A] computer data file that can include names, words, messages, pictures, sounds, and links to other information.

"Every web page has its own web site, which is its address, similar to a telephone number or street address."

> *Panavision Int'l, L.P. v. Toeppen,* 141 F.3d 1316, 1318 (9th Cir. 1998).

"[H]ypertext documents . . . that may incorporate any combination of text, graphics, audio and video content, software programs, and other data."

> *United States v. Microsoft Corp.,* 65 F. Supp. 2d 1, 5 (D.D.C. 1999) (Finding of Fact 12).

"[C]omputer data files in Hypertext Markup Language ('HTML')—which contain information such as text, pictures, sounds, audio and video recordings, and links to other web pages."

> *Brookfield Comm., Inc. v. West Coast Entertainment Corp.,* 174 F.3d 1036, 1044 (9th Cir. 1999).

Annotation. "Each has its own address—'rather like a telephone number.' Web pages frequently contain information and sometimes allow the viewer to communicate with the page's (or 'site's') author. They generally also contain 'links' to other documents created by that site's author or to other (generally) related sites."

> *Reno v. American Civil Liberties Union,* 521 U.S. 844, 852 (1997), *quoting American Civil Liberties Union v. Reno,* 929 F. Supp. 824, 836 (3d Cir. 1996) (footnotes omitted).

"When the web server receives an inquiry from the Internet, it returns the web page data in the file to the computer making the inquiry. The web page may comprise a single line or multiple pages of information and may include any message, name, word, sound or picture, or combination of such elements."

> *Intermatic, Inc. v. Toeppen,* 947 F. Supp. 1227, 1231 (N.D. Ill. 1996).

"Any Internet user anywhere in the world with the proper software can create a Web page, view Web pages posted by others, and then read the text, look at images and video, and listen to sounds posted at these sites."

> *American Library Ass'n v. Pataki*, 969 F. Supp. 160, 166 (S.D.N.Y. 1997).

"A user of a computer connected to the Internet can publish a page on the Web simply by copying it into a specially designated, publicly accessible directory on a Web server."

> *United States v. Microsoft Corp.*, 65 F. Supp. 2d 1, 5 (D.D.C. 1999) (Finding of Fact 12).

"Most Web pages are in the form of 'hypertext'; that is, they contain annotated references, or 'hyperlinks,' to other Web pages. Hyperlinks can be used as cross-references within a single document, between documents on the same site, or between documents on different sites."

> *United States v. Microsoft Corp.*, 65 F. Supp. 2d 1, 5 (D.D.C. 1999) (Finding of Fact 13).

Related issues. "There is no technical connection or relationship between a domain name and the contents of the corresponding web page."

> *Intermatic, Inc. v. Toeppen*, 947 F. Supp. 1227, 1231 (N.D. Ill. 1996).

"Each web page has a corresponding domain address, which is an identifier somewhat analogous to a telephone number or street address."

> *Brookfield Comm., Inc. v. West Coast Entertainment Corp.*, 174 F.3d 1036, 1044 (9th Cir. 1999).

See also **web; web site.**

web publishing *(Internet)*

"Web standards are sophisticated and flexible enough that they have grown to meet the publishing needs of many large corporations, banks, brokerage houses, newspapers and magazines which now publish 'online' editions of their materials, as well as government agencies, and even courts, which use the Web to disseminate information to the public. At the same time Web publishing is simple enough that thousands of individual users and small community organizations are using the Web to publish their own personal 'home pages,' the equivalent of individualized newsletters about the person or organization, which are available to everyone on the Web."

> *Reno v. American Civil Liberties Union*, 929 F. Supp. 830, 837 (3d Cir. 1996), *aff'd*, 521 U.S. 844 (1997).

"[T]he Web, like the rest of the Internet, is an important medium of non-commercial communications. The Web has made it easier for individuals and small organizations to publish information to the general public. Pub-

lication on the Web simply requires placing a formatted file on a host computer."
> *Lockheed Martin Corp. v. Network Solutions, Inc.,* 985 F. Supp. 949, 951 (C.D. Cal. 1997).

web rot *(Internet)*
The gradual decay of accuracy in web site references.

web server *(Internet)*
A computer system connected to the Internet that provides access for Internet users to the content stored on the system.

Related issues. "A content provider who makes files available on . . . a Web server has no way of knowing the identity of other participants who will have access to those servers."
> *Shea v. Reno,* 930 F. Supp. 916, 941 (S.D.N.Y. 1996).

"When the web server receives an inquiry from the Internet, it returns the web page data in the file to the computer making the inquiry."
> *Intermatic, Inc. v. Toeppen,* 947 F. Supp. 1227, 1231 (N.D. Ill. 1996).

See also **server.**

web site *(Internet)*
Also written as "Web site" or "website."

"A group of related documents sharing a Web 'address.' . . ."
> *Digital Equipment Corp. v. Altavista Technology, Inc.,* 960 F. Supp. 456, 459 n.2 (D. Mass. 1997).

". . . which is its [web page's] address, similar to a telephone number or street address. Every web site on the Internet has an identifier called a 'domain name.'"
> *Panavision Int'l, L.P. v. Toeppen,* 141 F.3d 1316, 1318 (9th Cir. 1998).

"[A]n interactive presentation of data which a user accesses by dialing into the host computer, can be created by any user who reserves an Internet location—called an Internet protocol address—and does the necessary programming."
> *Avery Dennison Corp. v. Sumpton,* 189 F.3d 868, 872 (9th Cir. 1999).

Annotation. "Any internet user can access any website, of which there are presumably hundreds of thousands, by entering into the computer the internet address they are seeking. Internet users can also perform searches on the internet to find websites within targeted areas of interest. Via telephone lines, the user is connected to the website, and the user can obtain any information that has been posted at the website for the user. The user can also interact with and send messages to that website. Upon connecting to a website, the information is transmitted electronically to the user's computer and quickly appears on the user's screen. This transmitted information can easily be downloaded to a disk or sent to a printer."

> *Maritz, Inc. v. CyberGold, Inc.,* 947 F. Supp. 1328, 1330 (E.D. Mo. 1996).

"Information on the Web can be presented on 'pages' of graphics and text that contain 'links' to other pages—either within the same set of data files ('Web site') or within data files located on other computer networks."

> *Lockheed Martin Corp. v. Network Solutions, Inc.,* 985 F. Supp. 949, 951 (C.D. Cal. 1997).

"With a website, one need only post information at the website. Any internet user can perform a search for selected terms or words and obtain a list of website addresses that contain such terms or words. The user can then access any of those websites."

> *Maritz, Inc. v. CyberGold, Inc.,* 947 F. Supp. 1328, 1333 (E.D. Mo. 1996).

"A specific web site is most easily located by using its domain name."

> *Brookfield Comm., Inc. v. West Coast Entertainment Corp.,* 174 F.3d 1036, 1044 (9th Cir. 1999).

"A web site can be programmed for multiple purposes. Some merchants maintain a form of 'electronic catalog' on the Internet, permitting Internet users to review products and services for sale. A web site can also be programmed for e-mail, where the provider licenses e-mail addresses in the format <alias@SLD.TLD>, with <alias> selected by the e-mail user [note: SLD refers to "second-level domain"; TLD to "top-level domain."] A person or company maintaining a web site makes money in a few different ways. A site that aids in marketing goods and services is an asset to a merchant. E-mail providers make money from licensing fees paid by e-mail users. Money is also made from advertising and links to other web sites."

> *Avery Dennison Corp. v. Sumpton,* 189 F.3d 868, 872 (9th Cir. 1999).

Related issues. "We agree that simply registering someone else's trademark as a domain name and posting a web site on the Internet is not sufficient to subject a party domiciled in one state to jurisdiction in another. . . . [T]here must be 'something more' to demonstrate that the defendant directed his activity toward the forum state."

> *Panavision Int'l, Inc. v. Toeppen,* 141 F.3d 1316, 1322 (9th Cir. 1998).

"[W]e have found as a fact that operation of a computer is not as simple as turning on a television, and that the assaultive nature of television . . . is quite absent in Internet use. The use of warnings and headings, for example, will normally shield users from immediate entry into a sexually explicit Web site or newsgroup message. The government may well be right that sexually explicit content is just a few clicks of a mouse away from the user, but there is an immense legal significance to those few clicks."

> *American Civil Liberties Union v. Reno,* 929 F. Supp. 824, 876 n.19 (E.D. Pa. 1996), *aff'd, Reno v. American Civil Liberties Union,* 521 U.S. 844 (1997).

See also **access.**

Whelan *(copyright; software)*

Citation: Whelan Assocs., Inc. v. Jaslow Dental Lab., Inc., 797 F.2d 1222 (3d Cir. 1986), *cert. denied,* 479 U.S. 1031 (1987).

This was one of the first cases that considered the protectability of the non-literal elements (namely, the "structure, sequence, and organization") of a computer program. In determining which elements of the program were protectable expression and which were nonprotectable ideas, the court stated the following concept:

> "[T]he line between idea and expression may be drawn with reference to the end sought to be achieved by the work in question. In other words, the purpose or function of a utilitarian work would be the work's idea, and everything that is not necessary to that purpose or function would be part of the expression of the idea. . . . Where there are various means of achieving the desired purpose, then the particular means chosen is not necessary to the purpose; hence, there is expression, not idea." *Id.* at 1236 (citations omitted).

While a few cases followed the *Whelan* decision (*see, e.g., Bull HN Infor. Sys., Inc. v. American Express Bank, Ltd.,* 1990 Copyright L. Dec. (CCH) ¶ 26,555, at 23,278 (S.D.N.Y. 1990)), most courts have found the analysis to be too simplistic and to have placed the boundary between idea and expression much too far toward the idea, giving the copyright owner excessive protection for what should be classified as unprotectable elements of its computer program. *See, e.g., Computer Assocs. Int'l, Inc. v. Altai, Inc.,* 982 F.2d 693, 705-06 (2d Cir. 1992) and the cases cited therein. As noted by the court in *Computer Associates:*

> "We think that *Whelan's* approach to separating idea from expression in computer programs relies too heavily on metaphysical distinctions and does not place enough emphasis on practical considerations." *Id.* at 706.

White Paper *(Internet)*

A document prepared by the Working Group on Intellectual Property Rights, chaired by U.S. Commissioner of Patents Bruce A. Lehman, on the need to modify existing intellectual property and contract laws to deal with the emergence of the National Information Infrastructure. The full title of the report is "Intellectual Property and the National Information Infrastructure: The Report of the Working Group on Intellectual Property Rights" (1995).

Whois *(Internet)*

A searchable database containing information about networks, networking organizations, domain names, and the contacts associated with them for the com, org, net, edu, and ISO 3166 country code top-level domains.

widow/widower *(copyright)*

"The author's 'widow' or 'widower' is the author's surviving spouse under the law of the author's domicile at the time of his or her death, whether or not the spouse has later remarried."

U.S. Copyright Act, 17 U.S.C. § 101.

willful infringement *(patent)*

Annotation. "A finding of willful infringement supports, but does not compel, enhancement of damages."

Brooktree Corp. v. Advanced Micro Devices, Inc., 977 F.2d 1555, 1581 (Fed. Cir. 1992).

winchester disk *(hardware)*

A "hard" disk that is completely enclosed, preventing contamination from the environment.

window *(technology)*

A rectangular portion of a video display in which visual images are displayed. There may be more than one window open on a display screen at the same time.

"[A] framing device on the computer screen that displays information and may set the displayed information apart from other information on the screen."

Apple Computer, Inc. v. Articulate Sys., Inc., 234 F.2d 14, 19 (Fed. Cir. 2000).

Annotation. "[M]enu bars or buttons are commonly understood to be types of windows by those skilled in the art."

> *Apple Computer, Inc. v. Articulate Sys., Inc.*, 234 F.2d 14, 21 (Fed. Cir. 2000).

Windows *(software)*

"WINDOWS is a graphical interface of MS-DOS developed and marketed by Microsoft, which is currently licensed for use on more than ten million personal computers worldwide."

> *Microsoft Corp. v. BEC Computer Co.*, 818 F. Supp. 1313, 1315 (C.D. Cal. 1991).

"Microsoft Windows ('Windows') is an operating system released by Microsoft Corp. It is the most widely used operating system for PCs in the United States, and its versions include Windows 95, Windows 98, Windows NT and Windows 2000."

> *Universal City Studios, Inc. v. Reimerdes*, 111 F. Supp. 2d 294, 305 (S.D.N.Y. 2000).

Annotation. "In 1985, Microsoft began shipping a software package called Windows. The product included a graphical user interface, which enabled users to perform tasks by selecting icons and words on the screen using a mouse. Although originally just a user-interface, or 'shell,' sitting on top of MS-DOS, Windows took on more operating-system functionality over time.

"In 1995, Microsoft introduced a software package called Windows 95, which announced itself as the first operating system for Intel-compatible PCs that exhibited the same sort of integrated features as the Mac OS running PCs manufactured by Apple Computer, Inc. ('Apple'). Windows 95 enjoyed unprecedented popularity with consumers, and in June 1998, Microsoft released its successor, Windows 98."

> *United States v. Microsoft Corp.*, 65 F. Supp. 2d 1, 4 (D.D.C. 1999) (Findings of Fact 7-8).

Related issues. Consumer demand for Windows enjoys positive network effects. . . . The fact that there is a multitude of people using Windows makes the product more attractive to consumers. The large installed base attracts corporate customers who want to use an operating system that new employees are already likely to know how to use, and it attracts academic consumers who want to use software that will allow them to share files easily with colleagues at other institutions. The main reason that demand for Windows experiences positive network effects, however, is that the size of Windows' installed base impels ISVs to write applications first and foremost to Windows, thereby ensuring a large body of applications from which

consumers can choose. The large body of applications thus reinforces demand for Windows, augmenting Microsoft's dominant position and
thereby perpetuating ISV incentives to write applications principally for
Windows. This self-reinforcing cycle is often referred to as a "positive feedback loop."

> *United States v. Microsoft Corp.*, 65 F. Supp. 2d 1, 11 (D.D.C. 1999) (Finding
> of Fact 39).

See also **operating system.**

window of opportunity *(business)*
The period of time a new technology or title has in which to become
profitable before better technology or newer titles are introduced.

windowing (fixed, sliding) *(Year 2000)*
A technique for handling the Year 2000 problem using logic rules to interpret a two-digit year. *Fixed* windowing logic goes like this: If the year is less
than 20, the century must be 2000; if the year is greater than 80, the century must be 1900. *Sliding* windowing uses a moving window of time,
based on the current year, plus or minus some number of years. Either
technique for windowing is designed to allow the company to retain current application code and data file formats. Windowing has several draw-
backs, such as added overhead, and being yet another piece of code that
could cause problems. (wsr)

WIPO *(organization)*
Acronym for "World Intellectual Property Organization." An international
intellectual property organization. Located at <http://www.wipo.int>.

wire communication *(telecommunications)*
"[A]ny aural transfer made in whole or in part through the use of facilities
for the transmission of communications by the aid of wire, cable, or other
like connection between the point of origin and the point of reception
(including the use of such connection in a switching station) . . . and such
term includes any electronic storage of such communication."

> 18 U.S.C. § 2510(1).

wire fraud *(criminal)*
"Whoever, having devised or intending to devise any scheme or artifice to
defraud, or for obtaining money or property by means of false or fraudulent pretenses, representations, or promises, transmits or causes to be transmitted by means of wire, radio, or television communication in interstate

or foreign commerce, any writings, signs, signals, pictures, or sounds for the purpose of executing such scheme or artifice, shall be fined not more than $1,000 or imprisoned not more than five years, or both. If the violation affects a financial institution, such person shall be fined not more than $1,000,000 or imprisoned not more than 30 years, or both."

18 U.S.C. § 1343.

Annotation. "The wire fraud statute was enacted to cure a jurisdictional defect that Congress perceived was created by the growth of radio and television as commercial media. In its report to the House of Representatives, the Committee on the Judiciary explained:

"'[T]he measure in amended form . . . creates a new, but relatively isolated area of criminal conduct consisting of the execution of a scheme to defraud or to obtain money or property by means of false or fraudulent pretenses, representations, or promises transmitted in writings, signs, pictures, or sounds via interstate wire or radio communications (which includes the medium of television). . . . The rapid growth of interstate communications facilities, particularly those of radio and television, has given rise to a variety of fraudulent activities on the part of unscrupulous persons which are not within the reach of existing mail fraud laws, but which are carried out in complete reliance upon the use of wire and radio facilities and without resort to the mails. . . . Even in those cases of radio fraud where the mails have played a role, it is sometimes difficult to prove the use of the mails to the satisfaction of the court, and so prosecutions often fail. Because of the greater facility in proving the use of radio, this bill if enacted might often rescue a prosecution which would otherwise be defeated on technicalities.'"

H.R. Rep. No. 388, 82d Cong., 1st Sess. 102 (1951).

"As the legislative history makes clear, the wire fraud statute was intended to complement the mail fraud statute by giving federal prosecutors jurisdiction over frauds involving the use of interstate (or foreign) wire transmissions."

United States v. LaMacchia, 871 F. Supp. 535, 540-41 (D. Mass. 1994).

"A scheme to defraud is the defining concept of the mail and wire fraud statutes. Because of the conjunctive use of the word 'or' in the statutory phrase 'any scheme or artifice to defraud, or for obtaining money or property by false or fraudulent pretenses, representations, or promises,' the federal courts (encouraged by prosecutors) have essentially bifurcated mail and wire fraud into two separate offenses; the first, the devising of a scheme to defraud, the second, the devising of a scheme to obtain money or property by false pretenses. While the latter crime comports with common law notions of fraud, '[t]he phrase, "a scheme to defraud" came to prohibit a plan, that is, to forbid a state of mind, rather than physical conduct.'

* * *

"[M]ail and wire fraud statutes do not require that a defendant be shown to have sought to personally profit from the scheme to defraud."
United States v. LaMacchia, 871 F. Supp. 535, 541 (D. Mass. 1994) (citations omitted).

word processing *(software)*
The form of data processing concerned with recording, editing, and storing written text and data for the purpose of creating printed reports and documents.

word wrap *(software)*
The capability to automatically move text entered on a line to a new line (if it would otherwise overrun the right margin), without having to type a carriage return.

work *(copyright)*
A copyrightable creation.

Related issues. "[I]t is equally important to remember that there exists a distinction between the work and the copyright. The work—in this case a computer program—is separate and distinct from the copyright; the copyright is the rights to which the copyrighted work is subject. It is the rights, not the work, that the copyright holder owns. This distinction is manifest in view of the fact that when the copyright expires, the erstwhile copyright holder no longer owns any exclusive rights, but the work continues to exist without change. The copyright owner never owns the work because copyright is a series of specified rights to which a designated work is subject for a limited period of time, after which the work enters into the public domain unencumbered by copyright. Hence, the use of the work and the use of the copyright are distinct. One may use the work without using the copyright, but one cannot use the copyright without using the work—one does not infringe the work, rather one infringes the copyright. . . . Therefore, the basic issue in all copyright defense is whether the use involved was a use of the work or a use of the copyright."
Bateman v. Mnemonic, Inc., 79 F.3d 1532, 1542 n.23 (11th Cir. 1995).

work made for hire *(copyright)*
". . . is—(1) a work prepared by an employee within the scope of his or her employment; or

(2) a work specially ordered or commissioned for use as a contribution to a collective work, as a part of a motion picture or other audiovisual work, as a translation, as a supplementary work, as a compilation, as an instructional text, as a test, as answer material for a test, or as an atlas, if the parties expressly agree in a written instrument signed by them that the work shall be considered a work made for hire. For the purpose of the foregoing sentence, a 'supplementary work' is a work prepared for publication as a secondary adjunct to a work by another author for the purpose of introducing, concluding, illustrating, explaining, revising, commenting upon, or assisting in the use of the other work, such as forewords, afterwords, pictorial illustrations, maps, charts, tables, editorial notes, musical arrangements, answer material for tests, bibliographies, appendixes, and indexes, and an 'instructional text' is a literary, pictorial, or graphic work prepared for publication and with the purpose of use in systematic instructional activities."

U.S. Copyright Act, 17 U.S.C. § 101.

work of authorship *(copyright)*

A copyrightable creation that originates from an author.

Annotation. "Copyright protection subsists . . . in original works of authorship fixed in any tangible medium of expression, now known or later developed, from which they can be perceived, reproduced, or otherwise communicated, either directly or with the aid of a machine or device."

17 U.S.C. § 102(a).

"Authors are continually finding new ways of expressing themselves, but it is impossible to foresee the forms that these new expressive methods will take. The bill does not intend either to freeze the scope of copyrightable subject matter at the present stage of communication technology or to allow unlimited expansion into areas completely outside the present congressional intent. Section 102 implies neither that that subject matter is unlimited nor that new forms of expression within that general area of subject matter would necessarily be unprotected."

H.R. Rep. 94-1476, 94th Cong, 2d Sess. 57 (1976).

"Some concern has been expressed lest copyright in computer programs should extend protection to the methodology or processes adopted by the programmer, rather than merely to the 'writing' expressing his ideas. Section 102(b) is intended, among other things, to make clear that the expression adopted by the programmer is the copyrightable element in a computer program, and that the actual processes or methods embodied in the program are not within the scope of the copyright law."

H.R. Rep No. 1476, 94th Cong., 2d Sess. 57 (1976).

See also ideas.

work of the United States Government *(copyright)*

"[A] work prepared by an officer or employee of the United States Government as part of that person's official duties."

U.S. Copyright Act, 17 U.S.C. § 101.

World Intellectual Property Organization *(organization)*

See WIPO.

World Trade Organization *(organization)*

See WTO.

World Wide Web *(Internet)*

Abbreviated as "WWW" and "W3C."

"The best known category of communication over the Internet is the World Wide Web, which allows users to search for and retrieve information stored in remote computers, as well as, in some cases, to communicate back to designated sites. In concrete terms, the Web consists of a vast number of documents stored in different computers all over the world."

American Civil Liberties Union v. Reno, 521 U.S. 844, 852 (1997), *aff'g Reno v. American Civil Liberties Union,* 929 F. Supp. 824 (E.D. Pa. 1996).

"[A] massive collection of digital information resources stored on servers throughout the Internet."

United States v. Microsoft Corp., 65 F. Supp. 2d 1, 5 (D.D.C. 1999) (Finding of Fact 12).

". . . refers to the collection of sites available on the Internet."

Zippo Mfg. Co. v. Zippo Dot Com, Inc., 952 F. Supp. 1119, 1120 n.2 (W.D. Pa. 1997); *Bensusan Restaurant Corp. v. King,* 937 F. Supp. 295 (S.D.N.Y. 1996).

Annotation. "Since the World Wide Web was introduced to the public in 1991, the resources available on the Web have multiplied at a near-exponential rate. The Internet is becoming a true mass medium. Every day Web resources are published, combined, modified, moved, and deleted. Millions of individuals and organizations have published Web sites, and Web site addresses are pervasive in advertising, promotion, and corporate identification."

United States v. Microsoft Corp., 65 F. Supp. 2d 1, 49 (D.D.C. 1999) (Finding of Fact 199).

"The economics of the Internet, along with the flexible structure of Web pages, have made the Web the leading trajectory for the ongoing convergence of mass communications media. Many television and radio stations make some or all of their transmissions available on the Web in the form of static multimedia files or streaming media. Many newspapers, magazines, books, journals, public documents, and software programs are also published on the Web. Multimedia files on the Web have emerged as viable substitutes for many pre-recorded audio and video entertainment products. Web-based E-mail, discussion lists, news groups, 'chat rooms,' paging, instant messaging, and telephony are all in common use. In addition to subsuming all other digital media, the Web also offers popular interactive and collaborative modes of communication that are not available through other media."

United States v. Microsoft Corp., 65 F. Supp. 2d 1, 49 (D.D.C. 1999) (Finding of Fact 200).

"The World Wide Web (W3C) was created to serve as the platform for a global, online store of knowledge, containing information from a diversity of sources and accessible to Internet users around the world. Though information on the Web is contained in individual computers, the fact that each of these computers is connected to the Internet through W3C protocols allows all of the information to become part of a single body of knowledge. It is currently the most advanced information system developed on the Internet, and embraces within its data model most information in previous networked information systems such as ftp, gopher, wais, and Usenet.

". . . W3C was originally developed at CERN, the European Particle Physics Laboratory, and was initially used to allow information sharing within internationally dispersed teams of researchers and engineers. Originally aimed at the High Energy Physics community, it has spread to other areas and attracted much interest in user support, resource recovery, and many other areas which depend on collaborative and information sharing. The Web has extended beyond the scientific and academic community to include communications by individuals, non-profit organizations, and businesses.

". . . The World Wide Web is a series of documents stored in different computers all over the Internet. Documents contain information stored in a variety of formats, including text, still images, sounds, and video. An essential element of the Web is that any document has an address (rather like a telephone number). Most Web documents contain 'links.' These are short sections of text or image which refer to another document. Typically the linked text is blue or underlined when displayed, and when selected by the user, the referenced document is automatically displayed, wherever in the world it actually is stored. Links for example are used to lead from overview documents to more detailed documents, from tables of contents to particular pages, but also as cross-references, footnotes, and new forms of information structure.

* * *

"The World Wide Web exists fundamentally as a platform through which people and organizations can communicate through shared information. When information is made available, it is said to be 'published' on the Web. Publishing on the Web simply requires that the 'publisher' has a computer connected to the Internet and that the computer is running W3C server software. The computer can be as simple as a small personal computer costing less than $1500 dollars or as complex as a multi-million dollar mainframe computer. Many Web publishers choose instead to lease disk storage space from someone else who has the necessary computer facilities, eliminating the need for actually owning any equipment oneself.

* * *

"The Web links together disparate information on an ever-growing number of Internet-linked computers by setting common information storage formats (HTML) and a common language for the exchange of Web documents (HTTP). Although the information itself may be in many different formats, and stored on computers which are not otherwise compatible, the basic Web standards provide a basic set of standards which allow communication and exchange of information. Despite the fact that many types of computers are used on the Web, and the fact that many of these machines are otherwise incompatible, those who 'publish' information on the Web are able to communicate with those who seek to access information with little difficulty because of these basic technical standards.

". . . Running on tens of thousands of individual computers on the Internet, the Web is what is known as a distributed system. The Web was designed so that organizations with computers containing information can become part of the Web simply by attaching their computers to the Internet and running appropriate World Wide Web software. No single organization controls any membership in the Web, nor is there any single centralized point from which individual Web sites or services can be blocked from the Web. From a user's perspective, it may appear to be a single, integrated system, but in reality it has no centralized control point.

* * *

". . . The World Wide Web has become so popular because of its open, distributed, and easy-to-use nature. Rather than requiring those who seek information to purchase new software or hardware, and to learn a new kind of system for each new database of information they seek to access, the Web environment makes it easy for users to jump from one set of information to another. By the same token, the open nature of the Web makes it easy for publishers to reach their intended audiences without having to know in advance what kind of computer each potential reader has, and what kind of software they will be using."

American Civil Liberties Union v. Reno, 929 F. Supp. 824, 836-38 (E.D. Pa. 1996), *aff'd, Reno v. American Civil Liberties Union*, 521 U.S. 844 (1997).

"Documents available on the Web are not collected in any central location; rather, they are stored on servers around the world running Web server software. To gain access to the content available on the Web, a user must have a Web 'browser'—client software, such as Netscape Navigator, Mosaic, or Internet Explorer, capable of displaying documents formatted in 'hypertext markup language' ('HTML'), the standard Web formatting language."

Shea v. Reno, 930 F. Supp. 916, 929 (S.D.N.Y. 1996).

See also **Internet; Web.**

worm

(criminal)

"[A] program that travels from one computer to another but does not attach itself to the operating system of the computer it 'infects.'"

United States v. Morris, 928 F.2d 504, 505 n.1 (2d Cir. 1991).

(hardware)

Acronym for "write once, read many." A type of CD-ROM technology in which digital information can be recorded on a blank disc and played back repeatedly. However, the disc cannot be erased nor the data written over.

(software)

"[S]elf-contained programs containing malicious code that copy versions of themselves across electronically connected nodes."

U.S. General Accounting Office, *Information Superhighway: An Overview of Technology Changes* 19 n.5 (Jan. 1995).

See also **network worm.**

wraparound *(multimedia)*

"To evade capture by a pursuing monster, the player can cause the central character to exit through one opening and re-enter through the other on the opposite side."

Atari, Inc. v. North American Philips Consumer Elecs. Corp., 672 F. Supp. 607, 610 (7th Cir.), *cert. denied,* 459 U.S. 880 (1982).

wrapper *(technology)*

"The wrapper—the digital envelope—is not encrypted. Anyone receiving a copy of a digital object will therefore be able to read the wrapper. What the wrapper contains is up to the owner of the object. The expected uses for the wrapper are to contain things like abstracts or summaries of the content; the name and address of the copyright owner; the fees, required by the owner to make the content available; and so on."

I. Trotter Hardy, *Project Looking Forward: Sketching the Future of Copyright in a Networked World* 71-72 (May 1998).

See also **digital object.**

write *(technology)*

To transfer data from internal to external memory.

writing *(contract)*

"[I]ncludes printing, typewriting or any other intentional reduction to tangible form."

U.C.C. § 1-201(46).

written *(contract)*

"[I]ncludes printing, typewriting or any other intentional reduction to tangible form."

U.C.C. § 1-201(46).

written warranty *(contract)*

"(A) any written affirmation of fact or written promise made in connection with the sale of a consumer product by a supplier to a buyer which relates to the nature of the material or workmanship and affirms or promises that such material or workmanship is defect free or will meet a specified level of performance over a period of time, or (B) any undertaking in writing in connection with the sale by a supplier of a consumer product to refund, repair, replace, or take other remedial action with respect to such product in the event that such product fails to meet the specifications set forth in the undertaking, which written affirmation, promise, or undertaking becomes part of the basis of the bargain between a supplier and a buyer for purposes other than resale of such product."

15 U.S.C. § 2301(6).

See also **express warranty.**

WTO *(organization)*

Acronym for "World Trade Organization." An organization established by GATT to resolve trade disputes. Located at <www.wto.org>.

WWW *(Internet)*

". . . which stands for 'World-Wide Web.'"

Avery Dennison Corp. v. Sumpton, 189 F.3d 868, 872 n.2 (9th Cir. 1999).

See **World Wide Web.**

WYSIWYG *(technology)*

Acronym for "What You See Is What You Get." Pronounced "wizzy-wig." This term means that what is displayed on a computer screen looks exactly as it will look if it is output to a printer, plotter, or other output device.

XCMD *(software)*

Acronym for "external command." A program to control a device in a manner not provided by the computer provider.

Year 2000 compliance *(Year 2000)*
Refers to two related components:
1. Process compliance, which is the ability for computer systems to perform as intended, regardless of the century.
2. Data compliance, meaning that all existing stored corporate data is accessible and will continue to be accessible in the Year 2000 and beyond. This may involve the use of logic bridges to convert dates on demand, or it may require physically changing the data as stored during the compliance process to include a century indicator.

Year 2000 compliant *(Year 2000)*
Information systems able to accurately process date data—including, but not limited to, calculating, comparing, and sequencing—from, into, and between the twentieth and twenty-first centuries, including leap year calculations.

Sample clause. "Licensor warrants that the occurrence in or use by the Software of dates on or after January 1, 2000 ('Millennial Dates'), will not adversely affect its performance with respect to date-dependent data, computations, output, or other functions (including, without limitation, calculating, comparing, and sequencing) and that the Software will create, store, process, and output information related to or including Millennial Dates without error or omissions and at no additional cost to Licensee. At Licensee's request, Licensor will provide evidence sufficient to demonstrate adequate testing of the Software to meet the foregoing requirements."

Year 2000 methodology *(Year 2000)*
A detailed process or road map for achieving compliance, including identifiable phases and steps, and relevant milestones and deliverables. Solution vendors typically have some methodology or approach for how they will deal with bringing a company into compliance. The best vendors will tailor their methodology to meet the specific situation and needs, rather than applying a process template.

Year 2000 overview committee *(Year 2000)*

A group of individuals from many areas of the organization, representing line functions, middle-management, and, most importantly, senior enterprise management. This cross-functional group will steer the commitment of enterprise management during the compliance process. Outside stakeholders may also be involved on the Year 2000 committee under certain conditions. Depending on the structure of the organization, there may be several project committees, with distinct groups representing, for example, individual lines of business, departments, or business units. This scenario may be especially true where these distinct entities maintain and have control over their own information systems, including budgets.

Year 2000 problem *(Year 2000)*

The potential problems and its variations that might be encountered in any level of computer hardware and software from microcode to application programs, files, and databases that need to correctly interpret year-date data represented in 2-digit-year format.

Annotation. "The Year 2000 problem has served to heighten the awareness of our nation's critical reliance on technology and permeates all industries through the interdependence of our infrastructures. These critical infrastructures include telecommunications, energy, banking and finance, transportation, water systems, and emergency services, both government and private."

Office of the Comptroller of the Currency, Infrastructure Threats from Cyber-Terrorists 5 (Mar. 19, 1999).

YYMMDD *(Year 2000)*

Abbreviation for "year, month, day." Standard abbreviation for dates in an automated system.

Y2K *(Year 2000)*

Acronym for "Year 2000."

zero-delay *(technology)*

". . . means that [the encryption software] can be used for interactive communications because it encrypts and decrypts on a character-by-character basis—the users need not complete the entire message before encrypting and sending."

Bernstein v. United States Dept. of Justice, 176 F.3d 1132, 1135 n.1 (9th Cir. 1999).

zero fill *(technology)*

To fill a field with the character zero in order to bring an item of data up to a specified size.

Zippo Mfg. *(jurisdiction)*

"In *Zippo Mfg.,* the district court for the western district of Pennsylvania formulated a 'sliding scale' test to determine whether a defendant's contact with the forum state through a site on the World Wide Web supported the exercise of specific personal jurisdiction. The court stated:

At one end of the spectrum are situations where a defendant clearly does business over the Internet. If the defendant enters into contracts with residents of a foreign jurisdiction that involve the knowing and repeated transmission of computer files over the Internet, personal jurisdiction is proper. At the opposite end are situations where a defendant has simply posted information on an Internet Web site which is accessible to users in foreign jurisdictions. A passive Web site that does little more than make information available to those who are interested in it is not grounds for the exercise [of] personal jurisdiction. The middle ground is occupied by interactive Web sites where a user can exchange information with the host computer. In these cases, the exercise of jurisdiction is determined by examining the level of interactivity and commercial nature of the exchange of information that occurs on the Web site."

Coastal Video Comm. Corp. v. Staywell Corp., 59 F. Supp. 2d 562, 570 n.7 (E.D. Va. 1999).